第一次就考好
英语四级

张宇泽　金姆 ◎著

吉林出版集团有限责任公司

图书在版编目(CIP)数据

第一次就考好英语四级 / 张宇泽，（美）金姆著. —
长春：吉林出版集团有限责任公司，2012.6
ISBN 978-7-5463-9455-8

Ⅰ.①第… Ⅱ.①张… ②金… Ⅲ.①大学英语水平
考试－自学参考资料 Ⅳ.①H310.42

中国版本图书馆CIP数据核字（2012）第103161号

第一次就考好英语四级

作　者	张宇泽　（美）金　姆	
选题策划	含章行文·易人英语	
责任编辑	王　平　齐　琳	
特约编辑	姜程程	
开　本	787mm×1092mm　1/16	
字　数	253千字	
印　张	23.5	
版　次	2012年11月第1版	
印　次	2012年11月第1次印刷	
出　版	吉林出版集团有限责任公司	
电　话	总编办：010-63109269	
	发行部：010-63329002	
印　刷	北京中振源印务有限公司	

ISBN　978-7-5463-9455-8　　　　　　定价：39.80元

前言
Preface

　　大学英语四级（以下简称"四级"）考试对于很多考生来说是一个"梦魇"，词汇量大（内含4000多个单词），考试题型多变，包括听力、阅读理解、完形填空、写作、翻译等。尽管历年的考题不同，但考察范围没变，不外乎这4000多个单词和基本的语法知识，不过每年还是有考生栽在这雷同的题目上。

　　人生没有捷径，学习知识也是如此。天道酬勤，付出才有回报。考试固然会牵涉到一些社会常识、英美文化背景知识和逻辑思辨能力，但更重要的考察对象还是基本的语言知识，也就是单词和语法，这是一切题型的基础。再者，考生还必须熟悉历年考试题型，了解应试技巧与策略。

　　针对广大读者认为的"四级难"状况，结合教育部最新颁布的《大学英语四级考试大纲》，我们编写了这本《第一次就考好英语四级》。书中第一部分罗列出四级考试需要用到的词汇，共计有4000多个单词。在单词排序方面，本书摒弃了其他单词书按字母顺序排序的弊端，采用按类别划分单词的方法，便于系统记忆。此外重点单词我们还添加了考点，配有历年出现的真题，并分析每个选项，让读者知悉考点，做到心中有数。书中第二部分我们以近两年的四级真题为例，分析题型结构，解析正确答案，并总结出做题技巧，给出应试策略，让读者熟悉考试题型，了解应试技巧。第三部分，我们给出一套大学英语四级考试模拟试题，此试题是我们在总结了历年四级考试出题规律的基础上编出的，并配有详细的答案解析。读者考前做一做，就如同亲历考场，可以找到自己的不足，并及时进行弥补，以便能一次性通过四级考试。

　　最后，希望本书能给广大读者带来切实的帮助，让您轻松顺利地通过四级！

编　者

1 按类别排序，方便记忆

本书摒弃了其他单词书按字母排序的弊端，按照类别划分单词。每一类别囊括与此相关的单词，这样读者可以系统地记忆单词，大大提高学习效率。

2 国际音标，让你准确读单词

国际标准语音，能够让你掌握单词的正确发音，在看到单词的同时就能把它准确地读出来。朗读单词有助于记忆，只有知道一个单词怎么读，并且经常地读，才能在听力里听到它时迅速地反应过来。除此之外，知道了单词的正确读音有助于拼写记忆。事实证明，按音标去记忆单词的方法比按字母顺序去记忆科学、有效得多。

3 一个单词，一个例句

根据单词的释义，造出相关的句子，让你在句子中背单词，活学活用，轻松、灵活地掌握该单词的用法。只有把单词放到一定的语境下，你才能更好地理解这个单词，也能了解该单词怎样运用。这些句子涉及了生活中的方方面面，不仅避免了单纯记单词的枯燥乏味，也在一定程度上帮您提高了阅读水平，甚至写作水平。

④ 添加考点，贴近考试

在一些重点单词后面，我们还添加了考点。根据类型，考点可分为三种：一是常用短语，二是历年真题，三是听力考点。本书中收录的跟单词相关的短语，能让你掌握地道的英文，并实现高分突破。如果一个单词在历年真题中出现过，我们会把真题列出，并分析每个选项，排除干扰项，为你找出正确答案。而所谓的听力考点，就是在听力中会考察该单词的哪些知识，通常是发音问题。

⑤ 分析考试技巧，加深对题型的理解

在本书的第二部分，我们以近两年的四级真题为例，分析了题型结构，解析了正确答案，并总结出了做题技巧。贴心的应试策略，让你不再畏惧四级考试，轻松上阵。

⑥ 模拟试题，让你进一步了解自己的实力

书中的第三部分，是一套大学英语四级考试模拟题。在总结了历年四级考试出题规律的基础上，我们编出了这套题，并配有详细的答案解析。考前做一做，看清自己的长处与短处，在实战时，可以做到扬长避短，考出好的成绩。

目 录

第一部分 | 单词

日常生活 Daily Life

衣

食

住

行

人际交往 Social Communication

沟通交流

日常联络

友好和睦

目 录

摩擦失和

教育 Education

学校

专业学科

校园生活

职场生涯 Career

求职面试

日常办公

人事管理

商务贸易 Business Trade

市场和销售

会见客户

谈判与签约

目 录

娱乐休闲 Entertainment

兴趣爱好

狂欢

运动锻炼

外出游玩

艺术欣赏

闲聊杂谈 Chatting

娱乐体育

人生梦想

医疗养生

科学技术

政府政治

和平与发展

其他

目 录

人与自然 Human and Nature

人

自然

环境保护

第二部分 │ 大学英语四级题型分析及考试技巧

第三部分 │ 大学英语四级考试模拟试题及答案解析

Contents

大学英语四级模拟试题答案解析

第 一 次 就 考 好 英 语 四 级

第一部分

单 词
Word

日常生活 | Daily Life

衣 服装服饰

bag [bæg] *n.* 袋,包,钱包,背包
I am frightened by the bag which is full of snakes.
我被那个装满蛇的袋子吓坏了。

belt [belt] *n.* 腰带,皮带,区
Hang on to the belt——we're off.
抓住吊带——我们要出发了。

boot [bu:t] *n.* 靴子,长统靴
She stood on her bare feet, with her boots thrown beside.
她光脚站着,靴子在一边扔着。

brim [brim] *n.* 边,边缘,帽沿
There is a little girl dancing at the fountain's brim.
有个小女孩在泉边跳舞。

button ['bʌtn] *n.* 扣子,按钮;*vt.* 扣紧
Mom, could you stitch a button on my skirt?
妈妈,你能给我的裙子钉上一颗纽扣吗?

cap [kæp] *n.* 帽子,便帽,帽状物
I know that cap; it's a service cap.
我认识那顶帽子,那是一顶军帽。

cloak [kləuk] *n.* 斗篷,覆盖(物)
The woman who wears a red cloak is the duchess.
穿着红色斗篷的那个女人是公爵夫人。

closet ['klɔzit] *n.* 壁橱,衣帽间,密室,厕所;*adj.* 隐藏的,不公开的,空谈的;*vt.* 把……关在房间里
There's still damp in the closet.
这个衣柜还是有点潮湿。

cloth [klɔθ] *n.* 布,衣料,桌布
Don't worry. This cloth is made of very durable material.
别担心,这种衣服是用非常耐用的料子做成的。

clothes [kləuðz] *n.* 衣服,服装,被褥
Could you take this heap of dirty clothes to the laundry?
你能把这堆脏衣服送到洗衣店吗?

clothing ['kləuðiŋ] *n.* 衣服,被褥
To the victims, what they need most is food, clothing and shelter.
对于灾民来说,他们最需要的是吃的、穿的和住的。

coat [kəut] *n.* 外套,上衣,表皮
If your coat is too large, the tailor can alter it to fit you.
如果你的上衣过大,裁缝可以依据你的体形给你修改。

collar ['kɔlə] *n.* 衣领,项圈
I recommend you this shirt, for a stiff collar may chafe your neck.
我向你推荐这件衬衣,因为硬领可能会磨疼你的脖子。

cotton ['kɔtn] *n.* 棉,棉线,棉布
According to these symptoms, I can conclude that these cotton plants have got the disease of blight.
根据这些症状,我可以推断出这些棉花得了枯萎病。

fabric ['fæbrik] *n.* 织物,布,构造,组织
We must find out the fabric of this machine.
我们必须弄明白这些机器的构造。

gown [gaun] *n.* 长袍,长外衣
Her mother made her a gown as a gift.
她妈妈给她做了件长袍作为礼物。

leather ['leðə] *n.* 皮革,皮革制品
My aunt likes the gloves best which are made of leather.
我阿姨最喜欢皮革手套。

material [mə'tiəriəl] *n.* 材料，素材
adj. 物质的，有形的，实质性的
These fatigue clothes are made of very durable material.
这些工装是用非常耐用的料子做的。

nylon ['nailən] *n.* 尼龙，耐纶
My coat is made of nylon.
我的外套是尼龙的。

overall ['əuvərɔ:l] *n.* 工装裤；*adj.* 全面的
The overall length of the highway is 1000 kilometers.
这条高速公路的全长是1000公里。

真题

The _____ goal of the book is to help bridge the gap between research and teaching, particularly the gap between researchers and teachers.
A) joint   B) intensive
C) overall   D) decisive

详 解：选C。题意为：这本书总的目标就是帮助消除科研与教学，尤其是科研人员与教师之间的隔阂。overall goal指的是"总体目标"。A) joint意思是"共同的，联合的"；B) intensive意思是"集中的，加强的"；D) decisive意思是"果断的"。

(CET-4 2003.12)

overcoat ['əuvəkəut] *n.* 外衣，大衣
It's hot today, but she is wearing an overcoat.
今天很热，但是她穿着一件长大衣。

pure [pjuə] *adj.* 纯粹的，纯洁的
Her sweater is made of pure wool.
她的毛衣是用纯羊毛做的。

rag [ræg] *n.* 破布，碎布，抹布
Look, the ragged man is dragging a wagon of rag fragments.
看，那个衣衫破烂的人拉着一货车破布碎片。

robe [rəub] *n.* 长袍，长衣，浴衣
The policeman dressed in a robe dipped in blood.
那个警察穿着溅了血的衣服。

rubber ['rʌbə] *n.* 橡皮（擦子）
adj. 橡胶的
I know you have no rubber band, but you can bind up your hair with a handkerchief.
我知道你没有皮筋，可是你可以用手绢把头发扎起来嘛！

shorts [ʃɔ:ts] *n.* 短裤
Nobody is allowed into the school in shorts.
任何人都不许穿短裤进入学校。

sole [səul] *n.* 脚底，鞋底，袜底
adj. 单独的，唯一的
His sole wish is to support his son for university.
他唯一的愿望是能供儿子上大学。

sweater ['swetə] *n.* 厚运动衫，毛线衫
Her mother knit her a new sweater before winter.
在冬天到来之前，她妈妈给她织了一件新毛衣。

textile ['tekstail] *n.* 纺织品；*adj.* 纺织的
A new textile emerged in the market.
一种新织物出现在市场上。

texture ['tekstʃə] *n.* 质地，手感，口感，组织，结构，纹理，特点
Cotton fabric has a pleasant texture and is very comfortable.
棉布的手感很好，而且也很舒适。

thermal ['θə:ml] *adj.* 热的，由热造成的，保暖的
This thermal underwear is in a high quality.
这件保暖内衣质量很好。

thick [θik] *adj.* 厚的，密的，浓的
My thick clothing made me tired when climing the mountain.
爬山时，我的厚衣使我感到不负重荷。

考点：through thick and thin 不顾艰难险阻，在任何情况下

tie [tai] *n.* 领带，联系；*vt.* 系，打结
vi. 不分胜负
His tie often does not match with his suit.
他的领带与他的西装总是不(相)配。

考点：tie down 限制，牵制；tie up 拴住，阻碍；tie...to... 把……拴在

uniform ['ju:nifɔ:m] *adj.* 一样的；*n.* 制服
He hardly wears the uniform at work.
工作时间他都不怎么穿制服。

veil [veil] *n.* 面纱，面罩，遮蔽物
She raised her veil to see what happened outside.
她掀起面罩看外面发生什么事。

🖱 考点：draw a veil over 避而不谈，隐瞒

wallet ['wɔlit] *n.* 钱包，皮夹子
I lost my wallet on my way to work.
在上班路上我把钱包丢了。

woollen ['wulən] *adj.* 羊毛制的，毛线的
My mum bought me a pretty woollen sweater.
妈妈为我买了一件漂亮的羊毛衫。

衣 设计制作 ✎

needle ['ni:dl] *n.* 针，缝补，编织针
Can I borrow your needle? Since my socks are broken.
你的针能借我用一下吗？我的袜子破了。

patch [pætʃ] *n.* 补钉，碎片；*vt.* 补缀
My trousers need a patch on the keen.
我的裤子膝盖上需要打个补丁。

🖱 考点：patch up 解决（争吵、麻烦等），
修补

pocket ['pɔkit] *n.* 衣袋；*adj.* 袖珍的
There is a hole on his pocket and the coin dropped on the ground from it.
他的口袋上有个洞，硬币就是从那里掉下去的。

ribbon ['ribən] *n.* 缎带，丝带，带
The dress which embellished with lace and ribbons is very beautiful.
那件有花边和丝带的连衣裙真的很漂亮。

rip [rip] *n.* 裂口，裂缝；*vi.&vt.* 扯破，撕坏
I think you should rip the cover off the box first.
我认为你首先应当把这个盒子的封套扯掉。

🖱 考点：rip apart 把……扯破，把……弄得
凌乱不堪；rip off 撕掉

scissors ['sizəz] *n.* 剪刀，剪子
Don't cut the hard thing, or you'll blunt the scissors.
别剪硬东西，否则你会把剪刀弄钝的。

sew [səu] *n.* 缝制；*vi.* 缝纫
Mother sewed a frill on the bottom of the blouse and it looks much beautiful now.
妈妈在衬衫的下摆缝了条褶皱，它现在看起来漂亮多了。

🖱 考点：sew up 缝合，使万无一失

strap [stræp] *n.* 带子；*vt.* 捆扎
The child's trousers were held on by an elastic strap.
这个小孩的裤子是用一根松紧带系着的。

stripe [straip] *n.* 条纹，条子
Lily has a lovely red dress with a hair stripe.
莉莉有一条好看的细条纹红色裙子。

tailor ['teilə] *n.* 裁缝；*vt.* 裁制衣服
The tailor cuts me a dress according to my measurement.
裁缝按照我的身材给我做了一条裙子。

thread [θred] *n.* 线，丝，螺纹，头绪
You need to snip off the end of a thread at last.
最后你得剪去线头。

typical ['tipikəl] *adj.* 典型的，代表性的
This building was a typical feature of the Rome period.
这个建筑是罗马时期的代表。

🖱 考点：be typical of 是……的特点，不出
所料

weave [wi:v] *vt.* 织，编；*vi.* 纺织
Better weave nets than covet fish.
临渊羡鱼不如退而结网。

alter ['ɔ:ltə] *n.* 祭坛
vt. 改做，改变，变更
I have to alter the wording of this text.
我得改一下这篇文章的措辞。

衣 颜色

black [blæk] *adj.* 黑色的，黑暗的

How about the black sweater?
那件黑色的毛衣怎么样？

blue [blu:] *n.* 蓝色；*adj.* 蓝色的

I like the blue roses most.
我最喜欢蓝色的玫瑰花（蓝色妖姬）。

🔍 考点：out of the blue 出乎意料地，突然

brown [braun] *n.* 褐色，棕色

The man with a brown hair seems to be waiting for you.
那个褐色头发的男子似乎在等你。

color ['kʌlə] *n.* 颜色，彩色，颜料

Every color in the spectrum stands for a meaning.
光谱中的每种颜色都代表了一层含义。

dark [dɑːk] *adj.* 暗的，黑色的

The car moved at a crawl in the dark.
汽车在黑暗中缓慢移动。

golden ['gəuldən] *adj.* 金色的，极好的

I have seen the film of "On Golden Pond" last year.
去年我就看过了"金色池塘"这部电影。

🔍 考点：golden与gold的区别：golden也
　　　　有"金制的"意思，但原则上gold
　　　　指"金制的"，golden常
　　　　指"金黄色的"。

pink [piŋk] *adj.* 粉红色的；*n.* 粉红色

I think pink curtain is better, for it can impart a certain elegance to the room.
我认为粉色的好，它能为房间增添几分雅致。

tan [tæn] *n.* 棕褐色，黝黑
　　　　adj. 棕褐色的
　　　　vi.&vt. 晒黑，晒成棕黑色，
　　　　　　　　鞣（革），<俚>痛打

She spends all her spare time on the beach so she can get a tan.
她一有空就待在沙滩上，因此她的皮肤被晒成棕褐色。

purple ['pəːpl] *n.* 紫色；*adj.* 紫的

Purple is quite in fashion this year.
紫色在今年很流行。

vivid ['vivid] *adj.* 生动的，鲜艳的

I saw a sunset with vivid coloring.
我看到了一轮绚丽的夕阳。

衣 清洗打理

laundry ['lɔːndri] *n.* 洗衣店，洗衣，要洗的
　　　　　　　　　　衣服

Please send these clothes to the laundry as soon as possible.
请尽快把这些衣服送到洗衣店去洗。

neat [niːt] *adj.* 整洁的，利索的，熟练的

Staying in the neat room, he felt relaxed and comfortable.
待在整洁的房间里，他感到既放松又舒服。

polish ['pɔliʃ] *vt.* 磨光，使优美

Don't polish your glasses with a handkerchief.
不要用手帕擦拭眼镜。

soak [səuk] *vt.* 浸，泡；*vi.* 浸泡

You can use a paper towel to soak up the water on your book.
你可以用纸巾把你书上的水吸干。

🔍 考点：soak up 吸收，摄取
　　　　be soaked in 沉浸在……中

spot [spɔt] *vt.* 认出，发现，玷污
　　　　n. 点，斑点，地点

America is the spot they have been longing for all the time.
美国是他们向往已久的地方。

🔍 考点：on the spot 在场，立即
　　　　spot on 恰好地，准确地

shrink [ʃriŋk] *vi.* 收缩，缩小，退缩

He did not shrink from the personal exertions required.
这个人对他应尽的个人努力是不会畏缩不前的。

考点: shrink from (doing) sth. 畏缩不敢做

真题

The advertisement says this material doesn't _____ in the wash, but it does.
A) dissolve   B) contract
C) slim   D) shrink

详 解: 选D。题意为: 广告说这种料子洗涤时不缩水, 但是实际上缩水了。A) dissolve意思是"溶解"; B) contract 意思是"(尺寸的)缩短, 压缩"; C) slim意思是"变苗条, 减肥"; D) shrink意思是"收缩, 起皱"。

(CET-4 2003.6)

sort [sɔ:t] *n.* 种类, 类别; *vt.* 整理
Can't you sort the goods on the bed?
你难道不能整理一下床上的物品吗?

考点: of sorts / of a sort 马马虎虎的, 较差的; out of sorts 身体不适, 精神不佳; sort of 有几分, 有那么点; sort out 整理, 解决

stain [stein] *vt.* 沾污, 给……着色
n. 污迹
Oil should take that stain out of your shoes.
油可洗去你鞋上的污迹。

tangle ['tæŋgl] *vt.* 使缠结, 使纠缠
I didn't know what I was saying because the bad news tangled my thoughts terribly.
我都不知道自己在说些什么, 这个坏消息使我的思想混乱极了。

考点: tangle with 与……争吵, 与……有纠葛

衣 穿衣打扮

clothe [kləuð] *vt.* 给……穿衣服
The young mother is busy with clothing her baby.
那个年轻的母亲在忙着给她的宝贝穿衣服。

comb [kəum] *n.* 梳子; *vt.* 梳理
The expensive comb bought abroad was broken, which made the girl unhappy.
那把从国外买回来的昂贵梳子断了, 这让女孩很不开心。

daily ['deili] *n.* 日报; *adj.* 每日的
When my mother went to France for travel, one of my friends there arranged my mother's daily life for me.
妈妈去法国旅游的时候, 那里的一个朋友帮我安排了妈妈的日常生活。

decent ['di:snt] *adj.* 正派的, 体面的
We all want to live a decent life.
我们都想过体面的生活。

loosen ['lu:sn] *vt.* 解开, 使松弛
Can you help me loosen the lid of this jar?
你能帮我把这个瓶盖打开吗?

mirror ['mirə] *n.* 镜子, 反射镜, 写照
vt. 反映, 反射
If we put a mirror in our room, the reflection will make it brighter.
如果我们在房间里放面镜子, 反射现象会让我们的房间更明亮。

naked ['neikid] *adj.* 裸体的, 无遮蔽的, 直率的
In my dream, I saw a naked child run towards me.
在梦里我看见一个裸体的孩子向我跑来。

pair [pɛə] *n.* 一对; *vi.* 成对, 配对
I have been knitting a pair of gloves for about two months.
我近两个月一直在织手套。

pierce [piəs] *vt.* 刺穿; *vi.* 穿入
Nowadays more and more girls have their ears pierced for earrings.
如今越来越多的女孩子为了戴耳环而穿耳洞。

pretty ['priti] *adj.* 漂亮的，标致的

The girl was very pretty, but I really was shocked by her foul words.
女孩很漂亮，可她的粗话让我感到震惊。

---

purse [pə:s] *n.* 钱包，小钱袋，手袋

He pushed me suddenly and tried to snatch my purse.
他猛地推了我一下，试图抢我的包。

---

rub [rʌb] *vt.* 摩擦，擦；*vi.* 摩擦

Please rub out these words and write them again.
请把这些字擦掉重写。

🔍 **考点**：rub it in 反复提起令人不愉快的事

---

shave [ʃeiv] *n.* 刮脸；*vt.* 剃，刮；*vi.* 修面

The girl shaved the hair on legs.
女孩刮掉了腿毛。

🔍 **考点**：a close shave 侥幸脱险

---

undo [ˌʌndu] *vi.* 解开，打开，取消

You had better undo this computational facility.
最好是删除计算机的这项功能。

---

wear [wɛə] *vt.* 穿着，戴，磨损

I hope one day I can wear the coat designed by myself.
我希望有一天我能穿上自己设计的大衣。

真题

This kind of glasses manufactured by experienced craftsmen _____ comfortably.
A) is worn   B) wears
C) wearing   D) are worn

详　解：选B。题意为：由经验丰富的匠人做成的眼镜戴着很舒服。本题考查wear的习惯用法。英语中有不少动词与well等副词连用，其主动形式表示被动意义。

(CET-4 2000.1)

---

perfume ['pə:fju:m] *n.* 香味，芳香，香料

The aroma of perfume penetrated the whole room.
满屋子散发着香水的香味。

---

powder ['paudə] *n.* 粉末，药粉，火药

The black powder is a kind of agent which can kill the mosquitos.
那种黑色粉末是种能杀死蚊子的化学药剂。

---

curl [kə:l] *n.* 卷毛，螺旋；*vi.* 卷曲

She likes to keep the hair in curl.
她喜欢让头发卷着。

🔍 **考点**：curl up 卷起，使卷曲

---

dye [dai] *n.* 染料，染色；*vt.* 染

That naughty boy dyed the white curtain colorful.
那个调皮的小男孩把白窗帘染得五颜六色。

🔍 **考点**：dye的现在分词与过去式（分词）分别是dyeing，dyed。

---

jewel ['dʒu:əl] *n.* 宝石，宝石饰物

The businessman guaranteed the jewel to be genuine.
那个商人保证这珠宝是真的。

🔍 **考点**：jewel是"宝石，宝石饰物"个体；jewellery是"珠宝，珠宝饰物"的总称，不可数名词。

---

necklace ['neklis] *n.* 项链，项圈

This luxury necklace is surplus to requirements.
这款奢侈项链供过于求。

---

ornament ['ɔ:nəmənt] *n.* 装饰物，装饰

The thief stole some ornaments and money from that mansion.
这个小偷从那所豪宅偷了一些饰物和钱财。

---

pearl [pə:l] *n.* 珍珠，珍珠母

My English teacher wears a pearl necklace today.
今天我的英语老师戴了一条珍珠项链。

---

seashell ['si:ʃel] *n.* 海贝，贝壳

The little girl walked along the beach and collected seashells.
那个小女孩沿海滩拾贝壳。

---

shell [ʃel] *n.* 壳，贝壳，炮弹

Tiny shells were spangled on that woman's dress.
那个妇女的礼服上装饰着小贝壳。

---

valuable ['væljuəbl] *adj.* 值钱的，有价值的

Please take the valuable things with you all the time.
请随身携带贵重物品。

🔍 **考点**：invaluable无价的，非常宝贵的valueless没有价值的

fantastic [fæn'tæstik] *adj.* 极好的，难以相信的，奇异的

She wore a fantastic dress in the party.
她在聚会上穿了一件惹眼的连衣裙。

---

fancy ['fænsi] *n.* 想象力，设想，爱好

I think most of girls like fancy clothes.
我认为大部分女孩子都喜欢穿新奇的服装。

🖱 考点：take a fancy to 喜欢上，爱上

衣 **流行时尚** ✏

current ['kʌrənt] *adj.* 当前的，通用的

His perspicacious remark about current events was well received by readers.
他对时事敏锐的评论得到了读者的好评。

真题

People's expectations about the future may have more influence on their sense of well-being than their ___ state does.
A) primitive　　B) modern
C) current　　　D) initial

详 解：选C。题意为：人们对未来的期望要比目前的生活状态给予他们的幸福感更有感染力。A) primitive意思是"原始的，远古的"；B) modern意思是"近代的，现代的"；C) current意思是"当前的"；D) initial意思是"最初的，原始的"。

(CET-4 2006.6)

---

fashionable ['fæʃənəbl] *adj.* 流行的，时髦的

The hair style becomes fashionable for a time.
那种发型风靡一时。

---

mainstream ['meinstri:m] *n.* 方式，样式，流行

In this city, bicycle is the mainstream of transport.
在这个城市，自行车是最重要的交通工具。

---

modern ['mɔdən] *adj.* 现代的，近代的，时髦的

They bought a new modern machine, and the production of their factory goes steadily upward.
他们买进一台新的现代化机器，所以工厂的生产量稳步上升。

---

new [nju:] *adj.* 新的，新近出现的

When will the new legislation begin to be enforced?
新法规何时开始实施？

---

newly ['nju:li] *adv.* 新近，最近

Have you seen the product that they have newly developed?
你见到他们最近开发出的新产品了吗？

---

popular ['pɔpjulə] *adj.* 民众的，流行的

TV has displaced movies as our most popular form of entertainment nowadays.
现在电视取代了电影的地位，成了我们最为普遍的娱乐方式。

---

present ['preznt] *n.* 目前，礼物；*adj.* 现在的；*vt.* 赠送，介绍，提出

I'm discontented with my present wages.
我对于目前的工资不满。

---

prevail [pri'veil] *vi.* 胜，优胜，流行

Suddenly the tide turned and the unfortunate prevailed.
突然之间情势改变了，弱者占了优势。

---

recent ['ri:snt] *adj.* 最近，新近

The famous editor was revising what he had written in recent days.
这个著名的编辑正在修改他最近所写的东西。

---

recently ['ri:səntli] *adv.* 最近，新近

Recently a new law passed which forbids smoking in public.
最近通过了一项禁止在公共场合吸烟的新法规。

---

style [stail] *n.* 风格，文体，式样

The style of this author is often obvious.
这位作者的文风常常很显著。

🖱 考点：in style 不过时的，时髦的

---

tide [taid] *n.* 潮，潮汐，潮流

The adverse tide was strong in those years.
那时这股逆流是十分强大的。

🖱 考点：tide over 使渡过（困难时期）

tendency ['tendənsi] *n.* 趋向，趋势，倾向

There is a growing tendency among them to accept this child.
他们渐渐倾向于接受这个孩子。

trend [trend] *n.* 倾向；*vi.* 伸向，倾向

Let's look the new trend of affairs.
让我们来看一看事情的新趋势吧。

真题

Crime is increasing worldwide, and there is every reason to be believe the ____will continue into the next decade.
A) pace   B) trend
C) schedule   D) emergency

详 解：选B。题意为：全球犯罪现象在增加，而且有理由相信这种趋势会延续到未来十年。A) pace 意思是"步伐"；B) trend意思是"（事物发展的）趋势"；C) schedule意思是"日程，计划表"；D) emergency意思是"紧急情况"。

(CET-4 2003.6)

up-to-date [ˌʌptəˈdeit] *adj.* 直到最近的，现代的

They plan to establish an up-to-date factory.
他们打算建一座现代化的工厂。

nowadays ['nauədeiz] *adv.* 现今，现在

Nowadays there are more and more people having the orthopedics.
现在做整形手术的人越来越多了。

衣 挑选试穿

loose [lu:s] *adj.* 松的，宽松的，不精确的，散漫的

After giving birth to her daughter, she became fat and had to wear loose clothes.
生了女儿后她胖了，于是不得不穿上宽松的衣服。

考点：break loose 松开了，（动物）跑掉了

measurement ['meʒəmənt] *n.* 衡量，测量，尺寸

My brother's waist measurement is 40 inches.
我哥哥的腰围是40英尺。

neither ['ni:ðə] *adj.* （两者）都不的

When something is neutral, it is neither acid nor alkaline.
中性的东西既非酸性也非碱性。

考点：neither...nor... 既不……也不……（后面的谓语动词用单数）

nor [nɔ:] *conj.* 也不，不

My father neither smokes nor drinks.
我爸爸既不抽烟也不喝酒。

option ['ɔpʃən] *n.* 选择，选择权

They have no option but to do so.
他们除了这样做以外别无选择。

考点：at option 随意

optional ['ɔpʃənəl] *adj.* 可以任意选择的

You needn't have this radio in your new car; it's an optional extra.
你不必非要为你的新车配这台收音机，它只是一个额外的选择。

or [ɔ:] *conj.* 或，否则，即

Which skirt do you like, the green one or the red one?
你喜欢哪件短裙，是绿色的还是红色的?

prefer [priˈfə:] *vt.* 宁可，宁愿

I prefer sightseeing to staying at home playing computer games.
比起在家打游戏，我喜欢观光旅游。

preferable ['prefərəbl] *adj.* 更可取的，更好的

The pink T-shirt is preferable to the yellow one.
那件粉红色的T恤要比黄色的那件好。

select ['silekt] *vi.&vt.* 选择，挑选

My teacher selected a particularly pleasing form from his sketches.
我的老师从草稿图中选了一个特别满意的图形。

selection [si'lekʃən] *n.* 选择，挑选，精选物

The short-answer test is a kind of compromise between the composition and selection types.
简答题是作文题和选择题折中的产物。

sensible ['sensəbl] *adj.* 可感觉得到的，明智的

The seriously wounded soldier was speechless but still sensible.
那个受了重伤的士兵不能说话但仍有知觉。

preference ['prefərəns] *n.* 偏爱，优先，优先权

This kind of birds has a preference for hot weather.
这种鸟喜欢热的天气。

真题

The findings paint a picture of the shopping habits of consumers, plus their motivation and _____.

A) possessions　　B) possibilities
C) privileges　　　D) preferences

详　解：选D。题意为：这些发现描绘了一幅关于消费者购物习惯、动机和偏好的独特画面。A) possession 意思是"所有，拥有"；B) possibility 意思是"可能性"；C) privilege 意思是"特权，特别待遇"；D) preference 意思是"偏爱，有限选择"。

(CET-4 2006.6)

choose [tʃuːz] *vt.* 选择，挑选，情愿

Of course you can choose to post the check to the payee.
当然，你也可以选择把支票寄给收款人。

衣 砍价退货

discount ['diskaunt] *n.* 折扣

I bought this umbrella at 30% discount.
这把伞我是7折买的。

price [prais] *n.* 价格，价钱，代价

The mother was disturbed to find that the toy's price was exorbitant for the size of her purse.
那位母亲看到玩具的价钱她付不起时，心里不安起来。

考点：at any price 无论如何，不惜任何代价

claim [kleim] *vt.* 声称，主张，索取

He claimed that he lost his diamond.
他声称他的钻石丢了。

考点：lay claim to 声称对……有权利

purchase ['pəːtʃəs] *n.* 买，购买；*vt.* 买

My company contracted with an electronics factory for the purchase of their electronic instruments.
我们公司与一家电子厂签约购买他们的电子仪器。

reasonable ['riːznəbl] *adj.* 合情合理的，公道的

Look at its superb quality; this price is quite reasonable.
看看它的高质量，这个价钱很合理了。

rise [raiz] *vi.&n.* 起立，升起，上涨

Price control is a good method to damp down the general rise in prices.
价格控制是控制物价普通上涨的好方法。

考点：give rise to 引起，导致
rise above 克服，不受……的影响
rise up 起义，起来

value ['væljuː] *n.* 价值，价格；*vt.* 评价

Quarrel has no value at all in preventing him smoking.
争吵对于阻止他吸烟没有任何作用。

考点：value for money 货真价实

receipt [ri'siːt] *n.* 收条，收据

If you can't produce the receipt, we can't take goods back.
如果你不能提供收据，我们无法予以退货。

standard ['stændəd] *n.* 标准；*adj.* 标准的

A product like this is considered below standard.
这样的产品被认为是不合格的。

食 厨具设备

barrel ['bærəl] *n.* 桶，圆筒，枪管

Susan, bring that wooden barrel to me.
苏珊，把那个木桶拿给我。

basin ['beisn] *n.* 盆，洗脸盆，盆地

Robert took off the dirty clothes and placed them in the basin.

罗伯特把脏衣服脱下来放在盆里。

---

basket [bɑ:skit] *n.* 篮，篓，筐

The little girl was too young to carry a basket of peaches.

那个小女孩太小了，拎不起来一篮子桃。

---

boiler ['bɔilə] *n.* 锅炉，汽锅，热水器

When you enter the boiler room in the summer, what you can only see is vapor.

夏天的时候当你走进锅炉房，你所能看到的全部是蒸汽。

---

bowl [bəul] *n.* 碗，钵，碗状物

This kind of abluent can remove oil stain from the bowls and plates.

这种洗涤剂能清除碗盘上的油渍。

---

chopsticks ['tʃɔpstiks] *n.* 筷子

The boy is teaching his American friend carefully how to use chopsticks.

那个男孩正在认真地教他的美国朋友如何使用筷子。

---

cup [kʌp] *n.* 杯子，（一）杯，奖杯

She drank two cups of beer on an empty stomach and she felt unwell now.

她空腹喝了两杯啤酒，现在感觉很不舒服。

---

cupboard ['kʌbəd] *n.* 碗柜，碗碟橱，食橱

You'd better lock the cupboard, or the baby will open it and steal the biscuits.

你最好把橱柜锁上，不然孩子会打开偷饼干吃。

---

fork [fɔ:k] *n.* 餐叉，叉，分叉

He stabbed the fruit with his fork.

他用叉子叉水果。

---

furnace ['fə:nis] *n.* 炉子，熔炉，鼓风炉

Most people complained this meeting room's like a furnace.

大部分人都抱怨这个会议室热得像火炉一样。

---

jar [dʒɑ:] *n.* 罐子，坛子，广口瓶

He fashioned the clay into a jar for his wife's gift.

他用黏土做成一个陶土罐子作为送给妻子的礼物。

---

lid [lid] *n.* 盖子，盖，囊盖

My father carefully tapped the lid down.

爸爸小心地将盖子敲紧了。

---

kettle ['ketl] *n.* 水壶，水锅

The baby upset the kettle on the table and the hot soup burned his hand.

婴儿打翻了桌子上的水壶，滚热的汤烫到了他的手。

---

mug [mʌg] *n.* 大杯

Bill swilled the pills down with a mug of water.

比尔就着一大杯水，把药丸冲了下去。

---

oven ['ʌvən] *n.* 炉，灶，烘箱

What are you baking in the oven? I seem to smell something burnt.

你在烤箱里烤什么？我好像闻到什么东西烧焦了。

---

pail [peil] *n.* 桶，提桶

The woman poured some water into the pail.

那个女人把一些水倒进提桶里。

---

pan [pæn] *n.* 平底锅，盘子

Knowing that you like eggs, she specially fried a large pan of that for you.

知道你喜欢吃鸡蛋，她特地为你煎了一大锅。

---

plate [pleit] *n.* 板，片，盘；*vt.* 电镀

You broke the plate on purpose; I know you didn't want to wash it.

你是故意摔坏盘子的，我知道你不想洗。

---

pot [pɔt] *n.* 锅，壶，罐，盆

When I entered the room, I saw a pot of water bubbling on the range.

一进屋，我就看见一壶水在炉子上沸腾着。

---

saucer ['sɔ:sə] *n.* 茶托，浅碟

She settled the cup into the saucer after drinking up the coffee.

她喝光了咖啡，把杯子放在托盘上。

---

stove [stəuv] *n.* 炉，火炉，电炉

The water is boiling on the stove.

水在炉子上沸腾着。

食品

apple ['æpl] *n.* 苹果，苹果树

Susan, bring me some apples, please.
苏珊，请给我拿些苹果来。

bacon ['beikən] *n.* 咸肉，熏肉

This restaurant offers pork chops, ham, bacon and sausage.
这家餐馆提供猪排、火腿、熏肉和香肠。

bean [bi:n] *n.* 豆，蚕豆

Nowadays bean curd is regarded as a healthy diet.
现在豆腐被认为是有益于健康的食物。

beef [bi:f] *n.* 牛肉，菜牛

I bought the beef at the butcher's shop.
我在肉铺买的牛肉。

berry ['beri] *n.* 果（草莓等）

These animals feed mainly on berries when winter comes.
冬天来临的时候，这些动物主要以浆果为食物。

biscuit ['biskit] *n.* （英）饼干，（美）软饼

I like chocolate biscuit very much.
我非常喜欢吃巧克力饼干。

bread [bred] *n.* 面包，食物，粮食

It tastes better if you spread the jam on your bread.
把果酱涂到你的面包上，这样味道会好一点。

bucket ['bʌkit] *n.* 水桶，吊桶，铲斗

Armed with a bucket and a mop, I started cleaning the room.
拿着水桶和抹布，我开始打扫房间。

butter ['bʌtə] *n.* 黄油，奶油

First you have to blend the butter and sugar together.
首先，你必须把奶油和糖混合在一起。

cabbage ['kæbidʒ] *n.* 洋白菜，卷心菜

Do you like eating cabbages?
你喜欢吃洋白菜吗？

cake [keik] *n.* 饼，糕，蛋糕

All kinds of cakes were displayed in the shopping window.
各式各样的糕点陈列在橱窗里。

candy ['kændi] *n.* 糖果，砂糖结晶

The little girl snatched the candy from her mother's hand.
小女孩从妈妈的手中抓去了糖果。

carrot ['kærət] *n.* 胡萝卜

The rabbit likes eating carrots.
兔子爱吃胡萝卜。

cereal ['siəriəl] *n.* 麦片粥，谷类食物 *adj.* 谷类的，谷物的

Those peasants barter cereal for cloth and fruits.
那些农民用谷物换布和水果。

cheese [tʃi:z] *n.* 乳酪，干酪

Do you know the book *Who Moves My Cheese*?
你知道《谁动了我的奶酪》这本书吗？

cherry ['tʃeri] *n.* 樱桃，樱桃树

I want to eat a cake with several cherries on.
我喜欢吃点缀有几颗樱桃的蛋糕。

chicken ['tʃikin] *n.* 小鸡，小鸟，鸡肉

Who ate the chicken I cooked in the casserole?
谁吃了我砂锅里炖的鸡肉？

chip [tʃip] *n.* 薄片，片屑，芯片；*vi.&vt.* 凑份子，切（成碎片），形成（缺口）

She had a hamburger and a portion of chip for her breakfast.
她早餐吃了一个汉堡包和一份炸薯条。

chocolate ['tʃɔkəlit] *n.* 巧克力，巧克力糖

I read information on the label before deciding which chocolate to buy.
我先看巧克力标签上的说明再决定买哪种。

corn [kɔ:n] *n.* 谷物，（英）小麦

They planted some red corns and yellow corns.
他们种了一些红玉米和黄玉米。

cream [kri:m] *n.* 奶油，乳脂，奶油色

Would you buy some cream for me when you go shopping?
你去逛街时能否给我买一些乳酪？

crust [krʌst] *n.* 面包皮，硬外皮，表层，外皮

Could you cut the crusts off the bread, please?

可以把面包皮给切了吗？

cucumber ['kju:kʌmbə] *n.* 黄瓜
The bald man is as cool as a cucumber in the rain.
那个秃顶的男人在雨中不慌不忙，泰然自若。

dessert [di'zə:t] *n.* 甜食，点心
I want some pudding for dessert.
我想吃一些布丁作为点心。

drink [driŋk] *n.* 饮料；*vt.* 饮，喝
After one-day rush work, I want to have a drink and relax myself.
一天紧张的工作之后，我想喝一杯放松放松。

eggplant ['egplɑ:nt] *n.* 茄子
When we take photos, we like to cry "eggplant" loudly.
照相的时候我们喜欢大声喊"茄子"。

flour ['flauə] *n.* 面粉，粉，粉状物质
"Blend the water and flour." Mom required.
"把水和面粉和在一起。"妈妈说道。

gum [gʌm] *n.* 口香糖，树胶
Many people like to chew gum in public.
许多人喜欢在公共场合嚼口香糖。

hotdog ['hɔt,dɔg] *n.* 热狗
Xiao Ming likes sandwiches and hotdogs.
小明喜欢吃三明治和热狗。

jam [dʒæm] *n.* 果酱；*vt.* 使塞满，使堵塞
Cover the jam! It's sure to split out.
盖上果酱瓶！要不准得洒出来。

lemon ['lemən] *n.* 柠檬，柠檬树，柠檬色
We can't find any lemons in this supermarket.
我们没能在这家超市找到柠檬。

loaf [ləuf] *n.* 一条面包，一个面包
vi. 游荡，闲逛
Could you get a loaf of French bread when you go to the bakery?
你去面包房时能帮我带一个法式面包吗？

meat [mi:t] *n.* 肉，肉类
Meat spoils more quickly without preservatives.
不加防腐剂，肉会坏得快。

melon ['melən] *n.* 瓜，甜瓜
Of all the fruits, I like melons best.
在所有水果中，我最喜欢甜瓜。

mushroom ['mʌʃrum] *n.* 蘑菇，菌类植物
We all know that some mushrooms are edible.
我们都知道有些蘑菇是可食用的。

mutton ['mʌtn] *n.* 羊肉
Mutton can substitute for pork in this recipe.
在这个食谱中，可用羊肉代替猪肉。

nut [nʌt] *n.* 坚果，干果，螺母
These nuts are delicious, but it's hard to crack them.
这些坚果很好吃，但弄掉它们的壳有点困难。

onion ['ʌnjən] *n.* 洋葱，洋葱头
I hate the soup with too much onion.
我讨厌在汤中放太多洋葱。

orange ['ɔrindʒ] *n.* 桔子，橙（树），柑（树），橙色的
I like to drink the concentrated orange juice.
我喜欢喝浓缩桔子汁。

pea [pi:] *n.* 豌豆，豌豆属植物
The princess couldn't fall asleep because of the pea on the bed.
床上的那颗豌豆搅得公主睡不着觉。

peach [pi:tʃ] *n.* 桃子，桃树
I am not comfortable after eating these raw peaches.
我吃了这些不熟的桃子后感觉很不舒服。

pear [pɛə] *n.* 梨子，梨树
Hebei province is known for its pears.
河北省以鸭梨而闻名。

pie [pai] *n.* （西点）馅饼
That pie your mother cooked tastes very good.
你妈妈做的那个馅饼味道不错。

pork [pɔ:k] *n.* 猪肉
How about we have pork chops for dinner tonight?
今晚我们吃猪排怎么样？

porridge ['pɔridʒ] *n.* 粥，麦片粥
You'd better have some porridge for breakfast; it's good for your stomach.

你早餐最好喝点粥，这对你的胃有好处。

potato [pə'teitəu] *n.* 马铃薯，土豆

Potatoes are planted in every vegetable garden in this area.
在这个地区，家家户户的菜园子里都种有土豆。

pudding ['pudiŋ] *n.* 布丁

She would like some pudding.
她想吃些布丁。

radish ['rædiʃ] *n.* 小萝卜

To my surprise, the radish has gone spongy.
让我吃惊的是，这个萝卜已经糠了。

sausage ['sɔsidʒ] *n.* 香肠，腊肠

They have garlic sausage and some bread for lunch.
他们午餐吃大蒜香肠肉加面包。

steak [steik] *n.* 牛排，肉排，鱼排

I'd like some steak and bread.
我要牛排和面包。

toast [təust] *n.* 烤面包；*vt.* 烘，烤

My mother likes to slather jam on toast.
妈妈喜欢在吐司上涂果酱。

watermelon ['wɔːtə,melən] *n.* 西瓜

Watermelon is one of my favourite fruits.
西瓜是我喜欢的水果之一。

yoghurt ['jəugəːt] *n.* 乳酸酪，酸奶

Which brand of yoghurt do you like best?
你最喜欢哪个牌子的酸奶？

pepper ['pepə] *n.* 胡椒，胡椒粉

Don't add any pepper to the dishes, since she is hypersensitive to it.
她对胡椒粉过敏，不要在菜里放了。

salt [sɔːlt] *n.* 盐，盐类；*vi.* 加盐于

My grandmother told me that salt can preserve food from decay.
我外婆告诉我盐能防止食物腐烂。

🔍 **考点**：worth one's salt 胜任的，称职的

sauce [sɔːs] *n.* 调味汁，酱汁

People from all over the country come to the small restaurant just for the unique sauce.

全国各地的人都来这家小餐馆，仅仅为了品尝这里风味独特的调味汁。

vinegar ['vinigə] *n.* 醋

Put in just a dash of vinegar; it will be very sour.
稍放一点点醋就会很酸。

 饮料

alcohol ['ælkəhɔl] *n.* 酒精，乙醇，含酒精的
饮料

Drinking too much alcohol does harm to the liver.
饮酒过多对肝有害。

beer [biə] *n.* 啤酒

Please fetch me a can of beer.
给我拿过来一罐啤酒。

brandy ['brændi] *n.* 白兰地酒

How about drinking some brand?
喝点白兰地怎么样？

café [kæ'fei] *n.* 咖啡，咖啡馆，小餐厅

Would you like a cup of café?
来杯咖啡怎么样？

coca-cola ['kəukə'kəulə] *n.* 可口可乐(财富
500强公司之一，
总部所在地美
国，主要经营
饮料)

Coca-cola is a household trade name throughout the world.
可口可乐是个全世界都家喻户晓的商标名。

coffee ['kɔfi] *n.* 咖啡，咖啡茶

When I sat down, the waiter served me a cup of coffee.
我坐下时，服务员给我端上了一杯咖啡。

dairy ['dɛəri] *n.* 牛奶场，乳制品

We bought milk at the dairy.
我们在奶品店买牛奶。

ice-cream ['aiskriːm] *n.* 冰激凌

Children always like eating ice-cream.
孩子们总是爱吃冰激凌。

juice [dʒuːs] *n.* （水果等）汁，液

If there is a bottle of cool juice, it will be much better.
如果能有一瓶冰凉的果汁就再好不过了。

liquor [ˈlikə] *n.* 酒，溶液，液剂

His wife divorced with him because he was always in liquor.
他妻子跟他离婚是因为他经常喝得醉醺醺的。

milk [milk] *n.* 乳，牛奶
　　　　　　vt. 挤（奶），榨取

Please help me turn off the gas; the milk will boil over.
请帮我把煤气关掉，牛奶要溢出来了。

soda [ˈsəudə] *n.* 碳酸钠，纯碱，汽水

Soda water is her favorite drink.
苏打水是她最喜欢的饮品。

 分量

bottle [ˈbɔtl] *n.* 瓶，酒瓶，一瓶

Please give me a bottle of wine.
请给我拿瓶酒。

handful [ˈhændful] *n.* 一把，少数，一小撮

Only a handful of students are late for school.
只有一小部分学生迟到。

heap [hiːp] *n.* （一）堆，大量

A heap of equipment is on the table.
桌子上堆了一堆东西。

lack [læk] *n.* 缺乏，无；*vt.* 缺少，没有
　　　　　vi. 缺少，不足，没有

What does the successful man lack?
成功人士缺少的是什么？

考点：for lack of 由于缺乏

liter [ˈliːtə] *n.* 升（容量单位）

According to the newspaper, this system can desalinate up to 300 liters of brackish water a day.
根据报纸上说，这个系统一天可以将多达300公升的盐水去盐。

mouthful [ˈmauθˌful] *n.* 满口，一口，少量

She bit off a mouthful of the moldy bread and then spat it out immediately.
她咬了一口发霉的面包，然后立刻吐了出来。

nothing [ˈnʌθiŋ] *n.* 没有东西　*adv.* 毫不

I know nothing about the phase of the moon.
我对月相是一窍不通。

ounce [auns] *n.* 盎司，英两

An ounce is one sixteenth of a pound.
一盎斯是十六分之一磅。

piece [piːs] *n.* 碎片，块；*vt.* 拼合

He found a piece of fossil of an ancient man.
他发现了一块古猿人的化石。

考点：go to pieces 崩溃，垮掉
　　　pick / pull to pieces 严厉批评

pint [paint] *n.* 品脱

My sister had a pint of milk yesterday.
昨天，我妹妹喝了一品脱牛奶。

quart [ˈkwɔːt] *n.* 夸脱（＝2品脱）

Don't you know that there are two pints in a quart?
你难道不知道一夸脱是两品脱吗？

several [ˈsevərəl] *adj.* 几个，数个

The black dog gave several fierce barks then ran away.
那只黑狗汪汪叫了几声后跑开了。

sip [sip] *v.* 小口地喝；*n.* 小口的量

The man was asked to have a sip of coffee.
那人被要求喝一小口咖啡。

bit [bit] *n.* 一点，一些，小片

At last, he decided to cut down smoking bit by bit.
最终，他决定一点一点把烟戒掉。

考点：a bit 多少，有点
　　　bit by bit 一点一点地
　　　every bit 完全，从头到尾

味道

acid ['æsid] *n.* 酸；*adj.* 酸的，酸性的
Learning from the last failure, this time he treats this substance with the acid more carefully.
从上次的失败中吸取了教训，这次他更加小心地用酸来处理这种物质。

appetite ['æpitait] *n.* 食欲，胃口，欲望
The pregnant woman has a poor appetite.
那个孕妇胃口不好。

fatty ['fæti] *adj.* 油腻的，脂肪含量高的
　　　　　　 n. 胖子
It's reported that most of the obese patients have a fatty diet.
据报道，大部分有肥胖症的病人吃的食物都比较油腻。

flavour ['fleivə] *n.* 味，味道，风味
This song has a flavour of ballad.
这首歌有民歌风味。

foul [faul] *adj.* 难闻的，发臭的，肮脏的，
　　　　　　　　　 下流的
　　　　　　 vt. 弄脏，污染，对……犯规
　　　　　　 n. 犯规
It was foul of him to cheat her for marrying.
他骗她结婚，真是卑鄙。
考点：foul up 把……搞乱，把……弄糟

fresh [freʃ] *adj.* 新的，新鲜的
Fresh eggs and fresh milk are not enough.
新鲜的鸡蛋和牛奶不够了。

odour ['əudə] *n.* 气味，香气，味道
The old man's room is filled with foul odour.
那个老人的房间里充满了难闻的气味。

oily ['ɔili] *adj.* 含油的，油腻的
The man always wears an oily old pair of jeans.
那人总穿着一条沾满油污的旧牛仔裤。

smelly ['smeli] *adj.* 发出难闻气味的，有臭味的
The river was so smelly that the near residents can not stand.
附近的居民难以忍受这条河散发出的一股臭味。

sour ['sauə] *adj.* 酸的，脾气坏的
The dishes turned sour in the heat usually.
饭菜通常在高温下会变酸。

stale [steil] *adj.* 陈腐的，走了气的
Nobody likes your stale theory of education.
谁也不喜欢听你那些陈旧的教育理论。

sweet [swi:t] *adj.* 甜的，甜美的
The flower sends out one kind of sweet smell that makes us happy.
这花散发出一种令人愉快的香味。

taste [teist] *vt.* 尝，尝到；*n.* 味觉
She has rather poor taste in clothes.
她对衣服的欣赏水平相当低。
考点：taste of 有……的味道

tasty [teisti] *adj.* 美味的，可口的
These fish are really tasty. Who sent them to you?
这些鱼真好吃。谁送你的?

yummy ['jʌmi] *adj.* 味道好的，好吃的
His cooking is superb, so the food he made is yummy.
他厨艺精湛，因此他做的饭很好吃。

rotten ['rɔtn] *adj.* 腐烂的，发臭的
The disappearance of the rotten institution won't outlast most of us.
我们大多数人将看到这一腐败机构的消亡。

 农业

crop [krɔp] *n.* 农作物，庄稼，一熟
　　　　　　 vt. 剪短，修短
We should not have planted crops in such barren land.
我们本不应该在如此贫瘠的土地上种植庄稼的。
考点：crop up 突然发生，突然出现

cultivate ['kʌltiveit] *vt.* 耕，种植，培养
It is estimated that more than half of the land can't be cultivated.
据估计，一半以上的土地不能耕种。

fertile ['fə:tail] *adj.* 肥沃的，多产的

It is a pleasant fertile spot and people live happily.
那是一个富饶的地方，人们生活得很幸福。

fertilizer ['fə:ti‚laizə] *n.* 肥料

They have accumulated a large amount of river mud for fertilizer.
他们累积了大量河泥当做肥料。

fruitful ['fru:tful] *adj.* 多产的，肥沃的

Governors asserted that the work was fruitful in the meeting.
政府官员们在会议中宣布这项工作还是富有成果的。

grain [grein] *n.* 谷物，谷粒，颗粒

Corn and wheat are feed grain.
谷类、麦子都是家畜的饲料。

irrigate ['irigeit] *vt.* 灌溉，冲洗（伤口）

The villagers irrigate their crops with water from the ocean.
村民们引海水灌溉庄稼。

irrigation [‚iri'geiʃən] *n.* 灌溉

An irrigation system should be selected carefully.
要谨慎选择灌溉系统。

peasant ['pezənt] *n.* 农民

Peasants here have to go to the town to buy the agriculture implements they need.
这里的农民不得不到城镇上买他们需要的农具。

plantation [plæn'teiʃən] *n.* 种植园，栽植

Many of the earliest immigrants into the United States established large plantations.
许多早期移民美国的人都建起了大的种植园。

plough [plau] *n.* 犁；*vi.&vt.* 犁，耕

He decided to plough the field first and then sow the seeds in the ground.
他决定先犁下地，然后在地里撒种。

pluck [plʌk] *vt.* 采，摘，拉下；*n.* 拉

I feared the flower would droop and drop into the dust, so I plucked it.
我怕这朵花会萎谢，掉在尘土里，所以我把它摘了下来。

pump [pʌmp] *n.* 泵；*vt.* 用泵抽

The farmers pumped water from the river.
农民从河里抽水。

raise [reiz] *vt.* 举起，引起，提高

The new measures have helped raise farm yields steadily.
新措施有助于农业产量的稳步提高。

rake [reik] *vi.* 耙，搜索；*n.* 耙子

A bad gardener quarrels with his rake.
一名糟糕的园丁抱怨他的耙子。

reap [ri:p] *vi.&vt.* 收割，收获

The peasants are busy reaping the wheat in the field.
农民们忙着在田里割麦子。

ripen ['raipən] *vt.* 使熟；*vi.* 成熟

Their seed ripened, and soon they turned brown and shriveled up.
它们的种子熟后，不久就变枯萎了。

scatter ['skætə] *vt.* 使消散，撒，散播

He was cremated and his ashes was scattered into the sea.
他死后被火化，骨灰撒到了海里。

sow [səu] *vt.* 播（种）；*vi.* 播种

It is not yet time to sow wheat.
现在还不是播种小麦的时候。

straw [strɔ:] *n.* 稻草，麦杆吸管

They laid straw over the yard after the big harvest.
大丰收后，他们将稻草铺在院子里。

acre ['eikə] *n.* 英亩（＝6.07亩）

He gives thousands of acres farmland to a stranger.
他把成千英亩的田地给了一个陌生人。

agriculture ['ægrikʌltʃə] *n.* 农业，农艺，农学

Our country values the development of agriculture very much.
我们国家非常重视农业发展。

加工

add [æd] *vt.* 添加，附加，掺加

Add some sugar to the coffee and it will taste better.
加一些糖到咖啡里，咖啡味道会好一些。

考点：add in 添加
add on 附加，另外加上去
add up to 合计达，意味着

---

bake [beik] *vt.* 烤，烘，焙，烧硬

I love the cakes baked by mom.
我特喜欢妈妈烤的面包。

---

boil [bɔil] *vi.* 沸腾，汽化；*vt.* 煮沸

Hurry up, please! The water is boiling!
快点，水开了！

考点：boil down to 意味着，归结为
boil over 激动，发怒

---

bubble ['bʌbl] *n.* 泡；*vi.* 冒泡，沸腾

A pot of water was bubbling on the stove.
一壶水在炉上沸腾着！

---

carve [kɑ:v] *vt.* 切，把……切碎（或切成片），雕刻

The sculptor carved an angel on the wall with his knife.
雕刻家用刀子在墙上刻了一个天使。

考点：carve out 创业，发财
carve up 分割，瓜分

---

burn [bə:n] *vi.* 烧，燃烧；*n.* 烧伤

You should know that dry wood burns easily.
你应该知道干柴易燃。

考点：burn down 烧毁，火势减弱
burn out 烧光，熄灭

---

chop [tʃɔp] *vi.&vt.* 砍，劈，切细；*n.* 砍

She cut down the sapling with one chop.
她一斧子就把树苗砍倒了。

---

cook [kuk] *vt.* 烹调，煮，烧菜；*n.* 厨师

She had grown up, but she was still ignorant about cooking.
她已经长大了，可还是不会做饭。

---

crush [krʌʃ] *vt.* 压碎，碾碎，镇压

The machine is used to crush the wheat grains to flour.
这种机器用于把小麦粒压碎制成面粉。

---

cut [kʌt] *vt.* 切，割，剪，减少

He cut off the flowers at the stalk with a pair of scissors.
他用剪子连花带茎都剪下来。

---

decay [di'kei] *vi.* 腐烂，衰败；*n.* 腐烂

That corpse begins to decay.
那具尸体开始腐烂。

---

dip [dip] *vt.* 浸，蘸；*vi.* 浸一浸

He likes to dip his head into water.
他喜欢把头浸入水中。

考点：dip into 浏览，从……中取得

---

dissolve [di'zɔlv] *vt.* 使溶解，解散

The salt dissolved in the warm water.
盐在温水中溶解了。

---

drain [drein] *vt.* 排去，放水；*n.* 耗竭

Drain the spinach that I have washed through the sieve.
用笊篱把我洗过的菠菜上的水控干。

---

filter ['filtə] *vt.* 过滤；*n.* 滤纸

The filter is now ready for operation after few months' researching and producing.
经过几个月的研制，这种滤器目前即将投入运转。

---

fry [frai] *vt.* 油煎，油炸，油炒

We fried eggs for breakfast.
我们煎蛋当早餐。

---

grind [graind] *vt.* 磨（碎），磨快

He used to grind his teeth when sleeping in the night.
他总是在晚上睡觉时磨牙。

考点：grind down 折磨，压榨

---

make [meik] *n.* 品牌，类型
vt. 使，做，制造

Before I make a decision I must consult with my wife.
我必须与妻子商量，才能做出决定。

manufacture [ˌmænjuˈfæktʃə] *vt.* 制造，加工
n. 制造，产品，制造业

This factory manufactures electronic products.
这家工厂制造电子产品。

manufacturer [ˌmænjuˈfæktʃərə] *n.* 制造商，制造厂

This recent tragedy has put the manufacturers of the drug squarely in the dock.
最近这一悲惨事件的发生使药品厂商受到指控。

melt [melt] *vi.* 融化，溶解
vt. 使融化，使软化

The snow on the ground began to melt after the sun rose.
太阳出来后，地面上的雪开始融化。

考点：melted ice 融化的冰
molten steel 熔化的钢

mill [mil] *n.* 磨坊，制造厂，工厂
vi. 磨，碾

My father used to work in a limber mill.
我爸爸以前在一个锯木厂工作。

考点：factory, mill, plant, works 都有"工厂"的意思：factory 指任何生产、制造产品的地方；mill 原意是"磨坊"，尤其指轻工业方面的制造，如纺织业、面粉业、造纸业；plant 多用于电气业或机械制造的工厂；works 多用于钢铁等重工业的工厂。

mix [miks] *vt.* 使混合，混淆，调制

I experimented until I succeeded in mixing the right colour.
我不断地进行实验，直至将所需颜色调配成功。

mixture [ˈmikstʃə] *n.* 混合，混合物

The mixture is allowed to hydrate for approximately 3 minutes.
混合物需进行大约3分钟的水合反应。

peel [pi:l] *vt.* 剥（皮），削（皮）

Mother told him to peel the onions and wash them.
妈妈让他把洋葱剥去皮，再洗干净。

考点：peel of 剥掉，脱去

pinch [pintʃ] *vt.* 捏，拧，掐掉

I like to pinch my little brother's pink cheek.
我喜欢拧弟弟的粉红脸颊。

考点：at / in a pinch 必要时；feel the pinch 感到手头拮据；a pinch of 一捏，一撮

process [prəˈses] *n.* 过程，工序；*vt.* 加工

It's a long process for the formation of one's character.
人的性格的形成是一个长期的过程。

考点：in (the) process of 进行中，在……的过程中

produce [prəˈdjuːs] *vt.* 生产，产生，展现

It's amazing that the earthworms can produce antibiotic substance.
真神奇，蚯蚓可以产生抗菌物质。

productive [prəˈdʌktiv] *adj.* 生产的，丰饶的

As far as I know, he is a productive writer of detective stories.
据我所知，他是写侦探小说的多产作家。

purify [ˈpjuərifai] *vt.* 使纯净，使洁净

Distilling can be used to purify water.
通过蒸馏可以净化水。

purity [ˈpjuəriti] *n.* 纯净，纯洁，纯度

At least you must ensure the purity of our drinking water.
至少你必须确保我们的饮用水是纯净的。

raw [rɔː] *adj.* 未煮过的，未加工的

We all know that raw tomatoes can be eaten.
众所周知，西红柿可以生吃。

考点：in the raw 处在自然状态的，裸体的

refine [riˈfain] *vi.&vt.* 精炼，提纯

The author would like to refine on his work of five years ago.
作者想要把他5年前的著作修改得更完美些。

refinery [riˈfainəri] *n.* 精炼厂，提炼厂

He used to work in a sugar refinery.
他曾经在一个制糖厂工作。

roast [rəust] *vi.&vt.* 烤，炙，烘
　　　　　　 n. 烤肉，烘，烤
　　　　　　 adj. 烤过的

The dogs and cats in the yard are lying in the sun and roasting.
院子里的狗和猫躺在太阳下取暖。

---

shake [ʃeik] *vt.* 摇，使震动
　　　　　 n. 摇动

Shake the bottle before you drink the juice.
喝果汁前先把瓶子摇一摇。

🔍 **考点**：shake down 敲诈，勒索
　　　　　 shake off 抖落，摆脱
　　　　　 shake up 使改组，激励

---

slice [slais] *n.* 薄片，切片，部分

The government has devoted a larger slice of its national budget to agriculture than most other countries.
该国政府用于农业的国家预算比大多数国家都多。

---

squeeze [skwi:z] *vi.&vt.* 榨，挤，压榨

It's a tight squeeze to get eight people in that small house.
8个人住在那个小屋子里真是太挤了。

真题

The opening between the rocks was very narrow, but the boys managed to _____ through.
A) press　　　 B) squeeze
C) stretch　　 D) leap

详　解：选B。题意为：石头间的缝隙很窄，但那些孩子还是挤过去了。A) press意思是"挤压"；B) squeeze意思是"挤进（狭小的空间）"；C) stretch意思是"拉伸"；D) leap意思是"跳跃"。

(CET-4 2003.12)

---

stir [stə:] *vt.* 动，拨动，激动
His dropping out created no small stir in school.
他的辍学在学校引起了不小的轰动。

🔍 **考点**：stir up 激起，挑起

---

swell [swel] *vi.* 膨胀，隆起，增长
His ankles began to swell two days later.
两天后他的脚踝肿起来了。

wrap [ræp] *vt.* 裹，包，捆
　　　　　 n. 披肩

She had wrapped this necklace with a white handkerchief before she gave it to him.
她先把这条项链用白手绢包好然后送给了他。

🔍 **考点**：wrap in 用……将某物包起来
　　　　　 wrap up 掩饰，围好围巾

---

blend [blend] *vi.&vt.&n.* 混和

Excuse me, which blend of coffee would you like to drink?
请问你要喝哪种混合咖啡？

🔍 **考点**：blend, mix的区别：blend侧重整体的统一性；mix侧重混合物或多或少保持原来的形状、性质；blend意味着和谐，mix则意味着混乱。

🍽 **储藏**

abundant [ə'bʌndənt] *adj.* 丰富的，大量的
Don't worry. We have abundant proof of that guy's guilt.
不用担心，我们有充分的证据证明那家伙有罪。

🔍 **考点**：be abundant in... 在什么方面丰富，富于某些东西

---

barn [bɑ:n] *n.* 谷仓，牲口棚
There is a large barn in Jack's farm.
杰克家的农场有一个大谷仓。

---

preserve [pri'zə:v] *vt.* 保护，保存，腌渍
Being a Chinese, you should take care to preserve our national heritage.
作为一个中国人，你应该保护我们的民族遗产。

---

provision [prə'viʒən] *n.* 供应，预备，存粮
I don't think the provision will sustain us for this winter.
我认为这些供给根本不够我们过冬。

---

storage ['stɔridʒ] *n.* 贮藏，贮藏量
The storage of food is not enough for the whole family in winter.
粮食的储存量不够一家人过冬。

store [stɔ:] *n.* 贮藏，贮存品，商店
I'll go to pick up some odds and ends at the store.
我要到商店买些零碎的东西。

🔍 **考点：** in store 储藏着，准备着
set store by 重视，尊重

uncover [ʌn'kʌvə] *vt.* 揭开……的盖子，揭露，暴露
The grave robber uncovered the hidden riches.
盗墓者找到了隐埋的宝藏。

食 进餐

breakfast ['brekfəst] *n.* 早饭，早餐
My father scanned the *China Daily* over breakfast.
父亲边吃早餐边浏览《中国日报》。

brunch [brʌntʃ] *n.* 早午餐
Brunch has become a fashion among teenagers.
在青少年中，早午餐合二为一成了一种时尚。

chew [tʃu:] *vt.* 咀嚼，嚼碎
This beef steak is difficult to chew.
这牛排很难嚼。

digest [di'dʒest] *vt.* 消化，领会；*n.* 文摘
The French fries is hard for me to digest.
炸土豆对我来说不易消化。

lick [lik] *vt.* 舔，舔吃，打败，克服，轻拍
n. 舔，少许
The man gave the stamp a lick.
那人舔了一下邮票。

meal [mi:l] *n.* 膳食，一餐；*vi.* 进餐
This ticket entitles you to a free meal in our new restaurant.
你可以凭此券在我们的新餐馆免费就餐一次。

starve [stɑ:v] *vi.* 饿死；*vt.* 使饿死
They would rather starve than surrender to the enemy.
他们宁愿饿死也不向敌人投降。

suck [sʌk] *vt.* 吸，吮，啜，吸收
She sucked back the milk that was going to flow down.
她吸了一下快要流下来的牛奶。

🔍 **考点：** suck up 奉承，拍马屁

swallow ['swɔləu] *vi.&vt.* 吞下，咽下
He took a long swallow of water as soon as he got home.
一到家他就喝了一大口水。

thirst [θə:st] *n.* 渴，口渴，渴望
A large number of refugees perished from hunger and thirst.
很多难民死于饥渴。

食 餐饮服务

bakery ['beikəri] *n.* 面包店
The bread is sold at half price in this bakery after six o'clock.
这家面包店6点之后，所有的面包都以半价出售。

grocer ['grəusə] *n.* 食品商，杂货商
You can not buy everything you want at the grocer.
你不可能在杂货店买到你想要的所有东西。

grocery ['grəusəri] *n.* 食品杂货店
He opened a grocery store last week.
上个星期他开了一家杂货铺。

menu ['menju:] *n.* 菜单，饭菜，菜肴
He didn't know any English words, so he couldn't read the menu.
他一个英语单词也不认识，所以看不懂这个菜单。

offer ['ɔfə] *vt.* 提供，提出；*n.* 提供
The police asked him to offer a document to certify his son's birth.
警察要求他为儿子的出生提供一份证明文件。

provide [prə'vaid] *vt.* 提供，装备，供给
The chicken provided in the small shop is always tender.
这家小商店出售的鸡肉总是很鲜嫩。

🔍 **考点：** provide for 作准备，供养
provide sb. with sth.=provide sth. to / for sb. 向某人提供某物

reservation [ˌrezə'veiʃən] *n.* 提供预订，保留，犹豫

When he tried to make a reservation, he found that the hotel that he wanted was completely filled because of a convention.
当他试图预订房间时，发现那个旅馆因为有一个会议已经客满了。

reserve [ri'zəːv] *vt.* 储备，保留，预定

Sorry, you can't sit here. These seats were reserved for special guests.
对不起，你不能坐这儿，这些座位是为特别来宾保留的。

真题

We'd like to _____ a table for five for dinner this evening.
A) preserve   B) sustain
C) retain   D) reserve

详　解：选D。题意为：我们想预订一张今晚5人用的餐位。A) preserve 意思是"保存，保护"；B) sustain 意思是"维持，支持"；C) retain 意思是"保持，保存"；D) reserve 意思是"预订，储存"。

(CET-4 2002.6)

restaurant ['restrɔnt] *n.* 餐馆，饭店，菜馆

He was employed as a waiter at his auntie's restaurant.
他在姑姑的饭店里做服务员。

snack-bar ['snæk'bɑː(r)] *n.* 小吃店；快餐店

We always have lunch at the snack-bar.
我们经常在小吃店吃午饭。

tip [tip] *vt.* 轻击，给……小费
　　　　n. 梢，末端，尖，尖端
　　　　vi. 给小费

The waiter received a handsome tip from that consumer.
侍者从那位顾客那里得到了数量可观的小费。

 考点：from tip to toe 从头至尾
　　　　 tip off 事先给警告，告密

cafeteria [ˌkæfi'tiəriə] *n.* 自助食堂

We can have delicious roast duck in this cafeteria.
我们可以在这家自助餐厅吃到美味的烤鸭。

canteen [kæn'tiːn] *n.* 小卖部，临时餐室

We invited our maths teacher to dine with us at the student canteen yesterday.
昨天我们邀请数学老师在学校餐厅和我们一起吃饭。

bar [bɑː(r)] *n.* 酒吧，间，条，杆，栅

He often has a drink in the bar.
他常在酒吧喝酒。

考点：behind bars 在狱中

食 餐桌礼仪

formal ['fɔːməl] *adj.* 正式的，礼仪上的

It was a formal embrace, a farewell.
这是一次正式的拥抱，一次告别。

occasion [ə'keiʒən] *n.* 场合，时刻，时机
　　　　　　vt. 引起，惹起

You should seize the occasion to invite your heart-throb home for dinner.
你应该抓住时机邀请你的心上人回家里吃饭。

proper ['prɔpə] *adj.* 适合的，本身的，合乎体统的，正派的

The traffic policeman told us that the proper intervals should be maintained between vehicles.
交警告诉大家，车辆之间要保持适当的间距。

考点：proper当"本身的"讲时，常作为后置定语。eg. China proper 中国本土；the dictionary proper 词典正文。

properly ['prɔpəli] *adv.* 适当地，彻底地

Make sure the machine's connected properly before you use it.
机器在使用前务必要接好电源。

taboo [tə'buː] *n.* 禁忌，禁止接近，禁止使用
　　　　　adj. 禁忌的；*vt.* 禁忌

Friday is a taboo for most westerners.
多数西方人忌讳星期五。

particular [pə'tikjulə] *adj.* 特殊的，特定的

The doctors said that some children who remain as dwarfs just because they lack a particular hormone.

医生说有些孩子长不高是因为他们身上缺少一种特殊的荷尔蒙。

真题

I went along thinking of nothing _____, only looking at things around me.
A) in brief   B) in doubt
C) in harmony   D) in particular

详 解：选D。题意为：我一路走着，什么都没想，只是看着周围的事物。A) in brief 意思是"简而言之"；B) in doubt 意思是"感到怀疑的"；C) in harmony 意思是"一般的，和谐的"；D) in particular 意思是"特别，尤其"。

(CET-4 2002.6)

particularly [pə'tikjuləli] *adj.* 特有的，特别的

Though he looks ugly, he is really a peculiar talent.
虽然他看上去其貌不扬，但确实是个怪才。

🗨 **考点**：be peculiar to 是……所特有的

party ['pɑ:ti] *n.* 派，聚会

After coming back from the party, she locked herself in the room for a whole day without one word.
从聚会上回来后，她一句话不说，一整天都把自己锁在房间里。

convention [kən'venʃən] *n.* 习俗，惯例，公约

"Lady first!" is a social convention in most of western countries.
在大多数西方国家，女士优先是一种社会习俗。

conventional [kən'venʃənl] *adj.* 普通的，习惯的

The child should be taught the conventional rules of etiquette.
要教会小孩一些通常的礼节。

🗨 **考点**：conventional medicine 常用的医学方法

住 房屋建筑 🖊

apartment [ə'pɑ:tmənt] *n.* 一套公寓房间

Jane has got a satisfying job in a company, but she dislikes the apartment it offers.
简在一家公司找到了满意的工作，但她不喜欢住在公司提供的公寓里。

castle ['kɑ:sl] *n.* 城堡，巨大建筑物

The duke in the castle was sick, but no doctor can cure him.
住在城堡里的公爵生病了，但是没有医生能治好他。

cell [sel] *n.* 细胞，小房间

The prisoner began to shout in his cell.
这个囚犯开始在他的牢房里大喊起来。

cellar ['selə] *n.* 地窖，地下室
          vt. 把……藏入地窖

Why don't you excavate a large hole to cellar the Chinese cabbages in it?
你为什么不挖个大洞把白菜窖进洞里呢？

chimney ['tʃimni] *n.* 烟囱，烟筒，玻璃罩

This gas fire doesn't need a chimney.
这种煤气不需要烟囱。

cottage ['kɔtidʒ] *n.* 村舍，小屋

This is the first time I have come to the country, and those simple cottages here attract me.
这是我第一次来到乡村，那些简朴的农舍吸引了我。

dormitory ['dɔ:mitri] *n.* 集体寝室，宿舍

The new dormitory has been building.
新的宿舍还在建设中。

flat [flæt] *adj.* 平的，扁平的
          n. 一套房间，单元住宅

She rents a furnished flat for her parents.
她给她父母租了一套备有家具的单元房。

hedge [hedʒ] *n.* 篱笆，树篱，障碍物

Beyond the hedge he pulled on his clothes and went away.
他在篱笆外把衣服穿上就走掉了。

housing ['hauziŋ] *n.* 房屋，住宅，供给，外罩

The housing problem is bound up with many other things.
住房问题涉及许多其他问题。

hut [hʌt] *n.* 小屋，棚屋

The old man lives in a hut.
老人住在小屋里。

lavatory ['lævətəri] *n.* 盥洗室，厕所

Is the lavatory vacant now?
厕所现在可以用吗？

lawn ['lɔːn] *n.* 草地，草坪，草场

Many children were playing on the lawn in front of your house.
许多孩子在你家门前的草坪上玩耍。

lobby ['lɔbi] *n.* 大厅，休息室
vi. 进行游说

A child is crying in the lobby because he couldn't find his mother.
一个孩子因为找不到妈妈，正在大厅里哭。

pillar ['pilə] *n.* 柱，柱子，栋梁

The pillars sustain the weight of the roof.
柱子支撑着房顶。

porch [pɔːtʃ] *n.* 门廊，入口处
There are plenty of colorful flowers on both sides of the porch to the city hall.
通往市政厅的门廊两侧摆有很多五颜六色的花。

真题

Several guests were waiting in the _____ for the front door to open.
A) porch   B) vent   C) inlet   D) entry

详 解：选A。题意为：几位客人正在门廊里等着开前门。A) porch意思为"门廊"；B) vent意思为"通风口，出气孔"；C) inlet意思为"入口，进口"；D) entry意思为"入口，大门"。

(CET-4 2002.6)

rail [reil] *n.* 横条，横杆，铁轨

That day she leaned on the rail of the second floor to see off her son who was going into the army.

那天她靠在二楼的栏杆上，目送她的儿子去参军。

shelter ['ʃeltə] *n.* 隐蔽处，掩蔽，庇护
We found shelter from the hurricane in a cave.
我们在一个山洞里躲藏飓风。

🔍 **考点：** shelter from 躲避，避开

terrace ['terəs] *n.* 平台，阳台，露台

In the evening we sat on the terrace listening to grandma telling stories.
晚上我们坐在平台上听奶奶讲故事。

yard [jɑːd] *n.* 院子，庭院，场地

On summer nights, mother often tells fairy stories to us in the yard.
在夏天的晚上，妈妈经常在院子里给我们讲神话故事。

construction [kən'strʌkʃən] *n.* 建造，建筑，建筑物

This is a perfect construction.
这是一个完美的建筑。

bathroom ['bɑːθrum] *n.* 浴室，盥洗室，（委婉语）洗手间

Could you mind my using your bathroom?
能用下你的洗手间吗？

barrier ['bæriə] *n.* 栅栏，屏障，障碍

Let us set a barrier to prevent the chicken from running away.
为了防止小鸡乱跑，咱们建一个栅栏吧！

真题

Deserts and high mountains have always been a _____ to the movement of people from place to place.
A) jam   B) barrier
C) fence   D) prevention

详 解：选B。题意为：沙漠和高山通常是阻止人们从一处向另一处迁移的障碍。A) jam意思是"阻塞物"；B) barrier意思是"障碍，隔阂"；C) fence意思是"栅栏，围栏"；D) prevention意思是"预防，阻止"。

(CET-4 2004.6)

building ['bildiŋ] *n.* 建筑物，大楼；建筑
The shape of the building is so unique.
那个建筑物的造型真独特。

basement ['beismənt] *n.* 根基，地下室
The vegetables were stored in the basement against the low temperature.
蔬菜储藏在地下室里以防低温。

column ['kɔləm] *n.* 柱，支柱，圆柱，专栏
The columns of this building make it look so spectacular.
这个建筑物的几根圆柱把它衬得很壮观。

住 施工建造

crane [krein] *n.* 起重机
        vi.&vt. 伸长，探头
The truck which dashed into the river was lifted from the water by a crane.
冲进河中的那辆卡车被一架起重机吊了出来。

depth [depθ] *n.* 深度，深厚，深处
More and more snow fell, and it accumulated to a depth of eight feet.
雪越下越大了，已经积到8尺深了。
🔍 考点：in depth 深入地，彻底地
       out of one's depth 为……所不理解

dig [dig] *vt.* 掘，挖，采掘
He digs a hole to bury his treasure.
他挖个洞把自己的宝藏埋了进去。
🔍 考点：dig out 挖出，发现
       dig up 挖掘出，找出

edge [edʒ] *n.* 边缘，边，刀口
The edge must be machined down to 1 mm.
侧边必须加工成一毫米。
🔍 考点：on edge 紧张不安，烦躁

enclose [in'kləuz] *vt.* 围住，圈起，附上
You could not pull apart two bowls which enclosed a vacuum.
如果两个碗之间是真空的，你就无法将它们分开。

erect [i'rekt] *vt.* 建造，使竖立
In a perfect square, the lines at the side are erect to the lines at the bottom.
在一完全正方形内，两条边线与底边成直角。

foundation [faun'deiʃən] *n.* 基础，地基，基金
His excellent performance laid a foundation for his career.
他出色的表现为他的事业打下了基础。
🔍 考点：lay solid foundation for 为……打下坚实的基础

layer ['leiə] *n.* 层，层次，铺设者
News about the hole in ozone layer can be seen on newspapers.
关于臭氧层空洞的新闻在报纸上可以看到。

link [liŋk] *vt.* 有环连接，联系
       n. 环，联系，纽带
It is necessary for us to link all the useful information together.
我们有必要把所有有用的信息连接起来。
🔍 考点：link up 连接，会合

mechanical [mi'kænikl] *adj.* 机械的，力学的，呆板的
We asked this machine works to produce the mechanical device for us.
我们请这家机械厂为我们生产这种机械装置。

mechanically [mi'kænikəli] *adv.* 机械地，无意识地
The old man advised us to apply advanced experience according to local conditions, instead of applying it mechanically.
老人建议我们对先进的经验应该因地制宜，而不是生搬硬套。

mechanics [mi'kæniks] *n.* 力学，技术性细节
He didn't pass the examination of mechanics.
他没有通过力学考试。

mould [məuld] *n.* 模子，模型；*vt.* 浇铸
The man moulded some dishes out of clay.
那个人用黏土浇铸成了几个盘子。

outlet ['autlet] *n.* 出口，出路，排遣

I need an outlet for my pent-up anger.
我的满腔怒火需要有机会发泄。

🔍 考点：inlet, outlet 特指流体的"入口"、"出口"；人们使用的"入口"、"出口"用entrance, exit。

pit [pit] *n.* 坑，地坑，煤矿

It is easy to hunt animals that are trapped in the pits.
猎取陷入坑中的动物很容易。

project ['prɔdʒekt] *n.* 方案，工程；*vi.* 伸出

Finally their project, which had been prepared for a long time, collapsed for lack of money.
最后，他们准备良久的计划还是因为缺钱而宣告失败。

pull [pul] *vt.* 拖，拉，拉力

I felt very cold at midnight and pulled the sheet over my body.
半夜里我感觉很冷，于是就拉起被单盖住身体。

🔍 考点：pull away 开走，使离开；pull down 拆毁；pull out 拔出，取出；pull up 使停下

removal [ri'mu:vəl] *n.* 移动，迁移，除掉

At last, the principal had to consent to the removal of the flags.
最终，校长不得不同意撤走旗帜。

remove [ri'mu:v] *vt.* 移动，搬开，脱掉

The criminal wanted to remove the tarnish from his file.
这个罪犯想除去他档案上的污点。

reverse [ri'və:s] *vt.* 颠倒，翻转；*n.* 背面

The result was just the reverse of what I expected.
结果正好与我期望的相反。

roll [rəul] *vi.&vt.* 滚动，转动

My grandpa told me they often rolled the trolley to carry heavy things in the past.
我爷爷告诉我，在过去他们经常用手推车搬重东西。

sharpen ['ʃɑ:pən] *vt.* 削尖，使敏锐，加剧

My pencil is blunt, but I don't have a knife to sharpen it.
我的铅笔钝了，但是我没有刀子削。

site [sait] *n.* 地点，地基，场所

Workers at the site must wear the safety helmet when they work.
工地上的工人在工作的时候必须带上安全帽。

smash [smæʃ] *n.* 破碎，猛击
vi.&vt. 粉碎，猛撞

My father began to smash things as soon as he got home.
一回家爸爸就开始砸东西。

storey ['stɔ:ri] *n.* （层）楼

You can find a building which is ten storey high in that street.
你可以在那条街找到一座10层高的楼房。

strip [strip] *vt.* 剥，夺去；*n.* 条、带

They carefully selected a strip of ground to build a house.
他们仔细地选择了一块地建房子。

🔍 考点：strip off 脱衣，剥落

stroke [strəuk] *n.* 打，击，鸣声，抚，摩，捋，中风
vt. 抚，摩，捋

He broke the vase with one stroke of the hammer.
他一锤就把花瓶砸碎了。

substantial [səb'stænʃəl] *adj.* 物质的，坚固的

The castle is substantial enough to last a hundred years.
这城堡很坚固，一百年也不会倒。

surround [sə'raund] *vt.* 围，围绕，圈住

Listen to the sounds of the insects that surround us.
仔细倾听周围昆虫的叫声。

sustain [sə'stein] *vt.* 支撑，供养，忍受

The branches could hardly sustain the weight of him.
树枝已经很难支撑他的重量。

tile [tail] *n.* 瓦片，瓷砖，贴砖

Many houses in the countryside are roofed in blue tiles.
农村很多房子都是用蓝瓦盖的。

tilt [tilt] *vi.&vt.* （使）倾斜

    vi. 抨击，争论

    n. 倾斜，车盖

The wall is not vertical but tilts to the north.
墙不是垂直的而是向北倾斜。

🔍 **考点**：at full tilt 全速地，极力地

underground ['ʌndəgraund] *adj.* 地下的，秘密的

There is an unknown underground room in their old house.
在他们的老房子里有一个不为人知的地下室。

weld [weld] *vt.&n.* 焊接，熔接

He is very skillful in welding metalwork.
他很擅长焊接金属制品。

base [beis] *n.* 基础，底层，基地

    vt. 建立在……基础上

That company has offices all over the country, but their base is in Zhengzhou.
那家公司在全国都有办公地，不过总部还是在郑州。

beam [bi:m] *n.* 梁，横梁，束，柱

We can see beams support the roof of a house.
我们可以看到横梁支撑着房顶。

build [biid] *vt.* 筑，立，创立

The hospital was built in one month.
那家医院在一个月内就建好了。

🔍 **考点**：build in 使成为固定部分，使成为组成部分；build into 使固定于 build up 逐步建立，增进，增强

construct [kən'strʌkt] *vt.* 建造，建设，构筑

The rich businessman has determined to construct a factory in his hometown.
那个富商决定在他的家乡建一个工厂。

enormous [i'nɔːməs] *adj.* 巨大的，庞大的

I have never seen such an enormous spider.
我从未见过这么大的蜘蛛。

angle ['æŋgl] *n.* 角，角度

    vt. 把……放置在一个角度

Don't look at the problem only from your own angle.
别只从自己的立场看问题。

🔍 **考点**：angle for 谋取，猎取

bottom ['bɔtəm] *n.* 底，底部，根基

The carpenter was asked to shave off a small amount from the bottom of the door.
请木匠过来刨去一点门的底边。

ground [graund] *n.* 地，场地，根据

The old man suddenly fell down on the ground.
老人突然倒在了地上。

🔍 **考点**：get off ground 开始；on (the) grounds of 以……为理由

住 结构材料

cement [si'ment] *n.* 水泥，胶泥；*vt.* 粘结

In modern society, cement is widely used in building.
在现代社会，水泥在建筑中应用很广。

clay [klei] *n.* 粘土，泥土，肉体

This kind of cans is made from clay.
这种罐子是粘土做成的。

compound ['kɔmpaund] *n.* 化合物，复合词

Water is a compound of hydrogen and oxygen.
水是氢和氧的化合物。

concrete ['kɔnkri:t] *n.* 混凝土，具体物

He always feels lonely and sad in the city built with steel rods and concrete.
在钢筋和混凝土建成的城市里他总是感到孤独悲伤。

🔍 **考点**：当"具体的"讲时，concrete与abstract（抽象）相对，specific与general（一般），vague（模糊）相对。

consist [kən'sist] *vi.* 由……组成，在于

This magazine consists mainly of reviews of new books and plays.
该杂志主要包括新书、新剧本的评论。

constitute ['kɔnstitjuːt] *vt.* 粘结构成，设立，任命

After consultation, a committee was constituted to investigate rising prices.
经过协商，成立了一个委员会来调查价格上涨问题。

constitution [ˌkɔnsti'tjuːʃən] *n.* 章程，体质，构造

According to the Chinese Constitution, the citizens have the right to vote.
按照中国宪法，公民有选举权。

copper ['kɔpə] *n.* 铜，铜币，铜制器

It's said that copper conducts electricity better than iron does.
据说，铜的导电性比铁强。

cord [kɔːd] *n.* 细绳，粗线，索

Have you got some cord that I can tie this baggage up with?
有一些可以让我把行李系在一起的绳子吗？

cordless ['kɔːdlis] *adj.* 无线（绳）的，不用电池供电的

A cordless telephone has been installed in our dormitory.
我们宿舍已安装了一部无线电话。

formation [fɔ:'meiʃən] *n.* 形成，构成，形成物

The maltreatments accelerate the formation of the child's negative mentality.
打骂加速了孩子逆反心理的形成。

frame [freim] *n.* 框架，框子，构架

The devise is to fix the frame of chair.
此装置是用于固定椅子框架的。

framework ['freimwə:k] *n.* 框架，构架，结构

He has to gild a picture framework today.
他今天要给一个画框镀金。

pane [pein] *n.* 窗格玻璃

The little girl blew on the window pane.
那个小女孩往玻璃窗上哈气。

ingredient [in'gri:diənt] *n.* 组成部分，原料，要素，因素

It needs kinds of ingredients in cooking this dish.
做这道菜需要好几种原料。

integrate ['intigreit] *vt.* 使……合体，使……成为一体

The peasants can not find it easy to integrate into the life of city.
农民们感到不易融入城市生活。

log [lɔg] *n.* 原木，木料，航海（飞行）日志 *vt.* 正式记录

The log in the yard has rotted away.
院子里的这条圆木已腐烂了。

🔍 **考点**：log in 进入计算机系统
log out 退出计算机系统

mud [mʌd] *n.* 软泥，泥浆

When the Yellow River rises, it deposits a layer of mud on the land.
当黄河泛滥时，河水在地上淤积起一层泥。

paper ['peipə] *n.* 纸，官方文件，文章

Can you write them down on a piece of paper?
你能把它们写在一张纸上吗？

part [pɑːt] *n.* 一部分，零件，本份

Our planet is only a small part of the cosmos.
我们的星球只是宇宙的一小部分。

partially ['pɑːʃəli] *adv.* 部分地

The driver is partially responsible for the accident.
司机对该事故负有部分责任。

partly ['pɑːtli] *adv.* 部分地，不完全地

I heard this ship was destroyed partly in the storm.
我听说这条船在风暴中部分被毁。

🔍 **考点**：看重数量上的"部分"，partly 与 wholly 相对；看重程度上的"有限"，partially 与 completely 相对。

pebble ['pebl] *n.* 卵石，细砾

The naughty boy dropped a pebble from the bridge and waited for the plop.
那个淘气的男孩从桥上扔下一颗卵石，然后等着听那扑通的一声。

plaster ['plɑːstə] *n.* 灰泥，硬膏，熟石膏

The plaster on the walls of his room began to flake.
他房间墙壁上的灰泥开始掉落了。

日常生活

住

plastic ['plæstik] *adj.* 可塑的；*n.* 塑料
This pair of glasses are made of plastic lens.
这副眼镜的镜片是用塑料做成的。

plentiful ['plentiful] *adj.* 丰富的，富裕的
Our hometown is blessed with plentiful rainfall and a mild climate.
我们家乡雨量充足，气候温和。

plenty ['plenti] *n.* 丰富，充足，大量
I think an itinerary which could leave us plenty of leeway would be better.
我觉得能给我们留下很多自由活动余地的旅行计划就是好计划。

🔍 **考点**：plenty of 很多，大量的

section ['sekʃən] *n.* 切片，一段，部门
I've already prefabricated sections of houses, and I have to ask the workers to assemble them.
我已经预制好房屋的各个部件，接下来就要找工人们把它们组装起来。

segment ['segmənt] *n.* 部分，片段，瓣，弓形；*vt.* 分割，划分
My son cleaned a small segment of the painting.
我儿子把画上的一小部分擦干净了。

semiconductor ['semikən'dʌktə] *n.* 半导体
Do you know what semiconductors are used for?
你知道半导体是用来做什么的吗？

stainless ['steinlis] *adj.* 没有污点的，不锈的
Nowadays most silver are made of stainless steel.
现在大部分的餐具是不锈钢制的。

stick [stik] *n.* 棍，棒；*vt.* 刺，粘贴
He cut nicks in a stick to mark his name.
他在一根杖上刻上自己的名字作为记号。

🔍 **考点**：stick by 忠于……
stick to 紧跟，粘贴在……上
stick together 团结一致
stick up for 支持，为……辩护

structure ['strʌktʃə] *n.* 结构，构造
vt. 建造
The architectural structure of the Palace Museum is unique.

故宫的建筑结构很别致。

stuff [stʌf] *n.* 原料，东西
The plates were made of a kind of plastic stuff.
这些盘子是用一种塑料制造的。

surplus ['sə:pləs] *n.* 过剩，盈余
adj. 过剩的，多余的
The surplus equipment should be handed in to the factory.
多余器材应该交回工厂。

synthetic [sin'θetik] *adj.* 综合的，合成的
Synthetic leather is widely used in making shoes.
人造皮革被广泛用于制鞋中。

timber ['timbə] *n.* 木材，木料
The settlers cut down the timber to build houses.
开拓者们砍下树木用于建房子。

transparent [træns'pɛərənt] *adj.* 透明的，易识破的
His lie was easily transparent in front of the police.
在警察面前，他的谎言很容易就被识破了。

vertical ['və:tikəl] *adj.* 垂直的，竖式的
He draws a lot of horizontal lines and vertical lines on the paper.
他在纸上画了很多水平的线和垂直的线。

🔍 **考点**：vertical, perpendicular的区别：
vertical指与水平面成直角的垂直线；perpendicular特指用于几何的任何与平面成直角的直线。前者只用 于比喻，而后者则多用于具体方面。

waterproof ['wɔ:təpru:f] *adj.* 不透水的，防水的
This piece of fibreboard is flexible and waterproof.
这块纤维板具有弹性还防水。

brick [brik] *n.* 砖，砖块，砖状物
To his surprise, the house was built with no bricks.
让他吃惊的是，这座房子建造时竟然没用一块砖。

comprise [kəm'praiz] *vt.* 包含，包括，构成
The class is comprised mainly of Chinese and French students.
课堂上大部分都是中国学生和法国学生。

考点：comprise, consist, compose, constitute的用法：comprise =constitute组成=consist of / be composed of由……组成

contain [kən'tein] *vt.* 包含，容纳，等于

Each galaxy contains myriads of stars.
每一星系都有无数的恒星。

bronze [brɔnz] *n.* 青铜，青铜制品

You mean this statue was cast in bronze.
你是说这尊塑像是用青铜铸造的。

circle ['sə:kl] *n.* 圆，圆周，圈子

Let's sit in a circle and then tell the stories one by one.
让我们围成圈坐在一起，然后一个接着一个讲故事。

circular ['sə:kjulə] *adj.* 圆的，循环的

She hopes she will have a circular tour around the world.
她希望有一天可以环球旅行。

cube [kju:b] *n.* 立方形，立方

I know a cube has six surfaces.
我知道立方体有6个面。

cubic ['kju:bik] *adj.* 立方形的，立方的

I can't believe that the volume of this big box is only 30 cubic centimeters.
我不敢相信如此大的一个箱子，体积只有30立方厘米。

curve [kə:v] *n.* 曲线，弯；*vt.* 弄弯

He bunted a curve and scored a point.
他打出了一个曲线球，并因此赢得了一分。

考点：take curves 转弯

form [fɔ:m] *n.* 形式，形状；*vt.* 形成

Water forms ice at low temperature.
水在低温下形成冰。

考点：in form 在形式上，在状态

round [raund] *adj.* 圆的；*n.* 兜圈，一轮

My niece has a round face.
我侄女有一张圆圆的脸。

考点：round off 完成，使完美

round up 把……聚拢起来

sector ['sektə] *n.* 部分，防区，扇形

Please figure out the area of this sector.
请计算出这个扇形的面积。

sphere [sfiə] *n.* 球，圆体，范围

The criminals only have a small sphere of activity.
罪犯只有很小的活动范围。

考点：sphere of influence 势力范围

shape [ʃeip] *n.* 形状，情况；*vt.* 形成

A dim shape loomed up in the dense fog.
浓雾中出现一个模糊的身影。

考点：in (good) shape 处于（良好）状况；shape up 发展顺利，表现良好；take shape 形成

住 装修布局

carpet ['kɑ:pit] *n.* 地毯，毡毯，毛毯

He is interested in the veivet carpet.
他对天鹅绒地毯很感兴趣。

ceiling ['si:liŋ] *n.* 天花板，顶蓬

Suddenly, he saw a fly on the ceiling.
突然，他看到天花板上有一只苍蝇。

corridor ['kɔridɔ:] *n.* 走廊，回廊，通路

They are drinking the wine in the corridor.
他们正在走廊里喝酒。

decorate ['dekəreit] *vt.* 装饰，装潢，修饰

I bought a new house, and prepared to decorate it.
我买了一个新房子，准备把它装修一下。

考点：decorate...with sth. 用……装饰……

decoration [ˌdekə'reiʃən] *n.* 装修，装饰（品）

I am excited when Halloween comes, because father can make many beautiful decorations.
每当万圣节前夕到来时，我总是很兴奋，因为父亲会做很多漂亮的装饰。

divide [di'vaid] *vt.* 分，分配，分开

The large yard was divided into two parts by the hedge which was set last year.

那个大院子被去年立起来的树篱分成了两部分。

downstairs [ˌdaun'stɛəz] *adv.* 在楼下
         adj. 楼下的

Hurry up! Your mate is waiting for you downstairs.
快点，你的同伴在楼下等你呢！

elegant ['eligənt] *adj.* 优美的，文雅的，简
         练的，简洁的

I want to buy an elegant vase to decorate my room.
我想买个别致的花瓶来装饰我的房间。

elevator ['eliveitə] *n.* 电梯，升降机

You can take the elevator to get the eleventh floor.
你可以乘电梯去11楼。

entrance ['entrəns] *n.* 入口，门口，进入

The soldier placed a mine at the entrance to the village.
那位战士在村口埋了一颗地雷。

entry ['entri] *n.* 入口处，登记，进入

I'll wait for you at the entry to the school.
我在校门口等你。

exterior [eks'tiəriə] *adj.* 外部的，对外的

The exterior surface of the hollow ball is green.
这个空心球的外表面是绿色的。

external [eks'tə:nl] *adj.* 外部的，外面的

Don't only owe your failure to the external causes.
不要只把错误归结到外因。

fasten ['fɑ:sn] *vt.* 弄弯扎牢，扣住

Use some nails to fasten that picture.
用几个钉子把那幅画钉上。

fence [fens] *n.* 栅栏

They set up a new fence around their house.
他们在房子周围建了一圈新栅栏。

🔍 **考点**：on the fence 保持中立

indoor ['indɔ:] *adj.* 室内的，户内的
      adv. 在室内，在户内

You can play some indoor games if you don't want to go out.
如果不想出去，你可以进行室内活动。

fit [fit] *vt.* 适合；安装；*vi.* 适合

This shirt that his girlfriend bought fits him very well.
他穿着他女朋友买的这件衬衣很合身。

🔍 **考点**：fit, suit的区别：fit 侧重指尺寸大
    小合适，因而引申为"吻合"；suit
    侧重合乎条件，身份，口味，需要
    等。

furnish ['fə:niʃ] *vt.* 供应，提供，装备

How are you going to furnish the room?
你将如何布置房间？

🔍 **考点**：furnish 表示"提供"时，要用
    furnish A with B或者furnish B
    toA的结构。

hang [hæŋ] *vt.* 挂，悬，吊死

Please hang out your clothes or they will never dry.
请把你的衣服挂出去，否则它们永远不会干的。

🔍 **考点**：hang about / around 闲逛，闲
    待着；hang on 坚持，（打电话
    时）不挂断；hang up 挂断（电
    话），悬挂

inside ['in'said] *prep.* 在……里面；*n.* 内部

The vase should be put inside the lobby.
花瓶应当放在门厅里。

🔍 **考点**：inside out 里面朝外，彻底地

install [in'stɔ:l] *vt.* 安装，设置

He installed an air-conditioner in their house last month.
上个月他给家里装了台空调机。

installation [ˌinstə'leiʃən] *n.* 安装，装置，
          设施

They still have an installation of the telephone this afternoon.
今天下午他们还有一个电话要安装。

interior [in'tiəriə] *adj.* 内的，内地的
       n. 内部

She specialized in interior design in university.
大学时，她专修室内设计。

internal [in'tə:nl] *adj.* 内的，国内的
This family didn't have an internal coherence.

这个家庭内部不和谐。

🔹 **考点**：internal, inner, inward均有"内部的"意思：internal"内部的"，用法比较广，eg. internal trade 国内贸易；inner本义是"较里面的"，如里外相连的房子，里面的是inner room；inward本义是"向内的"。引申义中，inner, inward通常都可以指人的内心方面。

knot [nɔt] *n.* （绳的）结，（树的）节
vt. 把……打成结，捆扎
vi. 打结

Could you help me tie the two ropes in a knot?
你能帮我把那两根绳子打成一个结吗？

layout ['leiaut] *n.* 布局，安排，设计

The layout of the park is designed by a Frenchman.
这个公园的布局是一个法国人设计的。

mess [mes] *n.* 混乱，混杂，肮脏

She was indeed good at cooking, but she would make a mess in the kitchen every time when she cooked.
她的确很会做饭，但她每次做饭都会把厨房弄得一团糟。

🔹 **考点**：mess about / around 闲逛，瞎忙，轻率地对待；mess up 把……弄糟（弄乱）；mess with 干预，介入

narrow ['nærəu] *adj.* 狭的，狭窄的

It's hard for him to wheel his bike through that narrow lane.
让他推着自行车穿过狭窄的巷子很不容易。

orderly ['ɔ:dəli] *adj.* 整洁的，有秩序的

The books are in orderly rows on shelves in the library.
图书馆里，书籍整齐地排列在书架上。

outer ['autə] *adj.* 外部的，外面的

The outer door needs to be repaired.
外面的门需要修理一下。

outward ['autwəd] *adj.* 外面的，向外的

The girl isn't interested in outward trappings.
那个女孩不喜欢装饰外表的物品。

outwards ['autwədz] *adv.* 向外，往海外

Can you tell me whether this door opens inwards or outwards?
你能告诉我这门朝里开还是朝外开吗？

space [speis] *n.* 空间，场地，空白

The goods take up more space of this warehouse.
这批货占用仓库太多的空间。

真题

Now in Britain, wines take up four times as much _____ in the storehouse as both beer and spirits.
A) block　　B) land
C) patch　　D) space

详　解：选D。题意为：现在在英国，仓库中葡萄酒所占的空间是啤酒和烈性酒的4倍。A) block意思是"街区"；B) land意思是"土地"；C) patch意思是"一片土地"；D) space意思是"空间，场地"。

(CET-4 2005.6)

whole [həul] *adj.* 完整的；*n.* 全部

I spent a whole day in watching television at home yesterday.
我昨天一整天都在家看电视。

🔹 **考点**：as a whole 整个看来；on the whole 总的来说，大体上

long [lɔŋ] *adj.* 长的，远的；*adv.* 长久
vi. 渴望，极想念

I found a long white scar on his leg, which to his souvenir of battle.
我发现他腿上有一条长长的白色伤疤，那是对他参战的纪念。

🔹 **考点**：as / so long as 只要，由于
so long 再见
before long 不久以后
no longer 不再，已不

proportion [prə'pɔ:ʃən] *n.* 比，比率，部分

The boy looks funny; you know his head is out of proportion to the size of his body.
男孩看上去很滑稽，他的头部和身体大小不成比例。

真题

It is clear that the dog has a much greater _____ of its brain devoted to smell than is the case with humans.
A) composition   B) proportion
C) compound   D) percent

详 解：选B。题意为：很显然，狗的大脑用于嗅觉的比例要比人在这方面的比例大得多。A) composition意思是"成分，合成物"；B) proportion 意思是"比例，比率"；C) compound意思是"混合物，化合物"；D) percent 意思是"百分比，百分数"。

(CET-4 2006.6)

panel ['pænl] *n.* 专门小组，面，板
The ceiling in the sitting room has a carved panel.
客厅的天花板上装有刻花镶板。

separate ['sepəreit] *adj.* 分离的，个别的
The children in this school have separate bedrooms.
这个学校的孩子都有单独的卧室。

set [set] *vt.* 放，安置；*vi.* 落
Fox is so sly; you have to set traps to catch it.
狐狸很狡猾，你必须设陷阱来捕捉它。

slam [slæm] *vt.* 使劲关，砰地放下
I was reading English when I heard someone slam the door.
我正在读英语时听到有人"砰"地一声把门关上了。

suspend [sə'spend] *vt.* 吊，悬，推迟
I don't know what suspends in the water.
我不知道什么悬浮在水中。

breadth [bredθ] *n.* 宽度，幅度，幅面
Our headteacher is a man of intellectual breadth.
我们班主任是个知识渊博的人。

住 光线

glow [gləu] *n.* 白热光；*vi.* 发白热光
The faint glow of a lamp shone through the room.
昏暗的灯光从房间里透出。

loop [lu:p] *n.* 圈，环，环孔，循环
        vt. 把……圈成环，缠绕
The little girl looped the curtain up to let the sunlight in.
小女孩卷起窗帘，让阳光照进来。

open ['əupən] *adj.* 开的，开放的；*vt.* 开
The candle blew out when I opened the window.
当我打开窗户的时候，蜡烛随之被风吹灭了。

dim [dim] *adj.* 昏暗的，朦胧的
I don't like a dim room.
我不喜欢光线暗的房间。

真题

"This light is too _____ for me to read by. Don't we have a brighter bulb somewhere?" said the elderly man.
A) mild   B) dim
C) minute   D) slight

详 解：选B。题意为："在这么昏暗的灯光下我没法看书，我们就没有亮点的灯泡吗？"。A) mild意思是"温和的，适度的"；B) dim意思是"昏暗的"；C) minute意思是"仔细的"；D) slight意思是"轻微的"。

(CET-4 2005.12)

penetrate ['penitreit] *vt.* 穿过；*vi.* 穿入
He died; here is a knife penetrating his chest.
他死了，有把刀刺穿了他的胸膛。

ray [rei] *n.* 光线，射线，辐射线
The room is so dark that there isn't a ray of sunshine all day long.
那个房间很暗，一整天都没有一丝阳光。

shade [ʃeid] *n.* 荫，遮光物；*vi.* 荫蔽
These trees can supply shade in summer.
这些树夏天可以供人们乘凉。

🔍 **考点**：shade in / into 逐渐变成；shade... from... 使……免受……的照射

---

streak [stri:k] *n.* 条纹，条痕，个性特征，一连串
        vi. 飞跑，疾驰
        vt. 在……加上条纹

A streak of lightning flashed through the sky in the deep night.
一道光闪过深夜的天空。

---

sunlight ['sʌnlait] *n.* 日光，阳光

Outdoor sunlight is very good for your headache.
户外的阳光对你的头痛很有好处。

---

visible ['vizəbl] *adj.* 看得见的，有形的

The car was not visible because of the brilliance of the light.
车是看不见的，因为光线太强。

住 家具家电

air-conditioning ['ɛəkən'diʃəniŋ] *n.* 空调设备，空调系统

Close the door and windows, please; the air conditioning is operating.
空调正开着，请关上门窗。

---

ampere ['æmpɛə] *n.* 安培

Owing to the electrician, I have mastered how to use an ampere meter.
多亏了电工师傅，我掌握了用安培表的方法。

---

appliance [ə'plaiəns] *n.* 器具，器械，装置

He sells a variety of medicine appliances.
他销售各种类型的医疗器械。

---

applicable ['æplikəbl] *adj.* 能应用的，适当的

The new equipments are applicable to all European countries.
新的设备适用于所有的欧洲国家。

---

bolt [bəult] *n.* 螺栓，插销；*vt.* 闩门

Dad told me to fasten the bolt.
爸爸让我把螺栓扭紧。

🔍 **考点**：a bolt from / out of the blue 晴天霹雳，意外事件

---

box [bɔks] *n.* 箱，盒，包箱
        vi. 拳击，打拳

He sends a box of books to me.
他给我送来一箱子的书。

---

broom [bru:m] *n.* 扫帚

In the fairy stories, the witch always flies about, riding a broom.
在童话故事里，女巫总是骑在一把扫帚上飞来飞去。

---

bulb [bʌlb] *n.* 电灯泡；球状物

The bulb was invented by Edison.
电灯泡是爱迪生发明的。

---

cabinet ['kæbinit] *n.* 橱，柜，内阁

Can you help me find the book with blue cover in the document cabinet?
能帮我在文件柜里找到那本蓝色封皮的书吗？

---

chair [tʃɛə] *n.* 椅子，主席

I couldn't see anything in the dark and my legs knocked against the chair.
黑暗中我看不见任何东西，两条腿就撞到了椅子上。

---

circuit ['sə:kit] *n.* 电路，环行，巡行

Maybe there is something wrong with the electric circuit; please check it carefully.
也许是电路出问题了，请仔细检查一下。

---

clean [kli:n] *adj.* 清洁的，纯洁的
        vt. 打扫

Dust soon accumulates if you don't clean the room regularly.
如果你不经常打扫房间，尘土很快就会积聚起来。

---

clear [kliə] *adj.* 清晰的；*vt.* 清除

First, you should be very clear about your business rivals.
首先，你应该很清楚你的商业竞争对手。

---

clock [klɔk] *n.* 钟，仪表

When I came through the customs at the airport, I had to pay duty on a clock I had bought.
在机场海关处，我不得不对我买的钟付税。

comfort ['kʌmfət] *n.* 舒适，安慰

vt. 安慰

We tried to comfort her, but she cried even harder.
我们试图安慰她，可是她却哭得更厉害了。

comfortable ['kʌmfətəbl] *adj.* 舒适的，安慰的

It's comfortable to make an overland journey.
做一次陆地旅行很惬意。

curtain ['kə:tən] *n.* 帘，窗帘，幕（布）

I want to buy a curtain to match the furniture.
我想买一个跟家具搭配的窗帘。

cushion ['kuʃən] *n.* 垫子，坐垫，靠垫

When I entered, I saw the old man kneeling on a cushion to pray.
我进去的时候，看到这个老人跪在垫子上祈祷。

drawer ['drɔ:ə] *n.* 抽屉

These drawers slide in and out easily.
这些抽屉很容易推进拉出。

fragment ['frægmənt] *n.* 碎片，破片，碎块

Please sweep up the fragments of that vase.
请清扫一下花瓶碎片。

handle ['hændl] *n.* 柄，把手

vt. 拿，触

Loose the handle of the door.
松开门把手。

refrigerator [ri'fridʒəreitə] *n.* 冰箱，冷藏库

The refrigerator in this cold drinks shop didn't work this morning.
今天上午，这家冷饮店的冰箱坏了。

shelf [ʃelf] *n.* 搁板，架子

He put many carvings on the shelf of his study.
他在书房的书架上摆放了许多雕刻品。

🔍 **考点：** on the shelf 被搁置

sofa ['səufə] *n.* 沙发

A cat lay coiled up on the sofa watching TV.
一只猫卷成一团地躺在沙发上看电视。

suitcase ['sju:tkeis] *n.* 小提箱，衣箱

She put all her possessions in one suitcase.
她把她的全部财物装在一个手提箱内。

switch [switʃ] *n.* 开关，转换；*vt.* 转换

His questing fingers found the light switch in the black.
黑暗中他用手指摸到了灯的开关。

🔍 **考点：** switch on （用开关）开启
switch off （用开关）关掉

table ['teibl] *n.* 桌子，餐桌，项目表

She likes sitting on the edge of the table dangling her legs.
她喜欢坐在桌子边上，摆动着双腿。

🔍 **考点：** on the table 提交议案，留待日后处理；turn the tables 扭转形势

volt [vəult] *n.* 伏特，伏

He didnt know the meaning of volt before the class.
课前他并不知道"伏特"的含义。

bench [bentʃ] *n.* 凳，条凳，工作台

There is a drunken man sleeping on the bench of the garden.
有个醉汉在公园的长椅上睡觉。

住 **起居用品** ✏️

blanket [blæŋkit] *n.* 毛毯，毯子，羊毛毯

She needs a blanket to keep warm.
她需要一条毛毯来保暖。

pillow ['piləu] *n.* 枕头

Could you spare some time to embroider a pillow cover for me?
你能否抽点时间帮我绣一个枕头套?

quilt [kwilt] *n.* 被（子）

Tom, go and fetch the guest a quilt and an overcoat.
汤姆，去给客人拿一床棉被和一件大衣来。

razor ['reizə] *n.* 刮脸刀，剃刀

I sent a razor to my boyfriend on his 28th birthday.
我男朋友28岁生日时我送了他一个剃须刀。

shaver ['ʃeivə] *n.* 剃须刀
Finally, he found his shaver under the bed.
最后，他在床底下找到了他的剃须刀。

sheet [ʃi:t] *n.* 被单，纸张，薄板
A blast of wind blew my sheet away.
一阵风把我的床单刮走了。

tissue ['tiʃu] *n.* 薄绢，薄纸，组织
He wrapped the gift with the tissue.
他用薄纸将礼物包起来。

住 其他器具

arrow ['ærəu] *n.* 箭，箭状物
Cupid always takes the arrow with him.
丘比特总是随身带着箭。

auxiliary [ɔ:g'ziljəri] *adj.* 辅助的，附属的
Due to lack of auxiliary verb, it became a wrong sentence.
由于缺少了助动词，它变成了一个错误的句子。

ax [æks] *n.* 斧子，削减
This ax is sharp enough to cut the tree.
这个斧子锋利得可以砍倒一棵树。

backup ['bækʌp] *n.* 后备，备用物
We should always have a backup plan in case of unpredictable trouble.
我们应该总是有备用的计划以免遇到未知的麻烦。

battery ['bætəri] *n.* 电池，一套，一组
Don't throw the used battery at your will.
不要随意乱扔用过的电池。

blade [bleid] *n.* 刀刃，刀片，叶片
I wanted to ask you whether you'd got any razor blades.
我正想问你还有刀片没有。

available [ə'veiləbl] *adj.* 可利用的，通用的
Are you available today? I want to treat you to dinner.
今天你有空吗？我想请你吃饭。

真题

There should be more money ____ to support people in establishing a sense of identity and finding constructive roles for the "third age".
A) reliable   B) considerable
C) available   D) feasible

详 解：选C。题意为：我们需要更多的资金来帮助老年人建立一种认同感，并找到"第三年龄人群"所扮演的建设性角色。A) reliable意思是"可靠的"；B) considerable意思是"可观的"；C) available意思是"可用的，可获得的"；D) feasible意思是"可行的"。

(CET-4 2009.12)

board [bɔ:d] *n.* 板；*vt.* 上（船、车等）
Look, your painting is on the board.
看，你的画儿在黑板上呢。

考点：across the board 全面地
above board 光明正大的，公开的
on board 在船（车或飞机）上

cage [keidʒ] *n.* 笼，鸟笼，囚笼
The bird tried to fly from the cage, but failed.
那只鸟试图飞出笼子，不过失败了。

chain [tʃein] *n.* 链，链条，项圈
This chain store opened last year and attracted a lot of customers.
这家连锁店去年开的业，吸引了不少顾客。

clip [klip] *n.* 夹子，别针，弹夹，片断
vt. 夹住；修剪
Our manager has just bought a box of clips for the company.
经理刚刚为公司买了一盒夹子。

clockwise ['klɔkwaiz] *adj.* 顺时针方向的
adv. 顺时针方向地
She ran clockwise three circuits of the track.
她沿跑道顺时针跑了3圈。

coil [kɔil] *n.* （一）卷，线圈；*vt.* 卷
The burnt coil should be renewed on time.
烧焦的线圈应及时换新的。

drill [dril] *n.* 钻头，操练；*vi.* 钻孔
My dog has taken my drill to the garden.
我的狗把电钻叼到花园去了。

dryer/drier ['draiə] *n.* 干燥机，吹风机
Don't use a dryer too often; it's not good to your health.
别经常使用吹风机，对你的健康没好处。

durable ['djuərəbl] *adj.* 耐久的，耐用的
I think the friendship between us is durable.
我认为我们之间的友谊是持久的。

electric [i'lektrik] *adj.* 电的，电动的
The solar cell can convert the energy of sunlight into electric energy.
太阳能电池能把阳光的能量转化为电能。

electrical [i'lektrikəl] *adj.* 电的，电气科学的
Refrigerators are available in any electrical shops.
冰箱在任何一家家电商场都能买到。

electron [i'lektrɔn] *n.* 电子
The electron microscope can give things much greater magnification.
电子显微镜能把物体放大好多倍。

electronic [iˌlek'trɔnik] *adj.* 电子的
My company contracted with an electronics factory for the purchase of their electronic instruments.
我公司与一家电子厂签约购买他们的电子仪器。

firewood ['faiəwud] *n.* 柴
I saw a bundle of firewood in the kitchen.
我在厨房看见了一捆劈柴。

function ['fʌŋkʃən] *n.* 功能，职务，函数
The function of this machine is tremendous.
这台机器的功能是非常强大的。

functional ['fʌŋkʃənl] *adj.* 实用的，正常运转的，有用途的
You must consider how different these functional elements are.
你必须考虑这些功能元素有何不同。

generator ['dʒenəreitə] *n.* 发电机，发生者
The generator could be back in service.
发电机可以重新使用了。

glue [glu:] *n.* 胶，胶水；*vt.* 胶合
Glue has stuck to his toes.
胶水粘在他脚趾上了。
🔎 **考点**：glued to 不愿离开，盯住不放

hammer ['hæmə] *n.* 锤，榔头；*vt.* 锤击
Please hand on the hammer to me.
请把锤子递给我。
🔎 **考点**：hammer away at 努力做
hammer out 竭力想出（办法等）

handy ['hændi] *adj.* 手边的，便于使用的
I think vacuum cleaner is a handy household.
我认为吸尘器是一种使用方便的家庭用具。

hardware ['hɑ:dwɛə] *n.* 五金器具，硬件
There is a hardware store at the corner of the street.
街角有一个五金店。

hook [huk] *n.* 钩，挂钩；*vt.* 钩住
Please help me hang this shirt on a hook.
请帮我把衬衣挂在挂钩上。
🔎 **考点**：hook up 将……接上电源，将……连接起来
off the hook 脱离困境

kit [kit] *n.* 成套工具，配备元件，工具箱
vt. 装备
Prepare a family emergency kit against unexpected needs.
要准备一个家庭应急工具箱以备不时之需。

lock [lɔk] *n.* 锁，船闸；*vt.* 锁上，锁住
You'd better lock your bicycle.
你最好把自行车锁上。
🔎 **考点**：lock up 把……监禁起来
lock in 紧闭

mat [mæt] *n.* 席子，草席，垫子
vt. 给……铺垫子，使缠结
The mat on your bed is too thick to double over.
你床上的垫子太厚了，不能折起来。

nail [neil] *n.* 钉，指甲；*vt.* 钉
Use some nails to fasten that picture.
用几个钉子把那幅画钉上。
🔎 **考点**：nail down 确定

日常生活

住

opener ['əupnə] *n.* 开启工具

Let's open the tin of food with a tin opener.
我们用起子来打开罐头。

paste [peist] *n.* 糊，酱，浆糊

My mother sealed the envelope with paste.
我妈妈用浆糊粘信封。

pin [pin] *n.* 针，饰针，大头针；*vt.* 别住

We need to buy a box of pin.
我们需要买一盒大头针。

pipe [paip] *n.* 管子，导管，烟斗

There is a block in the pipe and the liquid can't
flow away.
管子里有阻碍物，液体流不出去。

plug [plʌg] *n.* 塞子，插头；*vt.* 塞

She plugged her ears with cotton balls in order not
to be disturbed by the noise.
为了不受噪音的打扰，她用棉球塞住了耳朵。

practical ['præktikəl] *adj.* 实践的，实用的

The book is very practical, which has many figures
to help us understand the articles.
这本书很实用，它有许多图表帮助我们理解文
章。

procedure [prə'si:dʒə] *n.* 程序，手续，过程

According to the instruction, the next procedure is
to insert the battery.
依照说明书，下一步是安装电池。

rod [rɔd] *n.* 杆，竿，棒

My grandfather has a long finishing rod.
我爷爷有一根长长的鱼竿。

roller ['rəulə] *n.* 滚柱，滚筒，滚轴

I advise you to apply it with brush or roller.
我建议你使用毛刷或滚筒进行涂抹。

sack [sæk] *n.* 袋，麻袋，开除
　　　　　　 vt. 解雇，洗劫

An empty sack cannot stand upright.
空袋不能直立。

saw [sɔ:] *n.* 锯子；*vt.* 锯，锯开

My father sawed the wood into four.
我父亲把那木头锯成4段。

saddle ['sædl] *n.* 鞍子，马鞍
　　　　　　 vt. 给……装鞍，使承担任务

Before you ride the horse, please fasten the saddle
on its back.
骑马之前，先把鞍子系在马背上。

考点：in the saddle 在职，掌权

screw [skru:] *n.* 螺旋，螺丝；*vt.* 拧紧

Before putting it into the refrigerator, make sure
the top is screwed back tightly onto the jar.
把它放进冰箱之前，一定要把罐子盖拧紧。

考点：put the screw(s) on... 对……施
　　　加压力，强迫
　　　screw up 拧紧，扭歪

sharp [ʃɑ:p] *adj.* 锋利的，敏锐的
　　　　　　 adv. （时刻）整，准

The robber rushed into the bank, with a sharp knife
in his hand.
那个强盗手持一把锋利的刀闯进了银行。

考点：sharp 放在时间后面，表示"（时
　　　刻）整，准"。eg. at 8 o'clock
　　　sharp 8点整。

shield [ʃi:ld] *n.* 盾；防护物；*vt.* 保护

It's said that the car polish is an effective shield
against rust.
据说，汽车上光蜡有防锈的作用。

spade [speid] *n.* 铲，铁锹

We dig holes with spades to fill the trees.
我们用铁锹挖洞栽树苗。

sponge [spʌndʒ] *n.* 海绵；*vt.* 用海绵擦，揩

People soaks up new knowledge like a sponge!
人们像海绵一样吸收新知识！

考点：sponge off 依赖他人生活

sticky ['stiki] *adj.* 黏性的，胶粘的

We use sticky paper tape to stick pieces together.
我们用胶纸把碎片粘在一起。

string [striŋ] *n.* 线，细绳，一串

She took up the scissors to cut the string.
她拿起剪刀剪断绳子。

考点：string along 欺骗，跟随
　　　string out （使）成行地展开

tap [tæp] *vt.* 轻叩，开发，利用

n. 塞子，龙头，清口

vi. 开发

He left the tap running for a day.
他忘了关水龙头，让水流了一天。

thermos ['θə:mɔs] *n.* 保温瓶

There is no water left in that thermos bottle.
那个暖瓶里没有一点水。

torch [tɔ:tʃ] *n.* 火炬，火把，手电筒

Shine your torch into the dark house.
你用手电筒照一下这黑暗的房子。

tube ['tju:b] *n.* 管，电子管，显像管

I bought a tube of tooth paste to take to school.
我买了一管牙膏带去学校。

indispensable [ˌindis'pensəbl] *adj.* 必不可少的，必需的

A library is indispensable to a college.
大学里图书馆是必不可少的。

真题

First published in 1927, the chats remain an ____ source for researchers.
A) intelligent   B) indispensable
C) inevitable   D) identical

详　解：选B。题意为：这些首次出版于1927年的图标一直是研究人员必不可少的资料。A) intelligent意思是"聪明的"；B) indispensable意思是"必不可少的"；C) inevitable意思是"不可避免的"；D) identical意思是"相同的"。

(CET-4 2004.6)

wax [wæks] *n.* 蜡，蜂蜡

I used to draw with wax crayon when I was a child.
我小时候经常用蜡笔画画。

whip [wip] *n.* 鞭子；*vt.* 鞭笞，搅打

The shepherd flicked the sheep with his whip.
牧羊人用鞭子轻轻抽打羊。

考点：whip up 鞭打，激起

machinery [mə'ʃi:nəri] *n.* 机器，器械

Our factory has phased in new machinery for increasing automation.
我们工厂已开始逐步采用新机器以提高自动化程度。

考点：machine 是单称，可数名词；
machinery 是总称，不可数名词。

住 打扫整理

spill [spil] *vt.* 使溢出；*vi.* 溢出

Take care not to spill a drop of the water on the ground.
注意一滴水也不要洒在地上。

stack [stæk] *n.* 堆，垛；*vt.* 堆积

Don't stack tabs and scattered on the table.
不要把标签堆叠地散落一桌。

考点：pile, stack, heap都有"堆"的意思。pile是一般用语，指把同种类的东西比较整齐地堆起来；stack是指将同种类且同种大小的东西整齐地堆在一起；heap指不分种类、杂乱地堆放。

sweep [swi:p] *vt.* 扫，刮起，扫过

My mother has to sweep the floor every day.
我妈妈不得不每天打扫一次地板。

tidy ['taidi] *adj.* 整洁的，整齐的；整洁，（使）整齐

Please make your room tidy and we will leave soon.
请把你的房间收拾干净，我们很快就要走了。

trim [trim] *adj.* 整齐的；*vt.* 使整齐

The room is very trim after cleaning.
打扫后这房间甚为整洁。

vacuum ['vækjuəm] *vt.&n.* 揩，擦

There is too much powder on your nose; go back to wipe it off.
你鼻子上的粉太多了，快回去抹掉。

考点：wipe out 擦掉，消灭

close [kləuz] *vt.* 关，闭，结束
Please close the widow for me.
请帮我关上窗户。

住 保养维修

detail ['di:teil] *n.* 细节，枝节，零件
Can you give us more details about a solid?
你能给我们多讲点有关立体图形的东西吗？

🔍**考点**：go into details 详细叙说，逐一说
明；in detail 详细地

equip [i'kwip] *vt.* 装备，配备
Our troop is well equipped.
我们军队装备良好。

🔍**考点**：be well / poorly equipped 是常
用搭配，表示"装备好（不
好）"。

equipment [i'kwipmənt] *n.* 装备，设备，配备
It is necessary for us to purchase some modern
office equipment.
我们有必要去购买一些现代化的办公设备。

maintain [mein'tein] *vt.* 维持，赡养，维
修，主持，赡养
It is said that they maintained only formal unity.
据说，他们只在表面上保持一致。

maintenance ['meintinəns] *n.* 维持，保持，
维修，抚养费
It's said that maintenance costs have been reduced
substantially.
据说，维修费已大幅度降低了。

mend [mend] *vt.* 修理，修补，缝补
Would you please help me mend my umbrella?
你能帮我修一下伞吗？

leak [li:k] *vi.* 渗，漏，泄露
n. 漏洞，泄露
A drop of water is leaking from the pipe, so we
must take some measures to stop it.
管子正在渗水，所以我们必须采取措施来阻止
这种情况。

真题

A house with a dangerous gas _____ can be
broken into immediately.
A) leak   B) crack
C) split   D) mess

详 解：选A. 题意为：如果房子出现了煤
气泄漏的危险情况，可以立刻破门而入。A)
leak意思是"（气体、液体的）泄漏"；B)
crack意思是"裂缝"；C) split意思是"撕裂
的长缝"；D) mess意思是"混乱"。

(CET-4 2003.6)

operational [ˌɔpə'reiʃənl] *adj.* 操作上的，可
使用的
The refrigerator is fully operational again.
冰箱又完全可以使用了。

repair [ri'pɛə] *vt.&n.* 修理，修补
The faucet in the kitchen is leaking; I have to find
someone to repair it.
厨房的水笼头漏水，我得找个人修修它。

restore [ris'tɔ:] *vt.* 恢复，归还，修补
After a course of proper treatment, I restored my
health.
经过适当的治疗，我恢复了健康。

crack [kræk] *vi.* 爆裂
n. 裂缝，裂纹
How can there be a crack in the windscreen?
挡风玻璃上怎么会有裂纹？

🔍**考点**：crack down 对……采取严厉措施
crack up 崩溃

住 购房租房

landlord ['lændlɔ:d] *n.* 地主，房东，店主
My landlord informed us that the rent would be put
up by 50 *yuan* a week.
我的房东说要把每周租金提高50元。

lease [li:s] *n.* 契约，租契；*vt.* 出租，租得
I am afraid he has lost the lease, because he always
does such things.
恐怕他已经把租契弄丢了，他总是这样丢三落
四的。

lodge [lɔdʒ] *vi.* 暂住，借宿，嵌入

vt. 供……临时住宿

n. 乡间小屋，旅社

The doctor couldn't take out the bullet, because it lodged in my spine.
医生取不出子弹，因为它嵌在我的脊椎骨里。

考点：board and lodging 膳宿

accommodation [əˌkɔmə'deiʃən] *n.* 招待设备，预订，铺位住宿

I will supply you with food and accommodation if you want to stay with me for a few days.
如果你想和我在一起待一些日子的话，我会给你提供食宿。

register ['redʒistə] *vt.&n.* 登记，注册

Though you are a famous statesman, you need to register at the hotel.
尽管你是一个著名的政员，你也要在旅馆登记姓名。

真题

With two weeks of arrival, all foreigners had to _____ with the local police.
A) inquire   B) consult
C) register   D) resolve

详 解：选C。题意为：在入境两周后，所有的外国人都必须去公安机关登记。 A) inquire 意思是"询问"；B) consult 意思是"商谈"；C) register 意思是"登记"；D) resolve意思是"决定"。

(CET-4 2005.1)

registration [ˌredʒis'treiʃən] *n.* 登记，注册

You can find every visitor's message on the registration form.
你能在登记表上看到每个来访者的信息。

accommodate [ə'kɔmədeit] *vt.* 容纳，供应，供给，顺应

This hotel could accommodate seven hundred tourists.
这家酒店可以容纳700名观光游客。

住 住址

address [ə'dres] *n.* 地址，演说，谈吐

vt. 向……讲话，向……发表演说

In case I forget your address, I will jot it down in my notebook.
以防我忘了你的地址，我要把它记在我的笔记本上。

adjacent [ə'dʒeisənt] *adj.* 临近的，毗邻的

I know him very well, because my house is adjacent to his.
我和他很熟，因为我的房子和他的相邻。

考点：be adjacent to 与……毗邻，临近

block [blɔk] *vt.* 堵塞，拦阻； *n.* 街区

The supermarket is close; it is only two blocks away.
超市很近，距此只有两条街。

考点：block off 封锁，封闭
block up 堵塞，挡住

downtown ['dauntaun] *adj.* 商业区的，闹市区的； *adv.* 在（到）闹市区

I was born in downtown Zhengzhou.
我出生在郑州市区。

inhabitant [in'hæbitənt] *n.* 居民，住户

There are few inhabitants on this island.
这个岛上没有多少居民。

locate [ləu'keit] *vt.* 探明，找出，查出，使坐落于

We must spend time in locating the position of the enemy.
我们必须花时间确定敌人的位置。

live [liv] *vi.* 居住，活；['laiv] *adj.* 活的

Be realistic! Don't live in the dreams.
现实点，别活在梦想之中。

考点：live off 依赖……生活；live on 以……为食物；live through 度过，经受住；live up to 遵守，符合，不辜负

location [ləu'keiʃən] *n.* 位置，场所，外景拍摄地

My home is in a convenient location.
我家的地理位置很方便。

place [pleis] *n.* 地方，地点，住所
This place will subside into a sleepy and closed provincial city.
这个地方将衰退为一个死气沉沉、闭关自守的省城。

🔍 考点：in place 在合适的位置
　　　　in place of 代替，交换
　　　　take place 发生，进行
　　　　take the place of 取代，代替

residence ['rezidəns] *n.* 居住，驻扎，住处
Let's go to my temporary residence and have a rest.
去我的临时住处休息会儿吧。

resident ['rezidənt] *adj.* 居住的；*n.* 居民
They say residents of the area are unhappy about the noise.
他们说该地区的居民对这吵闹声很是不满。

settle ['setl] *vt.* 安排，安放，调停
At last a swarm settled in a hive.
终于有一群蜂落进了蜂巢。

🔍 考点：settle down 定居，平静下来
　　　　settle for 勉强认可
　　　　settle on / upon 决定，选定

community [kə'mju:niti] *n.* 社区，社会，公社
The young man was very diligent and went to the community library to study on weekends.
那个年轻人很勤奋，每周末都去社区图书馆学习。

住 作息 🖊

asleep [ə'sli:p] *adj.* 睡着的，睡熟的
I fell asleep while I was reading a novel.
我在读小说的时候睡着了。

🔍 考点：asleep不能用very修饰，
　　　　be fast / sound asleep
　　　　睡得快（香）。

bath [ba:θ] *n.* 浴，洗澡，浴缸
The mother stripped the kid and put her in the bath tub.
妈妈脱掉孩子的衣服给她洗澡。

bathe [beið] *vt.* 给……洗澡，弄湿
　　　　vi. 洗澡，游泳
The baby was happy when I was bathing him.
给宝宝洗澡的时候，他可高兴了。

exhaust [ig'zɔ:st] *vt.* 使筋疲力尽，用尽
After a whole day's exercise, I'm completely exhausted.
一天的运动下来，我精疲力竭。

fatigue [fə'ti:g] *n.* 疲劳，劳累
I hate to work overtime, for it always leaves me great fatigue.
我讨厌加班加点，因为我会感到疲惫不堪。

真题

I suffered from mental _____ because of stress from my job.
A) fatigue　　　B) damage
C) relief　　　　D) release

详 解：选A。题意为：由于工作压力大，我的精神极为疲惫。A) fatigue意思是"疲劳，劳累"；B) damage意思是"（物体的物理）损坏"；C) relief 意思是"放松"；D) release意思是"发行，释放"。

(CET-4 2003.6)

leisure ['li:ʒə] *n.* 闲暇，休闲
I'm busy now; I have no leisure for reading stories.
我现在很忙，没有空闲时间读故事。

🔍 考点：at leisure 有空，从容不迫地

nap [næp] *n.* 小睡，打盹，瞌睡
　　　　vi. 打盹，小睡
Do you want to take a nap at noon?
你中午想要小睡一下吗？

nightmare ['naitmɛə] *n.* 噩梦，可怕的事物
Her staying in the country is a total nightmare.
在那个国家待的日子对她来说纯粹是一场噩梦。

rest [rest] *n.* 休息，安静，静止，剩余部分，其余的人
There were 5 votes in favor of my suggestion, and the rest against.
只有5票赞成我的建议，其他的全是反对。

rouse [rauz] *vt.* 唤醒，唤起，惊起

We had to shake her several times to rouse her from sleep.
我们推了她几次才将她从梦中唤醒。

🔍 考点：rise, rouse多用于具体意义；
arise, arouse多用于抽象意义。

timetable ['taim,teibəl] *n.* 时间表，时刻表

The timetable is subject to alteration in summer time.
在夏季，时间表有可能更改。

wake [weik] *vi.* 醒，醒来；*vt.* 唤醒

Be quiet, or you will wake the sleeping baby.
安静点，不然会把那个孩子吵醒的。

🔍 考点：wake up 醒来
wake (up) to 认识到，意识到

waken ['weikən] *vi.* 醒来；*vt.* 弄醒

Waken up by a slight noise, he was unable to fall asleep again.
被一点轻微的噪音吵醒后，他再也无法入睡了。

yawn [jɔːn] *vi.* 打呵欠；*n.* 呵欠

My fourteen-month-old niece begins to yawn around nine o'clock every night.
我14个月大的侄女一到晚上9点就开始打哈欠。

awake [ə'weik] *adj.* 醒着的；*vt.* 唤醒

After one night's sleep, the drunkard was wide awake.
经过一晚上的休息，那个醉汉完全清醒了。

🔍 考点：awake和wake虽然同义，但awake通常用于"觉悟，觉醒"的比较意义。

🚗 能源动力

fuel [fjuəl] *n.* 燃料；*vt.* 给……加燃料
Convenience of fuel is a prime factor.
燃料的方便性是首要因素。

gasoline ['gæsəliːn] *n.* （美）汽油
The price of gasoline is higher and higher.

油价越来越高。

gallon ['gælən] *n.* 加仑

They need at least a gallon of petro to finish the last distance.
他们至少需要一加仑的汽油去走完剩下的路。

generate ['dʒenə,reit] *vt.* 给……加燃料

This machine can generate electricity.
这台机器能发电。

真题

Extensive reporting on television has helped to _____ interest in a wide variety of sports and activities.
A) gather   B) generate
C) assemble   D) yield

详解：选B。题意为：电视上的大量报道有助于人们对各类体育运动产生兴趣。A) gather意思是"收集，聚集"；B) generate意思是"引起（情感反应）"；C) assemble意思是"装配，集合"；D) yield意思是"生产，产生（结果，答案等）"。

(CET-4 2001.6)

horsepower ['hɔːs,pauə] *n.* 马力

The horsepower of the new automobile is increasing steadily.
新车的马力在不断增加。

oil [ɔil] *n.* 油，石油；*vt.* 加油于

The price of oil jumped sharply this year.
今年油价急剧上涨。

petrol ['petrəl] *n.* （英）汽油

We all know that the petrol is highly combustible.
众所周知，汽油极易燃烧。

petroleum [pi'trəuliəm] *n.* 石油

Our teacher told us that the petroleum is one-off, non-renewable resource.
老师告诉我们石油是一次性的非再生资源。

scarce [skɛəs] *adj.* 缺乏的，稀有的

It is estimated that the supply of cruel oil is scarce.
据估计，原油供应不足。

🔍 考点：make oneself scarce 溜走，躲开

scarcity ['skɛəsiti] *n.* 缺乏，不足，萧条
The scarcity of water caused the reduction in harvest.
缺水造成了粮食的减产。

shortage ['ʃɔ:tidʒ] *n.* 不足，缺少，不足额
The shortage of capital is a perennial phenomenon to my family.
资金短缺对我们家来说是终年不断的问题。

steam [sti:m] *n.* 蒸汽；*vi.* 蒸发；*vt.* 蒸
In 19th century，the motive power of car was steam.
19世纪时，汽车的动力是蒸汽。
考点： steam up （使）蒙上水汽

sufficient [sə'fiʃənt] *adj.* 足够的，充分的
Dad had sufficient confidence in his son.
老爸对儿子充满信心。

utility [ju:'tiliti] *n.* 效用，有用，实用
Their research project has little practical utility.
他们的研究项目没有多少实用价值。

utilize ['ju:tilaiz] *vt.* 利用
You must utilize all available resources to export this programme.
你必须利用一切可以得到的资源去开发这个项目。
考点： utilize与use的不同在于：utilize 往往指使本来无用的或者未开发的东西变为有用的。

行 交通工具

aircraft ['ɛəkra:ft] *n.* 飞机，飞行器
This is the first time for me to travel by aircraft.
这是我第一次坐飞机旅行。

airway ['ɛəwei] *n.* 航线，航空公司
Finland is the closest European country in airway from Asia to Europe .
芬兰是欧洲国家中空中航线与亚洲最接近的一个国家。

airline ['ɛə,lain] *n.* 航空公司，航线
Everyone hates airline changes schedules for no apparent reason.
每个人都讨厌航空公司无故改变班次。

airplane ['ɛəplein] *n.* 飞机；*vi.* 坐飞机
I am wondering why he is afraid of taking airplane.
我在想为什么他害怕坐飞机。

airport ['ɛəpɔ:t] *n.* 机场，航空站
A luxury airport will be built in this city.
这个城市将建造一个豪华的机场。

anchor ['æŋkə] *n.* 锚；*vi.* 抛锚，停泊
When we were on vacation, we saw a boat anchor in the vicinity of the coast.
当我们在度假的时候，我们看到了有船在附近的海岸抛锚。
考点： cast / weigh anchor 抛（起）锚
lie at anchor 停泊着

auto ['ɔ:təu] *n.* （口语）汽车
Who is the pioneer in the auto industry?
谁是汽车工业的先驱者?

automobile [ɔ:təmə'bi:l] *n.* 汽车，机动车
I will buy an automobile when I get enough money.
攒够钱的时候，我会买辆汽车。

bicycle ['baisikl] *n.* 自行车，脚踏车
This kind of electric bicycle is inferior.
这种类型的电动车质量很次。

bike [baik] *n.* 自行车；*vt.* 骑自行车
Police restored the stolen bike to its owner.
警察把被盗的自行车归还给了失主。

boat [bəut] *n.* 小船，艇，渔船
There is no boat. How could I cross the river?
这里没有一只船，我如何过河呢?

brake [breik] *n.* 闸，刹车；*vi.* 制动
The car in front of me suddenly braked to a stop.
我前面那辆车突然刹车停了下来。

bus [bʌs] *n.* 公共汽车
I got up late this morning, and didn't catch the bus.
今天早上起床晚了，没有赶上公交车。

cabin ['kæbin] *n.* 小屋，船舱，机舱
The support of the cabin is rigid.
小屋的支柱很坚固。

canal [kə'næl] *n.* 运河，沟渠，管

The canals take water to the rice fields.
水渠把水引到稻田里。

canoe [kə'nu:] *n.* 独木舟，皮艇，划子

He almost upset the canoe.
他差点把小船弄翻。

car [kɑ:] *n.* 汽车，小汽车，轿车

The victims of the car accident were buried yesterday.
车祸的遇难者昨天举行了葬礼。

carriage ['kærɪdʒ] *n.* 客车厢，四轮马车

We'll be sitting in the second carriage from the bottom of the train.
我们的座位在倒数第二节车厢。

carrier ['kærɪə] *n.* 运输工具，运载工具

The mail carrier in our neighborhood is a friend of all children.
我们这个街区的邮递员是孩子们的朋友。

carry ['kæri] *vt.* 携带，运载，传送

Seeing the sky was cloudy, mother told David to carry an umbrella.
看到天阴了，妈妈让大卫带着伞。

cart [kɑ:t] *n.* 二轮运货马车

William, lying in his cart with his feet sticking out, watched what happened in the street happily.
威廉坐在他的马车里，脚伸到外面，高兴地看着街上发生的一切。

charter ['tʃɑ:tə] *n.* 宪章，特许，（船、机、车等的）租赁
　　　　　　　　 vi. 包租，特许，发给……执照
　　　　　　　　 adj. 特许的

They are rich enough to charter a helicopter for the trip.
他们很富有，租了架直升飞机去旅行。

conductor [kən'dʌktə] *n.* 售票员，（乐队）指挥

This kind of bus is without bus conductor.
这种公交车是没有售票员的。

convey [kən'vei] *vt.* 传送，运送，传播

I can't convey my feelings in words.
我的情感难以言表。

cycle ['saikl] *n.* 自行车，循环

May heaven help anyone, car driver or pedestrian, who strays even momentarily into a cycle lane.
但愿老天保佑那些一时误入自行车道的汽车司机或行人吧。

cyclist ['saiklist] *n.* 骑自行车的人

Although the cyclist was unhurt, his bicycle was crushed between the lorry and the wall.
尽管骑车者没有受伤，但他的自行车在货车和墙壁之间被挤扁了。

deck [dek] *n.* 甲板，舱面，层面

There are four kinds of suits in a deck of playing cards.
在一副扑克牌里有4种花色。

engine ['endʒin] *n.* 发动机，引擎，机车

This engine would still not have the reliability of jet engines.
这个引擎仍不会具有喷气式发动机那样的可靠性。

flight [flait] *n.* 航班，飞行，逃跑

He can't catch the next flight.
他赶不上下一个航班了。

garage ['gærɑ:ʒ] *n.* 车库，加油站

He parked his car in the garage after shopping back.
购物回来后，他把车停在了车库。

helicopter ['helikɔptə] *n.* 直升机

There is a helicopter carrying out a task in the sky.
空中有一架直升机正在执行任务。

jet [dʒet] *n.* 喷气式飞机，喷嘴

The students learned the theory of jet this class.
这节课上，同学们学习了喷气式飞机的原理。

lorry ['lɔri] *n.* 运货汽车，卡车

The lorry was so heavy that the bridge was ruined.
这辆卡车太重了，把桥都给压坏了。

motor ['məutə] *n.* 发动机，机动车

Everytime we go out by plane, one of my friends will ask what we should do if the motor breaks.
每次我们坐飞机出去的时候，我的一个朋友就问如果飞机的发动机坏了我们该怎么办。

motorbike ['məutəbaik] *n.* 摩托车，轻型摩托车

We always see him going about by motorbike.
我们总是见他骑摩托车。

plane [plein] *n.* 平面，飞机

Lots of people were killed in the plane crash.
很多人在飞机坠毁中丧生了。

sailing ['seiliŋ] *n.* 航班，帆船运动

My outside interests are fishing and sailing.
我的业余爱好是钓鱼和航海。

steamer ['sti:mə] *n.* 轮船，汽船

He put her aboard a steamer bound for London.
他把她送上了一艘驶向伦敦的汽船。

submarine ['sʌbməri:n] *adj.* 水下的
n. 潜水艇

Submarine can submerge very quickly in the ocean.
潜水艇在海里的下潜速度非常快。

subway ['sʌbwei] *n.* 地道，地下铁路

An explosion happened in the subway this afternoon.
今天下午地铁里发生了爆炸事件。

tanker ['tæŋkə] *n.* 油船，空中加油飞机

The tanker taking on 200,000 barrels of crude oil sank and the oil polluted the sea.
那艘装载了20万桶原油的油轮沉没了，石油污染了海面。

van [væn] *n.* 大篷车，运货车

Their factory bought a van for sending goods last week.
他们工厂上周买了一辆运货车。

vehicle ['vi:ikl] *n.* 车辆，机动车

In general, the vehicles on the street are a lot in the rush hour.
通常在高峰时刻，街上的车辆会很多。

vessel ['vesl] *n.* 容器，船，飞船，管

When the vessel touched the strand, it was dark.
当小船停靠海滩时，天已黑了。

waggon ['wægən] *n.* 四轮运货马车

The waggon is on the way to farm.
货车正在去往农场的路上。

crew [kru:] *n.* 全体船员

The experienced old crew always throw their soul into the oars.
有经验的船员总是全神贯注地摇桨。

> 考点：crew作主语时，如看做整体，谓语用单数；如看做成员们，谓语用复数。

aeroplane ['ɛərəplein] *n.* 飞机

That famous star owns a private aeroplane.
那个明星有一架私人飞机。

行 交通状况

convenience [kən'vi:njəns] *n.* 便利，方便，厕所

Convenience stores can be found everywhere in this city.
在这个城市里，便利店随处可见。

convenient [kən'vi:njənt] *adj.* 便利的，近便的

It is convenient to use a digital camera.
数码相机用起来很方便。

crowd [kraud] *n.* 群，大众，一伙人

The old lady thrust herself through the crowd to look for her pet dog.
老妇人挤过了人群去寻找她的宠物狗。

facility [fə'siliti] *n.* 设备，容易，便利

There are no cooking facilities in my house.
我屋子里没有烹饪设备。

inevitable [in'evitəbl] *adj.* 多泥的，泥泞的，浑浊的

It is inevitable to be late when encountering such traffic jam.
遇到这样的交通拥挤状况，迟到是不可避免的。

facilitate [fə'siliteit] *vt.* 使顺利，使容易

Shopping on line facilitates people's life.
网上购物方便了人们的生活。

真题

Eisenhower's interstate highways bound the nation together in new ways and ____ major economic growth by making commerce less expensive.

A) facilitated   B) modified
C) mobilized   D) terminated

详 解：选A。题意为：艾森豪威尔的州际高速公路将全国以新的方式联系起来，并通过使贸易成本降低促进了主要的经济增长。A) facilitate意思是"推动，促进"；B) modify意思是"修改，改进"；C) mobilize意思是"移动，调动"；D) terminate意思是"停止，结束"。

(CET-4 2009.6)

traffic ['træfik] *n.* 交通，通行，交通量
Most cities in China have traffic problems.
中国人部分城市都存在交通问题。

考点：交通量的大小用heavy / light，或者a lot / a little表达，不用large / small表达。eg. The traffic is heavy. 交通很繁忙。

relief [ri'li:f] *n.* 减轻，救济，援救
Seeing my naughty nephew got high marks in the exam, I felt an inexpressible relief.
看到淘气的外甥考试得了高分，我感到一种说不出的宽慰。

真题

To our ____, Geoffrey's illness proved not to be as serious as we had feared.

A) relief   B) judgement
C) view   D) anxiety

详 解：选A。题意为：让我们欣慰的是，杰弗里的病不像我们担心的那样严重。本题考察介词的固定搭配，选项中只有relief能跟在to one's后面，表示"让人放心的是"。in one's judgement 表示"在某人看来"；in one's view 表示"以某人的看法"；in anxiety 表示"焦虑，担忧"。

(CET -4 2002.6)

relieve [ri'li:v] *vt.* 减轻，解除，救济
How to relieve the traffic congestion?
如何缓解交通拥挤？

考点：relieve sb. from 使某人从……解脱出来

行 **方向位置**

compass ['kʌmpəs] *n.* 罗盘，指南针，圆规
You can use the compass to find the right direction.
你可以用指南针找到正确的方向。

direction [di'rekʃən] *n.* 方向，方位，指导
The direction of the thrust of the rockets is controlled by computer.
火箭推力的方向是由电脑控制的。

downward ['daunwəd] *adj.* 向下的
　　　　　　　　　　　　adv. 向下地
He is on the downward path.
他正在走下坡路。

north [nɔ:θ] *n.* 北，北方；*adj.* 北方的
It's cold outside, and the north wind is blowing hard.
外面很冷，北风刮得很猛。

northeast ['nɔ:θ'i:st] *n.* 东北
　　　　　　　　　　　adj. 位于东北的
I'm afraid the Northeast Tigers are in danger of becoming extinct.
我担心东北虎有灭绝的危险。

northern ['nɔ:ðən] *adj.* 北方的，北部的
The president emphasized that they aren't going to militarize the northern border.
那位总统强调说，他们不会将北方的边界军事化。

northwest ['nɔ:θ'west] *n.* 西北
　　　　　　　　　　　adj. 位于西北的
We can see that Dutch lies in the northwest of Europe from the world map.
从世界地图上我们可以看到，荷兰位于欧洲的西北部。

sideways ['saidweiz] *adv.* 斜着，斜向一边地
The proud woman glanced, sideways, at the old beggar and kept silent.
那位傲慢的女士斜眼看了一眼老乞丐，依然默不作声。

towards [tə'wɔ:dz] *prep.* 向，对于，接近
Let us examine our attitudes towards the teacher.
我们先来检讨一下我们对老师的态度。

考点：to, towards都有"朝……"的意思：to强调到达目的地，towards强调方向。

among [ə'mʌŋ] *prep.* 在……之中
You may choose your favorite flavor among these candies.
你可以从这些糖果中选择你最喜欢的口味。

amongst [ə'mʌŋst] *prep.* 在……之中(= among)
It's difficult for me to choose amongst these beautiful clothes.
这么多漂亮的衣服，选起来可真难。

around [ə'raund] *prep.* 在……周围，环绕，绕过，在……各处，大约
Lots of children crowded around the tree.
许多孩子都围在那棵树的周围。

aside [ə'said] *adv.* 在旁边，到旁边
Let's have a rest and lay the problem aside for a while.
让我们休息一会，先把问题搁一搁。

考点：aside from 除……之外

anywhere ['eniwɛə] *adv.* 在什么地方，某处
I'm looking for my book, but I can't find it anywhere.
我在找我的书，可是到处都找不着。

before [bi'fɔ:] *prep.* 在……以前，在……前面
Check the brake before you drive the car.
开车前先检查一下刹车。

behind [bi'haind] *prep.* 在……后面
I live in a house left behind by my grandmother.
我住在外婆遗留下的房子里。

below [bi'ləu] *prep.* 在……下面（以下）
Winter is very cold here; it's always five to ten below zero.
这里的冬天很冷，气温总是在零下5度到10度。

beneath [bi'ni:θ] *prep.* 在……下
I'm so nervous beneath the gaze of so many eyes.
在这么多眼睛的注视下，我很紧张。

beside [bi'said] *prep.* 在……旁边
You can take your seat beside Lily.
你可以坐在莉莉的旁边。

考点：beside oneself 极度兴奋，对自己的感情失去控制

centre ['sentə] *n.* 中心，中枢
vt. 集中
In my opinion, universities should be centres of culture.
我认为大学应该是文化的中心。

corner ['kɔ:nə] *n.* 角落，角，犄角，边远地区
The girl stood at the street corner, racked by indecision, and began to cry.
女孩站在街角，犹豫不决，然后哭了起来。

考点：around the corner 在附近
turn the corner 出现转机

extent [iks'tent] *n.* 广度，范围，程度
Monopoly can hold back market competition to some extent.
垄断在一定程度上阻碍了市场竞争的发展。

between [bi'twi:n] *prep.* 在……中间
This matter increased the conflict between us.
这件事加剧了我们之间的冲突。

考点：in between 在……之间

真题

Reading _____ the lines, I would say that the Government are more worried than they will admit.
A) behind   B) between
C) along   D) among

详 解：选B。题意为：体会其言外之意，我认为政府担心的程度远比他们愿意承认的深。read between the lines是固定词组，意思是"体会言外之意，体会字里行间隐含的意思。

(CET-4 2002.1)

beyond [bi'jɒnd] *prep.* 在……的那边

Beyond question, you are the right person for this position.
毫无疑问，你是这份工作的合适人选。

central ['sentrəl] *adj.* 中心的，主要的

I'm glad that the central heating has been installed in our house.
我真高兴我们家安装了中央暖气系统。

middle ['midl] *n.* 中部
　　　　　　　　adj. 中部的，中等的

The ring on her middle finger shows that she is engaged.
她中指上的戒指表明她已经订婚了。

midst ['midst] *n.* 中部，中间

We have walked one hour in the midst of a heavy rain.
我们在大雨中走了一个小时。

🔍 考点：in the midst of 在……之中，正在……的时候

on [ɒn] *prep.* 在……上，在……旁

The dictionary is on the desk.
字典在课桌上。

underneath [ˌʌndə'ni:θ] *adv.* 在头顶

There's a crack on the underneath of the floor.
地板下面有一条裂痕。

overhead ['əʊvəhed] *adj.* 在头顶上的，架空的

She put the book in the overhead locker.
她把书放在上头的柜子里。

rear [riə] *n.* 后部，背面
　　　　　　vt. 抚养，培养

The hall is in the rear of the center building.
礼堂在中央大楼的后部。

🔍 考点：bring up the rear 处在（队列或者比赛中）最后的位置，殿后

over ['əʊvə] *prep.* 在……上方，超过

There is no bridge over the river.
河上面没有桥。

by [bai] *prep.* 在……旁，被，由

I was woken up by a loud noise last night.
昨晚我被一阵喧闹声吵醒。

行 驾驶&乘坐 ✐

gear [giə] *n.* 齿轮，排挡，设备
　　　　　　vt. 使适应，使适合

Change into first gear when you go down the hill.
下山时要换第一挡。

🔍 考点：gear up 准备好，作好安排
　　　　　be geared to 适用于
　　　　　gear...to... 使……适应于

high-speed [hai'spi:d] *adj.* 高速的

The computer is working at a high-speed loading.
电脑正在高速下载中。

move [mu:v] *vt.* 移动，感动；*n.* 动

The movie star was besieged by his fans and couldn't move forwards.
这个电影明星被粉丝们围在中间，前进不得。

overtake [ˌəʊvə'teik] *vt.* 追上，赶上，压倒
　　　　　　　　vi. 超车

Pursue quickly after them; I believe you can overtake them.
快去追，我相信你能追上他们。

passenger ['pæsindʒə] *n.* 乘客，旅客，过路人

All the passengers must board the ship before 8 a.m.
所有的乘客必须在早上8点前登船。

pause [pɔ:z] *vi.&n.* 中止，暂停

She made a pause when she heard that somebody called her name.
当听到有人叫她的名字时，她停顿了一下。

press [pres] *vt.* 压，按，揿，催促

If you need some help, please press this button.
如果你有什么需要，请按这个按钮。

🔍 考点：press on 加紧进行；be pressed for 缺少（时间，钱，空间）

queue [kju:] *n.* 行列；*vi.* 排队等候

I have no choice but wait in a long, slow queue.
我没有别的选择，只能在很长的、慢慢移动的队伍里等候。

🔍考点： jump the queue 不按次序排队，插队；queue up 排队等候

schedule ['ʃedju:l] *n.* 时刻表，清单
vt. 安排，排定

You can look up the train schedule.
您可以查询火车时刻表。

🔍考点： ahead of schedule 提前
on schedule 按时间表，及时

steer [stiə] *vi.&vt.* 驾驶

We must steer by those deer across the road.
我们要小心地绕过那些过马路的鹿。

🔍考点： steer clear of 绕开，避开

tow [təu] *vt.&n.* 拖引，牵引

My car's broken down; I had to tow it to the nearest garage.
我的车抛锚了，不得不把它拖到最近的修车厂。

🔍考点： in tow 被拖着，陪伴着
on tow （车辆）被拖（带）着

backward ['bækwəd] *adj.* 向后的，倒的
adv. 倒

Our teacher asked him to make a backward step.
我们老师让他后退一步。

🔍考点： know...backward(s) 对……极其熟悉

行 **步行**

out [aut] *adv.* 出，在外，出来

Having had supper, he went out for a walk.
晚饭后，他出去散步了。

pace [peis] *n.* 步，步速；*vi.* 踱步

The soldier took three paces forward.
士兵向前走了3步。

🔍考点： keep pace (with) （与……）齐步前进，（与……）并驾齐驱
set the pace 起带头作用

stride [straid] *vi.* 大踏步走
n. 大步，步伐，进展

In a big stride he came out of the room to run after his wife.
他一个箭步出了房间去追他的妻子。

🔍考点： take in (one's) stride 轻而易举地应付，轻松地胜任

wander ['wɔndə] *vi.* 漫游，迷路，离题

He had nothing to do and wandered in the streets.
他闲来无事可做，在街上闲逛。

行 **问路指路**

accessible [ək'sesəbl] *adj.* 可达到的，可接近的，易懂的

I know such information is not really accessible.
我知道这种信息不是很容易得到的。

across [ə'krɔs] *prep.* 横过，在……对面

The camels are carrying our goods across the desert.
骆驼正驮着我们的货物在沙漠里行走。

avenue ['ævinju:] *n.* 林荫道，道路，大街

Having a walk on the avenue after dinner is comfortable.
吃完饭在街上散步很舒服。

cross [krɔs] *vt.* 穿过，使交叉；*n.* 十字架

It was said that an expressway would cross their village.
据说，一条高速公路将穿过他们的村庄。

directly [di'rektli] *adv.* 直接地，立即

You can tell me what you think directly.
你可以直接告诉我你是怎么想的。

🔍考点： direct, directly的区别：direct用于具体意义："不拐弯，不转向"；directly用于抽象意义上的"直接地"。

distance ['distəns] *n.* 距离，间距，远处

We could see several smoking stacks in the distance.
我们可以看到远处好几个冒着烟的烟囱。

考点：in the distance 在远处

keep a distance 对……冷淡

---

access ['ækses] *n.* 接近，通道，入口

Don't worry. He has access to men who can help him get work.

别担心，他有办法接近帮助他找工作的人。

真题

For professional athletes, _____ to the Olympics means that they have a chance to enter the history books.

A) access   B) attachment
C) appeal   D) approach

详 解：选A。题意为：对职业运动员而言，能参加奥运会意味着他们有机会被载入史册。A) access to 意思是"进入"；B) attachment 意思是"附件"；C) appeal 意思是"兴趣"；D) approach 意思是"方法，途径"。

(CET-4 2005.6)

---

line [lain] *n.* 线，排，路线，线条；*vt.* 使成

一排，画线标出；*vt.* 排队，排齐

We could see I didn't know why he drew some lines in this document.

我不知道他为什么在这份文档上画一些线。

考点：in line 成一直线，成一排；in line

with 与……一致；line up 使成

行，使排队；on line 与计算机连

接的，联机的；out of line 不成一

条直线

---

lose [lu:z] *vt.* 失去，迷失，输掉，白费

When he lost his job, the whole family lived a precarious existence.

他失业后，全家人过着朝不保夕的生活。

考点：lose oneself in 专心致志于

---

map [mæp] *n.* 地图，图，天体图

When you want to go out for travel, I believe map is a good helper.

当你想出去旅行时，我坚信地图会是一个很好的帮手。

mile [mail] *n.* 英里

The church was located beside the river, five miles from my house.

这个教堂坐落在河边，离我家有5英里远。

---

near [niə] *adv.* 近，接近；*adj.* 近的

Do you often go to the bookstore near our school?

你经常去我们学校附近的书店吗？

---

nearby ['niəbai] *adv.* 在附近；*adj.* 附近的

He is going to raise funds to build a factory nearby.

他正准备筹集资金在附近建一个工厂。

---

next [nekst] *adj.* 下次的，紧接的，贴近的

The Whites are planning to go skiing in Switzerland next winter.

怀特夫妇正计划明年冬天去瑞士滑雪。

---

nowhere ['nəuhwɛə] *adv.* 任何地方都不

She is going to nowhere else.

她不准备再去别的什么地方了。

---

opposite ['ɔpəzit] *adj.* 对面的，相反的

n. 对立物

My house is opposite to the school.

我家在学校对面。

考点：the opposite directions 相反的方

向；live in the house opposite

住在对面的房子里

---

path [pɑ:θ] *n.* 路，小道，道路

Under the shine of the setting sun, there are a young couple ambling along the path.

夕阳下，一对年轻夫妇悠闲地在小路上漫步。

---

straight [streit] *adv.* 直；*adj.* 直的，正直的

Go straight down the road and you can find the bank.

顺着这条路一直走就到银行了。

---

wayside ['weisaid] *n.* 路边

When night comes, local inhabitants sell their handicrafts on the wayside.

到了晚上，当地居民在路边出售他们的手工艺品。

---

crossing ['krɔsiŋ] *n.* 交叉，十字路口

Go along this road and turn left when you reach a crossing, and then you can see it on your right.

沿着这条路一直走，走到一个十字路口时左转，它就在你的右侧。

crossroads ['krɔsrəudz] *n.* 交叉路，十字路口
I happened to meet him at the crossroads.
我碰巧在十字路口遇见了他。

destination [ˌdesti'neiʃən] *n.* 目的地，终点，目标
Oh, the letter was sent to a wrong destination.
噢，信被我送错了地方。

行 交通规则

driving-licence ['draiviŋ'laisəns] *n.* 驾照
The traffic policeman is looking at my driving-licence.
交警正在看我的驾照。

fine [fain] *adj.* 美好的，纤细的
　　　　　 n. 罚金，罚款
What he did is a fine display of courage.
他的所作所为是勇气的充分表现。
考点：fine是可数名词。
　　　　eg. pay a fine of 200 dollars
　　　　交200美元的罚款。

toll [tɔːl] *n.* 过路费，损失；*vi.&vt.* 敲钟
Anyone traveling across the road has to pay a toll.
过这条路的人都要付通行费。

limit ['limit] *n.* 限度，限制，范围，极限；
　　　　 vt. 限制，限定
Because of exceeding the speed limit, my brother was taken to the police box.
因为超速，我哥哥被带到了警察亭。
考点：set a limit to / set limits to
　　　　对……加以限制

limitation [ˌlimi'teiʃən] *n.* 限制，限度，局限
It is a truth that we can't transcend the limitations of the ego in some sense.
在一定程度上，我们无法超越自我的局限性是一个真理。

interval ['intəvəl] *n.* 间隔，休息，间距
An interval of a year elapsed when he came back.
隔了一年他才回来。

考点：at intervals 不时，每隔一段距离

 真题

It may be necessary to stop _____ in the learning process and go back to the difficult points in the lessons.
A) at a distance　　　　B) at intervals
C) at ease　　　　　　 D) at length

详　解：选B。题意为：学习过程中不时停下来学习里面的重点是很有必要的。
A) at a distance意思是"隔一段距离"；B) at intervals意思是"不时"；C) at ease意思是"安逸，自由自在"；D) at length意思是"最终，详细地"。

(CET-4 2005.12)

regulation [regju'leiʃən] *n.* 规则，规章，管理
Tom often attempts to escape being fined whenever he breaks traffic regulations.
每当汤姆违反交通规则时，他常常企图逃避罚款处分。

行 交通事故

accident ['æksidənt] *n.* 意外事故，（交通）事故
I hope there can be no car accident in the world. I hate that bad news.
我希望世界上不再有交通事故，我讨厌那些坏消息。

crash [kræʃ] *n.* 爆裂声，撞毁
　　　　　 vt. 撞毁，粉碎
　　　　　 vi. 猛撞，坠毁
Steve crashed his jeep when he drove it to visit his teacher.
史蒂芬开着他的吉普车去拜访他的老师时撞坏了他的车。
考点：crash into 与……相撞

danger ['deindʒə] *n.* 危险，危险事物
Of course there is always danger in a battle.
战场上总是有危险的。

dangerous ['deɪndʒərəs] *adj.* 危险的，不安全的

There is an old saying: a little knowledge is a dangerous thing.
有一句老话叫做：一知半解是很危险的事。

*

happen ['hæpən] *vt.* 发生，碰巧，恰好

In retrospect, the thing happened yesterday was a nightmare.
回想起来，昨天所发生的事真是一场噩梦。

🔑 考点：happen to do sth. 或it happens that... 碰巧……

*

slope [sləup] *vt.* 倾斜；*n.* 倾斜，斜面

They decided to slide down the grassy slope.
他们决定顺着这草坡滑下去。

*

smooth [smuːð] *adj.* 平滑的，平静的，圆滑的，调匀的
vt. 弄平，使平整

We hope the thing becomes smooth finally.
我们希望事情最终变得一切顺利。

🔑 考点：smooth over 缓和，减轻

*

scene [siːn] *n.* 发生地点，道具，场面

I don't like that movie; you know the comic scenes were overdone.
我不喜欢那个电影，里面的滑稽场面演得太过夸张。

🔑 考点：behind the scene 在幕后，不公开的

真题

Computer power now allows automatic searches of fingerprint files to match a print at a crime ____.
A) stage   B) scene
C) location D) occasion

详解：选B。题意为：现在计算机可以自动搜索指纹档案，以找到和犯罪现场相匹配的指纹。at a crime scene是固定搭配，意思是"在犯罪现场"。A) stage常与at/in搭配，意思是"阶段，时期"；C) location常与on搭配，意思是"电影的外景拍摄"；D) occasion常与on搭配，意思是"间或，偶尔"。

(CET-4 2005.6)

survival [sə'vaɪvəl] *n.* 幸存，幸存者，残存物

We need food and water for survival.
我们为了生存需要食物和水。

*

survive [sə'vaɪv] *vi.* 活下来，幸存，幸免于
vt. 幸免于，比……活得长

There is no one to survive the accident.
这次事故没有幸存者。

🔑 考点：survive本身已有"幸免，幸存"的意思，因而后面不需要再跟介词。
eg. survive the earthquake 从地震中幸存下来。

*

survivor [sə'vaɪvə] *n.* 幸存者，残存者

Being a survivor of a disaster, he decided to begin a new life with his family.
劫后余生的他决定和家人开始新的生活。

*

tumble ['tʌmbl] *vi.* 暴跌，跌倒，翻滚，弄乱，明白，突然发现
vt. 使跌倒，使暴跌，乱扔
n. 暴跌，跌跤，混乱

She tumbled down the stairs suddenly and got hurt.
她突然滚下了楼梯受伤了。

🔑 考点：tumble to（突然）明白，领悟

*

via ['vaɪə] *prep.* 经过，通过

He succeeded via illegal means.
他通过违法行为获得了成功。

*

wreck [rek] *n.* 失事，残骸；*vt.* 破坏

In spite of all his efforts, the ship wasn't saved from wreck.
尽管做了最大的努力，那条失事的船只仍未得到营救。

行 道路运输 🖊

freeway ['friːweɪ] *n.* 高速公路

One tire of our car blew out on the freeway last night.
昨晚我们的一个轮胎在高速公路上爆了。

*

expressway [ik'spresweɪ] *n.* 高速公路，快速干道

The expressway mars the beauty of the countryside.

日常生活 行

这条高速公路破坏了农村的田园美景。

highway ['haiwei] *n.* 公路，大路

A fast highway is being built.
一条高速公路正在修建。

incline [in'klain] *n.* 斜坡；*vt.* 使倾斜

Tad rolled the apple down the incline.
泰德让苹果从斜面上滚下。

motorway ['məutəwei] *n.* 高速公路，快车道

You drove above the speed limit on the motorway.
你在高速公路上超速驾驶了。

pave [peiv] *vt.* 铺，筑（路等）

The road from the garden to the gate is paved with bricks.
从花园到大门的路是用砖铺的。

🔍 **考点**：pave the way for 为……铺平道路，为……作准备

pavemen ['peivmənt] *n.* （英）人行道

The crazy car was forced to stop by the traffic policemen after knocking over four pedestrians on the pavement.
那辆疯狂的小轿车在人行道上撞到4个行人后，被交警强行拦下。

railroad ['reilrəud] *n.* 铁路；*vi.* 由铁路运输

My uncle's first job was working on a railroad.
我叔叔的第一份工作就是在铁路上干活。

railway ['reilwei] *n.* 铁路，铁道

Though the driver raced me to the railway station, I still missed the train.
虽然司机飞速送我到火车站，我还是误了火车。

ringroad ['riŋrəud] *n.* 环城公路

A terrible car accident happened on the ringroad just now.
刚刚环城公路上发生了一起可怕的车祸。

rough [rʌf] *adj.* 表面不平的，粗略的

I don't like the rough shirt because it prickles my skin.
我不喜欢这件粗布衬衫，因为它使我的皮肤感到刺刺的。

sidewalk ['saidwɔ:k] *n.* 人行道

The old man passed out on the sidewalk.
那个老人在人行道上晕倒了。

slip [slip] *vi.* 滑倒，滑落，溜

A snake slipped into their tent last night.
昨天晚上，一条蛇溜进了他们的帐篷。

🔍 **考点**：slip, glide, slide 都有"滑"的意思：slip表示不由自主地"滑"，"滑倒"；glide, slide表示有意地"滑"。

slippery ['slipəri] *adj.* 表面不平滑的，使人滑跤的

Many people fell down on that slippery sidewalk.
很多人在那条打滑的人行道上摔倒了。

surface ['sə:fis] *n.* 地面，表面，外表

The surface of the crystal is smooth.
水晶表面很光滑。

track [træk] *n.* 行踪，路径，轨道

They are laying a railroad track linking those two cities.
他们正在铺设一条连接两个城市的铁路轨道。

🔍 **考点**：keep track of 与……保持联系
lose track of 失去与……的联系
rack down 跟踪找到，追查到

trail [treil] *n.* 痕迹，小径；*vi.* 跟踪

A few people were chosen to scout the trail.
一些人被选去探路。

🔍 **考点**：trail away / off 逐渐减弱，缩小

transport [træns'pɔ:t] *vt.* 运输；*n.* 运输

You can go to Beijing by many means of transport.
你可以乘坐多种交通工具去北京。

transportation [ˌtrænspɔ:'teiʃən] *n.* 运输，运送，客运

Public transportation played a subsidiary role in city nowadays.
公共交通现在在城市中起辅助的作用。

tunnel ['tʌnl] *n.* 隧道，坑道，地道

The workers are digging through the hill to make a tunnel.

工人们正在凿山建一条隧道。

voyage ['vɔiidʒ] *vi.&n.* 航海，航空
It was the ship's maiden voyage in 1945.
1945年是该船的处女航。

wide [waid] *adj.* 宽阔的，广阔的
There was a wide river behind my home.
我家的后面有一条很宽的河。

🔍 **考点**：wide of the mark 远离目标，偏离

widen ['waidn] *vt.* 加宽；*vi.* 变宽
The road in front of my house is being widened.
我家门前的那条路正在拓宽。

width [widθ] *n.* 宽阔，广阔，宽度
Please gauge the width of the classroom and write it down on your note.
请测量一下教室的宽度，然后把结果记在你的笔记里。

passage ['pæsidʒ] *n.* 通过，通路，通道
I must seal off the passage from which the mice could enter my house.
我必须封死这个通道，老鼠会从这儿进入我家。

span [spæn] *n.* 跨距，一段时间
vt. 持续，包括，横跨
The explorer reckoned the span of a bridge last week.
勘探员在上周测量了桥的长度。

bridge [bridʒ] *n.* 桥，桥梁，桥牌
vi. 架桥于……，把……连接起来
Don't cross the bridge until you come to it.
不要杞人忧天，自寻烦恼。

真题

Actually, information technology can ___ the gap between the poor and the rich.
A) link   B) break
C) ally   D) bridge

详 解：选D。题意为：事实上，信息技术能够填补穷人和富人之间的鸿沟。bridge在此作动词，意思是"把……连接起来"。

(CET-4 2005.6)

日常生活

行

人际交往 | Social Communication

沟通交流 寒暄问候

clasp [klɑːsp] *n.* 扣子，紧抱，紧握
vt. 抱紧，握紧，扣住

Before parting, the two girls clasp hands tightly.
分别前，两个女孩紧紧地握了握手。

encounter [in'kauntə] *vt.* 遭遇，遇到
n. 遭遇

I encountered my old school friend when I was walking in the park.
我在公园散步的时候遇到了我的老同学。

greeting ['griːtiŋ] *n.* 问候，招呼，致敬

As I approached, Tad gave me a warm greeting.
我走近时，泰德向我热情问候。

hey [hei] *int.* 嗨，喂

Hey! What are you doing?
嗨！你在干什么？

kind [kaind] *n.* 种类；*adj.* 友好的，和蔼的

I really appreciate your kind words; they mitigated my suffering.
我很感激你亲切的话语，它减轻了我的痛苦。

🔍 **考点：** of a kind 同类的，徒有其名的
kind of 有几分，有点儿

Mister ['mistə] *n.* 先生（通常简写为Mr.）

Excuse me, Mister, would you mind my sitting here?
打扰了，先生。你介意我坐这里吗？

沟通交流 介绍应答

familiar [fə'miljə] *adj.* 熟悉的，冒昧的

He is quite familiar with French.
他十分精通法语。

🔍 **考点：** （人）be familiar with sb. / sth.
与某人亲密（通晓某物）

acquaint [ə'kweint] *vt.* 使认识，使了解，使熟悉

Although the professor is erudite, he isn't acquainted with Chinese literature.
尽管那个教授很博学，但他对中国文学不甚了解。

acquaintance [ə'kweintəns] *vt.* 认识，了解，相识的人，熟人

I don't think I'm good at English; I just have some acquaintance with it.
我不擅长英语，只是懂一点罢了。

🔍 **考点：** have an acquaintance with...
对……知悉，了解

impress [im'pres] *vt.* 给……深刻印象

He did not impress me well at all.
他没有给我留下丝毫好印象。

真题

I was impressed _____ the efficiency of the work done in the company.
A) in   B) about
C) with   D) for

详解： 选C。题意为：该公司较高的工作效率给我留下了深刻的印象。主语是人，所以impress与with搭配。

(CET-4 2005.6)

impressive [im'presiv] *adj.* 给人印象深刻的

That is the most impressive building I have ever seen.
那栋建筑物给我留下了最深刻的印象。

my [mai] *pron.* 我的

It seems that you are uneasy about my decision.
看上去你对我的决定感到不安。

introduce [ˌintrə'dju:s] *vt.* 介绍，引进，传入
Let me introduce you to your new colleague.
我来把你引荐给你的新同事。

introduction [ˌintrə'dʌkʃən] *n.* 介绍，引
进，引言
The introduction of Buddhism into China influenced Chinese greatly.
佛教传入中国，深深地影响了中国人。

impression [im'preʃən] *n.* 印，印象，印记
The accident left him indelible impression.
事故给他留下深刻的印象。

🔍 **考点**：under the impression of / that
有……的印象

真题

Almost all job applicants are determined to leave a good _____ on a potential employer.
A) illusion　　B) impression
C) reflection　　D) reputation

详 解：选B。题意为：几乎所有求职者都想给可能成为他们老板的人留下好印象。A) illusion意思是"错觉，幻觉"；B) impression意思是"印象"；C) reflection意思是"反映，反思"；D) reputation意思是"名誉，名声"。

(CET-4 2004.6)

myself [mai'self] *pron.* 我自己，我亲自
John, I appreciate you on behalf of my parents and myself.
约翰，我代表我的父母和我自己向你表示感谢。

name [neim] *n.* 名字，名誉；*vt.* 命名，说出
Can you tell me the names of some famous oligopolies?
你能告诉我一些有名的垄断组织的名字吗？

oneself [wʌn'self] *pron.* 自己，亲自
It takes some time to acquaint oneself with a new environment.
了解一个新环境是要花费些时间的。

roughly ['rʌfli] *adv.* 粗糙地，粗略地
She roughly outlined the plot of the opera.
她粗略地概述了歌剧的情节。

respective [ris'pektiv] *adj.* 各自的，各个的
The two methods he has described have their respective merits.
他陈述的两种方法都有它们各自的优点。

response [ris'pɔns] *n.* 作答，回答，响应
Seismic sections show the response of the earth to seismic waves.
地震剖面是地壳对地震波的响应。

🔍 **考点**：in response to 作为对……的反应

respectively [ri'spektivli] *adv.* 各自地，分别地
Three states of matter are solid, liquid and gas respectively.
物质的三种状态分别是固体、液体和气体。

respond [ris'pɔnd] *vi.* 作答，响应
Look at the teacher's eyes when you respond to her question.
回答老师问题时要看着她的眼睛。

stranger ['streindʒə] *n.* 陌生人，新来者
Don't open the door for the stranger when you are at home alone.
一个人在家时不要给陌生人开门。

namely ['neimli] *adv.* 即，也就是
Only one student failed the exam, namely Steven.
只有一个学生没有通过考试，也就是史蒂文。

so-called ['səu'kɔ:ld] *adj.* 所谓的，号称的
Where are your so-called friends now?
你那些所谓的朋友现在都到哪儿去了？

沟通交流 沟通谈话

approach [ə'prəutʃ] *vt.* 向……靠近；*n.* 靠近
Forget it! That guy is difficult to approach.
算了吧！那家伙难于接近。

contact ['kɔntækt] *vt.* 使接触，与……联系
Wait a minute! I will contact him by cellphone.
等一下，我用手机与他联系。

forum ['fɔ:rəm] *n.* 讨论，讨论会
They are holding a forum on juvenile education.
他们正举行一个有关青少年教育的讨论会。

conversation [ˌkɔnvə'seiʃən] *n.* 会话，非正式会谈

This *English Conversation Book* teaches me a wealth of phrase and sentences.
这本《英语会话书》教给我大量的短语和句子。

🔍 考点：have a conversation with 与……交谈

dialect ['daiəlekt] *n.* 方言，土语，地方话
There are many dialects in the movie, so most of us can't understand its content.
这部电影里有很多方言，所以我们中的大多数人理解不了它的内容。

exchange [iks'tʃeindʒ] *n.* 交换
vt. 交换，交流

The shop assistant finally agreed to exchange the goods for me.
售货员终于同意给我调换商品了。

fluent ['flu:ənt] *adj.* 流利的，流畅的

He is fluent in a few languages.
他能流利地说好几种语言。

真题

Though he was born and brought up in America, he can speak____Chinese.
A) smooth   B) fluent
C) fluid   D) flowing

详 解：选B。题意为：尽管他在美国出生长大，却能说一口流利的汉语。A) smooth意思是"平滑的，光滑的"；B) fluent意思是"流利的，流畅的"；C) fluid意思是"流体的，流动的"；D) flowing意思是"流体的，（文体）流畅的"。

(CET-4 2001.6)

implication [ˌimpli'keiʃən] *n.* 含义，暗示，暗指

He has not realized the full implication of the words.
他没有领悟到这些话语的全部含义。

implicit [im'plisit] *adj.* 含蓄的，内含的，无保留的

Mr. Lee's silence gave an implicit agreement.
李先生用沉默表示默许。

imply [im'plai] *vt.* 暗示，意指

Do you imply that he can go home?
你的意思是他可以回家了？

indirect [ˌindi'rekt] *adj.* 间接的，婉转的，不直截了当的

The indirect evidence proved his crime.
这一间接证据证明了他的罪行。

inform [in'fɔ:m] *vt.* 通知，向……报告

Please inform him that I have to go.
麻烦你通知他我必须得走了。

🔍 考点：inform sb. of sth. 把某事告知某人

真题

The president promised to keep all the board members____ of how the negotiations were going on.
A) informed   B) inform
C) be informed   D) informing

详 解：选A。题意为：总裁答应让所有董事会成员随时了解谈判的进展情况。keep sb. / sth. done "让……保持……"，其中keep的宾语是过去分词动作的受动者。本句中inform是及物动词，all the board members是它的动作对象，所以要用过去分词。

(CET-4 2001.6)

information [ˌinfə'meiʃən] *n.* 消息，信息，通知

You had better keep this information secret.
这条消息你最好保密。

🔍 考点：information是不可数名词。

interrupt [ˌintə'rʌpt] *vt.* 打断，打扰，中止

I'm sorry to interrupt your dialogue.
我很抱歉打断你们的谈话。

brief [bri:f] *adj.* 简短的，短暂的

I left a brief note to my father that I had to go to Beijing on a business trip.
我给父亲留了个便条，告诉他我必须去北京出差。

communicate [kə'mju:nikeit] *vi.* 通讯，传达，传播

Foreign languages help us to communicate with different foreigners.

外语帮助我们和不同的外国人进行交流。

🔍**考点：** communicate with sb. 和……通信；communicate sth. to sb. 把……传达给某人

communication [kə͵mjuːniˈkeiʃn] *n.* 通讯，传达，交通

A terrible earthquake disrupted the communication system in the city.
一场可怕的地震使这个城市的通讯系统中断。

mention [ˈmenʃən] *vi.&n.* 提及，说起

At the mention of exam, an expression of upset appeared on her face at once.
一提到考试，她脸上立刻出现一种难过的表情。

nonsense [ˈnɔnsəns] *n.* 胡说，废话，轻浮（冒失）的行为

Whatever nonsense newspapers print, some people always believe it.
无论报纸上刊登什么荒谬的东西，总有人相信。

🔍**考点：** talk nonsense 胡说，说废话

refer [riˈfəː] *vt.* 使求助于；*vi.* 谈到

He referred to the China's achievement in his paper.
在他的论文里，他提到了中国的成就。

真题

I didn't know the word. I had to _____ a dictionary.
A) make out　　B) look out
C) go over　　D) refer to

详　解： 选D。题意为：我不认识这个单词，得查一下字典。A) make out意思是"填写，认出来"；B) look out (for sb. / sth.) 意思是"当心，守候"；C) go over意思是"仔细检查，复习"；D) refer to 意思是"参考，咨询"。

(CET-4 2004.6)

seminar [ˈseminɑː] *n.* 研究班，教务研究会

They will have a painting seminar tomorrow.
明天他们有一堂绘画研讨课。

topic [ˈtɔpik] *n.* 题目，论题，话题

Let's end this topic and begin another.
让我们结束这个话题然后开始一个新的话题吧。

vague [veig] *adj.* 模糊的，含糊的

His thought was too vague after a high tense.
高度紧张之后，他的思路混混沌沌的。

whisper [ˈwispə] *vt.* 低声地讲；*vi.* 低语

They keep whispering in the corner for two hours.
他们在角落里悄悄说了两个小时。

hollow [ˈhɔləu] *adj.* 空的，空洞的

The words he spoke sounded hollow.
他所说的话很空洞。

沟通交流 批评建议

acceptable [əkˈseptəbl] *adj.* 可接受的，合意的

Your advice is acceptable.
你的意见是很可取的。

acceptance [əkˈseptəns] *n.* 接受，验收，承认

The research of that expert has received wide acceptance.
那位专家的研究已经得到了广泛的认可。

advice [ədˈvais] *n.* 劝告，忠告，意见

She accepted his advice with alacrity.
她欣然接受了他的建议。

advisable [ədˈvaizəbl] *adj.* 明智的，可取的

It is advisable to drink a little.
稍微喝点酒还是可以的。

advisory [ədˈvaizəri] *adj.* 咨询的，劝告的

Our college created the Mathematics Advisory Panel last year.
我们学校去年创立了数学顾问小组。

advise [ədˈvaiz] *vt.* 劝告，建议，通知

Learning that her daughter's boyfriend was not rich, she advised her daughter not to marry him.
了解到女儿的男友没有钱，她劝女儿不要嫁给他。

blame [bleim] *vt.* 责备，把……归咎于

If you fail the exam you'll only have yourself to blame.
你若考试不及格，只能怪你自己。

🔍 考点：be to blame 该受责备的
blame sb. for sth. 因……责备某人
blame sth. on / upon sb.
把……归咎于某人

真题

The mother didn't know who ＿＿＿ for broken glass.
A) will blame   B) to blame
C) blamed   D) blames

详 解：选B。题意为：母亲不知道谁该为打碎玻璃负责。to blame以主动形式表示被动意思，句中who是blame的宾语。

(CET-4 2002.1)

critic ['kritik] *n.* 批评家，爱挑剔的人

She worshipped that guy though he was a critic.
尽管那个男人总是吹毛求疵，她还是很崇拜他。

critical ['kritikəl] *adj.* 决定性的，批评的

Did you read the critical report?
你读了那篇批评性的报道了吗？

criticism ['kriti,sizəm] *n.* 批评，批判，评论

Though I hate him, I acknowledge his criticism is just.
尽管我讨厌他，但我承认他的批评是公正的。

criticize ['kritisaiz] *vt.* 批评，评论，非难

Nowadays most of people criticize the ideology of going after fame and wealth.
如今大多数人都批评追求名利的思想。

hint [hint] *n.* 暗示，示意，建议

There's a hint of fall in the air.
空气中有了一点秋天的味道。

🔍 考点：drop / give sb. a hint 给人暗示；
take a hint 会意

proposal [prə'pəuzəl] *n.* 提议，建议，求婚

After he finished speaking, his proposals were met by a storm of protest.
他刚说完建议，就遭到激烈的反对。

propose [prə'pəuz] *vt.* 提议；*vi.* 求婚

Tom proposed to his girlfriend yesterday, but she refused.
昨天汤姆向他的女朋友求婚了，但是她拒绝了。

recommend [rekə'mend] *vt.* 推荐，介绍，劝告

I recommend you to read up anthropology.
我建议你攻读人类学。

🔍 考点：It is recommended 后跟that从句，从句要用虚拟语气。类似的结构还有It is suggested / requested / ordered / proposed / decided / necessary。

recommendation [,rekəmen'deiʃən] *n.* 推荐，介绍，劝告

The student asked his teacher to write a recommendation letter for him.
那个学生请求老师给他写封推荐信。

reproach [ri'prəutʃ] *vt.&n.* 责备，指责

Grandmother has just reproached him for his bad behavior.
奶奶刚刚批评了他的不良表现。

🔍 考点：blame, scold, condemn和reproach都含有"责备，指责"的意思，但程度不同，各有侧重。blame表示"埋怨，责怪"；scold表示"责骂，训斥"；condemn通常用于比较正式的、严重的场合，表示从道义或原则上"谴责"；reproach往往只是一种表示不满的意见，表示、"责备"。

scold [skəuld] *vi.* 责骂；*vt.* 申斥

Please don't scold me in the face of my friends.
请不要当着朋友的面骂我。

suggest [sə'dʒest] *vt.* 建议，暗示，启发

I would suggest that you stay a few more days here to wait your mother back.
我主张你在这儿多待几天等你妈妈回来。

suggestion [sə'dʒestʃən] *n.* 建议，意见，暗示

His suggestion is not carried at all in the plan.
他的建议在计划中完全没有体现。

真题

The suggestion that the mayor＿＿ the prizes was accepted by everyone.
A) would present   B) ought to present
C) present   D) presents

详 解：选C。题意为：大家采纳了让市长颁奖的建议。suggestion等词的同位语从句或表语从句中，谓语动词也要用虚拟语气，即should + 动词原形（should可以省略），因此选C。

(CET-4 2000.6)

沟通交流 认可肯定

acknowledge [ək'nɒlidʒ] *vt.* 承认，告知收到，答谢

He was generally acknowledged to musical talent.
他是公认的音乐天才。

affirmative [ə'fɜ:mətiv] *adj.* 肯定的
n. 肯定词，肯定陈述

Can you give us an affirmative answer?
你能给我们一个肯定答复吗？

agree [ə'gri:] *vi.* 同意，持相同意见

I can't agree to your plan, here are so many people objected to it.
我不能同意你的计划，很多人都反对它。

🔍 **考点**：agree with 同意

agreeable [ə'griəbl] *adj.* 惬意的，同意的，愿意的

I don't think life is like a sequence of agreeable events. It still has bitter waves.
我不认为生活就是一连串愉快的事情，它也包含着苦涩。

certain ['sɜ:tn] *adj.* 确实的，肯定的

Sexism still exists in certain quarters.

在某些地方还存在着女性歧视。

🔍 **考点**：for certain 肯定地，确切地

advocate ['ædvəkit] *vt.* 拥护，提倡，主张
n. 拥护者，提倡者，律师

The mayor advocates reforming the economic system.
市长主张改良经济制度。

真题

Mr. Jones holds strong views against video games and＿＿ the closing of all recreation facilities for such games.
A) assists   B) acknowledges
C) advocates   D) admits

详 解：选C。题意为：琼斯先生强烈反对电子游戏，主张关闭所有经营此类游戏的娱乐场所。A) assist意思是"援助，帮助"；B) acknowledge意思是"承认，答谢"；C) advocate意思是"提倡，主张"；D) admit意思是"承认，接纳"。

(CET-4 2003.9)

approval [ə'pru:vl] *n.* 赞成，同意，批准，认可

I appreciate that you give your approval to this project which is the turning point of my career.
很感激你批准了这项工程，它对于我来说是个事业的转折点

🔍 **考点**：on approval 供试用的，包退包换的

approve [ə'pru:v] *vi.* 赞成，称许，批准

No matter what I want to do, my parents will approve.
无论我想做什么，父母总会同意。

certainly ['sɜ:tənli] *adv.* 一定，必定，当然

I am certainly right, whatever others may say.
无论别人怎么说，我确实是对的。

confirm [kən'fɜ:m] *vt.* 证实，肯定，批准

The legality of this action is confirmed by the public.
这一行为的合法性被公众所认可。

consensus [kən'sensəs] *n.* 意见一致，舆论
It seems we have a consensus.
看来我们的意见是一致的。

真题

Encouraged by their culture to voice their opinions freely, the Canadians are not afraid to go against the group ____, and will argue their viewpoints enthusiastically, though rarely aggressively.
A) consent   B) conscience
C) consensus   D) consciousness

详　解：选C。题意为：加拿大文化鼓励人们自由发表观点，他们不畏惧与团体立场相异，而是热切地就自己的观点进行辩论，但很少咄咄逼人。A) consent意思是"同意，赞同"；B) conscience意思是"良心"；C) consensus意思是"共识，一致同意"；D) consciousness意思是"意识"。

(CET-4 2005.1)

favour ['feivə] *n.* 好感，赞同，恩惠
　　　　　　　　vt. 支持，赞同
It is reported that an increasing number of people favour building more nuclear power plants.
据报道，越来越多的人赞同多修些核电站。

考点：in favour of 赞同，支持

favourable ['feivərəbl] *adj.* 有利的，赞成的
This newspaper produced so much favourable comment.
这份报纸赢得了广泛的好评。

consent [kən'sent] *n.* 同意，赞成
　　　　　　　　vi. 同意
Her father reluctantly consented to the marriage.
她父亲勉强答应了这桩婚姻。

考点：by common consent 经一致同意
consent, agree的区别：consent多用于上下级关系，只表示单方面地申请或要求；agree表示双方意见一致，无上下级之限。

真题

Because of his excellent administration, people lived in peace and ____ all previously neglected matters were taken care of.
A) conviction   B) contest
C) consent   D) content

详　解：选D。题意为：由于他的出色管理，人们生活得祥和满足，所有先前被忽视的问题都得到了解决。A) conviction意思是"信服"；B) contest意思是"比赛"，竞赛；C) consent意思是"同意，赞成"；D) content意思是"满足"。

(CET-4 2005.6)

sanction ['sæŋkʃən] *vt.&n.* 批准，认可
The law would not sanction his second marriage.
法律不会认可他的第二次婚姻。

考点：apply / take sanctions against
对……实行制裁

satisfaction [ˌsætis'fækʃən] *n.* 满意，乐事，赔偿
You know what? The success brought me great satisfaction.
你知道吗？成功给我带来了极大的快慰。

satisfactory [ˌsætis'fæktəri] *adj.* 令人满意的，良好的
I'm very glad that you've made a satisfactory bargain with him.
我很高兴你与他做了一次满意的交易。

satisfied ['sætisfaid] *adj.* 感到满意的
My parents are quite satisfied with my boyfriend, for he is eloquent and humorous as well.
父母对我男朋友很满意，因为他口才好，人又幽默。

satisfy ['sætisfai] *vt.* 满足，使满意
In order to satisfy most people, the singer decided to give a repeat performance.
为了满足众多朋友的要求，歌手决定再表演一次。

wholly ['həulli] *adv.* 完全地，全部
I wholly agree with you.
我完全同意你的观点。

考点：not wholly 表示部分否定

沟通交流 征询确认

ambiguity [ˌæmbi'gju:iti] *n.* 意义不明确，
歧义

The argument resulted from the ambiguities in the text.
这场争论是由文中含糊不清的歧义引起的。

ambiguous [ˌæm'bigjuəs] *adj.* 模棱两可
的，引起歧义的，含糊不清的

She gave me an ambiguous answer when I asked about her age.
当我问她年龄时，她给了我一个含糊不清的答案。

真题

The meaning of the sentence is _____; you can interpret it in several ways.
A) skeptical   B) intelligible
C) ambiguous   D) exclusive

详　解：选C。题意为：这句话有歧义，可以有几种不同的解释。A) skeptical意思是"怀疑的"；B) intelligible意思是"能被理解的"；C) ambiguous意思是"含糊的，不明确的"；D) exclusive意思是"专有的，独占的"。

(CET-4 2005.12)

apparent [ə'pærənt] *adj.* 表面上的，明显
的，显然的

It is apparent he is the thief.
很明显他是个小偷。

clarify ['klærifai] *vt.* 澄清，阐明

There are a lot of things you should clarify.
有很多事情需要你澄清。

clearly ['kliəli] *adv.* 明白地，清晰地

They talked in whispers and I couldn't hear clearly.
他们说话声很低，我听不清楚。

consultant [kən'sʌltənt] *n.* 顾问，咨询者，
会诊医生

The manager keeps her on as a consultant.
经理继续留用她当顾问。

真题

I think we need to see an investment_____before we make an expensive mistake.
A) guide   B) entrepreneur
C) consultant   D) assessor

详　解：选C。题意为：我认为我们需要请教投资顾问，以免犯代价高昂的错误。consultant顾问；A) guide意思是"想到，指南"；B) entrepreneur意思是"企业家"；D) assessor意思是"陪审法官"。

(CET-4 2000.6)

definite ['definit] *adj.* 明确的，肯定的

Our English teacher told us that the word "the" is the only definite article in English language.
我们的英语老师告诉我们，"the"这个词是英语中唯一的一个定冠词。

definitely ['definitli] *adv.* 一定地，明确地

The narcissuses are white or yellow, so this unknown red flower is definitely not narcissus.
水仙花是白色或者黄色的，所以这个不知名的红花肯定不是水仙。

demand [di'mɑːnd] *vt.* 要求，需要，询问

There aren't enough yoga schools in the town to satisfy the demand for them.
在这个城镇里，没有足够的瑜伽学校来满足大家的需要。

考点：in demand 非常受欢迎的
on demand 一经要求

inquiry [in'kwaiəri] *n.* 询问，打听，调查

Don't pay any attention to his inquiry of your family.
不要搭理他对你家庭情况的任何打听。

obvious ['ɔbviəs] *adj.* 明显的，显而易见的

It's obvious that your behavior is a breach of our agreement.
很明显你的行为违反了我们的协议。

inquire [in'kwaiə] *vt.* 打听，询问，调查

I recommend that you inquire about his address.
我建议你打听一下他的地址。

考点：inquire后不能跟双宾语，而且不能直接以人做宾语，常使用inquire sth. of sb. 或inquire of sb.

about sth. 的结构。

obviously ['ɔbviəsli] *adv.* 明显地，显然地
Obviously it is your fault to abuse your power to help her.
显然，滥用你的权利去帮她是你的错。

verify ['verifai] *vt.* 证实，查证，证明
I have been hunting through all sorts of materials to verify his point.
我查了好多资料来核实他的观点。

would [wud] *aux.&v.* 将，愿，总是
Would you like another cup of coffee?
再来杯咖啡怎么样？

another [ə'nʌðə] *adj.* 再一个的，别的
The cake is delicious; could you give me another one?
蛋糕太好吃了，可以再给我一块吗？

沟通交流 争吵辩论

argue ['ɑːgjuː] *vi.* 争论，争辩，辩论
I'm busy now; I don't have time to argue with you.
我现在很忙，没有时间与你争辩。

argument ['ɑːgjumənt] *n.* 争论，辩论，理由，论据
The argument resulted from the ambiguities in the text.
这场争论是由文中含糊不清的歧义引起的。

arise [ə'raiz] *vi.* 出现，由……引起，起源于
Could you tell me how the quarrel arises?
你能告诉我争吵是怎么发生的吗？

🔍 考点：arise from 由……引起

concede [kən'siːd] *vt.* 承认，让与
vi. 让步，认输
After investigation, people have to concede the president's incorruptible honesty.
经过调查，人们不得不承认总统的清白、诚实。

controversial [ˌkɔntrə'vəːʃəl] *adj.* 有争议的，争论的，可疑的
They say the topic of argument is controversial.

他们说这个议题是很有争议的。

contrary ['kɔntrəri] *adj.* 相反的；*n.* 相反
You are not ugly to me; on the contrary, I think you are beautiful.
对我来说你一点也不丑，相反，我认为你挺美。

🔍 考点：on the contrary 正相反
to the contrary 相反地

debate [di'beit] *vi.&n.* 争论，辩论
It is estimated that the debate will be televised live this weekend.
据估计，这个辩论赛这周末将会现场直播。

disagree [ˌdisə'griː] *vi.* 有分歧，不一致
Paul intended to name his baby after his grandfather, but his wife disagreed.
保罗打算给他的孩子取他祖父的名字，但他妻子不同意。

disapprove [ˌdisə'pruːv] *vt.* 不批准，不赞成
vi. 不同意
My parents disapprove of my marriage.
我父母不赞成我的婚姻。

dispute [dis'pjuːt] *vi.* 争论，争执
n. 争论
It is very troublesome to arbitrate a dispute.
为一项争执做仲裁很麻烦的。

🔍 考点：in dispute 在争论中，处于争议中

objection [əb'dʒekʃən] *n.* 反对，异议，不喜欢
We tried our best to prevent him, but he waved aside all our objection.
我们尽最大的努力去阻止他，可是他全然不顾我们的反对意见。

真题

I have no objection _____ your story again.
A) to hearing   B) to have heard
C) to hear   D) to having heard

详 解：选A。题意为：我不反对再听一遍你的故事。have no objection to sth. / doing sth. 反对做某事，to为介词。

(CET-4 2000.6)

人际交往

沟通交流

opinion [ə'pinjən] *n.* 意见，看法，主张

As a member of the jury, you must offer your opinion about the case.
作为陪审团的一员，你必须就此案件给予你的看法。

opposition [ɔpə'ziʃən] *n.* 反对，相反，反对者

I just don't understand why you remained consistent in your opposition to anything new.
我不明白你为什么始终反对一切新事物。

oppose [ə'pəuz] *vt.* 反对，反抗

All the peace-loving people in the world will oppose violence and war.
全世界爱好和平的人们都会反对暴力和战争。

🔍 考点：be oppose to 反对，相对

point [pɔint] *n.* 点，要点，细目，分

I exerted all my influence to make my parents accept my point.
我用尽了一切影响力使父母接受我的观点。

quarrel ['kwɔrəl] *n.* 争吵，吵架，口角

Don't get in the middle of it; you know your intervention would bring their quarrel to a climax.
不要卷入此事。要知道你的干预会使他们的口角更加激烈。

refute [ri'fju:t] *vt.* 驳斥，反驳，驳倒

I was able to refute the lawyer's argument to defend him.
我能驳倒那个律师的论点来保护他。

row [rau] *vi.&n.* 争吵，吵闹

The woman had a row with her new neighbour.
那个女人跟新来的邻居吵架了。

shout [ʃaut] *vi.&n.* 呼喊，喊叫

You'd better not touch any of his things, or he will shout at you.
你最好不要碰他的任何东西，否则他会冲你大吼的。

🔍 考点：shout down 用叫喊声淹没（压倒）
　　　　shout at 冲着……大嚷
　　　　shout to 朝……大声喊话

standpoint ['stændpɔint] *n.* 立场，观点

From the standpoint of the government, this plan is not practicable.
从政府的角度来看，这个计划不可行。

view [vju:] *n.* 视力，风景，观点

From a teacher's point of view, this book will be very useful.
以教师的观点来看，这本书很有用.

🔍 考点：in view of 鉴于，考虑到
　　　　with a view to 为了，为的是

viewpoint ['vju:,pɔint] *n.* 观点，看法，见解

We should look at this problem from a different viewpoint.
我们应该以不同的观点来看待这个问题。

yell [jel] *vi.* 叫喊

He yells at his girlfriend every time he gets drunk.
他每次喝醉就冲着女友大喊大叫。

fierce [fiəs] *adj.* 凶猛的，狂热的

A fierce debate on the tax cut is going on in the government building.
一场围绕着减税的辩论正在政府大楼中激烈进行。

真题

Owing to ＿＿＿ competition among the airlines, travel expenses have been reduced considerably.
A) eager　　　B) critical
C) strained　　D) fierce

详　解：选D。题意为：由于航空公司间的激励竞争，旅行费被用得大幅减少。A) eager意思是"急切的"；B) critical意思是"批评的，紧要的"；C) strained意思是"紧张的"；D) fierce意思是"激烈的"。
(CET-4 2002.12)

justification [,dʒʌstifi'keiʃən] *n.* 正当理由，借口

There is no justification for his absence for his daughter's birthday party.
他没有理由缺席他女儿的生日。

日常联络 电话&电报

booth [bu:θ] *n.* 货摊，公用电话亭

I'll give my mother a call from the phone booth on the corner.
我到街角的电话亭给妈妈打个电话。

nobody ['nəubədi] *pron.* 谁也不，无人

Nobody care that old man when he was alive, but many people attended his funeral.
那位老人活着的时候没有人关心他，死后却有很多人参加他的葬礼。

not [nɔt] *adv.* 不，没有

Learning that her daughter's boyfriend was not rich, she advised her daughter not to marry him.
了解到女儿的男友没有钱，她劝女儿不要嫁给他。

call [kɔ:l] *vt.* 把……叫做，叫，喊

Sorry, he is not here. You'd better call again this evening.
抱歉，他不在。你最好今晚再打电话过来。

考点：call at sp. / on sb.访问，拜访某地/某人；call for叫（某人）来；要求，需要；call off取消

真题

She _____ her trip to New York because she was ill.
A) went off   B) called off
C) put up   D) closed down

详 解：选B。题意为：因为生病，她取消了纽约之行。A) go off意思是"离开，消失，爆炸，发射"；B) called off 意思是"取消"；C) put up意思是"举起，建造，提名"；D) close down意思是"关闭，倒闭"。

(CET-4 2003.6)

operator ['ɔpəreitə] *n.* 操作人员，接线员

The radio operator sent out an appeal for help to headquarters.
无线电报务员向司令部发出求救信号。

pad [pæd] *n.* 垫，本子；*vt.* 填塞

The boss always keeps a pad of notes on his desk.
老板总是在他的桌子上留一个便笺簿。

phone [fəun] *n.* 电话，电话机，耳机

The regulations specify that you may not take a phone in the examination.
规则中指明考试时不可以带手机。

telecom ['telikɔm] *abbr.* (= telecommunication) 电信

China's telecom industry could still maintain a rapid growth despite global slowdown.
在全球电信业全面滑坡的情况下中国电信业依然能实现持续快速增长。

touch [tʌtʃ] *n.* 触；*vt.* 触摸，触动

He made up his mind never to touch a cigarette.
他决心不再吸烟。

考点：in touch with 联系，接触
touch down 降落，着陆
touch on / upon 谈到，谈及

urgent ['ə:dʒənt] *adj.* 紧急的，强求的

I want to talk to your parents about an urgent matter.
我想和你们父母谈一件紧急的事。

考点：It is urgent that...句型中，从句中用虚拟语气，即从句中的谓语动词用should + 动词原形。

videophone ['vidiəufəun] *n.* 可视电话

The videophone is not universal in our life now.
现在可视电话在我们的生活中还没有普及。

wireless ['waiəlis] *adj.* 不用电线的，无线的

He is the first man to use a wireless telephone in this village.
他是这个村里最早使用无线电话的人。

cable ['keibl] *n.* 缆，索，电缆，电报

I need a cable to tow this car.
我需要一个缆绳拖这辆车。

telegraph ['teligrɑ:f] *n.* 电报机，电报

The telegraph transmits messages to all parts of the country.
电报把信息传达到全国各地。

考点：telegram n. 一封电报
telegraph 电报（尤指通讯方式）

lately ['leitli] *adv.* 最近，不久前

I haven't heard any news from my sister lately.
我最近没听到我妹妹的任何音讯。

考点：lately, recently都有"最近的"意思：lately用来指某一段时间，常与现在完成时连用；recently既可以指一段时间，也可以指某一时刻。

日常联络 信件

attach [ə'tætʃ] *vt.* 缚，系，贴，使成为一部分，附加

The librarian attached a label to every book for better control.
为了便于管理，图书管理员把每本书上都贴上了标签。

anonymous [ə'nɔniməs] *adj.* 无名的，匿名的，无特色的

If the author chooses to remain anonymous, just let him be.
如果作者不愿署名，就随他吧。

intact [in'tækt] *adj.* 完整无缺的，未受损伤的

The packages are intact when they are sent here.
当送过来的时候这些包装完好无损。

letterbox ['letəbɔks] *n.* 邮箱

I saw her put the letter into the letterbox.
我看见她把信投送到信箱里。

message ['mesidʒ] *n.* 信息，消息，启示

You can find every visitor's message on the registration form.
你能在登记表上看到每个来访者的信息。

messenger ['mesindʒə] *n.* 送信者，信使

The messenger trekked in the mountain for several days to send the special letter.
邮递员在山中跋涉了数日，终于把这封特殊的信送到了。

package ['pækidʒ] *n.* 包裹，包，捆

A package can sometimes urge someone to buy a product.
一种包装有时可以促进人们购买某种产品。

考点：a package deal / offer 一揽子交易

packet ['pækit] *n.* 小包（裹），小捆

The mailman brought a small packet to me yesterday.
昨天邮差给我送来了一个小邮包。

parcel ['pɑːsl] *n.* 包裹，小包，邮包

The postman sealed the parcel with adhesive tape.
邮递员用胶带把包裹封住了。

personal ['pəːsənl] *adj.* 个人的，本人的

We have been told that under no circumstances may we use the telephone in the office for personal affairs.
我们被告知在任何情况下都不能用办公室的电话办私事。

post [pəust] *n.* 邮政，邮寄，岗位，柱
vt. 贴出，邮寄

I have checked again, but there is still no post for you.
我已经检查过了，仍然没有你的邮件。

postage ['pəustidʒ] *n.* 邮费，邮资

How much postage does the parcel cost?
寄这个包裹需要多少邮资？

receive [ri'siːv] *vt.* 收到，得到，接待

I wonder why my mother hasn't received my letter. I sent it off last month.
我在想妈妈为什么没有收到我的信，我上个月就寄出去了啊。

receiver [ri'siːvə] *n.* 收受者，收件人，听筒

When I finished talking with him on the phone, I replaced the receiver.
我和他通完话后，就把听筒放了回去。

stamp [stæmp] *n.* 戳子，邮票，标志
vt. 踩，盖上（字样）
vi. 踩脚，重步走

They didn't stamp my passport for my inadequate materials.
因为我的资料不足，他们没在我的护照上盖章。

考点：stamp on 用力踩，镇压
stamp out 消灭，踩灭

transmission [trænz'miʃən] *n.* 传送，传动，发射

The document was lost in transmission.
这份文件在传送中被弄丢了。

transmit [trænz'mit] *vt.* 传送，传达，发射

Mosquitoes transmit malaria.
蚊子传播疟疾。

真题

Some diseases are_____ by certain water animals.
A) transplanted   B) transformed
C) transported   D) transmitted

详 解：选D。题意为：某些疾病是由一些水生动物传播的。A) transplant意思是"移植（器官）"；B) transform意思是"改观"；C) transport意思是"运输"；D) transmit意思是"传递，传播"。

(CET-4 2000.1)

instant ['instənt] *n.* 瞬间；*adj.* 立即的

The letter asked for an instant reply.
这封信要求立即回复。

考点：for an instant 一瞬间
in an instant 很快，马上
on the instant 立即

友好和睦 邀请拜访

entertain [ˌentə'tein] *vt.* 使欢乐，招待

It is my time to entertain friends at dinner.
该我招待朋友们吃饭了。

entertainment [entə'teinmənt] *n.* 娱乐，文娱节目，招待，款待

We will attend a musical entertainment tonight.
我们今晚要出席一场音乐演奏会。

enthusiasm [in'θju:ziæzəm] *n.* 热情，热心，热忱

He is a kind-hearted merchant, and he is full of enthusiasm about charity.
他是一个心肠好的商人，他热衷于慈善事业。

考点：show enthusiasm for 表现出对……的热情

fellow ['feləu] *n.* 人，家伙，伙伴

He is my school fellow in my middle school.
他是我在中学时的同学。

host [həust] *n.* 主人，东道主

China is the host of the 29th Olympic Games.
中国是第29届奥林匹克运动会的主办国。

考点：host与guest相对应，而master与servant相对应。

invitation [ˌinvi'teiʃən] *n.* 邀请，招待，请柬

He declined an invitation from the palace of imperial.
他谢绝了一个皇室的邀请。

invite [in'vait] *vt.* 邀请，聘请，招待

You can invite anyone to your birthday party.
你可以邀请任何人参加你的生日宴。

mistress ['mistris] *n.* 女主人，夫人（通常简写为Mrs.），老板娘，情妇

I am afraid that the mistress isn't at home.
我担心女主人不在家。

knock [nɔk] *vi.&vt.&n.* 敲，击，打

Having heard that somebody was knocking, she pulled the door open but found that nobody was outside.
她听到有人敲门，但她拉开门时却发现没有人在外面。

考点：knock about / around 到处闲逛；knock off 下班，迅速而不费力地做成；knock at / on a door 敲门

neighbour ['neibə] *n.* 邻居，邻国，邻人

My neighbours come to congratulate me on winning the race.
邻居们来祝贺我比赛获胜。

neighbourhood ['neibəhud] *n.* 邻居关系，邻近的地方

They are living in the neighbourhood of the airport and suffering from the noise of the planes.

他们住在机场附近，深受飞机噪音的危害。

🔍 **考点**：in the neighbourhood of 在附近，大约

---

punctual [ˈpʌŋktjuəl] *adj.* 立即的

No one can guarantee the punctual arrival of trains in the snowy day.
下雪天没有人能保证火车准时到达。

---

treat [tri:t] *vt.* 对待，处理；*n.* 款待

It's my turn to treat us today.
今天，该轮到我请客了。

🔍 **考点**：treat of 探讨，论述

真题

Being out of work, Jane can no longer _____ friends to dinners and movies as she used to.
A) treat 　　B) appeal
C) urge 　　D) compel

详　解：选A。题意为：由于失业，简不能像以前一样请朋友吃饭和看电影了。A) treat 意思是"款待，请客"；B) appeal意思是"求助，申诉"；C) urge意思是"促使，催促"；D) compel意思是"迫使，强迫"。

(CET-4 2006.6)

友好和睦 *欢迎送别* ✎

apart [əˈpɑːt] *adv.* 相隔，分开，除去

The two brothers hugged each other tightly when they met after having been apart for thirty years.
相隔30年未见的兄弟，再见面的时候紧紧地抱在了一起。

🔍 **考点**：apart from 除……之外

---

appear [əˈpiə] *vi.* 出现，来到，似乎，显露

I saw a light appear at the end of the tunnel.
我看见隧道的末端出现了亮光。

---

arrival [əˈraivəl] *n.* 到达，到来，到达者

I learned of your arrival only this morning.
我今天早上才知道你来了。

🔍 **考点**：on / upon someone's arrival 在某人到达时

arrive [əˈraiv] *vi.* 到达，来临，达到

The book I ordered will arrive tonight.
我订购的书今晚会到。

🔍 **考点**：arrive in 后面接比较大的地点；arrive at 后面接比较小的地点

---

away [əˈwei] *adv.* 离开，远离，……去

My grandfather suggested that we keep a dog to scare away thieves.
爷爷建议我们养条狗来吓走小偷。

---

back [bæk] *adv.* 在后，回原处，回

Don't worry. I'll be back soon. That's only a brief trip.
别担心，我很快就会回来，那只是一个短暂的旅行。

---

come [kʌm] *vi.* 来，来到，出现

Two cotyledons have come out from the seedling.
小苗长出了两片子叶。

---

depart [diˈpɑːt] *vi.* 离开，起程，出发

We will depart on a journey tomorrow.
我们明天要去旅行。

---

departure [diˈpɑːtʃə] *n.* 离开，出发，起程

Everyone in the company was surprised by his sudden departure.
公司的每个人对他的突然离开都表示很吃惊。

---

ease [i:z] *n.* 容易，不费力，悠闲
　　　　　　 vi. 缓和，解除，减轻

The hostess greeted her guests with ease.
女主人大方地迎接她的客人。

🔍 **考点**：at ease 不拘束
　　　　　 easy off 减轻，减缓

---

embrace [imˈbreis] *vt.* 拥抱，包括，包围
　　　　　　　　 n. 拥抱，怀抱

When we met, we embraced each other warmly.
当我们相遇时，彼此相互热烈拥抱。

---

meet [mi:t] *vi.* 相遇；*vt.* 遇见，迎接

Seeing that her mother came, she immediately ran down to meet her.
看到她妈妈来了，她立刻跑下来迎接她。

---

off [ɔ:f] *adv.* （离）开，（停）止

Keep the children off the dangerous switch.

让孩子们远离那个危险的开关。

---

meeting ['mi:tiŋ] *n.* 聚集，会合，会见

The theme of our meeting is how to improve our work efficiency.
我们会议的主题是如何提高工作效率。

---

warmth [wɔ:mθ] *n.* 温暖，暖和，热烈，热心

I appreciate the warmth of their welcome very much.
我非常感谢他们的热烈欢迎。

友好和睦 礼貌教养

culture ['kʌltʃə] *n.* 文化，文明，教养

I wonder the origin of Chinese tea culture and plan to write an article about it.
我想知道中国茶文化的起源，并打算写出一篇相关的文章。

---

cultural ['kʌltʃərəl] *adj.* 文化（上）的，教养的

In my opinion, the screen plays an important part in enriching cultural life of citizen.
在我看来，影视在丰富人们精神文化生活方面起着重要的作用。

---

gentleman ['dʒentlmən] *n.* 绅士，有教养的人

A friend of mine is a cultured gentleman.
我的一个朋友是一位有修养的绅士。

---

grace [greis] *n.* 优美，文雅，雅致

She refused that man with stately grace.
她优雅地拒绝了那个男人。

考点：in good grace 欣然地

---

manner ['mænə] *n.* 方式，态度，礼貌

I don't want to make friends with her. You know her artificial manner really makes me sick.
我不想和她交朋友，她那装腔作势的样子实在令我恶心。

考点：all manner of 各种各样的，形形色色的
in manner of 不妨说，在某种意义上

The rapid development of communications technology is transforming the _____ in which people communicate across time and space.
A) route   B) transmission
C) vision   D) manner

详　解：选D。题意为：信息技术的快速发展正改变着人们跨时空交流的方式。A) route 意思是"路线"；B) transmission 意思是"传播，传递"；C) vision 意思是"视力，视觉"；D) manner 意思是"方式，方法"。

(CET-4 2003.12)

---

graceful ['greisful] *adj.* 优美的，优雅的

She performed graceful in the dance.
她在那支舞蹈中表现得很优雅。

---

polite [pə'lait] *adj.* 有礼貌的，有教养的

It's not polite to interrupt people when they are speaking.
打断别人说话是不礼貌的。

---

respect [ris'pekt] *vt.&n.* 尊敬，尊重

I showed my respect for ancient warriors when I watched the costume film.
当我看古装电影时我对勇士充满敬意。

考点：with / in respect to 至于，关于

友好和睦 赞美祝贺

admire [əd'maiə] *vt.* 钦佩，羡慕，赞赏

I really admire my little sister's diplomatic tact.
我真的很佩服我妹妹的外交手腕。

---

applaud [ə'plɔ:d] *vi.&vt.* 鼓掌，喝彩

When the performance was over, the dancers bowed to the audience who applauded loudly.
表演结束时，舞蹈演员们向热烈鼓掌的观众鞠躬致意。

---

applause [ə'plɔ:z] *n.* 鼓掌，喝彩

We welcome the famous professor with thunderous applause.
我们以雷鸣般的掌声欢迎这位著名的教授。

deserve [di'zə:v] *vt.* 应受，值得

I tried to hint my boss that I deserved a promotion.
我竭力暗示我的老板我应该得到晋升。

考点：deserve doing sth. 主动形式表被动意思。

excellence ['eksələns] *n.* 优秀，卓越，杰出，美德

She received a prize for excellence in Enlish.
她因在英语方面的卓越表现而获奖。

excellent ['eksələnt] *adj.* 优秀的，杰出的

The play was an excellent vehicle for my talents.
那出戏给了我一个展展才华的大好机会。

highly ['haili] *adv.* 有高度地，很，非常

She is a highly competent teacher.
她是一个十分称职的教师。

perfect ['pə:fikt] *adj.* 完美的，完全的

If you can coordinate everything well, you will find your life is perfect.
如果你能协调好所有事情，你就会发现你的生活很完美。

perfection [pə'fekʃən] *n.* 完美，完善

I am glad that your work is approaching perfection.
我很高兴你的工作日渐完美。

考点：to perfection 完美地，完全地

perfectly ['pə:fiktli] *adv.* 很，完全

The little girl always behaves perfectly and her teachers praise her with one accord.
这个小女孩一向表现很好，老师们都一致表扬她。

praise [preiz] *n.* 赞扬，赞美；*vi.* 赞扬

The teacher praises Tony that he is an assiduous student.
老师夸奖托尼是个勤奋的学生。

考点：heap praise upon 表示"大加赞扬"；praise sb. for 因……而赞扬某人

terrific [tə'rifik] *adj.* 可怕的，极好的，非常的

It's terrific that I passed the final exam without putting in a lot of effort.
我没有花费太大力气就通过了期末考试，真是棒极了。

wise [waiz] *adj.* 智慧的，聪明的

I think you are wise enough to know the connotation from what he said.
我很聪明，我想你会明白他的言外之意。

congratulation [kənˌgrætjuˈleiʃən] *n.* 祝贺，祝贺词

I couldn't attend my best friend's wedding, so I sent her a gift as a token of my congratulation.
我不能参加我最好朋友的婚礼，于是我给她寄去了一件礼物表示祝贺。

congratulate [kən'grætjuleit] *vt.* 祝贺，向……道喜

He congratulated me on having passed the examination.
他庆祝我通过了考试。

真题

I must congratulate you____ the excellent design of the new bridge.
A) with   B) at
C) on   D) of

详 解：选C。题意为：我就你对新桥所做的杰出设计向你表示祝贺。congratulate常与介词on搭配，表示"祝贺"。

(CET-4 2004.6)

toast [təust] *n.* 祝酒，祝酒词

I'd like to propose a toast to Ms Lin—the best actress.
我要请大家为林小姐干一杯酒，她获得最佳女主角。

bless [bles] *vt.* 为……祝福

May God bless you and all the people you love.
愿上帝保佑你和所有你爱的人！

友好和睦 请求帮助

ask [ɑ:sk] *vt.* 问，要求，邀请

May I ask you some questions about your new book?
可不可以就你的新书问几个问题？

beg [beg] *vi.&vt.* 乞求，请求

Dad, I beg you don't enforce your will on me, please.
爸爸，我请你不要把你的意愿强加于我。

考点：beg off 推辞（已答应的事）

borrow ['bɔrəu] *vt.* 借，借用，借入

How much money do you want to borrow from me?
你想向我借多少钱？

bother ['bɔðə] *vt.* 烦扰，迷惑；*n.* 麻烦

Don't bother me! I'm counting the money.
别打扰我，我正在数钱呢。

kneel [ni:l] *vi.* 跪，跪下，跪着

He knelt down and asked for forgiveness.
他跪下来乞求原谅。

me [mi:] *pron.* （宾格）我

Can you give me some examples to illustrate the superiority of socialism?
你能举出一些例子给我说明一下社会主义的优越性吗？

readily ['redili] *adv.* 乐意地，无困难地

I don't know why children are not readily to be familiar with me.
我不知道为什么孩子们不太乐意与我亲近。

request [ri'kwest] *vt.&n.* 请求，要求

The poor girl's request for a donation met with a rude repulse.
这个可怜女孩要求赞助却遭到粗暴拒绝。

考点：request只可接一个宾语，常见的句型为request sth. from / of sb. 向某人要求某物。

resort [ri'zɔ:t] *vi.&n.* 求助，凭借，诉诸

Meeting such matter you should have resorts to your friends.
碰到这种事你应该求助于你的父母。

真题

I would never have _____ a court of law if I hadn't been so desperate.
A) turned up   B) sought for
C) resorted to   D) accounted for

详　解：选C。题意为：如果当时我不是极度绝望的话，我是绝不会起诉到法院的。A) turn up 意思是"出现，找到"；B) seek for 意思是"寻找，追求"；C) resort to 意思是"求助于，诉诸"；D) account for 意思是"说明是……的原因"。

(CET-4 2002.6)

willing ['wiliŋ] *adj.* 愿意的，心甘情愿的

Are you willing to play chess with us after school?
你愿意放学后和我们下国际象棋吗？

appeal [ə'pi:l] *vi.* 呼吁，申述，有感染力，
有吸引力
n. 呼吁，要求，申诉，吸引力

He was trapped in the snare and appealed to me for help.
他掉进了陷阱，向我求援。

any ['eni] *adj.* 什么，一些，任何的

You can ask me if there is any question.
有什么问题都可以问我。

anybody ['eni,bɔdi] *prep.* 任何人

Is there anybody who can do me a favor?
有谁能帮我个忙吗？

友好和睦 道歉致谢

apologize [ə'pɔlədʒaiz] *vi.* 道歉，谢罪，认错

You must apologize to your mother for what you said just now.
你必须为刚才说过的话向妈妈道歉。

apology [ə'pɔlədʒi] *n.* 道歉，认错，谢罪

I owe you an apology for not going to your birthday party.
我没有出席你的生日聚会，我应该向你道歉。

consult [kən'sʌlt] *vt.* 请教，查阅

You had better find a travel agent to consult about your travel things.
你最好找一个旅行代理人咨询一下出行事宜。

真题

Please ____ dictionaries when you are not sure of word spelling or meaning.
A) search   B) seek
C) inquire   D) consult

详　解：选D。题意为：如果你对单词的拼写或词义拿不准，请查字典。A) search意思是"搜查，搜寻"；B) seek意思是"探索，追求"；C) inquire意思是"询问"；D) consult意思是"查阅，咨询以获取信息"。

(CET-4 2004.6)

forgive [fə'giv] *vt.* 原谅，饶恕，宽恕

Please forgive me—I didn't mean to that.
请原谅我，我不是有意的。

gratitude ['grætitju:d] *adj.* 感激，感谢，感恩

He wrote a letter of gratitude for me.
他写了一封感谢信给我。

pardon ['pɑ:dn] *n.* 原谅，赦免；*vt.* 原谅

The kind-hearted priest decided to pardon the guilty young man.
善良的牧师决定原谅这个有罪的年轻人。

repay [ri'pei] *vi.&vt.* 偿还，报答，报复

Now it is time for me to repay you for your kindness.
现在是我报答你好意的时候了。

reward [ri'wɔ:d] *vt.* 报答；*n.* 报答，报酬

She gave herself a reward or treat when she did well in Chemistry.
当自己的化学方面表现不错时，她就奖赏自己或好好吃一顿。

sincere [sin'siə] *adj.* 真诚的，真挚的

He made a sincere self-criticism at the meeting.
他在会议上作了诚恳的自我批评。

token ['təukən] *n.* 信物，纪念品
　　　　　　　　　 adj. 象征性的，装样子的

He wishes to make you a present in token of his gratitude.
他想送你一件礼物，以表示对你的感谢之情。

🔍 **考点：** by the same token 由于同样的原因，同样地；in token of 作为……的标记，成为……的纪念

tribute ['tribju:t] *n.* 贡物，献礼，贡献

She began by paying tribute to the people from whom she once received help.
她首先向给予她帮助的人们表示敬意。

unless [ən'les] *conj.* 除非，如果不

I won't forgive her unless she apologizes first.
除非她先道歉，否则我不原谅她。

真题

Many people believe we are heading for environmental disaster ____ we radically change the way we live.
A) but   B) although
C) unless   D) lest

详　解：选C。题意为：许多人认为：除非我们彻底改变自己的生活方式，否则我们将面临环境灾难。A) but意思是"但是"，常与to搭配；B) although意思是"尽管"；C) unless意思是"除非"；D) lest意思是"以免"。

(CET-4 2005.6)

友好和睦 公德爱心

bystander ['baistændə] *n.* 旁观者

Don't hit me! I was nothing more than an almost innocent bystander.
别打我，我只是个看热闹的。

---

care [kɛə] *vi.* 关心，介意；*n.* 小心

Just do whatever you like, and don't care what people say.
只管做你喜欢的任何事，别在乎他人会怎么说。

考点：care for照顾，照料，喜欢；take care当心，注意；take care of爱护，照料

真题

Areas where students have particular difficulty have been treated ___ particular care.
A) in   B) by
C) with   D) under

详 解：选C。题意为：对有特殊困难学生的地区已予以特别照顾。with care为固定搭配，表示"小心，慎重"。

(CET-4 2003.6)

---

charity ['tʃæriti] *n.* 施舍，慈善事业

The charity her husband worked in was a non-profit organization.
她丈夫工作的那个慈善团体是个非盈利性的组织。

---

conscience ['kɔnʃəns] *n.* 良心，道德心

As for this matter, I have a clear conscience.
对于这件事，我问心无愧。

考点：in (all / good) conscience凭良心，公正地；on one's conscience引起某人悔恨（或内疚）的

---

consider [kən'sidə] *vt.* 认为，考虑，关心

She is so selfish, and never considers others.
她很自私，从来不为他人着想。

---

concern [kən'sə:n] *n.* 关心，挂念，关系

My main concern is the safety of schoolchildren.
我最关心的是在校儿童的安全问题。

考点：as / so far as...be concerned 就……而言

真题

Dr. Smith was always ____ the poor and the sick, often providing them with free medical care.
A) reminded of   B) absorbed in
C) tended by   D) concerned about

详 解：选D。题意为：史密斯医生总是很关心穷人和病人，经常为他们提供免费的医疗服务。A) remind of意思是"提醒，使记起"；B) be absorbed in意思是"全神贯注于，专心于"；C) be tended by意思是"由……照管（护理）"；D) be concerned about意思是"对……关心"。

(CET-4 2005.12)

---

consideration [kənsidə'reiʃən] *n.* 考虑，思考，体贴

In consideration of his bad temper, she refused him.
考虑到他的坏脾气，她拒绝了他。

考点：in consideration of 考虑到，由于；作为……的报酬；take into consideration 考虑到，顾及

---

considerate [kən'sidərit] *adj.* 考虑周到的，体谅的

They should be more considerate to young people.
他们应该更体谅年轻人。

真题

It's very ____ of you not to talk aloud while the baby is asleep.
A) concerned   B) careful
C) considerable   D) considerate

详 解：选D。题意为：孩子睡觉时你没大声讲话，真是体贴啊。considerate这里指"体贴的，周到的"。

(CET-4 2003.12)

considering [kən'sidəriŋ] *prep.* 经 就……而论，照……说来，鉴于；*conj.* 考虑到

Considering his ill health, they asked him to stay in bed.
考虑到他身体不好，他们让他待在床上。

---

contribute [kən'tribju:t] *vt.* 捐献，捐助，投稿

I contributed all my money to the people of the disaster-stricken areas.
我把所有的钱都捐给了灾区人民。

真题

Eating too much fat can ___ heart disease and cause high blood pressure.
A) contribute to   B) attribute to
C) attend to   D) devote to

详　解：选A。题意为：摄入太多脂肪会导致心脏病和高血压。A) contribute to 意思是"促成"；B) attribute sth. to sth. 意思是"把……归因于……"，本句应该用被动；C) attend to 意思是"照顾，照料"；D) devote to意思是"献身于"。

(CET-4 2001.6)

---

contribution [ˌkɔntri'bju:ʃən] *n.* 贡献，捐献，捐款，捐献物

He made such a generous contribution to the university that they are naming one of the new buildings after him.
他曾慷慨地给这所大学捐过一笔钱，因而人们准备将一座大楼以他的名字命名。

考点：make contribution to 对……做出贡献

---

devote [di'vəut] *vt.* 将……奉献，致力于

He has devoted his whole life to composing music.
他一生都在致力于音乐创作。

---

donor ['dəunə] *n.* 赠送人，捐款人

The patient wants to know the donor's name.
病人想知道捐赠者的姓名。

---

pity ['piti] *n.* 怜悯，遗憾；*vt.* 同情

It's a pity that the car accident left the girl with paralysis of the limbs.
真遗憾，事故使女孩四肢瘫痪。

moral ['mɔrəl] *adj.* 道德的，合乎道德的 *n.* 寓意，道德，教训

It is said that moral taint has spread among young people.
据说，道德败坏在年轻人之间蔓延开来。

考点：draw a moral from... 从……中吸取教训

---

soul [səul] *n.* 灵魂，精神，人

Christians cleanse sin from the soul through chanting the Holy Bible.
基督徒通过诵读圣经涤荡心灵上的罪恶。

---

sympathetic [ˌsimpə'θetik] *adj.* 同情的，和谐的

It's easy to strike a sympathetic chord in his heart.
总是会很容易触及他的怜悯之情。

考点：be sympathetic with sb. 同情某人
be sympathetic to sth. 对某事赞同

---

sympathize ['simpəθaiz] *vi.* 同情，同感，共鸣

I sympathize with you; I understand that's what a feeling.
我很同情你，我知道那是一种什么样的感觉。

---

sympathy ['simpəθi] *n.* 同情，一致，同感

The stimulus of sympathy is very important to a man.
一种趣味相投、志同道合的相互鼓励对一个人来说是非常重要的。

---

virtue ['və:tju:] *n.* 善，美德，优点

His virtue had been rewarded good returns.
他的美德获得了好的回报。

考点：by virtue of 借助，由于

---

voluntary ['vɔləntəri] *adj.* 自愿的，志愿的

She is a voluntary worker at the Home for the Aged.
她是在这家养老院义务服务的。

友好和睦 鼓励安慰

encourage [in'kʌridʒ] *vt.* 鼓励，支持，助长

The teacher encouraged the little girl not to be coy and speak out her idea.
老师鼓励那个小女孩不要害羞，大胆地说出自己的想法。

* ⁻⁻⁻⁻⁻⁻⁻⁻⁻⁻⁻⁻⁻⁻⁻⁻⁻⁻⁻⁻⁻⁻⁻

encouragement [in'kʌridʒmənt] *n.* 鼓励，赞助，促进

We all need other's encouragement.
我们都需要别人的鼓励。

* ⁻⁻⁻⁻⁻⁻⁻⁻⁻⁻⁻⁻⁻⁻⁻⁻⁻⁻⁻⁻⁻⁻⁻

stimulate ['stimjuleit] *vt.* 刺激，激励，激发

Playing can stimulate children's imagination.
玩耍能促进孩子的想象力。

* ⁻⁻⁻⁻⁻⁻⁻⁻⁻⁻⁻⁻⁻⁻⁻⁻⁻⁻⁻⁻⁻⁻⁻

urge [ə:dʒ] *n.* 冲动；*vt.* 推进，催促

The urge to survive drove them to run very quickly.
求生的欲望驱使他们快跑。

🔍 考点：urge后接从句时，从句中用虚拟语气，即从句中的谓语动词用should + 动词原形的形式。

inspire [in'spaiə] *vt.* 鼓舞，给……以灵感

We should inspire the students to think in the study.
我们应启发学生在学习中多思考。

真题

_____ by the superstars on television, the young athletes trained hard and played intensely.
A) Imitated   B) Insured
C) Imposed   D) Inspired

详 解：选D。题意为：受到电视上超级明星的鼓舞，年轻的运动员们刻苦训练，认真比赛。A) imitate意思是"模仿"；B) insure意思是"确保"；C) impose意思是"强加，欺骗"；D) inspire意思是"鼓舞"。

(CET-4 2006.6)

motivate ['məutiveit] *vt.* 促动，激励，激发

She wanted to find some effective ways to motivate her son to study.
她想要找一些有效的方法来激励她的儿子学习。

友好和睦 理解信任

depend [di'pend] *vi.* 依靠，依赖，相信

Health depends on good food, enough sleep and regular exercise.
健康依靠的是好的食物，充足的睡眠和适当的运动。

🔍 考点：sb. depend on 某人依赖……
　　　sth. depend on 依……而定

* ⁻⁻⁻⁻⁻⁻⁻⁻⁻⁻⁻⁻⁻⁻⁻⁻⁻⁻⁻⁻⁻⁻⁻

dependence [di'pendəns] *n.* 依靠，依赖，相信

I like her self-dependence most.
我最欣赏她的自立。

* ⁻⁻⁻⁻⁻⁻⁻⁻⁻⁻⁻⁻⁻⁻⁻⁻⁻⁻⁻⁻⁻⁻⁻

dependent [di'pendənt] *adj.* 依靠的，依赖的

Generally speaking, China is heavily dependent on its exports of agricultural commodities.
通常来说，中国很大程度上依靠农产品的出口。

* ⁻⁻⁻⁻⁻⁻⁻⁻⁻⁻⁻⁻⁻⁻⁻⁻⁻⁻⁻⁻⁻⁻⁻

insight ['insait] *n.* 洞察力，领悟，洞悉，了解

She had a singular insight into this matter.
她对于此事件有一个不同的理解。

真题

The film provides a deep _____ into a wide range of human qualities and feelings.
A) outlook   B) imagination
C) insight   D) fancy

详 解：选C。题意为：该电影展现出对广泛的人性与情感的深刻洞察。an insight into sth. "对……的深入见解"，是固定搭配，其他三项都不与into搭配。

(CET-4 2002.12)

integrity [in'tegriti] *n.* 正直，诚实，诚恳，完整，完善

His reputation for integrity was permanently remembered.
他那刚正不阿的声誉将永远被记住。

loyal ['lɔiəl] *adj.* 忠诚的，忠心的

My husband is a good man and he is loyal to me.
我丈夫是个好男人，对我很忠诚。

loyalty ['lɔiəlti] *n.* 忠诚，忠心

His loyalty and support was steadfast, and I was sure of myself.
他对我的忠诚和支持是始终不渝的，我对自己满怀信心。

truthful ['tru:θfəl] *adj.* 诚实的，真实的

What you say will be accredited as long as you are always truthful.
只要你一向诚实人家就会相信你所说的话。

reliable [ri'laiəbl] *adj.* 可靠的，可信赖的

This kind of comparable and reliable data is often lacking, which can only be built up gradually.
这种可靠而又真实可信的资料常感缺乏，而它们又只能慢慢地积累起来。

rely [ri'lai] *vi.* 依赖，依靠，信赖

An erratic mind jump from one idea to another, you can't rely on such person.
心意不定的人反复无常，你不能依赖这类人。

🔍考点：rely on 依赖，依靠

trust [trʌst] *n.* 信任；*vt.* 相信，委托

She learnt not to trust anybody easily.
她认识到了不要轻易相信任何人。

🔍考点：trust表示"委托，托与"，不用双宾语，而采用"trust sb. with sth."或"trust sth. to sb."的结构。

understand [ˌʌndə'stænd] *vt.* 懂，获悉
vi. 懂得

You need understand what the customers think.
你需要了解顾客想什么。

🔍考点：make oneself understood 清楚表达自己的意见

understanding [ˌʌndə'stændiŋ] *n.* 理解，理解力，协定

Thank you for your understanding and cooperation in this matter.
谢谢你们对此事的理解和合作。

🔍考点：understanding与comprehension作"理解力"时能通用，但understanding有"同情，谅解"之意，而comprehension没有。

undoubtedly [ʌn'dautidli] *adv.* 毋庸置疑，肯定地

The vase undoubtedly is genuine.
这个花瓶无疑是真品。

友好和睦 团结合作

accompany [ə'kʌmpəni] *vt.* 陪伴，陪同，伴随，为……伴奏，伴随……发生

I believe I can conquer anything if you accompany me.
我相信有你的陪伴，我可以征服一切。

🔍考点：accompany on / at 为……伴奏（或伴唱），陪伴……

aid [eid] *vt.* 帮助，援助
n. 帮助，救护，助手

Please dial 110 for aid if you have any trouble.
有困难，请拨打110寻求帮助。

🔍考点：aid, assist, help的区别：aid（用金钱）援助一群人；assist常与help同义，但assist（协助）指受协助的人自己做一部分工作。

assist [ə'sist] *vt.* 援助，帮助，搀扶

I asked my sister to assist me in studying English.
我请求姐姐帮我学英语。

🔍考点：assist ab. in doing sth.= assist sb. to do sth. 帮助某人做某事

assistance [ə'sistəns] *n.* 帮助，援助

He is reluctant to give me assistance.
他很不情愿给我帮助。

associate [ə'səuʃieit] *n.* 伙伴，同事
vi. 交往

In America, people always associate turkey with Thanksgiving Day.
在美国，人们总是把火鸡与感恩节联系在一起。

🔍 考点：associate with 与……交往

collective [kə'lektiv] *adj.* 集体的，集合性的

These books are collective but the man took them home just now.
这些书是公用的，但是那个人刚刚把它们带回家了。

cooperate [kəu'ɔpəreit] *vi.* 合作，协作，配合

I would like to cooperate with you.
我愿意和你合作。

🔍 考点：cooperate with sb. in doing sth. 与某人合作某事

cooperation [kəu,ɔpə'reiʃən] *n.* 合作，协作，互助

I really calculate on your cooperation.
我真的指望你们的合作。

bond [bɔnd] *n.* 联结，联系，公债

I recommend you to buy this glue which makes a good firm bond.
我推荐你买这种胶水，它粘得很结实。

cling [kliŋ] *n.* 紧抓，紧贴
vi. 紧贴，附着，依恋，坚持

My deskmate and I are good friends and we cling together wherever we go.
我和同桌是好朋友，我们形影不离。

partner ['pɑ:tnə] *n.* 伙伴，搭挡，配偶

The man in black dinner-jacket is the dominant partner of the business.
那个穿黑礼服的男人是公司举足轻重的合伙人。

closely ['kləuzli] *adv.* 紧密地，接近地

The little girl clung closely to her elder sister.
那个小女孩紧紧地依偎着她的姐姐。

companion [kəm'pænjən] *n.* 同伴，共事者，伴侣

This time I will be your travelling companion on the train.
这次我会是你火车上的旅伴。

comrade ['kɔmrid] *n.* 同志，亲密的同伴

Many of his comrades were killed in the battle.
他的很多同伴都死在了战场上。

intimate ['intimeit] *adj.* 亲密的，个人的

Both of them felt that they had become very intimate during the training.
他俩在训练当中都感到彼此相当亲密了。

mutual ['mju:tjuəl] *adj.* 相互的，共同的

The little kingdom tried to confederate itself with others for mutual safety.
这个小王国为了共同安全，曾试图与其他的王国结盟。

our ['auə] *pron.* 我们的

Though my brother is older, he is junior to me in our company.
虽然哥哥比我年长，但在我们公司他级别比我低。

ours ['auəz] *pron.* 我们的

The football is yours; ours is over there.
这个足球是你的，我们的在那边。

ourselves [,auə'selvz] *pron.* 我们自己

We must introduce some systems into our office routine to constrain ourselves.
我们须在我们日常公务中建立一些制度来约束我们。

outsider [,aut'saidə] *n.* 局外人，外人，不大可能获胜的人

Don't treat him as an outsider.
别把他当做外人。

own [əun] *adj.* 自己的；*vt.* 有，拥有

No one wants his own country to become the colony of other countries.
没有人想要自己的国家变成其他国家的殖民地。

and [ænd] *conj.* 和，又，并，则

Susan and I are associates in business.

苏珊和我是生意上的合作伙伴。

strengthen ['streŋθən] *vt.* 加强，巩固

We must strengthen and increase the membership of the company.
我们必须加强并扩大公司组织。

teamwork ['ti:mwə:k] *n.* 合作，协作，配合

We have learned how important teamwork is in this match.
在这场比赛中，我们学到了团队精神的重要性。

together [tə'geðə] *adj.* 共同，一起

It is common interests that bind the businessmen together.
是共同的利益使商人结合在一起。

🔘 考点：together with 和……在一起

union ['ju:njən] *vi.* 联合；*vt.* 使联合

We must unite as many people as possible to against the oppression.
我们必须团结尽可能多的人反对压迫。

workmate ['wə:kmeit] *n.* 同事

My workmate Tony decided to go to night school to learn something about accounting.
我同事托尼决定去夜校学习一些有关会计学的知识。

友好和睦 劝说告诫

conviction [kən'vikʃən] *n.* 确信，说服，定罪

This was his third conviction for cheating.
这是他第3次被判犯有欺诈罪。

convince [kən'vins] *vt.* 使确信，使信服

I can't convince him to buy our company's product.
我无法说服他买我们公司的产品。

🔘 考点：convince sb. of sth. 使某人相信某事

persuade [pə'sweid] *vt.* 说服；*vi.* 被说服

I really don't know how I can persuade you of my sincerity.
我真的不知道如何能够让你相信我的诚意。

warn [wɔ:n] *vi.* 发出警告（预告）
　　　　　　 vt. 警告，告诫

She warned us not to take that road at night.
她提醒我们晚上不要走那条路。

🔘 考点：warn sb. of 警告某人注意；warn against doing 警告某人别做……

友好和睦 同意允许

accept [ək'sept] *vi.&vt.* 接受，领受，同意，认可

Sorry, I can't accept your gift.
对不起，我不能接受你的礼物。

grant [grɑ:nt] *vt.* 授予，同意
　　　　　 n. 拨款，补助金

Tom importuned me to grant his request.
汤姆纠缠着要我答应他的请求。

🔘 考点：take... for granted 认为……是理所当然；granted that... 即使……

let [let] *vt.* 让，允许，使

It is a fine day today; let's go for a picnic by the riverside.
今天天气不错，我们到河边野餐去吧。

nod [nɔd] *vt.* 点（头），点头表示

The general manager nodded his approval.
总经理点头表示同意。

permission [pə'miʃən] *n.* 允许，许可，同意

In order to launch a legal demonstration, you must first obtain permission from the police.
为了发动合法的游行，你们必须先得到警方的许可。

permit [pə'mit] *n.* 执照；*vt.* 允许

No vehicles are permitted into the special place.
这个特别的地方禁止任何车辆进入。

allow [ə'lau] *vt.* 允许，准许

Usually passengers are not allowed to smoke.
通常来说乘客们不允许吸烟。

🔘 考点：allow for 考虑到；allow of 容许，使有……的可能

友好和睦 保证承担

ensure [in'ʃuə] *vt.* 保证，保护，赋予
At least you must ensure the purity of our drinking water.
至少你必须确保我们的饮用水的纯净。

guarantee [ˌgærən'ti:] *n.* 保证，担保物
"Goods are sold with money-back guarantee." marketers said.
"售出商品质量不符保证退款。"商家说道。

真题

The Car Club couldn't _____ to meet the demands of all its members.
A) ensure   B) guarantee
C) assume   D) confirm

详　解：选B。题意为：这家汽车俱乐部不能保证满足所有会员的要求。A) ensure 意思是"保证"，但用于"ensure + that从句……"或者"ensure sth."的结构；B) guarantee意思是"保证"，guarantee to do sth. 保证做……；C) assume意思是"假设，认为"；D) confirm意思是"证实，确认"。

(CET-4 2001.6)

promise ['prɔmis] *vt.* 允诺
　　　　　　　　　　n. 诺言，指望
My father promised me a new bicycle for my birthday.
我爸爸许诺我过生日的时候送我一辆新的自行车。

考点：make a promise 答应，允诺；
　　　hold a promise sacred 信守诺言

swear [swɛə] *vi.* 诅咒；*vt.* 宣（誓）
Tom made everybody swear to keep the secret of him liking Lily.
汤姆叫大家立誓保守他喜欢莉莉的秘密。

考点：swear off 戒掉，保证放弃

undertake [ˌʌndə'teik] *vt.* 从事，承担，保证
I cannot undertake to accomplish that task.
我不能担保完成那件事。

摩擦失和 阻挠破坏

prevent [pri'vent] *vt.* 预防，防止，阻止
How can we prevent the spreading of the disease?
我们怎么样才能防止这种疾病的传播呢？

考点：prevent from 阻止，防止

prohibit [prə'hibit] *vt.* 禁止，阻止
I'm afraid that my prior engagement will prohibit me from joining your birthday party.
我有约在先，恐怕不能参加你的生日聚会了。

restrain [ris'trein] *vt.* 抑制，遏制，限制
He couldn't restrain his curiosity to study this strange toy.
他抑制不住自己的好奇心来研究这个奇怪的玩具。

考点：restrain sb. from doing sth. 阻止
　　　某人做

restraint [ris'treint] *n.* 抑制，遏制，克制
Hearing that her car was stolen, her anger was beyond restraint.
听说车被偷了，她怒不可遏。

restrict [ris'trikt] *vt.* 限制，限定，约束
I think education should not be restricted to any specific age group.
我认为教育不应限制在任何特定的年龄组上。

考点：be restricted to (doing) sth.
　　　限制做

restriction [ris'trikʃən] *n.* 限制，限定，约束
He wants to know if the bank has any other restriction regarding accepting loan.
他想知道关于接受贷款银行方面有没有什么其他限制。

interfere [ˌintə'fiə] *vi.* 干涉，干预，妨碍
He often interferes with my work.
他经常妨碍我的工作。

interference [ˌintə'fiərəns] *n.* 干涉，干预，
　　　　　　　　　　　　　　　　　　阻碍
He can't brook any interference when he is working.
他工作时不能容忍他人的任何干涉。

摩擦失和 矛盾冲突

against [ə'genst] *prep.* 倚在，逆，对着

The peasant leaned against the tree to have a rest.
农夫靠着树休息了一会儿。

compromise ['kɔmprəmaiz] *n.* 妥协，和解

You should make a compromise over this housing matter.
就房子事情上你应该做出让步。

concession [kən'seʃən] *n.* 让步，妥协，优惠

At last, I decided to make some concession.
最后，我决定让步。

accuse [ə'kju:z] *vt.* 控告，控诉，指责，归咎于

Believe it or not, our neighbor Mr. Huang was accused as a thief.
信不信由你，我们的邻居黄先生被指控为盗犯。

🔍 考点：be accused of 指控

真题

The shop assistant was dismissed as she was ____ of cheating customers.
A) cursed   B) charged
C) accused   D) scolded

详 解：选C. 题意为：该店员因被指责欺诈顾客而被解雇。A) curse意思是"诅咒，骂人"；B) charge sb. with sth. 意思是"以……指控某人"；C) be accused of意思是"指控"；D) scold sb. for sth. 意思是"因……斥责某人"。

(CET-4 2002.12)

conflict ['kɔnflikt] *n.* 争论，冲突，斗争

This matter increased the conflict between us.
这件事加剧了我们之间的冲突。

contradiction [ˌkɔntrə'dikʃən] *n.* 矛盾，不一致，否认

No one wants to escalate contradiction.
没有人想要把矛盾升级。

🔍 考点：in contradiction to 与……矛盾

conversely ['kɔnvə:sli] *adv.* 相反地

In real life, nobody was all bad, nor, conversely, all good.
现实生活中，不是所有人都坏，反过来说，也不一定都是好人。

counter ['kauntə] *vt.* 反对，反驳，抗辩
n. 反面，反对物，柜台，计数器

He countered my proposal with one of his own.
他以自己的一个建议来反对我的建议。

curse [kə:s] *n.* 诅咒，咒骂，天谴

The witch imprecated curses upon the prince and made him change into a frog.
这个巫婆诅咒这个王子，并把他变成了一只青蛙。

division [di'viʒən] *n.* 分，分配，除法

There was a division of opinion on the matter.
对于那件事有意见上的分歧。

offend [ə'fend] *vi.* 犯过错; *vt.* 冒犯

Sorry, I didn't mean to offend you.
对不起，我不是故意冒犯你的。

confront [kən'frʌnt] *vt.* 面临，正视，使对质

The judge didn't know how to do with it, just confronted the accused with his accuser.
法官不知道如何是好，只好让被告和原告对质。

真题

We need to create education standards that prepare our next generation who will be ____ with an even more competitive market.
A) tackled   B) encountered
C) dealt   D) confronted

详 解：选D. 题意为：我们需要设立教育标准，使我们的下一代做好面对竞争更为激烈的市场的准备。A) tackle 意思是"处理，解决"，是及物动词，后面直接跟宾语；B) encounter 意思是"遭遇，遇到"，尤指不期而遇；C) deal意思是"对付，应对"；D) confront意思是"面临，面对"，常与with搭配。

(CET-4 2005.6)

neutral ['nju:trəl] *adj.* 中立的，中性的，不偏不倚的

According to the history, Ireland was a neutral nation in World War II.
历史上，爱尔兰在第二次世界大战中是保持中立的。

reconcile ['rekənsail] *vt.* 使协调，使和解，使甘心

It's impossible for me to reconcile the two sisters, since I don't know them at all.
我不可能去调解那对姐妹的,因为我根本就不认识她们。

🔍 考点：reconcile with 与……和解

slap [slæp] *vt.&n.* 掌掴，掌击

The furious father gave his son a slap on the cheek.
暴怒的父亲一巴掌打在儿子的脸上。

insult ['insʌlt] *vt.&n.* 侮辱，凌辱

He had to swallow the insult from the boss in the company.
他在公司不得不忍受老板的侮辱。

misunderstand ['misʌndə'stænd] *vt.* 误解，误会，曲解

My boyfriend always misunderstands me and I feel sorrowful.
我男朋友总是误解我，我觉得很伤心。

摩擦失和 欺骗隐瞒

cheat [tʃi:t] *vt.* 骗取，哄；*vi.* 行骗

I won't cheat you; I'm a man of my word.
我不会骗你的，我是个信守诺言的人。

deceive [di'si:v] *vt.* 欺骗，蒙蔽，行骗

He used to deceive others by trickery.
他过去常常用诡计欺骗他人。

🔍 考点：cheat, deceive的区别：cheat侧重采取不诚实手段，获得某种个人利益或损害他人利益。deceive侧重将不真实情况告诉别人或以某种错误说法、理论、假象等使人上当。

deception [di'sepʃən] *n.* 欺瞒，欺诈

The man obtained their trust by deception.
那人靠欺骗获取了他们的信任。

disguise [dis'gaiz] *n.* 假装
vi. 隐瞒，掩埋

That guy made his escape in disguise.
那家伙化装后逃走了。

🔍 考点：in disguise 伪装，假扮

fraud [frɔ:d] *n.* 欺诈，诈骗，骗子

You must realize that all you see is a fraud.
你必须认识到你看到的所有都是欺骗。

hide [haid] *vt.* 把……藏起来，隐瞒

It must be him who has hidden the child.
一定是他把孩子藏起来了。

🔍 考点：hide sth. from sb. 对某人隐瞒某事

pretend [pri'tend] *vi.* 假装
vt. 假托，借口

I can see that you just pretend to be foolish intentionally.
我可以看出来你是有意装傻。

摩擦失和 强迫威胁

compel [kəm'pel] *vt.* 强迫，迫使屈服

The heavy rain compelled us to come into the house.
大雨迫使我们不得不回到屋里。

enforce [in'fɔ:s] *vt.* 实施，执行，强制

I can do nothing, you know the police department enforces the law.
我帮不上什么忙，你知道警察部门是按法律执行的。

impose [im'pəuz] *vt.* 把……强加，征（税）

Sam always imposes on Lucy's good nature.
塞姆总是欺负露西。

oblige [ə'blaidʒ] *vt.* 迫使，施恩惠于

A late meeting obliged me to change my plan.
迟到的会面使我不得不改变计划。

人际交往

摩擦失和

考点： oblige通常指按照法律、或道义等驱使某人去做某事；be obliged to do sth. 被迫做某事；be obliged to sb. for sth. 因……感激某人

---

oppress [ə'pres] *vt.* 压迫，压制，压抑

The people were oppressed by the colonialists.
人民受殖民者的压迫。

---

reluctance [ri'lʌktəns] *n.* 不愿，勉强

She showed the greatest reluctance to answer the question.
她表示很不愿意答复。

---

reluctant [ri'lʌktənt] *adj.* 不愿的，勉强的

He knew his own propensity to evil, but he was reluctant to change it.
虽然他意识到自己生性作恶，但并不愿意悔改。

---

resist [ri'zist] *vi.&vt.* 抵抗，抵制

I can say only a few people could resist the lure of money.
我敢说只有少数人能抵制金钱的诱惑。

---

resistance [ri'zistəns] *n.* 抵抗，抵制，抵抗力

The conservatives show stubborn resistance to change.
保守的人对改革采取顽抗态度。

---

resistant [ri'zistənt] *adj.* 抵抗的，反抗的

I wonder why he is resistant to have his hair cut.
我想知道他为什么那么拒绝剪发。

考点： be resistant to 抵抗……的，耐……的

---

threat [θret] *n.* 威胁，恐吓，凶兆

He blustered out a threat when he left.
他离开时气势汹汹地发出威胁之词。

---

threaten ['θretn] *vi.&vt.* 威胁，恐吓

Don't threaten me; I am not afraid of you.
别威胁我，我不怕你。

考点： threaten...with... 以……相威胁

摩擦失和　拒绝禁止

decline [di'klain] *vi.&vt.* 拒绝，谢绝，推辞，下垂

I declined to have dinner with that man, saying that I wasn't feeling well.
我说身体不舒服，婉拒了和那个男士共进晚餐。

考点： decline是"婉言谢绝"；refuse, reject是"拒绝"。

---

denial [di'naiəl] *n.* 否认，拒绝

I didn't know my denial of her request hurt her.
我不知道我的拒绝伤害了她。

---

deny [di'nai] *vt.* 否定，拒绝相信

This is not to deny that China has been overinvestment in some sectors, such as steel and cars.
这并不是要否认中国已经在一些行业，如钢铁业和汽车业，存在过度投资。

考点： deny sb. sth. 拒绝给予某人某物
deny doing sth. 否认做某事

---

no [nəu] *adv.* 不，并不；*adj.* 没有

There was no person learned enough to understand it.
没有人有足够的学识理解它。

---

refusal [ri'fju:zəl] *n.* 拒绝

My refusal to attend the ceremony is taken as an insult to the host.
我拒绝参加典礼，主人认为这是对他们的一种侮辱。

---

reject [ri'dʒekt] *vt.* 拒绝，丢掉，驳回

He was afraid she would reject him because he didn't satisfy the qualification.
他担心她会因他不满足要求而拒绝他。

---

ban [bæn] *n.* 禁令，禁止
v. 禁止，剥夺权利

Parking is banned in this street.
这条街禁止停车。

考点： ban sth. 取缔，查禁某物
ban sb. from doing sth. 对……开禁

forbid [fə'bid] *vt.* 禁止，不许，阻止
I can't forbid him going out on weekends.
我不能阻止他在周末外出。

 真题

Brazil's constitution_____ the military use of
nuclear energy.
A) withdraws   B) interrupts
C) objects   D) forbids

详 解：选D。题意为：巴西宪法禁止核
能应用于军事。A) withdraw意思是"撤回，
退出"；B) interrupt意思是"中断，中途打
断"；C) object意思是"反对，拒绝"，后
常跟介词to；D) forbid意思是"禁止"。

(CET-4 2006.6)

摩擦失和 引诱误导

induce [in'dju:s] *vt.* 引诱，劝，导致
Nothing in the world would induce me to commit.
什么也不能引诱我去犯罪。

考点：induce, tempt, elicit的区别：
induce指引导、诱导，不一定怀有
坏动机；tempt指通过试探性的引诱
而使对方脱离正轨或违背良心行
事；elicit指诱出（真理、回答）
等，引起（笑）等。

mislead [mis'li:d] *vt.* 使误入岐途，使误
解，给……错误印象
He was just misled by the woman's wiles.
他只是被那个女人的花言巧语给蒙混住了。

temptation [temp'teiʃən] *n.* 诱惑，引诱
We are easy to fall before strong temptation.
我们都容易在强烈的诱惑面前失足。

trap [træp] *n.* 陷阱，诡计；*vt.* 诱骗
No one has ever fallen into this trap till now.
直到现在没人掉入这个陷阱。

摩擦失和 命令指示

conformation [ˌkɔnfɔ:'meiʃən] *n.* 符合，一
致，构想
My son was potty about face and conformation of
cars when he was a child.
我儿子小的时候，对汽车的外观和构造都非常
着迷。

dictate [dik'teit] *vi.&vt.* 口授，命令
The boss dictated a letter to the typist.
老板向打字员口授了一封信。

dominant ['dɔminənt] *adj.* 支配的，统治性
的
What is the dominant theme of this conference?
这次会议的首要议题是什么?

dominate ['dɔmineit] *vt.* 统治，支配，占
优势
She has strong desire to dominate over others.
她很想支配别人。

domination [dɔmi'neiʃən] *n.* 支配，统治，
最主要特征
Nobody can stand others' domination.
没人能容忍别人的支配。

follow ['fɔləu] *vt.* 跟随，结果是
He followed her long distance in an alley.
他在小巷里跟了她很久。

考点：as follows 如下；follow through
把……进行到底；follow up 追
究，追查

indicate ['indikeit] *vt.* 标示，表示，表明
Government statistics indicates that prices have
gone up this year.
政府统计指出今年物价已经上升。

indication [ˌindi'keiʃən] *n.* 指示，表示，表明
His words have given indication of depression for
some weeks.
几个星期以来，他的话语都带有一些沮丧。

obey [ə'bei] *vi.* 服从；*vt.* 顺从
As a schoolchild, you should obey school rules.

作为一名学生，你应该遵守学校规定。

---*

submit [səb'mit] *vi.* 服从；*vt.* 使服从

vt. 呈送，提交

You're required to submit a resume when you come to that company.
你去公司时必须交一份个人简历。

order ['ɔ:də] *n.* 次序，整齐；*vt.* 命令

Who do you think you are? What entitles you to order us about?
你以为你是谁？你有什么权力命令我们做事？

考点：in order 按顺序，按次序；in order that 为了；in order to 为了；in short order 立即；out of order 不正常的，不按次序的

教育 | Education

学校 校园设施

campus ['kæmpəs] *n.* 校园，场地

There is a wide dissatisfaction among the students with the food on campus.
学生们普遍对学校的饭菜不太满意。

college ['kɔlidʒ] *n.* 学院，大学

Most college students here have no idea of the politics in Philippines.
这里大部分大学生不了解菲律宾的政治。

blackboard ['blækbɔːd] *n.* 黑板

You didn't know that? You must have missed the notice on the blackboard.
你不知道？你一定是没有注意到黑板上的布告。

chalk [tʃɔːk] *n.* 白垩，粉笔

The chalk had scrapes on the blackboard.
粉笔在黑板上发出刮擦声。

kindergarten ['kində,gɑːtn] *n.* 幼儿园

In the kindergarten, children are taught to put waste into dustbins by their teachers.
在幼儿园里，老师教孩子们把垃圾扔到垃圾箱里。

nursery ['nəːsəri] *n.* 托儿所，苗圃

Being a teacher in the nursery can be hard work.
在托儿所里当老师是件辛苦事。

multiple ['mʌltipl] *adj.* 复合的，并联的，多样的

This insect grasps a target with its multiple subterranean tentacles.
这只昆虫用它多条地下触手来抓住目标。

playground ['pleigraund] *n.* 操场，运动场

All the staff were assembled at the playground to honor the leader's visit.
所有员工聚集在操场上欢迎领导的来访。

stadium ['steidiəm] *n.* 露天大型运动场

As soon as the game ended, the stadium was almost vacant.
比赛一结束，体育馆几乎空了。

学校 领导管理

academic [ækə'demik] *n.* 大学教师，专业学者；*adj.* 学院的，学术的，纯理论的

Last year I got my academic degree.
去年我获得了学位。

academy [ə'kædəmi] *n.* 私立中学，专科院校，研究院，学会

Don't look down on that old man. He is an academic of Dunhuang Academy.
别小看那个老头儿，他可是敦煌研究院的学者。

assistant [ə'sistənt] *n.* 助手，助理，助教

The manager needs an assistant to help him solve problems.
经理需要一位助手帮他处理问题。

dean [diːn] *n.* 教长，学院院长，系主任

Most of the students like the new dean very much.
学生们大都很喜欢这位新系主任。

department [di'pɑːtmənt] *n.* 部，司，局，处，系

He said he was the successive head of personnel department.
他说他是新任的人事部负责人。

headmaster [,hed'mɑːstə] *n.* 校长

The headmaster is a powerful man.
校长是个强有力的人物。

headmistress [ˌhed'mistrəs] *n.* （中小学的）女校长

The headmistress spoke at a considerable length.
（女）校长讲话讲了好长一段时间。

head-teacher [hed'ti:tʃə] *n.* 中小学校长

His mother is the head-teacher of his school.
他妈妈是他们学校的校长。

institute ['institju:t] *n.* 研究所，学院

Their college has an institute of foreign languages.
他们学校有外国语学院。

schooling ['sku:liŋ] *n.* 学校教育，学费

The man was deprived of schooling when he was a boy.
这个男人小时候就失学了。

enroll [in'rəul] *vi.* 入学，加入
vt. 招收，吸收

That girl has a great talent for music, but why didn't you enroll her?
那个女孩很有音乐天赋，但你为什么不录取她呢？

expel [iks'pel] *vt.* 开除，除名，驱逐，排出

According to the school rules, he should be expelled from school.
按照校规，他应该被开除。

专业学科 划分

basic ['beisik] *adj.* 基本的，基础的

Firstly, we will learn it from basic principles.
首先，我们从它的基本原理学起。

basically ['beisikəli] *adv.* 基本上，从根本上说

Basically, they want more information about him before accepting it.
从根本上说他们在接收他之前，想了解更多关于他的事。

basis ['beisis] *n.* 基础，根据

They got the conclusions on basis of careful observation and detailed studies.
在细心细致研究的基础上，他们得出了结论。

classification [ˌklæsifi'keiʃən] *n.* 分类，分级，分类法

Do you understand the system of classification used in Chemistry?
你理解化学里的分类系统吗？

classify ['klæsifai] *vt.* 把……分类

The fruits in the fruit stall are classified according to quality.
水果摊上的水果是根据其品质分等级的。

elementary [ˌeli'mentəri] *adj.* 基本的，初级的

I think the elementary mathematics is very easy.
我认为基础数学很简单。

fundamental [ˌfʌndə'mentl] *adj.* 基础的，基本的

Students must grasp the fundamental knowledge.
学生必须掌握好基础知识。

真题

The computer revolution may well change society as _____ as did the Industrial Revolution.
A) certainly　　B) insignificantly
C) fundamentally　D) comparatively

详 解：选C。题意为：像工业革命一样，计算机革命也会给社会带来根本性变化。A) certainly意思是"当然，确定地"；B) insignificantly意思是"无关紧要地"；C) fundamentally意思是"根本性地"；D) comparatively意思是"比较地"。

(CET-4 2000.1)

similar ['similə] *adj.* 相似的，类似的

Taxonomy is a system for organizing similar things into groups.
分类学是把相同的事物组织在一起的体系

考点：be similar to 与……相似

similarly ['similəli] *adv.* 类似地，相似地

My deskmate was late this morning and I was similarly delayed.
我同桌早上迟到了，我也迟到了。

subject ['sʌbjekt] *n.* 题目，学科，主语

The students need to learn nine subjects this semester.
同学们这一学期要学九门课程。

---

regarding [ri'gɑ:diŋ] *prep.* 关于

I know nothing regarding the prosody.
我对韵律学一无所知。

专业学科 数学

addition [ə'diʃən] *n.* 加，加法，附加物

Please use the addition to solve this problem.
请用加法解决这个问题。

👉 考点：in addition 另外，加之；in addition to 除了……之外（还有）

---

arithmetic [ə'riθmətik] *n.* 算术，四则运算

I've never been interested in arithmetic.
我对算术从来不感兴趣。

---

axis ['æksis] *n.* 轴，轴线，中心线

Please find out axis to symmetry of this figure and mark it with a line.
请找出这个图形的对称轴，并用一条线把它标出来。

---

diameter [dai'æmitə] *n.* 直径

The diameter of the circle is 20 centimetres.
这个圆的直径是20厘米。

---

equation [i'kweiʃən] *n.* 方程（式），等式

Which number is the quotient in the equation?
在这个等式中，哪个数是商？

---

equivalent [i'kwivələnt] *adj.* 相等的，等量的

Do you believe the statement that the nutrition of an egg is equivalent to a pound of meat?
你相信一只蛋的营养相当于一磅肉这个说法吗？

---

formula ['fɔ:mjulə] *n.* 公式，式

This formula is very difficult to remember.
这个公式非常难记。

👉 考点：formula的复数形式是formulas或者formulae。

---

geometry [dʒi'ɔmitri] *n.* 几何，几何学

She did very well in geometry in school.
上学时，她的几何学得很好。

---

major ['meidʒə] *n.* 专业，专业学生；*adj.* 较大的，主要的，主修的；*vi.* 主修，主攻

An unknown conglomerate holds a major share in the company.
一家不知名的大联合企业持有该公司的大部分股份。

---

mathematical [ˌmæθi'mætikəl] *adj.* 数学的，数学上的

Some of the most important concepts in physics owe their success to these mathematical systems.
物理学上的一些最重要的概念的成功应归功于这些数学体系。

---

mathematics [ˌmæθi'mætiks] *n.* 数学

He displayed interest in mathematics when he was a little boy.
他从小就对数学有兴趣。

---

minus ['mainəs] *n.* 负数，减号；*prep.* 减（去）；*adj.* 负的，阴性的

Three minus one is two.
3减去1得数是2。

---

multiply ['mʌltiplai] *vt.* 使增加，乘

In order to multiply the chance of success, he practiced very hard every day.
为了增加成功的机会，他每天都刻苦训练。

---

number ['nʌmbə] *n.* 数，数字，号码；*vt.* 给……编号

I don't think it's hard to state the number of casualties with accuracy.
我认为准确地说出伤亡人数并不难。

👉 考点：a number of... 若干，许多

---

odd [ɔd] *adj.* 奇数的，单只的，奇特的，不固定的，剩余的

Three and five are odd numbers.
3和5是奇数。

---

parallel ['pærəlel] *adj.* 平行的，相同的

This road is running parallel to the railway.
这条路与铁路平行。

plus [plʌs] *adj.* 正的；*prep.* 加，加上
Three plus two equals five.
3加2等于5。

principle ['prinsəpl] *n.* 原则，原理，主义
Can you explain the principle of jet propulsion?
你能解释一下喷气推进的原理吗？

🔍考点：in principle 原则上，大体上
on principle 根据原则

radius ['reidjəs] *n.* 半径
The radius of the circle is two centimeters.
这个圆的半径是两厘米。

ratio ['reiʃiəu] *n.* 比，比率
Its overall sex ratio is 150 and this is very high.
其总体性别比例是150，这是非常高的。

statistics [stə'tistiks] *n.* 统计数值，统计学
Both sides offered statistics to bolster their arguments.
双方都拿出统计数字来支持他们的论点。

subtract [səb'trækt] *vt.* 减，减去，去掉
His daughter has begun to learn to add and subtract.
他女儿已在学做加减法了。

🔍考点：subtract...from... 从……中减去

theoretical [ˌθiə'retikəl] *adj.* 理论（上）的
I am not good at learning theoretical concepts.
我不擅长学理论概念。

triangle ['traiæŋ] *n.* 三角（形）
We all have learned a triangle has three sides.
我们都学过三角形有3条边。

circumference [sə'kʌmfərəns] *n.* 圆周，周长，圆周线
This circle is ten miles in circumference.
这个圆的周长是10英里。

centimetre ['sentiˌmi:tə] *n.* 公分，厘米
There is a three-centimeter scar in her face.
在她脸上有一个3公分长的疤痕。

dimension [di'menʃən] *n.* 尺寸，尺度，面积
There is a building of vast dimensions.
那儿有一个大面积的建筑。

inch [intʃ] *n.* 英寸
He can not exactly say how many inches the stick is.
他不能准确说出这根棍子有多少英寸。

🔍考点：every inch 完全，彻底

length [leŋθ] *n.* 长，长度，距离，一段
Please gauge the length of the classroom and write it down on your note.
请测量一下教室的长度，然后把结果记在你的笔记里。

🔍考点：at length 详细地，最终，终于
go to great lengths 竭尽全力

meter ['mi:tə] *n.* 米，计量器，计，表
He is the first Chinese who broke the record for the one-hundred meter dash.
他是第一个打破百米赛跑纪录的中国人。

metric ['metrik] *adj.* 公制的，米制的
Nowadays, a lot of countries have adopted metric system.
如今，很多国家都采用了米制。

millimetre ['miliˌmi:tə] *n.* 毫米
This kind of glass is less than two millimeters thick.
这种玻璃的厚度不足两毫米。

symbol ['simbəl] *n.* 象征，符号，记号
We don't know what the special symbols mean.
我们不知道这些特殊的符号是什么意思。

symbolic [sim'bɔlik] *adj.* 象征性的，符号的，记号的
Symbolic colour is very complicated in this book.
在这本书中符号的颜色是非常复杂的。

abstract ['æbstrækt] *adj.* 抽象的；*n.* 摘要
Sometimes it is very hard for me to understand some of his abstract theories.
有时候，我很难理解他的一些抽象理论。

🔍考点：in the abstract 抽象地，在理论上地

专业学科 自然地理

ash [æʃ] *n.* 灰，灰末，骨灰

She was hurt by the ash of the cigar.
他被雪茄烟的烟灰给弄伤了。

air [ɛə] *n.* 空气，空中，外观

The fresh air of the mountain is benefit to the health.
山里的新鲜空气对身体有好处。

area ['ɛəriə] *n.* 面积，地区，领域

The park that is being built will cover an area of 90 thousand square meters.
正在修建的这个公园将会占地90000平方米。

atmosphere ['ætməsfiə] *n.* 大气，空气，气氛

The classroom has a stuffy atmosphere.
教室里很闷热。

atmospheric [ˌætməs'ferik] *adj.* 大气（层）的，空气的

All the people on the earth should make every effort to prevent atmospheric pollution.
地球上所有的人都应该竭尽全力防止大气污染。

being ['bi:iŋ] *n.* 存在，生物，生命

How did this river come into being?
这条河流是如何形成的?

biology [bai'ɔlədʒi] *n.* 生物学，生态学

I am studying biology in university now.
我现在在大学学习生物学。

erode [i'rəud] *vt.&n.* 腐蚀，侵蚀，磨损

The sea has eroded the cliff face over the years.
海水长年累月冲刷着峭壁的表面。

erosion [i'rəuʒən] *n.* 侵蚀，磨损，削弱

Therefore, the corrosion is caused by erosion of rainwater during ocean shipping.
因此，这些腐蚀是海运途中雨水侵蚀造成的。

drip [drip] *n.* 水滴；*vi.* 滴下，漏水

The umbrella dripped moisture.
伞滴着水珠。

fluid ['flu:id] *n.* 流体，液体

He could only eat fluid food in a long time after the operation.
手术结束后的很长一段时间他只能吃流食。

fossil ['fɔsl] *n.* 化石，思想僵化的人

They found a pile of fossils of the ox on the hill.
他们在山上发现了一堆牛的化石。

geography [dʒi'ɔgrəfi] *n.* 地理，地理学

Don't you like geography till today?
直到今天，你还喜欢地理吗?

germ [dʒə:m] *n.* 微生物，细菌，幼芽

As we all know, mosquito are germ carriers.
众所周知蚊子是带菌体。

greenhouse ['gri:nhaus] *n.* 温室，玻璃暖房效应

The little boy doesn't know what greenhouse effect is.
小男孩不知道什么是温室效应。

liquid ['likwid] *n.* 液体；*adj.* 液体的，液态的，清澈的，流畅的

Cups, pots, bottles, etc, are vessels that hole liquids.
杯子、罐、瓶子等都是盛液体的容器。

Mercury ['mə:kjuri] *n.* 水星

Do you know if there are human beings on the Mercury?
你知道水星上是否有人类?

moon [mu:n] *n.* 月球，月亮，卫星

We all know that the moon goes round the earth.
我们都知道月亮绕着地球转。

natural ['nætʃərəl] *adj.* 自然界的，大然的，天生的

I think no one can change the natural course of the events.
我想没有人能改变事态的自然进程发展。

naturally ['nætʃərəli] *adv.* 自然地，天然地

She has never got her hair permed; her hair curls naturally.
她从来没有烫过头发，她的头发是自然卷曲的。

nature ['neitʃə] *n.* 大自然，本性，性质

Historically, the war between nature and humans has never stopped.
历史上，人与自然之间的战争从未停止过。

ocean ['əuʃən] *n.* 海洋，洋

This creature lives at the bottom of the ocean.
这种生物生活在海底。

Oceania [ˌəuʃi'einiə] *n.* 大洋洲

Oceania is separated from Asia by very shallow water.
大洋洲与亚洲之间只隔着很浅的水域。

orbit ['ɔ:bit] *n.* 运行轨道；*vt.* 环绕

It's said that the orbit of Mars is elliptic.
据说，火星的轨道是椭圆形的。

organic [ɔ:'gænik] *adj.* 有机体的，器官的

When I was in senior middle school, I did badly in organic chemistry.
当我上高中时，我有机化学学得很不好。

organism ['ɔ:gənizəm] *n.* 生物体，有机体

Germs may invade the organism.
细菌会侵入有机体。

outskirt ['autskə:t] *n.* 外边，郊区

They lived in the hotel which is situated in the outskirt of the city last night.
昨晚他们住在郊区的一个旅馆里。

pacific [pə'sifik] *n.* 太平洋；*adj.* 和平的

Both of the presidents are satisfied with the pacific relation between the two countries.
两国的总统对他们之间的和平关系感到很满意。

phenomenon [fi'nɔminən] *n.* 现象

The phenomenon was caused by the gravitational force.
这种现象是由地心引力引起的。

planet ['plænit] *n.* 行星

There are nine planets in the solar system.
太阳系有九大行星。

pole [pəul] *n.* 极（点），磁极，电极，杆，柱

The South Pole abounds with penguins.
南极有很多企鹅。

port ['pɔ:t] *n.* 港，港口

The former village has now become an important port and the economy here is very prosperous.
以前的那个村庄现在已经变成了一个很重要的港口，经济也很发达了。

Portuguese [ˌpɔ:tju'gi:z] *n.* 葡萄牙人，葡萄牙语；*adj.* 葡萄牙（人）的

The designer styled his house in the Portuguese manner.
设计师以葡萄牙的风格设计他的房子。

rotate [rəu'teit] *vi.* 旋转；*vt.* 使旋转

It is a natural rule that the earth rotates round the sun.
地球绕太阳转是一个自然规律。

rural ['ruərəl] *adj.* 农村的，田园的

Sickness was rampant in the rural areas of this nameless country.
疾病在这个不知名国家的农村地区流行开来。

solar ['səulə] *adj.* 太阳的，日光的

There is no doubt solar energy is enormous.
太阳的能量是巨大的，毫无疑问。

suburb ['sʌbə:b] *n.* 郊区，郊外，近郊

Nowadays people would like to live in the suburb and work in the city.
现在人们更愿意住在郊区，工作在城里。

territory ['teritəri] *n.* 领土，版图，领域

China ceded the territory to many countries at that time.
那时中国把领土割让给了许多国家。

urban ['ə:bən] *adj.* 城市的

There is a bulge in urban population in recent years.
近年都市人口有所急增。

westerner ['westənə] *n.* 西方人，美国西部人

He became the first Westerner to introduce Chinese culture to the western countries.
他是把中国文化介绍到西方的首位西方人。

zone [zəun] *n.* 地区，区域，范围

Don't get close to the danger zone.
不要靠近危险地带。

boundary ['baundəri] *n.* 分界线，界限，范围
There is no boundary of knowledge.
知识无界限。

tropical ['trɔpikl] *adj.* 热带的
These animals inhabit the tropical forest.
这些动物居住在热带森林中。

universe ['juːnivəːs] *n.* 宇宙，世界
At that time people believed the earth was the center of the universe.
当时人们相信地球是宇宙的中心。

vapour ['veipə] *n.* 汽，蒸气
Water will change to vapour after heated.
水经过加热就会变成蒸气。

volcano [vɔl'keinəu] *n.* 火山
The volcano is extinct in the past hundred years.
在过去的几百年里这座火山是座死火山。

Africa ['æfrikə] *n.* 非洲
Sahara desert which is the largest in the world is in Africa.
世界上最大的沙漠——撒哈拉沙漠，位于非洲。

African ['æfrikən] *n.* 非洲人；*adj.* 非洲的
This book is about the African history.
这是一本关于非洲历史的书。

America [ə'merikə] *n.* 美国，美洲
My grandparents have a bias against products made in America.
我外公外婆讨厌美国货。

American [ə'merikən] *n.* 美国人
adj. 美洲的
Professor Wang is going to lecture American literature for us.
王教授将给我们讲美国文学。

Arabian [ə'reibjən] *adj.* 阿拉伯的
Little Lucy likes to listen to the story of Arabian Nights.
小露西喜欢听《天方夜谭》里面的故事。

Asia ['eiʃə] *n.* 亚洲
Hong Kong is one of the financial centers of Asia.
香港是亚洲金融中心之一。

Asian ['eiʃən] *n.* 亚洲人；*adj.* 亚洲的
China is the largest Asian country.
中国是亚洲最大的国家。

Atlantic [ət'læntik] *adj.* 大西洋的
n. 大西洋
Do you know who the first to navigate the Atlantic Ocean is?
你知道是谁首先横渡大西洋的吗？

Australia [ɔs'treiljə] *n.* 澳大利亚
Australia is famous of the cotton.
澳大利亚以产羊毛而闻名。

Australian [ɔs'treiliən] *adj.* 澳大利亚的
The restaurant is special of the Australian dishes.
这家餐馆的招牌是澳大利亚菜。

Britain ['britən] *n.* 大不列颠，英国
Britain is a developed country.
英国是一个发达国家。

British ['britiʃ] *adj.* 大不列颠的，英联邦的
You know the American Congress corresponds to the British Parliament.
你知道吗？美国的国会相当于英国的议会。

Canada ['kænədə] *n.* 加拿大
The man has never been to Canada and he is regretful about this.
那人从没去过加拿大，他一直为此感到遗憾。

Canadian [kə'neidiən] *adj.* 加拿大的
Although he is Canadian, his Chinese is excellent.
尽管他是加拿大人，但是他的汉语非常出色。

China ['tʃainə] *n.* 中国
Poetry and essay were blooming in China in the Tang and Song dynasty.
诗歌和散文在中国唐宋时代十分盛行。

Chinese ['tʃai'niːz] *n.* 中国人；*adj.* 中国的
I am proud of being a Chinese.
我以身为一个中国人而骄傲。

county ['kaunti] *n.* 英国的郡，美国的县
Is the comprehensive health care of the county up to the standard?
这个县的综合医疗是否达到标准水平？

country ['kʌntri] *n.* 国家，国土，农村
Most part of our country lies in the temperate zone.
我们国家大部分都在温带。

countryside ['kʌntrisaid] *n.* 乡下，农村
Marsh gas is a kind of wonderful fuel in the
countryside these years.
这些年沼气在农村是种非常不错的燃料。

🔍 考点：country, countryside 的区别：在
强调区别于城市或城镇的乡村时用
country，泛指一切乡村时用
countryside。

district ['distrikt] *n.* 区，地区，区域
There are miles and miles marsh in this district.
这个地区有连绵数英里的沼泽。

native ['neitiv] *n.* 本地人
adj. 本土的，本国的
Keep away from the natives here; I heard they are
very brutal.
离这儿的本地人远点，我听说他们很野蛮。

density ['densiti] *n.* 密集，稠密，密度
Do you know the urban population density in this
province?
你知道这个省的城市人口密度吗?

真题

Britain has the highest _____ of road traffic in
the world–over 60 cars for every mile of road.
A) density   B) intensity
C) popularity   D) prosperity

详　解：选A。题意为：英国是世界上公
路交通密度最大的国家——平均每英里的
公路上有60辆汽车。A) density意思是"密
集，稠密"；B) intensity意思是"强度"；
C) popularity意思是"大众性，流行"；D)
prosperity意思是"繁荣"。

(CET-4 2002.6)

dense [dens] *adj.* 密集的，浓厚的
I can see nothing but the dense palls of smoke
hung over the site.
我什么也看不见，除了看到浓密的烟幕笼罩着
这个地方。

distribute [di'stribjut] *vt.* 分发，分送，分布
We must take measures to distribute these goods.
我们必须采取一些措施去分销这些商品。

distribution [ˌdistri'bjuːʃən] *n.* 分发，分
配，分布
We will try our best to increase the distribution of
the magazine.
我们要尽力增加这种杂志的发行量。

human ['hjuːmən] *adj.* 人的，人类的
n. 人
People are devoted in improving human situations.
人们正在致力于改善人类处境。

human being ['hjuːmən'biːiŋ] *n.* 人
Each human being in the world finally has to die.
世界上的每个人最终都会死。

humanity [hjuː'mæniti] *n.* 人，人类，博
爱，人文学科
The humanity has made a great achievement in the
field of science.
人类已经在科学领域取得了巨大的成就。

humankind [ˌhjuːmən'kaind] *n.* 人，人类
For humankind, it is important to protect the
nature.
对于人类，保护环境是非常重要的。

mankind [mæn'kaind] *n.* 人类，人
Our chief purpose is to serve mankind.
我们的主要目的是服务于人类。

people ['piːpl] *n.* 人民，民族，人
All people are born equally without regard to race,
creed or color.
所有人不管他们的种族、宗教信仰或肤色，生
下来都是平等的。

person ['pəːsn] *n.* 人，人身，本人
She is such a person with a rapacious and predatory
nature.
她是那种贪婪的、具有掠夺性格的人。

population [ˌpɔpju'leiʃən] *n.* 人口，全体居民
According to the latest census, the population of
Chiles has increased.
根据最近人口调查，智利的人口有所增加。

city ['siti] *n.* 城市，都市

Thousands of athletes came to our city for the field events.
成千上万的运动员到我们的城市来参加田赛。

----

mainland ['meinlənd] *n.* 大陆，本土

Do you know how many states there are on the mainland of the United States?
你知道美国本土有多少州吗？

Mediterranean [ˌmeditə'reinjən] *n.* 地中海
adj. 地中海的

Europe is separated from Africa by the Mediterranean.
地中海把欧洲与非洲分离开来。

Midwest ['midwest] *n.* 美国的中西部

Severe storms also rolled through the Midwest.
强风暴也席卷了美国中西部地区。

----

oriental [ˌɔːri'entl] *adj.* 东方的，东方国家的

The professor specializes in oriental history.
那位教授专门研究东方史。

----

region [ri'dʒən] *n.* 地区，地带，领域

Nowadays sports stores proliferate in this region.
如今体育用品商店在这个地区增加了。

🧭 考点：in the region of 在……左右，接近

----

remote [ri'məut] *adj.* 相隔很远的，冷淡的

The government is planning to pioneer the remote areas.
政府正在计划开发边远地区。

----

altitude ['æltitjuːd] *n.* 高，高度，高处，海拔

One of the team members felt uneasy when they reach higher altitude.
到达更高的海拔时，其中一个队员身体感觉不适。

----

universal [ˌjuːni'vəːsəl] *adj.* 宇宙的，普遍的

Contradiction is a universal exist; this is truth.
矛盾是普遍存在的，这是一个真理。

----

continent ['kɔntinənt] *n.* 大陆，陆地，洲

The remarkable animal only can be seen on the continent of Australia.
这种奇异的动物只在澳洲能看到。

border ['bɔːdə] *n.* 边，边缘，边界
vi. 接壤，近似
vt. 邻接，给……加上边

Her white handkerchief has a red border.
她的白手帕有一条红边。

🧭 考点：border on 接壤

专业学科　物理化学

atom ['ætəm] *n.* 原子，微粒，微量

A molecule is made up of atoms.
分子由原子组成。

----

atomic [ə'tɔmik] *adj.* 原子的，原子能的

Russia is researching and producing atomic weapon.
俄国正在研制原子武器。

----

chemical ['kemikəl] *n.* 化学制品
adj. 化学的

I tell you these are physical changes not chemical changes.
我告诉你这些是物理变化不是化学变化。

----

chemistry ['kemistri] *n.* 化学

Our chemistry teacher had informed us to go to laboratory to have an experiment this afternoon.
我们化学老师已通知我们今天下午去实验室做实验。

----

element ['elimənt] *n.* 成分，要素，元素

Food, water and air are necessary elements for people's living.
食物、水和空气是人们生活所必需的要素。

----

gravity ['græviti] *n.* 重力，引力，严重性

I don't think you realize the gravity of the situation.
我认为你没有意识到局势的严重性。

----

hydrogen ['haidrədʒən] *n.* 氢

Hydrogen bomb blasted because of their mistakes.
因为他们的疏忽，氢弹爆炸了。

molecule ['mɔlikjuːl] *n.* 分子，微小颗粒

A molecule of water is made up of two atoms of hydrogen and one atom oxygen .
水分子由两个氢原子和一个氧原子组成。

motion ['məuʃən] *n.* 运动，手势，提议

The teacher told us that kinetic energy is the energy arising from motion.
老师告诉我们动能就是由于运动而产生的能量。

真题

He gave a _____ to handle the affairs in a friendly manner.
A) motion   B) pledge
C) mission   D) plunge

详 解：选A。题意为：他提议用友好的方式来解决这些问题。give a motion "提议，示意"，其他3个词一般不与give 搭配使用。

(CET-4 2003.6)

nitrogen ['naitrədʒən] *n.* 氮（气）

The nitrogen in the roots of plants is indispensable for their growth.
植物根部的氮对植物的生长来说不可或缺。

nuclear ['njuːkliə] *adj.* 原子核的，核心的

The banners with the words "No Nuclear Weapons" stretched across the street.
"禁止使用核武器"的横幅悬挂街头。

nucleus ['njuːkliəs] *n.* 核，核心，（原子）核，细胞核

In every cell there is a part like a little ball. That is the nucleus.
在每一个细胞内，都有一个像球一样的部分，这叫细胞核。

考点：nucleus的复数形式是nuclei或者 nucleuses。

object ['ɔbdʒikt] *n.* 物，物体，目的
vi. 反对，抱反感

What's the strange object in your purse?
你包里的那个奇怪的东西是什么？

particle ['pɑːtikl] *n.* 粒子，微粒

The child was choked on a particle of food.

那个孩子让一小粒食物噎住了。

oxygen ['ɔksidʒən] *n.* 氧气

When something burns, the oxygen in the air will be used.
当东西燃烧时，空气里的氧气会被消耗掉。

physics ['fiziks] *n.* 物理学

Mary and I are twins, but her specialism is physics and mine is English.
玛丽和我是双胞胎，但是她的专业是物理，我的是英语。

radiate ['reidieit] *vi.* 发射光线，辐射

It is a truth that the sun radiates light and heat.
太阳散发光和热是真理。

radiation [ˌreidi'eiʃən] *n.* 放射，发射，辐射能

It is said that the cactus can absorb in radiation.
听说仙人掌能吸收辐射。

radioactive ['reidiəu'æktiv] *adj.* 放射性的

Computers are radioactive, so we'd better keep away from them.
电脑具有辐射性，我们最好远离它们。

radioactivity ['reidiəuæk'tiviti] *n.* 放射性，放射（现象）

It's reported that the site has been contaminated by radioactivity.
据报道，此地已经受到放射性污染。

radium ['reidjəm] *n.* 镭

I know radium can be used in the treatment of cancer.
我知道镭可以用来治疗癌症。

react [ri'ækt] *vi.* 起反应，有影响

I can't imagine how my father would react to this question.
我想象不出我爸爸对这个问题会有什么反应。

考点：react against 反对，反抗，反动；react on 对（某事物）有影响，起作用；react with sth 与……起化学反应

reaction [ri'ækʃən] *n.* 反应，反作用

Before taking measures, we have to put out some feelers to gauge people's reactions.

教育
专业学科

在采取措施之前，我们必须试探一下，看人们对这些措施的反应。

reflect [ri'flekt] *vt.* 反射，反映，思考

Your choice reflects your taste.
你的选择反映了你的品味。

reflection [ri'flekʃən] *n.* 反射，映象，反映

The naughty boy felt curious when he saw his own reflection in the mirror.
这个淘气的小男孩看到自己在镜子中的倒影，感到很好奇。

reflexion [ri'flekʃən] *n.* 反射，映象，反映

The difference among different cultural trades is the reflexion of their characteristics.
文化行业之间的差异正是不同文化行业特征的反映。

rust [rʌst] *n.* 锈；*vi.* 生锈，氧化 *vt.* 使生锈，使氧化

It is a common sense that iron gathers rust easily.
铁易生锈是一个常识。

static ['stætik] *adj.* 静的，静态的

House prices, which have been static for a short time, are now rising again.
房价稳定了一段时间，现在又上涨了。

substance ['sʌbstəns] *n.* 物质，实质，本旨

The world is consisted of substance.
世界是由物质组成的。

🔍 考点：in substance 大体上

relative ['relətiv] *adj.* 有关系的，相对的

We have just learned that motion is absolute while stagnation is relative.
我们刚刚学到：运动是绝对的，而静止是相对的。

专业学科 思想政治

citizen ['sitizn] *n.* 公民，市民，居民

I don't think our government brought tangible benefit to the citizens.
我认为政府没有给我们市民带来实际好处。

citizenship ['sitizn ʃip] *n.* 国籍，公民权，公民的身份

She was Chinese by birth but she is entitled to American citizenship.
她在中国出生但现在是美国公民。

civil ['sivl] *adj.* 公民的，文职的

Do you know what stirred the civil rights movement across the nation?
你知道是什么激起了全国的民权运动吗？

civilian [si'viljən] *n.* 民法专家，平民 *adj.* 平民的

It grieves us to see the loss of civilian life in Iraq.
看见伊拉克平民的伤亡我们很悲痛。

civilization [ˌsivilai'zeiʃən] *n.* 文明，文化，开化

When you finished this book, you will know the march of the civilization of a primitive society.
你读完这本书，你就会知道原始社会的进化过程了。

civilize ['sivilaiz] *vt.* 使文明，教育

It is very hard to civilize all the primitive tribes all over the world.
使世界上所有的原始部落变成文明社会是很难的。

nationwide ['neiʃənwaid] *adv.* 遍布全国 *adj.* 全国的

I heard they are going to open up a nationwide debate.
我听说他们正准备展开一场全国性的争论。

philosopher [fi'lɔsəfə] *n.* 哲学家

The philosopher is talking historical idealism with us.
这位哲学家正在和我们讨论唯心史观。

philosophy [fi'lɔsəfi] *n.* 哲学，哲理，人生观

Is philosophy an optional lesson or a compulsory one?
哲学是选修课还是每个人必修的课程？

political [pə'litikəl] *adj.* 政治的，政治上的

This is an academic problem, not a political one.
这是一个学术性的问题，不是政治性的。

politician [ˌpɔli'tiʃən] *n.* 政治家，政客
Generally speaking, a politician must be able to withstand public criticism.
一般说来政治家必须能经得起公众的批评。

politics ['pɔlitiks] *n.* 政治，政治学，政纲
It is no doubt that his ideas on politics are not well founded.
毋庸置疑，他的政治见解缺乏事实根据。

province ['prɔvins] *n.* 省，领域，部门
Henan has larger population than other provinces of China.
在中国，河南省的人口最多。

realm [relm] *n.* 王国，国土，领域
The president wanted to expand his realm.
总统想要扩张他们国家的领土。

reunification [ˌri:ju:nifi'keiʃən] *n.* 重新统一
We all know it takes time to bring about peaceful reunification.
众所周知，实现和平统一需要一定时间。

socialism ['səuʃəlizəm] *n.* 社会主义
China insists on the road of socialism.
中国坚持走社会主义道路。

socialist ['səuʃəlist] *adj.* 社会主义的
We are concentrating our efforts on socialist construction of civilization.
我们正集中力量建设社会主义文明。

society [sə'saiəti] *n.* 社会，团体，社交界
Some people think that our society is going backward.
一些人认为我们的社会在倒退。

sociology [ˌsəusi'ɔlədʒi] *n.* 社会学
For Judy, sociology was mysterious.
对于朱迪来说，社会学是神秘的。

transition [træn'ziʃən] *n.* 转变，变迁，过渡
I think nothing can affect her, let alone such a sudden transition.
我认为什么都影响不了她，更何况这样一个突然变化呢。

🔍 考点：transition from...to... 由……过渡到……，由……转化成
in transition 转变中的

unity ['ju:niti] *n.* 单一，统一，团结
It's not enough only to maintain a formal unity.
只在表面上保持一致是不够的。

nation ['neiʃən] *n.* 民族，国家
As Chinese, we have the duty to make the revitalization of the Chinese nation.
作为中国人，我们有责任去振兴中华。

national ['næʃənəl] *adj.* 民族的，国家的
When will the Republican national convention be held?
什么时候举行共和党全国代表大会？

nationality [ˌnæʃə'næliti] *n.* 国籍，民族
Do you know what that foreign teacher's nationality is?
你知道那个外教的国籍吗？

belief [bi'li:f] *n.* 信任，相信，信念
I have a firm belief that I can conquer English.
我坚信我能攻克英语。

🔍 考点：beyond belief 难以置信

believe [bi'li:v] *vt.* 相信，认为
I believe him because he always performs his duty faithfully.
我相信他，因为他总是忠实地履行自己的职责。

🔍 考点：believe in 信仰，认为……有益

Bible ['baibl] *n.* 圣经
Regard the dictionary as your Bible when you are studying English.
在学英语的时候，你要把字典当圣经一样。

cathedral [kə'θi:drəl] *n.* 总教堂，大教堂
My best friend will hold their wedding in the cathedral.
我最好的朋友将在大教堂举办婚礼。

Christian ['kristʃən] *n.* 基督教徒，信徒
The priest needs to preach Christian doctrine.
牧师需要布道基督教教义。

church [tʃə:tʃ] *n.* 教堂，礼拜堂，教会
The church was located beside the river, five miles from my house.
这个教堂坐落在河边，离我家有5英里远。

教育 专业学科

097

holy ['həuli] *adj.* 神圣的，圣洁的
Let us see the holy moment together.
让我们共同见证这一神圣的时刻吧。

minority [mai'nɔriti] *n.* 少数，少数民族
Only a minority of passengers survived in the car accident.
只有极少数的乘客在那次车祸中幸存下来。

pray [prei] *vi.&vt.* 请求，祈祷
I pray to God that you will be lucky enough to be admitted by a famous university.
我向上帝祈祷你会很幸运被一所著名大学所录取的。

prayer [prɛə] *n.* 祈祷，祈求
I don't know why they say "amen" at the end of each prayer.
我不知道为什么每句祈祷结束后，他们都要说"阿门"。

priest [pri:st] *n.* 教士，牧师，神父
The priest is preaching the doctrine of Christianity for us.
这个牧师正在给我们布道基督教道义。

religio [ri'lidʒən] *n.* 宗教，宗教信仰
Sometimes science is in conflict with religion.
有时科学和宗教是相抵触的。

religious [ri'lidʒəs] *adj.* 宗教的，虔诚的
Speaking of the religious fervor, no one can compare to you.
说起宗教热情，没人比得过你。

ritual ['ritjuəl] *n.* 宗教仪式，例行公事
　　　adj. 作为仪式的一部分，例行的
It's a pity that the ritual is just a fond memory.
很遗憾，这种仪式已成为美好的回忆了。

saint [seint] *n.* 圣徒，基督教徒，圣人
All the people in this country revered the saint.
这个国家的所有人都崇敬这位圣人。

temple ['templ] *n.* 圣堂，神殿，庙宇
The family visited the biggest temple in the country last week.
上周他们一家参观了全国最大的庙宇。

worship ['wə:ʃip] *n.* 拜，崇拜
　　　vt. 崇拜
She led her daughter to the church to worship God.
她带她女儿来教堂敬拜上帝。

ethnic ['eθnik] *adj.* 种族的
I advocate practicing the regional autonomy, because it ensures the rights of the ethnic minorities, and upholds the unification of the state.
我提倡实行民族区域自治，这样既保障了少数民族的权利，又维护了国家的统一。

Negro ['ni:grəu] *n.* 黑鬼，黑人（含有贬义）
The black boy hates being called "Negro" by the white.
那个黑人男孩痛恨被白人叫做"黑鬼"。

racial ['reiʃəl] *adj.* 种族的，人种的
She sued the company for racial discrimination.
她以种族歧视为由起诉公司。

communism ['kɔmjunizəm] *n.* 共产主义学说，共产主义制度
We should fight for the communism cause.
我们应该为共产主义事业而奋斗。

communist ['kɔmjunist] *n.* 共产主义者，共产党员
The speaker is an intellectual with communist ideology.
演讲者是一位具有共产主义思想的知识分子。

concept ['kɔnsept] *n.* 概念，观念，设想
Please tell me the concept of morpheme and find out the morphemes in the word.
请告诉我语素的概念，并找出这个单词里的语素。

Confucian [kən'fju:ʃiən] *n.* 儒家
　　　adj. 孔子的，儒教的
Do you know what Confucian assumptions were involved?
你知道都涉及了什么样的儒家思想吗？

conscious ['kɔnʃəs] *adj.* 意识到的，有意的
My girlfriend is conscious of a sense of guilt.
我女友感到内疚。

考点：be conscious of 意识到……
conscious表示内心所意识到的感觉；aware指感官上的知觉。

illusion [i'luːʒən] *n.* 幻想，错误的观念，错觉，假象

This physical phenomenon is just an illusion.
这个物理现象只是一个假象。

imaginary [i'mædʒinəri] *adj.* 想象中的，假想的

There are too many imaginary elements in this theory.
这个理论中有太多假想的因素。

imagination [i͵mædʒi'neiʃən] *n.* 想象，想象力，空想

Good film can arouse one's imagination.
好的电影作品能激发人的想象力。

imagine [i'mædʒin] *vt.* 想象，设想，料想

There are more in the book than you can imagine.
书中还有很多你想象不到的东西。

Marxism ['maːksizəm] *n.* 马克思主义

The students are studying the basic principles of Marxism now.
学生们正在学习马克思主义的基本原理。

Marxist ['maːksist] *adj.* 马克思主义的
n. 马克思主义者

I have no idea of the Marxist world outlook.
我对马克思主义世界观不是很了解。

materialism [mə'tiəriəlizəm] *n.* 唯物主义，唯物论

We advocate materialism and oppose idealism.
我们提倡唯物主义，反对唯心主义。

progress ['prəugres] *n.* 前进，进展，进步

Your progress will urge him to work hard.
你的进步会促进他努力学习。

theory ['θiəri] *n.* 理论，学说，意见

His theory was not accepted by most people.
他的学说不被大多数人接受。

besides [bi'saidz] *adv.* 而且
prep. 除⋯⋯之外

The Chinese nation includes more than 50 national minorities besides the Hans.
中华民族除了汉族外，还包括50多个少数民族。

专业学科 经济金融

economic [͵iːkə'nɔmik] *adj.* 经济的，经济学的

The government will implement robust monetary policy and maintain economic growth.
政府将采取积极稳健的货币政策，并保持经济增长。

economics [͵iːkə'nɔmiks] *n.* 经济学，经济状况，经济因素

She's in her third year of economics at Tsinghua university.
这是她在清华大学读经济学的第3年。

economical [͵iːkə'nɔmikəl] *adj.* 节约的，经济学的

My grandmother was economical with cooking oil when cooking.
外婆烹饪时总是用油很省。

🔍 **考点**：be economical of / with 节约⋯⋯

industrial [in'dʌstriəl] *adj.* 工业的，产业的

How to judge a city is an industrial city or not?
怎样判断一个城市是否是工业城市？

industrialize [in'dʌstriəlaiz] *vt.* 使工业化

Many townships in the coastal area have begun to industrialize a few years ago.
沿海地区的许多乡镇几年前已开始工业化了。

industry ['indəstri] *n.* 工业，产业

He wants to devote himself to the development of electronics industry.
他想致力于电子工业的发展。

inflation [in'fleiʃən] *n.* 膨胀，通货膨胀

Government brings up a hedge against inflation.
政府提出一项作为预防通货膨胀的对策。

prosperity [prɔs'periti] *n.* 繁荣，昌盛，兴旺

You know "Zhen Guan Zhi Zhi" is a period of wealth and prosperity.
贞观之治是一个富有和繁荣的时期。

prosperous ['prɔspərəs] *adj.* 繁荣的，昌盛的

What we should do now is to bring about prosperous economy.
我们现在应该做的事是繁荣经济。

recession [ri'seʃən] *n.* （经济）衰退，衰退期
It is said that during the economic recession the big factory terminated a large number of workers.
据说，经济衰退时期这家大工厂解雇了许多工人。

 真题

We should concentrate on sharply reducing interest rates to pull the economy out of ____.
A) retreat   B) rejection
C) recession   D) restriction

详 解：选C。题意为：我们应集中精力大幅度降低利率，以使经济摆脱不景气的局面。A) retreat意思是"从危险的地方撤回到安全的地方，不指经济"；B) rejection意思是"断然决绝"；C) recession 意思是"经济不景气"；D) restriction 意思是"限制"。

(CET-4 2003.6)

steady ['stedi] *adj.* 稳固的
                    vt. 使稳定
Have you got a steady group of friends around?
你有关系固定的朋友圈吗?

tariff ['tærif] *n.* 关税，价目表
                    vt. 交关税
There is a very high tariff on smoke.
烟类的税率很高。

tax [tæks] *n.* 税，税款，负担
                vt. 对……征税，使费尽力气
Their company fiddles an income tax return.
他们公司伪造所得税申报表。

tax-free ['tæks'fri:] *adj.* 免税的
Where is the tax-free shop in Sanya?
三亚的免税店在哪里?

thrive [θraiv] *vi.* 兴旺，繁荣，旺盛
They will survive and thrive under the humans' careful care.
在人类的精心照料下，他们会生存下来并兴旺繁殖的。

possess [pə'zes] *vt.* 占用，拥有（财产）
The child possessed an extraordinary memory.
这个孩子有着超常的记忆力。

wealth [welθ] *n.* 财富，财产，丰富
It's no worth exchanging honor for wealth.
牺牲荣誉以换取财富是不值得的。

⚲ 考点：a wealth of 大量的……

possession [pə'zeʃən] *n.* 有，所有，占有物
The New Concept English book is my most precious possession.
这本新概念英语是我最珍贵的财产。

property ['prɔpəti] *n.* 财产，资产，性质
According to the law, school property is exempt from all taxes.
依据法律，学校财产免除一切赋税。

treasure ['treʒə] *n.* 财富，珍宝
                    vt. 珍视
The pirates stole the treasure from a cave.
海盗把洞里的财宝偷走了。

earn [ə:n] *vt.* 赚得，挣得，获得
Everyone has such a lust that the more they earn, the more they seem to want.
每一个人都有这种欲望，挣得越多，好像想要的也越多。

income ['inkʌm] *n.* 收入，收益，进款
His income is inadequate to pay for his room rent.
他的收入不够支付房租的费用。

⚲ 考点：income, expense, fortune等词谈及多少时，不用much或little，而是用large或small。

loss [lɔs] *n.* 遗失，损失，失败，亏损，损耗
I had computed my loss in the accident last night.
我昨天晚上已经估算了一下我在这次事故中的损失。

⚲ 考点：at a loss 困惑，不知所措

profit ['prɔfit] *n.* 益处，利润；*vi.* 得益
If you want to get more profit, you should adopt the consumers' suggestion.
如果你想赢利更多的话，你应该接受用户的建议。

⚲ 考点："利润"只能用profit, 不能用benefit, 其他情况下两者用法相同。

additional [ə'diʃənl] *adj.* 附加的，额外的，追加的
I can assure you there will not be any additional charge.

我能向你保证没有任何额外的费用。

allowance [ə'lauəns] *n.* 津贴，补贴，零用钱
The meager monetary allowance from the government can't support the old couples.
政府的少量津贴根本无法让这对老夫妻生活。

🔍 考点：make allowance(s) for 考虑到，顾及

assess [ə'ses] *vt.* 对（财产等）估价
It's too early to assess the achievement of the new president.
现在来评价新总统的功绩还为时过早。

asset ['æset] *n.* 资产，财产，有价值的人（物），优点
You should know that good health is a great asset.
你应该知道健康就是莫大的财富。

bankrupt ['bæŋkrʌpt] *adj.* 破产的，道德败坏的，枯竭的
vt. 使破产
n. 破产者
Owing to his extravagance, his company went bankrupt in the end.
由于他挥霍无度，他的公司最终破产了。

🔍 考点：go bankrupt 破产
be bankrupt of / in 完全丧失

balance ['bæləns] *vt.* 使平衡，称；*n.* 天平
It is impossible to change the situation of balance of trade in a short time.
在短时间内改变国际贸易差额状况是不可能的。

🔍 考点：in the balance 在危急状态中，未定的；off balance 不平衡

真题

Companies are struggling to find the right_____ between supply and demand, but it is no easy task.
A) equation   B) formula
C) balance   D) pattern

详 解：选C。题意为：公司正致力于寻求供需平衡，但这很不容易。A) equation意思是"平均，相等"；B) formula意思是"公式，规则"；C) balance意思是"平衡，和谐"；D) pattern意思是"模仿，方案"。

(CET-4 2005.6)

belong [bi'lɔŋ] *vi.* 属于，附属
If the house really belongs to you, you can lay claim to it.
如果这套房子真是属于你的，你可以争取产权的。

belongings [bi'lɔːŋiŋz] *n.* 财产，所有物
Please protect your belongings from the thieves.
请照看好自己的财物，严防小偷扒手。

billion ['biljən] *num.* 十亿（英）
I guess there must be billions of stars in the sky.
我猜天上的星星肯定有几十亿个。

budget ['bʌdʒit] *n.* 预算，*vt.* 编预算，为……做预算；*vi.* 节省开支
The brokering budget has been overestimated by the government.
政府对经纪业的预算过分估计了。

calculate ['kælkjuleit] *vt.* 计算，估计，计划
The boss asked that the cost of production should be precisely calculated.
老板要求必须精确计算生产成本。

calculation [ˌkælkju'leiʃən] *n.* 计算，计算结果
I'm sorry; your calculation is way off beam.
抱歉，你的计算大错特错。

calculator ['kælkjuleitə] *n.* 计算器，计算者
Calculators are allowed to use in this exam.
这场考试可以用计算器。

capital ['kæpitl] *n.* 资本，资金，首都
In order to collect enough capital to build a factory, he turned to his uncle for help.
为了筹集到足够的资金建工厂，他向他叔叔求助。

cash [kæʃ] *n.* 现金，现款
I am short of cash now and I want to borrow some money from you.
我现在在缺钱，我想从你这里借点。

cent [sent] *n.* 分，分币，百
She took a twenty-five cent piece out of her pocket.
他从口袋里，掏出了两毛五分钱。

coin [kɔin] *n.* 硬币，铸造（硬币）
This convertible note can be exchanged into coins.
这张可兑换纸币可以兑换成硬币。

compute [kəm'pju:t] *vt.* 计算，估计，估算
She computed her loesses at five thousand dollars.
她估计她的损失有5000美元。

credit ['kredit] *n.* 信用贷款，信用，赊账
He bought the book on credit.
他赊账买了这本书。

考点：to one's credit 在……名下
on credit 赊账，挂账

expense [ik'spens] *n.* 花费，消费，费用
I lost my job, so I have to keep down my expenses this month.
我失业了，所以我这个月必须缩减开支。

考点：at the expense of 由……付费，以……为代价

fee [fi:] *n.* 费，酬金，赏金
I have to look for a part-time job for my tuition fee.
为了学费我不得不找兼职。

reduce [ri'dju:s] *vt.* 减少，减小，简化
To the government the paramount thing is to reduce the unemployment.
对政府来说最重要的事就是降低失业率。

reduction [ri'dʌkʃən] *n.* 减少，减小，缩减
The coat was very cheap, but Lucy still asked for a 10% reduction.
那件外套已经很便宜了，但是露西还要求降价10%。

insurance [in'ʃuərəns] *n.* 保险，保险费
She worked in insurance since she graduated from university.
大学毕业后，她就从事保险业。

insure [in'ʃuə] *vt.* 给……保险，确保
An insurance company will insure nearly what you want.
保险公司几乎可以保任何险。

loan [ləun] *n.* 贷款，暂借，*vt.* 借出，贷给
That's great, the bank made a loan of four hundred thousand *yuan* to our factory.
太棒了，银行贷给我们厂40万元。

考点：on loan 暂借的（地）

fare [fɛə] *n.* 票价；*vi.* 进展
Sorry, I don't have enough money for the fare.
对不起，我没钱付车费。

真题

Urban crowdedness would be greatly relieved if only the _____ charged on public transport were more reasonable.
A) fares　　B) costs
C) fees　　D) payments

详解：选A。题意为：只有当公共交通收费更合理时，都市的拥挤才会得到缓解。A) fare意思是"（交通工具的）票价"；B) cost意思是"（各类）费用"；C) fee意思是"（服务）费用"；D) payment意思是"付费"。

(CET-4 2002.12)

owe [əu] *vt.* 欠，应把……归功于
I remembered that I owed me one hundred *yuan*.
我记得你欠我100块钱。

考点：owe...to... 把……归功于……

stock [stɔk] *n.* 原料，库存品，股本
Losses on the stock market caused him to jump from the flat.
股票市场上的损失使他跳楼自杀。

考点：in stock 有现货的，有库存的
out of stock 无现货的，脱销的
stock up 备货，囤积

debt [det] *n.* 债，债务，欠债
I'm glad that I have already wiped off all my debt.
我很高兴，我已经还清了所有的债务。

考点：in debt 欠债，负债
in sb's debt 欠某人的人情

due [dju:] *adj.* 预期的，应给的
Her smile is affected due to nervousness.
由于紧张，她的笑也变得不那么自然了。

考点：due to 由于，因为
in due course 到时候，在适当的时候

finance [fai'næns] *n.* 财政，金融，财源
He got the position of manager on the strength of his skill in finance.
他凭着自己的理财本领得到了经理这个职位。

financial [fai'nænʃəl] *adj.* 财政的，金融的
These are involved financial affairs for him.
对他来说这些是错综复杂的金融事务。

fund [fʌnd] *n.* 资金，基金，存款
Mr. Lee gave the fund for victims of the earthquake.
李先生向地震灾民捐款。

input ['input] *n.* 输入，投入的资金
You had better provide direct manipulation and graphical input in the document.
你最好在文件中提供直接的操作和图形输入。

invest [in'vest] *vt.* 投资，投入
Astute salesmen know how to invest in the real estate.
精明的商人懂得如何做房地产投资。

investment [in'vestmənt] *n.* 投资，投资额，投入
It is sensible in terms of an investment.
从投资的角度来考虑这是合理的。

bank [bæŋk] *n.* 银行，库，岩，堤
I planned to deposit some money in the bank each month.
我计划每月都在银行里存一些钱。

deposit [di'pɔzit] *vt.* 使沉淀，存放
He wanted to deposit his money in bank.
他想把他的钱存在银行里。
考点：deposit sth. with sb. 把某物存放在某人处

withdraw [wið'drɔ:] *vt.* 收回，撤回；*vi.* 撤退
My sister want me to withdraw some money from the bank for her.
妹妹想让我在银行为她取些钱。

economy [i'kɔnəmi] *n.* 经济，节约，节省
The state of economy in Japan is very worring.
目前日本的经济状况令人担忧。

expensive [iks'pensiv] *adj.* 昂贵的，花钱多的
Under the influence of devaluation, we began to realize that the goods are very expensive.
在货币贬值的影响下，我们开始意识到商品的价格是昂贵的。

money ['mʌni] *n.* 货币，金钱，财富
I want to borrow some money—do I make myself plain?
我想借点钱——我的意思清楚吗？

luxury ['lʌkʃəri] *n.* 奢侈，奢华，奢侈品
It's impossible for her falling in love with you, you are poor and she has a penchant for luxury and opulence.
她不可能爱上你，你那么穷，而她又崇尚豪华阔绰的生活。

necessarily ['nesisərili] *adv.* 必然，必定
I don't think the possession of money necessarily brings happiness.
我认为有钱不一定幸福。
考点：not necessarily 未必，表示部分否定

necessary ['nesisəri] *adj.* 必要的，必然的
I believe it's necessary for everyone to learn some first aid course.
我坚信对于每个人来说学点急救课程是很必要的。

necessity [ni'sesiti] *n.* 必要性，必然性，需要，必需品
Here I have to emphasize the necessity for preserving our natural resources again.
在此，我必须再次强调保护自然资源的必要性。
考点：of necessity 必定，无法避免地

worth [wə:θ] *adj.* 值……的；*n.* 价值
It's no worth exchanging honor for wealth.
牺牲荣誉以换取财富是不值得的。
考点：of great worth 值钱的

真题

In the Mediterranean seaweed is so abundant and so easily harvested that it is never of great _____.
A) fare   B) payment
C) worth   D) expense

详 解：选C。题意为：在地中海地区，海藻丰富且很容易收割，因此从来都不值钱。A) fare意思是"车费"；B) payment意思是"支付的款项"；C) worth意思是"价值"；D) expense意思是"（时间、金钱、精力）的消耗"。
(CET-4 2005.6)

Franc [fræŋk] *n.* 法郎（货币单位）
He has only 5 Francs left.

他只剩下5法郎了。

 考点：Dollar 美元；Pound 英镑
Yen日元；Euro 欧元

needless ['ni:dlis] *adj.* 不需要的，无用的，
多余的 ＊
We are not rich, so buying a car is needless expense.
我们并不富裕，所以买车是一笔不必要的开支。

worthless ['wə:θlis] *adj.* 无价值的，无用的
His head is full of worthless ideas.
他满脑子都是无用的念头。

penny ['peni] *n.* （英）便士，（美）分
A penny saved is a penny earned.
省钱就是赚钱。

pound [paund] *n.* 磅，英镑 ＊
vt. 捣碎，舂烂，猛击
Do you believe that an egg is the equivalent of a pound of meat?
你相信一只蛋的营养相当于一磅肉吗？

euro [juərəu] *adj.* 欧洲的（尤指欧盟的） ＊
n. 欧元
There are seven euro notes and eight euro coins.
欧元总共有7种纸币和8种铸币。

accelerate [æk'seləreit] *vt.* （使）加快，促进 ＊
The policy will be carried out to accelerate the economic recovery.
这个政策的实施是为了促进经济的复苏。

acceleration [æk‚selə'reiʃən] *n.* 加速，加速度 ＊
I want to buy a car with a good acceleration.
我想买一辆加速性能很好的车。

account [ə'kaunt] *n.* 记述，解释，账目， ＊
报告；*v.* 解释，说明
The account shows that I have spent much money this month.
账目表明我这个月花了大量的钱。

 考点：on account of 因为……缘故
take account of 考虑到，顾及
take into account 考虑到，顾及

真 题

I'd _____ his reputation with other farmers and business people in the community, and then make a decision about whether or not to approve a loan.
A) take into account   B) account for
C) make up for   D) make out

详 解：选A。题意为：我想在考虑了他与社区其他农民和商人的交往的信誉后，再决定是否同意向他贷款。A) take into account 意思是"考虑到，顾及"；B) account for意思是"说明"；C) make up for意思是"补偿"；D) make out意思是"理解，辨认"。

(CET-4 2000.1)

专业学科 语言词汇

accent ['æksənt] *n.* 口音，腔调，重音，强调
His accent tells us where he comes from.
听他的口音就知道他是哪儿的人。

alphabet ['æːlfəbit] *n.* 字母表，字母系统 ＊
The teacher arranged his students' names in alphabetical order.
老师把他学生的名字按字母先后顺序排列。

branch [brɑ:ntʃ] *n.* 树枝，分部，分科 ＊
Stylistics is a branch of linguistics.
文体学是语言的一个分支。

 考点：branch out 扩充，扩大活动范围

conjunction [kən'dʒʌŋkʃən] *n.* 接合，连接， ＊
连接词
The moon is in conjunction with the sun.
月亮与太阳处在合点。

 考点：in conjunction with 与……共同，
连同

grammar ['græmə] *n.* 语法，语法书
He wrote a book on grammar.
他写了一本关于语法的书。

idiom ['idiəm] *n.* 习语，成语
The teacher is teaching students idioms.
老师正在教学生习语。

intensive [in'tensiv] *adj.* 加强的，精耕细作的
He spent a lot of money on the intensive course in English.
他花费很多钱在英语精读课程上。

noun [naun] *n.* 名词
I wonder that this noun is countable or uncountable.
我想知道这个名词是一个可数名词还是一个不可数名词。

oral ['ɔ:rəl] *adj.* 口头的，口的
The professor devised a new method of teaching oral English.
教授设计了一种新的教英语口语的方法。

phrase [freiz] *n.* 短语，习惯用语
This English Conversation Book teaches me a wealth of phrases and sentences.
这本英语会话书教给我大量的短语和句子。

plural ['pluərəl] *adj.* 复数的；*n.* 复数
Do you know what the plural of this word is?
你知道这个单词的复数形式是什么吗？

preposition [ˌprepə'ziʃən] *n.* 前置词，介词
Can you help me to find a preposition to collocate the word "home"?
你能帮我找到一个可以和"home"这个词搭配的介词吗？

pronoun ['prəunaun] *n.* 代名词
If you want me to tell you the part of speech of this word, my answer is pronoun.
如果你想要我告诉你这个单词的词性，我的答案是代词。

pronounce [prə'nauns] *vt.* 发……的音，宣布
Could you tell me how to pronounce this word?
你能告诉我这个单词怎么发音吗？

pronunciation [prəˌnʌnsi'eiʃən] *n.* 发音，发音法
My sister does not qualify as an English teacher as her pronunciation is terrible.
我姐姐当英语老师不称职，因为她的发音很差劲。

relate [ri'leit] *vt.* 叙述，使联系 *vi.* 有关联，符合，相适应
I want to ask you a question that relates to English.
我想问你一个与英语有关的问题。

sentence ['sentəns] *n.* 判决，句子；*vt.* 宣判
A period is used at the end of the sentence.
句号通常用在句尾。

singular ['siŋjulə] *adj.* 单一的，非凡的
The singular form of "children" is "child".
"Children"的单数形式是"child"。

specialize ['speʃəlaiz] *vi.* 成为……专家，专攻
After his first degree, he wishes to specialize in linguistics.
获得学士学位之后，他希望专攻语言学。

🔍 考点：to specialize in math 专攻数学

translation [træns'leiʃən] *n.* 翻译，译文，译本
This book is a literal translation from English.
这本书是从英文直译过来的。

speak [spi:k] *vi.* 说话，发言；*vt.* 说
We never speak seriously about the education of our children.
我们从没认真谈过孩子的教育问题。

🔍 考点：so to speak 可以说
speak for 代表……讲话，证明
speak out 大声说出来

真题

John cannot afford to go to university, _____ going abroad.
A) nothing but   B) anything but
C) not to speak of   D) nothing to speak of

详　解：选C。题意为：约翰没钱上大学，更不用说出国了。
A) nothing but 相当于only；　B) anything but是习语，意思是"绝对不"；C) not to speak of 意思是"更不用说"；D) nothing to speak of 意思是"没有什么，不值得一提"。

(CET-4 2005.12)

usage ['ju:sidʒ] *n.* 使用，对待，惯用法
A few of these idioms have received frequent usages.
其中有些习语已经得到了广泛应用。

vocabulary [və'kæbjuləri] *n.* 词汇表，词汇，语汇
Wide reading will increase your vocabulary.

博览群书会增加你的词汇量。

word [wə:d] *n.* 词，话，消息，语言
So far we have learned more than eight thousand English words.
迄今为止，我们学了8000多个单词。

🔍 考点：in a word 总之，一句话
in other words 换句话说
word for word 逐字地

Latin ['lætin] *adj.* 拉丁语的，拉丁人的，拉丁语系国家的；*n.* 拉丁语，拉丁人
As we all know, thousands of English words derive from Latin.
众所周之，英语中有成千上万的词源自拉丁文。

preliminary [pri'liminəri] *adj.* 预备的，初步的
If you want to learn English well, you have to lay a preliminary groundwork.
如果你想学好英语，你必须打好初步基础。

beginner [bi'ginə] *n.* 初学者，生手
This class may be a little difficult for the beginners.
这节课对于初学者或许有点难度。

adjective ['ædʒiktiv] *n.* 形容词
adj. 形容词的
In most situations, adjective is used to modify noun.
在大多数情况下，形容词用来修饰名词。

adverb ['ædvə:b] *n.* 副词
Please find the relative adverb of this sentence.
请找出句子的关系副词。

专业学科 文学历史 ✏️

compile [kəm'pail] *vt.* 汇编，编制，编纂
It took him three years to compile this dictionary.
编这本词典花了他3年时间。

🔍 考点：词典类编辑用compile, compiler，报刊类编辑用edit, editor。

cowboy ['kaubɔi] *n.* 牧童，牛仔
The boy is a sure-enough cowboy.
那个男孩是个地道的牛仔。

fiction ['fikʃən] *n.* 小说，虚构，杜撰
Mark Twain bought a new spirit into American fiction.
马克•吐温将一种新精神注入了美国小说。

fable ['feibl] *n.* 寓言，传说，神话
Most children like to listen to the fable.
大部分的孩子都喜欢听神话故事。

folklore ['fəuklɔ:] *n.* 民间传说，民间传统
His grandmother often told folklores to him.
他奶奶总是给他讲一些民间传说。

masterpiece ['mɑ:stəpi:s] *n.* 杰作，名著
Talking of oil paintings, I guess it is a masterpiece.
提起油画，我想它是幅精品画。

mysterious [mis'tiəriəs] *adj.* 神秘的，难以理解的
The police found that the wall is full of mysterious curves.
警察发现，那面墙上画满了神秘的曲线。

mystery ['mistəri] *n.* 神秘，神秘的事物
The experts unraveled the mystery of the tumulus.
专家们揭开了这个古墓的谜。

🔍 考点：in mystery 在秘密中

novel ['nɔvəl] *n.* 小说；*adj.* 新的
That novel didn't impress me at all.
那本小说没有给我留下任何印象。

prince [prins] *n.* 王子，亲王
My little son always has visions of being a prince himself.
我的小儿子总是幻想自己是个王子。

princess [prin'ses] *n.* 公主，王妃
The beautiful princess dropped her veil and exposed her pretty face.
这个公主摘下面纱，露出漂亮的脸蛋。

literally ['litərəli] *adv.* 照原文的，确实地，简直
You have to translate the passage literally.
你需要逐字逐句地翻译这段文字。

literary ['litərəri] *adj.* 文学（上）的，文人的，书卷气的
The number of literary magazines has accelerated recently.
最近，文学杂志的数目增加了。

literature ['litəritʃə] *n.* 文学，文献，图书资料
Professor Wang is going to lecture American literature for us.
王教授将给我们讲美国文学。

poem ['pəuim] *n.* 诗，韵文，诗体文
She is only fifteen years old, but her poems abound in imagery.
虽然她只有15岁，可是她的诗富于幻象。

poet ['pəuit] *n.* 诗人
The poet song a lyric love poem to his lover.
这位诗人唱了一首爱情抒情诗给他的爱人。

poetry ['pəuitri] *n.* 诗，诗歌，诗作
Shakespeare wrote a great deal of poetry.
莎士比亚写了大量诗篇。

version ['və:ʃən] *n.* 译文，说法，改写本
Lu Xun's works were translated into various versions in the world.
鲁迅的作品被译成多种版本留于全世界。

ancient ['einʃənt] *adj.* 古代的，古老的，年老的，老式的
There is an ancient custom that passes around in our village.
在我们的村庄里流传着一个古老的习俗。

colony ['kɔləni] *n.* 殖民地，侨居地
No one wants his own country to become the colony of other countries.
没有人想要自己的国家变成其他国家的殖民地。

emperor ['empərə] *n.* 皇帝
When this emperor was enthroned, he was only eight years old.
这位皇帝登基时只有8岁。

empire ['empaiə] *n.* 帝国
It's clear that collapse of the Empire can't be prevented.
很明显帝国的崩溃不可避免。

establish [is'tæbliʃ] *vt.* 建立，设立，确立
The new traffic rule is now established beyond recall.
新交通规则已制定，不得撤销。

establishment [is'tæbliʃmənt] *n.* 建立，设立，确立
The establishment of diplomatic relations is helpful to the development of the countries.
外交关系的建立有助于国家之间的发展。

event [i'vent] *n.* 事件，大事，事变
I think no one can change the natural course of the events.
我想没有人能改变事态的自然进程发展。

🔍 **考点：** in the event of 万一，倘若
　　　　in the event that 万一，倘若

historic [his'tɔrik] *adj.* 历史上著名的，具有重大历史意义的
This is a historic moment for the whole country.
对整个国家来说这是一个历史性的时刻。

historical [his'tɔrikəl] *adj.* 历史的，有关历史的
They recurred the historical situation in this play.
他们在这部剧中再现了那个历史情景。

imperial [im'piəriəl] *adj.* 帝国的，帝王的
She was invited to the Imperial Palace.
她被邀请去皇宫。

origin ['ɔridʒin] *n.* 起源，由来，出身
Could you tell me what the origin of the quarrel is?
能告诉我争吵的起因吗？

original [ə'ridʒənəl] *adj.* 最初的，新颖的
The bad weather hampered my original plan.
坏天气妨碍了我原来的计划。

primitive ['primitiv] *adj.* 原始的，粗糙的
When you finish this book, you will know the march of the civilization of a primitive society.
你读完这本书，你就会知道原始社会的进化过程了。

thereafter [ðɛə'ɑ:ftə] *adv.* 此后，以后
She went to America three years ago and we heard no more of her thereafter.
她3年前去了美国，自那以后再没有听到她的音讯。

tribe [traib] *n.* 部落，族，一伙人
As a matter of fact, people in the tribe lived a simple life as the barbarians.
事实上，这个部落的人像野蛮人一样过着简单的生活。

sequence ['si:kwəns] *n.* 连续，继续，次序
Historians deal with events in historical sequence.
历史学家按照历史上的先后顺序研究大事。

教育 专业学科

专业学科 其他学科

engineering [ˌendʒi'niəriŋ] *n.* 工程，工程学
He was very interested in engineering when he was in university.
大学时期，他对工程学很感兴趣。

forestry ['fɔristri] *n.* 林学，林务
His major is forestry in the college.
他大学主修林学。

architecture ['ɑːkitektʃə] *n.* 建筑学，建筑样式
My elder brother majors in architecture, but he doesn't like it at all.
我哥哥学的是建筑学，但是他一点都不喜欢它。

aviation [ˌeivi'eiʃən] *n.* 航空，航空学
Finally he decided to choose the aviation as his major.
最后他决定选航空学作为自己的专业。

校园生活 学业

absorb [əb'sɔːb] *vt.* 吸收，使专心，吸引……的注意
I like wearing cotton socks, because they absorb sweat.
我喜欢穿棉袜，因为他们吸汗。

真题

The writer was so _____ in her work that she didn't notice him enter the room.
A) absorbed   B) abandoned
C) focused   D) centered

详 解：选A。题意为：那位作家工作太投入了，没有察觉到他进入了房间。A) be absorbed in 是固定搭配，意思是"专心于"；B) abandon 意思是"抛弃，丢弃"；C) focus on意思是"集中"；D) center on 意思是"集中"。

(CET-4 2005.6)

absence ['æbsns] *n.* 缺席，不在场，缺乏
Tomorrow is my sister's wedding, no matter what happens I won't give her my absence.
明天是姐姐的婚礼，无论发生什么，我都不会缺席的。

 考点：in the absence of 在……不在时，在（物）缺乏或没有时

absent ['æbsənt] *adj.* 缺席的，不在场的，缺乏的，心不在焉的
I think you should tell me the reason why you were absent.
我想你应该告诉我你缺席的原因。

考点：be absent from 缺席

classroom ['klɑːsrum] *n.* 教室，课堂
We are having an English lesson in the classroom.
我们正在教室里上英语课。

absorbed [əb'sɔːbd] *adj.* 全神贯注的，一心一意的
Don't shout at him. He can't hear you; he's utterly absorbed in his book.
别喊了，他听不见，他正在全神贯注地看书呢。

考点：be absorbed in... 全神贯注于……

class [klɑːs] *n.* 班，班级，阶级
Most of the boys in my class are basketball fanatics.
我们班里大部分的男孩子都是篮球迷。

classmate ['klɑːsmeit] *n.* 同班同学
The girls performed a very graceful dance for their classmates.
女孩们为她们的同学们表演了优美的舞蹈。

define [di'fain] *vt.* 给……下定义，限定
It's difficult for us to define success.
我们很难给成功定义。

考点：define...as 把……定义为……

definition [ˌdefi'niʃən] *n.* 定义，释义，定界
If you don't know the definition of homonym, you can check it in this book.
如果你不知道同形异义词的定义，你可以在这本书里查一下。

dictation [dik'teiʃən] *n.* 口授笔录，听写
Let's have a dictation before the new lesson.
进行新课之前，我们先做一个听写测试。

discipline ['disiplin] *n.* 纪律，训练 *vt.* 训练
I think our company lack discipline.

教育
校园生活

我觉得我们公司很散漫。

distract [dis'trækt] *vt.* 分散，使分心
Don't try to distract my attention. I'm not fall for it.
不要试图分散我的注意力，我才不上当呢。

grasp [grɑːsp] *vt.* 抓紧，掌握；*n.* 抓
I have only a rudimentary grasp of English.
我只掌握了英语的初步知识。

instead [in'sted] *adv.* 代替，顶替，反而
Can you use this paragraph instead?
可以用这篇文章取代吗？

🔍 考点：instead of 代替，而不是

lecture ['lektʃə] *n.* 讲课，演讲，训话
vt. 训斥，讲课，教导
vi. 演讲，讲课
Professor Wang is going to lecture Enlish literature for us.
王教授将给我们讲英国文学。

method ['meθəd] *n.* 方法，办法，教学法
Who can give us a more accurate method to compute the average?
谁能给我们一个更精确的求平均数的方法？

monitor ['mɒnitə] *n.* 班长，监视器，劝告者，提醒物
Mom, tell you a good news; I was elected monitor of our class.
妈妈，告诉你一个好消息，我被选为班长了。

noisy ['nɔizi] *adj.* 嘈杂的，喧闹的
The teacher frowned angrily at the noisy class.
老师对那班吵吵嚷嚷的学生生气地皱起了眉头。

note [nəut] *n.* 笔记，便条，注释
She suggested me to take notes in class.
她建议我在课堂上记笔记。

🔍 考点：compare notes 交换意见
of note 重要的
take note of 注意，留意

notebook ['nəutbuk] *n.* 笔记本，期票簿
He wrote down what the teacher said in his notebook.
他把老师所讲的记在了笔记本上。

platform ['plætfɔːm] *n.* 平台，站台，讲台
The famous writer made a speech on the platform in the school hall.
那位著名的作家在学校礼堂的演讲台上做了演讲。

professor [prə'fesə] *n.* 教授
She was professor of chemistry at Beijing University.
她过去是北京大学化学系的教授。

pupil ['pjuːpl] *n.* 学生，小学生，瞳孔
In my eyes, he is always a studious pupil in our class.
在我眼里，他在我们班里一直是一个勤奋好学的学生。

recite [ri'sait] *vi.&vt.* 背诵，朗诵
The diligent boy recited the grammar by rote.
这个勤奋的男孩强记背诵了这个语法。

record ['rekɔːd] *n.* 记录，履历；*vt.* 记录
I have a good habit to keep a record of my daily expenses.
我有把日常开销都记录下来的好习惯。

row [rəu] *n.* （一）排，（一）行
vt. 划（船等）
vi. 划船
We sat in the middle row.
我们坐在中间一排。

🔍 考点：in a row 一个接一个，不断地

scholar ['skɒlə] *n.* 学者（尤指文学方面）
As a scholar, he is so modest and prudent that we all respect him.
作为一名学者，他如此谦虚谨慎以至于我们大家都尊敬他。

scrape [skreip] *vi.&vt.&n.* 刮，擦
Don't scrape feet on the floor.
不要用脚摩擦地板发出刺耳的声音。

🔍 考点：scrape through 勉强通过
scrape together / up 费力地获得

shed [ʃed] *vt.* 流出，散发，脱落，去除
n. 棚，小屋，贷棚
This method can help students shed inhibitions.
这一方法能帮助学生消除顾虑。

summarize ['sʌməraiz] *vt.* 概括，概述，总结
The teacher summarized the contents as follows.
老师将上述内容总结如下。

summary ['sʌməri] *n.* 摘要，概要，一览
A very brief summary is included in this note.
这本笔记里有十分简单的摘要。

🔍 **考点**：in summary 总的说来，概括起来

transcribe [træns'kraib] *vt.* 抄写，用音标标出，改编（乐曲），转录
The teacher let me transcribe the whole text as punishment.
老师让我把整篇课文抄写下来作为对我的惩罚。

accumulate [ə'kju:mjuleit] *vt.* 积累
vi. 堆积
More and more snow fell, and it accumulated to a depth of eight feet.
雪越下越大了，已经积到8尺深了。

acquire [ə'kwaiə] *vt.* 取得，获得，学到，养成
I'm very lucky; I have just acquired Zhou-jie-lun's autography.
我真是太幸运了，我刚得到周杰伦的亲笔签名。

🔍 **考点**：acquire, retain, gain, achieve的区别：acquire指获得（知识，习惯等）；retain指留住，保持 gain赢得（名声等）；achieve取得（成功，进步等）。

acquisition [ˌækwi'ziʃən] *n.* 习得，获得（物），采集
My sister spends much time on the acquisition of foreign language.
我姐姐花大量的时间学习外语。

analyse ['ænəlaiz] *vt.* 分析，分解，解析
Take it easy. Let's analyse the situation and find the way to solve this problem.
别急，让我们分析一下形势，找出解决这个问题的方法。

analysis [ə'nælisis] *n.* 分析，分解，解析
The analysis of characters of *Gone with the Wind* is my thesis title.
浅析《乱世佳人》中的人物是我的论文题目。

complicate ['kɔmplikeit] *vt.* 使复杂，使陷入
This problem can be solved easily. Don't complicate it.
这个问题很好解决，别复杂化了。

complicated ['kɔmplikeitid] *adj.* 复杂的，难懂的
What you said was too complicated for him to understand.
你所说的太复杂，他根本不理解。

comprehension [ˌkɔmpri'henʃən] *n.* 理解，理解力，领悟
The passage is beyond my comprehension.
这个段落超出我的理解力。

comprehensive [ˌkɔmpri'hensiv] *adj.* 全面的，综合的，广泛的，理解的
Is it true that your daughter has been studying at the local comprehensive school?
你女儿正在本地的一所综合学校学习是真的吗?

educate ['edjukeit] *vt.* 教育，培养，训练
You want to be a teacher, but remember an educator must first educate himself.
你想做一名老师，但是记住，教育者必须自己先受教育。

education [ˌedju'keiʃn] *n.* 教育，训导，教育学
I think education should not be restricted to any specific age group.
我认为教育不应限制在任何特定的年龄段上。

enlighten [in'laitn] *vt.* 启发，开导
The parents should enlighten the children properly.
父母应该对孩子做出适当的引导。

guidance ['gaidns] *n.* 引导，指导，领导
A new Travel Guidance has been published.
一本新的旅游指导书已出版了。

🔍 **考点**：under the guidance / leadership of 在……的领导下

instruct [in'strʌkt] *vt.* 教，指示，通知
I will instruct him whether to come or not.
我将通知他是否要来。

🔍 **考点**：teach, instruct的区别：teach后面可以跟双宾，eg. teach them English 教他们英语；instruct则用于instruct sb. in sth. 的结构，"教某人……"。

instruction [in'strʌkʃən] *n.* 命令，教学，教训
We have to lift the level of instruction in the coming years.
近几年内我们得提高教学水平。

intermediate [ˌintə'miːdjət] *adj.* 中间的，中级的
Lily takes an intermediate level English class.
丽丽上了一个中级英语班。

lead [liːd] *vi.&vt.* 引导，带路，带领，过……（的生活），导致
n. 铅，铅制品
She led me into the world of science.
她带我进入科学的殿堂。

🔍 **考点：** lead up to 作为……的准备（先导）

master ['mɑːstə] *n.* 主人，能手，硕士
vt. 掌握，精通
adj. 主要的，精通的
It is impossible for everyone to master a language overnight. We must learn it bit by bit.
对于任何一个人来说都不可能一夜之间掌握一门语言，我们必须一点一点地学。

practice ['præktis] *n.* 实践，练习，业务
The correct ideas are not innate in mind, but come from social practice.
正确的思想不是头脑中先天固有的，而是来源于社会实践。

🔍 **考点：** in practice 在实践中
out of practice 生疏的，荒废的
put into practice 实施，实行

practise ['præktis] *vt.* 练习，实习，训练
They always practise German together.
他们总是在一起练习德语。

reinforce [ˌriːin'fɔːs] *vt.* 增援，支援，加强
Public reaction will reinforce the effect of reformation.
社会反响会进一步增强改革的作用。

simplicity [sim'plisiti] *n.* 简单，简易，朴素
It's said that the essence of French savoir-vivre is simplicity.
据说，法国人的处世之道的实质就是淳朴。

simplify ['simplifai] *vt.* 简化，使单纯
Of course, you can do something to simplify this task.
当然，你可以做一些事来简化这项任务。

trainee [trei'niː] *n.* 受培训的人，学员
She was dispatched abroad as a trainee journalist.
她作为一个实习记者被派遣出国。

trainer ['treinə] *n.* 培训人，教练员
The trainer performed how to throw fish to the seals.
驯兽人表演了如何把鱼儿扔给海豹。

training ['treiniŋ] *n.* 培训，锻炼，培养
The policemen need undergo severe training when they are in school.
警察在警校时需要经受严格的训练。

tuition [tjuː'iʃən] *n.* 学费，教海，教学
Professor Wang who we once got much benefit from his tuition will retire soon.
王教授很快要退休了，我们曾在他那里受益匪浅。

tutor ['tjuːtə] *n.* 家庭教师，导师
Her tutor points out the mistakes in her essay.
她的导师指出了她论文中的错误。

tutorial [tjuː'tɔːriəl] *n.* 指南，教程，辅导班
adj. 辅导的，个别指导的
We have a tutorial every Tuesday afternoon.
每周二下午我们有一节辅导课。

course [kɔːs] *n.* 课程，过程，一道菜
We must attend a training course next Monday.
下周一我们必须参加一个培训课。

🔍 **考点：** of course 当然，自然
in the course of 在……的过程中

answer ['ɑːnsə] *vt.* 回答，响应，适应
n. 答案
I'm sorry; this question is difficult to answer.
不好意思，这个问题太难回答了。

assign [ə'sain] *vt.* 指派，分配，指定
Our maths teacher begins to assign homework for us now.
现在我们数学老师开始给我们布置家庭作业了。

assignment [ə'sainmənt] *n.* 任务，指定的
作业
He will get a new assignment every day.
他每天都会有一个新任务。

composition [kɔmpə'ziʃən] *n.* 构成，作品，
写作
First, you should find a good topic for your composition.
首先，你应该为你的作文找一个好题目。

examination [igˌzæmi'neiʃən] *n.* 考试，检
查，细查
I hope you can pass the examination without resort to cheating.
我希望你能不靠作弊而通过考试。

🔍 考点：take / do an examination 参加考试

lag [læg] *vt.* 落后，减退，缓慢进行
n. 落后，时间间隔
She is afraid that she will lag behind her classmates.
她害怕她会落在同学们的后面。

🔍 考点：lag behind 落后

memory ['meməri] *n.* 记忆，回忆，存储
She still had a vivid memory of that accident in which she lost her parents forever.
她仍然清楚地记得那场车祸，因为在车祸中她永远地失去了父母。

🔍 考点：in memory of 纪念

mark [mɑːk] *n.* 斑点，记号，考试分数
vt. 标明，纪念，给……打分
He got 70 marks for geography.
他的地理得了70分。

🔍 考点：mark down 记下，降低……的分数
（价格）；mark off 划出，画线分
割；mark up 提高……的分数（价
格）；wide of the mark 远离目
标，离谱

mistake [mis'teik] *n.* 错误；*vi.* 误解，弄错
I know it's the manager who altered the mistake on the price tag.
我知道是经理更正了价格标签上的错误。

modify ['mɔdifai] *vt.* 更改，修改，修饰
If you intend to persuade her, you'd better modify your tone.
如果你打算劝服她，你最好说得婉转一点。

outcome ['autkʌm] *n.* 结果，后果，成果
The general risked his whole campaign on the outcome of one battle.
将军孤注一掷，把整个战役的成败押在一场战斗上。

pass [pɑːs] *vt.* 经过，通过，度过
I hope you can pass the Enlish examination.
我希望你能通过英语考试。

preparation [ˌprepə'reiʃən] *n.* 准备，预备，
制备
What you should do is to try your best to make preparation for a bright future.
你所应该做的是尽力为你美好的未来做准备。

🔍 考点：make preparation for 为……做准备

prepare [pri'pɛə] *vi.&vt.* 准备，预备
We should prepare for the flood protection, for the river would inundate the valley any time.
我们应该做好防汛工作，因为这条河流随时都会泛滥。

🔍 考点：prepare 准备（不一定刚准备
好）；be prepared= be ready
准备好

problem ['prɔbləm] *n.* 问题，习题
I think the best way to solve this problem is to arrive at a compromise.
我认为解决这个问题最好的方法就是达成一个妥协。

question ['kwestʃən] *n.* 发问，问题，疑问
The question is so complex that I don't know how to answer it.
这个问题太复杂了，我不知道如何回答。

🔍 考点：in question 正在讨论的
out of question 没有问题
without question 毫无疑问

quiz [kwiz] *n.* 小型考试，测验
The teacher gave us a quiz in maths yesterday.
昨天老师给我们测验数学。

quote [kwəut] *vt.* 引用，引证，报价
He quoted a Chinese proverb to end his speech.
他引用一句汉语谚语来结束他的演讲。

ready ['redi] *adj.* 准备好的，愿意的
He is ready to propose his views in the coming colloquium.

他准备在将要到来的学术交流会上提出他的观点。

reference ['refrəns] *n.* 参考，出处，提及
It is hard to find the zoo without reference to a map.
如果不参照着地图的话，很难找到这个动物园。

🔍 **考点**：with reference to 关于，就……而论

result [ri'zʌlt] *n.* 成果；*vi.* 发生，结果
Before we make a decision, we have to consider the eventual results.
在我们做决定前，必须考虑到最终的结果。

🔍 **考点**：result in 导致；result from 起因于

review [ri'vju:] *vt.* 再检查，复习，回顾
n. 复习
I have a habit that I always review the day's happenings before falling asleep.
我有一个习惯，那就是入睡前总爱回顾一下一天所发生的事情。

🔍 **考点**：be / come under review
在复查或重新考虑中

revise [ri'vaiz] *vt.* 修订，校订，修改
Our teacher asked you to revise the errors in your composition.
我们老师要求你修改一下作文里的错误。

solution [sə'lju:ʃən] *n.* 解决，解答，溶解
It is an easy solution to this matter.
要解决该问题，这个办法很简单。

🔍 **考点**：solution to... 解决……的办法

solve [sɔlv] *vt.* 解答，解释，解决
In the first place, we should solve the problem of being late.
首先，我们应该解决迟到这个问题。

specify ['spesifai] *vi.* 指定，详细说明
We should specify the title of the competition.
我们应指定作文的题目。

terminal ['tə:minəl] *adj.* 末端的；*n.* 末端
The terminal examination is coming.
期终考试就要到了。

theme [θi:m] *n.* 主题，题目
He went to the theme park with a couple of classmates.
他和一帮同学去了主题公园。

thesis ['θi:sis] *n.* 论题，论点，论文
Before writing my thesis, I referred to many materials.
在写论文之前，我查阅了大量资料。

underline [,ʌndə'lain] *vt.* 画线于……之下
Underline the words the teacher read.
在老师读的词下面画线。

whatsoever [,wɔtsəu'evə] *pron.* 任何
The teacher found no mistakes in my homework whatsoever.
老师在我的家庭作业中未发现任何错误。

writing ['raitiŋ] *n.* 著作，写作
His writing shows his character.
他的作品体现了他的个性。

🔍 **考点**：in writing 以书面形式

admission [əd'miʃən] *n.* 允许进入，承认
We are excited to know that my sister has gained the admission to the Tsinghua University.
得知我妹妹被清华大学录取的消息，大家都很激动。

admit [əd'mit] *vt.* 承认，准许……进入
Though I don't like him, I have to admit that he's a good guy.
尽管我不喜欢他，可我不得不承认他是个好人。

bachelor ['bætʃələ] *n.* 未婚男子，独身汉，学士
I got my bachelor's degree in English three years ago.
我3年前取得了英语学士学位。

certificate [sə'tifikit] *n.* 证书，证件，执照
Show me your birth certificate, please.
请出示你的出生证明。

degree [di'gri:] *n.* 程度，度，学位
To my delight, I will get my degree in dentistry this June.
令我高兴的是，我今年6月份就要拿到牙医学位了。

graduate ['grædjueit] *n.* 毕业生
vi. 大学毕业
He was a graduate of the Peking University.
他是北京大学的毕业生。

undergraduate [ˌʌndə'grædʒuət] *n.* 大学肄业生

This is a high time that the undergraduates are seeking for job.
这正是毕业生们找工作的高峰期。

knowledge ['nɔlidʒ] *n.* 知识，学识，知道

Through further communication, she found that man had a wide knowledge of arts.
通过进一步的交流，她发现那个人在艺术方面知识广博。

👉 考点：to one's knowledge 据……所知

knowledgeable ['nɔlidʒəbl] *adj.* 有丰富知识的，消息灵通的

One of my friends is knowledgeable about the chemistry, and he chose it as his major.
我的一个朋友对化学知之甚多，他所选的专业也是化学。

learned ['lə:nid] *adj.* 有学问的，学术上的；
['lə:nd] *v.* learn的过去式与过去分词

Not all learned men are necessarily wise.
博学者未必都是聪明的。

💬 听力考点：learned当learn的过去式与过去分词时，读音为['lə:nd]；当"有学问的"时，读音为['lə:nid]。

learning ['lə:niŋ] *n.* 学习，学问，知识

A modest man will never boast of his learning.
谦虚的人从不夸耀自己的学识。

retell [ˌri:'tel] *vt.* 再讲，重述，复述

The Chinese teacher asked him to retell the story in his own words.
语文老师让他用自己的话复述这个故事。

pen [pen] *n.* 钢笔，自来水笔

My pen doesn't write well.
我的钢笔不好写。

pencil ['pensl] *n.* 铅笔

My son is doing his homework with a pencil in his hand.
我儿子手里拿着一支铅笔正在做家庭作业。

immense [i'mens] *adj.* 巨大的，极好的

They plunged into their studies with immense zeal.
他们以极大的热情投入学习。

bell [bel] *n.* 钟，铃，门铃，钟声

When the bell rang, the children swept out of the classroom.
下课铃声一响，孩子们就冲出教室。

transfer [træns'fə:] *vt.* 转移，调动
vi. 转移

We must transfer all active factors to stimulate students.
我们必须调动一切积极因素鼓励同学们。

真题

Jessica was _____ from the warehouse to the accounting office, which was considered a promotion.
A) delivered   B) exchanged
C) transferred   D) transformed

详　解：选C。题意为：杰西卡从仓库调到了会计室，这被认为是一次提升。A) deliver 意思是"运送（货物）"；B) exchange意思是"交换"；C) transfer意思是"调动"；D) transform意思是"改变，转变"。

(CET-4 2005.12)

校园生活 社团活动

association [əˌsəusi'eiʃən] *n.* 协会，团体，联合

This magazine was sponsored by the association.
这个杂志是由社团主办的。

chairman ['tʃɛəmən] *n.* 主席，议长，会长

The chairman is delivering a speech in a high tone.
主席正在大声地讲话。

league [li:g] *n.* 同盟，联盟，联合会，种类，社团

Name the universities which belong to the Ivy League.
列举出常春藤联合会中各大学的名字。

👉 考点：in league with 与……密谋（联合）

member ['membə] *n.* 成员，会员，部分

Do you know the members of the committee?
你认识那个委员会的成员吗？

of [ɔv] *pron.* ……的，由于

My father was accepted as a member of the club.
爸爸被接受为该俱乐部的成员。

organization [ˌɔːgənai'zeiʃən] *n.* 组织，团
体，机构

There are several organizations petitioned the government for cancelling the rules.
有好几个组织上书政府，请求取消规则。

organize ['ɔːgənaiz] *vt.* 组织，编组

It's said that the strike was organized by some political agitators.
据说，这次罢工是由一些政治鼓动者组织的。

participate [pɑː'tisipeit] *vi.* 参与，参加，分享

They will go to the town square to participate in the ceremony of raising national flag on the National Day.
他们将会在国庆节那天去市政广场参加升旗仪式。

🔍 考点：participate in 正式用语，"参与到……"；日常用语是 "take part in"。

participation [pɑːˌtisi'peiʃən] *n.* 参加，加入

It seemed that his participation is not welcomed.
看来他的参与不受欢迎。

scholarship ['skɔləʃip] *n.* 学业成绩，奖学金

I'm very glad I've been awarded a scholarship to study at Harvard.
我真高兴，我获得了去哈佛大学读书的奖学金。

sponsor ['spɔnsə] *n.* 发起者；*vt.* 发起

The cost of this programme is borne by an identified sponsor.
这个项目的费用由主办人承担。

club [klʌb] *n.* 俱乐部，夜总会

I want to join the club but I haven't enough time.
我想加入俱乐部，只是我没有时间。

activity [æk'tivəti] *n.* 活动，活力，行动

Because of my job, I can't participate in the activity held on this Saturday.
由于工作的原因，我不能参加这周六举行的活动了。

校园生活 假期兼职

part-time ['pɑːt'taim] *adj.* 兼职的，花部分时间的；*adv.* 花部分时间，兼职地

Maybe you can augment your income by doing some part-time job.
或许你可以做些兼职工作来增加你的收入。

semester [si'mestə] *n.* 半年，学期，半学年

How many subjects are you choosing this semester?
这学期你选了几门课程？

temporary ['tempərəri] *adj.* 暂时的，临时的

He found a temporary work in New York.
他在纽约找到了一个临时工作。

真题

Salaries for _____ positions seem to be higher than for permanent ones.
A) legal   B) optional
C) voluntary   D) temporary

详　解：选D。题意为：临时岗位的工资好像比固定岗位的高。A) legal意思是"法律的"；B) optional意思是"任选的，随意的"；C) voluntary意思是"自愿的"；D) temporary意思是"暂时的，临时的"。

(CET-4 2005.1)

term [təːm] *n.* 期，学期，条件，词

The summer term runs from March to June in China.
在中国夏季学期从3月份到6月份。

🔍 考点：in terms of 用……的话，按照
come to terms 妥协，和解

vacation [vei'keiʃən] *n.* 假期，休假

I give up the summer vacation to Europe.
我放弃了夏天去欧洲的休假。

🔍 考点：on vacation 在度假

although [ɔːl'ðəu] *conj.* 尽管，虽然，但是，然而

Although he is a minor, he has to seek for a job to support his family.
尽管他还未成年，却不得不找工作养家糊口。

校园生活 出国留学

abroad [əˈbrɔːd] *adv.* （在）国外，到处，传开，散开

My son couldn't return in time; he is still living abroad.
我儿子不能及时赶回，他仍然在国外。

---

adapt [əˈdæpt] *vt.* 使适应，改编

He changed his job. And now he tried hard to adapt himself to the new surroundings.
他换工作了，现在他正努力使自己适应新环境呢。

真题

It is too early to say whether IBM's competitors will be able to ____ their products to the new hardware at an affordable cost.
A) adapt   B) stick
C) yield   D) adopt

详 解：选A. 题意为：现在说IBM公司的竞争对手能否使他们的产品在可承受的成本上与新硬件兼容还为时尚早。A) adapt sth. to…意思是"使适合"；B) stick(to)意思是"坚持"；C) yield (to) 意思是"屈服"；D) adopt意思是"采用，采取"。

(CET-4 2003.9)

---

alien [ˈeiljən] *adj.* 外国（人）的，不相容的
n. 外国人，外侨，外星人

It's great to run into an old friend in the alien land.
在异国他乡遇到故知真是太好了。

---

check [tʃek] *vt.* 检查，制止；*n.* 检查，支票

Excuse me, could you cash this check for me?
劳驾，你能为我兑现这张支票吗？

考点：check in（在旅馆、机场等）登记，报到；check out结账离去，办妥手续离去；check up (on)检查，核实；in check受抑制的，受控制的

---

emigrate [ˈemigreit] *vi.* 移居外地（国外）

How long ago did your parents emigrate?
你父母多久前移居外地的啊？

---

immigrant [ˈimigrənt] *n.* 移民；*adj.* 移民的

This house is tenanted by an immigrant from Africa.
这所房屋为一个来自非洲的移民所有。

---

jet lag [ˈdʒet ˌlæg] *n.* 飞行时差反应，跨时区高速飞行后生理节奏的破坏

Owing to jet lag, we felt so tired to walk.
经过长时间的飞行，我们觉得疲倦得走不动了。

---

migrate [maiˈgreit] *vi.* 迁徙，移居，迁移

It is a common sense that some birds migrate from here to warmer places every winter.
这是个常识，有些鸟每年冬天从这里向温暖的地方迁徙。

---

overseas [ˌəuvəˈsiːz] *adv.* 海外
adj. 在海外的

Between 1974 and 1997, the number of overseas visitors expanded by 27%.
1974年至1997年之间，海外观光者的人数增加了27%。

考点：overseas作副词时与abroad用法基本相同，但作形容词时常放在名词前面。

---

passport [ˈpɑːspɔːt] *n.* 护照

I am afraid that your passport is overdue.
恐怕你的护照已经过期了。

---

visa [ˈviːzə] *n.* 签证

I didn't obtain a visa to visit England.
我没有获得访问英国的签证。

---

subsequent [ˈsʌbsikwənt] *adj.* 随后的，后来的

On the day subsequent to the earthquake he went abroad.
在地震发生的第二天，他出国了。

职场生涯｜Career

求职面试 职业

announcer [ə'naunsə] *n.* 报告员，广播员
Being a TV announcer is my dream.
成为一名电视播音员是我的梦想。

architect ['ɑ:kitekt] *n.* 建筑师，设计师
His father is an architect and always busy.
他爸爸是个建筑师，总是很忙。

artist ['ɑ:tist] *n.* 艺术家，美术家
The old artist is very gentle with his granddaughter, and now he is playing chess with her.
那位老艺术家对自己孙女非常慈祥，现在他正在跟她下棋。

astronomer [ə'strɔnəmə] *n.* 天文学家
It's amazing that the astronomers can calculate when there will be eclipses of the sun and moon.
天文学家可以算出何时发生月食及日食，真是太神奇了。

astronaut ['æstrənɔ:t] *n.* 宇宙航行员，宇航员
Being an astronaut may be the dream of every boy.
成为一名宇航员或许是每个男孩的梦想。

athlete ['æθli:t] *n.* 运动员，田径运动员
He will fight for his dream of being an excellent athlete.
他会为成为一名优秀的运动员的梦想而奋斗。

attorney [ə'tə:ni] *n.* 律师，代理人
The boy wants to be a prominent attorney when he grows up.
男孩长大后想当一名著名的律师。

author ['ɔ:θə] *n.* 作者，作家
The author of this detective novel must be a detective.
这本侦探小说的作者一定是一个侦探。

barber ['bɑ:bə] *n.* 理发师
The barber asked him which styling he required.
理发师问他想要什么样的造型。

butcher ['butʃə] *n.* 屠夫，屠杀者
My brother is willing to be a butcher.
我哥哥很乐意当个屠夫。

career [kə'riə] *n.* 生涯，职业，经历
I really appreciate your zeal for your career.
我真的很欣赏你对事业的热情。

carpenter ['kɑ:pəntə] *n.* 木工，木匠
My grandfather was apprenticed to a carpenter when he was a boy.
爷爷还是个孩子的时候就被送去学木匠了。

chemist ['kemist] *n.* 化学家，药剂师
The man who is wearing a black hat is a great chemist.
那个戴黑色帽子的人是个伟大的化学家。

commentator ['kɔmenteitə] *n.* 注释者，实事评论员
We hear that he is a clear-eyed commentator on the news.
我们听说他是一个目光锐利的新闻评论家。

accountant [ə'kauntənt] *n.* 会计，出纳
The middle-aged woman was defrauded of her money by a dishonest accountant.
这个中年女人的钱被一个奸诈的会计骗走了。

director [di'rektə] *n.* 指导者，理事，导演
That director made his daughter start as a junior clerk in the company.
那个董事让他的女儿从初级文员开始做起。

economist [i:'kɔnəmist] *n.* 经济学家
The dream of the boy is to be an economist.
这个孩子的梦想是成为一个经济学家。

117

engineer [ˌendʒi'niə] *n.* 工程师，技师

Now I am just a student engineer.
现在我还只是个见习技术员。

---

mechanic [mi'kænik] *n.* 技工，机械，机修工，过程，方法

James was a mechanic twenty years ago.
20年前，詹姆斯是个技工。

---

merchant ['məːtʃənt] *n.* 商人，零售商
adj. 商人的，商业的

It's the Liaoning merchant who endows this university.
是这位辽宁的商人捐资建造了这所大学。

---

model ['mɔdl] *n.* 模型，模式，模特儿；*vt.* 做……的模特，仿效；*vi.* 当模特示范

The attractive model had brown skin, which was owed to her Mexican blood.
那位迷人的模特儿有着棕色的皮肤，这得益于她的墨西哥血统。

---

novelist ['nɔvəlist] *n.* 小说家

The novel predisposed her to become a famous novelist.
那本小说使她轻松成为著名的小说家。

---

observer [əb'zəːvə] *n.* 观察员，观测者

We sent him there as an observer.
我们派他去那里做观察员。

---

occupation [ˌɔkju'peiʃən] *n.* 占领，占据，职业，消遣

Many young people have no enough respect for their occupations nowadays.
如今许多年轻人对自己的工作缺少足够的尊重。

---

physician [fi'ziʃən] *n.* 医生，内科医生

The physician prescribed him some medicine and told him to take it three times a day.
医生给他开了一些药，并叮嘱他一日服三次。

---

physicist ['fizisist] *n.* 物理学家

The physicist must think of an effective way to demonstrate his scientific assumption.
这位物理学家必须想出一个有效的方法来论证他的科学设想。

---

pilot ['pailət] *n.* 领航员，飞行员

Tommy's dad was once a pilot in the Royal Air Force.
汤米的爸爸曾经是皇家空军的一名飞行员。

---

porter ['pɔːtə] *n.* 搬运工人

She gave the porter some tips and thanked him.
她给了那个搬运工人一些小费，并感谢他的帮忙。

---

postman ['pəustmən] *n.* 邮递员

The duty of a postman is to deliver letters and parcels.
邮递员的职责是传递信件和包裹。

---

profession [prə'feʃən] *n.* 职业

Being a doctor is a challenging profession that requires a lifelong commitment.
从医是个很有挑战性的职业，需要终生奉献。

---

professional [prə'feʃənl] *adj.* 职业的
n. 专业人员

As the husband of a professional woman, he is responsible for all the housework.
作为一名职业女性的丈夫，他负责所有的家务活儿。

---

reporter [ri'pɔːtə] *n.* 记者，通讯员

The reporter had unearthed some intimacy about him.
那位记者发现了一些关于他的隐私。

---

reviewer [ri'vjuːə] *n.* 评论家

I heard the reviewer mercilessly took apart the young writer's novel.
我听说评论家把这位年轻作者的小说抨击得一无是处。

---

sailor ['seilə] *n.* 水手，海员，水兵

The experienced old sailor have no fear of the violent storms on the sea.
有经验的水手不会惧怕海上的狂风暴雨。

考点：be a good / bad sailor 翻译为"晕（不晕）船"，而不是"好（坏）水手"

---

seaman ['siːmən] *n.* 海员，水手，水兵

I dream of being a seaman and voyaging around the world.
我梦想成为一名海员，环游全世界。

---

spy [spai] *n.* 间谍，特务；*vt.* 侦察
vi. 当间谍，暗中监视

No one knew he was a spy during working with him.
与他共事时没人知道他是间谍。

考点：spy sth. / sb. 看见（发现）

　　　　spy on sth. / sb. 暗中监视

---

surgeon ['sə:dʒən] *n.* 外科医师，军医

Tom is the youngest surgeon in the hospital.

汤姆是医院里最年轻的医生。

---

technician [tek'niʃən] *n.* 技术员，技师

The technician had on a blue jacket and went to the room.

那个技术员穿着蓝色的夹克进入了房间。

---

violinist ['vaiəlinist] *n.* 小提琴手

He is the best violinist in the philharmonic orchestra.

他是这个交响乐队最棒的小提琴手。

求职面试 能力

ability [ə'biliti] *n.* 能力，能耐，本领，才智，才能

I think my sister has enough ability to manage that department.

我认为我姐姐完全有能力管理那个部门。

考点：ability for 有哪一方面的才能

　　　　ability to 有某种能力

真题

He soon received promotion, for his superiors realized that he was a man of considerable _____.

A) future　　　B) possibility

C) ability　　　D) opportunity

详 解：选C。题意为：他很快就得到了提升，因为他的上司们发现他是一个很有才能的人。A) future意思是"未来，前途"，但它不与considerable搭配；一个有前途的人，可译为a man with a future；B) possibility 意思是"可能性"，不能跟在of后面修饰人；可以说He has future possibility. 他前途远大；D) opportunity 意思是"机会"，也不常跟在of后面修饰人。

(CET-4 2002.6)

able ['eibl] *adj.* 有能力的，出色的，有才干的，能力出众的

I was able to refute the lawyer's argument to defend him.

我能驳倒那个律师的论点来保护他。

考点：be able to 有能力做某事

---

advantage [əd'vɑ:ntidʒ] *n.* 优点，优势，好处；*vt.* 有利于，有助于

He was an astute merchant, and nobody could take advantage of him.

他是个精明的商人，没有人能占他的便宜。

考点：take advantage of 利用，占便宜

　　　　to advantage 有利地，使优点突出地

---

can [kæn] *aux.v.* 能，会，可能 *n.* 罐头，听头，容器

What can I do for you?

有什么我可以帮忙的吗？

---

adequate ['ædikwit] *adj.* 足够的，可以胜任的，足够的

We can't accuse him, because we don't have adequate proof.

我们不能控告他，因为我们没有充分的证据。

真题

By law, when one makes a large purchase, he should have _____ opportunity to change his mind.

A) accurate　　　B) adequate

C) urgent　　　D) excessive

详 解：选B。题意为：根据法律，一个人购买大宗物品时，他应有充分的机会改变主意。A) accurate意思是"准确的，精确的"；B) adequate意思是"充分的，足够的"；C) urgent意思是"紧急的，急迫的"；D) excessive意思是"过多的，极度的"。

(CET-4 2000.6)

capable ['keipəbl] *adj.* 有能力的，有才能的

My brother is capable as a businessman.

我哥哥是一个有能力的商人。

---

capacity [kə'pæsiti] *n.* 容量，能力，能量

The seating capacity of the hall is five thousand.

这个大厅能坐5000人。

competent ['kɔmpitənt] *adj.* 有能力的，应该做的

In reality, he is more competent than what you see now.

事实上，他比你看到的更有能力。

考点：be competent for sth. / to do sth.= be capable of doing sth. = be able to do sth. 有能力做某事

真题

Mobile telecommunications _____ is expected to double in Shanghai this year as a result of a contract signed between the two companies.
A) capacity   B) potential
C) possession   D) impact

详 解：选A。题意为：这两家公司签署合同后，今年上海移动通信的容载量有望翻倍。句中通讯能力是以容载量衡量，所以用capacity。B) potential意思是"潜势，潜能"；C) possession意思是"拥有"；D) impact意思是"碰撞，冲击力"。

(CET-4 2002.1)

could [kud] *aux.v.* 能（can的过去式）

Could you help me watch my baby while I'm away?

我不在的时候你能不能帮忙看管一下我的孩子？

enable [i'neibl] *vt.* 使能够，使可能

Exercises enable you to keep healthy.

锻炼能使你保持健康。

考点：enable sb. to do sth. 使某人能做……；enable sth. 使某事成为可能

faculty ['fæklti] *n.* 才能，能力，系，科

The boy has a great faculty for language.

这个男孩具有很强的语言学习能力。

extraordinary [iks'trɔ:dnri] *adj.* 非同寻常的，特别的

The boy is an extraordinary genius.

这个男孩真是个惊人的天才。

genius ['dʒi:njəs] *n.* 天才，天赋，天资

Bill is a genius in the field of science.

比尔是个科学天才。

考点：genius指天赋，talent指才华。

instinct ['instiŋkt] *n.* 本能，直觉，生性

He seemed to have an instinct about the number.

他好像对数字有一种本能。

ordinary ['ɔ:dinəri] *adj.* 平常的，平凡的

She thinks as a sage, but she has to live as an ordinary woman.

她像哲人一样思考，却不得不像普通人一样生活。

考点：out of the ordinary 不寻常的，非凡的

outstanding [aut'stændiŋ] *adj.* 突出的，杰出的

You are an outstanding player and will probably become a champion.

你是一名出色的选手，很可能获得冠军。

potential [pə'tenʃəl] *adj.* 潜在的；*n.* 潜力

Their company gave a reception to the new potential customer.

他们公司为新的有潜力的客户举办了一场招待会。

power ['pauə] *n.* 能力，力，权，幂

They weren't satisfied with the verdict, but they had no power to resist.

他们对判决不服，但又无力反抗。

qualify ['kwɔlifai] *vt.* 使具有资格

I was thirty-four before I was qualified as a CPA(Certified Public Accountant).

我是34岁后才具备会计师资格的。

考点：qualify for 使合格，有……的资格

require [ri'kwaiə] *vt.* 需要，要求，命令

The witness was required to describe the appearance of the murderer he saw.

目击者被要求描述他看到的凶手的模样。

考点：向某人要求……可表示为：require sth. of sb. 或者 require of sb.

requirement [ri'kwaiəmənt] *n.* 需要，要求

It's said that the age requirement remains at 30.

据说，年龄要求还是30岁。

speciality [ˌspeʃi'æliti] *n.* 专长

Mary and I are twins, but her speciality is physics and mine is English.

玛丽和我是双胞胎，但是她的专业是物理，我的是英语。

skilled [skild] *adj.* 有技能的，熟练的

As we all know an army commander must be skilled in tactics.
大家都知道一名军事指挥官必须精通战术。

🔍**考点**：skilled 表示"熟练的"意思时，与 skillful 基本相同，都修饰人，但它还有"需要技能的"之义，用以修饰物。

strength [streŋθ] *n.* 力，力量，力气

He gathered up all of his strength for this hard job.
他集中精力去干这项艰巨的工作。

🔍**考点**：in strength 大量地；on the strength of 基于，依据

superb [sju:'pə:b] *adj.* 极好的，高质量的

What I really like about the film is the superb director.
我喜欢这部电影是因为导演十分出色。

talent ['tælənt] *n.* 天才，才能，人才

Jack's performance pointed up his unique talent for sport.
杰克的表现彰显了他独特的运动才能。

🔍**短语**：have a talent for 有……的才能

wisdom ['wizdəm] *n.* 智慧，才智，名言

The wisdom of the masses exceeds that of the wisest individual.
三个臭皮匠，赛过诸葛亮。

wit [wit] *n.* 智力，才智，智能

A fall into the pit, a gain in your wit.
吃一堑，长一智。

🔍**考点**：at one's wits' end 智穷计尽

求职面试 申请录用 ✎

applicant ['æplikənt] *n.* 申请人

Can you tell me your deepest impression to the applicant?
能告诉我你对申请人最深的印象是什么吗？

application [ˌæpli'keiʃən] *n.* 请求，申请，施用，应用程序

My boyfriend is writing application for admission.
我男朋友正在写入学申请。

employ [im'plɔi] *vi.&vt.* 雇用，用，使忙于

This company employs two hundred workers.
这家公司雇用了200名工人。

🔍**考点**：be employed in 从事于……；be employed to do sth. 被雇用来做……

employee [im'plɔi] *n.* 受雇者，雇员，雇工

That ignorant leader has no business to order his employees.
那个无知的领导根本无权命令他的员工。

employer [im'plɔiə] *n.* 雇佣者，雇主

The employer threatened that if the strikers didn't return to work, they would be dismissed.
雇主威胁罢工者，如果他们不返回工作，就会被解雇。

apply [ə'plai] *vt.* 应用，实施，使用，申请，要求

Sometimes these rules don't apply.
有时候这些规则行不通。

🔍**考点**：apply to 适用于；apply...to... 把……适用于，运用；apply to sb. for sth. 向某人申请某物

真题

The most successful post-career athletes are those who can take the identity and life skills they learned in sports and _____ them to another area of life.
A) apply   B) utilize
C) employ   D) exert

详 解：选A。题意为：退役后最成功的运动员莫过于那些能利用自己的身份，把从运动中所学的技能应用到其他生活领域中的人。A) apply…to…意思是"把……适用于"；B) utilize意思是"利用"；C) employ意思是"雇佣"；D) exert意思是"运用（力量，影响，技巧等）"，后跟动词不定式。

(CET-4 2006.6)

employment [im'plɔimənt] *n.* 工业，雇用，使用

I know you lost your job, but don't worry, you are entitled to unemployment benefit.
我知道你失去了工作，但是别担心，你有资格领取失业救济金。

engage [in'geidʒ] *vt.* 使从事于，聘用
We engage him as technical adviser.
我们聘请他担任技术顾问。

考点：be engaged to sb. 与某人订婚
be engaged to do sth. 被雇用
来做……

hire ['haiə] *vt.* 租借；*n.* 租用，雇用
They hire some costumes for a fancy ball.
他们租借服装参加化妆舞会。

labo(u)r ['leibə] *n.* 劳动；工作；劳工
I think it is time for us to enjoy the fruits of our labours.
我想是我们享受劳动果实的时候了。

need [ni:d] *vt.* 需要；*aux.v.* 需要
We need an English teacher, so please appoint one as soon as possible.
我们需要一名英语老师，请尽快委派一名过来。

position [pə'ziʃən] *n.* 位置，职位，姿势
Please reverse the positions of the two desks.
请把两张桌子的位置倒转过来。

recruit [ri'kru:t] *vt.* 招募，吸收（新成员）
n. 新兵，新成员
Some companies will take the gender of the applicants into considerations when they recruit.
有些公司在招聘时会考虑应聘者的性别。

resume [ri'zju:m] *vt.* 恢复，重新开始
n. 摘要，简历
A perfect resume will give the interviewer a deep impression.
一份漂亮的简历会给面试官留下很深刻的印象。

trial ['traiəl] *n.* 试，试验，审判
The editor is engaged for a week on trial.
那位编辑被试用了一周。

考点：by trial and error 反复试验，不断摸索

vacant ['veikənt] *adj.* 空的，未被占用的
There are some vacant rooms in this flat.
公寓里还有几间空住房。

日常办公 了解公司

boss [bɔs] *n.* 老板，上司；*vt.* 指挥
He could not understand why his boss fired him.
他不明白为什么老板炒了他鱿鱼。

colleague ['kɔli:g] *n.* 同事，同僚
The colleague next to me is humorous and always tells jokes to us.
坐我旁边那个同事很幽默，总是给我们讲笑话。

corporation [ˌkɔ:pə'reiʃən] *n.* 公司，企业，社团
It cost him seven years to become a senior executive in the corporation.
他花了7年时间才成为这家公司的高级主管。

deputy ['depjuti] *n.* 代理人，代表，副手
Our deputy manager is the virtual head of the business.
我们的副经理是公司的实际负责人。

考点：a deputy for sb. 某人的代理人

enterprise ['entəpraiz] *n.* 事业，计划，事业单位，事业心
The enterprise should pay more attention to the exploration and management of human resource.
企业应当更加关注人力资源的开发和管理。

executive [ig'zekjutiv] *adj.* 执行的，行政的
n. 主管，高级行政人员，行政部门
It only cost him two years to become an executive in the corporation.
他只花了两年时间就成为这家公司的主管。

headquarters ['hedˌkwɔ:təz] *n.* 司令部，总部
The international corporation's headquarters is in New York.
这家跨国公司的总部设在纽约。

leadership ['li:dəʃip] *n.* 领导，领导才干
He was elected to the leadership of the Labour Party.
他被选为工党的领导人。

leading ['li:diŋ] *adj.* 领导的，指导的，主要的，在前的
Who will play the leading role in our drama play?
谁将出演我们话剧里的主角呢？

manager ['mænidʒə] *n.* 经理，管理人
Our manager will warrant me an honest and reliable fellow.
我们经理可以保证我是一个诚实可靠的人。

shut [ʃʌt] *vt.&n.* 关上，闭上，关闭
The wind is strong and the window shut with a bang.
外面风很大，窗户"呼"地一声关住了。

🔍 考点：shut away 把……藏起来，隔离；shut down 关闭，使停工；shut off 切断（水，电等）；shut up 闭嘴，监禁

virtual ['və:tjuəl] *adj.* 实质的，事实上的
The company didn't give us a virtual promise.
公司并没有给我们一个实质上的承诺。

virtually ['və:tʃuəli] *adv.* 实际上，事实上
It's virtually risk-free for you to investigate in the real estates.
事实上对您而言，投资房地产是完全没有风险的。

日常办公 分配任务

appoint [ə'pɔint] *vt.* 任命，委任，约定
He is appointed to be our marketing manager to take charge the market promotion of this region.
他被任命为销售主管负责这一区域的市场推广工作。

appointment [ə'pɔintmənt] *n.* 任命，约定，委派，约会
I am glad to hear that you've got a good appointment.
很高兴听说你有了个好的职位。

change [tʃeindʒ] *n.* 改变，变化，零钱
Please change this active sentence into a passive sentence.
请把这个主动句改为一个被动句。

cite [sait] *vt.* 引用，传讯，表扬，举（例）
Let me cite another case to illustrate it.
让我再举个例子来说明。

importance [im'pɔ:təns] *n.* 重要，重要性
You must realize the importance of this document.
你必须认识到这份文件的重要性。

mission ['miʃən] *n.* 使命，任务，使团
It's impossible for me to accomplish the mission successfully in one week.
我不可能在一个星期内成功地完成任务。

🔍 考点：on a...mission 负有……使命

shortly ['ʃɔ:tli] *adv.* 立刻，简短地
Shortly after my supper, it began to rain heavily.
我吃过晚饭不久，就开始下大雨了。

split ['split] *vt.* 劈开；*vi.* 被劈开
They split up the work among a few people.
他们把这项工作分工给了好几个人。

🔍 考点：split up 断绝关系，离婚，划分

真题

His trousers _____ when he tried to jump over the fence.
A) cracked   B) split
C) broke   D) burst

详　解：选B。题意为：当他试图跨过篱笆时裤子撕裂了。A) crack意思是"裂缝"；B) split意思是"撕裂，使破裂"；C) break意思是"打碎，粉碎"；D) burst意思是"爆炸，爆裂"。
(CET-4 2003.12)

subdivide ['sʌbdi'vaid] *vi.&vt.* 再分，细分
They often subdivide the task into a few parts.
他们经常会把任务细分。

task [tɑ:sk] *n.* 任务，工作，作业
Though the task was difficult, we managed to accomplish it in time.
尽管任务困难，我们仍按时完成了。

日常办公 工作职责

busy ['bizi] *adj.* 忙的，繁忙的
Our teacher is busy doing a chemical experience.
我们老师正忙着做化学实验。

personnel [,pə:sə'nei] *n.* 全体人员，全体职员，人事部门
He said he was the successive head of personnel department.

他说他是新任的人事部负责人。

shove [ʃʌv] *n.* 猛推；*vi.&vt.* 乱推

The manager always shoves the boring jobs off onto other people.

经理总是把乏味的工作硬推给别人去干。

🔍 **考点**：shove off（命令）滚开

dull [dʌl] *adj.* 枯燥的，不鲜明的

I'm very sorry about that I killed two good years on that dull job.

我很遗憾的是我在那件无趣的工作上浪费了整整两年的时光。

（真题）

We don't know why so many people in that region like to wear dresses of such ____ colors.
A) low   B) humble   C) mild   D) dull

详　解：选D。题意为：我们不知道为什么那个地区有那么多人喜欢穿颜色如此暗淡的衣服。A) low意思是"低的"；B) humble意思是"谦逊的，恭顺的"；C) mild意思是"温和的，温柔的"；D) dull意思是"不鲜明的"。

(CET-4 2005.6)

manage ['mænidʒ] *vt.* 管理，操纵
vi. 设法对付

Thanks to her knowledge on obstetrics, she managed to deliver the triplets safely.

多亏了她有产科方面的知识，她才顺利接生了那三胞胎。

🔍 **考点**：manage to do sth. "成功做成某事"，含有成功、顺利之意；try to do sth. "设法做某事"，努力去做，但不一定成功；succeed in doing sth. "成功做成某事。

management ['mænidʒmənt] *n.* 管理，经营，处理，管理部分，管理人员

The enterprise should pay more attention to the exploration and management of human resource.

企业应当更加关注人力资源的开发和管理。

agenda [ə'dʒendə] *n.* 议事日程

As a secretary, one of my tasks is to let my boss know the agenda before 8:30 every day.

作为一个秘书，每天我的任务之一就是让我的老板在8点半之前知道日程安排。

arrange [ə'reindʒ] *vt.* 筹备，安排，筹划，整理，调解，布置

Don't worry. I have arranged everything for you.

别担心，我已经为你安排好了一切。

arrangement [ə'reindʒmənt] *n.* 整理，排列，安排

Arrangement of furniture in your apartment is very reasonable.

你公寓里的家具安排得很合理。

desktop ['desktɔp] *n.* 桌面，案头工作

I have dragged it into the desktop.

我把它拖到桌面上了。

disposal [dis'pəuzəl] *n.* 丢掉，处理，销毁

His disposal of the work pleased everybody.

他对工作的处理使大家都感到满意。

🔍 **考点**：at sb. disposal 任某人处理

dispose [dis'pəuz] *vi.* 去掉，丢掉，销毁

Many beggars disposed to solicit from this rich and generous man.

许多乞丐想向这个富有而大方的人乞讨。

🔍 **考点**：dispose of 处理，解决

document ['dɔkjumənt] *n.* 公文，文件，证件，文档

The secretary found the lost document on the doorstep at last.

秘书最终在门阶上找到了那份丢失的文件。

error ['erə] *n.* 错误，谬误，差错

I'm sorry I committed an error in handling the business.

对不起，我在处理业务时犯了一个错误。

fulfill [ful'fil] *vt.* 履行，满足，完成

We believe in ourselves we will fulfill the task without fail.

我们相信我们一定能完成任务。

immediate [i'mi:djət] *adj.* 立即的，直接的

His reflection to that crash was immediate.

他对碰撞立即做出了反应。

immediately [i'mi:djətli] *adv.* 立即，直接地

He would not inform Short immediately.

他是不会立即通知肖特的。

print [print] *vt.* 印刷；*n.* 印刷，正片

The boss asked us to print the posters.

老板吩咐我们印刷海报。

🔍 **考点**：in print 已出版的，以印刷的形式
out of print 已绝版的

incomplete [ˌinkəmˈpliːt] *adj.* 不完全的，不完善的，未完成的

She gave an incomplete account of the incident in the meeting.
会上，她对那次事件做了不完整的叙述。

office [ˈɔfis] *n.* 办公室，处，局，社

He promised to offer me a job in his office three days ago.
3天前，他许诺让我在他办公室工作。

prompt [prɔmpt] *adj.* 及时的，敏捷的
vt. 催促，提示；*n.* 提示

It's Jack's prompt action that saved the drowning boy.
杰克的及时行动救了那个溺水的男孩。

report [riˈpɔːt] *vi.&vt.&n.* 报告，汇报

The report has spotlighted real deprivation of the women's rights.
这篇报道披露了妇女权利被剥夺的真相。

🔍 **考点**：to report doing... 报道做过某事

staff [stɑːf] *n.* 工作人员，参谋

The staff is required to wear uniform clothing when they are working.
工作时间要求员工穿统一的制服。

🔍 **考点**：staff作主语时，若看做整体，则谓语动词用单数；若看做是个体，则谓语动词用复数。

work [wəːk] *n.* 工作；职业；*vi.* 工作

Play while you play; work while you work.
玩的时候就尽情玩，工作的时候就努力工作。

🔍 **考点**：at work 在工作，在运转；out of work 失业；work out 算出，理解，弄懂；work up 激起，制定出

copy [ˈkɔpi] *n.* 抄件；*vt.* 抄写，复制

We need a copy of your ID card to help you apply for a new credit card.
我们需要一张你的身份证复印件，然后才能帮你办银行卡。

briefcase [ˈbriːfkeis] *n.* 公文包

I'm afraid I left my briefcase on the train.

我担心我把公文包落在火车上了。

typewriter [ˈtaipraitə] *n.* 打字机

He had to change the old typewriter which was used for two years.
他不得不换掉那台用了两年的旧打字机。

routine [ruˈtiːn] *n.* 例行公事，惯例
adj. 日常的，常规的

It is our routine work to do a cleaning on Thursday afternoon.
周四下午大扫除是我们例行的工作。

rate [reit] *n.* 比率，速度，价格

The boss asked the secretary to show him that worker's attendance rate.
老板让秘书给他看那个工人的出勤率。

🔍 **考点**：at any rate 无论如何，至少
at this rate 既然这样
rate...as... 评为，列为

shift [ʃift] *vt.* 替换，转移；*n.* 转换，换班

This kind of job makes the workers tired, especially on night shift.
这项工作让工人们很累，尤其是上夜班的时候。

真题

Mass advertising helped to _____ the emphasis from the production of goods to their consumption.
A) vary   B) shift   C) lay   D) moderate

详　解：选B。题意为：大众广告有助于将重点从产品生产转向产品消费。shift sth. from…to…是固定搭配，意思是"使某事物由……向……改变位置或者方向"。A) vary意思是"改变，变化"；C) lay意思是"放置"；D) moderate意思是"协调，缓和"。

(CET-4 2005.6)

overtime [ˈəuvətaim] *adj.* 超时的，加班的

If I put in extra time, can I get overtime pay?
如果我加班，有加班费吗？

deadline [ˈdedlain] *n.* 限期，截止日期，最后期限

I am sure I can meet the deadline.
我确定我能在截止日期前完成。

initial [i'niʃəl] *adj.* 最初的，词首的

Her initial performance can be seen as an illusion.
她最初的表现看来是一种假象。

---

tackle [tækle] *n.* 阻截，用具
　　　　　　　 vt. 对付，处理，阻截，解决

What do you always tackle first in this task?
这个任务中哪些问题是你常常会最先解决的？

真题

Although many experts agree that more children are overweight, there is debate over the best ways to ____ the problem.
A) relate　　　B) file
C) attach　　　D) tackle

详　解：选D。题意为：尽管有很多专家认为有越来越多的儿童超重，但是关于解决这一问题的最好办法却一直存在争议。A) relate意思是"与……相连"，常与to搭配；B) file意思是"提出，归档"；C) attach意思是"贴上，使依附"；D) tackle 意思是"处理，解决"，宾语常为question，problem。

(CET-4 2006.6)

---

efficiency [i'fiʃənsi] *n.* 效率，功效，效能

In order to increase your study efficiency, you must make yourself have enough sleep.
为了提高你的学习效率，你必须让自己有充足的睡眠。

---

efficient [i'fiʃənt] *adj.* 效率高的，有能力的

We have to take measures to make the heating system more efficient.
我们必须采取措施提高供暖设备的效率。

日常办公 **公司会议**

ahead [ə'hed] *adv.* 在前，向前，提前

Owing to our joint efforts, we fulfilled our task ahead of schedule.
由于我们共同努力，我们提前完成了任务。

考点：ahead of 比……提前，比……更早

---

annual ['ænjuəl] *adj.* 每年的；*n.* 年报

The annual governmental conference will be held in the city hall this year.
一年一度的政府会议今年将在市政大厅举行。

---

assemble [ə'sembl] *vt.* 集合，召集，装配

All the staff assembled at the playground to honor the leader's visit.
所有员工聚集在操场上欢迎领导的来访。

---

announce [ə'nauns] *vt.* 宣布，宣告，发表

The results of the beauty contest will be announced this evening.
选美比赛的结果今晚就会宣布。

真题

Official created something called the German Green Card and ____ that they would issue 20 000 in the first year.
A) conferred　　　B) inferred
C) announced　　　D) verified

详　解：选C。题意为：政府官员设计了德国绿卡，宣布他们将在第一年发行20000张。A) confer意思是"赠与"；B) infer意思是"推断，推论"；C) announce意思是"宣布"；D) verify意思是"检查，查证"。

(CET-4 2008.6)

---

assembly [ə'sembli] *n.* 集合，集会，装配

When dose the assembly begin?
集会什么时候开始？

---

attendance [ə'tendəns] *n.* 出席，在场，出席人数，护理

My attendance at school is excellent and my father is pleased.
我在学校的出席情况极好，我爸爸很高兴。

---

attend [ə'tend] *vt.* 出席，照顾，护理

I didn't know why he didn't attend the meeting yesterday.
我不知道为什么他昨天没有来参加会议。

真题

This is the nurse who ____ to me when I was ill in hospital.
A) entertained　　　B) accompanied
C) attended　　　D) shielded

详　解：选C。题意为：在我生病期间照顾我的就是这位护士。A) entertain意思是"娱乐，款待"；B) accompany意思是"陪伴"；C) attend意思是"护理，精心照料"；D) shield意思是"保护，遮挡"。

(CET-4 2003.6)

bring [briŋ] *vt.* 带来，引出，促使
Please bring this problem forward at the next meeting.
请在下次会议上提出这个问题。

chamber ['tʃeimbə] *n.* 会议室，房间，腔
That famous singer will hold a chamber concert.
那个著名的歌唱家将举行一场室内音乐会。

concerning [kən'sə:niŋ] *prep.* 关于
Let me see all the official communities concerning the sale of this land.
让我看看所有有关这块土地出售的官方文件。

cancel ['kænsəl] *vt.* 取消，撤消，删去
I heard that the meeting had been canceled.
我听说会议已经取消了。

【真题】

As we can no longer wait for the delivery of our order, we have to ____ it.
A) delay　　　B) refuse
C) cancel　　　D) postpone

详　解：选C。题意为：既然我们无法再等所订购的货物，只好将其取消。A) delay 意思是"延误，延期"，（与postpone同义）；B) refuse意思是"拒绝，回绝"；C) cancel意思是"取消"；D) postpone意思是"推迟"。

(CET-4 2000.6)

conference ['kɔnfərəns] *n.* 会议，讨论会
Today our boss rent a new room for our conference room.
今天老板新租了个房间，作为我们的会议室。

delay [di'lei] *vt.* 推迟，耽搁，延误，删除
Don't worry; maybe he was delayed by the traffic jam.
别担心，或许他因为交通堵塞而耽误了。

考点：delay doing sth. 推迟做某事

lengthy ['leŋθi] *adj.* 冗长的，漫长的
We didn't solve the problem until we had several lengthy discussions.
经过多次长时间的讨论，那个问题才得以解决。

notify ['nəutifai] *vt.* 通知，告知，报告
Have you notified him that the meeting was put off?

你告诉他会议推迟了吗?

outlook ['autluk] *n.* 观点，看法，展望
The experience in Europe completely changed my outlook on life.
在欧洲的经历彻底改变了我对生活的看法。

考点：outlook for ……的远景，……的前途

postpone [pəust'pəun] *vt.* 延迟，推迟，延缓
After a long meditation, I decided to postpone delivering the lecture.
经过一番思量，我决定延期演讲。

presence ['prezns] *n.* 出席，到场，在
The movie star's presence greatly brightened up the whole party.
这个电影明星的出席使整个晚会大为活跃。

考点：in sb.'s presence 当着某人的面，有某人在场；presence of mind 镇定自若

proceed [prə'si:d] *vi.* 进行，继续进行
The old man paused for some minutes, and then proceeded with his speech.
老人暂停了几分钟，然后继续他的演讲。

【真题】

The work was almost complete when we received orders to ____ no further with it.
A) progress　　B) march
C) proceed　　D) promote

详　解：选C。题意为：工作就要做完时，我们接到了命令停止工作。proceed with 表示"继续进行"；march with 表示"交界，接界"；其他两个词不与with搭配使用。

(CET-4 2003.6)

proclaim [prə'kleim] *vt.* 宣告，宣布，表明
Your accent proclaims you are northlander.
你的口音表明你是北方人。

tentative ['tentətiv] *adj.* 不确定的，暂时的，试验性质的，犹豫不决的
We spent the whole day to discuss the problem and reached a tentative conclusion.
我们花了一天的时间来讨论这个问题，得出了一个暂时的结论。

feasibility [ˌfiːzəˈbiliti] *n.* 可行性
All the members in this team suspected the feasibility of the plan.
所有队员都怀疑这个计划的可行性。

tedious [ˈtiːdiəs] *adj.* 冗长乏味的，沉闷的
He gave us such a tedious lecture that we all left before the meeting end!
他的演讲这么沉闷乏味，以至于我们在结束之前都离开了。

真题

The lecture which lasted about three hours was so _____ that the audience couldn't help yawning.
A) tedious   B) clumsy
C) bored   D) tired

详 解：选A。题意为：长达3个小时的讲座实在太过乏味，听众都忍不住打起了呵欠。A) tedious意思是"令人厌烦的，冗长乏味的"；B) clumsy意思是"笨拙的，愚笨的"；C) bored意思是"对……感到厌烦"；D) tired意思是"对……感到厌烦"。

(CET-4 2004.6)

人事管理 绩效考评

estimate [ˈestimeit] *vt.* 估计，评价
n. 估计
The new system is estimated to be enforced at the end of this month.
新制度估计到这个月底会实施。

evaluate [iˈvæljueit] *vt.* 评价，估……的价
The government has send related person to evaluate the cost of the damage.
政府已经派出相关人员核定损害额。

fault [fɔːlt] *n.* 缺点，过失，故障
Obviously it is your fault to abuse your power to help her.
显然，滥用你的权利去帮她是你的错。

考点：at fault 有责任，出毛病
        find fault with 抱怨，找茬，挑剔

faulty [ˈfɔːlti] *adj.* 有错误的，有缺点的
He soon detected the faulty place.
他很快查到了出问题的地方。

inefficient [ˌiniˈfiʃənt] *adj.* 效率低的，无能的
The management in their company is inefficient.
他们公司的管理非常低效。

inspect [inˈspekt] *vt.* 检查，审查，检阅
He gave us permission to inspect his room.
他允许我们进入他的房间进行检查。

merit [ˈmerit] *n.* 长处，优点，美德，功过
vt. 应得，值得
We should elect someone who has a lot of merits as our monitor.
我们应该选举一位有众多优点的人来做我们的班长。

objective [əbˈdʒektiv] *adj.* 客观的，无偏见的；*n.* 目标，目的
Please rest assured that we will give an objective evaluation towards this matter.
请放心，就这件事情我们会给出客观评价的。

shortcoming [ˈʃɔːtˌkʌmiŋ] *n.* 短处，缺点
Being too lazy is his greatest shortcoming.
过于懒惰是他最大的缺点。

人事管理 薪水福利

bonus [ˈbəunəs] *n.* 红利，意外所得之物，奖金
In order to remunerate Peter for his hard work, the boss decides to give him an extra bonus.
为了酬谢皮特的辛勤工作，老板决定给他发一笔额外奖金。

welfare [ˈwelfɛə] *n.* 幸福，福利
If you would like to work for us, we will supply you with good welfare.
如果你愿意为我们工作，我们将为你提供很好的福利政策。

benefit [ˈbenifit] *n.* 益，恩惠，津贴
Anyway we will benefit from this government ordinance.
不管怎么说，我们会从这条政府法令中得到好处。

🔍 **考点**：benefit... 对……有益
benefit by/from 从……中得益

（真题）

Not only the professionals but also the amateurs will ____ from the new training facilities.
A) benefit　　　B) derive
C) reward　　　D) acquire

详　解：选A。题意为：不仅专业人员，而且业余人员也能受益于这些新的训练设施。四个选项中只有A和B选项能与from连用，而derive from表示"源自于，来自于"，所以可以排除，只能选A。

(CET-4 2003.6)

deduct [di'dʌkt] *vt.* 扣除，减去
The company deducts part of my pay because of my being late.
由于迟到，公司扣了我一部分工资。

beneficial [beni'fiʃəl] *adj.* 有利的，有益的
Amity between the two nations will be beneficial to their economy.
这两国友好相处有益于它们的经济增长。

exploit [iks'plɔit] *vt.* 剥削，利用，开拓
The mine owner was accused of exploiting child labor.
矿主被指控剥削童工。

pension ['penʃən] *n.* 抚恤金，年金
My grandpa doesn't want to live on his pension, so he begins to deal with others.
爷爷不想靠退休金生活，所以开始和别人做起了生意。

prize [praiz] *n.* 奖赏，奖金；*vt.* 珍视
This ugly woman was awarded the Nobel Prize for physiology and medicine.
这个丑陋的妇人获得了诺贝尔生理学奖和医学奖。

salary ['sæləri] *n.* 薪金，薪水
I think you are brave enough to protest to the boss that the salary was too low.
我认为你真勇敢，敢向老板抗议工资太低。

wage [weidʒ] *n.* 工资，报酬
vt. 开展（运动）
Prices are on the rise, while the wage is unchanged.
物价在上涨，而工资却不见涨。

人事管理　辞职解雇

dismiss [dis'mis] *vt.* 不再考虑，解雇
He has been dismissed from his post because of alcohol abuse.
他因为酗酒被撤销了职务。

quit [kwit] *vt.* 离开，退出，停止
In the interests of hygiene, please quit smoking.
为了健康着想，请把烟戒了吧。

🔍 **考点**：quit 后面接动名词作宾语，接不定式作目的状语。eg. quit working 停止工作；quit to go abroad 辞职去国外。

replace [ri'pleis] *vt.* 把……放回，取代
He picked up the waste battery and replaced them in the bag.
他把废旧的电池捡了起来，放回包里。

（真题）

Many in the credit industry expect that the credit cards will eventually ____ paper money for almost every purchase.
A) exchange　　　B) reduce
C) replace　　　D) trade

详　解：选C。题意为：许多信贷行业人士期待将来信用卡最终会取代纸币用于所有消费行为。A) exchange 意思是"交换，交易"；B) reduce 意思是"减少，简化"；C) replace意思是"取代，替换"；D) trade 意思是"用……进行交易"。

(CET-4 2003.9)

replacement [ri'pleismənt] *n.* 代替，取代，替代的人（物）
We need to find a replacement for her as soon as possible
我们必须尽快找人来代替她。

resign [ri'zain] *vt.* 放弃；*vi.* 辞职
I don't know why he resigned his position on the school paper.
我不知道他为什么辞去了校报的职务。

vanish ['væniʃ] *vi.* 突然不见，消失
He seemed to vanish into thin air after quit.
辞职后，他就消失得无影无踪了。

resignation [ˌrezigˈneiʃən] *n.* 放弃，辞职，反抗

I've never thought that my resignation caused much public debate.

我从来没有想到我的辞职竟然会引起公众议论纷纷。

-- *

retire [riˈtaiə] *vi.* 退下，引退，就寝

I retired and lived a life of ease.

我退休了，过着安逸的生活。

🔍 **考点**：retired 不表示被动意义，只表示完成意义。eg. a retired worker 一个退休工人

workforce [ˈwəːkfɔːs] *n.* 全体从业人员，劳动力

Because of the economic crisis they decide to reduce some of the workforce.

由于经济危机他们决定减少一些工人。

-- *

substitute [ˈsʌbstitjuːt] *n.* 代替人
vi.&vt. 用……代替

I don't like to substitute for anybody to finish this programme.

我不想替换任何人去完成这个项目。

🔍 **考点**：substitute A for B 用A代替B

商务贸易 | Business Trade

市场和销售 市场调研

market ['mɑ:kit] *n.* 市场，集市，销路
Before I knew it, there was an influx of goods into the market.
不知不觉地，大批商品涌入了市场。

supply [sə'plai] *vt.&n.* 供给，供应
Our supply can fully meet the demand of the public.
我们的供应可以充分满足公众的要求。

turnover ['tə:nˌəuvə] *n.* 营业额，流动，成交量，翻覆，半圆卷饼
The shopkeeper always kept his shop's turnover in secret.
店老板对他的营业额总是很保密。

feedback ['fi:dbæk] *n.* 回授，反馈，反应
The best time to give feedback to employee is when the event occurs.
给员工反馈信息的最佳时机是在问题发生时。

intention [in'tenʃən] *n.* 意图，意向，目的
He intimated his intention of leaving this industry.
他明确表示他想早点离开这个工厂。

市场和销售 营销策略

ad [æd] *n.* 广告
The baby is easily attracted by the colorful ads.
婴儿很容易被炫目的广告吸引。

advertise ['ædvətaiz] *vt.* 做广告，宣扬，公布；*vi.* 登广告，登公告
We plan to advertise our new products.
我们计划为我们的新产品做广告。

sell [sel] *vi.&vt.* 卖，销售
I think what they sold best is condiment.
我认为他们卖得最好的是调味品。

考点：sell off 廉价出售；sell out 售完，脱销；sell up 卖掉（全部家产）

advertisement [ædvər'taizmənt] *n.* 广告，公告，登广告
She complained that the airtime of advertisement was too long.
她抱怨说广告播放时间太长了。

promote [prə'məut] *vt.* 促进，发扬，提升
It's a good way to promote the products by discounting all its slow-selling goods.
削价出售所有滞销货是一个好的促销产品的方法。

真题

Techniques for _____ sleep would involve learning to control both mind and body so that sleep can occur.
A) cultivating   B) promoting
C) pushing   D) strengthening

详 解：选B。题意为：促进睡眠的技巧包括学会控制思维和身体以产生睡意。
A) cultivate 意思是"促进（生长）"；B) promote 意思是"促进，增进"；C) push意思是"推动"；D) strengthen 意思是"加强"。

(CET-4 2003.9)

sale [seil] *n.* 卖，拍卖，销售额
Our sales of new products are down compared with last month.
与上月相比，我们新产品的销售额下降了。

考点：for sale 待售，供出售
on sale 正在出售

technique [tek'ni:k] *n.* 技术，技巧，技能，手艺
He used stick-and-carrot negotiating technique to persuade the rival.
他使用威逼利诱的谈判技巧说服了对方。

会见客户 接见客户

given ['givn] *adj.* 特定的，假设的，有倾向的
    prep. 考虑到
They have made a given time and place to date.
他们已经约好了见面的时间与地点。

interview ['intəvju:] *n.* 接见，会见，面谈
The interview only lasted fifteen minutes.
会谈只持续了15分钟。

delegate ['deligeit] *n.* 代表（团成员）
    vt. 委派代表
As an official delegate, he will go to Shanghai for an important meeting.
作为一名正式代表，他将去上海参加一个重要会议。

delegation [ˌdeli'geiʃən] *n.* 代表团
All the streets were decorated with flags to welcome the Chinese delegation.
所有的街道都装饰着旗帜以欢迎中国代表团。

🔍 **考点**：delegation指代表团时，既可以看做单数，也可以看做复数，要视情况而定。

reception [ri'sepʃən] *n.* 接待，招待会，接受
We have a meeting in the reception room at six o'clock this afternoon.
今天下午6点钟，我们在会议室开会。

receptionist [ri'sepʃənist] *n.* 接待员，招待员
Go and leave a message with the receptionist.
去给前台留个口信。

represent [ˌrepri'zent] *vt.* 描绘，代表，象征
It is said that the rose represents England.
据说，玫瑰花是英格兰的象征。

representation [ˌreprizen'teiʃən] *n.* 表现，代表，抗议
They say all the minority nationalities are entitled to appropriate representation.
他们说各少数民族都应当有适当名额的代表。

representative [ˌrepri'zentətiv] *adj.* 代表性的；*n.* 代表
Could you tell me some representative figures who hold monism?
你能告诉我几个持有一元论的代表人物吗？

会见客户 参观公司

exclusive [iks'klu:siv] *adj.* 专门的
I want to apply for an exclusive right to sell this brand of shoes.
我想申请卖这种品牌鞋子的独家经营权。

🔍 **考点**：exclusive to 为……所独享

product ['prɔdʌkt] *n.* 产品，产物，（乘）积
We live in a secular age, and I'm a product of it.
我们生活在一个世俗的时代，我是这个时代的产物。

production [prə'dʌkʃən] *n.* 生产，产品，总产量
The manager offered some measures which could help decrease the cost of production.
经理提出的一些措施有助于降低生产成本。

workplace ['wə:kpleis] *n.* 工作场所
To get used to new workplace isn't too difficult for me.
适应新的工作环境对我来说并不太难。

workman ['wə:kmən] *n.* 工人，劳动者，工匠
That workman didn't have any complains because he likes his job.
那个工人没有抱怨，因为他乐于工作。

workshop ['wə:kʃɔp] *n.* 车间，工场创作室
Do you know how many workers in this workshop?
你知道这个车间里有多少个工人吗？

谈判与签约 产品介绍

brand [brænd] *n.* 商品，烙印；*vt.* 铭刻
What brand of handbag do you like?
你喜欢什么牌子的手提包？

manual ['mænjuəl] *adj.* 体力的，手工的
    n. 手册，指南
Machines have revolutionized manual work.
机器的运用彻底改变了手工作业。

logo ['ləugəu] *n.* 标识
The girl is proud to have a baseball cap with the Olympic logo.

有一顶带有奥运会标志的棒球帽让那个女孩感到很骄傲。

label ['leibl] *n.* 标签，标记，称号
        vt. 把……称为，贴标签于……
The librarian attached a label to every book for better control.
为了便于管理，图书管理员把每本书上都贴上了标签。

真题

The ____ stuck on the envelope says "By Air".
A) diagram   B) label
C) signal   D) mark

详 解：选B。题意为：信封上的标签写着"航空"字样。A) diagram意思是"图解，简图"；B) label意思是"标签"；C) signal意思是"信号"；D) mark意思是"记号，标记"。

(CET-4 2002.1)

quality ['kwɔliti] *n.* 质量，品质，特性
If you want to make your company have good public praise, you should elevate the quality of your products.
如果你想让你的公司有好的口碑，你就应该提高产品的质量。

sample ['sæmpl] *n.* 样品，实例，标本
        vt. 从……抽样，品尝，体验
This company gives away free samples of lotion.
这个公司免费赠送洗液样品。

specimen ['spesimən] *n.* 样本，标本，样品
Arthur brought out his specimen box to show for his friends.
亚瑟拿出了他的标本箱向他的朋友们展示。

考点：sample, specimen 都有"样品，样本"的意思：sample多用于指商业上的样品，样本"；specimen多指动植物以及矿物标本，用于科学技术研究等。

trademark ['treidmɑ:k] *n.* 商标，特征
Through a careful inspect, this is an unregistered trademark.
经检查这是一个未被注册的商标。

谈判与签约 谈判内容

bind [baind] *vt.* 捆绑，包扎，装钉
I know you have no rubber band, but you can bind up your hair with a handkerchief.
我知道你没有皮筋，可是你可以用手绢把头发扎起来嘛！

brittle ['britl] *adj.* 脆的，易损坏的，易怒的
Lie is like the brittle glass.
谎言就像易碎的玻璃

bunch [bʌntʃ] *n.* 束，球，串，一群
I caught a bunch of flowers thrown by the bride.
我接到了新娘扔的那一大束花。

bundle ['bʌndl] *n.* 捆，包，束，包袱
        vt. 收集，归拢
He took a bundle of clothes and ran away.
他拿了一包衣服跑了。

考点：bundle up 把……捆扎起来，使穿得暖和

cargo ['kɑ:gəu] *n.* 船货，货物
The ship was carrying a cargo of clothes from China to France.
这艘船载了一船的衣服，从中国运往法国。

checkpoint ['tʃekpɔint] *n.* 检查站
All import and export goods shall be subject to examination at the custom checkpoint.
所有进出口货物应当在海关检查站接受查验。

cheque [tʃek] *n.* 支票
Large transaction should be conducted with cheque.
大宗交易要以支票结算。

commerce [kə'mə:ʃəl] *n.* 商业，贸易，社交
I remembered that my uncle majored in international commerce in college.
我记得我叔叔大学时学的专业是国际贸易。

考点：trade贸易；dealing交易；commerce商业，范围广，常与industry（工业）并称。

commercial [kə'mə:ʃəl] *adj.* 商业的，商品化的
Commercial invoice is a document.

133

商业发票是一种单证。

commission [kə'miʃən] *n.* 委任状，委员会，佣金

Mr. Grantly had received a commission from his boss.
格伦雷先生收到了老板的委托书。

container [kən'teinə] *n.* 容器，集装箱
Seeing that goods are packed into the container, he was relieved.
看着货物被装进了集装箱，他松了一口气。

agent ['eidʒənt] *n.* 代理人，代理商
You can sent agents to agitate the local people.
你可以找人去煽动当地的民众。

auction ['ɔ:kʃən] *vt.&n.* 拍卖
We didn't know actual auction price at that time.
那个时候我们不知道实际的拍卖价格。

bargain ['bɑ:gin] *n.* 交易；*vi.* 议价，成交
My friend glimpsed at my new shoes and said it was a good bargain.
我朋友看了一眼我的新鞋，说买得很合算。

🔍考点：bargain for / on 企图廉价获取
drive a hard bargain 杀价，迫使对方接受苛刻条件

bid [bid] *vi.* （尤指拍卖中）喊价
How much will you bid for that?
你会为它出价多少呢？

bill [bil] *n.* 账单，招贴，票据，议案
The bill was voted through last month.
这项议案上个月已经表决通过了。

🔍考点：fill the bill 符合要求，适合需要

business ['biznis] *n.* 商业，生意，事务
Creativity is the locomotive of business development.
创新将是企业发展的推动力。

🔍考点：get down to business 认真着手办事；have no business 无权，没有理由；in business 经商；mind your own business 少管闲事

export ['ekspɔ:t] *vt.* 输出，出口，运走
This company exports raw material.

这家公司出口原料。

client ['klaiənt] *n.* 委托人，客户
I am a regular client of your company, so can you give me a discount?
我是你们公司的老客户了，能不能给我打个折呢？

coarse [kɔ:s] *adj.* 粗的，粗劣的，粗糙的，粗鲁的
Because of cold, he snuggled down beneath the coarse blankets.
因为冷，他就蜷缩到粗硬的毯子下面。

compensate ['kɔmpənseit] *vi.&vt.* 偿还，补偿，抵消
Please cherish your time because nothing can compensate it when you lose.
请珍惜你的时间，因为当你失去的时候任何东西都弥补不回来。

deal [di:l] *n.* 买卖，待遇；*vt.* 给予
If we can cooperate with that company, it will be a big deal.
如果我们能同那个公司合作，那可真是一桩大买卖。

🔍考点：deal in 经营；deal with 处理

draft [drɑ:ft] *n.* 草稿，汇票；*vt.* 起草
I don't know when we can draft a speech.
我不知道我们何时可以起草一份演讲。

freight [freit] *n.* 货运，货物，运费
The books that our library bought came by freight.
我们图书馆买的这些书是货运来的。

import [im'pɔ:t] *vt.&n.* 输入，进口
The country has to import most of its grain.
这个国家粮食大部分靠进口。

item ['aitem] *n.* 条，条款，一条
Even the smallest item is a new evidence to speak for it.
即使再小的枝节都会成为它新的证据。

negotiate [ni'gəuʃieit] *vt.* 洽谈，协商，顺利通过；*vi.* 协商，谈判
The general had no choice but to negotiate with those terrorists.
将军除了跟恐怖分子谈判外，没有其他的选择了。

compensation [kɔmpen'seiʃən] *n.* 补偿
（金），报酬

The dead man's wife asked for extra compensation.
死者的妻子要求额外的赔偿。

 真题

The relatives of those killed in the crash got together to seek____.
A) premium　　B) compensation
C) repayment　　D) refund

详 解：选B。题意为：事故中遇难者的亲属，聚集到一起寻求赔偿。A) premium意思是"奖金，保险（费）"；B) compensation意思是"赔偿，补偿（金）"；C) repayment意思是"偿还，报偿"；D) refund意思是"偿还，退还"。

(CET-4 2004 5.6)

negotiation [ni,gəuʃi'eiʃən] *n.* 谈判，协商
The Ministry of Foreign Affairs decided to suspend negotiation.
外交部决定中止谈判。

output ['autput] *n.* 产量，输出量，输出
They have decided to accelerate the output.
他们决定增加产量。

🔍 考点：output, production 指工业产量
yield多指农业产量或者矿物开采量

payment ['peimənt] *n.* 支付，支付的款项
They hold a meeting to stipulate a date of payment and a price.
他们举行了一个会议来规定偿付日和赔偿的金额。

🔍 考点：in payment for 以偿还，以回报

quotation [kwəu'teiʃən] *n.* 引用，引文，报价单
I hope that you can give me your quotation as quickly as possible.
我希望你尽快把你的报价单给我。

settlement ['setlmənt] *n.* 解决，殖民，殖民地
At last two parties negotiated a settlement through mediation.
最后经调解，双方当事人达成协议。

trade [treid] *n.* 贸易，职业；*vi.* 交易
China does a lot of trades with Japan.
中国与日本进行大量的贸易。

🔍 考点：trade sth. for 用……交换……
trade...with sb. 与某人交换……

transaction [træn'zækʃən] *n.* 交易，业务
To help us make this transaction possible, he devoted a lot.
为了促成这笔交易，他付出了很多。

unload [ʌn'ləud] *vt.* 卸（货），丢掉
vi. 卸货
I was reluctant to unload those clothes.
我不愿意丢弃那些衣服。

谈判与签约 签约

compact ['kɔmpækt] *vt.* 压缩，使密集
n. 契约，合同
vi. 签约，签合同
adj. 坚实的

The next day, I found the old snow has compacted into the hard ice.
第二天，我发现雪堆已经凝固成冰了。

真题

In mountainous regions , much of the snow that falls is ____ into ice.
A) dispersed　　B) embodied
C) compiled　　D) compacted

详 解：选D。题意为：在山区，大部分降雪被挤压成冰。（根据常识可知，雪经过挤压坚实后就变成了冰。）A) dispersed意思是"分散，消散"；B) embody意思是"包含，表达"；C) compile意思是"编撰，编译"。D) compact意思是"压紧"。

(CET-4 2004.6)

agreement [ə'gri:mənt] *n.* 协定，协议，同意，契约

There have a lot of wheeling and dealing before an agreement is reached.
要经过一番讨价还价才能达成协议。

🔍 **考点**：in agreement with 与……一致，同意；arrive at / come to an agreement 达成协议

---

sign [sain] *n.* 符号，招牌，签名
　　　　　　vi.&vt. 签名，用手势表示
The salesman persuaded me to sign the document by guile.
这个推销员用欺骗手段说服我在文件上签字。
🔍 **考点**：sign for 签收；sign off 停止播放，结束；sign out 签名离开

---

clause [klɔːz] *n.* 条款，[语]从句
I am sure that this sentence is an attributive clause.
我确信这个句子是一个定语从句。

contract ['kɔntrækt] *n.* 契约，合同，婚约
Now let's sign the contract.
现在我们来签订这份合同。

---

short-term ['ʃɔːt'təːm] *adj.* 短期的
We have to suffer short-term discomfort for long-term gain.
为了长期收益，我们不得不承受短期不适。

---

signature ['signitʃə] *n.* 署名，签字，签名
Sorry, I can't identify the signature.
对不起，我识别不出这是谁的签字。

---

terminate ['təːmineit] *vi.&vt.* 停止，终止，结束，满期，达到终点
Your contract will terminate next month.
你的合同下个月期满。

娱乐休闲 | Entertainment

兴趣爱好 上网

blog [blɔg] *n.* 博客，网络随笔，日志
I update my blog four times a week.
我每周更新4次博客。

broaden ['brɔ:dn] *vi.&vt.* 变宽，扩大，开阔
I recommend you to broaden your experience by travelling more.
我建议你应该多到各地走走以增长见识。

browse [brauz] *v.* 浏览，随意观看，吃草
     n. 嫩叶，浏览
I like to browse store windows in my free time.
不忙的时候，我喜欢逛街。

browser ['brauzə] *n.* [计]浏览器，浏览（书本等）的人，食草动物
Which is the best browser you have ever used?
哪个是你用过的最好用的浏览器？

CD-ROM [si:di:'rɔm] *abbr.* （只读）光盘驱动器（= Compact Disc Read–Only Memory）
You can find out Western table manners on this CD-ROM.
你可以在这张光盘里找到有关西方餐桌礼仪的信息。

computer [kəm'pju:tə] *n.* 计算机，电脑
My computer can't process so many tasks at the same time.
我的电脑不能同时处理这么多任务。

computerize [kəm'pju:təraiz] *vt.* 使计算机化
       vi. 引进电脑设备
He decided to computerize the wages department of his firm.
他决定用电脑管理公司发薪部门的工作。

download [,daun'ləud] *vt.* 下载
You can download the lastest movies and songs on the Internet.
你可以从网上下载最新的电影和歌曲。

e-Bay [ibei] *n.* 一家知名购物网站
I always buy clothes on e-Bay.
我常在e-Bay上买衣服。

firewall ['faiəwɔ:l] *n.* 防火墙
You had better install a firewall to guarantee the safety of the computer.
你最好安装一个防火墙以确保电脑的安全。

hacker ['hækə] *n.* 电脑黑客
The hacker broke into the police's computer system.
电脑黑客闯入了警察的计算机系统。

Internet ['intə:net] *n.* 互联网
Now there is a new development on the Internet.
现在，互联网又有了新的发展。

italic [i'tælik] *adj.* 斜体的；*n.* 斜体字
Most time we use bold italic to emphasize points.
我们大多时候都用粗斜体去强掉重点。

keyboard ['ki:bɔ:d] *n.* 键盘
You need to buy a new keyboard, because the old one doesn't work well.
你需要买一个新键盘，因为原来的那个不好用了。

laptop ['læptɔp] *n.* 笔记本电脑
He bought a new laptop for me as my birthday gift.
他给我买了一台新的便携式电脑作为我的生日礼物。

load [ləud] *vt.* 装，装满，载入，储存
    n. 负载，负荷，装载
    vi. 装货
Can you help me check my computer to see why the website loads so slowly?
你能帮我检查下电脑，看看为什么网页下载这么慢吗？

manipulate [mə'nipjuleit] *vt.* 操纵，控制

My father doesn't know how to manipulate a computer.
我爸爸不知道如何操纵电脑。

microcomputer ['maikrəukəm'pju:tə] *n.* 微型计算机，微机

We all know that the monitor is an essential output device of a microcomputer.
我们都知道显示器是微机必需的输出设备。

net [net] *n.* 网，网状物，通信网

If the net is not strong enough, the whale would have chance to escape.
如果网不够结实，鲸鱼就有机会逃脱。

network ['netwə:k] *n.* 网状物，网络，广播网，电视网

The spring travel peak always put great pressure on the rail network。
春运高峰总是给铁路交通网带来相当大的压力。

password ['pɑ:swə:d] *n.* 口令，密码

The password of this E-mail address has eight bytes at least.
这个电子邮箱的密码至少有8个字节。

portable ['pɔ:təbl] *adj.* 轻便的，手提的

I'm planning to save up money to buy a portable computer.
我计划攒钱买一台手提电脑。

software ['sɔftwɛə] *n.* 软件

Their company devotes in designing desktop software.
他们公司致力于设计桌面软件。

surf [sə:f] *n.* 拍岸的浪花
　　　　　　 vi. 冲浪，做冲浪运动
　　　　　　 vt. 浏览

I always surf the Internet for shopping on weekends.
周末我总是网购。

system [ˌsistəm] *n.* 系统，体系，制度

People can identify the book they want by using only the retrieval system.
人们可以通过使用检索系统确定自己想要的书。

systematic [ˌsisti'mætik] *adj.* 有系统的，有计划的

He is a systematic researcher in the eyes of others.
他在大家眼中是个按部就班的研究者。

webcast ['webˌkɑ:st] *n.* 网络广播，网络讲座

Have you listened to the webcast of the solar eclipse?
你听那个关于日食的网络广播了吗?

data ['deitə] *n.* 数据，资料

More and more data proved that ape is our forebear.
越来越多的资料证明猿就是我们的祖先。

database ['deitəbeis] *n.* 数据库，基本数据

What's the matter? The database list is empty!
怎么回事? 数据库列表为空!

digital ['didʒitl] *adj.* 数字的，计数的

It is convenient to use a digital camera.
数码相机用起来很方便。

兴趣爱好 影视广播

pastime ['pɑ:staim] *n.* 消遣，娱乐

His favorite pastime is playing basketball.
他最喜欢的消遣是打篮球。

recreation [ˌrekri'eiʃən] *n.* 娱乐活动，消遣

Proper recreation will make tired workers in high spirits.
适当的娱乐会使劳累的工人精神振奋。

actor ['æktə] *n.* 男演员，演剧的人

He is one of my favorite actors.
他是我最喜欢的男演员之一。

actress ['æktris] *n.* 女演员

My best friend is a famous actress now, and I am proud of this.
我最好的朋友现在是一个名演员，我感到很骄傲。

amusement [ə'mju:zmənt] *n.* 娱乐,文娱设施

My mother usually took me to the amusement park when I was a child.

小时候妈妈经常带我去游乐园玩。

---

audience ['ɔ:djəns] *n.* 听众，观众，读者
The lecturer bowed as the audience applauded.
那个演讲者向鼓掌的观众鞠躬。

---

audio ['ɔ:diəu] *adj.* 听觉的，声音的
He has bought a set of multimedia equipment which has both the video and audio components.
他买了一套由视频和音频组成的多媒体设备。

---

aural ['ɔ:rəl] *adj.* 耳的，听觉的
I prefer to receive information in an aural manner rather than in visual means.
我喜欢靠听觉方式而不是凭视觉手段接收信息。

---

brass [brɑ:s] *n.* 黄铜，黄铜器
The brass is being blown by the musicians in the concert.
音乐会上音乐家们正吹奏着铜管乐器。

---

cinema ['sinimə] *n.* 电影院，电影，影片
The poster stuck on the wall of the cinema is eye-catching.
电影院墙上贴的海报很引人注目。

---

enrich [in'ritʃ] *vt.* 充实，使丰富，使富裕
In my opinion, the screen plays an important part in enriching cultural life of citizen.
在我看来，影视在丰富人们精神文化生活方面起着重要的作用。

---

film [film] *n.* 影片，胶卷，薄层
He praised warmly on the subject of this film.
他热情赞扬了这部影片的主题。

---

ghost [gəust] *n.* 鬼，灵魂，鬼魂
People are usually asked "Have you ever seen a ghost?"
"你见过鬼吗？"人们总是被这样问道。

---

movie ['mu:vi] *n.* 电影，电影院
This movie was adapted from a novel.
这部电影是由一部小说改编而成的。

---

screen [skri:n] *n.* 屏，屏幕，银幕；*vt.* 掩蔽
She had never expected that she would appear on the screen one day.
她从没想到过有一天自己会出现在银幕上。

---

surge [sə:dʒ] *vi.* 蜂拥而出，汹涌
　　　　　　　n. 洋溢，急剧上升
The crowds surge out of the cinema after the end of the movie.
电影结束后观众从电影院涌出。

---

thriller [θrilə] *n.* 惊险小说，惊险电影
There's a new American thriller on these days.
最近一部新的美国恐怖片正在上映。

VCD = video compact disk *n.* 影视光碟
He likes to store the VCD of Chinese movies.
他喜欢收集中国电影的影视光碟。

---

watch [wɒtʃ] *vi.&vt.* 观看；*n.* 手表
I like washing movies in my spare time.
空闲时我喜欢看电影。

 考点： watch out (for) 密切注意，留神

---

broadcast ['brɔ:dkɑ:st] *n.* 广播，播音
The broadcast of BBC can be heard in most parts of the country.
BBC的广播节目国内大部分地区都能听到。

---

episode ['episəud] *n.* 片段，连续剧中的一集，（剧本或者小说中的）插曲
Receiving the wrong phone is one of the funniest episodes in my life.
接到打错的电话是我生活中最有趣的插曲之一。

---

insert [in'sə:t] *vt.* 插入，嵌入，登载
Inserting the advertisement in a newspaper is very common.
在报纸上插入广告是非常普遍的。

真题

Mr. Smith asked his secretary to ____ a new paragraph in the annual report she was typing.
A) inject　　　B) install
C) invade　　　D) insert

详　解：选D。题意为：史密斯先生让他的秘书在她正在打的年度报告中插入新的一段。A) inject意思是"注射，注入"；B) install意思是"安装，安置"；C) invade意思是"侵略，入侵"；D) insert意思是"插入"。

(CET-4 2005.12)

program ['prəugræm] *n.* 节目单，大纲，程序

This program could be applied to the most of salient pole machines.
该程序适用于大多数常规结构的凸极同步电机。

---

radio ['reidiəu] *n.* 无线电，收音机

Oh, please don't play your radio at full volume. You know it's midnight.
哦，请不要把收音机开到最大的音量，现在可是午夜时间。

---

series ['siəri:z] *n.* 连续，系列，丛书

Qing government had signed a series of unequal treaties in the old days.
清政府过去签订了一系列不平等的条约。

考点：a series of 一系列，一连串

---

short-wave ['ʃɔ:t'weiv] *n.* 短波

They use a short-wave radio to pick up English programmes in the morning.
他们上午用短波收音机收听英语节目。

---

viewer ['vju:ə] *n.* 电视观众，观察家

Every viewer has his personal point on this thing.
在这件事上，每一个观察者都有各自的观点。

---

heroine ['herəuin] *n.* 女主角，女英雄

She is the heroine in that film.
她是那部影片中的女主角。

---

last [lɑ:st] *adj.* 最近的，上一个的，末尾的，最后的
　　　　 adv. 最后；*vi.* 持续，耐久

We went to the cinema to see an exciting movie last night.
昨天晚上我们去电影院看了一场激动人心的电影。

真题

The words of his old teacher left a ____ impression on his mind. He is still influenced by them.
A) long　　　　B) lively
C) lasting　　　D) liberal

详　解：选B。题意为：老教师的话给他留下了深刻的印象，并依然影响着它。A) 与 C) 意思很像，但lasting指"长久的，能持续很长时间的"。

(CET-4 2000.1)

amplify ['æmplifai] *vt.* 放大（声音等），增强，扩大，详述

It's my father who told me that a tube or a transistor can amplify an incoming signal.
我父亲告诉我电子管或晶体管能放大输入的信号。

真题

By turning this knob to the right you can ____ the sound from the radio.
A) intensify　　　B) amplify
C) enlarge　　　　D) reinforce

详　解：选B。题意为：向右旋转按钮，收音机里的声音就会变大。A) intensify意思是"增强，加强"，通常指强度加大；B) amplify意思是"放大，增强"，通常指程度上详尽，还可指声音、电流等增强；C) enlarge意思是"扩大，放大"，主要指尺寸、规模的增加；D) reinforce意思是"加强，加固"，主要指给予更多的力量或效力。

(CET-4 2005.1)

兴趣爱好 游戏玩具

amusing [ə'mju:ziŋ] *adj.* 有趣的，逗乐的

I think you are an amusing contrast to your father.
我认为你和你父亲形成了有趣的对比。

---

balloon [bə'lu:n] *n.* 气球，玩具气球

The girl was very naughty, and she burst all the balloons.
这个女孩很淘气，她把所有的气球都给弄爆了。

---

bet [bet] *vi.&vt.&n.* 打赌

He bet that the red team could not win.
他打赌说红队不会赢。

---

chess [tʃes] *n.* 棋，国际象棋

Why don't you play chess with me tomorrow?
你明天为什么不来和我一起下象棋呢？

---

drag [dræg] *vt.* 拖，拉，拖曳

My friend dragged me out to a concert.
朋友硬拖我去听音乐。

考点：drag on / out 使拖延

fun [fʌn] *n.* 乐趣，娱乐，玩笑
Anyway, our journey was filled with great fun.
总之，我们的旅程十分有趣。

🔍 考点：for / in fun 取乐，闹着玩
make fun of 拿……开玩笑，取笑

gamble ['gæmbl] *vi.* 赌博，投机，冒险
vt. 赌，以……为赌注
n. 赌博，投机，冒险
Don't gamble with your rest money.
不要拿你剩下的钱做赌注了。

🔍 考点：gamble away 赌掉，输光
take a gamble 冒风险
gamble on 把赌注押在……

play [plei] *vi.* 玩，游戏，演奏
My little brother likes to play the merry-go-round.
我的弟弟喜欢玩旋转木马。

player ['pleiə] *n.* 玩游戏的人，比赛者
Losing such kind of player like you was a handicap to the team.
失去像你这样的运动员对我队很不利。

puppet ['pʌpit] *n.* 木偶，玩偶，傀儡
He is very fond of puppet play.
他很喜欢木偶戏。

riddle ['ridl] *n.* 谜，谜语
She advised us to guess riddles to kill our time.
她建议我们猜谜语来打发时间。

snowball ['snəubɔ:l] *n.* 雪球，打雪仗
v. 丢雪球，滚雪球般增长
The business of their family started to snowball.
他们的家族生意像滚雪球般不断扩大。

slide [slaid] *vi.* 滑；*vt.* 使滑动；*n.* 滑
The thief slid out of the door while no one was looking.
小偷趁没人注意的时候悄悄地溜了出去。

🔍 考点：let slide 放任自我，顺其自然

snowman ['snəumæn] *n.* 雪人
They build a snowman on the ground.
他们在地上堆了一个雪人。

stake [steik] *n.* 桩，赌金，奖品
I'd stake my life on that he didn't betray us.

我愿意拿我的生命打赌他没有背叛我们。

🔍 考点：at stake 在紧急关头，在危险中

strain [strein] *vt.* 拉紧；*vi.* 尽力
Please strain the boy or he will fall down.
请抓紧那个孩子否则他就要掉下去了。

throw [θrəu] *vt.* 投，掷，抛，扔
I'm unable to throw off this feeling of terror.
我无法摆脱这种恐怖的感觉.

🔍 考点：throw away 扔掉，抛弃，错过
throw in 外加，额外奉送
throw up 呕吐，产生（想法）

thrust [θrʌst] *vt.* 插，刺；*n.* 插，讽刺
He thrusts his hands into his trousers pockets waiting for his girlfriend.
他把双手插在裤子的口袋里等待他的女朋友。

toss [tɔs] *vi.&vt.* 扔，抛，掷
We'll toss a coin to see who goes to buy food.
我们将掷币决定谁来买饭。

tug [tʌg] *n.* 用力拉，拖船；*vi.&vt.* 用力拉
The barge was broken and we had to send a launch to tug it.
驳船坏了，我们不得不派一艘小汽船去拖拽它。

twist [twist] *vt.* 捻，拧；*vi.&n.* 扭弯
Dickens was the author of *Oliver Twist*.
狄更斯是《雾都孤儿》的作者。

magic ['mædʒik] *n.* 魔法，巫术，戏法
adj. 有魔力的，魔术的
It's the magician who thrilled the audience with his feats of magic.
这位魔术师用其魔术技艺让观众激动不已。

狂欢 逛街购物 ✏

afford [ə'fɔ:d] *vt.* 买得起，花得起，担负得起，给予，提供
I couldn't afford to take a taxi, so I take bus to go to work every day.
我负担不起出租车费，所以每天上班只能乘坐公交车。

🔍 考点：afford sb. sth. 给某人提供某物

buy [bai] *vt.* 买，购买；*vi.* 买
My parents bought me a computer last year.
去年我父母给我买了一台电脑。

charge [tʃɑːdʒ] *vt.* 索价，控告；*n.* 费用
The shopkeeper charged me three *yuan* for the cup.
这个杯子店主向我要了3元钱。

考点：in charge (of) 管理，负责（主动意义）；in the charge of 受……管理，由……负责（被动意义）；take charge 接管；free of charge 免费

cheap [tʃiːp] *adj.* 廉价的，劣质的
Vegetables are cheaper when they're in season.
蔬菜当令时比较便宜。

clerk [klɑːk] *n.* 店员，办事员，职员
These clerks surveyed the land from a helicopter.
这些办事员从直升飞机上勘测了这块土地。

consumer [kən'sjuːmə] *n.* 消费者，消耗者，用户
Hundreds of consumers were poisoned after drinking the milk bought from the supermarket.
几百名消费者喝了这家超市卖出的牛奶后中毒了。

cost [kɔst] *n.* 价格，代价，成本 *v.* 花费
Be careful! You know sometimes the folly has cost you dearly.
小心啊！有时候你的愚蠢会让你损失惨重的。

costly ['kɔstli] *adj.* 昂贵的，价值高的
Speculating in the commodities market can be a costly venture.
在商品市场中投机是一种代价很高的冒险。

customer ['kʌstəmə] *n.* 顾客，主顾
This chain store opened last year and attracted a lot of customers.
这家连锁店去年开业的，吸引了不少顾客。

pay [pei] *vt.* 支付，付给，给予
You should pay one thousand *yuan* for the television.
这个电视机价值1000元。

考点：pay back 偿还，回报；pay off 还清，向……行贿；pay out 出钱

retail ['riːteil] *adv.&vt.&n.* 零售
Believe me, the retail price is very reasonable.
相信我，这个零售价非常合理。

scale [skeil] *n.* 天平，磅秤，标度，比例，大小
Can you tell me what the scale, dial, gauge read?
你能告诉我刻度尺、刻度盘和量规显示的计数是多少吗？

考点：on a... scale ……规模地
scale down 缩减

spur [spə:] *n.* 刺激物；*vt.* 刺激
She went to shopping on the spur of the moment.
她一时兴起就去购物了。

考点：on the spur of the moment 一时冲动之下，当即

tag [tæg] *n.* 附加语，标签 *vt.* 给……加上标签
Every articie has a price tag in the shopping mall.
超市里每件商品上都有标价签。

考点：tag along 尾随，跟随

weigh [wei] *vt.* 称……的重量，掂量
The weigh machine was broken as soon as the fat woman stood on it.
那个胖妇人一站上去，那个称体重的机器就坏了。

weight [weit] *n.* 重，砝码，重担
You become much heavier recently, so you must begin to loose weight now.
你最近变得更重了，现在必须开始减肥。

考点：lose weight 减肥；carry weight 有分量，有影响；pull one's weight 干好本分工作

cashier [kæ'ʃiə] *n.* 出纳员，收银员 *vt.* 解雇，丢弃
She worked as a cashier in the local bank after graduation.
她毕业后在当地银行做出纳。

square [skwɛə] *n.* 正方形，广场
There is a huge fountain surrounding the square.
这里有一个大喷泉环绕着这个广场。

meantime ['miːn,taim] *n.* 其时，其间 *adv.* 当时，同时
I was washing clothes. Meantime, my mother cooked the supper.
我在洗衣服，这期间，妈妈做了晚饭。

meanwhile ['miːn'wail] *n.&adv.* 同时，当时
In the meanwhile, I will go to the supermarket to buy some food.
在此同时，我将去超市买点食品。

狂欢 节日庆典

birthday ['bəːθdei] *n.* 生日，诞生的日期
That girl danced with wild abandon at her birthday party.
那个女孩在她的生日舞会上狂放地跳舞。

anniversary [ˌæni'vəːsəri] *n.* 周年纪念日
They went snorkelling in Hawaii to celebrate their 10th wedding anniversary.
为了庆祝结婚10周年，他们去夏威夷潜水了。

banner ['bænə] *n.* 旗，旗帜，横幅
The national banner fluttered in the breeze.
国旗在微风中飘扬。

banquet ['bæŋkwit] *n.* 宴会；*vi.* 参加宴会 *vt.* 宴请，设宴
The king held a state banquet in honor of the general with a triumphant return.
国王为凯旋而归的将军举办了国宴。

candle ['kændl] *n.* 蜡烛，烛形物，烛光
The candle blew out when I opened the window.
当我打开窗户的时候，蜡烛随之被风吹灭了。

card [kɑːd] *n.* 卡，卡片，名片
I intend to send my girlfriend a beautiful card on Christmas Day.
我打算在圣诞节那天送给女友一张漂亮的贺卡。

celebrate ['selibreit] *vt.* 庆祝，歌颂，赞美
The girl bought a black suit for her father to celebrate his 50th birthday.
为了庆祝父亲的50岁生日，那个女孩给他买了一套黑色西装。

ceremony ['seriməni] *n.* 典礼，仪式，礼节
This ceremony is quite an occasion, you must attend it.
这个典礼是一次重大的活动，你一定要参加。

tradition [trə'diʃən] *n.* 传统，惯例
This is a college saturated with tradition.

这是一个传统气息浓厚的大学。

calendar ['kælində] *n.* 日历，历书，历法
You can download a perpetual calendar from the internet.
你可以从互联网上下载一个万年历。

opening ['əupniŋ] *adj.* 开始的；*n.* 开始
Now the museum is closed and the opening time will be announced later.
博物馆正在闭馆，稍后通知开馆时间。

parade [pə'reid] *n.* 游行，检阅，陈列 *vi.* 游行，夸耀，检阅
Oh, God! The parade jammed traffic all over town.
噢，天啊！游行堵塞了全城的交通。

procession [prə'seʃən] *n.* 队伍，行列
The procession passed right by our school.
游行队伍正好经过我们学校。

solemn ['sɔləm] *adj.* 庄严的，隆重的
She gave a solemn undertaking to take their home.
她郑重地保证会将他们送回家。

Christmas ['krisməs] *n.* 圣诞节
We would feel more Christmassy if there was a Christmas tree in the sitting room.
如果客厅有一个圣诞树，就能感受到更浓的圣诞氛围了。

gift [gift] *n.* 礼物，赠品，天赋
Dad gave Lily a gift on her ten years' birthday.
莉莉10岁时，爸爸送给她一个礼物。

mask [mɑːsk] *n.* 面具，伪装，面膜 *vt.* 掩饰，遮盖
On Halloween, Tom intends to wear a very terrible mask.
万圣节那天，汤姆打算戴一个非常恐怖的面具。

mid-autumn [mid'ɔːtəm] *n.* 中秋
We eat moon cakes at the Mid-autumn Festival.
我们中秋节吃月饼。

mooncake [muːn'keik] *n.* 月饼
It is a Chinese tradition to eat mooncakes on Mid-autumn Festival.
在中秋节吃月饼是中国人的传统。

Thanksgiving [ˌθæŋks'giviŋ] *n.* 感恩节
Thanksgiving is on the last Thursday in November.

11月的最后一个星期四是感恩节。

reunion [ri'ju:njən] *n.* 重聚，团聚，聚会
The last time we had a family reunion was at my brother's wedding ceremony four years ago.
上一次全家团聚是4年前在我弟弟的婚礼上。

reunite [ˌri:ju:'nait] *vi.&vt.* （使）再结合，（使）重聚
The girl is trying her best to reunite with her family.
那个女孩想方设法与家人团聚。

custom ['kʌstəm] *n.* 习惯，风俗，海关
It's a custom to have soup with goose blood on November 22nd here.
每年的11月22日喝鹅血汤是这里的风俗。

institution [ˌinsti'tju:ʃən] *n.* 协会，制度，习俗
Giving presents on Thanksgiving Day is an institution.
感恩节送礼是一种风俗。

运动锻炼 跑步

outdoor ['autdɔ:] *adj.* 户外的，室外的
You can enjoy snowboarding and many other outdoor activities here.
在这里你可以尽情滑雪也可以做其他的户外活动。

outdoors [aut'dɔ:z] *adv.* 在户外，在野外
My son likes to play outdoors.
我儿子喜欢在户外玩耍。

sweat [swet] *n.* 汗；*vi.* 出汗
My shirt was sodden with sweat after running one thousand meters.
跑了1000米后，我的衬衫被汗水湿透了。

运动锻炼 球类

badminton ['bædmintən] *n.* 羽毛球
No one knows why the boy excels at badminton.
没有人知道男孩为什么擅长打羽毛球。

ball [bɔ:l] *n.* 球，球状物，舞会
You can catch the ball on the bounce.
你可以在球弹起时抓住它。

basketball ['bɑ:skitbɔ:l] *n.* 篮球，篮球运动
Basketball is the most popular sport in this city.
在这座城市里，篮球是最流行的一项运动。

bat [bæt] *n.* 球拍，短棍，蝙蝠
Have you got a pair of tennis bats?
你有网球拍吗？

golf [gɔlf] *n.* 高尔夫球
Can I interest you in a game of golf?
你有兴趣和我打高尔夫球吗？

pitch [pitʃ] *vi.&vt.* 投，掷；*n.* 沥青
The tall player tends to pitch the ball too high.
那个高个子队员往往把球掷得过高。
考点：pitch in 协力，做出贡献

racket ['rækit] *n.* 球拍
His son begged him to buy a pair of badminton rackets.
儿子乞求他买一副羽毛球拍。

softball ['sɔftbɔ:l] *n.* 垒球（运动）
The UN. softball team won in this match.
英国垒球队赢得了比赛。

volleyball ['vɔlibɔ:l] *n.* 排球，排球运动
Volleyball is a sport which I am very tired of.
排球是我很讨厌的运动。

运动锻炼 其他

stretch [stretʃ] *vt.* 伸展；*vi.* 伸；*n.* 伸展
Can't you stretch the rope longer?
你难道不能把绳子拉长一点吗？
考点：at a stretch 不停地，连续地

yoga ['jəugə] *n.* 瑜伽（术）
There aren't enough yoga schools in the town to satisfy the demand for them.
在这个城镇里，没有足够的瑜伽学校来满足大家的需要。

plunge [plʌndʒ] *vt.* 使投入，使陷入
I saw a diver plunge into the deep water suddenly.

我看见一个潜水员猛然跳进了深水里。

---

pool [puːl] *n.* 水塘，游泳池，水池，共用物
　　　　 vt. 共有
Let's enjoy a dip in the heated swimming pool.
我们在温水游泳池里泡一泡吧。

---

submerge [səb'məːdʒ] *vt.* 浸没
　　　　　　　　 vi. 潜入水中
To find the treasure one must submerge the bottom of a body of water.
要想找到财宝必须潜入这片水域的底部。

外出游玩 观光旅行

aboard [ə'bɔːd] *adv.* 在船（车）上，上船
　　　　　　 prep. 在船（飞机、车）上
I was informed that they had gone aboard.
我被告知他们已经上船了。

---

pack [pæk] *vt.* 捆扎，挤满；*n.* 包
Okay, time to go! Have you packed all your things?
好了，该走了。你所有的东西都打包好了吗？

🔍 考点：pack off 把……打发走
　　　　　 pack up 打包，收拾

---

agency ['eidʒənsi] *n.* 经办，代理，代理处
The travel agency is famous for its good service.
这家旅行社以良好的服务而出名。

🔍 考点：by / through the agency of 凭
　　　　　 借……的帮助，由于……的作用

---

appealing [ə'piːliŋ] *adj.* 吸引人的，招人喜欢的
His theory isn't appealing, but it may be partly right.
他的理论并不十分吸引人，但恐怕在一定程度上是对的。

---

attractive [ə'træktiv] *adj.* 有吸引力的
He is an attractive person.
他是一个有魅力的人。

---

baggage ['bægidʒ] *n.* 行李
Could you do me a favor? My baggage is too heavy.
能帮我个忙吗？我的行李太重了。

---

attract [ə'trækt] *vt.* 吸引，引起，诱惑
Her beauty attracted my notice.
她的美貌引起了我的注意。

真题

This new NSF network ＿＿＿ more and more institutional users, many of which had their own internal networks.
A) expanded　　　B) contracted
C) attracted　　　D) extended

详解：选C。题意为：这种新的NSF网络吸引了越来越多的机构用户，其中许多用户有自己的内部网。A) expand意思是"扩张，扩展"；B) contract意思是"签约，订约"；C) attract意思是"吸引"；D) extend意思是"延伸，伸展"。

(CET-4 2009.6)

---

attraction [ə'trækʃən] *n.* 吸引，吸引力，引力
The Great Wall is a great tourist attraction drawing millions of visitors every year.
长城是个大的旅游景点，每年都吸引数百万的观光者。

---

camp [kæmp] *n.* 野营，营地，兵营
I want to go to Summer Camp. What about you?
我想参加夏令营，你呢？

---

excursion [iks'kəːʃən] *n.* 远足，短途旅行
We are planning to go on an excursion.
我们打算做一个短途旅行。

---

picnic ['piknik] *n.* 郊游，野餐
　　　　　　 vi. 野餐
The Browns intended to have a picnic in the woods yesterday, but the weather ruled it out.
布朗一家昨天本打算去野餐，但是天气状况使得计划告吹。

---

plan [plæn] *vt.&n.* 计划，打算
This summer, we plan to take a vacation to seaside resort.
今年夏天，我们计划去海滨胜地度假。

---

pressure ['preʃə] *n.* 压力，压，按
Please release your pressure after getting the lesson.
得到这个教训后请释放下你的压力。

tourism ['tuərism] *n.* 旅游业，观光业
Yunnan is famous for its tourism.
云南以旅游业闻名。

scenery ['si:nəri] *n.* 舞台布景，风景
The scenery of the new development area is amazing and I want to live there.
新开发区的景色很迷人，我想住在那里。

🔍 考点：scenery, scene, sight, view
的区别：scenery是总称，指自然
风光；scene是"景色，景象"的
意思，指某一处的自然风光，
scenery是由多个scene组成的景
色；sight是"风景，名声"的意
思，用复数形式，多指人文景观；
view是"景色，风景"的意思，是
从人的角度，一眼所看到的景色。

seaside ['si:said] *n.* 海滨，海滨城镇
adj. 海滨的，海边的
Which seaside city do you want to go most?
你最想去哪一座海滨城市？

sightseeing ['saitsi:iŋ] *n.* 观光，游览
I decide to go to Beijing to have a sightseeing this weekend.
这个周末我决定去北京观光旅游。

🔍 考点：go sightseeing 去观光
do some sightseeing 观光

tour [tuə] *vi.&n.* 旅行，游历
It will certainly be interesting for you to tour in France.
去法国旅游你一定会感兴趣。

🔍 考点：tour表示旅行一周再转回原出发
地，在强调这种意思时不能用
journey, trip等词。

tourist ['tuərist] *n.* 旅游者，观光者
Most scenery spots provide restaurant caterings to tourists.
大部分景点都有专供旅游者就餐的饭店。

other ['ʌðə] *adj.* 另外的，其余的
I really admired him, he journeyed frequently to America and other places.
我真的很羡慕他，他常到美国及别的地方去旅行。

trunk [trʌŋk] *n.* 树干，大衣箱，皮箱
She stowed all her clothes in the trunk.
她把她所有的衣服藏入箱内。

stress [stres] *n.* 压力，重音
vt. 着重
He couldn't bear the immense stress and finally left the firm.
他无法承受巨大的压力最终离开了那家公司。

travel ['trævl] *vi.&vt.&n.* 旅行
We have not decided where we should travel to.
我们还不知道要到哪里去旅行。

🔍 考点：travel, journey, trip, tour,
excursion, voyage的区别：travel
是"旅行"的统称，当名词时
是不可数；journey指（陆地上
的）旅行；trip指（短途）旅行；
tour指访问几个地方后返回到出发
地的旅行；excursion 指（结伴或
团体）短途旅行；voyage指（水
上）旅行，航行。

外出游玩 爬山

climb [klaim] *vi.* 攀登，爬；*vt.* 爬
He puffed a little after climbing onto the top of the mountain.
爬上山顶后，他有些气喘。

mount [maunt] *vt.* 登上，爬上；*n.* 山
Though normally I can walk for miles without taking any rest, I found today's walk to Mount Tai very tiring.
虽然平时我可以不间歇地走上很多路，但今天爬泰山我还是觉得很疲惫。

onto ['ɔntu] *prep.* 到……上
She set her mind to climb onto the top of the moutain.
她下定决心要爬到山顶。

pant [pænt] *n.* 气喘，心跳，短裤（通常用复数）；*vi.* 喘气
He began to pant before he reached the top of the hill.
在到达山顶之前他已经开始喘气了。

peak [pi:k] *n.* 山顶，巅；*adj.* 最高的
They have reached the peak of the mountain before dark.
他们在天黑之前到达了山顶。

puff [pʌf] *vi.* 喘气，趾高气扬
n. （一）喷，（一）吹
He didn't puff at all after arriving the peak of this mountain.
爬到山顶后，他一点儿也不喘。

reach [ri:tʃ] *vt.* 抵达，伸出；*vi.* 达到
We managed to reach the top of the mountain, and half an hour later we began to descend.
我们成功地到达山顶，半小时后开始下山。

steep [sti:p] *adj.* 险峻的，陡峭的
He toiled up a steep slope to see the sunrise.
为了看日出他很吃力地走上一个陡峭的斜坡。

summit ['sʌmit] *n.* 最高点，顶峰，顶点
He's too tired to make the summit.
他已经疲倦得到不了山顶了。

外出游玩 探险考察

explore [iks'plɔ:] *vi.&vt.* 探险，探索
These scientists explored the Arctic regions last year.
去年，这些科学家们探测了北极地带。

risky ['riski] *n.* 危险的，冒险的
He was mad; he had staked all his money on the risky business.
他疯了，他将所有的钱都押在这个有风险的生意上。

search [sə:tʃ] *vi.&vt.&n.* 搜寻，寻找，探查
In rudderless despair, he began to search for ideological sustenance.
在失去航向的绝望中，他开始寻找思想寄托。

🔍 考点：search 表示"搜查"；search for 表示"寻找，搜寻"；search... for... 表示"搜查……以寻找……:"

traverse ['trævə:s] *vt.* 横越，横切，横断
They traversed hundreds of miles of desert on foot.
他们徒步穿过数百英里的沙漠。

venture ['ventʃə] *vi.&n.* 冒险；*vt.* 敢于
I won't venture a step farther to ask her.
我没勇气再上前一步去问她。

worthwhile [ˌwə:θ'wail] *adj.* 值得花时间的
It is worthwhile to take a risk.
冒险是值得的。

🔍 考点：worth one's while 值得（去花时间、金钱等）的

艺术欣赏 阅读

article ['ɑ:tikl] *n.* 文章，条款，物品
I was asked to contribute an article on American culture.
我被约稿写一篇有关美国文化的文章。

book [buk] *n.* 书，书籍；*vt.* 预订
I love books, in evenings I bury myself in them.
我喜欢读书，每天晚上我都埋头读书。

bookmark ['bukmɑ:k] *n.* 书签
I use the beautiful card he gave me as a bookmark.
我用他送我的漂亮卡片做书签。

catalog ['kætəlɔ:g] *n.* 目录，目录册
A library catalogue tells readers the names of all books in the library.
图书目录会告诉读者图书馆内所有书的书名。

chapter ['tʃæptə] *n.* 章，回，篇
Jack can recite chapter 1 of this book.
杰克会背这本书的第一章。

content [kən'tent] *n.* 内容，目录，容量
adj. 满意的，满足的
The teacher asked him to summarize the main content of that article.
老师要他总结一下文章的主要内容。

🔍 考点：content, satisfy的区别：satisfy 表示使人的要求、希望得到完全的满足，若只表示使人在一定程度上感到满足，要用content。

edit ['edit] *vt.* 编辑，校订，主编，剪辑
He spent three months in editing this book.

他编这本书花了3个月时间。

edition [i'diʃən] *n.* 版，版本，版次
The famous singer has many pairs of limited
edition shoes.
那个著名的女歌星有很多双限量版的鞋子。

editorial [edi'tɔ:riəl] *adj.* 编辑的，编者的，
社论的
n. 社论，重要评论
This is our editorial assistant.
这位是我们的编辑助理。

essay ['esei] *n.* 短文，散文，小品文
Yesterday I came across an interesting essay on
Dante.
昨天我偶然地读到一篇关于但丁的有趣文章。

extensive [iks'tensiv] *adj.* 广阔的，广泛的
You can get extensive knowledge by reading.
读书可以得到很多知识。

heading ['hediŋ] *n.* 标题，题词，题名
What is the heading of this passage?
这篇文章的标题是什么？

index ['indeks] *n.* 索引，指数，指标
Every book has an index in the front of it.
每本书开头都会有一个索引。

考点：index当"索引"讲时，复数形式
是indexes；当"指标，指数"讲
时，复数形式是indices。

journal ['dʒə:nl] *n.* 日报，杂志，日志
He kept a journal of his wanderings around the
world.
他记录了一本自己环游世界的日记。

newspaper ['nju:speipə] *n.* 报纸，报
The newspaper provides not only foreign news but
also domestic news.
这家报纸不仅刊登国外新闻也刊登国内新闻。

page [peidʒ] *n.* 页
Pleased do the exercises on page 10.
请做第10页上的练习题。

paragraph ['pærəgrɑ:f] *n.* （文章的）段，节
Can you translate this paragraph into English?
你能把这段译成英文吗？

margin ['mɑ:dʒin] *n.* 页边的空白，余地，
利润
When I read books, I always make some notes in
the margin.
我读书的时候，总在页边空白处做笔记。

真题

You shouldn't have written in the ____ since
the book belongs to the library.
A) edge   B) border
C) interval   D) margin

详　解：选D。题意为：你不该在页边空白
处写东西，因为这本书是从图书馆借的。
A) edge意思是"刀刃，物体的边缘"；B)
border意思是"边界，边缘"；C) interval意
思是"时间间隔"；D) margin意思是"页边
空白"。

(CET-4 2003.6)

preface ['prefis] *n.* 序言，前言，引语
I want to know what the writer says in the preface
of the book.
我想知道作者在这本书的序言里说了些什么。

publication [ˌpʌbli'keiʃən] *n.* 公布，出版，
出版物
This book he has written is ready for publication.
他写的这本书准备出版了。

考点：publication 是publish的名词形
式，而publicity 是public的名词
形式。

publish ['pʌbliʃ] *vt.* 公布，发表，出版
This book will be published soon.
这本书不久将会发行。

punctuate [ˌpʌŋktjueit] *vt.* 在……中间加标
点，强调，突
出，不时打断
vi. 使用标点，加
标点
Please punctuate the transcription of this speech
correctly.
请给这段讲话文本加上正确的标点符号。

read [ri:d] *vt.* 读，看懂；*vi.* 读
Do you know who read this memorial speech?
你知道念这篇悼词的人是谁吗？

reader ['ri:də] *n.* 读者，读物，读本
The story is full of surprises which cause the reader to catch his breath.
这个故事充满紧张情节，使读者透不过气来。

reading ['ri:diŋ] *n.* 读，阅读，读书
I've benefited a lot from the extensive reading.
广泛的阅读使我受益匪浅。

skim [skim] *vt.* 掠过，擦过，略读
The teacher asked us to skim the text to grasp its main idea.
老师要求我们通篇快速浏览，抓住文章大意.

specially ['speʃəli] *adv.* 特别地，明确地
Lu Xun's work was especially characteristic of the age.
鲁迅的作品具有时代的特征。

supplement ['sʌplimənt] *vt.&n.* 增补，补充
Sunday supplement is her favorite.
星期天附刊是她的最爱。

🕐考点：the supplement to the book 翻译为 "该书的增刊"

worthy ['wə:ði] *adj.* 有价值的，值得的
This is a book worthy of intensive reading.
这是一本值得专心阅读的书。

🕐考点：worth, worthy用法的区别：be worth + n. = be worthy of + n. 值得……be worth doing sth. = be worthy of being done= be worthy to be done. 值得做……

context ['kɔntekst] *n.* 背景，上下文
I advice you to guess the meaning of words from the context of this article.
我建议你从文章的语境中猜出词义。

copyright ['kɔpirait] *n.* 版权，著作权
Copyright is very important to the writer at present.
如今，版权对作者很重要。

contemporary [kən'tempərəri] *adj.* 当代的，同时代的
Is it a coincidence that many contemporary writers published articles to attack his cruelty?
许多同时代的作家们发表文章抨击他的残酷行径，这难道是巧合吗?

about [ə'baut] *prep.* 关于，在……周围
I know something about savages from books.
我从书上得知一些有关野蛮人的事情。

艺术欣赏 古玩字画

art [ɑ:t] *n.* 艺术，美术，技术
His major is English，but he is very interested in art.
他的专业是英语，却对美术特别感兴趣。

brush [brʌʃ] *n.* 刷子，毛刷，画笔 *vt.* 刷，拂；*vi* 触到
I need a brush to pain this picture.
我需要一支画笔来画画。

🕐考点：brush aside 不理，不顾
brush off 不愿见，打发掉
brush up 重温，再练

canvas ['kænvəs] *n.* 油画，粗帆布
The old painter's canvases were sold out as soon as he took them out.
那位老画家的油画刚一拿出来就出售完了。

china ['tʃainə] *n.* 瓷器，瓷料
Sometimes a piece of china is worth millions *yuan*.
有时候一件瓷器会值上百万元。

collect [kə'lekt] *vt.* 收集；*vi.* 收款
She likes to collect all kinds of artworks.
她喜欢收集各种艺术品。

collection [kə'lekʃən] *n.* 搜集，收集，收藏品
It took me ten years to collect those stamps.
收集那些邮票花费了我10年的时间。

draw [drɔ:] *vt.* 画，划，拖，拨出
What conclusions can you draw from all the facts that we have collected?
从我们所收集到的所有事实中你可以得出什么结论来呢?

🕐考点：draw in 天渐黑；draw on 利用
draw up 起草，拟定

drawing ['drɔ:iŋ] *n.* 图画，素描，绘图
Our maths teacher is drawing two parallel lines on the blackboard.
我们数学老师正在黑板上画两条平行线。

delicate ['delikit] *adj.* 纤细的，易碎的
Rose broke the delicate glass that her father likes best, so she dared not tell him.
罗丝打破了那只爸爸最喜欢的精品玻璃杯，所以她不敢告诉他。

真题

During the process, great care has to be taken to protect the ____ silk from damage.
A) tender   B) delicate
C) sensible   D) sensitive

详　解：选B。题意为：在加工时应格外小心，不要弄坏这精美的丝绸。A) tender意思是"柔嫩的，脆弱的"；B) delicate 意思是"精美的"；C) sensible意思是"明智的，明显的"；D) sensitive意思是"敏感的，灵活的"。

(CET-4 2002.6)

fake [feik] *n.* 假货，赝品，骗子；*adj.* 假冒的，冒充的；*vt.* 伪造，伪装
He isn't really sick; he's just faking.
他没有真的生病，只是假装而已。

forge [fɔ:dʒ] *vt.* 伪造，假冒，锻造，锤炼
Forging an official document is forbade in law.
法律规定，禁止伪造官方文件。

gallery ['gæləri] *n.* 长廊，游廊，画廊
The gallery is a treasure of modern art.
这个画廊是现代艺术的宝库。

genuine ['dʒenjuin] *adj.* 真的，真正的
He held a bottle of genuine vintage wine.
他拿着一瓶真正的佳酿品牌葡萄酒。

handwriting ['hænd,raitiŋ] *n.* 笔迹，手迹，书法
He's the student whose handwriting is the best in my class.
他就是我班里书法最好的那个学生。

outline ['əutlain] *n.* 轮廓，略图，大纲 *vt.* 概述，概括
What can you find from the outline of the painting?
从这幅画的轮廓图里你能发现什么东西吗？

paint [peint] *vt.* 画，油漆；*vi* 绘画
My mother doesn't allow me to paint my nails.

妈妈不准我染指甲。

🔹 考点：paint in oils / water colors 画油画（水彩画）

painter ['peintə] *n.* 漆工，画家，绘画者
The painter made a sketch of the queen immediately.
画家立刻给女王画了张素描。

painting ['peintiŋ] *n.* 油画，绘画，着色
Do you think it's right to make a bid of five thousand *yuan* for a painting?
你觉得为一幅油画出价5000元合适吗？

picture ['piktʃə] *n.* 画，图片；*vt.* 画
How about giving a tint to the picture drawn by him?
给他画的这幅画着一下色怎么样？

portrait ['pɔ:trit] *n.* 肖像，画像
The gallery is exhibiting a series of portraits.
这座画廊正在展示一系列的肖像画。

seal [si:l] *n.* 封蜡，印记，海豹；*vt.* 封
My father impressed his seal on the painting.
爸爸在那幅画上盖上了自己的印章。
🔹 考点：seal off 封闭，封锁

sketch [sketʃ] *n.* 略图，速写，概略
The sketch is apparently viable in finding the buried treasure.
从表面来看这个草图在寻找宝藏时是可行的。
🔹 考点：sketch out 简要地叙述

studio ['stju:diəu] *n.* 画室，录音室，播音室
The kitchen was filled with the rich odour of dishes.
厨房里充满了浓郁的饭香。

艺术欣赏 音乐

band [bænd] *n.* 乐队，带，波段
He wanted to join in the jazz band when he was a student at school.
他还是在校生时，想加入爵士乐队。

cassette [kə'set] *n.* 盒式录音带，盒子
I bought a lot of cassettes to learn singing songs when I was in middle school.

初中的时候，我买了很多磁带来学唱歌。

classic ['klæsik] *n.* 杰作，古典作品，第一流艺术家
adj. 最优秀的，传统的，古典的

It is a classic sanctuary in which the rationalist fancy may take refuge.
这是一所古雅的圣殿，理性主义者可以躲在其中。

classical ['klæsikəl] *adj.* 古典的，经典的
We have enjoyed the classical ballet in the concert.
我们在音乐会中欣赏到了古典芭蕾舞。

考点：classic, classical的区别：classic的主要意思是"第一流的，最上等的"；This is a really classic French champagne.这确实是上等的法国香槟；classical指古希腊、罗马的文学、艺术，在文学艺术上，他分别与romantic（浪漫主义）或popular music（流行音乐）相对。

component [kəm'pəunənt] *n.* 组成部分，分，组件
Theses things are the components of an engine.
这些东西是机车的部件。

compose [kəm'pəuz] *vt.* 组成，构成，创作
You don't know that water is composed of hydrogen and oxygen?
你不知道水是由氢和氧组成的？

考点：be composed of由……组成

composer [kɔm'pəuzə] *n.* 作曲家，创作者
Although he is deaf, Beethoven is a famous composer.
尽管耳朵聋了，贝多芬还是成为了一位著名的作曲家。

concert ['kɔnsət] *n.* 音乐会，演奏会
vt. 使协调
Would you like to go to a concert with me tomorrow?
明天你想和我一起去看音乐会吗？

考点：in concert 一齐，一致

drum [drʌm] *n.* 鼓，鼓状物，圆桶
We are very familiar with the percussion, such as drums, gongs, xylophones and so on.
我们对打击乐器非常熟悉，比如鼓、铜锣、木琴等等。

考点：drum up 竭力争取，招揽生意

guitarist [gi'tɑːrist] *n.* 吉他手
He is a genius guitarist.
他是一个天才吉他手。

hobby ['hɔbi] *n.* 业余爱好，癖好
Reading is my only hobby.
读书是我唯一的爱好。

horn [hɔːn] *n.* 号角，警报器，角
He used to blow the horn in the school orchestra.
他曾经在校管弦乐队中负责吹号。

instrument ['instrumənt] *n.* 仪器，工具，乐器
He can play nearly every musical instrument.
他几乎会弹奏每一种乐器。

microphone ['maikrəfəun] *n.* 话筒，麦克风
He gave a tap at the microphone before singing.
他在唱歌前先轻叩了一下话筒。

music ['mjuːzik] *n.* 音乐，乐曲，乐谱
The boy is endowed with a gift in music, and he promises to be a fine singer.
这个男孩天生有音乐才能，他很有可能成为一名优秀的歌手。

musical ['mjuːzikəl] *adj.* 音乐的，和谐的
I am invited to attend a musical soiree this evening.
我被邀请参加今天晚上的音乐晚会。

musician [mjuː'ziʃən] *n.* 音乐家，作曲家
The musician has composed more than 1000 songs in his whole life.
这个音乐家一生当中创作了1000多首歌曲。

orchestra ['ɔːkistrə] *n.* 管弦乐队
Who is going to conduct the orchestra tonight?
谁指挥今晚的管弦乐队呢？

pop [pɔp] *n.* 流行音乐，流行歌曲
n. 砰的一声，爆破声
The eccentric boy has a rage for pop music.
这个古怪的男孩对流行音乐有狂热爱好。

rhythm ['riðəm] *n.* 韵律，格律，节奏
The poetry has cadence or rhythm in most situations.
在大多数情况下诗歌都有韵律或节奏。

tone [təun] *n.* 音，腔调，声调
You shouldn't use the commanding tone to irritate him.
你不该用命令式的口吻激怒他。
考点：tone down（使）缓和

tune [tju:n] *n.* 调子，和谐；*vt.* 调谐
He played the tune from time to time.
他把那支曲子演奏了一遍又一遍。
考点：in tune with 与……协调，与……一致；out of tune 不协调，不一致；tune in (to) 收听，收看

vocal ['vəukəl] *adj.* 声音的，口头的，声乐的，直言不讳的；*n.* 元音，声乐作品
The tongue is one of the important vocal organs.
舌头是重要的发声器官之一。

volume ['vɔlju:m] *n.* 卷，册，容积，音量
Please turn down your speaker's volume.
请关小麦克风音量。

piano [pi'ɑ:nəu] *n.* 钢琴
You should tune your piano before you start playing.
在开始演奏之前你应该先给钢琴调调音。

trumpet ['trʌmpit] *n.* 喇叭，小号
Now the bird is singing with the trumpet.
现在这只鸟正在和着喇叭唱歌。

violin [ˌvaiə'lin] *n.* 小提琴
He has played the violin for nine years.
他拉小提琴已经9年了。

turnout ['tə:'naut] *n.* 生产量，出席，到场人数，岔道，清理，打扮
This year's concert attracted a record turnout.
今年的演唱会吸引的观众之多创下了纪录。

aloud [ə'laud] *adv.* 出声地，大声地
Please read this poem aloud.
请大声地读这首诗。

艺术欣赏 舞蹈

dance ['dɑ:ns] *vi.* 跳舞，摇晃；*n.* 舞
Would you mind dancing with me?
能和我跳支舞吗？

disco = discotheque ['diskəu] *n.* 迪斯科
I guess you can dance to the disco music.
我想你可以跟着迪斯科乐曲跳舞。

imitate ['imiteit] *vt.* 模仿，仿效，仿制
Tom often imitates his father.
汤姆总是模仿他的父亲。

真题

At yesterday's party, Elizabeth's boyfriend amused us by _____ Charlie Chaplin.
A) modeling   B) imitating
C) following   D) copying

详　解：选B。题意为：昨天的派对上，伊丽莎白的男朋友模仿查理·卓别林逗乐了我们。A) model意思是"以……为模式"；B) imitate意思是"模仿"；C) follow意思是"追随"；D) copy意思是"复制"。

(CET-4 2004.6)

spin [spin] *vt.* 纺，使旋转；*n.* 旋转
A dancer can usually spin on toes.
舞者通常能够踮着脚尖旋转。
考点：spin out 拖长时间，使尽可能多维持一段时间

艺术欣赏 戏剧

comedy ['kɔmidi] *n.* 喜剧，喜剧作品
The comedy actor wore a tartan skirt, which made the audience laugh.
那个喜剧演员穿了一条方格花纹的裙子，逗得观众们都笑了。

comic ['kɔmik] *adj.* 喜剧的，令人发笑的
n. 滑稽品，令人发笑的成分
I don't like that movie, you know the comic scenes were overdone.
我不喜欢那个电影，里面的滑稽场面演得太过夸张了。

dramatic [drə'mætik] *adj.* 引人注目的，戏剧的
Britain varies in scenery. In particular, there is a dramatic contrast between "highland" and "lowland".
英国自然风光丰富多彩，高地与低地的对比尤其鲜明。

opera ['ɔpərə] *n.* 歌剧
To tell you the truth, I prefer opera to drama.
说实话，与戏剧比起来，我比较喜欢歌剧。

perform [pə'fɔ:m] *vt.* 履行，执行，演出
The girls performed a very graceful dance for their classmates.
女孩们为同学们表演了优美的舞蹈。

performance [pə'fɔ:məns] *n.* 履行，演出，行为
She is a versatile person in her team and usually gives performance to the public.
她在该小组里是一个多才多艺的人，经常在公众面前演出。

 真题

Numerous studies already link the first meal of the day to better classroom＿＿＿.
A) function   B) behavior
C) performance   D) display

详　解：选C。题意为：大量研究表明早餐对改进课堂表现有帮助。A) function意思是"智能，功能"；B) behavior 意思是"行为，举动"；C) performance意思是"表现，表演"；D) display意思是"展示，陈列"。

(CET-4 2006.6)

plot [plɔt] *n.* 小块土地，情节；*vt.* 密谋
We have to admit that the plot of the novel is ingeniously conceived.
我们不得不承认小说情节的构思相当巧妙。

render ['rendə] *vt.* 表示，表演，给予，使得
I am afraid that he is not competent to render Othello.
我害怕他演不了奥赛罗。

script [skript] *n.* 剧本，字母表，笔记
The script staged pretty well.
这剧本舞台演出效果甚好。

setting ['setiŋ] *n.* 安装，调整，环境
The story in the novel has its setting in ancient Rome.
小说中这个故事的背景是在古罗马。

stage [steidʒ] *n.* 舞台，戏剧，阶段
She has a sense of fear to the stage.
她有舞台恐惧感。

🔍 考点：go (on) the stage 当演员

tragedy ['trædʒidi] *n.* 悲剧，惨事，惨案
I saw a genuine tragedy yesterday.
我昨天见证了一场真正的悲剧。

tragic ['trædʒik] *adj.* 悲剧性的，悲惨的
We felt sympathy for her tragic story.
我们对她的悲惨遭遇深表同情。

艺术欣赏 美术雕塑

artistic [ɑ:'tistik] *adj.* 艺术的，艺术家的
The Louvre is one of the world's famous artistic centers.
卢浮宫是世界有名的艺术中心之一。

artwork ['ɑ:twə:k] *n.* 插图，艺术品
She likes to collect various artworks.
她喜欢收集各种艺术品。

artificial [,ɑ:ti'fiʃəl] *adj.* 人工的，娇揉造作的
I found her eyebrow is artificial in a glance.
我一眼就看出她的眉毛是假的。

craft [krɑ:ft] *n.* 工艺，手艺，行业
He spent ten years to learn the craft of wood carver.
他花了10年时间学习雕木者的技艺。

design [di'zain] *vt.* 设计；*n.* 设计，图样
Your room is designed with good proportion.
你房间的设计比例很均衡。

🔍 考点：by design 有意地

elaborate [i'læbərət] *adj.* 复杂的，精心制作的
They plan an elaborate scheme to kill that man.
他们策划了一个周密的阴谋来杀掉那个男人。

handmade ['hændmeid] *adj.* 手工制作的
She bought some delicate handmade baby dresses.
她买了几件精致的手工婴儿服装。

* * *

knit [nit] *vt.* 把……编结，结合，皱眉
vi. 编织
I have been knitting a pair of gloves for about two months.
我近两个月一直在织手套。

* * *

precious ['preʃəs] *adj.* 珍贵的，宝贵的
The feathers of peacock are very precious for us.
孔雀毛对我们来说很珍贵。

* * *

statue ['stætju:] *n.* 塑像，雕像，铸像
The Statue of Liberty, located in US., embodies the spirit of freedom.
坐落在美国的自由女神像体现了其热爱自由的精神。

艺术欣赏 摄影

adjust [ə'dʒʌst] *vt.* 调整，调节，校正，
（改变……以）适应
You should adjust the focus of your camera before you take photos.
你应该在拍照之前调节下照相机的焦距。

真题

People need opportunities to make a "midlife review" to _____ to the later stage of employed life, and to plan for the transition to retirement.
A) transform   B) yield
C) adjust   D) suit

详　解：选C。题意为：人们需要有机会对人生做一个"中期检查"以便调整适应后期的职业生活，并计划一下退休前的过渡阶段。A) transform意思是"转换，改变"；B) yield意思是"生产，产出"；C) adjust to 意思是"调整，适应"；D) suit to意思是"适合"。

(CET-4 2009.12)

* * *

amateur ['æmətə:] *n.* 业余爱好，业余活动，外行；*adj.* 业余爱好的，业余的，外行的
You shouldn't let an amateur actor play such an important role.
你不应该让一个业余演员来扮演这样一个重要角色。

* * *

background ['bækgraund] *n.* 背景，后景，经历
My father took a picture of me with the pine tree in the background.
我爸爸以这个松树为背景给我照了一张相片。

* * *

camera ['kæmərə] *n.* 照相机，摄影机
Every camera we sell comes with a three-year guarantee.
我们出售的每台相机都有一张3年的保修单。

* * *

flash [flæʃ] *n.* 闪光；*vi.* 闪，闪烁
Jack gave a camera with a flash attachment to Tom.
杰克送给汤姆一架内置闪光装置的照相机。

* * *

lens [lenz] *n.* 透镜，镜片，镜头
This pair of glasses is made of plastic lens.
这副眼镜的镜片是用塑料做的。

* * *

photograph ['fəutəgra:f] *n.* 照片，相片
I enclose her photograph with this letter and hope you can get it.
我把她的照片放在这封信里，希望你能收到。

* * *

photographic [ˌfəutə'gra:fik] *adj.* 摄影的，摄影用的
You can ask the bank for help; it can provide photographic evidence of who used the machine.
你可以向银行求助，他们能提供使用过这台机器的人的录像资料。

* * *

posture ['pɔstʃə] *n.* 姿势，态度，情形
vt. 作……姿势，摆架子
vi. 摆出姿势，装模作样，故作姿态
I was attracted to those soldiers' erect posture.
我被这些站得笔直的士兵吸引住了。

* * *

shot [ʃɔt] *n.* 发射，拍摄，射门，铅球，尝试
A shot in which figures appear small against their background is a long shot.
人在画面中显得很小的镜头叫远景镜头。

考点：in a shot 立即，飞快地

艺术欣赏 参观展览

museum [mju:'ziəm] *n.* 博物馆，展览馆
There are lots of insect specimens on display in the museum.
博物馆里陈列着许多昆虫标本。

palace ['pælis] *n.* 宫，宫殿
In the past, royal palace was filled with intrigue.
在过去，皇宫里充满了勾心斗角。

park [pɑ:k] *n.* 公园，停车场
                vt. 停放，放置
The layout of the park is designed by a Frenchman.
这个公园的布局是一个法国人设计的。

display [dis'plei] *vt.* 陈列，展览，显示
On Sunday, the traditional Chinese painting is on display in the park.
星期日，公园里有国画展出。
🔍 **考点**：on display 在展览

exhibit [ig'zibit] *vt.* 显示，陈列，展览
He always exhibits calmness and alertness.
他总是表现得沉着机敏。

exhibition [ˌeksi'biʃən] *n.* 展览，陈列，展览会
Last Sunday, I went to see the exhibition of paintings by Picasso.
上星期日，我去参观了毕加索画展。
🔍 **考点**：make an exhibition of oneself 出洋相；on exhibition 在展览中

闲聊杂谈|Chatting

娱乐体育 明星艺人

comment ['kɔment] *v.* 评论，注释
I don't know what's in his mind, for he didn't comment on what I said.
我不知道他是怎么想的，因为他对我的话未作评论。

fame [feim] *n.* 名声，名望
The doctor's fame spread all over the country.
这位医生名震全国。

fan [fæn] *n.* （运动等）狂热爱好者，扇子，风扇；*vt.* 扇
There must be something wrong with the fan, it's making loud noises.
风扇一定出了什么故障，因为它发出很大的噪声。

influence ['influəns] *n.* 影响，势力
vt. 影响
School life has a great influence on the formation of a child's character.
学校生活对小孩个性的形成有很大影响。

🔍 考点：have an influence on sth. 对……有影响

influential [ˌinflu'enʃəl] *adj.* 有影响的，有权势的
In his day, he was a very influential writer.
在他那个年代，他是位非常有影响力的作家。

reputation [ˌrepju'teiʃən] *n.* 名誉，名声，好名声
Your reputation would be blemished if you take bribes.
如果你受贿，你的名声就会受到玷污。

🔍 考点：reputation, fame 都有 "名声" 的意思。reputation可指好名声，也可指坏名声，强调人心中的印象；fame 仅指好名声，强调较高的知名度。

succession [sək'seʃən] *n.* 连续，继任，继承
She has been awarded the best actress three years in succession.
她已连续3年获得最佳女主角了。

successive [sək'sesiv] *adj.* 连续的，接连的
He behaved nearly perfect in the successive rounds.
在相继几轮比赛中他表现得几乎完美。

throughout [θru:'aut] *prep.* 遍及
adv. 到处
The temple is famous throughout the world.
这个寺庙闻名于世界。

well-known ['wel'nəun] *adj.* 众所周知的，出名的
A well-known professor will give us a lecture about language the day after tomorrow.
一位知名的教授后天将给我们做一个关于语言的报告。

🔍 考点：well-known的最高级是best-known，而不是most well-known。

worldwide ['wə:ldwaid] *adj.* 遍及全球的
His dream is to be a poet of worldwide fame.
他的梦想是做一位举世闻名的诗人。

娱乐体育 花边新闻

expose [iks'pəuz] *vt.* 使暴露，揭露
When she smiled she exposed a set of perfect white teeth.
她笑时露出了一口漂亮的白牙。

exposure [iks'pəuʒə] *n.* 暴露，揭露，曝光
That movie star has got good exposure.
那位电影明星有很高的曝光率。

headline ['hedlain] *n.* 大字标题，新闻提要
The case became a headline in local news.
此案件成了当地头条新闻。

impact ['impækt] *n.* 影响，作用，冲击
There's no question that the news had a real impact on the public.
毫无疑问，这些新闻对公众确实产生了影响。

🔍考点：an impact / effect on
对……的影响

incident ['insidənt] *n.* 发生的事，事件
The incident did not affect him any more.
这件事对他的影响不大。

insider [in'saidə] *n.* 内部的人，知情者
They may had insider knowledge but didn't reported.
他们可能知道内情但是没有上报。

journalist ['dʒə:nəlist] *n.* 记者，新闻工作者
Xiaomei is a budding journalist in this field.
小美还是新闻界初出茅庐的记者。

media ['mi:djə] *n.* 新闻媒介，传播媒介
He suggested us not to neglect the power of the media.
他建议我们不要忽视媒体的力量。

真题

This research has attracted wide coverage in the _____ and has featured on BBC television's Tomorrow's World.
A) data　　　B) source
C) message　　D) media

详　解：选D。题意为：这项研究已经吸引了媒体的广泛报道，英国广播公司的电视节目"明天的世界"中也有专题报道。A) data 意思是"数据，资料"；B) source 意思是"消息，源泉"；C) message 意思是"通讯，消息"；D) media 意思是"媒体，媒介"。

(CET-4 2003.9)

medium ['mi:djəm] *n.* 媒质，中间
adj. 中等的，中间的
Most broadcasters argue that the power of the medium is exaggerated.
大多数播音员争论说媒体的作用被夸大了。

🔍考点：by / through the medium of...
通过，以……为媒介

news [nju:z] *n.* 新闻，消息
The CCTV news is broadcast at 19:00 every night.
新闻联播每晚7点钟播出。

private ['praivit] *adj.* 私人的，私下的
n. 士兵，列兵
I bitterly resent his attempts to interfere in my private affairs.
我非常讨厌他企图干涉我的私人事件。

🔍考点：in private 在私下，秘密地

remark [ri'ma:k] *vi.&vt.&n.* 评论，谈论
It's Tony's intemperate remarks got him into trouble.
托尼的言语肆无忌惮，惹出了是非。

rumour ['ru:mə] *n.* 谣言，谣传，传闻
The rumour percolated through the whole village.
那谣言在村子里慢慢流传开来。

scandal ['skændl] *n.* 丑事，丑行，流言飞语
I'll brand this scandal on my mind for ever.
我要永远把这个丑闻铭记在心。

spread [spred] *vt.* 伸开，传播
n. 传播
He spread the news that Helen has killed her husband around the town.
他在镇上到处传播海伦杀死她丈夫这一消息。

🔍考点：spread out 散开，伸展

widespread ['waidspred] *adj.* 分布广的，普遍的
He had to resign as manager for the widespread rumor of defalcation.
由于到处散布着他挪用公款的谣言，他不得不辞去经理的职位。

circulate ['sə:kjuleit] *vt.* 使循环；*vi.* 循环
People who circulate false news are to be punished.
散布流言者该受惩罚。

nightclub ['naitklʌb] *n.* 夜总会
I still haven't been to a nightclub yet.
我还没有去过夜店。

157

娱乐体育 体育赛事

coach [kəutʃ] *n.* 教练，长途公共汽车
The coach tried to analyse the cause of our defeat.
教练设法分析我们失败的原因。

compete [kəm'pi:t] *vi.* 比赛，竞争，对抗
He didn't compete in the finals of the race because of illness.
因为生病，他没有参加决赛。

competition [kɔmpi'tiʃən] *n.* 竞争，比赛
I was eliminated from the competition in the second round.
我在第二轮比赛中被淘汰。

competitive [kəm'petitiv] *adj.* 竞争的，比赛的
English language teaching is a very competitive market in China.
在中国，英语教学是一个充满竞争的市场。

competitor [kəm'petitə] *n.* 竞争者，对手
I think it's a good thing to have a preeminent competitor.
我认为有一个出类拔萃的对手对我们来说是一件幸事。

contest ['kɔntest] *vt.* 争夺，争取，辩驳
n. 竞赛，比赛
What is your final score in the contest?
你在比赛中的最后得分是多少？

contestant [kən'testənt] *n.* 竞争者，参加竞赛者
All contestants are required to wear helmets to assure their safety.
所有参赛者都必须戴上头盔以确保安全。

defeat [di'fi:t] *vt.* 战胜，击败，挫败
At the news that their army was defeated, all the people fell in gloomy silence.
听到他们军队战败的消息，所有人都感到沮丧沉默不语。

match [mætʃ] *n.* 比赛，对手，火柴
vt. （和）相配，（和）相称
vi. 相配，使适合
She thought she could beat anyone at tennis, but she's met her match in him.
她以为她打网球所向无敌，但遇到他却是旗鼓相当。

medal ['medl] *n.* 奖章，勋章，纪念章
As an athlete, she has won five gold medals and two silver ones for her country.
作为一名运动员，她已经为自己的国家赢得了5枚金牌，两枚银牌。

opponent [ə'pəunənt] *n.* 对手，敌手，对抗者
He taught his students how to wrestle with their opponents.
他教他的学生们如何同对手摔跤。

quick [kwik] *adj.* 快的，敏捷的
The boy wants to win the game and he runs as quickly as a deer.
男孩想赢得比赛，跑得像鹿一样快。

quicken ['kwikən] *vt. & vi.* 加快
Hearing this, the man quickened his pace.
听到这些，那个人加快了脚步。

quickly ['kwikli] *adv.* 快，迅速
The girl gave a snort of disgust, and went away quickly.
女孩厌恶地哼了一声，快速离开了。

race [reis] *n.* 比赛，竞争，人种，民族
Some girls were lagging behind in the race.
一些女孩子在比赛中落在了后面。

rapid ['ræpid] *adj.* 快的；*n.* 急流
The runner was so rapid that nobody could catch up with him.
这个运动员跑得太快了，没有人能追上他。

rapidly ['ræpidli] *adv.* 迅速地
I worried so much about her; you know her health is degenerating rapidly.
我很担心她，她的健康状况在迅速恶化。

vital ['vaitl] *adj.* 极其重要的，充满生机的
It is absolutely vital that we must win the match.
我们必须赢得这场比赛，这是至关重要的。

whistle ['wisl] *n.* 口哨；*vi.* 吹口哨
I heard the wind whistling outside the window.
我听见风在窗外呼呼地刮着。

win [win] *vi.* 获胜，赢；*vt.* 赢得
Our team has won the game after two months' practice.

经过两个月的训练，我们队获得了胜利。

🔍 **考点**：win, beat, defeat都有"战胜，打败"的意思：win后面只接事或物，beat, defeat后面接人。
eg. win a game / war 赢得比赛（战争）；beat / defeat a team / nation 打败一个队（国家）。

---

award [ə'wɔ:d] *n.* 奖，奖品，判定
vt. 奖赏

You know my naughty son received an award yesterday.
我那调皮的儿子昨天得了一个奖。

真题

The mayor _____ the police officer a medal of honor for his heroic deed in rescuing the earthquake victims.
A) rewarded   B) awarded
C) credited   D) prized

详　解：选B。题意为：市长授予那位警察荣誉奖章，以表彰他在抢救地震受害者时的英勇行为。A) reward sb. with…意思是"酬劳（奖赏）某人……"，泛指付给一项明确的有利行为的钱；B) award意思是"奖赏"，后跟双宾；C) credit sb. / sth. with意思是"认为某人（某事）具有……"；D) prize意思是"对优胜者或胜利者的奖励"。

(CET-4 2005.6)

---

champion ['tʃæmpjən] *n.* 冠军，得胜者
She is a table tennis champion of the world, and her parents are proud of it.
她是个世界乒乓球冠军，她的父母以此为荣。

---

challenge ['tʃælindʒ] *n.* 挑战，要求，需要
He received our challenge to game.
他接受了我们进行比赛的挑战。

---

ending ['endiŋ] *n.* 结尾，结局，死亡
A burst of hand-clapping followed the ending of the speech.
演讲过后响起一阵掌声。

人生梦想 恋爱家庭

abandon [ə'bændən] *vt.* 丢弃，放弃，抛弃
n. 放纵，放情

That woman wanted a son, so she abandoned her own daughter.
那个女人想要个儿子，于是就把自己的亲生女儿给抛弃了。

🔍 **考点**：abandon oneself to 沉溺于；with abandon 放任地，放纵地

---

adopt [ə'dɔpt] *vt.* 采用，收养，采取，正式通过，批准
If you want to get more profit, you should adopt my suggestion.
如果你想赢利更多的话，就应该接受我的建议。

---

baby ['beibi] *n.* 婴儿，孩子气的人
The baby of yours is so cute.
你家小孩真可爱。

---

bear [bɛə] *vt.* 容忍，负担，生育
It's hard for you to raise a child by yourself. You know you must bear all expenses.
一个人抚养孩子很难，你必须承担一切费用。

🔍 **考点**：bear down 竭尽全力，压倒；bear out 证实；bear up 坚持下去，振作起来；bear with 忍受，容忍

---

beloved [bi'lʌvid] *adj.* 为……所爱的
n. 爱人

The book is for my beloved.
这本书献给我所爱的人。

---

betray [bi'trei] *vt.* 背叛，辜负，泄漏
I think it's out of character to betray our friend.
我认为出卖我们的朋友不合适。

---

birthright ['bə:θrait] *n.* 生来就有的权利，长子继承权
Freedom is our birthright.
自由是我们与生俱来的权利。

---

birth [bə:θ] *n.* 分娩，出生，出身
Though he was of humble birth, he achieved great results.
虽然他出身卑微，却取得了巨大成就。

🔍 **考点**：give birth to 生（孩子），产生

born [bɔːn] *adj.* 天生的，出生的
The baby was born without mother.
那个宝宝生下来就没了妈妈。

brother ['brʌðə] *n.* 兄弟，同事，同胞
My brother is a lawyer as well as an interpreter.
我哥哥是名翻译，也是名律师。

chase [tʃeis] *n.* 追逐，追赶，追求
He doesn't have the courage to chase the girl he has adored for ages.
他没有勇气去追求那个他爱慕多年的女孩子。

couple ['kʌpl] *n.* 夫妇，（一）对，几个
It was a shock to the couple that their youngest daughter had contracted tuberculosis.
最小的女儿患了肺结核，那对夫妇十分震惊。

cousin ['kʌzn] *n.* 堂（或表）兄弟（姐妹）
Having nothing else to do on the weekend, she was delighted to go shopping with her cousin.
她周末无事可做，所以很乐意跟她的表姐去购物。

darling ['dɑːliŋ] *n.* 亲爱的人，宠儿
Why are you crying, my darling?
亲爱的，你为什么哭啊？

daughter ['dɔːtə] *n.* 女儿
The merchant's mind reeled when he learned that his daughter had been abducted.
得知女儿被人拐走，这个商人只觉得一阵眩晕。

discard [dis'kɑːd] *vt.* 丢弃，抛弃，遗弃
He discards his wife for another woman.
他为了另外一个女人遗弃了他的妻子。

divorce [di'vɔːs] *n.* 离婚，离异；*vi.* 离婚
The woman had a lot of lovers, so her husband divorced her.
那女的有很多情人，所以她丈夫与她离婚了。
🔍 考点：divorce from sb. 与某人离婚

engagement [in'geidʒmənt] *n.* 订婚，婚约，约会
Owing to a previous engagement, I can't be able to come.
因事先另有约会，我无法前来。
🔍 考点：engagement with sb. 与某人的约会，邀请
engagement to sb. 与某人的婚约

folk [fəuk] *n.* 人们，家属，亲属
The aged are taken care of in the old folk's home.
老年人在养老院里受到照顾。

gay [gei] *adj.* 同性恋的，快乐的，鲜明的 *n.* 男同性恋者
She looked young, beautiful and gay.
她看上去很年轻、漂亮、快乐。

generation [ˌdʒenə'reiʃən] *n.* 一代，一代人，产生
He is arguably the best actor of his generation.
他是那个时代最好的演员。

heir [ɛə] *n.* 后嗣，继承人
This old man didn't give his possessions to his heirs.
老人并没有把财产留给自己的继承人。

honeymoon ['hʌnimuːn] *n.* 蜜月
My colleague, Mary, became more beautiful when she returned from the honeymoon.
我的同事玛丽度蜜月回来变得更漂亮了。

household ['haushəuld] *n.* 家庭，户，家务
Joyfulness enveloped the household.
快乐的气氛环绕着这一家子。

housewife ['hauswaif] *n.* 家庭主妇
She is a luxurious housewife.
她是一个奢侈的家庭主妇。

inherent [in'hiərənt] *adj.* 固有的，内在的，生来就有的
This design solves the problem of the inherent stability of this product.
这个设计解决了该产品内在稳定性的难题。

inherit [in'herit] *vt.* 继承，遗传得来
He intended that his son should inherit the possessions.
他打算让他的儿子继承他的财产。

lesbian ['lezbiən] *n.* 女同性恋者 *adj.* 女同性恋的
She denied she had a lesbian love affair with her secretary.
她否认和自己的秘书有同性恋情。

marriage ['mæridʒ] *n.* 结婚，婚姻，婚礼
The biggest obstacle of my marriage is my parents' opposition.

我结婚的最大障碍是父母的反对。

married ['mærid] *adj.* 已婚的，婚姻的
She was accused of adultery with a married man by her husband.
丈夫控告她与一个已婚男人通奸。

marry ['mæri] *vt.* 娶，嫁；*vi.* 结婚
Having heard that her daughter decided to marry a commoner, the lady nearly fainted on the ground.
听到女儿要嫁给一个平民，那位夫人差点晕倒在地上。

punch [pʌntʃ] *vt.* 冲出，用拳猛击 *n.* 冲压机，拳打
The crazy man gave a punch in his wife's chest.
那个疯狂的人对着自己妻子的胸部打了一拳。

pursue [pə'sju:] *vt.* 追赶，追踪，进行
It's quite common that boys like to pursue elusive girls.
男孩们喜欢追求那些让人难以捉摸的女孩，这很正常。

pursuit [pə'sju:t] *n.* 追赶，追求，事务
The cruel murderer was captured without much pursuit.
那个残忍的杀人犯没有经过多少追捕就被捉住了。

真题

There are many people who believe that the use of force ＿＿＿ political ends can never be justified.
A) in search of   B) in pursuit of
C) in view of   D) in light of

详　解：选B。题意为：许多人认为运用武力实现政治目的永远不可能是正当的。A) in search of意思为"寻找"；B) in pursuit of意思为"追求，实行"；C) in view of意思为"鉴于，考虑到"；D) in light of意思为"根据，鉴于，考虑到"。
(CET-4 2003.12)

romantic [rə'mæntik] *adj.* 浪漫的，传奇的
I think Mr. Smith is a romantic man.
我认为史密斯先生是一个浪漫的男士。

widow ['widəu] *n.* 寡妇
The poor widow lives a hard life.

这个可怜的寡妇过着艰苦的生活。

mate [meit] *n.* 伙伴，同事，配偶 *vt.* 结伴，使交配
They work very well; the male hunts for food while his mate guards the nest.
他们合作得很好，雄鸟出去觅食的时候，它的配偶就守护着鸟窝。

mother ['mʌðə] *n.* 母亲，妈妈
My mother is bargaining with the street vendor over the price.
妈妈正在与街贩讨价还价呢。

nephew ['nefju:] *n.* 侄子，外甥
I can say Mr. Smith's nephew is a cautious investor.
我认为史密斯先生的侄子是一个小心谨慎的投资者。

niece [ni:s] *n.* 侄女，外甥女
My fourteen-month-old niece begins to yawn around nine o'clock every night.
我14个月大的侄女一到晚上9点就开始打哈欠。

only ['əunli] *adv.* 只，仅仅 *adj.* 唯一的
Though he is only a child, he performed many daring exploits.
虽然他只是个孩子，可他却有许多大胆之举。

parent ['pɛərənt] *n.* 父亲，母亲
Parents may never understand their children's strange mind.
父母们可能永远理解不了孩子奇特的思维方式。

relation [ri'leiʃən] *n.* 关系，联系，家属
After the venerable scholar died, all of his friends and relations attended his funeral.
那位德高望重的学者死后，他所有的朋友与亲戚都参加了葬礼。

考点：in relation to 关于，涉及，与……比

relationship [ri'leiʃənʃip] *n.* 关系，联系
You must know some bad words will destroy the relationship between friends.
你必须清楚一些不好的话会伤害朋友间的关系。

考点：relation, relationship 都有"关系，联系"的意思：relation 多指事物之间的联系；relationship 既可以指事物之间的联系，也可以指人与人之间的密切关系。

spouse [spauz] *n.* 配偶
Don't consider too many realistic conditions when choose a spouse.
择偶的时候，不要考虑得太现实。

*

pregnant ['pregnənt] *adj.* 怀孕的，妊娠的，丰富的
Abstention from smoking is essential for you while your wife is pregnant.
当妻子怀孕的时候，你必须得戒烟。

⏱ 考点：be pregnant with 充满……

*

supervise ['sju:pəvaiz] *vi.&vt.* 监督，管理，指导
He had left her at home to supervise the children.
他让她留在家里看管孩子。

*

support [sə'pɔ:t] *vt.* 支撑，支持，供养
He can't support the family any more due to his fewer salary.
他越来越少的工资再也无法支撑这个家了。

*

trifle ['traifl] *n.* 小事，琐事，少许
Don't trouble yourself with such a trifle in daily life.
生活中不要因为这样的小事而烦恼。

⏱ 考点：a trifle 有点，稍微

*

stereotype ['stiəriəutaip] *n.* 模式化观念
vt. 使形成固定看法
The old woman always holds a stereotype to look the relationship between his grandson and his girlfriend.
老人总是用自己固有的观念看待她孙子与女朋友之间的关系。

*

responsible [ris'pɔnsəbl] *adj.* 有责任的，尽责的
You shall be responsible for the loss of the goods in transit if you can't work seriously.
如果你工作不认真，你就来承担货物运输中的损失。

⏱ 考点：responsible 做前置定语与后置定语的意义不同。eg. a responsible man 可靠的人；the person responsible 负责人

responsibility [ris,pɔnsə'biliti] *n.* 责任，责任心，职责
Don't shuffle your own responsibility onto others.
不要把你的责任推诿给他人。

*

preceding [pri'si:diŋ] *adj.* 在前的，在先的
She gave birth to her son in the preceding winter.
她去年冬天生下了儿子。

*

spoil [spɔil] *vt.* 损坏，糟蹋，宠坏
Parents shouldn't spoil their children.
父母不应该纵容他们的孩子。

*

burden ['bə:dn] *n.* 担子，重担，装载量
vt. 加重压于……，烦扰，负重
I know he bears a heavy burden, but he never told me about it.
我知道他承载着很重的担子，可是他从来都不跟我说。

⏱ 考点：burden sb. with sth. 使某人负担……

真题

American college students are increasingly ____ with credit card debt and the consequences can be rather serious.
A) discharged   B) dominated
C) boosted   D) burdened

详 解：选D。题意为：越来越多的美国大学生背负着信用卡债务，其后果会非常严重。A) discharge 意思是"卸下，放出"；B) dominate 意思是"支配，占优势"；C) boost 意思是"增进，改善"；D) burden 意思是"使负担"。

(CET-4 2006.6)

人生梦想 成功荣耀

accomplish [ə'kɔmpliʃ] *vt.* 达到（目的），完成，做成功
I'm afraid I can't accomplish my ideal in my life.
我恐怕一生都实现不了我的梦想了。

achieve [ə'tʃi:v] *vt.* 完成，实现，达到
Due to his laziness, it is impossible for him to achieve success.
他懒惰，是不可能获得成功的。

achievement [ə'tʃi:vmənt] *n.* 完成，成就，成绩
I admire all the achievements you've got.
我很羡慕你所取得的成就。

aim [eim] *n.* 目标；*vi.* 瞄准，针对，致力
The young girl's aim is to become an excellent publicist.
这个年轻女孩的目标是成为一名出色的公关。

anticipate [æn'tisipeit] *vt.* 预料，预期，期望
It's difficult to anticipate which team will win.
很难预料哪个队会赢。

aspiration [ˌæspə'reiʃən] *n.* 强烈的愿望，志向，抱负
She has an aspiration to become a teacher.
她的志愿是当老师。

attain [ə'tein] *vt.* 达到，（经过努力）获得，完成
In order to attain this aim, she would rather sacrifice her husband and children.
为了达到这个目标，她宁愿牺牲她的丈夫和孩子。

attempt [ə'tempt] *vt.* 尝试，试图
n. 企图
Last night, that prisoner attempted to escape, but failed.
昨晚，那个囚犯企图逃跑，但未能成功。

bright [brait] *adj.* 明亮的，聪明的
I hope all my classmates have a bright future.
希望我所有的同学都拥有一个美好的未来。

brighten ['braitn] *vt.* 使发光，使快活
The new teacher brightened the atmosphere of class.
新来的老师使课堂气氛变得活跃起来。

brilliant ['briljənt] *adj.* 光辉的，卓越的
Look, the moon is brilliant tonight.
看，今晚的月亮明亮极了。

confidence ['kɔnfidəns] *n.* 信任，信赖，信心
Do you have confidence to pass the IELTS?
你有信心通过雅思考试吗？

🔍 **考点**：in confidence 私下地，秘密地
take into one's confidence 把……作为知己

confident ['kɔnfidənt] *n.* 确信的，自信的
I'm confident that these obstacles can be superable.
我有信心可以超越这些障碍。

conquer ['kɔnkə] *vt.* 征服，战胜，破除
The book showed many examples to teach you how to conquer laziness.
这本书有许多实例教你如何克服懒惰。

conquest ['kɔnkwest] *n.* 攻取，征服，克服，战利品
Her beauty won her many conquests.
她的美貌赢得许多崇拜者。

decide [di'said] *vt.* 决定，决心，解决
I decided to draw a diagram in proper position.
我决定在合适的地方画一张图表。

decision [di'siʒən] *n.* 决定，决心，果断
We will make a decision after studying the topography here.
研究地形之后我们再做决定。

derive [di'raiv] *vt.* 取得；*vi.* 起源
You know we can derive knowledge from books.
你知道我们能从书中获得知识。

🔍 **考点**：derive...from 源自，来自

desirable [di'zaiərəbl] *adj.* 值得相望的，可取的
It is desirable that we provide for the poor.
施舍穷人是可喜的事。

desire [di'zaiə] *vt.* 渴望，要求；*n.* 愿望
She has strong desire to dominate over others.
她很想支配别人。

考点：desire后接that从句时，从句中的谓语动词要用 "should + 动词原形" 表示虚拟。

---

determination [diˌtə:mi'neiʃən] *n.* 决心，决定，确定

He is a man of determination
他是一个有决断力的人。

---

determine [di'tə:min] *vt.* 决定，查明，决心

She determined to give up her schooling and go to earn money.
她决定放弃学业去挣钱。

考点：determine to do sth. 决心做某事

---

dream [dri:m] *n.* 梦，梦想；*vi.* 做梦

He did his best to finish this project just for his dream, not for profit.
他尽最大努力去完成这项工程是为了他的梦想，而不是为了利益。

考点：dream up 凭空想出

---

exert [ig'zə:t] *vt.* 尽（力），运用

You'll have to exert yourself more if you want to get high marks.
如果你想考高分，就必须更加努力。

考点：exert oneself 尽力

---

expectation [ˌekspek'teiʃən] *n.* 期待，期望，预期

The result is out of my expectation.
结果出乎我的意料。

---

fantasy ['fæntəsi] *n.* 想象，想象的产物

The young man lives in a world of fantasy.
这个年青人生活在幻想的世界里。

---

gain [gein] *vt.* 获得，增加；*n.* 增进

No pain, no gain.
一分耕耘，一分收获。

考点：gain on 赶上，逼近

---

glorious ['glɔ:riəs] *adj.* 光荣的，壮丽的

We won a glorious victory in building up our country.
在建设祖国中，我们赢得了辉煌胜利。

---

glory ['glɔ:ri] *n.* 光荣，荣誉的事

Her crowning glory is her white skin.
她最引以为荣的是她白皙的皮肤。

---

failure ['feiljə] *n.* 失败，失败的人

He tried his best to defend himself in court but ended in failure.
他竭力在法庭上为自己辩护，但是以失败而告终。

真题

She keeps a supply of candles in the house in case of power ____.
A) drop   B) lack
C) failure   D) absence

详　解：选C。题意为：她在房间里存了一些蜡烛，以防停电。power failure "停电"，是固定搭配。

(CET-4 2004.6)

---

grab [græb] *vt.* 抓取，攫取，赶紧做，抓住机会
vi. 抓，夺
n. 抓，夺

I managed to grab hold of the door before falling.
我设法抓住了那个门才未跌落。

---

heroic [hi'rəuik] *adj.* 英雄的，英勇的

The heroic exploits of these soldiers will go down in history.
战士们的英雄业绩将被载入史册。

---

heroism ['herəuizəm] *n.* 英雄主义，勇气

That is an act of great heroism.
那是一种了不起的英勇行为。

---

honourable ['ɔnərəbəl] *adj.* 诚实的，光荣的

He's a thoroughly honourable man.
他是个极为正直的人。

---

honour ['ɔnə] *n.* 光荣，尊敬，敬意

He won honour for his generosity.
他因慷慨而赢得人们的尊敬。

考点：do the honours 尽地主之谊
in honour of 为了向……表示敬意，为纪念

---

ideal [ai'diəl] *adj.* 理想的，观念的

This is an unattainable ideal.
这是一个难以达成的理想。

insist [in'sist] *vi.* 坚持，坚持要求
Dad insists that I shall go to school.
爸爸要求我一定去学校。

🔍 **考点**：insist that... 从句并非都用虚拟
语气。表示"坚持应该做……"
时，从句的谓语动词为"should +
动词原形"表示虚拟语气；表示
"坚持某一事实时"则用陈述语气。

真题

Mike's uncle insists _____ in this hotel.
A) staying not   B) not to stay
C) that he would not stay   D) that he not stay

详　解：选D。题意为：麦克的叔叔坚持不
留在旅馆里。insist后接从句，从句谓语为
"should + 动词原形"表示虚拟语气。

(CET-4 2000.1)

motive ['məutiv] *n.* 动机，目的
In case of murder, the police questioned everyone
who might have a motive.
在谋杀案的调查中，警方要查问每一个可能有
谋杀动机的人。

obtain [əb'tein] *vt.* 获得，得到，买到
vi. 通用，流行
His capability of obtaining information is the best
in our company.
在我们公司，他获取信息的能力是最强的。

pride [praid] *n.* 骄傲，自豪；*vt.* 自夸
The young man touched his car with pride.
年轻人得意地抚摸着自己的车。

🔍 **考点**：take pride in 以……而自豪
pride oneself on 以……而自豪

proud [praud] *adj.* 骄傲的，自豪的
Since you've won the first swimming certificate,
you are proud as a peacock.
自从你获得了第一个游泳证书后就变得非常骄
傲了。

purpose ['pə:pəs] *n.* 目的，意图，效果
His remarks left me wondering about his real
purpose.
他的一番话让我一直在琢磨他的真正意图。

🔍 **考点**：one's purpose in doing sth. 某
人做某事的目的
on purpose 故意
to no purpose 无效，无果

quest [kwest] *n.* 寻求，搜索，追求
Can you tell me what his ultimate quest is?
你能告诉我他追寻的最终目标是什么吗？

🔍 **考点**：in quest of 寻找

realize ['riəlaiz] *vt.* 实现，认识到
The boy lay down in a hurry and he realized that
he was being shot at.
男孩赶紧卧倒，接着意识到自己正是射击的目
标。

sake [seik] *n.* 缘故，理由
James once betrayed his friend for money's sake.
吉姆斯曾经为了钱而出卖自己的朋友。

🔍 **考点**：for the sake of 为了……起见，
看在……的份上

seek [si:k] *vt.* 寻找，探索，试图
It began to rain heavily, and people ran to seek
shelter from the rain.
雨开始下大了，人们都跑去寻找避雨之所。

🔍 **考点**：seek out 挑出，想获得

success [sək'ses] *n.* 成功，成就，胜利
Make people happy, and your performance will be
a success.
只要观众满意，表演就算成功。

tremendous [tri'mendəs] *adj.* 极大的，非
常的
This event stands as one of the tremendous facts of
all the time in this country.
这件事成了全国有史以来的大事之一。

triumph ['traiəmf] *n.* 凯旋，胜利
vi. 成功，获胜
He won a triumph without (a) parallel in this
match.
在这次比赛中，他取得了无与伦比的大胜利。

🔍 **考点**：triumph over 战胜

ultimate ['ʌltimit] *adj.* 最后的，最终的
He finally reached his ultimate destination.
最后，他到达了目的地。

will [wil] *aux.v.* 将要，会，愿

I will go to the playground to find him soon.
我马上去操场找他。

🏹 考点：at will 任意，随意

wish [wiʃ] *vt.* 想要；渴望

I wish I could have more free time to do my own things.
我希望有更多的自由时间来做自己的事。

真题

Sometimes I wish I _____ in a different time and a different place.
A) believing   B) were living
C) would live   D) would have lived

详 解：选B。题意为：有时我希望我生活在不同的时代和地方。本题考查的是虚拟语气的运用。根据题意，这种不可能的现实与现实情况相反，因此选B。

(CET-4 2000.1)

utmost ['ʌtməust] *adj.* 最远的；*n.* 极限

He has reached his utmost in the match.
他已经在比赛中达到自己的极限了。

🏹 考点：do one's utmost 竭尽全力

succeed [sək'si:d] *vt.* 继……之后
vi. 成功

Persevere and you'll succeed.
只要你坚持不懈，你会成功。

big [big] *adj.* 大的，巨大的

Could you tell me what your biggest accomplishment on the job is?
能告诉我你在工作上最大的成就是什么吗？

人生梦想 **人生命运**

adult ['ædʌlt] *n.* 成年人；*adj.* 成年的

He has been an adult, but often acts like a child.
他已经成年了，可他的行为举止却常常像孩子一样幼稚。

die [dai] *vi.* 死，死亡，灭亡

Knowing that he was about to die, the old man began to prepare his coffin secretly.

知道自己将不久于人世，老人开始偷偷地为自己准备棺材。

ego ['i:gəu] *n.* 自我，自己，自尊

Susan abandon egos just for her dream.
苏珊为了梦想而放弃自我。

elderly ['eldəli] *adj.* 年长的，年老的

I like to talk with my elderly sister.
我喜欢跟我姐姐聊天。

fatal ['feitl] *adj.* 致命的，命运的

The boy cycling in the street was knocked down by a minibus and received fatal injuries.
这个男孩在街上骑自行车时被一辆小型汽车撞倒，受了致命伤。

fortunate ['fɔ:tʃənit] *adj.* 幸运的，侥幸的

A fortunate encounter brought Jack and Lily together.
一次幸运的邂逅使杰克和莉莉相识。

真题

In Africa, educational costs are very low for those who are _____ enough to get into universities.
A) fortunate   B) substantial
C) aggressive   D) ambitious

详 解：选A。题意为：在非洲，对有幸进入大学的人来说，教育费用是很低的。A) fortunate意思是"幸运的"；B) substantial意思是"富裕的，大量的"；C) aggressive意思是"有进取心的"；D) ambitious意思是"有抱负的"。

(CET-4 2002.12)

fortunately ['fɔ:tʃənitli] *adv.* 幸运地，幸亏

Fortunately he was safe in the accident.
他遇到了意外，幸而没有怎么样。

🏹 考点：fortunately作插入语，表明说话人的态度，修饰全句。

fortune ['fɔ:tʃən] *n.* 命运，运气，财产

A fortune was divided among the nine grandchildren.
9个孙子孙女分享一笔财产。

🏹 考点：make a fortune 发财，致富
try one's fortune 碰运气

dilemma [di'lemə] *n.* 困境，窘迫，进退两难

He seems to be in a dilemma.
他似乎身陷困境。

hardship ['hɑːdʃip] *n.* 艰难，困苦

He has suffered a period fraught with hardship.
他经历了一段充满苦难的时期。

heaven ['hevən] *n.* 天堂，天，天空

She visualized an angel coming from heaven.
她想象一位天使从天而降。

hell [hel] *n.* 地狱，极大的痛苦

He made her life a hell.
他使她的生活像地狱般痛苦。

🔑 考点：like hell 拼命地；the hell 到底，究竟；to hell with 让……见鬼吧

impossible [im'pɔsəbl] *adj.* 不可能的，办不到的

At last she felt it is impossible to accomplish this task.
她最终感到无法完成这项任务。

🔑 考点：impossible意思是"不可能的"时，不能修饰人；修饰人时意思为"难对付的"。

individual [ˌindi'vidjuəl] *adj.* 个别的，独特的

Every individual has a physiological requirement for water.
每个人对水都有一种生理上的需要。

infant ['infənt] *n.* 婴儿；*adj.* 婴儿的

The death rate of infants and children is inclined.
婴儿和儿童的死亡率有所降低。

intend [in'tend] *vt.* 想要，打算，意指

For the future I intend to look after my parents myself.
今后我打算亲自照顾我的父母。

mean [miːn] *vt.* 做……解释，意指，打算
adj. 自私的，吝啬的，平均的
n. 平均值

It means our young people must have a relatively high level of responsibility.
这意味着我们年轻人要有更高的责任感。

🔑 考点：mean to do sth 有意做……，存心做……

meaning ['miːniŋ] *n.* 意义，意思，意图

I don't think his composition was good because the meaning in it was obscure.
我认为他的作文写的不好，因为文字意义晦涩。

miracle ['mirəkl] *n.* 奇迹，令人惊奇的人（或事）

The Great Wall in China is really a miracle.
中国的长城真是一个奇迹。

🔑 考点：do / work a miracle 创造奇迹

mortal ['mɔːtl] *adj.* 终有一死的，致死的

The police were told that though the victim was poisoned, the mortal reason was a heavy hit on his head.
警察被告知死者虽然被人下了毒，但致命原因却是头部被人重击。

orphan ['ɔːfən] *n.* 孤儿

He treats the orphan as his own child.
他对待那个孤儿就像对待自己的亲生孩子一样。

paradise ['pærədaiz] *n.* 伊甸乐园，天堂

Where there are you, there is a love paradise.
哪里有你，哪里就有爱的天堂。

poor [puə] *adj.* 贫穷的，贫乏的

Mr. Black has a big estate, where many poor men are hired and work for him.
布莱克先生拥有一个大庄园，在那里他雇用了很多穷人为他干活。

poverty ['pɔvəti] *n.* 贫穷，贫困

It's said that it's easy to conceal the wealth but difficult to conceal the poverty.
据说藏富容易，掩饰贫穷则难。

promising ['prɔmisiŋ] *adj.* 有希望的，有前途的

I hear the man who is sitting there is a promising artist.
我听说坐在那里的那个人是一位有前途的艺术家。

prospect ['prɔspekt] *n.* 展望，前景，前程

I was disappointed in her, as there was no prospect of an improvement in her condition.
我对她很失望，因为她没有任何改进的希望。

考点：prospect of sth. / doing sth.
有……的希望，可能性

real ['ri:əl] *adj.* 真的，现实的
I've never seen a real automatic rifle in my life.
我还从来没有见过真正的自动步枪是什么样子的。

reality [ri'æləti] *n.* 现实，真实
I will try my best to make it a reality.
我会尽最大的努力使这成为现实。

考点：in reality 实际上，事实上

recollect [ˌrekə'lekt] *vt.* 回忆，追忆，想起
She tried to calm her turbulent thoughts and recollect her attention.
她试图平息一下紊乱的思绪并重新集中注意力。

realistic [riə'listik] *adj.* 现实的，现实主义的，逼真的
Be realistic, we don't have enough money for the car.
现实点，我们没钱买车。

真题

I'm ____ enough to know it is going to be a very difficult situation to compete against three strong teams.
A) realistic   B) conscious
C) aware   D) radical

详　解：选A。题意为：我很实际地认识到与3个强队竞争是多么困难。be realistic to know sth. 是固定用法，表示"很实际地认识到"。

(CET-4 2005.1)

recall [ri'kɔ:l] *vt.* 回想，叫回，收回
I have only a dim memory and couldn't recall the exact circumstances.
我记忆模糊，回忆不起确切的情况。

考点：recall, remember 都有"记起"的意思：recall指经过努力后的"想起"；remember指自然而然的"想起"

scheme [ski:m] *n.* 计划，规划，诡计
Trust you to dream up a crazy scheme like this!

亏你想得出这种异想天开的计划！

remember [ri'membə] *vt.* 记得，想起，记住
I remembered that I made the acquaintance of Robert at that small hotel.
我记得我是在那个小旅馆里认识罗伯特的。

考点：remember to do sth. 记着要做某事（还没做）；remember doing sth. 记着做过某事（已经做了）

remind [ri'maind] *vt.* 提醒，使想起
First I have to remind you to see things in perspective.
首先我要提醒你必须正确地观察事物。

考点：remind sb. to do sth. 提醒某人做某事

significance [sig'nifikəns] *n.* 意义，意味，重要性
You won't refuse that job if you realize its significance.
如果你意识到那份工作的意义，你就不会拒绝它。

struggle ['strʌgl] *vi.&n.* 斗争，奋斗
The little girl struggled for a long time in the river but no one came.
小女孩在河里挣扎了好久还是没人来。

suicide ['su:isaid] *n.* 自杀，自取灭亡
Her suicide was motivated by breaking up with her boyfriend.
她自杀的诱因是与男友分手。

考点：commit suicide 自杀
attempt suicide 寻死

transform [træns'fɔ:m] *vt.* 改变，改造，变换
It seems to me that a reform can transform a whole community.
我觉得，一次革命可以改变整个社会。

transient ['trænʃənt] *adj.* 短暂的 *n.* 短期居留者，<电>顺变电流
Life is transient but precious.
人生虽短，但却珍贵。

young [jʌŋ] *adj.* 年轻的；*n.* 青年们
Young as she is, she is a sophisticated woman.

尽管她很年轻，但是一个老于世故的人。

🔑 **考点：** 做名词时是总称，常与the连用，the young做主语时，谓语常用复数。

---

significant [sig'nifikənt] *n.* 有意义的，重要的

I can recall the features of the significant leader.
我回忆得起这个有重大意义的领导人的容貌。

真题

Research shows that there is no ____ relationship between how much a person earns and whether he feels good about life.
A) successive　　B) sincere
C) significant　　D) subsequent

详　解：选C。题意为：研究表明个人收入多少与对生活是否满足没有重要关系。A) successive意思是"继承的，连续的"；B) sincere 意思是"诚挚的，真诚的"；C) significant意思是"重要的，重大的"；D) subsequent意思是"后来的"。

(CET-4 2006.6)

---

unfortunate [ʌn'fɔːtʃənit] *adj.* 不幸的，可取的

It was unfortunate that she lost her parents in this accident.
这场事故使她失去了父母，真不幸。

---

youngster ['jʌŋstə] *n.* 青年，年轻人，孩子
Youngsters are always self-absorbed till they become parents themselves.
年轻人总是只关心自己，直到他们自己做了父母。

---

youth [juːθ] *n.* 青春，青年们，青年
It is a truth that youth is the most precious age of one's life.
青年时代是人一生当中最宝贵的时期。

---

opportunity [ˌɔpə'tjuːniti] *n.* 机会，良机
What a pity! I missed a great opportunity to shoot at goal.
真可惜，我失去了一次极佳的射门机会。

---

obstacle ['ɔbstəkl] *n.* 障碍，障碍物，妨害
You should believe that you can defeat all the obstacles.

要相信，你能战胜所有的障碍。

真题

Not having a good command of English can be a serious ____ preventing you from achieving your goals.
A) obstacle　　B) fault
C) offense　　D) distress

详　解：选A。题意为：英语掌握得不好将严重影响你实现目标。A) obstacle 意思是"障碍"；B) fault 意思是"过错，缺点"；C) offense 意思是"冒犯，过失"；D) distress 意思是"痛苦，悲伤，忧虑"。

(CET-4 2003.12)

---

scope [skəup] *n.* 范围，余地，机会
Though he is endowed with a gift in music, he has no scope for his talents.
虽然他天生有音乐才能，可却没有施展自己才能的机会。

🔑 **考点：** give scope to / for 给予充分发挥……的天地（或机会）

---

seize [siːz] *vt.* 抓住，逮捕，夺取
The girl seized the leg of a broken chair as a weapon to defend herself.
女孩抓起一只破椅子腿当做武器自卫。

🔑 **考点：** seize on / upon 利用
　　　　seize up 卡住，停顿

---

overcome [ˌəuvə'kʌm] *vt.* 战胜，克服
You have still tremendous obstacles to overcome before you achieve your goal.
要想实现你的目标，你就必须克服很多障碍。

---

retreat [ri'triːt] *vi.* （被迫）退却，后退
The enemy was forced to retreat because of consequence of failure.
敌人失败后被迫撤退。

---

rid [rid] *vt.* 使摆脱，使去掉
n. 摆脱，除掉
How could I get rid of the man whom I don't love?
我怎样才能摆脱这个我不爱的男人啊?

🔑 **考点：** get rid of 摆脱，除掉

---

suffering ['sʌfəriŋ] *n.* 痛苦，不幸，苦恼
I hoped that this medicine might end my suffering.

我希望这种药物可能结束我的痛苦。

stoop [stu:p] *vi.* 俯身，弯身；*n.* 弯腰
The tall man had to stoop his head to get through the tunnel.
那个大个子只好低头以穿过隧道。

考点：stoop to do... 降低身份以求……；stoop to (doing) sth. 堕落到……的地步

suffer ['sʌfə] *vt.* 遭受，忍受，容许
He might suffer horrible cruelties in abroad.
他可能在国外遇到可怕的残酷待遇了。

考点：suffer with 遭受

vain [vein] *adj.* 徒劳的，自负的
All his attempts in educating his children were in vain.
他的一切教育孩子的尝试全部无效。

考点：in vain 徒劳，白费力

whatever [wɔt'evə] *pron.* 无论什么
Whatever we met, we should not lose the optimistic attitude towards life.
不论我们遇见了什么困难，都不能失去对生活的乐观态度。

withstand [wið'stænd] *vt.* 抵挡，反抗
I couldn't withstand this much heat.
我受不了这样的高温。

yield [ji:ld] *vi.* 屈服，倒塌，产生，让出
　　　　　　vt. 结出（果实），产生（效益），使屈服
　　　　　　n. 产量，收益
We will never yield to any difficulties.
我们绝不会向任何困难屈服。

考点：yield to sth. 屈服于……

cause [kɔ:z] *n.* 原因，理由，事业；*n.* 引起
Do you know what the cause of the accident was?
你知道造成这一事故的原因吗?

chaos ['keiɔs] *n.* 混乱，无秩序，混沌
The long war left the country in chaos.
长期战争使国家陷入一片混乱。

chaotic [kei'ɔtik] *adj.* 混乱的
The city traffic was chaotic during rush hour.
上下班时间市内交通混乱。

clash [klæʃ] *n.* 冲突，抵触，撞击声
　　　　　vt. 使……发出撞击声
　　　　　vi. 引起冲突
It is not only a clash of opinions between them but a clash of national interests.
这不仅是他们观点的冲突，也是两国利益的冲突。

collapse [kə'læps] *vi.* 倒坍，崩溃，瓦解
It's lucky that the collapse of the building caused no casualties.
幸运的是建筑物倒塌没有造成伤亡。

collision [kə'liʒən] *n.* 碰撞，冲突
After the collision, he examined the considerable damage to his car.
撞车后，他检查到车子受到了严重的损害。

真题

It is reported that thirty people were killed in a _____ on the railway yesterday.
A) collision　　　B) collaboration
C) corrosion　　　D) confrontation

详　解：选A。题意为：据报道，30人在昨天的火车相撞事故中丧生。A) collision意思是"相撞，碰撞"；B) collaboration意思是"合作，写作"；C) corrosion意思是"腐蚀，侵蚀"；D) confrontation意思是"面临，对峙"。

(CET-4 2003.12)

damage ['dæmidʒ] *vt.* 损害，毁坏
　　　　　　　n. 损害
These worms do damage to our vegetables.
这些小虫会毁坏我们的青菜。

disaster [di'zɑ:stə]] *n.* 灾难，灾祸，天灾
These difficulties are caused by natural disasters.
这些困难都是由自然灾害造成的。

drown [draun] *vi.* 淹死，溺死
After the boy was drowned, his mother got mad.
在那个男孩淹死后，他妈妈疯了。

考点：drown oneself in 埋头于……

emerge [i'mə:dʒ] *vi.* 出现，涌现，冒出
He emerged from the accident unharmed.
他在这次事故中侥幸脱险没有受伤。

explode [iks'pləud] *vt.* 使爆炸；*vi.* 爆炸
Watch out! The time bomb may explode at any time.
小心，定时炸弹可能随时会爆炸。

emergency [i'mə:dʒnsi] *n.* 紧急情况，突发事件
Not everyone can keep as cool as a cucumber in emergency .
并不是每一个人在紧急情况下都能保持冷静。

(真题)

A fire engine must have priority as it usually has to deal with some kind of ___ .
A) crisis　　　　B) precaution
C) urgency　　　D) emergency

详　解：选D。题意为：消防车应该有优先行驶权，因为它们常要应对一些紧急情况。A) crisis意思是"危机"；B) precaution意思是"预防措施"；C) urgency意思是"紧急，紧迫"；D) emergency意思是"紧急情况"。

(CET-4 2002. 12)

explosion [iks'pləuʒən] *n.* 爆炸，爆发，炸裂
The explosion blasted the house down.
这次爆炸把房屋炸倒了。

explosive [iks'pləusiv] *adj.* 爆炸的
Today I heard an explosive news that Lisa was my boss's daughter.
今天我听到个爆炸性新闻，丽莎竟然是我老板的女儿。

extinguish [iks'tingwiʃ] *vt.* 熄灭，扑灭，使身亡
The failure on his marriage extinguishes his faith in future.
婚姻的失败让他对未来的信念都破灭了。

fireman ['faiəmən] *n.* 消防队员；司炉工
A fireman has a dangerous way of life.
消防队员的谋生方式很危险。

missing ['misiŋ] *adj.* 缺掉的，失去的，失踪的
At last, they found the missing girl in the forest.
最后，他们在森林里找到了走失的那个小女孩。

occur [ə'kə:] *vi.* 发生，出现，存在
Whereas the following incidents have occurred, I think you should give us an explanation.
鉴于下列事件已经发生，我想你应该给我们一个解释。

考点：it occurs to sb. that... 使某人想起了……

occurrence [ə'kʌrəns] *n.* 发生，出现，事件
The fundamental principles which govern all physical processes are also related to many everyday occurrences.
解释所有物理过程的基本原理也与许多日常现象相关。

rescue ['reskju:] *vt.&n.* 援救，营救
The climber was buried by an avalanche, and so far, he has not been rescued.
那位登山者遇雪崩被埋住了，目前仍生死未卜。

(真题)

All their attempts to ____ the child from the burning building were in vain.
A) regain　　　B) recover
C) rescue　　　D) reserve

详　解：选C。题意为：要把这个孩子从燃烧的大楼里营救出来的所有努力都是徒劳的。A) regain 意思是"重新获得"；B) recover 意思是"恢复"；C) rescue 意思是"营救，救援"；D) reserve 意思是"预订，储存"。

(CET-4 模拟)

sink [siŋk] *vi.* 下沉，下垂，降低
If there are no writers and artists, the cultural life of the country will sink into atrophy.
如果没有作家和艺术家，一个国家的文化生活将枯萎衰落。

考点：sunk, sunken是sink的两种过去分词，作定语时用sunken（沉没的），不用sunk。

spark [spɑ:k] *n.* 火花，火星
A spark set the house on fire.
一点火星使房子烧了起来。

timely ['taimli] *adj.* 及时的，适时的
The girl got timely treatment for her ailment, and she is now released from the hospital.

女孩的疾病得到了及时治疗，目前已经出院。

burial ['beriəl] *n.* 埋葬，葬礼，坟墓
Many celebrities attended his burial.
许多名人参加了他的葬礼。

bury ['beri] *vt.* 埋葬，葬，埋藏
Nobody knows where the treasure is buried.
没人知道宝藏被埋在哪儿了。

🔍 考点：bury oneself in (doing) sth. 专心做……

funeral ['fju:nərəl] *n.* 葬礼，丧礼，丧葬
Funeral customs vary in different countries.
葬仪的习俗因国家不同而不同。

grave [greiv] *n.* 坟墓；*adj.* 严重的
The archaeologist found an ancient grave.
考古学家发现了一个古墓。

memorial [mi'mɔ:riəl] *adj.* 纪念的，记忆的，追悼的
n. 纪念碑，纪念堂，纪念仪式
Over thousand people attended the memorial meeting of my grandfather.
有1000多人来参加了爷爷的追悼会。

mourn [mɔ:n] *vi.* 哀痛，哀悼
Many students gathered in the hall spontaneously to mourn for their most respectable teacher.
学生们自发地聚集在礼堂悼念他们最尊敬的老师。

circumstance ['sə:kəmstəns] *n.* 情况，条件，境遇
He was obliged to leave you by force of circumstance.
他也是被形势所逼，不得不离开你。

🔍 考点：in / under the circumstance 在此情况下，（情况）既然如此 under no circumstance 决不，无论如何不

outset ['autset] *n.* 开始，开端
At the outset of my career, I was full of ambition.
在事业刚开始时，我踌躇满志。

🔍 考点：at / from the outset 开端，开始

chance [tʃɑ:ns] *n.* 机会，机遇，可能性
I met my ex-husband by chance when I was in London.

我在伦敦时碰巧遇到了我的前夫。

🔍 考点：by chance 偶然，碰巧；by any chance 万一，也许；take a chance 冒险，投机；stand a chance of 有……的希望，有……的可能

past [pɑ:st] *adj.* 过去的；*n.* 过去
She thought about the past years, sighing for her lost youth.
她想着过去的岁月，为逝去的青春而惋惜。

医疗养生 疾病伤害

AIDS [eidz] *n.* 艾滋病
AIDS is a serious infectious disease.
艾滋病是一种严重的传染病。

cancer ['kænsə] *n.* 癌，癌症，肿瘤
It was cancer that took away his father's life.
癌症夺去了他父亲的生命。

acute [ə'kju:t] *adj.* 严重的，尖的，锐的，敏锐的，急性的
What a pity! You suffer from acute depression.
真遗憾，你患有严重的抑郁症。

cough [kɔ:f] *vi.* 咳，咳嗽
n. 咳嗽
The girl began to sniffle and cough.
女孩开始抽噎和咳嗽。

ancestor ['ænsistə] *n.* 祖宗，祖先
He is amused to learn that his ancestors came here as refugees.
得知他的祖先是因为避难来这的，他觉得很好笑。

aunt [ɑ:nt] *n.* 伯母，婶母，姑母
My aunt controls the whole company.
我姑姑掌管着整个公司。

bacteria [bæk'tiəriə] *n.* 细菌
Of course you can't see most of the bacteria; you know they are too small to see with the naked eyes.
大多数细菌你都看不见，因为他们太小了，肉眼看不见。

bandage ['bændidʒ] *n.* 绷带
vt. 用绷带包扎
Please get a bandage and bind up his bleeding wound.
请拿一个绷带来，包扎一下他流血的伤口。

bleed [bli:d] *vi.* 出血，流血，泌脂
I think he's going to die. Look, he is bleeding badly.
我认为他快要死了，看，他流血流得很厉害。

blood [blʌd] *n.* 血，血液，血统
In my opinion, plasma is used for blood transfusions.
在我看来，血浆是用来输血的。

bloodshed ['blʌdʃed] *n.* 流血，杀人
They tried their best to prevent further bloodshed, but more and more people died in succession.
他们尽最大努力避免人员伤亡，但是越来越多的人还是相继死亡。

broken ['brəukən] *adj.* 被打碎的，骨折的
Your words make my heart broken.
你的话让我很伤心。

bruise [bru:z] *n.* 青肿，伤痕，擦伤
After the accident, the truck driver was treated for cuts bruises.
事故发生后，司机的创伤得到治疗。

choke [tʃəuk] *vt.* 使窒息，塞满
The boy was choked with smoke.
男孩被烟呛着了。

cigarette [sigə'ret] *n.* 香烟，纸烟，卷烟
Quit smoking please! You know the lung cancer is a consequence of cigarette smoking.
请戒烟吧！你知道肺癌就是吸烟的结果。

clinic ['klinik] *n.* 诊所，门诊部，科室
He planned to go to a private clinic to treat his illness instead of a hospital.
他计划去一个私人诊所治病而不是一家医院。

case [keis] *n.* 情况，事实，病例，箱（子），盒（子），套
I thought I had already got rid of him, but that was not the case.
我以为我已经甩掉了他，可是事实并非如此。

🔍 考点：in case (of) 假使，以防
in any case 无论如何，不管怎样
in no case 决不

真题

Don't let the child play with scissors ____ he cuts himself.
A) only if   B) in case
C) now that   D) so that

详 解：选B。题意为：别让孩子玩剪刀，以防他伤着自己。in case表示"以防，万一"，引导的从句时态一般为一般时或should do句型。

(CET-4 模拟)

clinical ['klinikəl] *adj.* 临床的，冷静的
The new drug is undergoing clinical trials now.
这种新药现在正在进行临床试验。

complementary [ˌkɔmpli'mentəri] *adj.* 补充的
Why are yellow and blue complementary colors?
为什么说黄与蓝是互补色？

deadly ['dedli] *adj.* 致命的，死一般的
He got a deadly disease.
他得了致命的疾病。

dizzy ['dizi] *adj.* 使人眩晕的，过快的
We were dizzy by the strong wind.
我们被大风刮得头晕目眩。

epidemic [ˌepi'demik] *n.* 流行病，流行盛行
adj. 流行性的，流传极广的
You know SARS is a highly infectious epidemic.
你知道非典是传染性很强的流行病。

HIV [ˌeitʃˌai'vi:] *n.* 人体免疫缺损病毒，艾滋病病毒（是Human Immunodeficiency Virus的缩写）
HIV can be infected through the blood.
HIV病毒可通过血液传染。

incidence ['insidəns] *n.* 发生率
There's a high incidence of heart attack in old age.
老年人心脏病的发病率很高。

infect [in'fekt] *vt.* 传染，感染
I don't want to infect you with my cold.
我可不想把我的感冒传染给你。

考点：infect...with 使某人（某物）感染，传染

---

infection [in'fekʃən] *n.* 传染，影响，传染病
His right leg was swollen with infection.
他的右腿受到感染，已经肿起来了。

---

injure ['indʒə] *vt.* 伤害，损害，损伤
You will injure your health by drinking too much.
喝酒太多，有伤身体。

---

injury ['indʒəri] *n.* 损害，伤害，受伤处
He demands reparation for the injury of his body.
他要求身体损害的赔偿。

---

lump [lʌmp] *n.* 团，块，肿块
　　　　　vt. 把……归并在一起
　　　　　vi. 结块

The doctor told her there is a lump in her left breast.
医生告诉她，她的左乳有个硬肿块。

---

matter ['mætə] *n.* 事情，物质
　　　　　　vi. 要紧，有关系

Tina is a popular girl in our school, so it is a difficult matter to choose a boy as her boyfriend among so many pursuers.
蒂娜在我们学校很受欢迎，所以要在众多追求者中挑一个人作为她男朋友也是一件很头疼的事。

考点：as a matter of fact 事实上，其实
　　　　for that matter 就此而言，而且
　　　　no matter how 不论

---

sore [sɔː] *adj.* 痛的，恼火的
　　　　　n. 疮

He had a sore throat and found it difficult to speak.
他嗓子疼，觉得说话困难。

---

stomachache ['stʌməkeik] *n.* 胃疼
The child squirmed with stomachache on bed for eating bad food.
这孩子吃错东西，肚子疼得在床上滚来滚去。

---

tuberculosis [tjuˌbəːkjuˈləusis] *n.* 肺结核
The person who had tuberculosis could hardly survive at that time.
那个时候结核病人很难活下来。

---

wound [wuːnd] *n.* 创伤，伤；*vt.* 使受伤

A nurse is bandaging the wound of the patient.
一位护士正在为病人包扎伤口。

---

symptom ['simptəm] *n.* 症状，征兆
A symptom of rabies is foaming at the mouth.
得狂犬病的症状之一就是口吐泡沫。

真题

Lung cancer, like some other cancers, often doesn't produce _____ until it is too late and has spread beyond the chest to the brain, liver or bones.
A) symbols　　B) symptoms
C) trails　　　D) therapies

详　解：选B。题意为：肺癌跟其他癌症一样，直到晚期才会表现出症状，此时它已从胸腔扩散到大脑、肝或骨头。A) symbol 意思是"符号，象征"；B) symptom意思是"征兆，症候"；C) trail意思是"踪迹，痕迹"；D) therapy 意思是"治疗"。

(CET-4 模拟)

医疗养生　身体状况

condition [kən'diʃən] *n.* 状况，状态，环境
I can't deny that my health is not in a good condition.
我不能否认我的健康状况不太好。

考点：on condition (that) 如果
　　　　out of condition 健康状况不佳

真题

We can accept your order _____ payment is made in advance.
A) in the belief that　　B) in order that
C) on the excuse that　　D) on condition that

详　解：选D。题意为：如预先付款，我们可接受你方订单。A) in the belief that 意思是"相信"；B) in order that意思是"为了"；C) on the excuse that意思是"以……为借口"；D) on condition that意思是"条件是，如果……"。

(CET-4 2003.9)

cripple ['kripl] *n.* 跛子，残废的人
vt. 削弱，使残废

What a pity! The accident crippled the pretty girl for life.
真可惜，这一事故使这个漂亮女孩终身残废。

deaf [def] *adj.* 聋的，不愿听的

The optimistic deaf man believes that physical disability will never cause mental anguish.
那位乐观的耳聋人相信身体上的残疾并不会引起心理的苦闷。

考点：turn a deaf ear to 不愿听

disable [dis'eibl] *vt.* 使丧失能力，使伤残

The terrible earthquake disabled the pretty girl, but she never gave up hope.
那次可怕的地震使这位可爱的女孩残疾了，但她从没放弃过希望。

考点：disable sb. from doing
使……不能做

faint [feint] *adj.* 微弱的，虚弱的

I guess her sudden fall in a faint is induced by the heat of the weather.
我猜想她突然晕倒是因为天气炎热导致的。

lively ['laivli] *adj.* 活泼的，逼真的，热烈的

The old professor is still vigorous and lively even in his 90s.
即使90多岁了那个老教授依然精力充沛。

pale [peil] *adj.* 苍白的，浅的

Hearing the bad news, Jim's face turned deathly pale.
听到那个坏消息后，吉姆的脸色变得惨白。

powerful ['pauəful] *adj.* 强有力的，有权威的

Some small states can be unified into one country to resist the invasion from powerful countries.
一些小的国家可以统一成一个国家来抵御大国的侵略。

vigorous ['vigərəs] *adj.* 朝气蓬勃的

He never cherished the time in his vigorous youth.
在精力充沛的年轻时代他从未珍惜过时间。

weak [wi:k] *adj.* 弱的，软弱的

Because of long illness she becomes very weak.
由于长期生病她变得很虚弱。

考点：be weak in 在……方面弱

state [steit] *n.* 状态，国家，州

He didn't has a good state these days.
这些天他状态不好。

（真题）

An important factor in determining how well your perform in an examination is the _____ of your mind.
A) case   B) circumstance
C) state   D) situation

详 解：选C。题意为：决定你考试发挥的一个重要因素就是你的心态。A) case意思是"情形，场合"；B) circumstance意思是"情况，情形"；C) state 意思是"情形，状态"；D) situation意思是"形式，事态"。

(CET-4 模拟)

sound [saund] *adj.* 健康的，完好的
n. 声音；*vi.* 响，发声

A sound sleep would make you a good work next day.
良好的睡眠有助于你第二天的工作。

（真题）

The situation described in the report _____ terrible, but it may not happen.
A) inclines   B) maintains
C) sounds   D) remains

详 解：选C。题意为：报告中描述的情景听起来很可怕，但可能不会发生。A) incline意思是"认为，倾向"；B) maintain 意思是"维持"；C) sound意思是"听起来"；D) remain意思是"保持"。A) B) D) 三个选项都含有事情已经发生的意思，只有选项C)符合题意。

(CET-4 模拟)

weaken ['wi:kən] *vt.* 削弱；*vi.* 变弱

My eyesight weakens with the increase of study stress.
我的视力随着学习压力的增加而减弱。

weary ['wiəri] *adj.* 疲倦的；*vt.* 使疲乏

After being a housewife for about two years, she was weary of staying at home.
做了两年的家庭主妇后，她很厌倦待在家里。

disorder [dis'ɔ:də] *n.* 混乱，杂乱，骚乱
He's suffering from severe mental disorder.
他患有严重的精神病。

---

handicap ['hændikæp] *n.* （身体或智力方面的）缺陷，不利条件；*vt.* 妨碍，使不利
Her mother is a person with a severe visual handicap.
她妈妈是一个有严重视觉障碍的人。

真题

Million of people around the world have some type of physical, mental, or emotional _____ that severely limits their abilities to manage their daily activities.
A) scandal   B) misfortune
C) deficit   D) handicap

详 解：选D。题意为：全球上百万的人都有身体上、精神上或者情感上的缺陷，这严重限制了他们应对日常生活的能力。A) scandal意思是"丑行，丑闻"；B) misfortune意思是"不幸，灾祸"；C) deficit意思是"缺乏，不足"；D) handicap意思是"障碍，缺陷"。

(CET-4 2005.12)

---

hearing ['hiəriŋ] *n.* 听力，听觉，意见听取会，申辩的机会
He bought a hearing aid to his grandmother.
他给奶奶买了一个助听器。

---

hinder ['hində] *vt.* 阻碍，妨碍
Don't hinder him in his work.
不要妨碍他的工作。

考点：hinder sb. from doing sth. 妨碍某人做某事

---

limp [limp] *v.* 软弱的，无生气的，软的
vi. 蹒跚，一瘸一拐地走
n. 跛行
The accident left the girl with a permanent limp.
那场事故后，女孩就一直瘸了。

---

mental ['mentl] *adj.* 智力的，精神的，内心的
My father's mental decay is really distressing.
父亲的智力衰退真令人苦恼。

考点：mental labor 脑力劳动
physical labor 体力劳动

mind [maind] *n.* 头脑，理智，记忆
vi.&vt. 注意，照顾，介意
Juridical ideas should be implanted in the mind of citizens.
法的观念应该被灌输进公民脑海中。

---

mute [mju:t] *adj.* 缄默的，哑的；*n.* 哑巴
I can't believe that the damp and mute boy became a musician at last.
我不敢相信那个又聋又哑的男孩最后竟成了音乐家。

---

optical ['ɔptikəl] *adj.* 眼的，光学的
I think that's only an optical illusion, for there is no ghosts in the world.
我觉得那只是一种幻觉，因为这个世界上根本没有鬼。

---

psychological [ˌsaikə'lɔdʒikəl] *adj.* 心理的，心理学的
The boy quitted school because he had a psychological disease.
那个男孩因为有心理疾病而退学了。

---

spirit ['spirit] *n.* 精神，气魄，情绪
She wants to marry a man with the spirit of enterprise.
她想嫁给一个有事业心的男人。

考点：in spirits 兴致勃勃
out of spirits 无精打采

---

spiritual ['spiritjuəl] *adj.* 精神的，心灵的
Which one would you think highly of between material and spiritual welfare?
物质幸福和精神幸福，你更重视哪一个呢？

---

vision ['viʒən] *n.* 想象，幻觉，视力
His vision appears limited on investigation.
在投资上他的目光短浅。

---

visual ['viʒuəl] *adj.* 视觉的，看得见的
Using different colors can enforce visual comparisons.
使用不同的颜色能加强视觉对比。

---

weakness ['wi:knis] *n.* 虚弱，软弱；弱点
Could you tell me what your greatest weakness is?
请问你最大的缺点是什么？

医疗养生 检查治疗

cure [kjuə] *vt.* 医治，消除；*n.* 治愈
The vet gave him some medicine to cure his kitten.
医生给他一些药用来给他的小猫治病。

diagnose ['daiəgnəuz] *vt.* 诊断，判断
Our challenge is how to diagnose this kind of disease in unborn children.
我们的挑战是如何诊断出未出生的孩子患有这种疾病。

heal [hi:l] *vt.* 治愈，使和解
Eating the ribs can help to heal the wound.
吃排骨有助于治愈伤口。

injection [in'dʒekʃən] *n.* 注射，注入，充满
She performed nervously when she gave the little boy an injection.
她给小男孩打针时表现得很紧张。

laser ['leizə] *n.* 激光，镭射
I wonder if the laser eye surgery has side effects on our eyes.
我想知道激光手术对我们的眼睛有没有副作用。

measure ['meʒə] *vt.* 量，测量
n. 分量，度量单位，尺寸，措施
A new type of machine was invented to measure people's heart rate.
人们发明了一种新型的仪器来测量心率。

🔑 考点：beyond measure 无可估量，极度
for good measure 额外地，另外
measure up 合格，符合标准

medical ['medikəl] *adj.* 医学的，内科的
My colleague advised me to arrange for insurance in case I need medical treatment.
同事建议我考虑投保事宜，以备治疗需要。

operate ['ɔpəreit] *vi.* 操作，施行手术
Do you know how to operate this machine?
你会操作这台机器吗？

🔑 考点：operate...on sb. 对某人实施手术
operate on sb. for some disease 给某人动手术治某病

remedy ['remidi] *vt.&n.* 治疗，补救
This kind of medicine is a good remedy for a cold.

这种药是治疗感冒的良药。

physical ['fizikəl] *adj.* 物质的，物理的，身体的
Last month we had a physical examination.
上个月我们进行了一次体检。

operation [ɔpə'reiʃən] *n.* 操作，手术，运算
Doctors will give patients a general anaesthesia before they perform an operation.
医生们在动手术之前会给病人们施予全身麻醉。

🔑 考点：perform an operation on sb. 对某人实施手术

phase [feiz] *n.* 阶段，方面，相位
It's lucky that my disease was discovered in an early phase.
幸运的是，我的病在早期就被发现了。

🔑 考点：phase in 逐步引入；phase out 逐步停止使用；in phase 同时协调地

pulse [pʌls] *n.* 脉搏，脉冲，脉动
There is something wrong with you; your pulse is not very regular.
你的身体出了点问题，你的脉搏跳动得很不稳定。

thermometer [θə'mɔmitə] *n.* 温度计，寒暑表
The thermometer recorded 42℃, send him to hospital quickly.
温度计上指明是42摄氏度，赶快送他去医院。

thorough ['θʌrə] *adj.* 彻底的，详尽的
Dad promises me to have a thorough check-up tomorrow.
爸爸答应我明天去彻底检查一下身体。

🔑 考点：be thorough in 对……仔细

treatment ['tri:tmənt] *n.* 待遇，治疗，疗法
He didn't want to submit to the unjust treatment.
他不愿屈服于这种不公平的待遇。

X-ray ['eks'rei] *n.* X射线，X光
The X-ray of his lungs showed that he was likely to have a lung cancer.
他肺部的X光照片显示他很可能患了癌症。

surgery ['sə:dʒəri] *n.* 外科，外科手术
The professor told them many aspects of new trends in surgery.

教授讲了许多外科手术方面的新动向。

dose [dəus] *n.* 剂量，用量，一剂
As for this medicine, you should take a dose per day.
至于这种药，一天吃一剂。

drug [drʌg] *n.* 药，药物，药材
The boy was forced to help the drug dealers to carry drugs.
这个男孩被迫帮助这个毒贩贩毒。

harm [hɑːm] *n.* 伤害，损害；*vt.* 损害
This kind of disease will not cause you any fatal harm.
这种病不会对你有致命的伤害。

🔍 考点：come to no harm 未受到伤害
　　　　do harm to 损害，对……有害

harmful ['hɑːmful] *adj.* 有害的
Freezing winter is harmful to fruit trees.
冰冻天气对果树是有害的。

medicine ['medisin] *n.* 内服药，医学
The doctor told him to take medicine after meals.
医生叮嘱他饭后要吃药。

pill [pil] *n.* 药丸，丸剂
Hold the pill in your mouth, which is very effective to release the sore of your pharynx.
嘴里含一粒药片，这对缓解你咽喉的疼痛十分有效。

prescribe [pris'kraib] *vt.* 命令，处（方）
　　　　　　　　　　vi. 规定，指示
You have to keep in mind that the law prescribes heavy penalties for this offence.
你必须牢记法律规定从严惩处这种不法行为。

tablet ['tæblit] *n.* 药片，匾，片状物，平板电脑
Take these tablets and you will feel better.
把这些药吃了吧，你会感觉好一些。

presently ['prezəntli] *adv.* 一会儿，目前
Don't worry; the doctor will be here presently.
别着急，医生马上就来。

ambulance ['æmbjuləns] *n.* 救护车，野战医院
Get an ambulance and send the injured in the accident to hospital.

喊一辆救护车，把事故中受伤的人送到医院去。

effect [i'fekt] *n.* 结果，效果，效力
We were suffering effects of the cold weather.
我们饱受寒冷气候之苦。

🔍 考点：take effect 生效，起作用
　　　　to the effect that 大意是

effective [i'fektiv] *v.* 有效的，有影响的
Don't take too many painkillers. It is bad for your body.
不要服太多的止疼片，对你的身体有害。

真题

Showing some sense of humor can be a(n) _____ way to deal with some stressful situations.
A) effective　　　　B) efficient
C) favourable　　　 D) favorite

详　解：选A。题意为：在处理某种让人感觉到紧张的情况时，表现出幽默感是特有效的方式。A) effective意思是"有效的"；B) efficient意思是"效率高的"；C) favourable意思是"赞成的"；D) favorite意思是"喜爱的"。

(CET-4 模拟)

医疗养生 护理休养

healthcare ['helθkɛə] *n.* 医疗保健，健康护理
It is an essential problem to hence the establishment of the healthcare.
加强医疗保健建设是一个非常重要的问题。

nurse [nəːs] *n.* 保姆，护士；*vt.* 看护
I still remembered the nurse who took care of me carefully when I was in hospital for illness.
我仍然记得那个在我生病住院时精心照顾我的护士。

recover [ri'kʌvə] *vt.* 重新获得，挽回
　　　　　　　　　vi. 恢复，痊愈
You should value your time; you know it's hard to recover the lost time.
你必须珍惜时间，要知道失去的时间是难以弥补的。

recovery [ri'kʌvəri] *n.* 重获，痊愈，恢复
The economy of this country has started to show signs of recovery.
这个国家的经济已经开始显示出复苏迹象。

refresh [ri'freʃ] *vt.* 使清新
　　　　　　　　vi. 恢复精神
Having a cool drink in hot summer will refresh you.
在炎热的夏天喝点冷饮会使你感到精神清爽。

tend [tend] *vt.* 照管，照料，护理
　　　　　　vi. 走向，趋向，倾向
She gave up the holiday to tend her patients.
她放弃节假日去照顾她的病人。
🔍考点：tend to 注意，倾向

therapy ['θerəpi] *n.* 治疗，理疗
The therapy worked very well on her; she recovered quickly.
这种治疗对她很管用，她很快就恢复了。

ward [wɔ:d] *n.* 病房，受监护人
The nurse came into the ward and started work.
护士走进病房开始工作。
🔍考点：ward off 防止，避开（危险，疾病等）

hourly ['auəli] *adj.* 每小时的，每小时一次的
　　　　　　　　adv. 每小时，随时
The doctor had to observe his patient hourly.
医生每小时都要去查看他的病人一次。

医疗养生 养生保健

diet ['daiət] *n.* 议会，国会，饮食
Could you recommend some diet for old people to me?
你能向我推荐一些适合老年人的饮食吗？
🔍考点：on a diet 节食

immune [i'mju:n] *adj.* 免疫的，不受影响的，免除的，豁免的
The mistakes he made were immune to the whole plan.
他所犯的错误对整个计划是没有影响的。

essential [i'senʃəl] *adj.* 必要的，基本的
For the human, essential vitamin and mineral requirements must be met .
对于人类来说，基本的维生素和矿物质的需求，必须得到满足。
🔍考点：essential后接that从句时，从句中的谓语要用"should + 动词原形"表示虚拟。

protein ['prəuti:n] *n.* 蛋白质，朊
To human beings, carbohydrate, fat and protein are the basic nutrition.
对人类来讲，碳水化合物、脂肪与蛋白质是基本营养成分。

vitamin ['vaitəmin] *n.* 维生素
Vegetables contain a large amount of vitamin C.
蔬菜里含有大量维生素C。

科学技术 科学实验

microscope ['maikrəskəup] *n.* 显微镜
These cracks can be seen under a microscope.
这些裂纹在显微镜下能看得见。

microwave ['maikrəuweiv] *n.* 短波，超短波
　　　　　　　　　　vt. 以短波传送
He is now studying on microwave attenuation of clear sky atmosphere.
他正在研究晴朗天气下短波的衰减情况。

precise [pri'sais] *adj.* 精确的，准确的
The athlete was precise and quick in her movements.
这个运动员的动作准确、迅速。

precision [pri'siʒən] *n.* 精确，精密，精密度
I don't think you are fit for the job, you know it entails precision.
我认为你不适合这个工作，因为它需要精确性。

radar ['reidə] *n.* 雷达，无线电探测器
After a few minutes' searching, the radar quickly pinpointed the attacking planes.
经过几分钟搜索，雷达很快确定了来袭敌机的精确方位。

scanner ['skænə] *n.* 扫描仪
Do you know the significance of the scanner?
你知道扫描仪的意义吗?

subtle ['sʌtl] *adj.* 微妙的, 狡诈的, 头脑灵活的
We have to make a subtle observation to this experiment.
我们需要对这个实验作精细入微的观察。

laboratory ['læbrətɔːri] *n.* 实验室, 研究室
Our chemistry teacher had informed us to go to laboratory to have an experiment this afternoon.
我们化学老师已通知我们今天下午去实验室做实验。

device [di'vais] *n.* 器械, 装置, 设计
He wants to invent a new device for catching mice
他想发明新的捕鼠器

🔍 考点: leave to one's own devices 听任……自便, 任……自行发展

experiment [iks'perimənt] *n.* 实验, 试验
We make experiments on animals not on human.
我们用动物而非用人做试验。

experimental [iks͵peri'mentl] *adj.* 实验的, 试验的
The experimental farm is near the waterpower station.
实验农场在水电站附近。

research [ri'sə:tʃ] *vi.&n.* 调查, 探究
The scientist devoted the entirety of his life to medical research.
这位科学家把毕生精力贡献给医学研究工作。

researcher [ri'sə:tʃə] *n.* 调查者, 探究者
His grandfather used to be a university professor and researcher.
他爷爷曾是大学教授和研究员。

科学技术 科技成就

discovery [dis'kʌvəri] *n.* 发现, 被发现的事物
That man has made many discoveries in science.
那个男人已经在科学领域有了很多发现。

advance [əd'vɑːns] *vi.* 前进, 提高
n. 进展, 预付, 预支
The bear advanced on the little boy silently.
那头熊悄悄地向男孩走去。

🔍 考点: in advance 预先, 事先

advanced [əd'vɑːnst] *adj.* 先进的, 高级的
Our company will introduce lots of advanced technology from abroad every year.
每年我们公司会从国外引进许多先进的技术。

automate ['ɔːtəmeit] *vt.* 使自动化
Automate the control process of the lathes has become very easy these years.
这些年来, 机床的控制过程自动化已变得很容易。

automatic [͵ɔːtə'mætik] *adj.* 自动的, 机械的
You will get an automatic promotion after two years.
两年之后你会得到自动升职的。

automation [͵ɔːtə'meiʃən] *n.* 自动, 自动化
The technology of automation has been widely used in many fields.
自动化技术已经广泛应用于很多领域。

breakthrough ['breikθruː] *n.* 突破
The invention of the computer is nothing less than a breakthrough.
计算机的发明无疑是个突破。

clone [kləun] *n.* 克隆, 无性繁殖, 复制品
vi.&vt. 克隆, 复制
It would be terrible to clone a person like you.
克隆一个和你一样的人一定很可怕。

DNA [͵diːen'ei] *n.* 脱氧核糖核酸
DNA confirmed he was the child's father.
DNA检测确认他就是孩子的父亲。

gap [gæp] *n.* 缺口, 间隔, 差距
Our findings in this field filled the gap in history.
我们在这个领域的发现填补了其在历史上的空白。

gene [dʒiːn] *n.* 基因
The scientists have intensified their search for a new gene.
科学家们加紧搜寻一种新的基因。

genetic [dʒi'netik] *adj.* 基因的，遗传（学）的
n. 遗传学
These differences are generally genetic.
这些差别大多是遗传上的差别。

grand [grænd] *adj.* 宏伟的，重大的
Government announced that a grand field of inquiry will be opened.
政府宣布一片广大的研究领域将被开辟。

invent [in'vent] *vt.* 发明，创造，捏造
She invented an excuse when being late.
她编造了一个迟到的借口。

invention [in'venʃən] *n.* 发明，创造，捏造
Edison is accredited with the invention of the bulb.
爱迪生被认为是发明电灯泡的人。

rocket ['rɔkit] *n.* 火箭，火箭发动机
The launch of a rocket received much media coverage.
火箭的发射广获传媒报道。

satellite ['sætəlait] *n.* 卫星，人造卫星
Nowadays, people receive television pictures by satellite.
如今，人们通过人造卫星接收电视图像。

scientific [saiən'tifik] *adj.* 科学（上）的
Scientific experiment proved it a sterile debate.
科学实验证明这是一个毫无结果的辩论。

shoot [ʃuːt] *vt.* 发射，射中，拍摄
vi. 射击，射门，拍摄
n. 发芽
Could you tell me when the rocket would be shoot up into the sky?
能告诉我火箭什么时候发射吗？

🔍 **考点**：shoot down 击落，击毙，驳倒
shoot up 迅速上升，猛增

spacecraft ['speiskrɑːft] *n.* 航天器，宇宙飞船
Spacecraft is carrying on a task in outer space.
宇宙飞船正在外太空执行任务。

spaceship ['speisʃip] *n.* 航天飞船
The spaceship had successfully made a travel in outer space.
航天飞船已成功在外太空环游。

launch [lɔːntʃ] *vt.* 发射，投射，发动
n. 下水，汽艇，发射
We witnessed a missile being launched into outer space.
我们目睹了一枚导弹向外太空发射的过程。

technical ['teknikəl] *adj.* 技术的，工艺的
Now that the technical problems have been settled, you should start the work again.
既然有关技术问题已经解决，你应该重新开始工作了。

technology [tek'nɔlədʒi] *n.* 工艺学，工艺，技术
Where is the University of Science and Technology of China?
中国科学技术大学在哪？

🔍 **考点**：technology, technique都有"技术"的意思。technology是"技术，工艺"在学术理论上的总称；technique常指某种具体的技术、技艺。

科学技术 创新灵感

create [kri'eit] *vt.* 创造，引起，产生
I believe we can create the miracle together.
我相信我们能一起创造奇迹。

creative [kri'eitiv] *adj.* 创造性的，创作的
This job needs enough creative enthusiasm.
这项工作需要足够的创作热情。

creator [kri:'eitə] *n.* 创造者，设立者
Who is the creator of the novel?
这本小说的作者是谁？

devise [di'vaiz] *vt.* 设计，发明
As for this project, you should devise a new plan.
对于这个工程，你要设计一个新计划。

originality [ˌəridʒi'næliti] *n.* 独特，新颖
His books show great originality.

他写的书极其独特。

---

inspiration [ˌinspə'reiʃən] *n.* 灵感，鼓舞人心的人或事

Writers cannot write without inspiration.
作家没有灵感写不出东西。

政府政治 国家制度

queen [kwi:n] *n.* 王后，女王

The painter made a sketch of the queen immediately.
画家立刻给女王画了张素描。

---

republic [ri'pʌblik] *n.* 共和国，共和政体

Can you describe the character of the Republic?
你能描述一下共和国的性质吗?

---

republican [ri'pʌblikən] *adj.* 共和国的

There is a significant drop in backing up the Republican Party.
民众对共和党的支持率已经大副下降。

---

session ['seʃən] *n.* 会议，一段时间

You know the importance of this session cannot be exaggerated.
你知道，这次大会极为重要。

---

throne [θrəun] *n.* 王位，君主

We all know that the king was forced to give up the throne and hand over power to others.
我们都知道国王是被迫退位，把政权交给他人的。

---

local ['ləukəl] *adj.* 地方的，局部的，狭隘的 *n.* 当地人，本地人

The drastic shortage of food drove the local people away.
当地的人因为食物的严重匮乏而选择离开。

---

parliament ['pɑ:ləmənt] *n.* 议会，国会

She is the first woman to go into the parliament.
她是第一个进入议会的女人?

🖊 考点：英国的议会称parliament
美国的议会称congress
日本的议会称diet

police [pə'li:s] *n.* 警察局，警务人员，治安

The police found the hiding place of the escaped convict by the trace of his blood.
警方通过血迹找到了逃犯的藏身之地。

---

policeman [pə'li:smən] *n.* 警察

I asked the policeman who is in charge of household registration to postdate my day of birth.
我请求这个户籍警察把我的生日往后填。

---

governor ['gʌvənə] *n.* 州长，主管人员

The governor persuaded both sides to continue their talks.
州长劝双方继续洽谈。

---

mayor [mɛə] *n.* 市长，镇长

The mayor advocates reforming the economic system.
市长主张改良经济制度。

---

minister ['ministə] *n.* 部长，大臣，公使

The minister was forced to resign by his illness.
部长因病被迫辞职。

---

officer ['ɔfisə] *n.* 官员，干事，军官

The officer is found guilty of negligence.
那个官员被判犯有玩忽职守罪。

---

official [ə'fiʃəl] *adj.* 官员的，官方的

Don't abuse your official power, or you will be punished.
不要滥用职权，要不然你会受到惩罚的。

---

premier ['premjə] *n.* 总理，首相

The encouragements from the premier aroused great enthusiasm of the workers.
总理鼓励的话激发了工人们的巨大热情。

---

president ['prezidənt] *n.* 总统，校长，会长

The president championed the cause of civil rights.
总统积极支持民权运动。

---

secretary ['sekrətri] *n.* 秘书，书记，大臣

The secretary was asked to supervise the refurbishing.
秘书被派去监督整修工作。

---

senate ['senit] *n.* 参议院，上院

I recommend you not to campaign for the senate.
我建议你不要去参加参议员的竞选。

senator ['senətə] *n.* 参议员
At last, he managed to go on to become a senator.
最终，他得以继续担任参议员。

ministry ['ministri] *n.* （政府的）部，任期
The Ministry of Foreign Affairs decided to suspend negotiation.
外交部决定中止谈判。

vote [vəut] *n.* 选举，投票，表决
Most people cast the negative votes on this plan.
对于这个计划大多数人投反对票。

考点：vote in 选出；vote for 投票赞成
vote against 投票反对

bureau ['bjuərəu] *n.* 局，司，处，社，所
He works in census bureau.
他在人口调查局工作。

council ['kaunsil] *n.* 理事会，委员会
The local council gave awards for these young people who saved the drowning boy.
当地委员会为这几个勇救落水儿童的年轻人颁了奖。

federal ['fedərəl] *adj.* 联邦的，联盟的
They sent these documents by Federal Express.
他们使用联邦快递运送这些文件。

administration [ədminis'treiʃən] *n.* 管理，实行，执行，管理部门，行政机关
She is experienced in the administration.
她在管理方面很有经验。

administrative [əd'ministrətiv] *adj.* 管理的，行政的，执行的，实施的
All the teaching and administrative staff are on the playground now.
全体教职工现在都在操场上。

bulletin ['bulitin] *n.* 公报，期刊，快报，公示 *vt.* 发表，用公告通知
Here is the latest bulletin about the president's election.
这里是有关总统选举的最新公报。

candidate ['kændidit] *n.* 候选人
That man is the candidate of the parliament.
那个人就是议会的候选人。

congress ['kɔngres] *n.* 大会，国会，议会
He is afraid of losing the support of the congress.

他害怕失去国会的支持。

affair [ə'fɛə] *n.* 发生的事情，大事，事件，事务
As a monarch, he always occupies with myriad affairs every day.
作为一个君王，他总是日理万机。

真题

The lawyers advised him to drop the ____ since he stands little chance to win.
A) event   B) incident
C) case   D) affair

详 解：选C。题意为：律师劝他放弃这个案子，因为他几乎没有胜诉的可能。A) event意思是"重要事件"； B) incident意思是"小事，政治事件"； C) case意思是"案子，案件"； D) affair意思是"事情，事物"。

(CET-4 模拟)

crown [kraun] *n.* 王冠，冕，花冠
Getting the crown means seizing the sovereignty of the country.
获得王冠意味着获得了这个国家的统治权。

democracy [di'mɔkrəsi] *n.* 民主，民主制
What do you think of the Western democracy?
你认为西方的民主制度怎么样呢？

democratic [,demə'krætik] *adj.* 民主的，民主政体的
These measures are taken to reinforce democratic centralism and oppose decentralism.
这些措施是用来加强中央集权制和反对分裂的。

elect [i'lekt] *vt.* 选举，推选，选择
He was elected as the new foreign minister which made him thrilled.
他被选为新一任的外交部长，这令他激动不已。

election [i'lekʃən] *n.* 选举，推举，当选
How about having a bet on the result of the election?
我们就选举结果打个赌怎么样？

govern ['gʌvən] *vt.* 统治，治理，支配
The king didn't do anything on governing the country.
国王对于国家治理不管不问。

government ['gʌvənmənt] *n.* 治理，政治
Her dad is a competent government official.
她爸爸是个称职的政府官员。

kingdom ['kiŋdəm] *n.* 王国，领域，界
The king who ruled his kingdom with violence was killed by the people in the end.
那个用暴力统治国家的国王最后被人民杀死了。

left-wing ['leftwiŋ] *adj.* 左翼的，左派的
Left-wing groups suffered defeat in the coup against the military government.
左翼团体在推翻军政府的政变中遭受失败。

liberate ['libəreit] *vt.* 解放，释放，放出
It's the Communist Party of China who liberated China.
是中国共产党解放了中国。

政府政治 政策措施

authority [ɔː'θɔriti] *n.* 当局，官方，权力
The municipal authorities want to implement a new set of traffic regulations.
市政当局想要实施一套新的交通法规。

combination [ˌkɔmbi'neiʃən] *n.* 结合，联合，化合
It facilitates the combination of the different schools.
它有利于把学校联合起来。

combine [kəm'bain] *vt.* 使结合，兼有
In the study, we must combine theory with practice.
在学习中，我们必须把理论和实践结合起来。

committee [kə'miti] *n.* 委员会，全体委员
After consultation, a committee was constituted to investigate rising prices.
经过协商，成立了一个委员会来调查价格上涨问题。

confine ['kɔnfain] *vt.* 局限，限制，禁闭
She had to confine to bed because of poor health.
因为身体不好，她必须卧床休息。

declare [di'klɛə] *vt.* 断言，声明，表明
I now declare this meeting open.
我现在宣布会议开幕。

declaration [ˌdeklə'reiʃən] *n.* 宣告，声明，宣言
Do you know who drafted *The Declaration of Independence*?
你知道是谁起草的《独立宣言》吗?

eliminate [i'limineit] *vt.* 消灭，消除，排除
How could you eliminate this possibility?
你是如何排除这种可能性的?

guideline ['gaidlain] *n.* 指导方针，准则
Can you give me an evident guideline?
你能给我一个明确的指示吗?

implement ['implimənt] *vt.* 使生效，履行，实施
n. 工具，用具，器具
We should implement the policies of the company actively.
我们应该积极执行公司的政策。

means [miːnz] *n.* 方法，手段，工具
The government adapted severe means to repress the rising.
政府采取了一些措施来镇压叛乱。

考点：by all means 当然可以
by means of 用，依靠
by no means 决不，并没有

policy ['pɔlisi] *n.* 政策，方针
The views of board of directors coalesced to form a coherent policy.
董事会的各种观点已统一为一致的政策。

reform [ri'fɔːm] *vt.&n.* 改革，改良
The progressive party made a clamor for reform.
激进党强烈要求改革。

slavery ['sleivəri] *n.* 奴隶制度，苦役
It's Abraham Lincoln who abolished slavery in the United Sates.
是亚伯拉罕·林肯废除了美国的奴隶制度。

tack [tæk] *n.* 大头钉，行动方针
vt. 以大头针钉住，附加
vi. 改变航向，改变方针
He came up with a new tack to solve the problem.
他想出了一个解决问题的新方法。

regulate ['regjuleit] *vt.* 管理，控制，调整
The clock in our office is always slow; it needs to be regulated.
我们办公室里的钟表总是走得慢，需要校准一下。

政府政治 法律案件

bound [baund] *adj.* 一定的，有义务的
I feel bound to tell you that you're drinking too much.
我觉得有必要跟你说，你酒喝得太多了。

🔍 考点：易混词形变化：bind—bound—bound 捆，绑（不规则动词）；bound—bounded—bounded 跳跃（规则动词）。

entitle [in'taitl] *vt.* 给……权利（或资格）
Who do you think you are? What entitles you to order us about?
你以为你是谁？你有什么权力命令我们做事？

🔍 考点：entitle sth. to sb. 给某人……的权利或资格

equal ['i:kwəl] *adj.* 相等的，平等的
I adhere to the principle that all men are equal before the law.
我坚持法律面前人人平等的原则。

equality [i:'kwɔliti] *n.* 等同，平等，相等
The business should be based on the principle of equality and mutual benefit.
生意应该建立在平等互利的原则上。

must [mʌst] *aux.v.* 必须，必然要
We must infuse new blood into the club.
我们必须给俱乐部注入新鲜血液。

obligation [ˌɔbli'geiʃən] *n.* 义务，责任
They have fulfilled their obligation to support you, so don't complain about that.
他们已经尽到了抚养你的责任，所以不要抱怨了。

🔍 考点：be under an obligation to do sth. 有义务做……

ought [ɔ:t] *aux.v.* 应当，应该
It's raining outside; you ought to wear a raincoat.

外面下雨了，你应该穿件雨衣。

ownership ['əunəʃip] *n.* 所有（权），所有制
I don't know why she disclaimed ownership of the house.
我不知道为什么她放弃了房子的所有权。

privilege ['privilidʒ] *n.* 特权，优惠
A good leader is supposed to make himself naked of all privileges.
一个好的领导应该消除自己的一切特权。

rights [raits] *n.* 权利
Contract parties should know their rights and duties.
合同双方当事人应该知道彼此的权利和义务。

code [kəud] *n.* 代码，准则，法典
I can tell you the postal code of this postal district.
我能告诉你这个邮政区的邮政编码。

commit [kə'mit] *vt.* 犯（错误）；干（坏事）
For one reason or another, she committed suicide.
不知什么原因，她自杀了。

🔍 考点：commit a crime 犯罪

commitment [kə'mitmənt] *n.* 犯罪，委托，承认
I don't like the man who always shrinks back from actual commitment.
我不喜欢老是不敢承担实际义务的男人。

condemn [kən'dem] *vt.* 谴责，指责，判刑
The man condemned to be shot because he killed three persons.
这个人被处以枪决，因为他杀了3个人。

confess [kən'fes] *vt.* 供认，承认，坦白
He is innocent, but the police tortured him to confess his crime.
他是无辜的，但是警察却拷打他，逼他招供。

convict ['kɔnvikt] *n.* 罪犯，囚犯
vt. 证明……有罪，判……有罪
The convict beseeched the warden to let him attend his mother's funeral and say goodbye to her.
囚犯恳求监狱长让他参加母亲的葬礼，跟她告别。

🔍 考点：to convict sb. of sth. 判决某人犯有……罪

crime [kraim] *n.* 罪，罪行，犯罪
According to the law, stealing cultural relics is a crime.
法律规定，偷窃文物是一种犯罪行为。

criminal ['kriminl] *n.* 犯人，罪犯，刑事犯
The police puts the arrested criminal in manacles.
警察给被捕的罪犯带上手铐。

evidence ['evidəns] *n.* 根据，证据，证人
Spring is coming! The signs are in evidence.
春天来了！迹象已经明显可见。

考点：in evidence 可看见的，明显的

exception [ik'sepʃən] *n.* 例外，除外
Most children like sweets, but there are some exceptions.
大多数孩子喜欢吃糖果，但也有一些例外。

考点：take exception to 反对，表示异议

exclude [iks'klu:d] *vt.* 把……排除在外
We must go to work every day, Sundays excluded.
除星期天外，我们每天都要去上班。

execute ['eksikju:t] *vt.* 处死，处决，实施，完成
The soldier had no choice but to execute the colonel's orders.
士兵除了执行上校的命令外，别无选择。

fair [fɛə] *adj.* 公平的，相当的
n. 定期集市，博览会
He is an upright man, so I believe he will make a fair judgement.
他是一个正直的人，所以我相信他会做出公正的判决。

innocence ['inəsns] *n.* 清白，天真，单纯
He maintained his innocence before the judge.
他在法官面前坚持自己是无辜的。

innocent ['inəsnt] *adj.* 清白的，幼稚的，无辜的
Everyone believes that he is innocent of murder in court.
法庭上，大家都认为他没有犯谋杀罪。

考点：be innocent of 没有……罪
be guilty of 有……罪

illegal [i'li:gəl] *adj.* 不合法的，非法的
Such an illegal act should be treated seriously.

这样的违法行为应该严重对待。

真题

In the US, 88 percent of smokers had started before they were 18, despite the fact that it is _____ to sell cigarettes to anyone under the age.
A) illegal   B) irrational
C) liberal   D) liable

详　解：选A。题意为：在美国，尽管把香烟卖给18岁以下的人是非法的，但88％的烟民在18岁之前就开始吸烟了。A) illegal意思是"违法的"；B) irrational意思是"无理性的"；C) liberal意思是"自由的，慷慨的"；D) liable意思是"易于……的，有……倾向的"，常与to连用。

(CET-4 模拟)

instance ['instəns] *n.* 例子，实例，事例
He provided an authentic instance for this case.
他为这个案件提供了可靠的实例。

考点：in the first instance 首先，起初
for instance 例如，比如

investigate [in'vestigeit] *vi.&vt.* 调查
The police began at once to investigate the case.
警察立即开始调查此案。

involve [in'vɔlv] *vt.* 使卷入，牵涉
This incident would involve Greece in a fearful strife.
这个事件将使希腊卷入一场可怕的战争。

真题

Putting in a new window will _____ cutting away part of the roof.
A) contain   B) comprise
C) include   D) involve

详　解：选D。题意为：装一扇新窗户就得截去部分屋顶。A) contain指容纳的东西是其组成的一部分；B) comprise指包含的人或物构成整体的全部；C) include所包含的人或事物整体中的一个组成部分；D) involve指根据整体性质决定应包含某些成分或结果，后接动名词作宾语。

(CET-4 模拟)

involved [in'vɔlvd] *adj.* 有关的，复杂的，混乱的
Jack was involved in a chain of matters.
杰克被卷入一连串的事件中。

judge [dʒʌdʒ] *n.* 法官，裁判员
The judge suspected the witness didn't speak out the truth.
法官怀疑证人没有说实话。

judgement [ˈdʒʌdʒmənt] *n.* 意见，审判，判断
My judgement is different from theirs about this question.
在这个问题上，我的意见与他们的不同。

jury [ˈdʒuəri] *n.* 陪审团，评奖团
He was convicted by the jury in court.
法庭上，陪审团宣判他有罪。

justice [ˈdʒʌstis] *n.* 正义，公正，司法
The society is lack of justice nowadays, he thinks.
他认为当今社会缺乏公正。

考点：bring...to justice 把……交付审判，使归案受审；do justice to 公平地对待，公平地评判

killer [ˈkilə] *n.* 杀人犯，杀手，屠宰者
The killer would appear because it was a good chance to take action as he planned.
杀手会出现，因为这是一个按照他的计划采取行动的好机会。

legalization [ˌliːgəlaiˈzeiʃən] *n.* 合法化
It still needs to make a deep investigation about the legalization of this document.
关于这份文件的合法性还需要做深度调查。

legal [ˈliːgəl] *adj.* 法律的，合法的
According to the law in our country, legal personal property should be protected.
按照我国法律规定，个人的合法财产应该受到保护。

legislation [ˌledʒisˈleiʃən] *n.* 法律，法规，立法
When will the new legislation begin to be enforced?
新法规何时开始实施？

murder [ˈməːdə] *vi.&n.* 谋杀，凶杀
The muder was still at large.
凶手仍然在逃。

liberty [ˈlibəti] *n.* 自由，释放，许可，放肆
The Statue of Liberty is a symbol of independence, democracy and freedom.
自由女神像是独立、民主和自由的象征。

考点：at liberty 自由的，不受囚禁的

murderer [ˈməːdərə] *n.* 杀人犯，凶手
The murderer thrust a dagger into her heart.
凶手把匕首刺进她的心脏。

partial [ˈpɑːʃəl] *adj.* 部分的，不公平的
As a judge, you should not be partial whichever part.
作为一名法官，你不应当偏颇任何一方。

考点：be partial to 对……有偏心，偏爱……

prison [ˈprizn] *n.* 监狱，监禁
The man was sent to prison on a narcotics charge.
那个男的因为被指控贩卖毒品而被关进监狱。

prisoner [ˈpriznə] *n.* 囚犯
The prisoner who escaped from prison last night had been hunted down.
昨晚越狱的那个囚犯已经被抓获了。

proof [pruːf] *n.* 证据，证明，校样
Do you have any proof to substantiate your alibi?
你有证据表明你当时不在犯罪现场吗？

prove [pruːv] *vt.* 证明；*vi.* 结果是
Fortunately, those methods have proved quite effective.
幸运的是那些方法证明是有效的。

punish [ˈpʌniʃ] *vt.* 罚，惩罚，处罚
I think it is cruelty to the innocent not to punish the guilty.
在我看来，不惩罚罪犯对无辜者来说就是残忍的。

punishment [ˈpʌniʃmənt] *n.* 罚，惩罚，处罚
We should inflict severe punishment on criminals.
我们应该对罪犯施加严厉的惩罚。

relativity [ˌreləˈtiviti] *n.* 相关性，相对性
I think there is no relativity between the two matters.
我认为这两件事毫无关系。

rob [rɔb] *vi.&vt.* 抢劫，劫掠，使丧失
You know that my brother's friend tempted him to rob the bank.
你知道吗，我弟弟的朋友竟然怂恿他去抢劫银行。

考点：比较 cheat, steal, rob的用法：cheat sb. (out) of sth. 骗某人某物；steal sth. from sb. / some place 从某人（某处）偷某物；rob sb. / some place of sth 抢某人（某处）某物。

snap [snæp] *vi.* 啪嗒一声，厉声说话，猛咬
　　　　　　 vt. 使咔嚓一声折断，给……拍快照
　　　　　　 n. 啪嗒声，快照
　　　　　　 adj. 仓促的，突然的
It is risky to make snap judgements for this case.
匆忙对这个案件作判断是有冒险性的。

考点：snap out 迅速从……中恢复过来
　　　snap up 抢购，抢先弄到手

release [ri'li:s] *vt.* 释放，放松，发表
The man concerned the case secured the release of the hostages.
关心这个案子的人已经设法使人质获释。

真题
The energy ＿＿＿ by the chain reaction is transformed into heat.
A) conveyed　　 B) released
C) transferred　 D)delivered

详　解：选B。题意为：在连锁反应中释放的能量转化成了热。A) convey 意思是"运送，传送"；B) release意思是"释放，解除"；C) transfer 意思是"转移，调任"；D) deliver意思是"递送，传送"。

(CET-4 模拟)

robber ['rɔbə] *n.* 强盗，盗贼
The girl was scared when the robber threatened her with a revolver.
当劫匪用一只左轮手枪威胁那个小女孩时，她十分恐惧。

sin [sin] *n.* 罪，罪孽；*vi.* 犯罪
God will forgive all sins.
神会宽恕一切的罪恶。

suit [sju:t] *n.* 起拆，诉讼；*vt.* 适合
People need suit themselves to the things around.
人们需要适应周围的事物。

supreme [sju:'pri:m] *adj.* 最高的，最大的
The Supreme Court will give the final ruling next week.
下周最高法庭将作出最后的裁决。

theft [θeft] *n.* 偷窃，失窃
Our security against theft is very adequate.
我们对窃盗的防备工作做得十分充分。

torture ['tɔ:tʃə] *n.* 拷问，折磨
　　　　　　　　　 vt. 拷打
The police used torture to extort a confession from the criminals.
警方用刑逼罪犯招供。

valid ['vælid] *adj.* 有效的，正当的
He declared the document legally valid.
他宣布这份文件有法律效力。

violate ['vaiəleit] *vt.* 违反，亵渎，侵犯
His behaviour has violated the privacy of others.
他的行为已经侵害了他人的隐私。

trace [treis] *n.* 痕迹，丝毫；*vt.* 跟踪
They disappeared without leaving a trace for the police.
他们不见了，没有给警察留下一点可循的痕迹。

考点：a trace of 一丝，少许
　　　trace back 追溯以往

真题
The physical difference between men and women can be ＿＿＿ directly to our basic roles as hunters and childbearers.
A) switched　　 B) traced
C) pursued　　 D) followed

详　解：选D。题意为：男人和女人体质的差异可以直接追溯到（早期的）基本角色：男人狩猎，女人生儿育女。A) switch意思是"转换，转变"；B) trace意思是"追踪，追溯"；C) pursue意思是"追赶，从事"；D) follow意思是"跟随，追随"，常与after连用。

(CET-4 模拟)

abolish [ə'bɔliʃ] *vt.* 彻底废除，废止
He advised me to abolish some bad customs.
他建议我废除一些不良的习俗。

*

public ['pʌblik] *adj.* 公众的；*n.* 公众
Police warned the public to be on the alert for suspected terrorist.
警方警告群众警惕涉嫌的恐怖分子。

*

commute [kə'mju:t] *vt.* 交换，兑换，偿付，减轻；*vi.* 通勤，补偿；*n.* 往返的路程
Is it possible for the pregnant woman to be given commuted sentence?
这个孕妇有可能获得减刑判决吗？

*

witness ['witnis] *n.* 证据，证人；*vt.* 目击
The witness was intimidated, so he dared not to tell the truth.
目击者被人威胁不敢说出实情。

真题

The defense lawyer was questioning the old man who was one of the _____ of the murder committed last month.
A) observers   B) witnesses
C) audiences   D) viewers

详　解：选B。题意为：辩护律师正在询问那位老人，他是上个月谋杀案的目击证人之一。A) observer意思是"（会议、课堂的）观察员"；B) witness意思是"证人"；C) audience意思是"听众，观众"；D) viewer意思是"电视观众"。

(CET-4 模拟)

*

clue [klu:] *n.* 线索，暗示，提示
A passer-by gave the police an important clue which helped them to solve the case.
一个过路人给了警方一条重要线索帮助他们破了案。

*

accessory [ək'sesəri] *n.* 同谋，从犯，附件
It is surprised to us that the little boy was an accessory to the murder.
让人吃惊的是那个小男孩竟然是谋杀案的从犯。

*

assert [ə'sə:t] *vt.* 声称，断言；维护，坚持
The young man most positively asserted the charge to be incorrect.
这个年轻人斩钉截铁地声称这一指控是不正确的。

考点：assert oneself 坚持自己的权利，显示自己的权威

*

bribe [braib] *n.* 贿赂，贿赂物
　　　　　 vi.&vt. 贿赂
The judge is an impartial and incorruptible one, and he's never taken bribes.
这个法官铁面无私，他从来不收贿赂。

*

court [kɔ:t] *n.* 法院，法庭，庭院
Mr. Green was summoned to appear in the court.
格林先生被传唤出庭。

考点：at court 在宫中
　　　 in court 在法庭上

*

courtroom ['kɔ:tru:m] *n.* 法庭，审判室
I can't stand the atmosphere in the courtroom.
我不能忍受法庭里的气氛。

*

arrest [ə'rest] *vt.&n.* 逮捕，拘留，阻止
Could you give me a just excuse if you want to arrest me?
如果你想逮捕我，那请给我一个正当的理由好吗？

考点：arrest sb. for... 因……而逮捕某人
　　　 under arrest 被捕
　　　 place sb. under arrest 逮捕某人

*

gang [gæŋ] *n.* 一帮，一伙
The gang knocked off a bank last night.
这帮匪徒昨晚抢了一个银行。

和平与发展 军事

army ['ɑ:mi] *n.* 军队，陆军
　　　　　 vt. 以武器装备，配备，支持
The people in the town are fighting against the invading army.
城镇中的人们正在抗击入侵的军队。

*

arm [ɑ:m] *n.* 臂，臂状物，武器，备战
My little sister's arm was hurt by the cat's sharp claws.
我小妹的胳膊被猫的利爪抓伤了。

考点：arm in arm 臂挽臂

attack [əˈtæk] *vi.&vt.&n.* 攻击，进攻，（病）发作

The enemy attacked us last night.
敌人昨晚攻击我们。

🔍 考点：have an attack of（……病）发作；launch / make an attack on 攻击

bullet [ˈbulit] *n.* 枪弹，子弹，弹丸

Imagine what will happen next when he carefully fits a bullet.
当他小心翼翼地装上一颗子弹时，试想一下将会发生什么事。

cannon [ˈkænən] *n.* 大炮，火炮，榴弹炮

They want to use cannons to reduce the city to rubble.
他们想要用大炮将这座城市夷为平地。

captain [ˈkæptin] *n.* 陆军上尉，队长

My brother is the captain of a football team.
我哥哥是一支足球队的队长。

colonel [ˈkə:nl] *n.* 陆军上校，中校

The soldier had no choice but to execute the colonel's orders.
士兵除了执行上校的命令外，别无选择。

command [kəˈmɑ:nd] *vt.* 命令，指挥，控制

It is said that he was in command of the air force in the World War II.
据说，在二战期间他是空军指挥官。

commander [kəˈmɑ:ndə] *n.* 司令官，指挥员

The commander regretted making this irrevocable order.
指挥官后悔下了这个不可改变的命令。

defence [diˈfens] *n.* 防御，防务，辩护

As Commander-in -Chief of the armed forces, I have directed that all measures be taken for our defence.
我作为武装部队的总司令命令采取一切措施进行防御。

detection [diˈtekʃən] *n.* 察觉，发觉，侦查

The detection of his crime took the police two months.
对他罪行的侦查花了警察两个月的时间。

detect [diˈtekt] *vt.* 察觉，发觉，侦察

I detected sadness from his expression.
我从他的表情中察觉到他的忧伤。

defend [diˈfend] *vt.* 保卫，防守

If the enemy army dares to invade, we must defend to the death our motherland.
如果敌军敢来侵犯，我们必须誓死保卫我们的国家。

detective [diˈtektiv] *n.* 侦探

His wife employed a private detective to investigate him.
他的妻子雇了一名私人侦探调查他。

disarm [disˈɑ:m] *vi.&vt.* 解除武装，放下武器

It is not easy to persuade them to disarm.
要说服他们放下武器是很不容易的。

fleet [fli:t] *n.* 舰队，船队，机群

The fishing fleet came back in the late evening.
直到深夜，渔船队才回来。

guard [gɑ:d] *vt.* 守卫，看守；*n.* 卫兵

The guard was punished for leaving his work without permission.
卫兵因擅离职守而受到处罚。

🔍 考点：guard against 提防，预防
　　　on guard 站岗，值班

marshal [ˈmɑ:ʃəl] *n.* 元帅，司仪，执法官

The old man used to be a marshal before retirement.
那个老人退休前是个元帅。

military [ˈmilitəri] *adj.* 军事的，军人的 *n.* 军人，军队

In some countries every young man must do three years' military service.
在有些国家，每个年轻男子都必须服3年兵役。

naval [ˈneivəl] *adj.* 海军的，军舰的

My uncle is a naval officer, and I haven't seen him for about two years.
我叔叔是个海军军官，我大概两年都没有见到他了。

navigation [ˌnæviˈgeiʃən] *n.* 航行，航海术，导航

This new system will facilitate the navigation of the seas.
这套新系统将会促进海上航行技术的发展。

navy ['neivi] *n.* 海军
The army, navy and air force are coordinate branches of the armed services.
陆、海、空三军是部队的3个平等的军种。

rifle ['raifl] *n.* 步枪，来复枪
The man accidentally triggered his rifle, and killed his lover.
男人无意中扣动了他步枪的扳机，误杀了他的爱人。

rightist ['raitist] *n.* 右派人士，保守党员
　　　　　　　　 adj. 右翼的，右派的
These mistakes here arose from a rightist viewpoint.
这些错误是从右倾的观点产生的。

right-wing [,rait'wiŋ] *adj.* 右翼的，右派的
The police suspected the bomb was planted by right-wing extremists.
警方怀疑这颗炸弹是右翼极端分子放置的。

safety ['seifti] *n.* 安全，保险，安全设备，安全场所
The careless driver is quite reckless of his own safety.
这个粗心的司机完全不顾及自己的安全。

scout [skaut] *n.* 侦察，侦察员，侦察机
He had a scout round to see what he could find.
他四处搜寻看看能找到些什么。

secure [si'kjuə] *adj.* 安心的，安全的
The danger is passed and the city is now secure.
危险过去了，城市现在安全了。

security [si'kjuəriti] *n.* 安全，安全感
Don't worry. I'll undertake for your security.
别担心，我将保证你的安全。

siege [si:dʒ] *n.* 包围，围困
After two year's siege, the small country surrendered.
经过一年的围攻，那个小国家投降了。

strategic [strə'ti:dʒik] *adj.* 关键的，战略上的
This is a tremendously strategic moment for him.
这对他来说是非常关键的时刻。

strategy ['strætidʒi] *n.* 战略，策略
We formulated our own strategy against our rivals.
我们制订了对付对手的策略。

telescope ['teliskəup] *n.* 望远镜
Who is the first person to use a telescope?
谁是第一个使用望远镜的人？

trench [trentʃ] *n.* 深沟，壕沟，战壕
During the war, trenches were dug to keep the soldiers' safety when they were fighting with the enemies.
战争时期，当战士们与敌人交战时，战壕可以保护他们的安全。

troop [tru:p] *n.* 军队，一群，大量
A troop of boys were playing in the swimming pool.
一群男孩在泳池玩耍。

pistol ['pistl] *n.* 手枪
The policeman dashed out the robber's brains with a pistol.
警察一枪就把劫匪打了个脑袋开花。

raid [reid] *n.* 袭击，突然搜查
　　　　 vt. 袭击，劫掠，劫夺
The troop of enemy raided the docks where our troop stayed.
敌军突然袭击了我军所在的码头。

🎯 考点：make a raid on 对……进行袭击

sword [sɔ:d] *n.* 剑，刀
He cut off the branch of the tree with one stroke of his sword.
他一刀就砍断了树枝。

tank [tæŋk] *n.* 坦克，大容器，槽
That country bought a large amount of light tanks.
那个国家买进大批轻型坦克。

trigger ['trigə] *n.* 扳机
　　　　　 vt. 触发，引起
Popular indignation was triggered by a chain of police arrest.
警方一连串的逮捕行动激起民愤。

weapon ['wepən] *n.* 武器，兵器
The warriors with weapons are ready to rush to the battlefield.
带着武器的勇士们准备奔赴战场。

archive ['ɑ:kaiv] *n.* 档案，档案管理处
He opened the archive to search for some militant information.
他打开档案，找一些军事资料。

file [fail] *n.* 档案；*vt.* 把……归档
The undergraduates need to draw out their files when they leave the college.
毕业生需要在离校前取出自己的档案。

考点：on file 存档

missile ['misail] *n.* 发射物，导弹，飞弹
We must try to intercept the missiles coming towards us.
我们必须设法拦截住飞过来的导弹。

dawn [dɔ:n] *n.* 黎明，开端
　　　　　 vi. 破晓，开始
I just want to remind you that the enemy will strike at dawn.
我就是想告诉你敌人会在拂晓时发起进攻。

考点：dawn on / up 开始明白，醒悟

signal ['signl] *n.* 信号；*vi.* 发信号
There is no signal in the mountain; the message can't be sent to her husband.
山中没有信号，不能把信息发给她丈夫。

和平与发展　战争&和平

campaign [kæm'pein] *n.* 战役，运动
The campaign to capture this fortress is proved to be a successful one.
攻破这个堡垒的战役被证明是成功的。

考点：campaign for / against 支持 / 反
　　　对……的活动

真题

We have planned an exciting publicity_____ with our advertisers.
A) battle　　　 B) struggle
C) conflict　　 D) campaign

详　解：选D。题意为：我们已经计划与我们的广告商一起举行一次激动人心的宣传活动。campaign常表示政治或商业性活动；election campaign竞选活动；campaign for equal rights争取平等权利的运动。A) battle意思是"战斗，争夺"；B) struggle意思是"斗争，奋斗"，struggle for independence争取独立；struggle against cancer同癌症的斗争；C) conflict意思是"冲突"。

(CET-4 模拟)

destroy [dis'trɔi] *vt.* 破坏，消灭，打破
You must know some bad words will destroy the relationship between friends.
你必须清楚一些不好的话会伤害朋友间的关系。

destruction [dis'trʌkʃən] *n.* 破坏，毁灭，
　　　　　　　　　　　　　 消灭
Drinking was thereason of his destruction.
酗酒是他毁灭的原因。

destructive [dis'trʌktiv] *adj.* 破坏性的，否
　　　　　　　　　　　　　　 定的
We can do nothing to this kind of destructive malfunction.
对于这种破坏性故障我们一点办法也没有。

exile ['eksail] *n.* 流放，流亡，流亡者，背井
　　　　　 离乡者
　　　　　 vt. 流放，放逐
He was exiled from his own country.
他被逐出自己的国家。

hostile ['hɔstail] *adj.* 敌方的，不友善的
They neither offend us, nor can we deem them hostile.
他们既不触犯我们，我们也不认为他们怀有敌意。

invade [in'veid] *vt.* 入侵，侵略，侵袭
The cancer cells may invade other parts of the body if you don't have an operation.
如果不动手术，癌细胞可能侵袭你身体的其他部分。

invasion [in'veiʒən] *n.* 入侵，侵略，侵犯
England itself was threatened with invasion in the World War II.
二战中英国自身也受到入侵的威胁。

monument ['mɔnjumənt] *n.* 纪念碑，纪念馆
This monument is in remembrance of the heroes died in the battle.
这座纪念碑是为怀念在这次战斗中牺牲的英雄而建的。

考点：the monument to the People's
　　　Heroes 人民英雄纪念碑

peace [pi:s] *n.* 和平，和睦，平静
I think world peace is a cause we should all work for.
我认为争取世界和平是一项我们都应该为之而努力的事业。

peaceful ['pi:sful] *adj.* 和平的，安静的
If the world is to remain peaceful, the utmost effort must be made by nations to limit local conflicts.
要想让世界保持安宁，各国必须尽最大的努力减少地区冲突。

refuge ['refju:dʒ] *n.* 避难，庇护，庇护者
I can find a refuge in music when I sad.
我伤心时会在音乐中寻找慰藉。

remain [ri'mein] *vi.* 剩下，余留，保持
In spite of the panic, she remained serene and in control.
尽管人心惶惶，但她却泰然自若。

remains [ri'meinz] *n.* 残余，余额，废墟
During my summer holiday, I visited the remains of ancient Rome.
暑假时，我参观了古罗马遗迹。

revenge [ri'vendʒ] *vt.* 替……报仇
n. 报仇
The man vowed to revenge on the people who had looked down upon him.
那人发誓一定要报复所有瞧不起他的人。

真题

The Spanish team, who are not in superb form, will be doing their best next week to _____ themselves on the German team for last year's defeat.
A) remedy   B) reproach
C) revive   D) revenge

详　解： 选D。题意为：不是最佳阵容的西班牙队下周将尽力向去年打败自己的德国队报仇。A) remedy意思为"医治，补救"；B) reproach意思为"责备"；C) revive意思为"使复活，再现"；D) revenge意思为"报仇，报复"。

(CET-4 2003.12)

ruin [ruin] *n.* 毁灭，废墟；*vt.* 毁坏
He ruined his prospects by cheating in the exam.
他因在考试中作弊而断送了前途。

🔍 **考点：** ruin, destroy, damage都有"破坏"的意思。ruin"毁坏，损坏"，指经过长时间的侵蚀而毁坏；destroy 指彻底的毁坏，摧毁；damage 是一般的部分损坏。

sacrifice ['sækrifais] *vt.&n.* 牺牲，献祭
The man sacrificed his life to save a girl from drowning.
那个男人为了救溺水的姑娘而牺牲了自己的生命。

stability [stə'biliti] *n.* 稳定，稳定性，巩固
The social stability can accelerate the development of economy.
社会安定能加速经济发展。

veteran ['vetərən] *n.* 老兵，老手
He is a veteran in playing football.
他是位足球老将。

surrender [sə'rendə] *vt.* 交出，放弃
vi. 投降，屈服于，让步
n. 投降，放弃
As we all know, the white flag is a symbol of a truce or surrender.
众所周知，白旗表示停战或投降。

terrorist ['terərist] *n.* 恐怖分子
adj. 恐怖主义的
The three terrorists involved in the embassy upheaval.
这3个恐怖分子被卷入到大使馆的动乱当中。

terrorism ['terə,rizəm] *n.* 恐怖主义，恐怖行动
The two countries have a reciprocal agreement to combat terrorism.
这两个国家有相互配合的协定，共同与恐怖主义作斗争。

turbulence ['tə:bjuləns] *n.* 骚乱，动荡，喧嚣，狂暴，湍流
This almost caused an unprecedented turbulence in the world situation.
这几乎导致了世界局势的空前大混乱。

undermine [,ʌndə'main] *vt.* 暗中破坏，侵蚀……的基础
Incidents like these can undermine his credibility.
这一类事情可能会损毁他的声誉。

violence ['vaiələns] *n.* 猛烈，激烈，暴力
Violence has erupted in the factory last week.
上周工厂突然发生了暴乱。

violent ['vaiələnt] *adj.* 猛烈的，狂暴的
He gave him a violent blow on the face.

他对准他的脸猛击一下。

------

progressive [prə'gresiv] *adj.* 进步的，向前进的

I believe all progressive human beings love peace.
我相信所有的进步人士都热爱和平。

------

confuse [kən'fju:z] *vt.* 使混乱，混淆

I always confuse Australia with Austria.
我总是把澳大利亚和奥地利混淆。

------

confusion [kən'fju:ʒən] *n.* 混乱，骚乱，混淆

After one day's confusion, I summoned up all my courage to telephone him.
一天的迷茫过后，我鼓足勇气给他打了个电话。

------

crisis ['kraisis] *n.* 危机，存亡之际

Affected by the economic crisis, this company was forced to fire half of its employees.
受经济危机的影响，这个公司被迫解雇了一半的员工。

------

rebel ['rebəl] *vi.* 造反； *n.* 造反者

The colonists took up weapons to rebel against the British ruler in the end of the movie.
电影的结尾部分是殖民地的人们拿起武器反抗英国统治者。

🔍**考点**：rebel against exploitation 反抗剥削；rebel at the very idea of 想到……就有反感

------

rebellion [ri'beljən] *n.* 造反，叛乱，反抗

There is a rule that every riot predicts a rebellion.
每一次骚动都预示着一场反叛，这是规律。

------

revolt [ri'vəult] *vi.&n.* 反抗，造反

The ruler convened his troops to put down the revolt of farmers.
统治者召集他的部队去镇压农民们的叛乱。

------

revolution [ˌrevə'lu:ʃən] *n.* 革命，旋转，绕转

Those rioters are planning to launch a revolution to overthrow the monarch.
那些暴民们正准备发动革命推翻君主。

------

revolutionary [ˌrevə'lu:ʃənəri] *adj.* 革命的 *n.* 革命者

There are many secret revolutionary societies in the city.
这个城市里有很多秘密的革命组织。

riot ['raiət] *n.* 暴乱，骚乱，极度丰富 *vi.* 聚众闹事

When the massive wave of student riots happened, I was sick in bed.
当那次大规模的学生骚乱发生时，我正卧病在床。

🔍**考点**：run riot 撒野，胡作非为

------

protest [prə'test] *vi.&vt.&n.* 抗议

It turned out that his proposal has raised squawks of protest in congress.
结果是他的建议在国会里引起了大声抗议。

------

strike [straik] *vi.&vt.* 打，击； *n.* 罢工

Strike while the iron's hot.
趁热打铁，趁机行事。

🔍**考点**：strike sb. doing sth. 撞见（偶然发现）某人做某事；to strike sb. as... 给某人留下……的印象；it strike sb. that...使某人忽然想起

真题

I was about to _____ a match when I remembered Tom's warning.
A)scrape　　B)strike
C)rub　　D)hit

详　解：选B。题意为：我正要划火柴时想起了汤姆的警告。strike a match 固定搭配，意思是"划火柴"。

(CET-4 模拟)

------

battle ['bætl] *n.* 战役，斗争； *vi.* 作战

After a fierce battle, we occupied the enemy's capital.
一场激烈的战斗之后，我们占领了敌国首都。

------

blast [blɑ:st] *n.* 爆炸，冲击波； *vt.* 炸

Lots of people were killed by this blast.
许多人在这次爆炸中丧生。

🔍**考点**：(at) full blast 大力地，全速地

------

blaze [bleiz] *vi.* 熊熊燃烧，着火，迸发 *n.* 火焰，烈火，光辉，爆发

Before the blaze was put out, there were seven buildings which had been burnt to the ground.
大火扑灭前，已经有7座大厦被烧成平地。

🔍**考点**：blaze a trail 开拓道路，先导

bomb [bɔm] *n.* 炸弹；*vt.* 轰炸
Watch out! The time bomb may explode at any time.
小心，定时炸弹可能随时会爆炸。

burst [bə:st] *vt.* 使爆裂；*vi.&n.* 爆炸
I want to know why the balloon burst.
我想知道这个气球为什么爆了。

考点：burst in / on 突然出现
burst into 闯入，突然……起来
burst out 大声喊叫，突然……起来
burst into + n. = burst out doing 突然做……

真题

In a sudden ____ of anger, the man tore up everything within reach.
A) attack　　B) burst
C) split　　D) blast

详　解：选B。题意为：一气之下，这个男人把触手可及的东西全撕毁了。burst用于情感的爆发，这里指发脾气。

(CET-4 模拟)

captive ['kæptiv] *n.* 俘虏，被监禁的人
The captive was confined in a dungeon.
俘虏被关在地牢里。

考点：be taken captive 被俘

capture ['kæptʃə] *vt.* 捕获，俘获，夺得
In order to avoid capture, the Communist went underground.
为了避免被抓，这个共产党员转入了秘密工作状态。

occupy ['ɔkjupai] *vt.* 占领，占有，使忙碌
It's not polite for young people to occupy the priority seats and ignore the weak standing nearby.
对于年轻人来说，霸占老弱病残孕专座，不给他们让座是不礼貌的。

combat ['kɔmbət] *vi.&vt.* 与……作斗争，搏斗，打
n. 斗争，搏斗
Police are planning sterner measures to combat crime.
警方正在制订更严厉的措施来打击犯罪活动。

真题

The university has launched a research center to develop new ways of ____ bacteria which have become resist.
A) regulating　　B) halting
C) interrupting　　D) combating

详　解：选D。题意为：这所大学已创办了一个科研中心，致力于开发新方法来对抗已产生抗药性的细菌。A) regulate 意思是"管理，为……制定规章"；B) halt意思是"停止，使终止"；C) interrupt意思是"打断，插话"；D) combat (= fight / battle with) the enemy / diseases 战胜敌人/疾病。

(CET-4 2003.12)

和平与发展　外交

domestic [də'mestik] *adj.* 本国的，家庭的
The newspaper provides not only foreign news but also domestic news.
这家报纸不仅刊登国外新闻也刊登国内新闻。

diplomat ['dipləmæt] *n.* 外交官（家），圆滑的人
Zhou Enlai was known as a famous statesman and diplomat.
周恩来是一位著名的政治家和外交家。

diplomatic [ˌdiplə'mætik] *adj.* 外交的，有手腕的
I really admire your little sister's diplomatic tact.
我真的很佩服你妹妹的外交手腕。

embassy ['embəsi] *n.* 大使馆，大使的住宅，大使及其随员
I am proud that my brother will be sent on an embassy.
我很骄傲我的弟弟出任大使。

global ['gləubəl] *adj.* 全球的，总的，完整的
Global economy is more and more common nowadays.
如今，全球化经济越来越普遍了。

globe [gləub] *n.* 地球，世界，地球仪
The world is a globe of substance.
世界是由物质构成的一个整体。

frontier ['frʌntjə] *n.* 边境，边疆，新领域
A lot of people can not adapt to the life in the frontier.
很多人都难以适应边疆生活。

🔍 考点：frontier, border的区别：frontier指某一国家单方面提及的边境；border可以用来指国与国之间的边界。

international [ˌintə'næʃənəl] *adj.* 国际的，世界（性）的
International trade reflects the evolution of global economy.
国际贸易反映了全球化经济的演变。

spokesman ['spəʊksmən] *n.* 发言人
He is the spokesman of the newspaper office.
他是这个报社的发言人。

spokesperson ['spəʊkspɜːsn] *n.* 发言人，代言人
The spokesperson said: "We have learned that they all were safe in this accident."
这名发言人说：“我们听说他们在这次事故中都是安全的”。

tact [tækt] *n.* 机智，手法
He showed great diplomatic tact in dealing with this conflict.
在解决这次冲突的过程中，他表现出了高超的外交手腕。

treaty ['triːti] *n.* 条约，协议，协定
France required appending a new clause to the treaty.
法国要求在条约上附加了一项新条款。

expert ['ekspɜːt] *n.* 专家；*adj.* 熟练的
My father is an expert in foreign affairs.
我父亲是一个外交事务专家。

alliance [ə'laiəns] *n.* 结盟，联盟
Many countries tried to seek economical alliance with other countries in order to develop economy.
为了发展经济，许多国家试图寻求与其他国家结成经济联盟。

🔍 考点：in alliance with 与……联盟

ally [ə'lai] *vt.* 使结盟，使联合
vi. 结盟，联合
n. 结盟者，联合者

We all know that England and Russia were allies in the Second World War.
大家都知道英国和俄国在第二次世界大战中是盟国。

ambassador [æm'bæsədə] *n.* 大使，使节，派驻国际组织的代表
American ambassador will visit China next month.
美国大使下个月将来访中国。

behalf [bi'hɑːf] *n.* 利益，维护，支持
I gave a speech on my family's behalf.
我代表我家人做了发言。

🔍 考点：in / on behalf of 代表，为了

其他　天气时令

blow [bləʊ] *vi.* 吹，吹动，吹响
n. 一击，打击
The wind is blowing hard outside.
外面风吹得很大。

🔍 考点：blow up 爆炸，（被）炸飞，充气，发脾气

breeze [briːz] *n.* 微风，和风
The flag was stirring in the morning breeze.
旗子在早上的微风中摇动。

centigrade ['sentigreid] *adj.* 摄氏的
According to the weather report, the temperature will be at zero degree centigrade and water will freeze tomorrow.
天气预报说，明天气温会在零度以下，水会结冰。

chill [tʃil] *vt.* 使变冷；*n.* 寒冷
There is a little chill in the air this morning.
今天早晨的空气颇有寒意。

climate ['klaimit] *n.* 气候，风土，地带
His wife couldn't adapt to the climate there and fell ill.
他妻子不能适应那里的气候因而病倒了。

cloud [klaud] *n.* 云，云状物，阴影
I can't see the mountain clearly, because the clouds cap it.
我看不清那座山，因为云层笼罩着它。

cloudy ['klaudi] *adj.* 多云的，云一般的
It's cloudy outside. You'd better stay at home.
外面乌云密布，你最好待在屋里。

* * *

cold [kəuld] *adj.* 冷的，冷淡的；*n.* 冷
It is an absurd idea for you to go to swim in such a cold day.
在这样冷的天你要出去游泳，你的想法可真是荒谬不堪啊。

* * *

cool [ku:l] *adj.* 凉的，冷静的
The little girl pursed her lips to blow hard towards the hot soup to cool it.
小女孩撅起嘴使劲儿对着热汤吹气以使它凉下来。

* * *

damp [dæmp] *adj.* 潮湿的，有湿气的
I don't want the damp wood which doesn't burn well.
我不要潮湿的木头，它们不好烧。

* * *

forecast ['fɔːkɑːst] *n.* 预测，预报
vt. 预示
The weather forecast was finished when he got home.
当他回家的时候，天气预报已经结束了。

* * *

freeze [friːz] *vi.* 冻，结冻
vt. 使结冰
It will freeze if you put it outside.
你把它放在外面会结冰的。

* * *

frost [frɔst] *n.* 冰冻，严寒，霜
The plants suffered frost damage these days.
这些天这些植物遭受了霜害。

* * *

general ['dʒenərəl] *adj.* 总的，一般的
n. 将军
In general, weather is cold in Britain in the winter.
英国冬天的气候一般是寒冷的。

🔍 考点：in general 一般来说，大体上

hail [heil] *n.* 一阵，雹；*vi.* 下雹
vt. 招呼，高呼，为……喝彩
"Hail to Dad"! The children cried out.
"老爸万岁！"孩子们高喊着。

🔍 考点：hail from 来自，出生于

lightening ['laitniŋ] *n.* 闪电
Heavy rain always comes on the heels of the lightening.

大雨总要紧跟着闪电而来。

* * *

mist [mist] *n.* 薄雾，朦胧，模糊不清
vt. 使蒙上薄雾，使不清
She peers through the mist, trying to find the right path.
她透过雾眯着眼看，想找出正确的路。

* * *

moist [mɔist] *adj.* 湿润的，多雨的
Their skin produces a slime that helps to keep it moist.
它们的皮肤能产生一种帮助其保持润湿的黏液。

* * *

moisture ['mɔistʃə] *n.* 潮湿，湿气，温度
The sun will take some of the moisture out of the atmosphere.
太阳会蒸发掉大气中的部分水分。

* * *

predict [pri'dikt] *vi.&vt.* 预言，预告，预测
You can't predict what will happen in the future.
你不能预言将来会发生什么。

真题

JAMA (Japan Automobile Manufacturers Association) _____ a further sales decline of 1.2 percent this year.
A) concludes   B) predicts
C) reckons   D) prescribes

详 解：选B。题意为：日本汽车制造商协会预测今年汽车销售量会再下降1.2个百分点。A) conclude 意思是"得出结论"；B) predict 意思是"预测，预报"；C) reckon 意思是"猜想，估计"；D) prescribe 意思是"规定，开药方"。

(CET-4 模拟)

rain [rein] *n.* 雨，雨水；*vi.* 下雨
It began to rain heavily, and people ran to seek shelter from the rain.
雨开始下大了，人们都跑去寻找避雨之所。

* * *

rainbow ['reinbəu] *n.* 虹，彩虹
Do you remember the story about the rainbow?
你还记得那个关于彩虹的故事吗？

* * *

rainy ['reini] *adj.* 下雨的，多雨的
The peasants try to harvest the wheat before the rainy season.
农民们尽量在雨季来临之前收割小麦。

sandstorm ['sændstɔ:m] *n.* 沙尘暴
My book was dirty from the dust that came from the sandstorm.
我的书被沙尘暴带来的灰尘弄脏了。

shower ['ʃauə] *n.* 阵雨，（一）阵，淋浴
In order to watch the football game on time, he showered in haste.
为了准时观看足球比赛，他匆忙地洗了洗澡。

thunder ['θʌndə] *n.* 雷；*vi.* 打雷 *vt.* 吼出
Tom is very afraid of thunder and lightning.
汤姆非常害怕雷声和闪电。

temperature ['tempəritʃə] *n.* 温度，体温
At what temperature does ice melt?
冰在什么温度下融化？
考点：take one's temperature 给……量体温；have (run) a temperature 发烧

wind [wind] *n.* 风，气息，呼吸
Our national flag is waving in the wind.
我们的国旗在风中飘扬。
考点：in the wind 即将发生

already [ɔ:l'redi] *adv.* 早已，已经
The kid has already apologized for his fault sincerely, so I think that we should give him another chance.
孩子已经为自己犯的错真诚地道歉了，所以我认为我们应当再给他一次机会。

also ['ɔ:lsəu] *adv.* 亦，也，而且，还
You needn't admire me of having a happy family, because you can also get one in the future.
你不需要羡慕我有一个幸福的家庭，因为你将来也会有的。

a.m. [,ei'em] *abbr.* （缩）上午，午前
John has to return to the company before 10 o'clock a.m.
约翰得在上午10点之前回到公司。

April ['eiprəl] *n.* 四月
We all like to fool others to celebrate the April Fool's Day.
我们都喜欢通过愚弄别人来庆祝愚人节。

as [æs] *conj.* 当……的时候
You will get more experiences as you grow older.
随着年纪的增长你会有更多的经验。

at [æt] *prep.* 在……里，在……时
I will be there at 9 o'clock.
我会在9点钟到那儿。

August ['ɔ:gəst] *n.* 八月
August Rush is a touching film.
《八月迷情》是一部感人的电影。

autumn ['ɔ:təm] *n.* 秋，秋季
Most people like the autumn.
大部分人都喜欢秋天。

B.C. ['bi: si:] （缩）公元前
It is curious that the little boy knows what happened in the B.C.
那个小男孩知道公元前都发生了什么事，真奇怪。

beginning [bi'giniŋ] *n.* 开始，开端，起源
I hate learning English in the beginning.
起初，我讨厌学英语。
考点：at the beginning of 在……之初，开始；from beginning to end 从头到尾，自始至终

century ['sentʃuri] *n.* 世纪，百年
That tribe decayed in the eighteenth century.
那个部落在18世纪时衰落了。

date [deit] *n.* 日期，约会；*vt.* 注……日期
We concluded our date at ten o'clock that night.
那晚我们10点钟结束了约会。

decade ['dekeid] *n.* 十年，十年期
Two decades have elapsed since she gave birth to her first baby.
自从她生下第一个孩子，20年已经过去了。

era ['iərə] *n.* 时代，年代，纪元
The fall of the Berlin wall marked the end of an era.
柏林墙的倒塌标志着一个时代的结束。

March [mɑ:tʃ] *n.* 三月
My sister will travel to France next March.
我姐姐明年3月要去法国旅游。

May [mei] *n.* 五月
Normally the tourist season extends from May till October.
通常旅游季节从5月份延续到10月份。

midday ['middei] *n.* 正午，中午
The terrible earthquake happened at midday.
那次可怕的地震发生在中午。

midnight ['mid,nait] *n.* 午夜，子夜，夜半
I heard a loud scream in the midnight.
我午夜时听到了很大的尖叫声。

midweek ['midwi:k] *n.* 一周之半（尤指星期三）；*adv.* 一周的中间
If you traveled midweek, the fare should be higher than usual.
如果周中去旅游，车票价格就会比平时高点。

minute ['minit] *n.* 分，分钟，一会儿
adj. 微细的，详细的
There are nearly twenty buttons on her dress, so she always spends several minutes putting it on.
她的礼服上有近20个扣子，所以她总要花好几分钟穿好它。

🔍 考点：up to the minute 最新的，最新式的

moment ['məumənt] *n.* 片刻，瞬间，时刻，现今
Excuse me, can I speak to you for a moment?
请问，我可以和你说会儿话吗？

🔍 考点：at the moment 此刻，目前；for the moment 暂时，目前；for a moment 片刻，一会儿；the moment (that) 一……就

Monday ['mʌndi] *n.* 星期一
The teacher told the naughty boy to ask his parent to come to school on Monday.
老师让那个淘气的小男孩星期一请家长到学校。

month [mʌnθ] *n.* 月，月份
The manager demanded me to finish the task at the end of this month.
经理要求我这个月底完成任务。

monthly ['mʌnθli] *adj.* 每月的
adv. 每月
n. 月刊
Could you tell me whether the magazine comes out in monthly issue?
能否告诉我这本杂志是不是月刊？

morning ['mɔ:niŋ] *n.* 早晨，上午
Tomorrow morning I'm going to a fashion display.
明天早上我要去看时装展览。

night [nait] *n.* 夜，夜间
The roof of the cottage was blown away by the strong wind last night.
昨晚的大风把茅舍的屋顶给刮走了。

noon [nu:n] *n.* 正午，中午
The meeting broke up at noon yesterday.
昨天的会议开到中午就散了。

November [nəu'vembə] *n.* 十一月
I wil marry tom on November 20th.
我11月20日就要和汤姆结婚了。

now [nau] *adv.* 现在，立刻，于是
She is now a bank clerk and teaching has lost its glamour for her.
她现在是一名银行职员，教学对于她来说已经没有吸引力了。

o'clock [ə'klɔk] *adv.* ……点钟
The sun rose at six o'clock in the morning.
太阳早上6点升起。

October [ɔk'təubə] *n.* 10月
Tourism is at its peak in October in this city.
10月份是这个城市的旅游高峰。

overnight [,əuvə'nait] *adv.* 一夜，突然
She complained that her husband had gambled away all his money overnight.
她抱怨说她丈夫一夜之间赌博输掉了他所有的钱。

quarter ['kwɔ:tə] *n.* 四分之一，一刻钟
It's a quarter to eight o'clock.
差一刻钟就8点了。

quarterly ['kwɔ:təli] *adj.* 季度的
adv. 季度地
Finally, they agreed to pay the rent quarterly.
最终他们同意按季度付租金。

season ['si:zn] *n.* 季，季节，时节
Spring is my favourite season.
春天是我最喜欢的季节。

🔍 考点：in season 当令的，在旺季；out of season 不当令的，不在旺季的

after ['ɑ:ftə] *prep.* 在……以后，次于
Shall we go to the cinema after dinner?
吃完饭我们去看电影吧？

---

spring [spriŋ] *vi.* 跳，跃
　　　　　　n. 跳跃，泉，春天，春季
Most flowers bloom in the spring and wither in the fall.
大部分花在春天开放，秋天枯萎。

🔍 考点：spring up 涌现，跳出来

真题

As the old empires were broken up and new states were formed, new official tongues began to _____ at an increasing rate.
A) bring up　　　B) build up
C) spring up　　 D) strike up

详　解：选C。题意为：随着古老帝国的瓦解，新的国家建立，新的官方语言也加速涌现。A) bring up意思是"抚养，培养"；B) build up意思是"建立，积累"；C) spring up 意思是"快速出现"；D) strike up意思是"认识，交谈"。

(CET-4 模拟)

---

alternate [ɔ:l'tə:nit] *vi.&vt.* （使）轮流，
　　（使）交替；*adj.* 交替的，轮流的，间隔的
The weather report says that there will be a week of alternate rain and sunshine.
天气预报说，下礼拜将会时雨时晴。

真题

Professor Smith and Professor Brown will _____ in presenting the series of lectures on American literature.
A) alter　　　　　B) alternate
C) substitute　　 D) exchange

详　解：选B。题意为：史密斯教授和布朗教授会轮流做关于美国文学的系列讲座。A) alter意思是"改变"；B) alternate意思是"轮流"；C) substitute意思是"取代，代替"；D) exchange意思是"交换，交流"。

(CET-4 2003.12)

---

afternoon ['ɑ:ftə'nu:n] *n.* 下午，午后
Since he has an important visitor, he will not be out this afternoon.

因为有个重要的客人要来，今天下午他就不出去了。

---

afterward ['ɑ:ftəwəd] *adv.* 后来，以后
The princess and the prince lived happily ever afterward.
后来，公主和王子过着幸福的生活。

---

ago [ə'gəu] *adv.* 以前
A ship sank in the Pacific Ocean ten days ago.
10天之前，有一艘船沉在了太平洋底。

其他　性别年龄

age [eidʒ] *n.* 年龄，时代；*vt.* 变老
He lied about his age to join the army.
他为了参军谎报了年龄。

---

boy [bɔi] *n.* 男孩，少年，家伙
The boy did the reverse of what his parents told him to do.
男孩做的与父母要求的相反。

---

child [tʃaild] *n.* 小孩，儿童，儿子
It's hard for you to raise a child by yourself. You know you must bear all expenses.
一个人抚养孩子很难，你必须承担一切费用。

---

childhood ['tʃaildhud] *n.* 童年，幼年，早期
Childhood was the most difficult period of my life.
童年是我一生中最艰难的时期。

---

gender ['dʒendə] *n.* 性，性别
The babies begin to identify their genders normally at three years old.
小孩子大概在3岁时才开始识别他们的性别。

---

male [meil] *adj.* 男的，雄的
　　　　　　n. 男子，雄性动物
In this company, male employees must wear jackets and ties.
在这家公司，男性员工必须穿夹克，戴领带。

---

man [mæn] *n.* 男人，人，人类
The man professed that he was a baronet, but the girl didn't believe him.
男子声称自己是个准男爵，但女孩并不相信他。

old [əuld] *adj.* 老的，……岁的
That old woman can walk only at a very slow pace.
那位老太太只能慢慢地走。

sexual ['seksjuəl] *adj.* 性的，性别的
Don't be indiscriminate in the choice of sexual partners, or you would catch the sexually transmitted diseases.
在选择性伴侣的时候要谨慎，否则你会感染性病的。

其他 变化&状态

descend [di'send] *vi.* 下来，下降，下倾
I saw the balloon descend on the river.
我看见气球落在了河面上。

decrease [di:'kri:s] *vi.&n.* 减少
The manager offered some measures which could help decrease the cost of production.
经理提出了一些有助于降低生产成本的措施。

🔍 考点：an increase / decrease in sth. 某事的增长（减少）

downside ['daun,said] *adj.* 下侧的，有下降趋势的；*n.* 下边，底侧，不利
I didn't find a downside to buy this new kind of computer.
我找不出这种新电脑的不利因素。

double ['dʌbl] *adj.* 两倍的，双的
If we can finish this task on schedule, our boss will double our salary.
如果我们按期完成这项任务，我们老板会给我们发双倍工资。

🔍 考点：double up 把……折叠起来

drop [drɔp] *vt.* 使落下，降低
They choose to drop bombs to blow up this fort.
他们选择扔炸弹来炸毁这个堡垒。

🔍 考点：drop in / by 顺便访问
drop off 睡着，下降
drop out 退出，退学

enlarge [in'lɑ:dʒ] *vt.* 扩大，扩展，放大
We need to enlarge the foreign trade to promote economic development.
我们需要扩大对外贸易以促进经济增长。

evolution [,i:və'lu:ʃən] *n.* 进化，演化，发展
In the course of evolution, some animals have lost their hard shells.
在演化过程中，一些动物失去了它们原有的硬壳。

evolve [i'vɔlv] *vt.* 使进化，使发展
Do you know that birds probably evolved from reptiles?
你知道鸟类可能是由爬行类动物进化而来的吗?

expand [iks'pænd] *vt.* 扩大，使膨胀
You know the metals expand when they are heated.
金属遇热就会膨胀。

expansion [iks'pænʃən] *n.* 扩大，扩充，扩张
The board turned down his expansion plans.
董事会否决了他的扩张计划。

extend [iks'tend] *vt.* 延长，扩大，致
He is busy with extending his garden.
他正忙于扩建花园。

extension [iks'tenʃən] *n.* 延长部分，伸展
The reform and open policy is beneficial to the extension of our foreign trade.
改革开放政策对我国外贸的扩大很有益。

fall [fɔ:l] *vi.* 落下，跌倒，陷落
He passed the ball to his teammate when he was going to fall.
他在快要摔倒时把球传给了队友。

🔍 考点：fall asleep 入睡；fall ill 病倒

fluctuate ['flʌktjueit] *vi.* 波动，起伏
The stock fluctuates hugely in couples of months.
近几个月股票波动非常大。

fade [feid] *vi.* 褪色，逐渐消失
The stars faded from the sky.
星星从天边消失。

enhance [in'hɑ:ns] *vt.* 提高，增加，加强
It is necessary for us to enhance the flexibility of our diplomacy.
加强我们在外交上的灵活性是很必要的。

gradual ['grædjuəl] *adj.* 逐渐的，渐进的
We must follow the principle of gradual improvement in learning a language.
学习语言必须遵循循序渐进的原则。

harden ['hɑːdn] *vt.* 使变硬；*vi.* 变硬
Harden up the rope or the clothes will drop down.
拉紧绳子，否则衣服会掉下来的。

improve [im'pruːv] *vi.&vt.* 改进，改善
Talking with foreigners could help you improve your competence in English.
同外国人讲话能够帮助你提高英语水平。

🔍 考点：improve on / upon 改进，胜过

improvement [im'pruːvmənt] *n.* 改进，改善，改进处
I can see the improvement in your study.
我能看出你的学习情况有所改善。

increase [in'kriːs] *vi.&vt.&n.* 增加
He asked for an increase in salary for his extra work.
他为自己额外的工作要求增加薪水。

🔍 考点：on the increase 正在增加，不断增长

increasingly [in'kriːsiŋli] *adv.* 日益，越来越多地
The living conditions of people are increasingly improved.
人们的生活条件日益提高。

intensify [in'tensifai] *vt.* 增强，加剧
The government needs to intensify structural adjustment in this item.
政府需要在这个项目中加大结构调整力度。

intensity [in'tensiti] *n.* 强烈，剧烈，强度
At night, the intensity of the light is not enough to work.
晚上光线太暗，不能工作。

minimum ['miniməm] *n.* 最小量
adj. 最小的
The weather forecast says that the minimum temperature today is 10℃, so remember to put on your thick clothes.
天气预报说今天的最低气温是10摄氏度，记着穿上你的厚衣服。

variable ['vɛəriəbl] *adj.* 易变的；*n.* 变量
His temper is much more variable than before.
他的脾气比以前更多变了。

variation [ˌvɛəri'eiʃən] *n.* 变化，变动，变异
The variation of the price is very large this year.
今年的价格变动非常大。

variety [və'raiəti] *n.* 多样化，种类，变种
It's important to keep the variety of species.
保持物种多样性很重要。

🔍 考点：a variety of 多种多样的

mobile ['məubail] *adj.* 运动的，流动的，多变的
My mother is on a mobile cinema team.
妈妈在巡回电影队工作。

真题

In order to make things convenient for the people, the store is planning to set up some _____ shops in the residential area.
A) flowing   B) mobile
C) drifting   D) unstable

详　解：选B。题意为：为了给居民提供方便，商店计划在该居民区设立移动售货亭。A) flowing 意思是"流动的，飘动的"；B) mobile 意思是"移动的"；C) drifting 意思是"漂流的"；D) unstable 意思是"不稳定的"。

(CET-4 模拟)

various ['vɛəriəs] *adj.* 各种各样的，不同的
Owing to various things, we arrived two days late.
由于种种事情，我们迟到了两天。

vary ['vɛəri] *vt.* 改变，使多样化
The styles of architectures vary widely from one area to another.
不同地区的建筑风格迥然不同。

🔍 考点：vary with 随……而变化
vary from 不同于……

continual [kən'tinjuəl] *adj.* 不断的，连续的
Continual dripping wears away the stone.
滴水穿石。

continue [kən'tinjuː] *vt.* 继续，连续，延伸
We continued working until it grew dark outside.
我们一直工作到外面天色变暗。

continuous [kən'tinjuəs] *adj.* 连续不断的，持续的
The continuous noise is driving us crazy.
这连续不断的噪声快把我们逼疯了。

endless ['endlis] *adj.* 无止境的

The endless speech makes me sleepy.
冗长的讲话让我都觉得困了。

*

eternal [i'tə:nəl] *adj.* 永久的，无休止的，
永恒的

We are talking about the topic of eternal love.
我们正在谈论永恒的爱情这一话题。

*

existence [ig'zistəns] *n.* 存在，实在，生存

Maybe most people don't believe the existence of telepathy.
或许大多数人不相信心灵感应的存在。

🔍 **考点**：bring...into existence 使……出现；come into existence 出现，产生

*

halt [hɔ:lt] *vi.* 停止，立定；*n.* 停住

We only have a few minutes to halt, then we have to march again.
我们只能停几分钟，然后得继续前进。

🔍 **考点**：bring...to a halt 使……停止
come to a halt 停止

*

invisible [in'vizəbl] *adj.* 看不见的，无形的

It is a common sense that air is invisible.
空气是看不见的，这是一个常识。

*

ongoing ['ɔngəuiŋ] *adj.* 持续的，继续的

She has an ongoing headache these days.
她最近总头疼。

*

permanent ['pə:mənənt] *adj.* 永久的，持久的

I've been on the run for so many years and decided to buy a permanent abode in Beijing.
我奔波了多年，想在北京买一处永久性的居所。

*

permanently ['pə:mənəntli] *adv.* 永久地，持久地

Female workers are made permanently sterile by this pesticide.
这种杀虫剂使得女性工人终生不育。

*

nevertheless [ˌnevəðə'les] *conj.* 然而
adv. 仍然

He was sick, nevertheless, he insisted on sending his daughter to school.
他病了，然而还是坚持送女儿去上学。

真题

The London Marathon is a difficult race. _____, thousands of runners participate every year.
A) Therefore　　　B) Furthermore
C) Accordingly　　D) Nevertheless

详　解：选D。题意为：伦敦马拉松比赛很有挑战性，不过，每年都有成千上万的人参加。A) Therefore 意思是"因此，所以"；B) Furthermore 意思是"此外，而且"；C) Accordingly 意思是"因此，相应地"；D) Nevertheless 意思是"不过，然而"。

(CET-4 模拟)

*

solid ['sɔlid] *adj.* 固体的，实心的，结实的，可靠的
n. 固体

He proved his innocence with solid facts.
他用确凿的事实证明了自己的清白。

真题

There is no____ evidence that people can control their dreams, at least in experimental situations in a lab.
A) rigid　　　B) solid
C) smooth　　D) harsh

详　解：选B。题意为：没有可靠的证据证明人们能控制自己的梦，至少在实验室做实验的情况下是如此。A) rigid 意思是"死板的，严格的"；B) solid 意思是"可靠的，稳固的"；C) smooth意思是"光滑的，流畅的"；D) harsh意思是"严厉的，手感粗糙的"。

(CET-4 模拟)

*

still [stil] *adj.* 静止的；*n.* 寂静
adv. 还，依旧

This proposal still fails for solving this problem.
这个方案仍然不能解决此问题。

🔍 **考点**：still less "更不用说"，是一种追加否定。

其他 可能性

assume [ə'sju:m] *vt.* 假定，承担，呈现
I assumed my mother had received my letter.
我想妈妈已经收到我的信了。

assumption [ə'sʌmpʃən] *n.* 假定，假象，承担
The facts proved your assumption wrong.
事实证明你的推断是错误的。

🔍 考点：on the assumption that 假定，如果

liable ['laiəbl] *adj.* 易于……的，可能的，有义务的，有……倾向的
I think your article is liable to give offence to many officers.
我认为你的文章可能会得罪很多官员。

🔍 考点：be liable for 对……有责任
be liable to 易于……的

likely ['laikli] *adj.* 可能的，适合的
adv. 很可能
On the evidence of their recent matches, it's likely the Spanish team will win the cup.
从西班牙队最近的比赛来看，他们很有可能在比赛中夺冠。

may [mei] *aux.&v.* 可能，可以，祝
The cry of the neonate may be the most exciting sound in the world.
新生儿的哭声大概是这世上最令人激动的声音了。

maybe ['meibi] *adv.* 大概，或许，也许
Maybe I wrong him.
或许我错怪他了。

odds [ɔdz] *n.* 可能性，差异，投注赔率
I think this kind of odds is very few here.
我认为在这里这种几率很少。

🔍 考点：against all the odds 尽管有极大的困难；odds and ends 零星杂物

perhaps [pə'hæps] *adv.* 也许，可能，多半
Perhaps, you should take the expert's advice.
或许，你应该听取专家的建议。

possibly ['pɔsəbli] *adv.* 可能地，也许
He can't possibly solve the problem himself.
他自己解决不了那个问题。

possibility [ˌpɔsi'biliti] *n.* 可能，可能的事
There is a distinct possibility that she'll never return your money.
她不还你钱的可能性非常大。

possible ['pɔsəbl] *adj.* 可能的，可能存在的
We've already prepared for any possible aggression.
我们已经为可能的侵犯做好了准备。

🔍 考点：probable, likely, possible都有"可能的"意思：probable 表示主观上有几分根据的推测，十有八九的可能；likely 比probable的可能性要小，比possible的要大，十之五六的可能；possible 表示客观上潜在的可能，十之二三的可能。

probability [ˌprɔbə'biliti] *n.* 可能性，概率
The probability of getting his instruction will increase if you visit him in person.
如果你亲自拜访他，得到他指导的机会就会增加。

probable ['prɔbəbl] *adj.* 或许的，大概的
It's highly probable that we'll win the match.
我们很可能会赢这场比赛。

probably ['prɔbəbli] *adv.* 或许，大概
She will probably arrive in Beijing next Friday
她可能下周五到达北京。

其他 异同

differ ['difə] *vi.* 不同，相异
The twins look alike, but their tastes differ from each other.
这对双胞胎长相相似，可是嗜好却不同。

🔍 考点：differ from 与……不同
differ with 不同意

distinct [dis'tiŋkt] *adj.* 与其他不同的
Australia and Austria are two distinct countries.
澳大利亚和奥地利是两个截然不同的同家。

🔍 考点：be distinct from 与……截然不同

distinction [dis'tiŋkʃən] *n.* 差别，不同，区分
There is no appreciable distinction between the twins.

在这对孪生子之间看不出有什么明显的差别。

distinctive [dis'tiŋktiv] *adj.* 有区别的，有特色的

Students wear a distinctive uniform in this school.
这个学校的学生们穿着特制的校服。

distinguish [dis'tiŋgwiʃ] *vt.* 区别，辨别，认别

I know that color-blind people can't distinguish between colors.
我知道色盲不能辨别颜色。

真题

Many personnel managers say it is getting harder and harder to _____ honest applicants from the growing members of dishonest ones.
A) dissolve   B) disguise   C) discount
D) distinguish

详　解：选D。题意为：许多人事经理认为，要把诚实的应聘者和数量渐增的不诚实的应聘者分开越来越难了。A) dissolve意思是"分解，解散"；B) disguise意思是"假装，伪装"；C) discount意思是"不重视，不理会"；D) distinguish意思是"区分"。

(CET-4 模拟)

former ['fɔ:mə] *adj.* 在前的；*n.* 前者

His former boss recommended him warmly to a new company.
他从前的老板热心地推荐他去一个新公司。

考点：the former 前者；the latter 后者

identical [ai'dentikəl] *adj.* 完全相同的，同一的

He is in the identical predicament with you.
他和你处于同样的窘境之中。

考点：be identical with / to... 和……完全相同

latter ['lætə] *adj.* （两者中）后者的

I prefer the latter book to the former.
我喜欢后一本书甚于前一本。

likewise ['laik,waiz] *adv.* 同样地，也，又

Mary wants to play tennis, and Lily likewise.
玛丽想要打网球，莉莉也想打。

both [bəuθ] *pron.* 两者（都）

His parents are both engaged in research on biology.
他的父母都在从事生物学的研究。

comparative [kəm'pærətiv] *adj.* 比较的，相对的

You should use comparative adjective in this sentence.
这句话应该用形容词的比较级。

contrast ['kɔntræst] *n.* 对比，对照，悬殊

You will find how agreeable the farm life when contrast with city life.
跟城市生活对比之下，你就会发现乡村生活有多惬意。

考点：by / in contrast 对比之下；in contrast to / with 与……比起来

comparable ['kɔmpərəbl] *adj.* 可比较的，类似的

This kind of comparable and reliable data is often lacking, which can only be built up gradually.
这种可靠而又真实可信的资料常常很缺乏，而这样的资料又只能慢慢地积累才行。

compare [kəm'pɛə] *vt.* 比较，对照，比作

It is very foolish of you to compare the advantages of others with the disadvantages of yours.
你很傻，竟然拿别人的优点和你的缺点相比较。

考点：beyond / without compare 无与伦比

comparison [kəm'pærisn] *n.* 比较，对照，比拟

There is no comparison between them.
两者不可以同日而语。

考点：by / in comparison 相比之下
in comparison with 与……比较起来

其他 原因结果

consequence ['kɔnsikwəns] *n.* 结果，后果
It rained today and in consequence our plan to go camping was canceled.
今天下雨了，所以我们出去野营的计划取消了。

🔍 **考点**：in consequence 因此，结果
in consequence of 由于，因为……的缘故

consequently ['kɔnsikwəntli] *adv.* 因此，因而，所以
I've never been to Japan. Consequently, I know very little about it.
我从未去过日本，所以对它了解得很少。

eventually [i'ventʃuəli] *adv.* 终于，最后
Eventually he was elected to be the king of the country for his bravery.
最终，由于他的英勇他被推举为这个国家的国王。

somehow ['sʌmhau] *adv.* 不知什么原因
Conditions of flood vary somehow on different time.
不知道什么缘故，各时段洪水情形大不相同。

hence [hens] *adv.* 因此，所以，今后
This ring is very important to her; hence she keeps it in this little box.
这个戒指对她非常重要，所以她把它保存在这个小盒子里。

🔍 **考点**：hence, therefore的区别：hence, therefore都是连接副词，表示因果关系；两词后面都可以接句子，但hence后可直接接名词，therefore通常不能。

therefore ['ðɛəfɔː] *adv.* 因此，所以
I repeat, therefore, we must accomplish this task tonight.
所以我再重复一句，我们今晚必须完成此项任务。

attribute [ə'tribjuːt] *vt.* 把……归因于
n. 属性
I have no secrets; I attribute my success to hard work.
我没有什么秘诀，我的成功归因于艰苦努力。

🔍 **考点**：attribute sth. to sb. 认为某事物是某人创造的；把某事归功于

because [bi'kɔz] *conj.* 由于，因为
Because of you, I learnt how to love others.
因为你，我学会了怎么爱别人。

owing ['əuiŋ] *adj.* 应付的，未付的；归因……于
Owing to his extravagance, his company went into bankruptcy in the end.
由于他挥霍无度，他的公司最终破产了。

🔍 **考点**：owing to 由于，因为

其他 身份地位

chief [tʃiːf] *adj.* 主要的，首席的
Our chief purpose is to serve mankind.
我们的主要目的是服务于人类。

dignity ['digniti] *n.* 庄严，尊严，高贵
The old man was once conferred the dignity of a peerage by the queen.
老人曾经被女王授予贵族头衔。

giant ['dʒaiənt] *n.* 巨人，巨物
Shakespeare is a giant among poets.
莎士比亚是诗人中的大文豪。

identification [ai,dentifi'keiʃən] *n.* 身份证明，鉴定，认出，认同
Do you have any identification?
你有任何证明文件吗？

identity [ai'dentiti] *n.* 身份，个性，同一性
Please affirm your identity before entering the conference hall.
请在进入会场前确认你的身份。

intellectual [,inti'lektjuəl] *n.* 知识分子
adj. 智力的
She is rarely a young intellectual in her day.
在那个年代，她是位罕见的年轻知识分子。

junior ['dʒuːnjə] *adj.* 年少的；*n.* 晚辈
After graduating from the junior middle school, he went to work.
他初中毕业后就去工作了。

考点：be junior to 比……年少（低级）

inferior [in'fiəriə] *adj.* 下等的，劣等的
She feels inferior to others in many aspects.
她感到在许多方面不如别人。

真题

Their products are frequently overpriced and
_____ in quality.
A) influential　　B) subordinate
C) inferior　　　D) superior

详　解：选C。题意为：他们的产品经常
是价高质劣。A) influential意思是"有影响
的"；B) subordinate意思是"下级的，次
要的"；C) inferior意思是"劣势的，下等
的"；D) superior意思是"上级的，上好
的"。

(CET-4 模拟)

lower ['ləuə] *adj.* 较低的，下面的；*vt.* 放下
Hotel prices are lower out of season.
在淡季，旅馆价格比较便宜。

measurable ['meʒərəbl] *adj.* 可测量的，相当的，重要的
We all know he is a measurable figure in Chinese history.
我们都知道他是中国历史上一个举足轻重的人物。

middle-class ['midl'klɑ:s] *adj.* 中等的
We all belong to the middle-class professional women.
我们都来是中产阶级职业妇女。

minor ['mainə] *adj.* 较小的，较次要的
n. 未成年人，副修科
vi. 副修
Luckily it is only a minor error and it doesn't affect overall situation.
幸好，它只是一个小错误，并不影响全局。

mostly ['məustli] *adv.* 主要的，大部分
The students in our class are mostly from Henan province.
我们班的大部分同学都来自河南省。

noble ['nəubl] *adj.* 贵族的，高尚的
n. 贵族
I really admire her. She is a woman of noble bearing.
我真的很钦佩她，她是一个举止端庄的女人。

pioneer [ˌpaiə'niə] *n.* 拓荒者，先驱者
Even today, we still remember those pioneers of the American West.
直到今天，我们依然记得那些美国西部的开拓者。

primarily ['praimərili] *adv.* 首先，主要地
He was primarily a teacher and then became a lawyer.
他原来是教师，后来成了一名律师。

primary ['praiməri] *adj.* 最初的，基本的
I know love and hatred are primary emotions.
我知道爱和恨是基本的情感。

prime [praim] *adj.* 首要的；*n.* 春天，青春
The children's prime need is a new school.
孩子们的最需要的是一所新学校。

考点：in / at the prime of 在鼎盛时期，正当壮年

principal ['prinsəpəl] *adv.* 主要的
n. 负责人
Electronic products are Japan's principal exports.
电子产品是日本的主要出口商品。

rank [ræŋk] *n.* 排，横行，社会阶层
The restaurant caters for everyone no matter what social rank you are.
宾馆为所有人服务，不管你的社会地位如何。

真题

His temper and personality show that he can
become a soldier of the top _____ .
A) circle　　　B) rank
C) category　　D) grade

详　解：选B。题意为：他的脾气和个性
表明他能成为一等兵。A) circle 意思是"领
域，范围"；B) rank 意思是"等级（尤指
部队中的军衔），阶层"；C) category 意思
是"种类，范畴"；D) grade 意思是"等
级"。

(CET-4 模拟)

prominent ['prɔminənt] *adj.* 实起的，突出的
I envy him very much, because his work allows him to access to some prominent people.

207

我很羡慕他，因为他的工作可以让他接近一些名人。

secondary ['sekəndəri] *adj.* 第二的，次要的
Such considerations are secondary to our main aim of improving efficiency.
对于我们提高效率的主要目的来说，这些想法都是次要的。

senior ['si:njə] *adj.* 年老的，地位较高的
It cost him seven years to become a senior executive in the corporation.
他花了7年时间才成为这家公司的高级主管。

servant ['sə:vənt] *n.* 仆人，佣人，雇工
This servant was always promiscuous and superficial.
这个佣人总是很随便、很浅薄。

specialist ['speʃəlist] *n.* 专家
The peasants looked up to him as a specialist on agriculture.
农民们把他看做农业专家。

🖈 **考点**：a specialist in history 历史专家

status ['stetəs] *n.* 地位，身份
What's your official status in the institute?
你在学院里的正式职位是什么？

（真题）
The clothes a person wears may express his ____ or social position.
A) curiosity   B) determination
C) significance   D) status

详　解：选D。题意为：一个人的着装也许能表明他的社会地位。A) curiosity意思是"好奇，奇物"；B) determination意思是"决定，决心"；C) significance 意思是"重要性，重大意义"；D) status意思是"身份，地位"。
(CET-4 模拟)

superior [su:'piəriə] *adj.* 较高的，优越的
Tad is a superior, trustworthy boy.
泰德是个优秀而可靠的男孩。

🖈 **考点**：superior to 比……好，优于

upper ['ʌpə] *adj.* 上面的，比较高的
Please take the upper book down.
请把上面的那本书拿下来。

wealthy ['welθi] *adj.* 富的，富裕的
She made a snap decision to marry a wealthy man.
她做了一个仓促的决定，她要嫁给一位富人。

white-collar [wait'kɔlə] *n.* 白领阶层的，从事脑力工作的
It seems that white-collar workers are lacking in physical exercises.
白领阶层似乎缺乏体育锻炼。

prior ['praiə] *adj.* 在先的，优先的
No one had a prior knowledge that the plan crash occurred only minutes after take-off.
事先没有人知道飞机在起飞几分钟后就会遇难。

🖈 **考点**：prior to 在……之前（to为介词）

（真题）
All the arrangements should be completed ____ your departure.
A) prior to   B) superior to
C) contrary to   D) parallel to

详　解：选A。题意为：所有的安排都应该在你离开前完成。A) prior to意思是"在……之前"；B) superior to 意思是"比……好"；C) contrary to 意思是"与……相反"；D) parallel to意思是"与……平行"。
(CET-4 模拟)

其他 程度频率

absolute ['æbsəlu:t] *adj.* 绝对的，纯粹的，不受任何限制的，专制的
Don't believe him. What he said is absolute libel.
别相信他，他所说的完全是诽谤。

absolutely ['æbsəlu:tli] *adv.* 完全地，绝对地，肯定地
What she said was not absolutely right.
她说的不完全正确。

accuracy ['ækjurəsi] *n.* 准确（性），准确度
I don't think it's hard to state the number of casualties with accuracy.
我认为准确地说出伤亡人数并不难。

accurate ['ækjərət] *adj.* 准确的，正确无误的
Please trust me. My information is accurate.
相信我，我的情报是准确的。

almost ['ɔːlməust] *adv.* 几乎，差不多
You may feel surprised that almost every idiom has a story behind it.
几乎每一个习语背后都有一个故事，你可能会对此感到惊奇。

altogether [,ɔːltə'geðə] *adv.* 完全，总而言之
Taken all passage into consideration, this sentence may be omitted altogether.
综合整段来看，这个句子完全可以省略。

🔍 **考点**：altogether 修饰句子，译作 "总体来说，总之"；修饰形容词、副词、动词时，译作 "完全，全部"。

always ['ɔːlweiz] *adv.* 总是，一直，永远
My family's debt was always a great worry to me.
家里的债一直以来都是我最担忧的事。

anyhow ['enihau] *adv.* 无论如何
Anyhow you must carry out the plan today.
无论如何你今天要把计划给实施了。

anyone ['eniwʌn] *pron.* 任何人
You can trust me; I will not tell anyone.
你要相信我，我不会告诉任何人的。

anything ['eniθiŋ] *pron.* 任何事物，一切
She worshipped that guy and refused to listen to anything about his criticism.
她崇拜那个男人，对任何批评他的语言都听不进去。

anyway ['eniwei] *adv.* 无论如何
Anyway I will instruct you to how to use the fax machine.
不管怎样，我都会教你使用传真机的。

best [best] *adj.* 最好的
My best friend is my junior by two years.
我最好的朋友比我小两岁。

🔍 **考点**：try / do one's best 尽力，努力；make the best of 充分利用

better ['betə] *adj.* 较好的；*adv.* 更好地
Compare these two pictures and take the better one.

比较这两幅画，选出较好的一个。

🔍 **考点**：for the better 好转，向好的方向发展；had better 最好，还是……好

complete [kəm'pliːt] *adj.* 完整的，完成的
They are very excited by the news of a complete triumph.
听到大获全胜的消息他们都很高兴。

completely [kəm'pliːtli] *adv.* 十分，完全地
After a whole day's study, I'm completely exhausted.
学习了一整天，我感到特别疲惫。

considerable [kən'sidərəbl] *adj.* 相当大的，重要的
The considerable ruin has been caused to the country after the disaster.
灾难之后，这个村子受到了很大的毁坏。

much [mʌtʃ] *adv.* 非常，很；*adj.* 许多的
It would take much time and toil to compile an encyclopedia.
汇编一本百科全书很花费时间和精力。

nearly ['niəli] *adv.* 几乎，差不多，密切地
Wait a minute. The water has nearly come to the boil.
等一下，水快开了。

practically ['præktikəli] *adv.* 实际上，几乎
The bombing raid practically leveled the tiny town.
空袭几乎把这座小城镇夷为平地。

purely ['pjuəli] *adv.* 纯粹地，完全地
I doubt his conclusions are purely speculative.
我怀疑他的结论完全是推测而来的。

quite [kwait] *adv.* 完全，相当，的确
It's quite common for children to imitate adults.
孩子们喜欢模仿成年人，这很常见。

rather ['rɑːðə] *adv.* 宁可，宁愿，相当
My teacher's criticism left me feeling rather abashed.
老师批评了我，我感到有些难为情。

remarkable [ri'mɑːkəbl] *adj.* 异常的，非凡的
The remarkable animal only can be seen on the continent of Australia.
这种奇异的动物只能在澳大利亚看到。

scarcely ['skɛəsli] *adv.* 仅仅，几乎不
The cat lay so still that it scarcely seemed animate.
那只猫卧着一动也不动，看起来简直不像是活的。

🔍 考点：scarcely...when... 一……就……
（相当于hardly...when...
no sooner... =than... ）

sheer [ʃiə] *adj.* 完全的，陡峭的，透明的
　　　　　adv. 垂直地，陡峭地
　　　　　vi. 急转向，偏离
The disabled boy lacks talent, but he won the game by sheer dogged persistence.
这个残疾男孩缺少天分，但却凭坚韧的毅力赢得了胜利。

slight [slait] *adj.* 细长的，轻微的
I have a slight acquaintance with the old coins.
我对古钱币有些许了解。

📕 真题

Can you give me even the ＿＿＿ clue as to where her son might be?
A) simplest　　B) slightest
C) least　　　D) utmost

详　解：选B。题意为：你能给我透漏一点她儿子可能在哪里的线索吗？B) slightest 是 slight的最高级，常用最高级形式修饰clue。A) simplest和D) utmost与句子不吻合。C) least是 little的最高级，只能修饰不可数名词。

(CET-4 2005.1)

somewhat ['sʌmwɔt] *pron.* 一点儿
　　　　　　　adv. 有点
He is somewhat of a connoisseur, you should believe him.
他也算是一个鉴定家，你应该相信他。

utter ['ʌtə] *adj.* 完全的，彻底的
　　　　　vt. 发出，说，讲
She asked for four days leave but met an utter refusal.
她要求请4天假，但遭到断然拒绝。

barely ['bɛəli] *adv.* 几乎不；刚刚；勉强，
　　　　　　　　　　少量地
We barely had time to rest during the busy time.
忙时我们几乎没空休息。

mere [miə] *adj.* 仅仅的，纯粹的
I know your love is a mere sham.
我知道你的爱情是虚假的。

merely ['miəli] *adv.* 仅仅，只不过
If man did not weave the web of life, he is merely a strand in it.
如果人类不把生命组织在一起，那么他就仅仅是岸边一只搁浅的小船。

again [ə'gein] *adv.* 又一次，而且
It depressed her to see her son fail the exam again.
看到她儿子考试又不及格，她感到很沮丧。

never ['nevə] *adv.* 永不，决不，从来没有
I've never cheated anybody; you know my conduct has been entirely above board.
我从来没有欺骗过任何人，我的一切行为都是光明正大的。

repeatedly [ri'pi:tidli] *adv.* 重复地，一再
She was repeatedly subjected to torture.
她不断地受到折磨。

especially [is'peʃəli] *adv.* 特别，尤其，格外
The girl loves literature, especially polite literature.
女孩喜欢文学，尤其是风雅文学。

🔍 考点：specially，especially的区别：
specially 多指为某一特别目的
而做；especially侧重达到异常的
程度。

exceedingly [ik'si:diŋli] *adv.* 极端地，非常
This is an exceedingly difficult book to buy.
这是一本很难买到的书。

extreme [iks'tri:m] *adj.* 极度的，尽头的
Mr. Smith can be very sad in private though in public he is extremely cheerful.
史密斯先生虽然在大庭广众之下显得极为开心，可私下里可能会很忧郁。

🔍 考点：go to extremes 走极端
in the extreme 非常，极其

frequency ['fri:kwənsi] *n.* 屡次，次数，频率
He speaks at a high-speed frequency.
他说话语速非常快。

frequent ['fri:kwənt] *adj.* 时常发生的，经常的
A few of these sentences have received frequent usage.

其中有些句子已经得到广泛应用。

further ['fə:ðə] *adv.* 更远地；*adj.* 更远的
We will further discuss in this chapter.
我们将在本章中继续讨论。

furthermore [ˌfə:ðə'mɔ:] *adv.* 而且，此外
Furthermore, he has to leave for a date tonight.
而且，他今晚要离开去赴约。

hardly ['hɑ:dli] *adv.* 几乎不，简直不
She could hardly say a word.
她几乎说不出话了。

really ['riəli] *adv.* 真正地，实在
It's Bobby's wife who really rules the roost in that family.
在鲍比家里，真正当家的是他的老婆。

common ['kɔmən] *adj.* 普通的，共同的
This is a common phenomenon in developed countries.
在发达国家这是个普遍现象。
🔍**考点**：in common 共用的，共有的

commonly ['kɔmənli] *adv.* 普通地，一般地
We commonly go to park on Sundays.
我们星期天通常会去公园。

complex ['kɔmpleks] *adj.* 结合的，复杂的
It's a complex sentence.
这是一个复合句。

alike [ə'laik] *adj.* 同样的，相同的，相像的
adv. 同样地
I was amazed that the two twin brothers looked exactly alike.
看到这两个孪生兄弟长得一模一样，我感到很惊奇。

actual ['æktjuəl] *adj.* 实际的，现行的
n. 实际，现状
What you said just now contradicts the actual result that we all have seen.
你刚才所说的与我们大家所看到的实际结果有矛盾。

actually ['æktʃuəli] *adv.* 实际上，竟然
To tell you the truth, I actually want you to accept my new concept of promoting products.
实话告诉你，我确实想要你接受我关于促销产品的新观念。

其他 数量表达 ✎

a [ə] *art.* 一（个），每一（个）
This is a good place for the patients to recover.
这是一个有助于病人康复的好地方。

all [ɔ:l] *adj.* 全部的；*prep.* 全部
He is a man of great resource and able to solve all kinds of problems.
他是一个足智多谋的人，能够解决各种各样的问题。

approximate [ə'prɔksimit] *adj.* 近似的，大概的
v. 接近，近似
I think the woman wearing a red dress is approximate 30-year-old.
我觉得那个穿红裙子的女人大概有30岁。

amount [ə'maunt] *n.* 总数，数量，和
As an interpreter, she needs to interpret a large amount of materials every day.
作为一个口译员，她每天都要口译大量的资料。
🔍**考点**：amount to 达……之多

approximately [ə'prɔksimitli] *adv.* 近似地，大约
It will take you approximately 30 minutes to walk there.
你走到那大约要半小时。

average ['ævəridʒ] *n.* 平均数；*adj.* 平均的
My income is very low which is even below the average.
我的收入很低，甚至低于平均水平。
🔍**考点**：on an / the average 按平均值，通常

exceed [ik'si:d] *vt.* 超过，胜过，超出
The result really exceeds my expectation.
这个结果却是超出了我的预料。

excess [ik'ses] *n.* 超越，过量，过度
Last month's profit were in excess of twenty thousand *yuan*.
上个月的利润超过了2000元。
🔍**考点**：in excess of 超过；to excess 过度，过分

excessive [ik'sesiv] *adj.* 过多的，极度的
I hate his excessive confidence.
我讨厌他的过度自信。

extra ['ekstrə] *adj.* 额外的；*adv.* 特别地
I am sorry; I have no extra money to lend you.
不好意思，我没有多余的钱借给你。

fraction ['frækʃən] *n.* 小部分，片断，分数
I only read a fraction of his passage.
我只读了他文章的一小部分。

inadequate [in'ædikwit] *adj.* 不充分的，不能胜任的，不适宜的
His income is inadequate to support his family.
他的收入不够养家。

infinite ['infinit] *adj.* 无限的，无数的
It takes infinite patience to teach the children to learn something.
教小孩子学东西需要极大的耐心。

largely ['lɑːdʒli] *adv.* 大部分，大量地
His successes were largely due to his diligence.
他的成功主要靠勤奋。

majority [mə'dʒɔriti] *n.* 多数，大多数
The majority of girls like reading love stories.
大部分女孩子都喜欢读爱情小说。

🔑 考点：the majority of...的谓语动词应与of后的名词一致。

many ['meni] *adj.* 许多的
pron. 许多，许多人
She tried her best to get invitation to that party which many personages would attend.
她想尽办法得到了参加派对的邀请，因为那个派对有很多名人参加。

🔑 考点：a great / good many of 相当多（后跟可数名词复数形式，做主语时谓语动词用复数），很多；
many a 许多（后跟可数名词单数形式，做主语时谓语用单数）。

mass [mæs] *n.* 众多，团，群众
vi. 聚集，集中
The main argument was submerged in a mass of tedious detail.
大量单调乏味的细节掩盖了主要论点。

maximum ['mæksiməm] *n.* 最大限度，最大量，顶点
adj. 最大的，顶点的
In China, a driver must not exceed a maximum of 80 miles an hour.
在中国，司机开车的最大时速不得超过每小时80英里。

million ['miljən] *num.* 百万；*n.* 许多
If I win five million in a lottery, I have to pay one million for my personal tax.
如果我能在抽奖中500万，我得付100万的个人所得税。

more [mɔː] *adj.* 更多的；*adv.* 更
More and more young people go to the city to work and it has a certain impact on the demography of the villages.
越来越多的年轻人去城市打工，这对农村的人口统计带来了一定的影响。

moreover [mɔː'rəuvə] *adv.* 再者，加之，此外
Moreover, doing extra-curricular activities is good to our health.
另外，做课外活动对我们的健康很有益处。

most [məust] *adj.* 最多的；*adv.* 最，很
Most Chinese people are friendly toward foreigners.
大部分中国人对外国人是很友好的。

nine [nain] *num.* 九，九个
You'd better be here by nine o'clock at the latest.
你最迟9点钟到这儿。

nineteen ['nain'tiːn] *num.* 十九，十九个
There are nineteen girls in our class.
我们班有19个女孩。

ninety ['nainti] *num.* 九十，九十个
I got ninety marks in Enlish.
我英语考了90分。

ninth [nainθ] *num.* 第九，九分之一
I had an apartment on the ninth floor.
我在9楼有一套房子。

none [nʌn] *pron.* 没有人，没有一点
adv. 毫不，一点也不
The pregnant woman waved to the taxies passing by, but none of them stopped.

孕妇向过往的出租车招手，但是没有一辆停下来的。

🔍 **考点**：none but 除……之外没有，只有；none too 一点也不

---

numerous ['njuːmərəs] *adj.* 为数众多的，许多

Numerous necessities were sent to Wenchuan after the earthquake.
地震发生后，数不清的生活用品被送往了灾区汶川。

🔍 **考点**：numerous 修饰可数名词。

---

one [wʌn] *num.* 一
pron. 一个人

He was blind in one eye after a fire accident.
在一次火灾事故后，他的一只眼睛失明了。

---

percent [pə'sent] *n.* 百分之……

Ninety percent of students have passed this exam.
90%的学生通过了这次考试。

---

trillion ['triljən] *n.* 大量，兆，万亿
adj. 兆的

The net income of the company is expected to reach 1.25 trillion *yuan* by the end of this year.
预计到年底该公司的纯收入将达到1.25万亿人民币。

---

triple ['tripl] *adj.* 有三部分的，三倍的
vt. （使）成三倍
n. 三个一组，三倍之数

In the past five years the company has tripled its profits.
过去5年中，该公司利润增至3倍。

---

quantity ['kwɔntiti] *n.* 量，数量，分量

I think we should put emphasis on quality rather than on quantity.
我认为我们应该重质而不是重量。

🔍 **考点**：in quantity 大量

---

portion ['pɔːʃən] *n.* 一部分，一分

The man left the major portion of his property to his son.
那个人把大部分的财产留给了儿子。

真题

The major ____ of our education budget is spent on people below the age of 25.
A) measure   B) ratio
C) area   D) portion

详 解：选D。题意为：教育经费主要用在25岁以下人口的经费方面。A) measure 意思是"尺度，衡量"；B) ratio 意思是"比例，比率"；C) area 意思是"地方，地区"；D) portion 意思是"部分，分配额"。

(CET-4 模拟)

---

sum [sʌm] *n.* 总数，金额；*vi.* 共计

The thief just stole an insignificant sum of money.
小偷只偷走了一笔小钱。

🔍 **考点**：in sum 总而言之
sum up 总结，概括

---

percentage [pə'sentidʒ] *n.* 百分比，百分率

The percentage has increased by 25 to 40.
百分比已由25增加到了40。

人与自然｜Human and Nature

 外貌长相

appearance [ə'piərəns] *n.* 出现，来到，外观
We are twins, and my appearance is identical to my sister's.
我们是双胞胎，我的相貌和姐姐的一模一样。

> 考点：to all appearance 就外表看来，根据观察推断

aspect ['æspekt] *n.* 方面，样子，外表
Modern people have much pressure from all aspects of life nowadays.
如今，现代人有很多来自生活方方面面的压力。

bare [bɛə] *adj.* 赤裸的，仅仅的
Little Susan was warned by her mother not to walk on the floor in bare feet.
小苏珊的妈妈警告她别光着脚在地板上走。

beard [biəd] *n.* 胡须，络腮胡子
His false beard fell off, which embarrassed him.
他的假胡须掉了下来，这让他很尴尬。

beautiful ['bju:təful] *adj.* 美的，美丽的
You don't know how beautiful you are.
你都不知道自己有多美。

beauty ['bju:ti] *n.* 美，美丽，美人
The beauty of a person consists in his virtue.
一个人的美丽在于品德。

beggar ['begə] *n.* 乞丐，穷人
My grandmother showed mercy to the beggar and gave him a lot of food.
奶奶对那个乞丐很是怜悯，给了他很多食物。

blind [blaind] *adj.* 瞎的，盲目的
This cat is blind in one eye.
这只猫的一只眼睛失明了。

> 考点：be blind to 对……视而不见
> turn a blind eye (to) 对……视而不见

dwarf [dwɔ:f] *n.* 矮小，侏儒；*adj.* 矮小的
The skyscraper dwarfs all the other buildings in the city.
这座摩天大楼使城市里其他的建筑物都显得矮小了。

feature ['fi:tʃə] *n.* 特征，特色，面貌
Her features remain young though she is forty five years old.
虽然已经45岁了，她的容貌依然年轻。

female ['fi:meil] *n.* 雌性的动物，女子
Migrants, both male and female, seem to come from all over the world.
似乎来自各个国家的男女移民都有。

handsome ['hænsəm] *adj.* 英俊的，相当大的
He is a handsome young man.
他是一个英俊的小伙子。

height [hait] *n.* 高，高度，高处
He couldn't hide his height when he took part in the interview.
面试的时候他无法掩盖自己的身高了。

image ['imidʒ] *n.* 像，形象，映象
The image was absolutely terrible.
这种形象非常可怕。

manly ['mænli] *adj.* 男子气概的，果断的
My brother looked manly in his new uniform.
哥哥穿着新制服，看起来很有男子气概。

mustache [mə'sta:ʃ] *n.* 小胡子，触须
The man with small mustache is suffering from some remnant feeling of disgrace.
留着小胡子的这个人还在为残留的耻辱感到苦恼。

resemble [ri'zembl] *vt.* 像，类似
The ball resembles an egg in shape.
这个球看上去像个鸡蛋。

slender ['slendə] *adj.* 细长的，微薄的
She is a slender, graceful ballet-dancer.
她是一个苗条而动作优美的芭蕾舞演员。

真题

Mrs. Morris's daughter is pretty and _____, and many girls envy her.
A) slender   B) light
C) faint   D) minor

详　解：选A。题意为：莫里斯夫人的女儿苗条又漂亮，许多女孩都嫉妒她。A) slender 意思是"苗条的"；B) light 意思是"轻的，不重的"；C) faint意思是"虚弱的，无力的"；D) minor意思是"较小的，较少的"。

(CET-4 模拟)

slim [slim] *adj.* 苗条的
　　　　　　 vi.&vt. 变苗条，缩小
You can't imagine that the slim girl is keen on weight-lifting.
你不能想象，那个苗条的女孩竟然爱好举重。

trait [treit] *n.* 特征，显著的特点
It didn't show more detailed traits in his performance.
在他的表演中并没有展现更多细节特点。

unlike [,ʌn'laik] *adj.* 不同的
　　　　　　 prep. 不像……
Jack is unlike Tom in almost every way.
杰克与汤姆几乎完全不同。

wrinkle ['riŋkl] *n.* 皱纹；*vi.* 起皱纹
Looking her face covered in wrinkles, could you imagine that she was a beauty when she was young?
看着她布满皱纹的脸，你能想象她年轻时是个美人吗？

bulk [bʌlk] *n.* 物体，容积，大批
Look! The elephant lowered its huge bulk.
看，大象蹲下了它庞大的身躯。
考点：in bulk 大批，大量

broad [brɔːd] *adj.* 宽的，阔的，广泛的
My dad's shoulders are broad.
我爸爸肩很宽。

short [ʃɔːt] *adj.* 短的，短期的
Sweet discourse makes short days and nights.
话若投机嫌日短。
考点：cut short 中断，打断；for short 缩写，简称；in short 简而言之，总之

figure ['figə] *n.* 数字，外形，人物
She has a wonderful figure.
她拥有一个完美的身材。
考点：figure out 想出，理解，明白

人 身体部位

ankle ['æŋkl] *n.* 踝，踝关节
I fell down from the bicycle and twisted my ankle.
我从自行车上摔了下来，扭伤了脚踝。

body ['bɔdi] *n.* 身体，主体，尸体
I felt very cold at midnight and pulled the sheet over my body.
半夜里我感觉很冷，于是就拉起被单盖住身体。

bone [bəun] *n.* 骨，骨骼
The dog ran over here when it heard my sound, with a bone in its mouth.
狗听到我的声音就跑了过来，嘴里还叼着一块骨头。
考点：have a bone to pick with 与……争辩；make no bones about 对……直言不讳（毫不犹豫）

bosom ['buzəm] *n.* 胸，胸部，内心
She clutched the little cat to her bosom.
她把小猫搂在怀里。

bowel ['bauəl] *n.* 肠，内部
The doctor says that eating plenty of fresh fruit and vegetables can reduce the risk of bowel cancer.
医生说多吃新鲜的水果和蔬菜可以减少患肠癌的危险。

brain [brein] *n.* 脑，脑髓，脑力
I racked my brains for an answer, but still couldn't find it.
我绞尽脑汁寻找答案，可仍然未果。
🔍 考点：pick sb.'s brains 向……请教
rack one's brains 绞尽脑汁

breast [brest] *n.* 乳房，胸脯，胸膛
She gives the breast to her baby.
她给婴儿吃奶。
🔍 考点：make a clean breast of 彻底坦白，把……和盘托出

brow [brau] *n.* 额，眉，眉毛
Do you know the function of the brow brush?
你知道眉刷的用途吗？

cheek [tʃi:k] *n.* 面颊，脸蛋
Having been told that the infant had been asleep, she entered the room quietly and kissed his cheek gently.
得知孩子已经睡着了，她悄悄地进了房间，在孩子的面颊上亲了一下。

chest [tʃest] *n.* 胸腔，胸膛，箱子
He folded his arms across his chest.
他把胳膊叠放在胸前。

chin [tʃin] *n.* 颏，下巴
Chin up! We can win this game.
打起精神来，我们会赢得这场比赛的。

dental ['dentl] *adj.* 牙齿的，牙科（用）的
n. 齿音
You should have a dental checked-up.
你应该去牙科做一次检查。

dentist ['dentist] *n.* 牙医
The dentist told the boy not to eat too many sweets.
牙医告诫这男孩不要吃太多糖果。

elbow ['elbəu] *n.* 肘，肘部，弯管
Oh, it hurts! You know I banged my elbow on the corner of the cupboard.
噢，疼死了，我的胳膊撞着柜子角了。

facial ['feiʃəl] *adj.* 面部的，脸上的
n. 面部美容
The pretty girl moisturizes her skin by applying the facial mask every night.
那个漂亮的女孩每天晚上都贴面膜使自己的皮肤湿润。

fist [fist] *n.* 拳（头）
He banged the desk with his fist because of the losing in match.
比赛失败，他用拳头在桌上砰地重击。

flesh [fleʃ] *n.* 肉，肌肉，肉体
The monster only eats the flesh of animals.
这只怪物只吃动物的肉。
🔍 考点：in the flesh 本人

head [hed] *n.* 头，上端；*vt.* 率领
There is a fly on his head, but he doesn't know it at all.
他头上有只苍蝇，而他浑然不知。
🔍 考点：head表示牲畜单位通常只用单数，eg. five head of pigs 5头猪。

heel [hi:l] *n.* 脚后跟，踵，后跟
This kind of shoes has a high heel which doesn't fit for middle-aged woman.
这种鞋子的后跟很高,不适合中年妇女。

hip [hip] *n.* 臀部
This dress completely shows out her wonderful hip.
这条裙子完全展现了她完美的臀部。

joint [dʒɔint] *n.* 接头，接缝，关节
Tom had a bad fall and his leg was out of joint.
汤姆跌下来负了重伤，腿也脱臼了。
🔍 考点：out of joint 脱臼，出了问题

lap [læp] *n.* 膝部，一圈
I fell asleep with a book on my lap.
我睡着了，膝上放着一本书。
🔍 考点：knee和lap都译作"膝"，但所指不同：knee指"膝盖"，lap指人坐下时腰到两膝的地方。

left-hand ['lefthænd] *adj.* 左手的，左边的，左撇子的，惯用左手的
Do you always write left-handed?
你一向用左手写字吗？

limb [lim] *n.* 肢，臂，翼，树枝
The monkey sat on a limb of the tree and looked down.
猴子坐在一根大树枝上往下看。

liver ['livə] *n.* 肝，肝脏，居住者
Drinking too much alcohol does harm to the liver.

饮酒过多对肝有害。

lung [lʌŋ] *n.* 肺脏，肺

The contour of the lung can be straight, slightly concave or slightly convex.
肺的形状可以是直的、轻微凹下或轻度突出的。

mouth [mauθ] *n.* 嘴，口，口腔

He opened his mouth, but he was too thirsty to say one word.
他张开嘴想说话，但因为太渴，一句话都说不出来。

muscle ['mʌsl] *n.* 肌肉，肌，体力

She was very proud of her boyfriend for his well-developed muscles.
她为男友有一身发达的肌肉而感到骄傲。

neck [nek] *n.* 颈，脖子

The boy strained his neck to see over the fence.
男孩伸着脖子看篱笆那边。

nose [nəuz] *n.* 鼻子，突出部分

It is very impolite to blow your nose in front of a lady.
当着女士的面擤鼻子是非常不礼貌的行为。

organ ['ɔ:gən] *n.* 器官，机构，管风琴

Considering her present state of health, she is not suitable for the organ transplantation.
考虑到她目前的健康状况，她不适合做器官移植。

palm [pɑ:m] *n.* 手掌，手心，掌状物

The nail went right through the worker's palm.
一个钉子正好穿透了那个工人的手掌。

🔑 考点：palm off 用欺骗的手段把……卖掉

skeleton ['skelitən] *n.* 骨骼，框架，提要

The professor has been studying the structure of skeleton these days.
教授这些天正在研究骨骼构造。

spine [spain] *n.* 脊柱，脊椎，刺毛

He sustained an injury to his spine when he fell off the hill.
他从山上摔下来，伤了脊梁骨。

thigh [θai] *n.* 股，大腿

He jumped from the tree and broke his thigh.
他从树上跳下来摔断了大腿骨。

throat [θrəut] *n.* 咽喉，喉咙，嗓音

A fishbone stabbed in my throat.
一根鱼刺刺伤了我的喉咙。

thumb [θʌm] *n.* （大）拇指

She prodded me on the shoulder with her thumb to warn me.
她用大拇指在我肩上戳了一下来警告我。

🔑 考点：all thumbs 笨手笨脚

toe [təu] *n.* 脚趾，足尖

My toe is very sore due to the uncomfortable shoes.
都是因为那不舒服的鞋子，我脚趾很痛。

🔑 考点：toe the line 服从，听从

tongue [tʌŋ] *n.* 舌，舌头，语言

His daughter has a facile tongue.
他的女儿口舌伶俐。

waist [weist] *n.* 腰，腰部

He hadn't seen his son for one year and felt surprised when he found that he had grown to his waist.
他一年没见儿子了，看到儿子长得跟他齐腰高了，他感到十分惊讶。

wrist [rist] *n.* 腕，腕关节

He got his wrist broken at the sports meeting.
在运动会上他扭伤了手腕。

人 **动作心理**

gesture ['dʒestʃə] *n.* 姿势，手势，姿态

His gesture relieves me before I step on the stage.
在我上台前，他的手势使我放松下来。

grip [grip] *vt.* 握紧，抓牢；*n.* 紧握

The dog seized the chicken in a tenacious grip.
狗紧紧抓住了小鸡。

🔑 考点：come / get to grips 认真对待（处理）

accord [ə'kɔ:d] *vt.* 使一致，给予
n. 一致，符合，协议

I don't buy your story. Your conduct doesn't accord with your words.
我才不相信你的鬼话，你的言行总不一致。

考点：in accord with 与……一致
with one's accord 主动地，自愿地

---

accordance [ə'kɔːdəns] *n.* 一致，和谐，授予
You must learn to act in accordance with the rules in our company.
在我们公司你必须学会按章程行事。

考点：in accordance with "与……一致，根据"；in accordance with 能做表语，状语；according to 只能做状语。

---

accordingly [ə'kɔːdiŋli] *adv.* 因此，所以，照着
He was told to marry the girl by his parents and accordingly married her.
父母让他跟那个女孩结婚，他就跟她结婚了。

---

act [ækt] *vi.* 行动，见效
vt. 扮演，效仿，学，充当
n. 行为
The old man sometimes acts like a child.
老年人有的时候表现得像个孩子。

考点：act on 奉行，影响；act out 表现出来；in the act of 正做……的过程中

---

action ['ækʃən] *n.* 行动，作用，功能
They conspired to blast the railway station but were arrested before action.
他们阴谋炸掉火车站，但是还没有行动就被抓获了。

考点：out of action 不起作用，不运转
take action 采取行动

---

amuse [ə'mjuːz] *vt.* 逗……乐，给……娱乐
I really enjoy his company. You know he always amuses me.
我很喜欢跟他在一块，他总是逗我开心。

---

avoid [ə'vɔid] *vt.* 避免，躲开，撤消
It cannot be avoided to make mistakes.
犯错在所难免。

考点：avoid后接动名词

---

await [ə'weit] *vt.* 等候，期待
He's anxiously awaiting the competition results.
他焦急地等待着比赛结果。

考点：await=wait for

---

aware [ə'wɛə] *adj.* 知道的，意识到的
I know you are not aware of the difficulty in front of you.
我知道你没有意识到前面的困难。

考点：be aware of sth. 意识到某事

---

awareness [ə'wɛənis] *n.* 意识，注意
Time always glides past without our awareness.
时间总是在我们不知不觉中逝去。

---

beat [biːt] *vi.&vt.* 打，敲，打败
Don't be nervous. I bet you can beat him.
别紧张，我肯定你会打败他的。

考点：beat down 平息，打倒；beat it 跑掉，走开；beat up 痛打，狠揍

---

become [bi'kʌm] *vi.* 变成，成为，变得
Trust yourself, and believe you can become No.1.
要相信自己能成为最好的那一个。

考点：become of 使遭遇，发生于

---

begin [bi'gin] *vi.* 开始；*vt.* 开始
Now, let's begin our class.
现在，让我们开始上课。

考点：to begin with 首先，第一

---

bend [bend] *vt.* 弯曲；*vi.* 曲
He bent to pick up all the coins he had dropped on the ground carelessly.
他弯下腰把自己不小心掉到地上的硬币都捡了起来。

考点：bend over backwards 竭尽全力

---

bite [bait] *vt.* 咬，叮，螫刺，穿
Oh, my God! That dog bit me.
噢，天呐！那只狗咬到我了。

---

blur [blə:] *v.* 弄脏，使……模糊
Her eyes blurred with tears after listening to the woman's misfortune.
听完这个女人的不幸遭遇泪水模糊了她的视线。

---

bounce [bauns] *vi.* 反跳，弹起，跳起
That little boy likes to bounce up and down on the bed.
那个小男孩喜欢在床上蹦跳。

---

break [breik] *vt.* 打破，损坏，破坏
He broke the law and should be punished.

他犯了法，应该受到惩罚。

🔍 考点：break down 损坏，垮掉；break into 非法闯入，强行进入；break out 爆发，脱逃；break through 突围，取得突破性成就

（真题）

Modern forms of transportation and communication have done much to _____ the isolation of life in America.
A) break through   B) break down
C) break into   D) break out

详 解：选A。题意为：现代化的交通与通讯方式打破了美国与世隔绝的生活状态。只有A符合题意。

(CET-4 2003.9)

breath [breθ] *n.* 气息，呼吸，气味
He opened the door and took a deep breath.
他打开门，深深地吸了口气。

🔍 考点：make one's breath 喘息，屏息 hold one's breath 屏息；out of breath 喘不过气来；under one's breath 压着嗓子，低声地

breathe [bri:ð] *vi.* 呼吸；*vt.* 呼吸
The wind was so fierce that we could hardly breathe.
风刮得很猛以至于我们几乎无法呼吸。

bump [bʌmp] *vi.* 碰撞，颠簸而行，提高 *n.* 肿块，撞击，表面隆起
I saw a bus bumped into the car in front on my way to school.
上学路上我看见一辆巴士撞上了前面的那辆汽车。

🔍 考点：bump into 偶然遇见，碰见

cast [kɑ:st] *vt.* 投，扔，抛，浇铸
Thanks to the wonderful performance of the cast, our film got the Golden Horse Prize.
多亏了全体演员的完美表演，我们的电影才获得了金马奖。

🔍 考点：cast about / around for 到处寻找，试图找到；cast aside 把……丢一边，丢掉；cast off 抛弃，丢弃

catch [kætʃ] *vt.* 捉住，赶上，领会
He caught me by the arm and asked me to return his money.
他抓住我的胳膊要我还他的钱。

cease [si:s] *vi.&vt.&n.* 停止，停息
In the end, the old man ceased breathing.
最后，老先生停止了呼吸。

cheer [tʃiə] *vt.* 使振作，欢呼
What a good news; everyone was cheered by it.
真是个好消息，它令每个人都感到兴奋。

choice [tʃɔis] *n.* 选择，抉择
I can't help you; you must make a choice by yourself.
我帮不了你，你必须自己做个选择。

clap [klæp] *vi.* 拍手；*vt.* 拍，轻拍
When she finished her speech, the audience clapped.
她演讲结束时，听众们都为其鼓掌。

compress [kəm'pres] *vt.* 压紧，压缩
Today my boss made me compress the material into 2 pages.
今天老板让我把这份材料压缩成两页。

condense [kən'dens] *vt.* 压缩，使缩短
Steam is condensed to water when it touches a cold surface.
水蒸气触及冷的表面即凝结成水。

cover ['kʌvə] *vt.* 盖，包括；*n.* 盖子
He decided to buy a toupee to cover his bald head.
他决定买一副假发来掩盖自己的秃顶。

arouse [ə'rauz] *vt.* 引起，唤起，唤醒
These English cartoons may arouse my daughter's interest in English.
这些英语动画片也许会引起我女儿对英语的兴趣。

conceal [kən'si:l] *vt.* 把……隐藏起来
She had to conceal her mixed emotions before her little son.
她必须在年幼的儿子面前隐藏自己复杂的感情。

🔍 考点：hide / conceal sth. from sb. 对某人隐瞒某事；hide (vi. / vt.) 不一定有"故意"的含义。conceal (vt.) 常指有目的地、非常巧妙地"掩藏"或"隐瞒"。

creep [kri:p] *vi.* 爬行，缓慢地行进
The thief crept along the corridor.
那贼偷偷地在走廊上潜行。

haul [hɔ:l] *vt.&n.* 拖，拉，运送
They hauled the cow to the market for sale.
他们把牛拉到集市上去卖。

heave [hi:v] *vt.* 举起，提起，扔，发出（叹息等）
vi. 举起，提起，扔，呕吐
n. 举起，升降
With one more heave, we will get the furnish onto the truck.
我们再使把劲，就能把家具抬到卡车上了。

hit [hit] *vt.* 打，碰撞；*n.* 击
Their car hit a stone when running in the deep night.
深夜行进时他们的车撞上一块石头。
考点：hit back 反击，抵抗；hit on / upon 忽然想出，无意中发现

jump [dʒʌmp] *vi.* 跳，暴涨；*vt.* 跳过
Students took an active activity in the high jump.
同学们踊跃报名参加跳高比赛。
考点：get the jump on 抢在……前面，较……占优势

kick [kik] *vi.&vt.* 踢；*n.* 踢，极大的乐趣
The old man's stall was kicked down by the police.
那个老人的摊位被警察踢倒了。
考点：kick off 开始，开球
kick up 引起，激起

lean [li:n] *vi.* 倾斜，屈身，依靠
adj. 瘦的，贫乏的，无脂肪的
The peasant leaned against the tree to have a rest.
农夫靠着树休息了一会儿。

leap [li:p] *vi.* 跳，跃；*n.* 跳跃
I leapt for joy at the good news he brought to us.
我一听到他带来的好消息高兴得跳了起来。
考点：by leaps and bounds 极其迅速地

lay [lei] *vt.* 置放，产（蛋，卵），铺设；（lie的过去式）
Lay your bag on the table and sit down to have a cup of tea.
把你的背包放在桌上，坐下喝杯茶。

考点：lay aside 把……搁置一旁；lay off 解雇，停止做；lay out 摆出，展开；lay up 使卧床不起

真题

With the increasing unemployment rate, workers who are 50 to 60 years old are usually the first to be _____.
A) laid aside   B) laid up
C) laid out   D) laid off

详　解：选D。题意为：随着失业率的上升，50到60岁的工人通常最先被解雇。只有B选项符合题意。

(CET-4 模拟)

pat [pæt] *vt.&n.* 轻拍
My grandmother patted me to make me go to sleep.
外婆拍我入睡。
考点：pat on the back 赞扬，鼓励

pick [pik] *vt.* 拾，摘；*vt.* 采摘
n. 镐，鹤嘴锄
She has picked more apples than me.
她摘的苹果比我多。
考点：pick in 吃一点点；pick on 找……岔子，挑选；pick out 挑出，分辨出；pick up 捡起，好转，继续

shrug [ʃrʌg] *v.&n.* 耸肩
I saw him dismiss the event with a most unsympathetic shrug.
我看见他无所谓地耸耸肩就把这件事情打发了。
考点：shrug off 对……满不在乎，对……不屑一顾

demonstrate ['demənstreit] *vt.* 说明，论证，表露
The physicist must think of an effective way to demonstrate his scientific assumption.
这位物理学家必须想出一个有效的方法来论证他的科学设想。

depict [di'pikt] *vt.* 刻画，描写，叙述
In the book, the character of the heroine is depicted to a nicety.
在这本书里，主人公的性格被刻画得非常细腻。

describe [dis'kraib] *vt.* 形容，描写，描绘
Can you describe the character of the Republic?
你能描述一下共和国的性质吗？

description [dis'kripʃən] *n.* 脚本，描写，形容
Our teacher gave us a vivid description.
我们老师给我们做了一番生动的描述。

evident ['evidənt] *adj.* 明显的，明白的
There are a lot of evident changes in our country.
我们国家有很明显的变化。

evidently ['evidəntli] *adv.* 明显地，显然
Don't argue with me, evidently you are in the wrong.
别和我争辩，这分明是你的错。

exact [ig'zækt] *adj.* 确切的，精确的
Susan said she'll come, but I can't nail down the exact time.
苏珊说她会来，但我不知道确切的时间。

exemplify [ig'zemplifai] *vt.* 作为……的典型，示例，举例证明
This work perfectly exemplifies the writing style of the writer.
这部作品充分体现了作者的写作风格。

explicit [iks'plisit] *adj.* 明确的，明晰的，直言的，露骨的
The contrast could not have been made more explicit .
差别已经再明显不过了。
🔍 考点：be explicit about 对……是明确的

illustrate ['iləstreit] *vt.* （用图等）说明
That example can illustrate the point.
那个例证可以说明这一点。

illustration [ˌiləs'treiʃən] *n.* 说明，图解，例证
He gave an illustration of his theory on math.
他对他的数学理论做了一个说明。

interpret [in'tə:prit] *vt.* 解释，说明，口译
We have to interpret his words in a different way.
我们得换一种方法来解释他的话。
🔍 考点：translate指的是口头和书面的"翻译"；interpret仅指"口头翻译"

interpretation [inˌtə:pri'teiʃən] *n.* 解释，口译
That's an interpretation against my own.
那种解释与我的解释相悖。

justify ['dʒʌstifai] *vt.* 证明……是正当的
How can you justify your being late?
你如何解释你的迟到呢？
🔍 考点：justify doing sth. 证明……正当，为……辩护

reveal [ri'vi:l] *vt.* 展现，揭示，揭露
Usually this kind of utterance could reveal your emotions.
通常这种语调能显露出你的感情。

show [ʃəu] *vt.* 表明，显示，指引，演出
vi. 显现，放映
n. 演出，上映，展览（会）
The account shows that I have spent much money this month.
账目表明我这个月花了很多钱。
🔍 考点：show off 炫耀，卖弄；show up 暴露，来到；on show 在展览中，展出；show sb. around / round 领某人参观

state [steit] *vt.* 陈述，说明，阐明
Please state exactly what you did in this room at such a night.
请准确地说明你今晚在这个房间都干了些什么。

statement ['steitmənt] *n.* 陈述，声明
The specialist are assessing the statement at its true worth.
专家们正在评估这个陈述的真正价值。

emphasis ['emfəsis] *n.* 强调，重点，重要性
I think we would put emphasis on quality rather than on quantity.
我认为我们应该注重质量而非数量。

emphasize ['emfəsaiz] *vt.* 强调，着重
He emphasized the importance of environment protection over and over again.
他反复强调环境保护的重要性。

pass [pa:s] *vi.* & *vt.* 通过，经过
She passed in English. but failed in Japanese.
她通过了英语，但日语却没通过。

221

highlight ['hailait] *vt.* 强调，突出
    n. 最精彩的部分，最重
      要的事件
You must highlight the points.
你必须强调重点。

inference ['infərəns] *n.* 结论，推论，推断
He came up with an unfounded inference from the evidence.
他从证据中得出一个没有根据的推测。

inward ['inwəd] *adj.* 里面的；*adv.* 向内
We should pay more attention to children's inward thoughts and feelings.
我们应该更多地关注孩子内心的思想和感情。

logic ['lɔdʒik] *n.* 逻辑，推理，逻辑性
Everyone has his set of logic in dealing with things.
每个人都有一套自己处理问题的逻辑。

logical ['lɔdʒikəl] *adj.* 逻辑的，符合逻辑
    的，合乎常理的
It's logical to assume that they will conceal the truth from the public.
按理说他们会向公众隐瞒事实。

reason ['ri:zn] *n.* 理由，理性
    vi. 推理
For some special reasons she repulsed his proposal.
因为某种特殊的原因她拒绝了他的求婚。

🔍**考点：** by reason of 由于
      with reason 理智的，合理的

speculate ['spekju,leit] *vi.&vt.* 推测，投
    机，推断
They speculate the outcome of negotiations will be unsatisfactory.
他们推测谈判的结果将会不尽如人意。

recognition [,rekəg'niʃən] *n.* 认出，识别，
    承认
They say the recognition might make some students more likely to study hard.
他们说这种认可可能会使学生更有可能努力学习。

recognize ['rekəgnaiz] *vt.* 认识，认出，
    承认
I can't recognize which one are you from the photo, for all the faces are elongated.
我认不出照片中哪个是你，因为这些脸都照得变长了。

exaggerate [ig'zædʒəreit] *vi.&vt.* 夸大，
    夸张
Don't be afraid, he just exaggerated the difficulties.
别害怕，他只是夸大了那些困难。

真题

Mr. Smith says: "The media are very good at sensing a mood and then ___ it."
A) exaggerating   B) overtaking
C) widening   D) enlarging

详 解： 选A。题意为：史密斯先生说：
"媒体非常善于捕捉人们的情绪，然后渲染它。"。A) exaggerate意思是"夸大"；
B) overtake意思是"超过"；C) widen意思是"拓宽"；D) enlarge意思是"扩大，开阔"。

(CET-4 模拟)

movement ['mu:vmənt] *n.* 动作，活动，
    移动
I love her. To me her every movement is very graceful.
我爱她，对我来说她的一举一动都很优美。

flee [fli:] *vi.* 逃走，逃掉，*vt.* 逃离，逃避
The thieves tried to flee, but they were caught.
小偷试图逃跑，但被抓获了。

fling [fliŋ] *n.* 逃跑，溃退
He dropped one important thing during the fling.
逃跑途中他落下一件很重要的东西。

🔍**考点：** fling oneself into 投身于……
      fling oneself against/on 猛扑向
      have a fling 纵情享乐

gaze ['geiz] *vi.* 凝视，盯，注视
He turned his gaze to the beautiful girl.
他把目光移到那个漂亮的女孩身上。

glance [glɑ:ns] *vi.* 看一下；*n.* 一瞥
Jack's glance was hostile.
杰克的眼光是带着憎恨的。

🔍**考点：** at a glance 一看就
      at first glance 乍一看

infer [in'fə:] *vt.* 推论，推断，猜想
I infer that my essay has passed.
我推测我的论文已经通过了。

人与自然

人

glimpse [glimps] *vt.* 瞥见； *n.* 一瞥，一看
I caught a glimpse of that boy when he came into the house.
那个男孩我只在他进入那栋房子时看过一眼。

考点：glimpse, glance的区别：
glimpse无意识 "瞥见"；
glance多指有意识的 "一瞥"。

notice ['nəutis] *vt.* 注意，意识到
n. 通知，注意
Don't you notice that he is behaving in a strange fashion?
你没有注意到他行为古怪吗？

考点：notice "注意"（无意识的行为）；take notice of "注意"（有意识的行为）

noticeable ['nəutisəbl] *adj.* 显而易见的，重要的
Her boyfriend's good humour was particularly noticeable.
她男朋友的幽默感是显而易见的。

observation [ˌəbzə'veiʃən] *n.* 注意，观察，观察力，观察资料
He is a good scriptwriter with keen observation and rich knowledge.
他是有着敏锐观察力和丰富知识的优秀剧作家。

考点：keep...under (close) observation 对……（密切）监视

observe [əb'zə:v] *vt.* 遵守，观察，说，遵守
If you observe carefully, you will find that they are asymmetric actually.
如果你仔细观察，你会发现它们实际上是不对称的。

peep [pi:p] *vi.*（从缝隙中）偷看
The thief is peeping through the glass hole in their door.
那个贼正从他门上的玻璃孔中看过去。

perceive [pə'si:v] *vt.* 察觉，发觉，理解
I perceive there are some changes in my husband's behavior.
我感觉到丈夫的行为有些变化。

考点：perceive sb. do / doing sth. 察觉某人做某事

perspective [pə'spektiv] *n.* 透视，远景，观点
First I have to remind you to see things in perspective.
首先我要提醒你必须正确地观察事物。

scan [skæn] *vt.* 细看，浏览，扫描
A fire lookout scanned the hills carefully.
火警监视员仔细地查看山区。

sight [sait] *n.* 视力，见，情景
The thief darted away at the sight of the policeman.
小偷一看到警察就飞奔而逃。

考点：at the first sight 乍一看，初看起来；catch sight of 突然看见
lose sight of 看不见，忘记
out of sight 看不见，在视野之外

stare [stɛə] *vi.* 盯，凝视； *n.* 凝视
Her stare made me feel a little scared.
她的凝视使我害怕。

考点：stare at 盯着……

survey ['sə:vei] *vt.* 俯瞰，检查，测量
From the top of the hill you can survey the whole city.
从山顶上你可以俯瞰整个城市。

reckon ['rekən] *vi.* 认为，估计，指望，测算
The readers reckon the book as one of the old poet's best works.
读者们认为这本书是这位老诗人的优秀作品之一。

考点：reckon on 依靠，指望
reckon with 估计到，处理

regard [ri'ga:d] *vt.* 把……看作，尊敬
Nowadays bean curd is regarded as a healthful diet.
现在豆腐被认为是有益于健康的食物。

考点：regard as 把……认为是……
with / in regard to 关于，就……而论

thought [θɔ:t] *n.* 思想，思维，想法
I thought the hotel's fee is rather high.
我认为那个旅馆收费很高。

🧭 考点：on second thoughts 经重新考虑，继而一想

provided [prə'vaidid] *conj.* 以……为条件
We will go to the park tomorrow provided it doesn't rain.
如果明天不下雨，我们就去公园。

suppose [sə'pəuz] *vt.* 猜想，假定，让
Suppose it rained, we would not go out.
假如下雨的话，我们就不出去了。

conclude [kən'klu:d] *vt.* 推断出，结束
From the evidence, I concluded that my boyfriend cheated on me.
我从证据上推断我男友对我不忠。

conclusion [kən'klu:ʒən] *n.* 结论，推论，结尾
I got a conclusion from his sophistry that he wanted to shirk the responsibility.
我从他的诡辩中得出一个结论：他想要推卸责任。

🧭 考点：come to / arrive at / reach / draw a conclusion 得出结论
make a conclusion 下结论
bring...to a conclusion 使……结束

identify [ai'dentifai] *vt.* 认出，识别，鉴定
He didn't identify his classmate many years later.
多年后他没有认出来他的同学。

🧭 考点：identify oneself with 与……打成一片，到……中去

inner ['inə] *adj.* 内部的，内心的
Good books and films can enrich man's inner life.
好书和好电影可以丰富人的精神生活。

spit [spit] *vi.* 吐，吐唾沫
He's used to spitting on the ground.
他习惯性地往地上吐唾沫。

🧭 考点：spit out 厉声说出

👤 **态度情绪** ✏️

temper ['tempə] *n.* 韧度；心情，情绪
vt. 调解，使缓和
He is a man of cheerful temper.
他是一个性格开朗的人。

🧭 考点：lose one's temper 发脾气，发怒

temperament ['tempərəmənt] *n.* 气质，性情
The present life style was well suited to his temperament.
当前的生活方式很适合他的性格。

impatient [im'peiʃənt] *adj.* 不耐烦的，急躁的
He is impatient to the children.
他对孩子们感到很不耐烦

🧭 考点：be impatient of 对……不耐烦，不能忍受；be impatient for / to do 急切……

impulse ['impʌls] *n.* 冲动，推动，驱使
She killed her husband on impulse last night.
昨晚她一时冲动杀了她丈夫。

🧭 考点：on impulse 一时冲动，心血来潮

restless ['restlis] *adj.* 不安定的，焦虑的
The sick child passed a restless night.
这患病的孩子一夜未眠。

🧭 考点：be uneasy about sb. / sth. 对……担心（不安）；be uneasy in doing sth. 对做……担心（不安）

anger ['æŋgə] *n.* 怒，愤怒；*vt.* 使发怒
I can't control my anger when I see him.
我一看见他就抑制不住自己的愤怒。

angry ['æŋgri] *adj.* 愤怒的，生气的
Having waited outside for three hours, he felt extremely angry when he was told to come tomorrow.
在外面等了3个小时后被告知明天再来，他感到非常愤怒。

annoy [ə'nɔi] *vt.* 使恼怒，打搅
He always annoyed me; you know last night he stood me up again.

他总是让我气愤，你知道吗，昨天晚上他又放我鸽子。

complain [kəm'plein] *vi.* 抱怨，诉苦，控告
She is always complaining and inclining to magnify difficulties.
她总是抱怨，总是夸大困难。

🗨 考点：complain that... 抱怨……
complain to sb. of / about sth. 向某人抱怨某事；complain of doing sth. 抱怨做某事

complaint [kəm'pleint] *n.* 抱怨，怨言，控告
I can't bear her perpetual complaints any more.
我再也受不了她不绝于耳的唠叨了。

cynical ['sinikəl] *adj.* 愤世嫉俗的，玩世不恭的
I don't like his cynical attitude.
我不喜欢他那愤世嫉俗的态度。

irritate ['iriteit] *vi.&vt.* 使恼怒，使不适，使疼痛
Don't irritate her; she's a bad temper.
别惹她，她脾气很坏。

moan [məun] *n.* 呻吟声
vi. 呻吟
vt. 抱怨
The patient let out a moan when the doctor bound up his wound.
当医生包扎伤口时，病人呻吟了一声。

mutter ['mʌtə] *vi.* 轻声低语，抱怨
She always mutters to herself, so nobody knows what she is thinking.
她老是一个人唧唧咕咕的，没有人知道她在想什么。

rage [reidʒ] *n.* （一阵）狂怒，盛怒
The boy exploded with rage when he heard the bad news.
听到这个坏消息，男孩勃然大怒。

resent [ri'zent] *vt.* 怨恨，对……表示愤恨
I resent being interrupted while I am working.
我讨厌工作时被打扰。

resentment [ri'zentmənt] *n.* 怨恨，愤恨
The unequal treatment provoked his resentment.

不平等的待遇激起了他的愤恨。

spite [spait] *n.* 恶意，怨恨
She pushed her brother down the hill out of spite.
出于怨恨，她把哥哥推下了山。

🗨 考点：in spite of 不顾，不管

disgust [dis'gʌst] *n.* 厌恶，憎恶
When the girl saw him, she turned away in disgust.
女孩一看见她，就厌恶地转过脸去。

🗨 考点：in disgust 厌恶地

disgusting [dis'gʌstiŋ] *adj.* 让人恶心的，可憎的
It's disgusting that snakes are considered a great delicacy in this area.
在这里，人们把蛇肉当作一道美食，这真让人恶心。

hatred ['heitrid] *n.* 憎恨，憎恶
Race hatred is common in the time of war.
战争年代，种族仇恨很普遍。

nuisance ['nju:sns] *n.* 讨厌的东西
He is such a nuisance; I hate his guts.
他真讨厌人，我对他恨之入骨。

真题

A lot of ants are always invading my kitchen. They are a thorough ____.
A) nuisance B) trouble
C) worry D) anxiety

详　解：选A。题意为：很多蚂蚁侵入我的厨房，它们真让人心烦。A) nuisance 意思是"讨厌的人或物"，符合题意。

(CET-4 模拟)

tired ['taiəd] *adj.* 疲劳的，厌倦的
I'm tired of your perpetual nagging.
我对你无休止的唠叨厌烦了。

🗨 考点：be tired with / from 因……而疲劳；be tired of 对……感到厌烦

wicked ['wikid] *adj.* 坏的，令人厌恶的
I hear that you have done something wicked. Can you tell me what they are?
我听说你做了一些缺德的事，你能告诉我是什么吗？

anxiety [æŋ'zaiəti] *n.* 焦虑，忧虑，渴望
Speech in the public causes him great anxiety.
公开演讲让他感到很焦虑。

anxious ['æŋkʃəs] *adj.* 忧虑的，渴望的
All his families looked very anxious when they
were waiting outside of the operating theatre.
他所有的家人都在手术室门外等待着，看起来
十分焦虑。

bore [bɔ:] *vt.* 使厌烦，钻，挖
The noise really bores me.
噪音真是让我心烦。

disturb [dis'tə:b] *vt.* 打扰，扰乱，弄乱
Don't disturb him! He is disciplining his little son.
别打扰他，他正在训他的小儿子呢。

puzzle ['pʌzl] *n.* 难题，谜；*vi.* 使迷惑
The crossword puzzle totally bewildered me.
这个纵横字谜完全把我弄糊涂了。
👉考点：puzzle out 苦苦思索而弄清楚

trouble ['trʌbl] *n.* 烦恼，困难；*vi.* 烦恼
He lied to the enemy out of trouble.
他骗过敌人从而摆脱了困境。
👉考点：in trouble 陷入困境，倒霉

troublesome ['trʌblsəm] *adj.* 令人烦恼的，
麻烦的
He has been a troublesome child from early age.
从小他就是一个令人头痛的孩子。

upset [ʌp'set] *vt.* 弄翻，打翻，倾覆
adj. 心烦的，苦恼的
He's upset over his own failure in the basketball
match.
他因为自己在篮球比赛中的失败而闷闷不乐。

endurance [in'djurəns] *n.* 忍耐力，持久力
Your behavior has come to the end of my
endurance.
你的行为已经让我忍无可忍。

endure [in'djuə] *vt.* 忍受，容忍
She is the most tolerant woman I have seen, and
she can endure her husband's betrayal.
她是我见过的最宽容的女人，竟然能忍受丈夫
的背叛。

tolerance ['tɔlərəns] *n.* 忍受，容忍，公差
His behaviour has gone beyond the range of her
tolerance.
他的行为已远远超出她的忍受范围。

tolerate ['tɔləreit] *vt.* 忍受，容忍，宽恕
I can not tolerate your irresponsibility.
我不能宽容你的不负责任。

undergo [ˌʌndə'gəu] *vt.* 经历，经受，忍受
Elevators must be undergone a regular safety
inspection.
电梯必须作一个定期安全检查。

agony ['ægəni] *n.* 极度痛苦
She was in agony of losing her baby.
她处于失去孩子的极度痛苦中。

awful ['ɔ:ful] *adj.* 令人不愉快的
People in Wenchuan had an awful earthquake last
year.
去年汶川人民经历了一次可怕的地震。

bitter ['bitə] *adj.* 痛苦的，严寒的
You know black coffee leaves a bitter taste in the
mouth.
不加奶的咖啡在嘴里留下了一些苦味。

bitterly ['bitəli] *adv.* 苦苦地，悲痛地
My mom wept bitterly as if her heart were broken.
妈妈哭得很悲痛，好像心都碎了一样。

sad [sæd] *adj.* 悲伤的
He is very sad of losing her car.
他还沉浸在丢车的悲伤之中。

excite [ik'sait] *vt.* 刺激，使兴奋
He is excited about his brother's wedding.
他因为哥哥婚礼而兴奋。

delight [di'lait] *n.* 快乐；*vt.* 使高兴
To our delight, we are progressing in the writing
skills.
令我们高兴的是，我们的写作技能在不断提
高。

frown [fraun] *vi.* 皱眉，蹙额

人与自然

人

She frowned on his late apology.
她因为他迟到的道歉而不高兴。

🔍 考点：frown at / upon 对……皱眉，不赞许

distress [dis'tres] *n.* 忧虑，悲伤，不幸
His ex-wife's visit caused him more distress than pleasure.
前妻的来访给他带来更多的痛苦，而不是愉快。

enjoyable [in'dʒeiəbl] *adj.* 使人快乐的，有乐趣的
Thank you for the most enjoyable weekend.
谢谢你给我带来这么愉快的周末。

grief [gri:f] *n.* 悲伤，悲痛，悲伤的事
Grief and disappointment are hastening the old man's death.
悲哀和失望在加速老人的死亡。

🔍 考点：come to grief 失败，遭受不幸
bring sb. to grief 使……遭受失败或者不幸

merry ['meri] *adj.* 欢乐的，愉快的
I wish all of you a merry Christmas.
我希望你们每个人圣诞快乐。

miserable ['mizərəbl] *adj.* 痛苦的，悲惨的，贫困的，让人难受的
Talking of feudalism, the old man seemed to have a lot of miserable stories to tell me.
提起封建制度，这位老人似乎有很多悲惨的故事要告诉我。

nice [nais] *adj.* 美好的，令人愉快的
You are a nice couple, I really admire you.
你们真是美满的一对，我真羡慕你们。

pain [pein] *n.* 疼，疼痛；辛苦
The old man was driven crazy by the extremity of pain.
极度的痛苦使老人发狂。

painful ['peinful] *adj.* 疼痛的，痛苦的，费力的
You will be painful during the operation.
手术期间你会感到疼痛。

pleasant ['plezənt] *adj.* 令人愉快的，舒适的
A pleasant recall always brings you much happiness.
一个令人愉悦的回忆总是给你带来快乐。

mood [mu:d] *n.* 心情，情绪，语气
He was in a good mood as the canoe slowly advanced.
当独木舟缓缓前进，他的心情十分轻松。

真题

After working all day, he was so tired that he was in no ____ to go to the party with us.
A) mood   B) emotion
C) sense   D) taste

详 解：选A。题意为：在工作了一整天后，他太累了，以至于没心情和我们一块去参加宴会。be in no mood for sth. / to do sth. 没心情做……

(CET-4 模拟)

please [pli:z] *vt.* 使高兴，请；*vi.* 满意
Please replenish a glass with wine to the honoured guest.
请再为这个尊贵的客人斟满一杯酒。

pleasure ['pleʒə] *n.* 愉快，快乐，乐事
Next month the whole family will visit a resort in order to get some pleasure.
下个月全体家庭成员将会去一个旅游胜地娱乐一下。

🔍 考点：take (a) pleasure in 以……为乐
with pleasure 乐意地，愿意地

rack [ræk] *n.* 搁物架，行李架
vt. 使苦痛，折磨
The girl stood at the street corner, racked by indecision, and began to cry.
女孩站在街角，犹豫不决，然后哭了起来。

🔍 考点：rack one's brains 绞尽脑汁

rejoice [ri'dʒɔis] *vi.* 欣喜，高兴
My parents sincerely rejoice over my victories.
父母为我的胜利感到由衷地高兴。

sorrow ['sɔrəu] *n.* 悲痛，悲哀，悲伤
His sorrow was concealed in his heart.
他的悲哀隐藏在内心。

sorry ['sɔri] *adj.* 难过的，对不起的
I'm sorry to interrupt your performance.
我很抱歉打断你们的表演。

tear [tiə] *n.* 眼泪，泪珠；*vt.* 撕开，撕裂
She tears up the composition and starts over again.
她把这篇作文撕掉，从头开始写。

真题

The old paper mill has been _____ to make way for a new shopping centre.
A) cut down   B) kept down
C) torn down   D) held down

详　解：选C。题意为：为了腾出地方盖新的购物中心，拆掉了老造纸厂。A) cut down 意思是"降低，减少"；B) keep down 意思是"压制或镇压（人民，国民）"；C) tear down 意思是"弄倒，拆除"；D) hold down 意思是"限制某人的自由，压制某事物"。

(CET-4 模拟)

weep [wi:p] *vi.* 哭泣，流泪
Laugh, and the world laughs with you; Weep, and you weep alone.
[谚]欢笑时，整个世界伴你欢笑。哭泣时，只有你独自向隅而泣。

depress [di'pres] *vt.* 使沮丧，按下
Bad weather always depresses me.
坏天气总会使我心情抑郁。

depression [di'preʃən] *n.* 低落，消沉，萧条
Our company sheared a lot of employees during the great depression.
在经济大萧条期间我们公司削减了很多员工。

真题

Many people lost their jobs during the business ____.
A) despair   B) decrease
C) desperation   D) depression

详　解：选D。题意为：许多人在经济萧条时期丢掉了工作。depression指（经济）萧条，该词的程度及范围比recession要小。

(CET-4 模拟)

despair [dis'pɛə] *n.* 绝望；*vi.* 绝望
In rudderless despair, he began to search for ideological sustenance.
在失去航向的绝望中，他开始寻找思想寄托。

🔸 **考点**：in despair 在绝望中

desperate ['despərit] *adj.* 拼死的，绝望的
He was desperate when he knew he got cancer.
当他得知自己患上癌症时，他绝望了。

disappoint [ˌdisə'pɔint] *vt.* 使失望，使受挫折
She was very disappointed with her lazy husband.
她对她的懒丈夫很失望。

disappointing [ˌdisə'pɔintiŋ] *adj.* 让人失望的
What he has done is disappointing.
他的所作所为让人失望。

discourage [dis'kʌridʒ] *vt.* 使泄气，使灰心
She is never discouraged by difficulties.
她从没因困难而泄气。

🔸 **考点**：discourage sb. from doing sth. 阻止某人做某事

frustrate [frʌs'treit] *vt.* 使沮丧，挫败，使受挫
This is the place that he frustrated enemy.
这是他挫败敌人的地方。

gloomy ['glu:mi] *adj.* 黑暗的，令人沮丧的
He studied in the gloomy light till dawn.
他在昏暗的灯光下学习到黎明。

energetic [ˌenə'dʒetik] *adj.* 精力充沛的，充满活力的
It would be very interesting to be an energetic campaigner.
做一名积极的活动家一定很有趣。

optimistic [ˌɔpti'mistik] *adj.* 乐观的，乐观主义的
Be optimistic! You know downhearted thoughts would hinder progress.
乐观一些！消沉的思想会妨碍进步。

positive ['pɔzətiv] *adj.* 确定的，积极的
We should watch some films that can have positive effect on us.
我们应该看一些对我们有积极影响的电影。

initiative [i'niʃiətiv] *n.* 主动性，主动权，倡议，提案
Some people think that the initiative comes from man throughout in nature.

有些人认为人在自然界中自始至终占主导地位。

🔍 **考点**：take the initiative (in doing sth.)
采取主动，起带头作用

真题

I told the German official at the time that I was
sure the _____ would fail.
A) adventure   B) response
C) initiative   D) impulse

详 解：选C。题意为：那时我告诉这个德
国官员这一提案会失败。A) adventure意思是
"冒险（经历）"；B) response意思是"回
答，反应"；C) initiative意思是"提议，提
案"；D) impulse意思是"刺激，冲动"。

(CET-4 模拟)

idle ['aidl] *adj.* 空闲的，懒散的
He has a lot of idle time at that moment.
那个时候他有很多的空闲时间。

negative ['negətiv] *adj.* 否定的，消极的，
反面的，阴性的
My father gave me a negative answer, which really
disappointed me.
爸爸给了我一个否定的答案，这真让我失望。

passive ['pæsiv] *adj.* 被动的，消极的
The man plays a passive role in his marriage.
那人在婚姻中扮演着被动的角色。

pessimistic [ˌpesi'mistik] *adj.* 悲观的，厌
世的
I am pessimistic about my chances of passing the
examination.
我对通过考试感到很悲观。

abnormal [æb'nɔ:məl] *adj.* 不正常的，反
常的，变态的
There is something wrong with my grandmother.
She looks abnormal today.
我奶奶有些不对劲，她今天看上去有些反常。

alarm [ə'lɑ:m] *n.* 惊恐，忧虑，警报
vt. 使惊慌，警告，警示
In case of fire, ring the alarm bell quickly.
如遇失火，请尽快按警铃。

amaze [ə'meiz] *vt.* 使惊奇，使惊愕
What you said really amazed me.

你所说的实在令我很惊讶。

alert [ə'lə:t] *adj.* 警觉的，注意的
vt. 向……报警，使意识到
n. 警戒，戒备，警报
From the telescope, I saw an alert leopard go up to
an antelope quietly.
从望远镜里，我看到一只警觉的豹子静悄悄地
接近一只羚羊。

🔍 **考点**：on the alert for / against 警戒
着，随时准备着

amazing [ə'meiziŋ] *adj.* 令人惊愕的，使人
惊叹的
It's amazing that the earthworms can produce
antibiotic substance.
真神奇，蚯蚓可以产生抗菌物质。

astonish [əs'tɔniʃ] *vt.* 使惊讶，使吃惊
I confess to being astonished at his unexpected
coming.
我承认我对他这次始料不及的来访感到吃惊。

crazy ['kreizi] *adj.* 疯狂的，荒唐的
The old man was driven crazy by the extremity of
pain.
极度的痛苦使老人发狂。

curiosity [ˌkjuəri'ɔsiti] *n.* 好奇，好奇心，
珍品
The cover of this book arises his curiosity.
这本书的封面引起了他的好奇心。

curious ['kjuəriəs] *adj.* 好奇的，稀奇古怪的
The children were curious about the photosensitive
paper.
孩子们对感光纸很感兴趣。

exclaim [iks'kleim] *vi.* 呼喊，惊叫
The children exclaimed with excitement.
孩子们兴奋地大叫。

fuss [fʌs] *vi.* 小题大做，烦恼，过于忧虑
n. 忙乱，大惊小怪
He always likes making a fuss on this kind of thing.
他总是喜欢在这种事情上小题大做。

🔍 **考点**：make a fuss of / over 对……关怀
备至，过分注意

startle ['stɑ:tl] *vt.* 使大吃一惊；*n.* 吃惊
I didn't mean to startle you by playing a ghost.

我扮鬼不是想吓你的。

🔎 考点：startle, surprise都有"使吃惊"的意思：startle特指吓得猛地一动，跳起来或者往后退；surprise强调内心吃惊，不一定伴有动作。

---

incredible [in'kredəbl] *adj.* 不能相信的，难以置信的，惊人的

The plot of novel is incredible nowadays.
现在的小说情节叫人难以置信。

---

marvelous ['mɑːviləs] *adj.* 奇迹般的，惊人的，了不起的

It's marvelous that elements can combine in many different ways to form thousands of compounds.
真是神奇，元素以多种形式结合成数千种化合物。

---

ridiculous [ri'dikjuləs] *adj.* 荒谬的，可笑的

It is ridiculous to politicize the strike and ruin the reputation.
使这次罢工带上政治色彩并破坏其声誉是很荒谬的。

---

stagger ['stægə] *vi.&vt.&n.* 摇晃，蹒跚，使吃惊，使交错

He gave a stagger on hearing the news that his son had sacrificed in the war.
他听到儿子战死的消息时，两腿摇晃了起来。

---

surprise [sə'praiz] *vt.* 使惊奇，突然袭击

What do you think the surprise will be?
你想会是什么样的意外惊喜？

🔎 考点：take...by surprise 使措手不及，使吃惊

---

unexpected [ʌniks'pektid] *adj.* 想不到的，意外的

Her approval was quite unexpected.
她的赞同是完全出人意料的。

---

weird [wiəd] *adj.* 离奇的，怪诞的

It is weird that no one attends the class.
没有人来上课真是太奇怪了。

---

wonder ['wʌndə] *n.* 惊异，惊奇，奇迹
vi.&vt. 想知道，（对……）感到奇怪

I wonder why you must perjure yourself.
我想知道你为什么非要作伪证。

🔎 考点：no wonder 并不奇怪，难怪

---

ache [eik] *vi.* 痛，想念；*n.* 疼痛

My heart ached when I knew the little girl's story.
知道了那个女孩的故事之后，我心里隐隐作痛。

---

lonely ['ləunli] *adj.* 孤独的，荒凉的，人迹罕至的

He always feels lonely and sad in the city built with steel rods and concrete.
在钢筋和混凝土建成的城市里他总是感到孤独悲伤。

---

miss [mis] *n.* （大写）小姐
vt. 未看到，惦念

He really missed his dead wife, especially on Tomb-sweeping Day.
他很思念去世的妻子，尤其是在清明节的时候。

---

emotion [i'məuʃən] *n.* 情感，感情，激动

You know love and hatred are both emotions.
爱恨都是情感。

---

emotional [i'məuʃənl] *adj.* 感情的，情绪的

The teacher's emotional pep talk stirred the students.
老师的激情鼓动刺激了同学们。

---

excitement [ik'saitmənt] *n.* 刺激，兴奋，令人兴奋的事，刺激的因素

Her even breathing showed that she had got over her excitement.
她均匀的呼吸显示出她已经由兴奋转为平静了。

---

intense [in'tens] *adj.* 强烈的，紧张的

She looks so terribly intense before the match.
比赛前，她看上去是那么紧张。

---

nervous ['nəːvəs] *adj.* 紧张的，神经的，易激动的

She stared at the young man for a long time, which made him very nervous.
她盯着那个年轻人看了很久，这让他很不自在。

---

tense [tens] *n.* 时态，时
adj. 拉紧的，绷紧的

He lowered his head with a tense anxiety.
他紧张焦虑地低下了头。

tension [tenʃən] *n.* 紧张，拉紧，拉力

Her nervous tension relaxed after an hour.
一小时后，她紧张的神经松弛了下来。

🔊 **考点**：strain, tension都有 "紧张" 的意思：strain通常指过分吃力、影响健康的紧张状态；tension一般指双方或各方关系不好所造成的紧张状态

thrill [θril] *n.* 一阵激动

He felt a thrill when he got on the stage.
他一上台就很激动。

affection [əˈfekʃn] *n.* 喜爱，慈爱，爱，爱慕

I have a great affection for my new Math teacher.
我很喜欢新来的数学老师。

affect [əˈfekt] *vt.* 影响，感动

The weather really affects us so directly—what we wear, what we do, and even how we fell.
天气对我们穿衣、做事、甚至心情都有直接的影响。

fascinate [ˈfæsineit] *vt.* 强烈地吸引，迷住

The changing vivid colours of the sunset fascinated the eye.
日落时变化分明的色彩使人看得入迷。

fascinating [ˈfæsineitiŋ] *adj.* 迷人的

The scenery there is quite fascinating.
那里的景色真迷人。

fond [fɔnd] *adj.* 喜爱的，溺爱的

I am not so fond of studying as I was at first.
我对学习已没有起初那么大的兴趣了。

magnetic [mægˈnetik] *adj.* 磁的，有磁性的，有吸引力的

I was ravished by her magnetic personality.
我为她迷人的风度所倾倒。

passion [ˈpæʃən] *n.* 激情，热情，爱好

He showed his zealous passion to the Radical Party.
他对激进党表现出狂热的激情。

🔊 **考点**：fly / get into a passion 大怒，大发雷霆；have a passion for 喜爱

keen [ki:n] *adj.* 热心的，激烈的，精明的

When I was a child, I was very keen on cartoons.
当我还是个孩子时，我非常喜欢漫画。

🔊 **考点**：be keen on (doing) sth. 对……热心，渴望

真题

My grandfather had always taken a _____ interest in my work, and I had an equal admiration for the stories of his time.
A) splendid   B) weighty
C) vague   D) keen

详 解：选D。题意为：爷爷总是对我的工作很感兴趣，而我也对他那个时代的故事充满了兴趣。A) splendid意思是 "极好的，杰出的"；B) weighty意思是 "重要的"；C) vague意思是 "含糊不清的"；D) keen意思是 "热烈的"。

(CET-4 模拟)

kind [kaind] *n.* 种类；*adj.* 友好的，和蔼的

I really appreciate your kind words; it mitigated my suffering.
我很感激你亲切的话语，它减轻了我的痛苦。

🔊 **考点**：of a kind 同类的，徒有其名的
kind of 有几分，有点儿

kindness [ˈkaindnis] *n.* 仁慈，好意

I am greatly appreciating your kindness.
我非常感激您的好意。

beg [beg] *vi. & vt.* 乞讨

The old man beg for his living.
那个老人靠乞讨为生。

🔊 **考点**：beg for/of 请求，恳求

harsh [hɑːʃ] *adj.* 严厉的，刺耳的

Mr. Wang is a harsh teacher, but everyone likes him.
王先生是一个严厉的老师，不过每个人都喜欢他。

indifferent [inˈdifərənt] *adj.* 冷漠的，不积极的

The friendship between gentleman appears indifferent but is pure like water.
君子之交淡如水。

isolate [ˈaisəleit] *vt.* 使隔离，使孤立

We can't isolate our classmates in school.
我们不可以孤立学校的同学。

ignore [igˈnɔː] *vt.* 不顾，不理，忽视

He is often ignoring anything around him.
他总是能忽视周围的一切。

真题

Some research workers completely ____ all those facts as though they never existed.
A) ignore   B) leave
C) refuse   D) miss

详 解：选A。题意为：一些研究人员完全忽视了这些事实，好像它们从来不存在似的。由"好像它们从来不存在似的"推断出他们"忽视"了某些东西。

(CET-4 模拟)

rigid ['ridʒid] *adj.* 刚硬的，僵硬的
Habits have ossified into rigid dogma.
习惯已僵化为不可更动的教条。

serious ['siəriəs] *adj.* 严肃的，认真的
Unfortunately a serious car accident made her lose her consciousness.
不幸的是，一场可怕的车祸使她失去了意识。

severe [si'viə] *adj.* 严格的，严厉的
We should inflict severe punishment on criminals.
我们应该对罪犯施加严厉的惩罚。

afraid [ə'freid] *adj.* 害怕的，担心的，恐惧的
I'm afraid of being at home alone.
我害怕一个人待在家里。

考点：be afraid of 害怕做某事

awfully ['ɔ:fuli] *adv.* 令人畏惧的，很
The teacher is awfully strict.
那个老师很严格。

fear [fiə] *n.* 害怕，担心；*vt.* 害怕
The man never feared hardship and he finally became a leader of the company.
那个人从不怕困难，最终成了公司的一个领导。

考点：for fear of doing / that 生怕，以免

fearful ['fiəful] *adj.* 害怕的，可怕的
The doctor was fearful that the patient should get worse.
医生担心病人的情况会恶化。

frighten ['fraitn] *vt.* 使惊恐，吓唬

He was frightened into cry before the tiger.
他被眼前的老虎吓哭了。

考点：frighten sb. into doing sth. 威胁某人做某事

horrible ['hɔrəbl] *adj.* 可怕的，骇人听闻的，极讨厌的，糟透的
He might have heard some horrible news.
他可能听到了什么可怕的消息。

真题

The other day, Mom and I went to St. James's Hospital, and they did lots and lots of tests on me, most of them ____ and frightening.
A) cheerful   B) horrible
C) hostile   D) friendly

详 解：选B。题意为：前天我和妈妈去了圣·詹姆斯医院，他们给我作了多项检查，多数结果是可怕的。A) cheerful意思是"愉快的，高兴的" B) horrible意思是"可怕的"；C) hostile意思是"有敌意的，不友好的"；D) friendly意思是"友好的"。

(CET-4 2005.6)

horror ['hɔrə] *n.* 战栗，憎恶
She went away in horror at the sight of so much blood.
她一看见这么多血就立刻吓得走开了。

scare [skɛə] *vt.* 惊吓；*vi.* 受惊
vt. 吓，使害怕
The body buried beneath the plastic bags really scared me.
塑料袋下面的尸体着实把我吓坏了。

quiver ['kwivə] *vi.* 颤动，抖动
n. 颤动，抖动
There is a slight quiver in her voice as she speaks.
她说话时声音有些颤抖。

考点：shake, tremble, quiver 都有"抖动"的意思：shake 可用于任何运动，常有粗鲁或不规则的含义；tremble 多用于胆怯、愤怒地发抖；quiver 表示类似琴弦振动的轻微的、迅速的振动，多用于事物。

人与自然

人

lest [lest] *conj.* 恐，以免

Tie the rope fast lest it should come loose.
把绳子系紧，免得它松脱。

（真题）

> While crossing the mountain area, all the men carried guns lest they ＿＿＿＿ by wild animals.
> A) had been attacked   B) must be attacked
> C) should be attacked   D) would be attacked
>
> 详　解：选C。题意为：在跨越山区时，所有人都带着枪以防遭到野兽的攻击。Lest引导的状语从句常用"should + 动词原形"表示虚拟；本题从句中主语they是动词attack的受动者，因此用被动形式。
>
> （CET-4 模拟）

shiver ['ʃivə] *vi.* 颤抖，哆嗦
　　　　　　　　 n. 冷颤

Having rushed home in the rain, he got drenched to the skin and shivered with cold constantly.
他冒雨赶回家，浑身都湿透了，冻得直发抖。

🔍 考点：shiver with 因……而发抖

terror ['terə] *n.* 惊骇

She was seized with a nameless terror when came in this house.
在进入这房子时她感到一种不可名状的恐惧。

timid ['timid] *adj.* 胆怯的，羞怯的

Lily is too timid to venture upon a new work.
莉莉太胆小，不敢从事新的工作。

🔍 考点：be timid of 害怕……

tremble ['trembl] *vi.* 发抖，哆嗦，摇动

Lotte heard the door open; all her limbs began to tremble.
绿蒂听见门开，她全身发抖。

🔍 考点：tremble with 因……而颤抖

nerve [nə:v] *n.* 神经，勇敢，胆量

My brother always drives fast, so you need plenty of nerve to sit beside him when he is driving.
我哥哥开车总是很快，所以他开车的时候，你得有足够的胆量才敢坐在他旁边。

🔍 考点：get on sb.'s nerves 惹得某人心烦

persist [pə'sist] *vi.* 坚持，固执，持续

If you persist in violating the traffic rules, one day you would get hurt in the car accident.
如果你再继续违反交通法规的话，总有一天你会在交通事故中受伤的。

🔍 考点：persist in doing sth 坚持做某事

regardless [ri'gɑ:dlis] *adv.* 不顾一切地

The plucky girl is determined to do it regardless of all consequences.
这个有毅力的女孩不顾一切后果，决心这样做。

🔍 考点：regardless of 不顾，不惜

（真题）

> Research universities have to keep up with the latest computer and scientific hardware ＿＿＿＿ price.
> A) on account of   B) regardless of
> C) in addition to   D) not to mention
>
> 详　解：选B。题意为：研究型大学必须不惜代价地使其计算机和研究设备保持领先水平。A) on account of 意思是"由于"；B) regardless of 意思是"不管，无论如何"；C) in addition to 意思是"除此之外"；D) not to mention意思是"更不用说"。
>
> （CET-4 2003.9）

resolution [ˌrezə'lu:ʃn] *n.* 坚决，坚定，
　　　　　　　　　　　　 决定

I am not confident to shake his resolution.
我没把握能够动摇他的决心。

🔍 考点：make a resolution to do sth. 下决心做某事

resolve [ri'zɔlv] *vt.* 解决，决心；*n.* 决心

He kept his resolve to get a good job.
他决心找到一个好工作。

🔍 考点：resolve to do sth. 或 resolve on doing sth. 下决心做某事

ashamed [ə'ʃeimd] *adj.* 惭愧（的）；羞耻
　　　　　　　　　　　 （的）羞愧，惭愧

His father worked as a waiter and he is ashamed of it.
他为父亲是一个服务员而感到丢脸。

awkward ['ɔ:kwəd] *adj.* 笨拙的，尴尬的

The boy is very awkward, he always keeps dropping things.

这个男孩很笨，总是丢东西。

disgraceful [dis'greisful] *adj.* 可耻的，丢脸的

It's disgraceful to spit here.
在这里吐痰真是丢脸。

embarrass [im'bærəs] *vt.* 使窘迫，使为难
The girl seemed embarrassed by the question.
女孩似乎被这个问题弄得有些窘迫。

shame [ʃeim] *n.* 羞耻，羞愧，羞辱
That man had no sense of shame and never felt guilty.
那个男人没有羞耻心，从来都不觉得内疚。

考点：feel shame at 因……感到羞愧

independence [ˌindi'pendəns] *n.* 独立，自主，自立
I am not willing to give up my independence to submit to them.
我不愿意丧失自己的独立性去屈从于他们。

independent [indi'pendənt] *adj.* 独立的，自主的
I'm pretty independent in daily life.
我在生活中是独立性很强的人。

neglect [ni'glekt] *vt.* 忽视，忽略，疏忽
I know you are busy, but you shouldn't neglect your health for it.
我知道你很忙，但你也不该因此而忽视自己的健康。

omit [əu'mit] *vt.* 省略，省去，遗漏
It's okay to omit the minor details.
可以省掉无关紧要的细枝末节。

overlook [ˌəuvə'luk] *vt.* 眺望，看漏，放任
He just put all his heart on it, and totally overlooked the enormous risks involved.
他一心扑在这事上，完全忽略了其中牵涉的极大危险。

contempt [kən'tempt] *n.* 轻视，轻蔑
I guess you could be cited for contempt of court.
我猜你会因藐视法庭而受到传讯的。

考点：hold...in contempt 轻视，认为……不屑一顾

assure [ə'ʃuə] *vt.* 使确信，向……保证
He assured me that he would return the book in three days.
他跟我保证3天以内还书。

真题

He was proud of being chosen to participate in the game and he _____ us that he would try as hard as possible.
A) assured   B) insured
C) assumed   D) guaranteed

详 解：选A。题意为：他很自豪能被选中参加这次比赛，并向我们保证他会尽最大努力。A) assure sb. of sth.或者assure sb. that...意思是"向……保证"；B) insure意思是"保险，使无风险"；C) assume意思是"假定，假象"；D) guarantee意思是"保证，确保"，后面直接跟名词或that从句。

(CET-4 模拟)

defy [di'fai] *vt.* 蔑视，不管，不怕
Anyone who defies the law would get punished.
任何无视法律的人都会受到惩罚。

考点：sth. defy description / understanding 某物难以描述（理解）

doubt [daut] *n.* 怀疑，疑虑；*vt.* 怀疑
It is no doubt that he is a faithful believer of Judaism.
毫无疑问，他是犹太教的忠实信徒。

考点：in doubt 不能肯定的
no doubt 很可能，无疑地

doubtful ['dautful] *adj.* 难以预测的，怀疑的
The result is doubtful.
这个结果很可疑。

prejudice ['predʒudis] *n.* 偏见，成见
The actress has deep-rooted prejudice against homosexuals.
那个女演员对同性恋者有根深蒂固的偏见。

考点：with prejudice (to) 没有不理，无损于……

sceptical ['skeptikəl] *adj.* 表示怀疑的
I am sceptical about the solution.

人与自然

人

我对这个解决办法表示怀疑。

🔍 考点：be sceptical about 对……表示怀疑

suspect [sə'spekt] *vt.* 怀疑；*vi.* 疑心
I rather suspect we're making a big mistake on that case.
我有些怀疑我们可能在那个案件上犯了个大错。

🔍 考点：suspect sb. of (doing) sth. 怀疑某人（做过）某事；suspect sb. to be 怀疑某人是……

suspicion [sə'spiʃən] *n.* 疑，疑心，猜疑
His crazy actions generated a good deal of suspicion.
他疯狂的行为招来不少的猜疑。

deliberate [di'libəreit] *vt.* 考虑，熟思，讨论
vi. 思考，协商
adj. 故意的，早有准备的
I think it's a deliberate crime not an accident.
我认为这是蓄意的罪行，而并非意外事故。

真题

Mr. Smith was the only witness who said that the fire was ____.
A) meaningful   B) deliberate
C) innocent   D) mature

详　解：选B。题意为：史密斯先生是唯一声称这是故意纵火案的目击者。deliberate 在这里指的是"有准备的，故意的"。

(CET-4 模拟)

demanding [di'mɑ:ndiŋ] *adj.* 需要技能的，苛求的
We all know teaching is a demanding profession.
我们都知道教学工作是个要求很高的工作。

tease [ti:z] *vt.* 逗乐，戏弄，强求
It's too bad of you to tease the child because he stutters.
因为一个孩子口吃而取笑他，你真是太不应该了。

envious ['enviəs] *adj.* 羡慕的，嫉妒的
She stares the diamond necklace on the duchess with envious looks.

她用羡慕的眼光盯着公爵夫人的钻石项链。

jealous ['dʒeləs] *adj.* 妒忌的，猜疑的
I was very jealous of Lily's new dress.
我很嫉妒莉莉的新裙子。

🔍 考点：be jealous of 嫉妒……，羡慕……

flexibility [ˌfleksə'biliti] *n.* 灵活性，柔韧性
In some cases, however, flexibility is very critical.
不过在有些情况下，灵活绝对是非常重要的。

flexible ['fleksəbl] *adj.* 易弯曲的；灵活的
He has a flexible mastery of the knowledge.
他对知识有一个灵活的掌握。

真题

We have arranged to go to the cinema on Friday, but we can be ____ and go another day.
A) reliable   B) probable
C) feasible   D) flexible

详　解：选D。题意为：我们计划星期五去看电影，但计划很灵活，我们也可以改天去。A) reliable意思是"可靠的，靠谱的"；B) probable意思是"大概的，可能的"；C) feasible意思是"可行的，行得通的"；D) flexible意思是"可变通的"。

(CET-4 模拟)

intelligence [in'telidʒəns] *n.* 智力，理解力，情报
In intelligence, most people are about equal.
人们的智力大致相同。

🔍 考点：intelligence, information都有"情报"的意思：information是强调提供给别人的情报；intelligence则不一定传给别人。

intelligent [in'telidʒənt] *adj.* 聪明的，理智的
The professor made a very intelligent comment.
教授做了很有见地的评论。

smart [smɑ:t] *adj.* 巧妙的，洒脱的
Don't worry, he is smart and can take care of himself.
别担心，他很聪明，也可以照顾好自己。

swift [swift] *adj.* 快的，反应快的
She did a swift mental calculation whether the business is workable.

她头脑敏捷地盘算了一下这笔生意是否可做。

scene [si:n] *n.* 场景，场面（事件发生的）地点
What a beautiful scene!
多美的风景啊！

真题

Computer power now allows automatic searches of fingerprint files to match a print at a crime _____ .
A) stage   B) scene
C) location D) occasion

详　解：选B。题意为：现在计算机可以自动搜索指纹档案，以找到和犯罪现场相匹配的指纹。at a crime scene是固定搭配，意思是"在犯罪现场"。A) stage常与at / in搭配，意思是"阶段，时期"；C) location常与on搭配，意思是"电影的外景拍摄"；D) occasion常与on搭配，意思是"间或，偶尔"。

(CET-4 2005.6)

fool [fu:l] *n.* 蠢人，傻子
vt. 欺骗
"She's a fool," said Jack bitterly.
"她是个糊涂虫。"杰克狠狠地说。
考点：fool about / around 虚度光阴，闲逛；make a fool of 愚弄，使出丑

ignorance ['ignərəns] *n.* 无知，愚昧
Her ignorance appeared completely on this thing.
她的愚昧无知在这件事情上体现得淋漓尽致。

ignorant ['ignərənt] *adj.* 不知道的，无知的
He felt himself very ignorant.
他感到自己很无知。

insane [in'sein] *adj.* 愚蠢的，荒唐的，疯狂的
He must have been insane to quit his decent job.
他竟把那么体面的工作辞了，真是疯了。

funny ['fʌni] *adj.* 古怪的，滑稽的
His behaviors are very funny in the film.
他在电影中的行为非常滑稽。

humorous ['hju:mərəs] *adj.* 富于幽默的，诙谐的
His humorous remarks made our conversation joyful.
他幽默的话语给谈话增添了不少愉悦。

humour ['hju:mə] *n.* 幽默，诙谐，幽默感
He has a sense of humour.
他很有幽默感。

laughable ['lɑ:fəbl] *adj.* 可笑的，有趣的
It is how laughable to mispronounce these characters!
读错这些字多可笑！

guilty ['gilti] *adj.* 内疚的，有罪的
He felt guilty by breaking the vase.
因为打破花瓶，他感到非常内疚。

regret [ri'gret] *vt.* 懊悔，抱歉；*n.* 懊悔
I immediately regretted what I said.
我说过话后立即就感到后悔了。
考点：with regret 遗憾地，抱歉地

stiff [stif] *adj.* 硬的，僵直的
His father was kind of stiff about his score.
他的父亲对他的成绩有点执拗。

bearing ['bɛəriŋ] *n.* 轴承，举止，忍受，支撑物，方面，方向
Her kind bearing caused all the children to like her.
她那种和蔼的态度使所有的孩子都喜欢她。
考点：have a bearing on 与……有关，对……有影响

expression [iks'preʃən] *n.* 词句，表达，表情
I find sadness from his expression.
我从他的表情中察觉到他的忧伤。

人 个性品质

character ['kæriktə] *n.* 性格，特性，角色
I don't know him very well; you know he has a changeable character.
我不太了解他，你知道的他性格多变。

🔍 考点：in character（与自身特性）相符；out of character（与自身特性）不相符

characteristic [ˌkæriktə'ristik] *adj.* 特有的 *n.* 特性
I like the characteristic flavor of apples.
我喜欢苹果所特有的那个味道。

🔍 考点：character, characteristic的区别：一个人可能只有一种"性格"(character)，但可能有多种"特征、特点"(characteristic)，所以这些"特征、特点"便构成了一个人"总的特征、特点，品质"(character)。

characterize ['kæriktəraiz] *vt.* 表示……的典型，赋予……特色
We shouldn't characterize people by their appearances.
我们不应以貌取人。

adventure [əd'ventʃə] *n.* 冒险，惊险活动 *vt.* 敢于，大胆提出
My father often chattered to us about his adventures as a young man.
父亲总是喋喋不休地跟我们讲他年轻时的冒险经历。

aggressive [ə'gresiv] *adj.* 侵略的，好斗的，敢作敢为的，有进取精神的
The politician always puts forward some aggressive policies.
那位政客总是提出一些富有侵略性的政策。

alive [ə'laiv] *adj.* 活着的，活跃的，有活力的，有生气的
In his will, he left all his fortune to the nurse who took care of him carefully when he was alive.
在他的遗嘱中，他把所有的财产都留给了生前细心照看他的护士。

bold [bəuld] *adj.* 大胆的，冒失的
That day Susan made a bold speech in front of everyone.
那天苏珊在众人面前做了一次大胆的演讲。

brave [breiv] *adj.* 勇敢的，华丽的
Be brave! There is nothing to fear.
勇敢点！没什么可怕的。

brisk [brisk] *adj.* 活泼的，清新的
The doctor told me a brisk massage could restore the body's vigor.
医生告诉我说轻快的按摩能恢复体力。

charming ['tʃɑ:miŋ] *adj.* 迷人的，可爱的
We had dinner with our boss and his charming wife.
我们跟老板和他迷人的妻子共进晚餐。

childlike ['tʃaildlaik] *adj.* 孩子似的，天真烂漫的
Here stands a girl with an air of childlike innocence.
站在面前的这位女孩有着一副孩子般天真无邪的神态。

clever ['klevə] *adj.* 聪明的，机敏的
My little sister is very clever but rather backward in expressing her ideas.
我妹妹很聪明，不过在表达思想时却有些脑腆。

contented [kən'tentid] *adj.* 知足的，满足的
I'm contented with my present wages.
我对于目前的工资很满意。

cordial ['kɔ:diəl] *adj.* 热情友好的，热诚的
My uncle is so handsome and always got cordial greeting from young ladies.
我叔叔很英俊，总能得到年轻女士的热忱问候。

chase [tʃeis] *vi. & vt.* 追逐
She never stopped to chase her dream when she was yourg.
当她年轻的时候，从未停止过追求梦想。

dare [dɛə] *vt.&aux.v.* 敢，竟敢
I can't believe it! How dare you accuse me of stealing her wallet.
我真不敢相信，你竟敢控告我偷她的钱包。

daring ['dɛəriŋ] *n.* 大胆，胆量
           adj. 大胆的，勇敢的，震惊的

I really admired those daring action of the parachutists.
我真的很钦佩那些跳伞者大胆的冒险动作。

dynamic [dai'næmik] *adj.* 有活力的，动力的

He is a dynamic boy who attracts a lot of girls.
他是个有活力的男孩，很吸引女孩子。

真题

He was such a _____ speaker that he held out attention every minute of the three-hour lecture.
A) specific   B) dynamic
C) heroic   D) diplomatic

详 解：选B。题意为：他讲话生动有趣，因此在三个小时的讲座中我们的注意力时时刻刻都为他所吸引。A) specific 意思是"具体的，明确的"；B) dynamic 意思是"有活力的"；C) heroic意思是"英勇的"；D) diplomatic意思是"圆通的，有策略的"。

(CET-4 模拟)

earnest ['ə:nist] *adj.* 认真的，诚恳的
My grandfather is an earnest Christian.
我祖父是一个虔诚的基督教徒。

考点：in earnest 认真地，坚定地

easy-going [ˌi:zi'gəuiŋ] *adj.* 随和的，容易相处的

I am an easy-going girl.
我是一个很容易相处的女孩。

patience ['peiʃəns] *n.* 忍耐，容忍，耐心
There is an old saying in China, "Patience is a virtue".
中国有句古老的谚语"宽容是美德"。

patient ['peiʃənt] *adj.* 忍耐的；*n.* 病人
You must be patient, because the cure woks slowly.
你必须要有耐心，因为这种疗法见效慢。

考点：be patient of 能容忍（物）；patient with 对……（人）耐心

generous ['dʒenərəs] *adj.* 慷慨的，宽厚的
Bob is a generous man, because he often gives money to the poor.

鲍勃是一个慷慨的人，因为他经常给穷人钱。

考点：be generous to sb. 对某人大方
      be generous with 对（钱）大方

liberal ['libərəl] *adj.* 心胸宽大的，不受限制的，自由主义的，慷慨的
My sister returned from abroad with very liberal ideas.
我姐姐带着非常开明的思想从国外回来了。

attention [ə'tenʃən] *n.* 注意，留心，注意力
The little boy concentrated his whole attention on the toy.
这个小男孩把全部注意力都集中在玩具上。

考点：pay attention to 注意

attentive [ə'tentiv] *adj.* 注意的，有礼貌的，专心的
Have you noticed that he is an attentive audience?
你注意到他是个聚精会神的听众了吗？

attitude ['ætitju:d] *n.* 态度，看法，姿势
I think you should maintain a humble attitude.
我觉得你应该保持谦逊的态度。

concentrate ['kɔnsentreit] *vt.* 集中，聚集，浓缩
The little girl concentrated her whole attention on the doll.
这个小女孩把全部注意力都集中在洋娃娃上。

考点：concentrate / focus on...集中（……）；指"集中（精神、精力）"时两词可以换用，但focus一般不以具体事物作宾语，而concentrate可以。

concentration [ˌkɔnsen'treiʃən] *n.* 集中，专注，浓缩
Too much concentration on one aspect of a problem is dangerous.
过度专注于问题的一面是危险的。

humble ['hʌmbl] *adj.* 谦逊的，地位低下的
He was just a humble civilian who couldn't marry that princess.
他只是一个地位低下的平民，不可能与公主结婚。

cautious ['kɔ:ʃəs] *adj.* 谨慎的
I can say Mr. Smith's nephew is a cautious investor.

我认为史密斯先生的侄子是一个小心谨慎的投资者。

考点：be cautious of 注意，小心；careful, cautious的区别：cautious比careful语气强，指"十分小心"，防止出危险和差错，带有"提防"的意味。

真题

They are ____ investors who always make thorough investigations both on local and international markets before making an investment.

A) indecisive   B) implicit
C) cautious   D) conscious

详 解：选C。题意为：他们是谨慎的投资者，在投资之前总是对国内、国际市场做全面、细致的调查。根据语境投资者应该是cautious（谨慎的）。A) indecisive意思是"不果断的"；B) implicit意思是"不言明的，含蓄的"；D) conscious意思是"清醒的，有意识的"。

(CET-4 2003.6)

modest ['mɔdist] *adj.* 有节制的，谦虚的，适度的
Don't be so modest, you deserve a pat on the back.
别这么谦虚了，你应该受到表扬。

modesty ['mɔdisti] *n.* 谦虚，虚心
Modesty is a kind of virtue.
谦虚是一种美德。

precaution [pri'kɔːʃən] *n.* 预防，警惕
Please take a raincoat as a precaution.
带上雨衣吧，有备无患。

mature [mə'tjuə] *adj.* 成熟的，成年的，慎重的；*vt.* 使成熟
When the peach trees begin bearing fruit, they are mature.
当桃树开始结果的时候，它们就成熟了。

考点：mature 应用比较广泛，不仅指果实、庄稼的成熟，而且还可以指动物的成熟；ripe 主要指果实、庄稼的成熟。

arbitrary ['ɑːbitrəri] *adj.* 随心所欲的，专断的

Putting the books in arbitrary is OK.
随意把书放在那里就可以了。

sophisticated [sə'fistikeitid] *adj.* 老于世故的，高级的
She is sophisticated for her ways of solving problems.
就处事方式而言她是世故了一点。

naughty ['nɔːti] *adj.* 顽皮的，淘气的
You know my naughty son received an award yesterday.
我那调皮的儿子昨天得了一个奖。

careful ['kɛəfəl] *adj.* 仔细的，细致的
Be careful, this matter concerns every one of us.
小心些，这件事影响到我们每个人。

upright ['ʌprait] *adj.* 直立的，正直的 *adv.* 挺直地，直立地
His father is a tall upright old man.
他父亲是一个个头高，腰笔挺的老人。

faint [feint] *a.* 头晕的，昏厥的
He fainted at once when he hearing the bad news of his brother.
当他听到关于哥哥的坏消息时，立刻晕倒了。

badly ['bædli] *adv.* 坏，差，严重地
Her left foot was badly hurt in this accident.
在这场事故中，她的左脚严重受伤。

考点：badly off... 贫困的，情况不好的

boast [bəust] *vi.* 自夸；*vt.* 吹嘘
Parents are always boasting about their children's success at school.
父母总是夸耀自己孩子的好成绩。

考点：boast of / about 自夸，夸耀
       boast that 夸口说，吹嘘
       boast sth. 以拥有……而自豪

childish ['tʃaildiʃ] *adj.* 孩子的，幼稚的
Hearing her husband's childish words, she burst into laughter.
听到丈夫孩子气的话语，她大笑了起来。

clumsy ['klʌmzi] *adj.* 笨拙的，愚笨的
The panda looks so cute and clumsy.
熊猫看起来可爱又笨拙。

coward ['kauəd] *n.* 懦夫，胆怯者

239

He is a coward.
他是个懦夫。

---

conservative [kən'sə:vətiv] *adj.* 保守的
         n. 保守的人
From my point of view, the young are less conservative than the old.
在我看来，年轻人没有老年人保守。

---

crude [kru:d] *adj.* 粗鲁的，简陋的，天然的
It's said that the scientist had born in a crude hut.
据说，那个科学家生于一个简陋的小棚子里。

真题

Petrol is refined from the _____ oil we take out of the ground.
A) fresh B) original
C) rude   D) crude

详　解：选D。题意为：汽油是由我们从地下获得的原油提炼而成的。A) fresh意思是"相等的"；B) original意思是"原先的，有独创性的"；C) rude意思是"粗暴的，粗鲁的"；D) crude意思是"粗糙的，天然的"。

(CET-4 模拟)

---

cruel ['kruəl] *adj.* 残忍的，残酷的
Although Hart has a good-natured face, he is cruel to animals.
尽管哈特长着一张善良的面孔，但他对动物十分残忍。

---

cunning ['kʌniŋ] *adj.* 狡猾的，狡诈的
One day the cunning fox wanted to eat grapes in the vineyard.
一天，狡猾的狐狸想吃葡萄园里的葡萄。

---

defect [di'fekt] *n.* 缺点，缺陷，欠缺
He wanted to find some ways to make up for a defect of his character.
他想找一些方法来弥补他性格上的缺点。

---

devil ['devl] *n.* 魔鬼，恶魔
Satan is a devil in the Bible.
撒旦是圣经里的一个魔鬼。

---

greedy ['gri:di] *adj.* 贪吃的，贪婪的
He's terribly greedy on money.
他非常贪钱。

---

nasty ['næsti] *adj.* 龌龊的，淫猥的，恶意的
There is a nasty swelling on the girl's face.
那个女孩的脸上有一个讨厌的肿块。

---

vice [vais] *n.* 罪恶，恶习，缺点
    n. （老）虎钳
She is a stupid woman and can't tell vice from virtue.
她是一个不辨善恶的蠢女人。

---

haste [heist] *n.* 急速，急忙，草率
Make haste, or you will be late for school.
动作快一点，否则你上课就迟到了。

🔍 **考点**：in haste = in a hurry 急忙，慌忙

---

careless ['keəlis] *adj.* 粗心的，漫不经心的
Because of carelessness, her tongue was bitten when having a dinner with her client.
由于粗心大意，她在和客户吃饭时咬到了舌头。

---

rational ['ræʃənl] *adj.* 理性的，出于理性的
Is there a rational explanation for what you have done?
你对自己所做的事有什么合理的解释吗？

---

active ['æktiv] *adj.* 活跃的，积极的
He always takes an active part in his class.
他在课堂上总是很活跃。

---

tough [tʌf] *adj.* 坚韧的，健壮的
I am well aware that this is a tough job, but I will never give up.
我深知这是一件棘手的工作，但我不会放弃的。

---

solitary ['sɔlitəri] *adj.* 单独的，唯一的，孤独的
He is naturally solitary, he thinks.
他认为他是天生的孤僻性格。

---

mild [maild] *adj.* 和缓的，温柔的，味淡的
My cousin is irritable while her boyfriend is mild.
我表姐脾气很暴躁，但是她男朋友却很温和。

---

moderate ['mɔdərit] *adj.* 温和的，适度的，有节制的
My demand is moderate; I'm only asking for a small increase in my wage.
我的要求并不过分，我只是要求增加少量的工资。

---

thoughtful ['θɔ:tful] *adj.* 沉思的，体贴的

She is very obliging and thoughtful to her host.
她对主人真是殷勤体贴。

tender ['tendə] *adj.* 嫩的，脆弱的
vt. 正式提出
vi. 投标
n. 投标

The plot in the film awakened a tender emotion in me.
电影里的情节在我心里唤起一脉柔情。

【真题】

She cooked the meat for a long time so as to make it ____ enough to eat.
A) mild   B) slight
C) light   D) tender

详 解：选D。题意为：她将肉烧了很久，使它软烂而易咀嚼。A) mild意思是"温和的"；B) slight意思是"轻微的"；C) light意思是"轻的"；D) tender意思是"嫩的"。

(CET-4 模拟)

shallow ['ʃæləu] *adj.* 浅的，浅薄的
We won't accept his advice because his views are always shallow.
我们不会接受他的建议，因为他的观点总是很肤浅的。

 行为习惯

accustom [ə'kʌstəm] *vt.* 使习惯
Thought he was a newcomer, he soon got accustom to the new surroundings.
尽管他是新手，但他很快就习惯了新环境。

🔍考点：accustom要用反身代词作宾语或用被动语态。

accustomed [ə'kʌstəmd] *adj.* 惯常的，习惯的
I am accustomed to napping after lunch.
我习惯了午饭后小睡一会。

🔍考点：be accustomed to 后面多跟名词或动名词，表示"习惯于"，偶尔也跟不定式。

constant ['kɔnstənt] *adj.* 经常的，永恒的

I hate my mother's constant nagging.
我讨厌妈妈的唠叨不休。

bow [bau] *n.* 鞠躬，弓，蝴蝶结
vi.&vt. 鞠躬，弯曲
I saw him and acknowledged him with a bow.
我看到了他，点头向他打招呼。

🔍考点：bow out 退出，辞职

consistency [kən'sistənsi] *n.* 坚韧，一致性
There is no consistency between the beginning and the ending of your composition.
你这篇作文的开始与结尾不连贯。

consistent [kən'sistənt] *adj.* 坚持的，一贯的
He is not consistent in his action.
他的行动前后不一致。

control [kən'trəul] *vt.* 控制，克制；
n. 控制
It seems that only you can control this machine.
似乎只有你会操作这台机器。

conversion [kən'və:ʃən] *n.* 转变，转化，改变
After hearing the lecture, he underwent a religious conversion.
听了那个讲座后，他的宗教信仰转变了。

convert [kən'və:t] *vt.* 使转变，使改变
They converted the theater into a supermarket.
他们把这个戏院改成了一家超市。

coordinate [kəu'ɔ:dinit] *vt.* 使协调，调节
It's not easy for a baby to coordinate his movement.
对婴儿来说协调自己的动作不容易。

cope [kəup] *vi.* 对付，应付
How could I cope with such a pile of work in one day?
我如何在一天之内处理这么多工作啊？

🔍考点：cope with 对付，应付

correct [kə'rekt] *adj.* 正确的；*vt.* 纠正
Who can give me the correct answer?
谁能给我正确答案？

correction [kə'rekʃən] *n.* 改正，纠正，修改
The correction of this design took a lot of the designer's time.
修改这个设计花去了设计师很多时间。

correspond [ˌkɔris'pɔnd] *vi.* 相符合，相当

Don't make friends with him. His actions don't correspond with his words.
不要和他交朋友，他是个言行不一的人。

🔍 考点：correspond to 相当于
correspond with 与……通信，相一致

---

correspondent [ˌkɔris'pɔndənt] *n.* 通信者，通讯员
adj. 相应的，一致的

The result was correspondent with our expectation.
该结果与我们所预料的一致。

---

corresponding [ˌkɔris'pɔndiŋ] *adj.* 相应的；符合的

All rights carry with them corresponding responsibilities.
所有的权利都带有相应的义务。

---

casual ['kæʒjuəl] *adj.* 偶然的，随便的

Do you think that's only a casual meeting?
你认为那只是一次偶然的邂逅吗？

---

deed [di:d] *n.* 行为，功绩，契约

Though we can't recall his feature, we still remembered the good deeds he had done.
虽然我们已经记不起他的容貌，但我们依然清晰地记得他做的好人好事。

---

habit ['hæbit] *n.* 习惯，习性

Every man has his own habit in the life.
生活中每个人都有他特有的习惯。

🔍 考点：in the habit of 有……的习惯

---

habitual [hə'bitjuəl] *adj.* 习惯性的，惯常的

An apple and a bowl of rice is her habitual dinner.
一个苹果和一碗米饭是她通常的晚餐。

---

conduct ['kəndʌkt] *v.* 领导，操纵

Our company decided to use the Internet to conduct our business.
我们公司决定用互联网来做业务。

---

normal ['nɔ:məl] *adj.* 正常的，普通的，正规的

It's normal that pretty girls attracted men's attention.
美丽的女孩吸引男人的眼球，这是很正常的。

---

normally ['nɔ:məli] *adv.* 通常，正常地

We need not repair the machine, for it operates quite normally.
我们不必修理这台机器，它运转得十分正常。

---

occasional [ə'keiʒnəl] *adj.* 偶然的，临时的

My new job involves occasional journey.
新工作需要我偶尔出差。

---

occasionally [ə'keiʒənəli] *adv.* 偶然，非经常地

She went on weeping, occasionally wiping at her face with a towel.
她继续哭着，偶尔用毛巾擦一下脸。

---

often ['ɔ:fən] *adv.* 经常，常常

I often recite poetry as possible as I can in my spare time.
在我有空时，我经常尽可能多地背诗。

---

once [wʌns] *adv.* 一次，曾经；*n.* 一次

The lady goes to hairdressing salon once a month.
那位女士每个月都要做一次美发。

---

pattern ['pætən] *n.* 型，式样，模，模型

The guy is stubborn, and he has a fixed pattern of behavior.
这家伙很固执，有着一套不变的行为方式。

---

queer [kwiə] *adj.* 奇怪的，古怪的

Last night he heard some queer footsteps.
昨天晚上他听到了一些可疑的脚步声。

---

regular ['regjulə] *adj.* 规则的，整齐的，匀称的

She is a beautiful girl with regular features.
她是个五官端正的漂亮女孩。

🔍 考点：regular as clockwork 极有规律

---

repeat [ri'pi:t] *vt.* 重说，重做；*n.* 重复

Susan said she didn't quite catch on and asked me to repeat what I had said.
苏珊说她不大明白，要我再说一遍。

---

repetition [ˌrepi'tiʃən] *n.* 重复，反复

Can't you talk with others without repetition?
你在跟别人谈话时就不能不重复吗？

---

retain [ri'tein] *vt.* 保持，保留，保有

Lily strove valiantly to retain a serene interest towards dead men.
莉莉鼓起勇气对死人保持一种冷静的兴趣。

人与自然

人

真题

The most basic reason why dialects should be preserved is that language helps to _____ a culture.
A) retain   B) relate
C) remark   D) review

详 解：选A。题意为：方言需要保护的最根本原因是语言有助于保存文化。A) retain 意思是"保持，保留"；B) relate 意思是"与……有关"；C) remark 意思是"讨论"；D) review意思是"审查，复习"。

(CET-4 模拟)

spontaneous [spɔn'teiniəs] *adj.* 自发的，本能的
Seeing his funny behavior, we burst into spontaneous laughter.
看到他的滑稽行为，我们不由自主地大笑起来。

used [ju:st] *vi.* 过去常常
adj. 旧的，习惯于……的
He was used to work by bike.
他过去经常骑自行车上班。

考点：容易混淆的3个used结构：used to do sth. 过去常常做某事；be used to doing sth. 习惯于做某事；be used to do sth. 被用来做某事

previous ['pri:vjəs] *adj.* 先前的
adv. 在前
This event shattered all my previous ideas.
这件事把我以前所有的想法都摧毁了。

考点：previous to 在……之前（to为介词）

previously ['pri:viəsli] *adv.* 先前，预先
Gradually their previously opposed views are beginning to converge.
渐渐地他们原来相互对立的观点开始趋于一致。

allergic [ə'lə:dʒik] *adj.* 过敏的
Some people are allergic to seafood.
有的人对海鲜过敏。

alone [ə'ləun] *adj.* 单独的；*adv.* 单独地
I like staying at home alone and amusing myself with a book.
我喜欢一个人待在家里，看书消遣。

考点：leave alone 让……独自待着，不打扰，不干预；let alone 更别提，更不用说

appropriate [ə'prəupriit] *adj.* 适当的，恰当的
If you want to use metaphor, you have to find an appropriate one.
如果你要用隐喻，你必须找个贴切的。

rudely ['rudli] *adv.* 无礼地
The girl in the yellow dress behaves very rudely toward the disabled boy.
那个穿黄裙子的女生无礼的对待那个残疾男孩。

考点：behave towards 对待……的表现，举止

behavior [bi'heivjə] *n.* 行为，举止，态度
Your behavior was celebrated by people.
你的行为为人们所赞颂。

behavio(u)ral [bi'heivjərəl] *adj.* 行为的
Last year, I studied behavioral psychology in the college.
去年，我在大学里学习了行为心理学。

generally ['dʒenərəli] *adv.* 一般地，通常地
Generally speaking, you need professional knowledge to accomplish this task.
通常来说，你需要具备专业的知识才能完成这项任务。

indeed [in'di:d] *adv.* 真正地，确实
Indeed, we have covered a great deal of fields.
我们的确涉及到了广泛的领域。

while [wail] *conj.* 当……的时候；而
Play while you play; study while you study.
玩就玩个痛快，学就学个踏实。

考点：all the while 始终
once in a while 偶尔

243

自然 动物

animal ['ænɪməl] *n.* 动物，兽；*adj.* 动物的
Which animal do you like best, dog, cat or pig?
你最喜欢哪种动物，狗、猫还是猪?

ant [ænt] *n.* 蚂蚁
My little brother regards an ant as his pet.
我小弟弟把蚂蚁当成他的宠物。

bear [bɛə] *n.* 熊，粗鲁的人
He saw an ugly bear in the zoo last weekend.
上周末，他在动物园见了一只特别丑的熊。

beast [bi:st] *n.* 兽，野兽，牲畜
The witch's magic changed the prince into a beast.
女巫施展魔法把王子变成了野兽。

bee [bi:] *n.* 蜂，蜜蜂，忙碌的人
You are as busy as a bee.
你忙得跟只蜜蜂似的。

bird [bə:d] *n.* 鸟，禽
Generally speaking, the wings of a bird correspond to the arms of a man.
一般来说，鸟的翅膀就相当于人的手臂。

breed [bri:d] *n.* 品种；*vt.* 使繁殖
Hey! I want to order the finest breed of pig.
嘿，我想要订购最优品种的猪。
🔍 考点：breed尤指动植物的品种；kind / sort指一般的种类；type 类型

bristle ['brisl] *n.* 短而硬的毛，鬃毛
Bristles are used to make brushes in the old days.
以前猪鬃用以做刷子。

brood [bru:d] *n.* 同窝幼鸟；*vt.* 孵（蛋）
My mother bought a brood of chickens yesterday.
昨天妈妈买了一窝小鸡。

brute [bru:t] *n.* 禽兽，畜生；*adj.* 残酷的
She is a brute to her children.
她虐待子女。

bug [bʌg] *n.* 臭虫，窃听器，（计）漏洞
v. 窃听，打扰，失去（镇定）
I guess it is a bug under the stone.
我猜石头下面是个臭虫。

bull [bul] *n.* 公牛，雄的象
Bull fight is popular in Spanish.
在西班牙很流行斗牛。

butterfly ['bʌtəflai] *n.* 蝴蝶
The little girl couldn't tell the difference between a butterfly and a moth.
这个小女孩说不出蝴蝶和飞蛾的区别。

camel ['kæməl] *n.* 骆驼
The camels are carrying our goods across the desert.
骆驼正驮着我们的货物在沙漠里行走。

cat [kæt] *n.* 猫，猫科，猫皮
Susan wants to buy a cat as her pet.
苏珊想买个猫当她的宠物。

cattle ['kætl] *n.* 牛，牲口，家畜
I want to herd cattle on the Qinghai-Tibetan Plateau.
我想去青藏高原上放牧。

claw [klɔ:] *n.* 爪，脚爪，螯
My little sister's arm was hurt by the cat's sharp claws.
我小妹的胳膊被猫的利爪抓伤了。

cock [kɔk] *n.* 公鸡，雄禽，旋塞
The little girl is drawing a cock absorbedly.
这个小女孩正在专心致志地画一只公鸡。

cow [kau] *n.* 母牛，奶牛，母兽
How many cows are there in the byre?
牛棚里有多少头牛?

crawl [krɔ:l] *vi.* 爬，爬行
Only the man who crawled out of the burning house survived.
只有从房子里爬出来的那个男人活了下来。
🔍 考点：crawl with 爬满

creature ['kri:tʃə] *n.* 生物，动物，家畜
This creature lives at the bottom of the sea.
这种生物生活在海底。

crow [krəu] *n.* 鸦，乌鸦；*vi.* 啼
It is said that the crow is a symbol of an evil augury.
据说，乌鸦是恶兆的象征。

flock [flɔk] *n.* 羊群，群，大量
He drove a flock of sheep into the sheepcote.
他把羊群赶到了羊圈里。

🔍 **考点：** in flocks 成群地，大量地

giraffe [dʒi'rɑːf] *n.* 长颈鹿
Tom likes giraffe very much till today.
直到今天，汤姆都非常喜欢长颈鹿。

herd [həːd] *n.* 兽群，牧群；*vt.* 放牧
I saw a herd of sheep on the hill from a long distance.
大老远我就看见山上有一群羊。

insect ['insekt] *n.* 昆虫，虫
As we all know, the bee is a diligent insect.
众所周知，蜜蜂是勤劳的昆虫。

lamb [læm] *n.* 羔羊，小羊，羔羊肉
My brother runs a restaurant which sells lamb soup.
我哥哥经营着一家羊肉汤馆。

monkey ['mʌnki] *n.* 猴子，猿
The monkeys in the circus amused all of us.
马戏团里的猴子们把大家都逗乐了。

mosquito [məs'kiːtəu] *n.* 蚊子
The purpose of a screen door is to keep mosquitos and flies out.
纱门的作用就是不让蚊子和苍蝇飞进来。

mouse [maus] *n.* 鼠，耗子
I have a great fear of mice.
我很怕老鼠。

nest [nest] *n.* 巢，窝，穴
If you stir up a hornet's nest, you will be stung by them.
如果你捅了马蜂窝，你会被蜇的。

owl [əul] *n.* 猫头鹰，枭
We know that an owl can see in the dark.
我们知道猫头鹰在黑暗中能看见东西。

panda ['pændə] *n.* 熊猫
The panda was eating the young shoots of bamboo.
这只熊猫正在吃竹笋。

paw [pɔː] *n.* 脚爪，爪子
When cats fight, they use their paws.
猫用爪子打架。

pet [pet] *n.* 爱畜，宠儿；*adj.* 宠爱的
The old lady thrust herself through the crowd to look for her pet dog.
老妇人挤过了人群去寻找她的宠物狗。

pig [pig] *n.* 猪，小猪，野猪
The peasants sacrificed one pig every month.
农民们每个月都要献祭一头猪。

pigeon ['pidʒin] *n.* 鸽子
A wounded pigeon was standing on the tree.
一只受伤的鸽子站在树上。

rat [ræt] *n.* 老鼠，耗子
My cousin has a pet rat which is very funny.
我堂兄就有只宠物老鼠，很有趣。

reproduce [ˌriːprə'djuːs] *vi.&vt.* 繁殖，生殖
Animals can reproduce their own kind.
动物能够繁殖同类。

scratch [skrætʃ] *vi.&vt.&n.* 搔，抓
Her hands were covered with scratches from the thorns.
她手上有很多棘刺划的伤痕。

🔍 **考点：** from scratch 从零开始，从头做起；up to scratch 合格，处于良好状态

seagull ['siːgʌl] *n.* 海鸥
I saw a seagull flutter down with an injured wing.
我看见一只海鸥拍打着翅膀飞落下来。

sparrow ['spærəu] *n.* 麻雀
I can see a sparrow eating worms.
我看见一只麻雀在吃小虫。

specific [spi'sifik] *adj.* 特有的，具体的
Panda is the specific animal in China.
熊猫是中国的特有物种。

spider ['spaidə] *n.* 蜘蛛
I saw a spider weaving a web under the eaves in a rainy day.
雨天我看到蜘蛛在屋檐下织网。

stable ['steibl] *adj.* 稳定的，不变的
n. 厩，马厩，牛棚
From the stable came the snuffle and stamp of a feeding caw.
牛棚里传来一头正在进食的牛的鼻声和蹄声。

stag [stæg] *n.* 成年雄鹿

I saw a stag come to a pool to quench his thirst one day.
有一天，我看见一只公鹿来到池边喝水。

sting [stiŋ] *vt.* 刺，刺痛；*vi.&n.* 刺

When you slice a chili, it makes your eyes sting.
切辣椒辣眼睛。

tail [teil] *n.* 尾巴，末尾部分；*vt.* 盯梢

At last he got hold of the dog's tail and pulled it out.
最后他总算抓住了狗的尾巴并把它抓了出来。

🔍 短语：tail off 变得越来越少（弱）

tame [teim] *adj.* 驯服的，顺从的，乏味的
vt. 制服，驯化，驯服

The little horse is very tame to his host.
这只小马驹对主人非常驯服。

真题

_____ elephants are different from wild elephants in many aspects, including their tempers.
A) Cultivated   B) Regulated
C) Civil   D) Tame

详 解：选D。题意为：驯养的大象和野生象在许多方面不同，包括脾性。A) cultivated 意思是"栽培的，有教养的"；B) regulated 意思是"调节的"；C) civil意思是"文明的"；D) tame意思是"驯养的"。

(CET-4 模拟)

wild [waild] *adj.* 野生的，野蛮的

There are several kinds of wild animals in this forest.
这片森林里有好几种野生动物。

wing [wiŋ] *n.* 翼，翅膀，翅

The hunter shot the eagle's left wing with arrows.
这个猎人用箭射中鹰的左翼。

🔍 考点：in the wings 准备就绪的，随时可以使用的

worm [wə:m] *n.* 虫，蠕虫

These worms will do damage to our vegetables.
这些小虫会损害我们的青菜。

hunt [hʌnt] *n.* 打猎，搜寻；*vt.* 追猎

They want to go on a hunt this weekend.
他们打算周末去打猎。

🔍 考点：hunt down 对……穷追到底，追捕到

🟦 **自然** 植物 ✏️

bamboo [bæm'bu:] *n.* 竹，竹子

Do you want to portray a bamboo grove in the picture?
你想在画中描绘一片竹林吗？

banana [bə'nɑ:nə] *n.* 香蕉，芭蕉属植物

Banana abounds in the south of China, such as Hainan, Guangdong, etc.
中国的南方，比如海南、广东等地都盛产香蕉。

bloom [blu:m] *n.* 花，开花，开花期

Those roses have beautiful blooms.
那些玫瑰花开得真美。

blossom ['blɔsəm] *n.* 花，开花；*vi.* 开花

A lot of flowers are blossoming in the valley in spring.
春天山谷里好多花都开了。

🔍 考点：in (full) blossom 正开着花

bough [bau] *n.* 树枝

There are many large boughs on the tree.
树上有很多大的树枝。

bud [bʌd] *n.* 芽，萌芽，蓓蕾

The grasses begin to bud in the spring.
小草在春天开始发芽。

bush [buʃ] *n.* 灌木，灌木丛，矮树

I think the new rose bush has taken root.
我认为新栽的玫瑰已经长根了。

🔍 考点：beat around / about the bush 转弯抹角，旁敲侧击

cane [kein] *n.* （藤，竹等的）茎，料，手杖，甘蔗

The blind man was walking with a cane.
那个盲人在拄着拐走路。

core [kɔ:] *n.* 果实的心，核心，中心部分

Please cut out the core of the apple.
请削掉苹果核。

🔍 考点：to the core 透顶的，十足的

flourish ['flʌriʃ] *vi.* 繁荣，茂盛，兴旺

Plants will not flourish without water.
没有水植物就不会长得茂盛。

hay [hei] *n.* 干草

Stacks of hay were in the field in the season of harvest.
收获季节，一堆堆干草堆在田里。

pine [pain] *n.* 松树，松木

The pine trees defy severe cold.
松树不畏严寒。

plant [plɑ:nt] *n.* 植物，工厂；*vt.* 栽种

This type of plant flourishes in the subtropics.
这种植物在亚热带地区生长茂盛。

seaweed ['si:wi:d] *n.* 海藻，海草

I know this substance is extracted from seaweed.
我知道这种物质是从海藻中提取的。

species ['spi:ʃiz] *n.* 种，类

There are many species of roses all over the world.
世界上玫瑰品种有很多。

🔍 考点：species是单复同形；a species of + 复数主语，谓语要用单数。

stem [stem] *n.* 茎，（树）干；*vi.* 起源

I've watched this series from stem to stern.
这部电视剧我已从头至尾看完了。

🔍 考点：stem from 起源于

thorn [θɔ:n] *n.* 刺，荆棘

There's no rose without a thorn.
玫瑰皆有刺。

自然 声音 🖊

bang [bæŋ] *n.* 巨响，枪声，猛击

The door shut with a bang.
门砰地一声关上了。

bark [bɑ:k] *n.* 吠叫声；*vi.* 吠，叫

A barking dog seldom bites.
会叫的狗很少咬人。

click [klik] *n.* 咔嗒声，[计]点击
vt. （使）发出咔嗒声，点击
vi. 一拍即合，成功，突然明白

Please click this icon to save the document.
请按这个图标保存一下这个文档。

echo ['ekəu] *n.* 回声，反响；*vi.* 发出回声
vt. 模范，重复，附和

He echoed every word of his superior.
他随声附和着上级的每一句话。

真题

Nancy is only a sort of _____ her husband's opinion and has no ideas of her own.
A) shadow   B) sample
C) reproduction   D) echo

详解：选D。题意为：南希只是附和她丈夫的观点，没有自己的主张。A) shadow意思是"影子"；B) sample意思是"样品"；C) reproduction意思是"再生，复制"；D) echo意思是"回声"。

(CET-4 模拟)

laughter ['lɑ:ftə] *n.* 笑，笑声

There was a burst of laughter in the next room.
隔壁房间里突然爆发出一阵笑声。

noise [nɔiz] *n.* 喧闹声，响声，噪声

The noise of the children who lived upstairs really irritated me.
楼上孩子的吵闹声真的让我很恼火。

tick [tik] *n.* 滴答声，记号；*vi.* 发出滴答声

They could hear the regular tick of the clock from far away.

他们很远还能听见时钟有规律的滴答声。

🔍 **考点**：tick away/by（时间一分一秒）过去

---

roar [rɔ:] *vi.* 吼叫，呼喊；*n.* 吼

The roar of the traffic made us very annoyed.
往来车辆的喧闹声使我们很烦。

真题

The _____ of airplane engines announced a coming air raid.
A) roar　　　B) scream
C) whistle　　D) exclamation

详解：选A。题意为：飞机发动机的轰鸣声预示了新一轮空袭的到来。A) roar 意思是"怒吼，轰鸣"；B) scream 意思是"尖叫声"；C) whistle 意思是"耳语，私语"；D) exclamation意思是"惊叫，惊呼"。

(CET-4 模拟)

自然 自然风光

appreciate [ə'pri:ʃieit] *vt.* 欣赏，领会，感谢，重视

Though someone doesn't like living in the village, I appreciate the peace and quiet of it.
尽管有些人不愿意生活在农村，可是我却欣赏农村的安定平静。

---

coast [kəust] *n.* 海岸，海滨（地区）

They had been wrecked off the coast of Europe.
他们的船在欧洲沿海遇难损毁。

---

coastal ['kəustl] *adj.* 沿海的，海岸的，沿岸的

Do you know how many coastal cities we opened last century?
你知道上世纪我们开放了几个沿海城市吗？

---

desert ['dezət] *n.* 沙漠；*vt.* 离弃，擅离

There is no sign of vegetation in the desert.
沙漠中寸草不生。

---

gulf [gʌlf] *n.* 海湾

Which year did the Gulf War happen?
海湾战争发生在哪一年？

---

harbour ['hɑ:bə] *n.* 海港，港口；*vt.* 庇护

Our boat left the harbour two days ago.
我们的船两天前离港了。

---

horizon [hə'raizn] *n.* 地平线，眼界，见识

I can see the horizon on top of the mountain.
我在山顶能看到地平线。

🔍 **考点**：on the horizon 即将发生的

---

horizontal [ˌhɔri'zɔntl] *adj.* 地平的，水平的

The machine is doing horizontal movements.
这台机器正在做水平运动。

---

jungle ['dʒʌŋgl] *n.* 丛林，密林，莽丛

They decided to skirt round the deep jungle to assemble in the village.
他们决定绕过那片茂密的丛林在村子里集合。

---

lane [lein] *n.* （乡间）小路，跑道

I am driving carefully on the rugged lane.
我正小心地行驶在这条崎岖的小路上。

---

marsh [mɑ:ʃ] *n.* 沼泽，湿地

There are miles and miles marsh here.
这有连绵数英里的沼泽。

---

meadow ['medəu] *n.* 草地，牧草地

There are some cattle grazing on the meadow.
有一些牛在草地上吃草。

---

peninsula [pə'ninsjulə] *n.* 半岛

Living on the peninsula, they were subjected to high winds.
因为住在半岛地区，他们受到了大风的影响。

---

plain [plein] *n.* 平原；*adj.* 清楚的

Have you ever been to the Great Plains?
你去过北美大平原吗？

🔍 **考点**：make oneself plain 表达清楚

---

shore [ʃɔ:] *n.* 滨，岸

Huge waves were breaking on the shore.

巨大的浪花拍打着海岸。

terrain ['terein] *n.* 地带，地形

He had made a detailed study of the terrain about western district.

他对西部地区地形做了缜密的研究。

bay [bei] *n.* 湾，山脉中的凹处

Do you know that in small bay big waves will never build up?

你知道吗？在小的港湾里永远也形不成大的波涛。

🔍**考点**：keep / hold sth. at bay 使无法近身

beach [bi:tʃ] *n.* 海滩，湖滩，河滩

The Blacks had a good holiday on the beach.

布莱克一家在沙滩上度过了一个愉快的假期。

bed [bed] *n.* 床，床位，圃，河床

The doctor said you should have a good rest on the bed.

医生说你需要躺在床上好好地休息。

brook [bruk] *n.* 小河，溪流

We can get some water to drink from the brook.

我们可以从小溪里弄点水喝。

cave [keiv] *n.* 山洞，洞穴，窑洞

Because of the heavy rain, the road has caved in.

暴雨使道路塌陷成穴。

channel ['tʃænl] *n.* 海峡，渠道，频道

Do you know something about English Channel?

你知道有关英吉利海峡的事情吗？

cliff [klif] *n.* 悬崖，峭壁

I scrambled up the cliff for a better look at the sea.

我很快地爬上峭壁，饱览大海的景色。

dam [dæm] *n.* 水坝，水堤，障碍物

They reinforced the dam with sandbags when the flood came.

洪水到来时，他们用沙袋加固堤坝。

ditch [ditʃ] *n.* 沟，沟渠，渠道

The drainage ditch of our bathtub needs repairing.

我们家浴盆的下水道需要修理。

drift [drift] *vi.* 漂流，漂泊；*n.* 漂流

Several clusters of white clouds are drifting across the blue sky.

蔚蓝的天空中飘过几朵白云。

float [fləut] *vi.* 漂浮；*vt.* 使漂浮

To the passengers, the fish appear to float in air.

在乘客看来，鱼好像悬浮在空中。

iceberg ['aisbəg] *n.* 浮山，冰块

The mighty iceberg came into my view.

巨大的冰山出现在我眼前。

landscape ['lændskeip] *n.* 风景，景色，全景　*vt.* 美化……的景观

It is said that Guilin's landscape is number one in the world.

据说，桂林山水甲天下。

magnificent [mæg'nifisnt] *adj.* 壮丽的，雄伟的，华丽的，极好的

You know the view from the hilltop is so magnificent.

从山顶看到的景色真是非常壮观。

marine [mə'ri:n] *adj.* 海的，海上的，航海的，海运的　*n.* 船只，海军

This kind of remote sensor is widely used in the marine science and technology field.

这种遥感器在海洋科技领域应用得非常广泛。

mountain ['mauntin] *n.* 山，山岳，山脉

I'm sitting at the foot of the mountain, and seeing the moonlight illuminate the valley.

我坐在山脚下，看到月光照亮了山谷。

pond [pɔnd] *n.* 池塘

Water lying stagnant in ponds and ditches is very smelly.

池塘和沟中的死水很臭。

ridge [ridʒ] *n.* 脊，岭，山脉，垄

It's exciting to walk along the mountain ridge.

走在山脊上真让人兴奋。

range [reɪndʒ] *n.* 排，行，山脉，范围
What did you find when you searched the range of woods?
你搜索那片林子时发现了什么东西？

真题

For more than 20 years, we've been supporting educational programs that ____ from kindergartens to colleges.
A) spread　　B) shift　　C) move　　D) range

详　解：选D。题意为：20多年来，我们一直支持从幼儿园到大学的教育项目。range from sth. to sth. 是固定搭配，意思是"从……到……"，表示范围。A) spread 意思是"传播，扩散"；B) shift 意思是"转换"；C) move 意思是"移动，挪开"。

(CET-4 模拟)

source [sɔːs] *n.* 河的源头，根源
Where is the source of that river?
那条河的源头在哪里？

真题

It is said in some parts of the world, goats, rather than cows, serve as a vital ____ of milk.
A) storage　　B) reserve
C) resource　　D) source

详　解：选D。题意为：据说，在世界上一些地方，奶的主要来源是山羊而不是奶牛。A) storage 意思是"货物的储存"；B) reserve 通常用复数形式，意思是"储藏量"；C) resource意思是"资源，财力"；D) source意思是"来源，源泉"。

(CET-4 模拟)

spectacular [spek'tækjulə] *adj.* 壮观的，引人注目的
n. 壮观的演出，惊人之举
Everyone is deeply appealed by the spectacular grandeur of the scenery at the Three Gorges.
每个人都被三峡壮观的景象深深吸引了。

splash [splæʃ] *vt.&n.* 溅，泼，飞溅
There's a splash of mud on her dress.
她身上溅了一片泥。

splendid ['splendid] *adj.* 壮丽的，显著的
My ambition is to make a splendid career.
我的志向是轰轰烈烈地干一番事业。

spray [spreɪ] *n.* 浪花，喷雾；*vt.* 喷
A spray of salt water hit her in the depressed face.
飞溅的海水打在她沮丧的脸上。

stream [striːm] *n.* 河，流；*vi.&vt.* 流
There is a stream issued from the bottom of the huge stone.
一条小溪自巨石下流出。

wave [weɪv] *n.* 波；波涛；*vi.* 波动
I can say in a small bay big waves will never build up.
我敢说，在小的港湾里永远也形不成大的波涛。

考点：wave aside 对……置之不理

quiet ['kwaɪət] *adj.* 寂静的，安静的
The sea was quiet before the storm struck.
暴风雨来袭前海面很平静。

考点：on the quiet 秘密地，私下地

dash [dæʃ] *vt.* 使猛撞，溅；*n.* 猛冲
Little mountain stream is dashing down to the plain.
小山涧奔腾而下，流向平原。

考点：dash off 迅速离去

above [ə'bʌv] *prep.* 在……上面，高于
adv. 在上文，在上游，在天上
Those birds are wheeling about in the sky above us.
那些鸟儿在我们上空盘旋着。

考点：above all 首先，尤其是

unique [juː'niːk] *adj.* 唯一的，独一无二的
The custom is unique in Yunnan.
这种风俗是云南特有的。

calm [kɑːm] *adj.* 静的，平静的
The surface of the river is calm.
河面很平静。

sway [swei] *vi.* 摇动；*vt.* 摇，摇动
The tree swayed from one side to the other in the wind.
树在风中从一边摇向另一边。

swing [swiŋ] *vi.* 摇摆，回转；*n.* 摇摆
The branches of the tree swung in the wind.
树枝在风中摇摆。

🔍 **考点**：in full swing 正在全力进行中

自然 金属矿产 ✎

alloy ['ælɔi] *n.* 合金；*vt.* 把……铸成合金
These typewriters are made of a light and hard alloy.
这些打字机是用轻质和硬质合金制造的。

aluminium [ˌælju:'minjəm] *n.* 铝
Aluminium cans can be recycled.
铝制的罐子是可回收利用的。

coal [kəul] *n.* 煤，煤块
The country is rich in oil and coal.
这个国家石油和煤资源丰富。

consume [kən'sju:m] *vt.* 消耗，消费，消灭
I consumed most of my time in playing computer games.
我把大部分时间都花在打电子游戏了。

🔍 **考点**：consume...on sth. / in doing sth.
花费……在……

真题

In Britain people _____ four million tons of potatoes every year.
A) swallow   B) dispose
C) consume   D) exhaust

详 解：选C。题意为：在英国，人们每年要消耗掉400万吨土豆。只有C）项能满足题意的需要。A) swallow吞咽；B) dispose处理，销毁；D) exhaust用尽，使筋疲力尽。

(CET-4 模拟)

consumption [kən'sʌmpʃən] *n.* 消耗量，消耗
The petrol consumption of the big car is very high.
这辆大汽车耗油量很大。

crystal ['kristl] *n.* 水晶，结晶体，晶粒
My cousin likes the crystal ornaments very much, so I plan to buy her one this time.
我的堂姐非常喜欢水晶饰品，所以我打算这次给她买一个。

deficiency [di'fiʃənsi] *n.* 缺乏，不足，缺陷
We can see the deficiency in this plan.
我们可以看到这个计划的不足之处。

deficit ['defisit] *n.* 不足，缺陷，亏损
The surcharge may change the composition of our country's trade deficit.
附加税可能会改变我国贸易赤字的组成结构。

diamond ['daiəmənd] *n.* 金钢石，钻石，菱形
In order to find the lost diamond, he searched everybody in the bus.
为了找到丢失的钻石，他对车上的每个人进行了搜身。

iron ['aiən] *n.* 铁，烙铁；*vt.* 烫（衣）
A magnet attracts iron. This is a common sense.
磁石吸引铁是一个常识。

🔍 **考点**：iron out 消除（困难等）

limited ['limitid] *adj.* 有限的
Don't be prodigal with water; you know water resource on the earth is limited.
别浪费水，你知道水资源是有限的。

marble ['mɑ:bl] *n.* 大理石
The table in our sitting room is made of marble.
我们客厅里那张桌子是用大理石制成的。

mercury ['mə:kjuri] *n.* 水银，汞
Look, the mercury in the thermometer rises to 38.5℃; you have a temperature.
看，温度计里的水银柱升到了38.5摄氏度，你发烧了。

metal ['metl] *n.* 金属，金属制品
　　　　　　　adj. 金属制的

Most of the spare parts of this machine are made of mental.

这台机器的大部分零部件都是由金属制成的。

mine [main] *pron.* 我的；*n.* 矿，矿山，地雷
　　　　　　　vt. 开矿，开采

It was terrible that I mistook other's baggage for mine at the carousel in the airport.

在机场的行李传送带上我把别人的行李错当自己的了，太糟糕了。

miner ['mainə] *n.* 矿工，开矿机

Being a miner is dangerous to him.

在他看来，当矿工很危险。

mineral ['minərəl] *n.* 矿物；*adj.* 矿物的

For the human, essential vitamin and mineral requirements must be met.

对于人类来说，必要的维生素和矿物质的需求，必须得到满足。

ore [ɔ:] *n.* 矿，矿石，矿砂

They can abstract metal from ore.

他们可以从矿石中提炼金属。

rare [rɛə] *adj.* 稀薄的，稀有的

This kind of heavy-metal ooze is rare.

这种重金属软泥很稀有。

🔎**考点**：rare, scare 都有 "少的" 意思：因长期缺少而珍贵的用rare；因暂时缺乏而不足的用scare；指时间和频率用rare，不用scare。

rarely ['rɛəli] *adv.* 很少，难得

Those unrealistic expectations will rarely come true.

那些不切实际的期望很少能实现。

renew [ri'nju:] *vt.* 使更新；*vi.* 更新

Jane wanted to renew her wardrobe.

简想要添置新衣。

silver ['silvə] *n.* 银，银子，银器

The princess wears several silver hairpins today.

公主今天戴了几个银制的发夹。

resource [ri'sɔ:s] *n.* 资源，物力，办法

Economics is the study of how people choose to use scarce or limited productive resources.

经济学研究人们如何进行抉择，以使用稀缺的或有限的生产性资源。

silicon ['silikən] *n.* 硅

Zhong Guan-cun can be called Silicon Valley of China.

中关村可以说是中国的硅谷。

vast [vɑ:st] *adj.* 巨大的，大量的

There are a vast number of firms located around.

有很多公司坐落在周边。

环境保护 相互关系

compatible [kəm'pætəbl] *adj.* 适宜的，能共存的，兼容的

What the official says is not compatible with his deeds.

那个政府官员所说的和他所做的一点都不符合。

真题

Don't trust the speaker any more since the remarks he made in his lectures are never _____ with the facts.
A) comparative　　B) compatible
C) harmonious　　D) symmetrical

详 解：选B。题意为：别再相信那个演讲者了，他发表的言论与事实从不相符。A) comparative意思是 "相当的，相对的"；C) harmonious意思是 "和谐的，和睦的"；D) symmetrical意思是 "对称的，均衡的"。

(CET-4 2005.6)

connection [kə'nekʃən] *n.* 连接，联系，连贯性

There is no connection between them.

他们之间没有什么关系。

🔎**考点**：in connection with 关于，与……有关

conservation [ˌkɔnsəˈveiʃən] *n.* 保存，保护，守恒

There is a need for the conservation of trees, or there will soon be no forests.
有必要保护树木，否则不久将会没有森林了。

connect [kəˈnekt] *vt.* 连接，连结，联系

This bridge connects the school and my home.
这座桥连接着学校和我家。

真题

Today, an information superhighway has been built–an electronic network that _____ libraries, corporations, government agencies and individuals.
A) merges   B) connects
C) relays   D) unifies

详　解：选B。题意为：现在，已建成了信息高速公路——连接图书馆、公司、政府机构和个人的电子网。connect连接，联系。A) merge意思是"合并，并入"，常用merge A with B；C) relay意思是"接替，转播"；D) unify意思是"统一，使成一体"。

(CET-4 2009.6)

contaminate [kənˈtæmineit] *vt.* 弄脏，污染，玷污

Flies are pests; they contaminated food.
苍蝇是害虫，它们会弄脏食物。

interact [ˌintərˈækt] *vi.* 相互作用，相互影响

These elements interact with each other in this experiment.
在这个实验中，这些元素是相互作用的。

interaction [ˌintərˈækʃən] *n.* 相互作用，干扰

His thought expressed the concept of interaction design.
他的想法体现了交互设计的理念。

harmony [ˈhɑːməni] *n.* 调合，和声，协调，和谐

Though we were not good at singing, we won in the singing contest by singing the song in harmony.
尽管我们不擅长唱歌，我们通过唱和声在歌唱比赛中取胜。

考点：in harmony with 与……一致，与……和睦相处

真题

The native Canadians lived in _____ with nature, for they respected nature as a provider of life.
A) coordination   B) acquaintance
C) contact   D) harmony

详　解：选D。题意为：加拿大当地的人与大自然和谐相处，因为他们将大自然视为供给者而予以尊敬。A) coordination意思是"协调，协和"，指各部分之间的配合；B) acquaintance意思是"熟悉，熟知"；C) contact意思是"接触，联系"；D) harmony意思是"和谐，调合"。

(CET-4 模拟)

relevant [ˈrelivənt] *adj.* 有关的，相对的，贴切的

Can you tell me why copyrights are relevant versus patents?
你能告诉我为什么版权和专利是对立的吗？

真题

Color and sex are not relevant _____ whether a person is suitable for the job.
A) on   B) for   C) to   D) with

详　解：选C。题意为：一个人是否适合这份工作与肤色和性别无关。be relevant to 固定搭配，表示"与……有关的"。

(CET-4 模拟)

环境保护 自然灾害

famine [ˈfæmin] *n.* 饥荒，严重的缺乏

Most persons of the country died of famine.
那个国家的人大部分都是饿死的。

hazard [ˈhæzəd] *n.* 危险，公害

All kinds of natural hazards happened frequently these years.
近年各种自然灾害频繁发生。

考点：at / in hazard = in danger 处于危险中

vibrate [vai'breit] *vt.* 使颤动；*vi.* 颤动
When the little girl plucks the strings, they vibrate without stopping.
小女孩拨弄琴弦时，它们颤动不停。

victim ['viktim] *n.* 牺牲者，受害者
He is one of the victims in this earthquake.
他是这次地震中的一名遇难者。

🔍 考点：fall (a) victim to 成为……的牺牲品

环境保护 污染与治理

carbon ['kɑːbən] *n.* 碳
Nowadays our government is taking measures to reduce the carbon emissions.
国家正在采取措施减少碳排放量。

consciousness ['kɔnʃəsnis] *n.* 意识，觉悟，知觉
It is necessary for us to popularize environmental consciousness among citizens.
很有必要在市民中间推广环保意识。

discharge [dis'tʃɑːdʒ] *vt.* 释放，排出，解雇 *n.* 释放
Do you know the reason why he was discharged?
你知道他被解雇的原因吗?

dump [dʌmp] *vt.* 倾倒，倾销
A lot of sewage was dumped into the river.
大量污水被排入河水中。

dumping ['dʌmpiŋ] *n.* 倾倒，倾销
Dumping is to sell the products at the price lower than the cost.
倾销就是指以低于成本的价格销售商品。

dustbin ['dʌstbin] *n.* 垃圾筒
We should put waste into the dustbin.
我们应该把废弃物扔进垃圾筒里。

dusty ['dʌsti] *adj.* 灰蒙蒙的，粉状的
The air is very dusty in this city.
这个城市的空气里灰尘很大。

emit [i'mit] *vt.* 散发，发射，发表
The sun emits light.
太阳发光。

真题
The beam that is _____ by a laser differs in several ways from the light that comes out of a flashlight.
A) emitted   B) transported
C) motivated   D) translated

详　解：选A。题意为：激光发出的光束和闪光灯所发出的光束在很多方面不同。A) emit意思是"发射"；B) transport意思是"传送"；C) motivate意思是"激发"；D) translate意思是"翻译"。

(CET-4 模拟)

garbage ['gɑːbidʒ] *n.* 垃圾，污物，废料
He threw the newspaper into the garbage can.
他将报纸扔到垃圾桶里。

pile [pail] *n.* 堆；*vt.* 堆叠，累积
I saw there were piles of litter in the yard.
我看见院子里堆着成堆的垃圾。

poison ['pɔizn] *n.* 毒，毒药；*vt.* 毒害
I doubt whether the antidote is strong enough to expel the poison.
我怀疑这种解药药力不足以驱散毒素。

poisonous ['pɔiznəs] *adj.* 有毒的，有害的
We should do something to prevent the poisonous waste to pollute the river.
我们应该阻止这些有毒废料污染河流。

pollute [pə'luːt] *vt.* 弄脏，污染，沾污
Some factories' chimneys poured a large volume of smoke to pollute the air.
一些工厂的烟囱排放烟雾污染空气。

pollution [pə'luːʃən] *n.* 污染
Many young people could not resist the spiritual pollution of this kind.
很多年轻人不能抵制这样的精神污染。

pour [pɔː] *vt.* 灌，倒；*vi.* 倾泻
Don't pour hot water into the glass or it will crack.
不要把热开水倒进玻璃杯里，否则它会炸裂的。

🔍 考点：pour into（使）川流不息地涌入
　　　　pour out 倾诉，倾吐

protect [prə'tekt] *vt.* 保护，保卫，警戒

He volunteered to protect his girlfriend as she looked so vulnerable.
他的女朋友看上去很脆弱，他就主动去保护她。

🔍 考点：protect...against (from) 保护……免遭

protection [prə'tekʃən] *n.* 保护，警戒

The girl raged when her jewels were stolen under police protection.
在有警察保护的情况下这个女孩的珠宝被偷了，她十分生气。

protective [prə'tektiv] *adj.* 保护的，防护的

As a mother, she naturally feels protective towards her children.
作为一名母亲，她天生要保护自己的孩子。

🔍 考点：be protective of sb. 保护某人

surroundings [sə'raundiŋz] *n.* 周围的事物，环境

He is such a person out of tune with his surroundings.
他是一个与环境格格不入的人。

sustainable [sə'steinəbəl] *adj.* 可持续的

China persists in the course of sustainable development.
中国坚持走可持续发展的道路。

toxic ['tɔksik] *adj.* 有毒的；*n.* 有毒物质

The atmosphere is seriously polluted by the toxic gases released by the factory.
工厂排放的有毒气体严重地污染了大气。

trash [træʃ] *n.* 垃圾，社会渣滓
vt. 捣毁，破坏

Lily threw the orange into the trash can.
莉莉将橘子扔进垃圾筒。

waste [weist] *n.* 浪费，废物，垃圾

A lot of poisonous waste has been taken away in trucks.
很多有毒的废料被装在大卡车里运走了。

🔍 考点：waste time (in) doing sth. 浪费时间做……；waste money on sb. / sth. 浪费金钱在……上；waste away 日渐消瘦，日益衰弱

真题

As he has ＿＿＿ our patience, we'll not wait for him any longer.
A) torn   B) wasted
C) exhausted   D) consumed

详　解：选C。题意为：因为他让我们失去了耐心，所以我们不再等他了。A）tear意思是"扯破"；B）waste意思是"浪费"；C）exhaust意思是"耗尽"；D）consume可以指"耗费时间和精力"，也可以指"身体被疾病摧毁"。

(CET-4 模拟)

environment [in'vaiərənmənt] *n.* 环境，外界，绕

The government urged on industry the importance of protecting the environment.
政府向工商业强调保护环境的重要性。

第二部分

大学英语四级题型分析及考试技巧

College English Test of Band Four analysis and examination techniques

Part I   Writing   (30 minutes)

　　写作是历年大学四级考试的必考内容，但一些考生在看到作文题目时不知如何提笔进行写作。想写出优秀的作文，首先要熟悉英语四级写作的具体要求，其次平时要注意积累英语素材。

　　英语四级考试要求考生在30分钟内写出120字的文章。体裁主要有议论文（分为"Topic题型"和A&B又称"正反观点题"）、应用文（主要是书信）、图表文等。针对不同的体裁，写作思路是不同的。但不管是哪一种体裁，一般都可以按以下的步骤来展开。

　　一、审清题意，草拟提纲。文章一定要有准确、鲜明的主题，在审好题，立好意后，就要写提纲，打造文章的骨架。这要求我们安排好层次段落，铺设好过渡，处理好开头和结尾。如命题作文中有提示句，还要从提示句的关键词出发，围绕关键词开拓思路，发挥联想，记录下联想到的东西，可以是句子或单词词组，可以是英语或汉语。

　　二、写出段落主题句。主题句就是英语文章的中心思想句，能概括出作者的写作目的或意图。看到段落主题句，读者就能大致了解段落所要阐述的内容。段落主题句通常是一个语法结构完整、内容概括、用词简洁明了的单句。通常将段落主题句置于段落的开头，可使文章结构更清晰，更有说服力。

　　三、参照提纲，紧扣主题句，完成各段落。有了段落主题句后，还需要顺着段落主题句的方向，参照提纲中的思路，进而完成各个段落。引导段要能引起读者的注意和兴趣，为主题段铺路架桥。主题段应围绕文章和该段的主题展开。展开的方式包括：顺序法、举例法、比较法、对比法、说明法、因果法、推导法、归纳法和下定义等。可以根据需要任选一种或几种方式。

　　四、把好检查关。文章写完后，要检查上下文是否连贯，是否有语法错误，主谓是否一致，动词的时态、语态、语气的使用是否正确，是否有大小写、拼写、标点错误，并注意卷面整洁。

　　当然，好的文章不是一蹴而就的，最根本的是要大量实践，必须多读多写，注意博览和精读相结合，也可以适当背诵一些名句名篇。中国有句古话，叫"熟读唐诗300首，不会作诗也会吟"。另外，还可选些范文，悉心领悟，多加模仿，以逐步达到运用自如。在平时的学习中，自己也要多练习写作，可以采用循序渐进、灵活多样的练习方式。从根据提示词写单句开始，然后到写几句话，最后到写完整的文段。在练习时，要充分体会所提供的情景素材，注意使用常见的连接词来表示顺序和逻辑关系，使句意表达连贯、语法正确、符合逻辑。

第一次就考好英语四级

下面是2011年6月份的大学英语四级作文考试题目

> Directions: *For this part, you are allowed 30 minutes to write a short essay on the topic of* Online Shopping. *You should write at least 120 words following the outline given below:*
> 1. 现在网上购物已成为一种时尚
> 2. 网上购物有很多好处，但也有不少问题
> 3. 我的建议

作文范文

With the help of the rapid development of Internet technology, online shopping is coming into fashion in most of cities.

Online shopping is welcomed by most people due to various reasons. From the perspective of the consumer, it can save some time for people who don't have much spare time. Just click the mouse, they can get whatever they want while staying at home. For the retailers, it can cut some costs for those who don't have much circulating funds. They don't have to rent a house and spend money on employees compared with the traditional trade mode. However, there are still some defects in online shopping. First, lack of face-to-face deal makes online shopping less reliable and trustworthy. Second, people will lose the fun of bargain.

It is undeniable that shopping on the Internet has become an irresistible trend in modern society. It's of great urgency that we need to regulate the relative laws with the rapid growth of online shopping. Only in this way can we enjoy the pleasure and convenience of online shopping without less concern of being cheated.

点评

今年的作文选择了年轻人比较熟悉的"网购"为话题，要求考生列出网购的优缺点，再写出自己的建议。因此作文体裁属于议论文中的A&B，又称"正反观点题"。这种体裁不需要考生过多陈述自己的观点与主张，因此难度不太大，只要按照要求一步步来写，一定能得到高分。

该考生在第一段总述现象并引出话题，说明网购在很多城市已成为一种时尚，满足了作文的第一个要求。

第二段从正反两方面来论述网购，分别写了其优缺点。关于优点，网购的优点很多，比如说网购可以节省很多时间，网购可以节省很多成本开支等。其次，缺点方面考生可以把重心放在诚信方面。为了不至于跟优点相比，缺点方面太少，考生可以考虑稍微提一下其他缺点，比如说与传统购物相比，网购少去了很多砍价的乐趣。

根据作文要求，考生必须给出自己的建议，根据第二段列出的缺点方面给出相应的防范应对措施，该考生在第三段交待了一些解决"网购"问题建议。该文章紧扣作文要

求，不仅列出了网购的优缺点，还顺畅地表达了自己的建议，不失为一篇佳作。

下面是2010年12月的大学英语四级作文考试题目

Directions: *For this part, you are allowed 30minutes to write a short essay on the topic of How Should Parents Help Children to Be Independent? You should write at least 120 words following the outline given below:*
1. 目前不少父母为孩子包办一切
2. 为了孩子独立，父母应该……

作文范文 ✎

Nowadays, there is a great concern over such a phenomenon. That is, some parents takc care of almost everything concerned with their children, including study, work, marriage and so on. Some parents believe that this is love.However, it is only to destroy children's independence thoroughly.

For the future of the next generation, more efforts should be made by parents to help their children to be independent. The fundamental method is to cultivate the awareness, namely, the importance and necessity of being independent, which is supposed to begin from childhood. Children should be taught that no one can be stronger and more helpful than themselves in this world.

The awarenss of independence is so indispensable for us that parents had better act as a tutor, not a dictator. And only with parents' trust, can the next generation gain confidence step by step.

点评 ☀

今年的作文题目贴近广大考生的生活，给了考生很大的发挥空间。考生可以根据自己的特长，用几句话勾勒父母对于子女的过度关爱，或者阐述父母怎样的行为才可以培养子女独立的品格，而过度宠爱正导致了他们独立精神的消失。

范文的第一段，考生描述了现实状况，即父母对孩子的溺爱造成了孩子的不独立。

第二段，针对孩子过分依赖父母的现状，说明父母应该从小让孩子养成独立的习惯。

第三段，呼吁父母亲引导孩子走向独立。

该文章基本上没有偏离主题，但美中不足的是，第二段描写父母如何培养孩子独立的习惯时，内容太少。如果多写几条父母亲帮助子女独立的策略，文章会更好。

Part II Reading Comprehension (Skimming and Scanning) 🕐(15 minutes)

快速阅读是新增题型，阅读材料总字数一般在800-1200之间，可以是一大篇文章，也可以是长度不等的几小篇。体裁主要是说明文，内容涉及自然科学、人文社科等，答题时间为15分钟。文章后面共有10道题，其中包括7道选择题和3道填空题。快速阅读不要求考生理解文章的每一个单词每一个句子，而是考查考生对文章的整体把握能力。再加上时间上的限制，考生不可能逐字逐句读完材料，然后做题。那么如何迅速有效地完成这种题型呢？

考生平时阅读一般会采取两种阅读方法。一种是先看问题，带着问题读文章。另一种是先看文章，然后再做题。究竟哪一种方法好呢？实践证明，第一种阅读方法效果要好一些。先看问题，就可以对出题人的出题意图有所了解。而且问题中的"线索词"，也有助于我们迅速准确地在原文中找到问题的出处，节省时间。具体的阅读方法总结如下：略读(skimming)与查读(scanning)。

所谓略读，就是快速浏览全文的阅读方法。略读的对象是文章的开始段、结束段、每段的段首句和结尾句，文章内容的概括性陈述一般都在这些位置。略读的目的在于了解文章的主题后，对文章的结构获得一个整体概念，并对各部分的内容获得一个粗略的印象。对快速阅读而言，略读最重要的意义在于对各部分的内容获得一个粗略印象，以便迅速确定答案所在的部分或段落。对于带有小标题的文章，把握住了小标题就把握住了文章的主要内容。而对于没有小标题的文章，需要通过把握文章的开头或结尾部分来把握文章的主题与写作目的；更重要的是，浏览每段的段首和段尾，会有助于对每一段的主题和内容获得一个粗略的印象。

所谓查读，是指以问题为线索、带着问题去寻找某一特定信息的阅读。对于四级考试的快速阅读来说，查读就是在读过文章后面的题目后，以题干中的某些词为线索，到原文中去寻找出处的过程。可是，以什么样的词为线索词到原文中去查找呢？一般是表示时间、地点、数字的词，或者是又长又难的名词。线索词找2-3个就行，而且最好位置不同。

在了解了什么是略读与查读后，我们就来说说快速阅读的具体步骤：

一、运用查读的方法，在扫描完题目后，找出题干的关键词。

二、运用略读的方法，快速浏览全文，把握文章的主旨大意。

三、定位原文，剖析句子。在略读完文章后，再看一遍问题，带着题干中的线索词迅速回原文定位，也就是找出这个问题出现在原文的第几段第几行。需要注意的是，四级的出题顺序一般与原文的行文顺序一致，就是说下一道题的出处一般位于前一道题出处后面。把握题目顺序与行文顺序一致的基本规律，将节省我们的查读时间。

四、比较选项定答案。在读懂文章句子的基础上，再回到问题上来，看一下ABCD

四个选项哪一项符合原文意思。如果第一个问题就是考察文章中心思想或作者写作意图时，可以先跳过去做其他的。因为这时候对文章还没有形成比较全面的理解，此时做出选择的正确率不太高。

下面是2011年6月份的大学英语四级考试快速阅读题目

> Directions: *In this part, you will have 15 minutes to go over the passage quickly and answer the questions on* Answer Sheet 1. *For questions 1-7, choose the best answer from the four choices marked A), B), C) and D). For questions 8-10, complete the sentences with the information given in the passage.*

British Cuisine: the Best of Old and New

British cuisine（烹饪）has come of age in recent years as chefs（厨师）combine the best of old and new.

Why does British food have a reputation for being so bad? Because it is bad! Those are not the most encouraging words to hear just before eating lunch at one of Hong Kong's smartest British restaurants, Alfie's by KEE, but head chef Neil Tomes has more to say.

"The past 15 years or so have been a noticeable period of improvement for food in England,"

The English chef says, citing the trend in British cuisine for better ingredients, preparation and cooking methods, and more appealing presentation. Chef such as Delia Smith, Nigel Slater, Jamie Oliver and Gordon Ramsay made the public realise that cooking – and eating – didn't have to be a boring thing. And now, most of the British public is familiar even with the extremes of Heston Blumenthal's molecular gastronomy, a form of cooking that employs scientific methods to create the perfect dish.

"It's no longer the case that the common man in England is embarrassed to show he knows about food," Tomes says.

There was plenty of room for improvement. The problems with the nation's cuisine can be traced back to the Second World War. Before the war, much of Britain's food was imported and when German U-boats began attacking ships bringing food to the country, Britain went on rations（配给）.

"As rationing came to an end in the 1950s, technology picked up and was used to mass-produce food," Tomes says. "And by then people were just happy to have a decent quantity of food in their kitchens."

They weren't looking for cured meats, organic produce or beautiful presentation; they were looking for whatever they could get their hands on, and this prioritisation of quantity over quality prevailed for decades, meaning a generation was brought up with food that couldn't compete with neighbouring France, Italy, Belgium or Spain. Before star chefs such as Oliver began making cooking fashionable, it was hard to find a restaurant in London that was open after 9p.m. But in recent years the capital's culinary（烹饪的）scene has developed to the point that it is now confident of its ability to please the tastes of any international visitor.

With the opening of Alfie's in April, and others such as The Pawn, two years ago, modern British food has made its way to Hong Kong. "With British food, I think that Hong Kong restaurant are keeping up," says David Tamlyn, the Welsh executive chef at The Pawn in Wan Chai. "Hong Kong diners are extremely responsive to new ideas or presentations, which is good news for new dishes."Chefs agree that diners in Hong Kong are embracing the modern British trend. Some restaurants are modifying the recipes（菜谱）of British dishes to breathe new life into the classics,while other are using better quality ingredients but remaining true to British traditional and tastes.

Tamlyn is in the second camp. "We select our food very particulary. We use US beef, New Zealand lamb and for our custards（牛奶蛋糊）we use Bird's Custard Powder," Tamlyn says. "Some restaurants go for custard made fresh with eggs, sugar and cream, but British custard is different, and we stay true to that."Matthew Hill, senior manager at the two-year-old SoHo restaurant Yorkshire Pudding, also uses better ingredients as a means of improving dishes. "There are a lot of existing perceptions about British food and so we can't alter these too much. We're a traditional British restaurant so there are some staples（主菜）that will remain essentially unchanged."

These traditional dishes include fish and chips, steak and kidney pie and large pieces of roasted meats. At Alfie's, the newest of the British restaurants in town and perhaps the most gentlemen's club-like in design, Neil Tomes explains his passion for provenance（原产地）. "Britain has started to become really proud of the food it's producing. It has excellent organic farms, beautifully crafted cheeses, high-quality meats."

However, the British don't have a history of exporting their foodstuffs, which makes it difficult for restaurants in Hong Kong to source authentic ingredients.

"We can get a lot of our ingredients once a week from the UK," Tamlyn explains. "But there is also pressure to buy local and save on food miles, which means we take our vegetables from the local markets, and there are a lot that work well with British staples."

The Phoenix, in Mid-Levels, offers the widest interpretation of "British cuisine", while still trying to maintain its soul. The gastro-pub has existed in various locations in Hong Kong since 2002. Singaporean head chef Tommy Teh Kum Chai offers daily specials on a blackboard, rather than sticking to a menu. This enables him to reinterpret British cuisine depending on what is available in the local markets.

"We use a lot of ingredients that people wouldn't perhaps associate as British, but are presented in a British way. Bell peppers stuffed with couscous, alongside ratatouille, is a very popular dish."

Although the ingredients may not strike diners as being traditional, they can be found in dishes across Britain.

Even the traditional chefs are aware of the need to adapt to local tastes and customs, while maintaining the Brutishness of their cuisine.

At Yorkshire Pudding, Hill says that his staff asks diners whether they would like to share their meals. Small dishes, shared meals and "mixing it up" is not something commonly done in Britain, but Yorkshire Pudding will bring full dished to the table and offer individual plates for each dinner. "That way, people still get the presentation of the dishes as they were designed, but can carve them up however they like," Hill says.

This practice is also popular at The Pawn, although largely for rotisseries（烤肉馆）, Tamlynsays. "Some tables will arrive on Sunday, order a whole chicken and a shoulder of lamb or a baby pig, and just stay for hours enjoying everything we bring out for them."

Some British traditions are too sacred（神圣的）to mess with, however, Tomes says. "I'd never change a full English breakfast."

注意：此部分试题请在答题卡1上作答。

1. What is British food generally known for?

A) Its unique flavor.

B) Its bad taste.

C) Its special cooking methods.

D) Its organic ingredients.

2. The Second World War led to _____ in Britain.

A) an inadequate supply of food

B) a decrease of grain production

C) an increase in food import

D) a change in people's eating habits

3. Why couldn't Britain compete with some of its neighboring countries in terms of food in the post-war decades?

A) Its food lacked variety.

B) Its people cared more for quantity.

C) It was short of well-trained chefs.

D) It didn't have flavorful food ingredients.

4. With culinary improvement in recent years, London's restaurants are now able to appeal to the tastes of _____.

A) most young people

B) elderly British diners

C) all kinds of overseas visitors

D) upper-class customers

5. What do Hong Kong diners welcome, according to Welsh executive chef David Tamlyn?

A) Authentic classic cuisine.

B) Locally produced ingredients.

C) New ideas and presentations.

D) The return of home-style dishes.

6. While using quality ingredients, David Tamlyn insists that the dishes should _____.

A) benefit people's health

B) look beautiful and inviting

C) be offered at reasonable prices

D) maintain British traditional tastes

7. Why does Neil Tomes say he loves food ingredients from Britain?

A) They appeal to people from all over the world.

B) They are produced on excellent organic forms.

C) They are processed in a scientific way.

D) They come in a great variety.

8. Tamlyn says that besides importing ingredients from Britain once a week, his restaurant also buys vegetables from _____.

9. The Phoenix in Mid-Levels may not use British ingredients, but presents its dishes _____.

10. Yorkshire Pudding is a restaurant which will bring full dishes to the table but offer plates to those diners who would like to _____.

答案分析：

1. **B**. Its bad taste

解析：题干中generally known for 可以作为线索词，查询原文，根据原文Why does British food have a reputation for being so bad? Because it is bad! 可知关键词为bad，故选B。

2. **A**. an inadequate supply of food

解析：由题干线索词Second World War可以定位到原文第六段。二战之前，英国的食品都是进口的，二战之后，食品供应船只遭到攻击，只能依靠配给，故选A。

3. **B**. Its people cared more for quantity

解析：由线索词compete with some of its neighbouring countries可以定位到原文第6段，they weren't looking for..., they were looking for..., this prioritization of quantity over quality prevailed for decades. 可见他们对数量的追求高于质量，故选B。

4. **C**. all kinds of overseas visitors

解析：由题干线索词culinary定位到原文第八段，根据最后一句its ability to please the tastes of any international visitor. 其中any international visitor就等同于all kinds of overseas visitors。故选C。

5. **C**. New ideas and presentations

解析：根据David Tamlyn这个线索词定位到原文第九段，根据第三句话Hong Kong diners are extremely responsive to new ideas or presentations, 这里的are extremely responsive to在意思上等于题干中的welcome，故选C。

6. **D**. maintain British traditional tastes

解析：一些饭店修改菜谱，采用新样式，而另外一些则保留英式口味，再根据Tamlyn is in the second camp，可知Tamlyn属于后者，即保留原汁原味。故选D。

7. **B**. They are produced on excellent organic farms

解析：由线索词Neil Tomes定位到原文第十一段，根据最后两句话It has excellent organic farms, beautifully crafted cheeses, high-quality meats可选出答案B。

8. the local markets

解析：根据原文，which means we take our vegetables from the local markets, 即除了从英国直接进口，还有部分蔬菜是从本地市场购买的，因此可知答案是the local markets。

9. in a British way

解析：先定位到The Phoenix那一段，再找到下一段，We use a lot of ingredients that people wouldn't perhaps associate as British, but are presented in a British way，因此可知答案是in a British way。

10. share their meals

解析：At Yorkshire Pudding, Hill says that his staff asks diners whether they would like to share their meals. 餐厅之所以在上菜之后再供应碟子，原因就在于可能会有人愿意和别人分享食物，因此可知答案是share their meals。

下面是2010年12月份的大学英语四级考试快速阅读题目

Directions: *In this part, you will have 15 minutes to go over the passage quickly and answer the questions on Answer Sheet 1. For questions 1-7, choose the best answer from the four choices marked A), B), C) and D). For questions 8-10, complete the sentences with the information given in the passage.*

A Grassroots Remedy

Most of us spend our lives seeking the natural world. To this end, we walk the dog, play golf, go fishing, sit in the garden, drink outside rather than inside the pub, have a picnic, live in the suburbs, go to the seaside, buy a weekend place in the country. The most popular leisure activity in Britain is going for a walk. And when joggers (慢跑者) jog, they don't run the streets. Every one of them instinctively heads to the park or the river. It is my profound belief that not only do we all need nature, but we all seek nature, whether we know we are doing so or not.

But despite this, our children are growing up nature-deprived (丧失). I spent my boyhood climbing trees on Streatham Common, South London. These days, children are robbed of these ancient freedoms, due to problems like crime, traffic, the loss of the open spaces and odd new perceptions about what is best for children, that is to say, things that can be bought, rather than things that can be found.

The truth is to be found elsewhere. A study in the US: families had moved to better housing and the children were assessed for ADHD—attention deficit hyperactivity disorder（多动症）. Those whose accommodation had more natural views showed an improvement of 19%; those who had the same improvement in material surroundings but no nice view improved just 4%.

A study in Sweden indicated that kindergarten children who could play in a natural environment had less illness and greater physical ability than children used only to a normal playground. A US study suggested that when a school gave children access to a natural environment, academic levels were raised across the entire school.

Another study found that children play differently in a natural environment. In playgrounds, children create a hierarchy（等级）based on physical abilities, with the tough ones taking the lead. But when a grassy area was planted with bushes, the children got much more into fantasy play, and the social hierarchy was now based on imagination and creativity.

Most bullying（恃强凌弱）is found in schools where there is a tarmac（柏油碎石）playground; the least bullying is in a natural area that the children are encouraged to explore. This reminds me unpleasantly of Sunnyhill School in Streatham, with its harsh tarmac, where I used to hang about in corners fantasising about wildlife.

But children are frequently discouraged from involvement with natural spaces, for health and safety reasons, for fear that they might get dirty or that they might cause damage. So, instead, the damage is done to the children themselves: not to their bodies but to their souls.

One of the great problems of modern childhood is ADHD, now increasingly and expensively treated with drugs. Yet one study after another indicates that contact with nature gives huge benefits to ADHD children. However, we spend money on drugs rather than on green places.

The life of old people is measurably better when they have access to nature. The increasing emphasis for the growing population of old people is in quality rather than quantity of years. And study after study finds that a garden is the single most important thing in finding that quality.

In wider and more difficult areas of life, there is evidence to indicate that natural surroundings improve all kinds of things. Even problems with crime and aggressive behaviour are reduced when there is contact with the natural world.

Dr William Bird, researcher from the Royal Society for the Protection of Birds, states in his study, "A natural environment can reduce violent behaviour because its restorative process helps reduce anger and impulsive behaviour." Wild places need encouraging for this reason, no matter how small their contribution.

We tend to look on nature conservation as some kind of favour that human beings are granting to the natural world. The error here is far too deep: not only do humans need nature for themselves, but the very idea that humanity and the natural world are separable things is profoundly damaging.

Human beings are a species of mammals（哺乳动物）. For seven million years they lived on the planet as part of nature. Our ancestral selves miss the natural world and long for contact with non-human life. Anyone who has patted a dog, stroked a cat, sat under a tree with a pint of beer, given or received a bunch of flowers or chosen to walk through the park on a nice day, understands that.

We need the wild world. It is essential to our well-being, our health, our happiness. Without the wild world we are not more but less civilised. Without other living things around us we are less than human.

Five ways to find harmony with the natural world

Walk: Break the rhythm of permanently being under a roof. Get off a stop earlier, make a circuit of the park at lunchtime, walk the child to and from school, get a dog, feel yourself moving in moving air, look, listen, absorb.

Sit: Take a moment, every now and then, to be still in an open space. In the garden, anywhere that's not in the office, anywhere out of the house, away from the routine. Sit under a tree, look at water, feel refreshed, ever so slightly renewed.

Drink: The best way to enjoy the natural world is by yourself; the second best way is in company. Take a drink outside with a good person, a good gathering: talk with the sun and the wind with birdsong for background.

Learn: Expand your boundaries. Learn five species of bird, five butterflies, five trees, five bird songs. That way, you see and hear more, and your mind responds gratefully to the greater amount of wildness in your life.

Travel: The places you always wanted to visit: by the seaside, in the country, in the hills. Take a weekend break, a day-trip, get out there and do it: for the scenery, for the way through the woods, for the birds, for the bees. Go somewhere special and bring specialness home. It lasts forever, after all.

注意：此部分试题请在答题卡1上作答。

1. What is the author's profound belief?

   A) People instinctively seek nature in different ways.

   B) People should spend most of their lives in the wild.

   C) People have quite different perceptions of nature.

   D) People must make more efforts to study nature.

2. What does the author say people prefer for their children nowadays?

   A) Personal freedom.

   B) Things that are natural.

C) Urban surroundings.

D) Things that are purchased.

3. What does a study in Sweden show?

    A) The natural environment can help children learn better.

    B) More access to nature makes children less likely to fall ill.

    C) A good playground helps kids develop their physical abilities.

    D) Natural views can prevent children from developing ADHD.

4. Children who have chances to explore natural areas _____.

    A) tend to develop a strong love for science

    B) are more likely to fantasise about wildlife

    C) tend to be physically tougher in adulthood

    D) are less likely to be involved in bullying

5. What does the author suggest we do to help children with ADHD?

    A) Find more effective drugs for them.

    B) Provide more green spaces for them.

    C) Place them under more personal care.

    D) Engage them in more meaningful activities.

6. In what way do elderly people benefit from their contact with nature?

    A) They look on life optimistically.

    B) They enjoy a life of better quality.

    C) They are able to live longer.

    D) They become good-humoured.

7. Dr William Bird suggests in his study that _____.

    A) humanity and nature are complementary to each other

    B) wild places may induce impulsive behaviour in people

    C) access to nature contributes to the reduction of violence

    D) it takes a long time to restore nature once damaged

8. It is extremely harmful to think that humanity and the natural world can be

    _____.

9. The author believes that we would not be so civilised without

    _____.

10. The five suggestions the author gives at the end of the passage are meant to
    encourage people to seek _____ with the natural world.

答案分析：

1. **A**. People instinctively seek nature in different ways.
解析：由题干中的线索词profound belief 可以定位到原文的第一段最后一句，
It is my profound belief that not only do we all need nature, but we all seek nature,
whether we know we are doing so or not. whether 引导的从句对应答案中的
instinctively，故选A。

2. **D**. Things that are purchased.
解析：由题干中的线索词prefer for可以定位到第二段最后一句，rather than 对应
题目中的prefer, that is to say作为暗示直接引出之后的things that can be bought, 故
选D。

3. **B**. More access to nature makes children less likely to fall ill.
解析：题干中的线索词是study，Sweden show，定位到第四段第一句，结合语
义可知B是正确答案。

4. **D**. are less likely to be involved in bullying.
解析：A选项具有干扰性，第三段结尾给出自然熏陶能够提高学生学科水平的
线索，但考虑到快速阅读题的传统，即题目顺序对应文章的行文顺序，所以应
该定位到第四段之后的内容，即大段有关bullying的段落，得出D是正确答案。

5. **B**. Provide more green spaces for them.
解析：该题目对应第八段内容，根据第二句中indicates that contact with nature
give huge benefits to ADHD to children,得出B是正确答案。

6. **B**. They enjoy a life of better quality.
解析：由第九段第二句可知老龄人口增长的侧重点是在高质量的生活水平上，
紧接着又指出绿色的生活方式是达到该种高质量生活水平的最重要因素，故选
B。

7. **C**. access to nature contributes to the reduction of violence
解析：由原文中第11段的can reduce violent behavior，可知C选项为正确答案。

8. separated
解析：题干是有关人们错误观念的问题，倒数第三段的关键词error引导的内
容，再对应到humanity and the natural world are separable things is profoundly

damaging，得出正确答案是separated。

9. the wild world
解析：由最后一段第二句可知，正确答案是the wild world。

10. harmony
解析：由最后几段内容的小标题可知答案是harmony。

Part III Listening Comprehension 🕐(35 minutes)

英语的五大基本技能是"听、说、读、写、译"，"听"位居第一，对英语学习起着至关重要的作用。但是对于很多考生来说，英语听力是他们的弱项。听力部分的分值在四级考试中占35%，录音播放时间在35分钟左右。除了复合式听写外，其它的内容都只放一遍，没有复听的机会，因此会使很多考生紧张。考生在听力考试进行时，应该尽量放松心情，这样可以保证考生发挥大脑最大的潜能。由于听力录音播放后没有再听的机会，这就要求考生在进行听力时要高度集中注意力，一旦有丝毫的分神，都会影响至少一个题目甚至多个题目的答案的选择。下面就听力部分的3种题型来具体讲述听力题目的做题方法。

一、对话题(short conversations)。这一部分含有10个短对话，每个题目只播放一遍，涉及的话题较广，但是涉及的单词不难，句子结构相对简单，语速略低于正常语速。做这一部分题目时，首先考生要预读选项，提前预览一下题目的四个选项，带着问题去听，就能将注意力集中在对话的关键信息点上，从而减轻听的负担。其次，考生要把握关键词和关键句，注意听一些表示转折关系的词汇，或者一些表示建议或劝告的句子。最后，考生要会判断相关场景，通过捕捉听力题目和听力录音中出现的关键词来判断相关场景。听力常考的场景一般有：天气场景、娱乐场景、选课场景、工作场景、学习场景、天气场景、医院场景、租房场景等。考生在平时应多积累一些场景中的高频词汇和习惯表达，以提高听力理解能力。

二、短文理解(short passages)。短文理解包括3篇文章，每篇文章后面有 2到4个题目，一共是10个题目。文章信息量大，题材范围广，涉及社会、生活、政治、历史、文化、艺术等多个领域。这一部分的内容虽然逻辑结构复杂，生词难句多，但如果注意分析和总结，还是可以驾驭的。由于西方人说话喜欢开门见山，所以很多情况下，一篇文章的开头就是全文的主题句，即使不是主题句，也包含很多信息。而结尾又是文章的总结句，概括归纳了全文的中心，所以一定要"重两头轻中间"。另外，要注意标志性细节，听力材料中出现的时间、数字、地点等信息以及表示原因和转折的重点词汇和句子都值得注意。

　　三、复合式听写(compound dictation)。复合式听写部分的文章长度在250个单词左右，一共播放3遍。其题型由两部分组成，前7个空是单词听写，所写单词必须是原文的单词，后3个空是补全内容，考生既可以按原文填写，也可以用自己的语言写出大概意思。全文朗读3遍，第一遍没有停顿，考生掌握大意；第二遍在空格后有停顿，要求考生把听到的内容填入空格；第三遍没有停顿，供考生核对内容。大家在复习时，重点仍旧是前两种题型。复合式听写的绝大部分文字已经在卷面给出，所以只要有时间先预览一遍，而且重点看空格上下文的内容，就可以基本知道文章的内容了。考生在第一遍听的时候，就可以尽量把听到的单词写下来，最后一定要再检查一遍所写的内容，尤其要防止在最后3题需要填写句子的部分，出现单复数和时态的错误。

下面是2011年6月份的大学英语四级听力考试题目
Section A

> Directions: *In this section, you will hear 8 short conversations and 2 long conversations. At the end of each conversation, one or more questions will be asked about what was said. Both the conversation and the questions will be spoken only once. After each question there will be a pause. During the pause, you must read the four choices marked A), B), C) and D), and decide which is the best answer. Then mark the corresponding letter on Answer Sheet 2 with a single line through the centre.*

注意：此部分试题请在答题卡2上作答。

11. A) He is careless about his appearance.

B) He is ashamed of his present condition.

C) He changes jobs frequently.

D) He shaves every other day.

12. A) Jane maybe caught in a traffic jam.

B) Jane should have started a little earlier.

C) He knows what sort of person Jane is.

D) He is irritated at having to wait for Jane.

13. A) Training for the Mid-Atlantic Championships.

B) Making preparations for a trans-Atlantic trip.

C) Collecting information about baseball games.

D) Analyzing their rivals' on-field performance.

14. A) He had a narrow escape in a car accident.

B) He is hospitalized for a serious injury.

C) He lost his mother two weeks ago.

D) He has been having a hard time.

15. A) The woman has known the speaker for a long time.

B) The man had difficulty understanding the lecture.

C) The man is making a fuss about nothing.

D) The woman thinks highly of the speaker.

16. A) He has difficulty making sense of logic.

B) Statistics and logic are both challenging subjects.

C) The woman should seek help from the tutoring services.

D) Tutoring services are very popular with students.

17. A) Her overcoat is as stylish as Jill's.

B) Jill missed her class last week.

C) Jill wore the overcoat last week.

D) She is in the same class as the man.

18. A) A computer game.

B) An imaginary situation.

C) An exciting experience.

D) A vacation by the sea.

Questions 19 to 21 are based on the conversation you have just heard.

19. A) Beautiful scenery in the countryside.

B) Dangers of cross-country skiing.

C) Pain and pleasure in sports.

D) A sport he participates in.

20. A) He can't find good examples to illustrate his point.

B) He can't find a peaceful place to do the assignment.

C) He doesn't know how to describe the beautiful country scenery.

D) He can't decide whether to include the effort part of skiing.

21. A) New ideas come up as you write.

B) Much time is spent on collecting data.

C) A lot of effort is made in vain.

D) The writer's point of view often changes.

Questions 22 to 25 are based on the conversation you have just heard.

22. A) Journalist of a local newspaper.

B) Director of evening radio programs.

C) Producer of television commercials.

D) Hostess of the weekly "Business World".

23. A) He ran three restaurants with his wife's help.

B) He and his wife did everything by themselves.

C) He worked both as a cook and a waiter.

D) He hired a cook and two local waitresses.

24. A) He hardly needs to do any advertising nowadays.

B) He advertises a lot on radio and in newspapers.

C) He spends huge sums on TV commercials every year.

D) He hires children to distribute ads in shopping centers.

25. A) The restaurant location.

B) The restaurant atmosphere.

C) The food variety.

D) The food price.

Section B

Directions: *In this section, you will hear 3 short passages. At the end of each passage, you will hear some questions. Both the passage and the questions will be spoken only once. After you hear a question, you must choose the best answer from the four choices marked A), B), C) and D). Then mark the corresponding letter on Answer Sheet 2 with a single line through the centre.*

注意：此部分试题请在答题卡2上作答。

Passage One

Questions 26 to 28 are based on the conversation you have just heard.

26. A) Its protection is often neglected by children.

   B) It cannot be fully restored once damaged.

   C) There are many false notions about it.

   D) There are various ways to protect it.

27. A) It may make the wearer feel tired.

   B) It will gradually weaken the eyes of adults.

   C) It can lead to the loss of vision in children.

   D) It can permanently change the eye structure.

28. A) It can never be done with high technology.

   B) It is the best way to restore damaged eyesight.

   C) It is a major achievement in eye surgery.

   D) It can only be partly accomplished now.

Passage Two

Questions 29 to 31 are based on the passage you have just heard.

29. A) They think they should follow the current trend.

   B) Nursing homes are well-equipped and convenient.

   C) Adult day-care centers are easily accessible.

   D) They have jobs and other commitments.

30. A) They don't want to use up all their life savings.

   B) They fear they will regret it afterwards.

   C) They would like to spend more time with them.

   D) They don't want to see their husbands poorly treated.

31. A) Provide professional standard care.

   B) Be frank and seek help from others.

   C) Be affectionate and cooperative.

   D) Make use of community facilities.

Passage Three

Questions 32 to 35 are based on the passage you have just heard.

32. A) Health and safety conditions in the workplace.

   B) Rights and responsibilities of company employees.

   C) Common complaints made by office workers.

   D) Conflicts between labor and management.

33. A) Replace its out-dated equipments.

   B) Improve the welfare of affected workers.

   C) Follow the government regulations strictly.

   D) Provide extra health compensation.

34. A) They requested to transfer to a safer department.

   B) They quit work to protect their unborn babies.

   C) They sought help from union representatives.

   D) They wanted to work shorter hours.

35. A) To show how they love winter sports.

   B) To attract the attention from the media.

   C) To protect against the poor working conditions.

   D) To protect themselves against the cold weather.

Section C

> Directions: *In this section, you will hear a passage three times. When the passage is read for the first time, you should listen carefully for its general idea. When the passage is read for the second time, you are required to fill in the blanks numbered from 36 to 43 with the exact words you have just heard. For blanks numbered from 44 to 46 you are required to fill in the missing information. For these blanks, you can either use the exact words you have just heard or write down the main points in your own words. Finally, when the passage is read for the third time, you should check what you have written.*

注意：此部分试题请在答题卡2上作答。

Contrary to the old warning that time waits for no one, time slows down when you are on the move. It also slows down more as you move faster, which means astronauts（宇航员）someday may (36) so long in space that they would return to an Earth of the (37) future.

If you could move at the speed of light, your time would stand still. If you could move faster than light, your time would move (38).

Although no form of matter yet (39) moves as fast as or faster than light, (40) experiments have already confirmed that accelerated (41) causes a traveler's time to be stretched. Albert Einstein (42) this in 1905, when he (43) the concept of relative time as part of his Special Theory of Relativity. A search is now under way to confirm the suspected existence of particles of matter (44)_____

_____.

An obsession（沉迷）with time-saving, gaining, wasting, losing, and mastering it—(45) _____

_____. Humanity also has been obsessed with trying to capture the meaning of time. Einstein (46) _____

_____. Thus, time and time's relativity are measurable by any hourglass, alarm clock, or an atomic clock that can measure a billionth of a second.

听力原稿及答案

Section A

11. M: Shawn's been trying for months to find a job. But I wonder how he could get a job when he looks like that.

W: Oh, that poor guy! He really should shave himself every other day at least and put on something clean.

Q: What do we learn about Shawn?

答案：**A.** He is careless about his appearance.

解析：从I wonder推断出男士对肖恩能否找到工作表示怀疑，因为他邋遢。女士接着提到肖恩应该每隔一天刮一次胡子，把自己弄得整洁干净一点。由此可知，肖恩是一个对外表不太注重，比较粗线条的人。be careless about不在乎，不介意，故选A。

12. W: I wish Jane would call when she know she'll be late. This is not the first time we've had to wait for her.

M: I agree. But she does have to drive through very heavy traffic to get here.

Q: What does the man imply?

答案：**A.** Jane maybe caught in a traffic jam.

解析：女士说："Jane已经不是第一次迟到让我们等了，我希望她能事先打电话告诉我们一下"，可见女士对Jane迟到的作法是不满的。男生又说："I agree. But she does have to drive through very heavy traffic to get here." "我同意。但是她到这里的确要遭受很拥堵的交通"。由此得出，男生对此事的态度是理解或宽容的。Jane可能被堵在半路了，故选A。

13. M: Congratulations! I heard your baseball team is going to the Middle Atlantic Championship.

W: Yeah, we're all working real hard right now!

Q: What is the woman's team doing?

答案：**A.** Training for the Mid-Atlantic Championship.

解析：对话开头男士提到女生所在的棒球队要参加Mid-Atlantic Championship.女士说："we're all working real hard right now!""我们现在正在加紧练习呢！"由此可知，女生所在的棒球队正在进行赛前训练。此题还有一个迷惑选项B，因开头的"Mid-Atlantic" 故选A。

14. W: John's been looking after his mother in the hospital. She was injured in a car accident two weeks ago and still in critical condition.

   M: Oh, that's terrible. And you know his father passed away last year.

   Q: What do we learn about John?

答案：**D.** He has been having a hard time.

解析：根据听力原文可知，"John's mother is in the hospital and his father died last year." "约翰的母亲出车祸住院了，父亲一年前也过世了。"由此可知，John的近况很悲惨，故选D。

15. M: What a boring speaker! I can hardly stay awake.

   W: Well, I don't know. In fact, I think it's been a long time since I've heard anyone is good.

   Q: What do we learn from the conversation?

答案：**D.** The woman thinks highly of the speaker

解析：根据听力原文可知，男士觉得演讲无趣，女士却说："其实我已经很久没有听到那么好的发言了"。由此可见，女士对发言还是很肯定的，故选D。

16. W: I'm having a lot of trouble with logic and it seems my professor can't explain it in a way that makes sense to me.

   M: You know, there is a tutoring service on campus. I was about to drop statistics before they helped me out.

   Q: What does the man mean?

答案：**C.** The woman should seek help from tutoring services.

解析：女士说她学逻辑学有点吃力，接受不了老师的讲课方式也理解不了课程内容。而男士说学校有辅导班，他在参加之前几乎要挂科了，辅导班帮了他大忙。暗含的意思是推荐女士也去上辅导班，故选C。

17. M: This is a stylish overcoat. I saw you wearing it last week, didn't I?

   W: Oh, that wasn't me. That was my sister Jill. She's in your class.

   Q: What does the woman mean?

答案：**C.** Jill wore the overcoat last week.

解析：男士问女士上周是否穿过拉风外套，女生回答说："That was my sister

Jill. She's in your class." "那是我姐姐Jill，她和你同班。" 也就是那个穿着拉风外套的人是女生的姐姐Jill，故选C。

18. M: Jane, suppose you lost all your money while taking a vacation overseas, what would you do?

   W: Well, I guess I'd sell my watch or computer or do some odd jobs till I could afford a return plane ticket.

   Q: What are the speakers talking about?

答案：**B**. An imaginary situation.

解析：男士说："Jane, suppose you lost all your money while taking a vacation overseas, what would you do?" 这里的"suppose"表明"假定、料想"，由此可见，两人谈论的是一个虚拟场景，故选B。

Conversation One

听力原文

M: Hello, professor Johnson.

W: Hello, Tony. So what shall we work on today?

M: Well, the problem is that this writing assignment isn't coming out right. What I thought I was writing on was to talk about what particular sport means to me when I participate in.

W: What sport did you choose?

M: I decided to write about cross-country skiing.

W: What are you going to say about skiing?

M: That's the problem. I thought I would write about how peaceful it is to be out in the country.

W: So why is that a problem?

M: As I start describing how quiet it is to be out in the woods. I keep mentioning how much effort it takes to keep going. Cross-country skiing isn't as easy as some people think. It takes a lot of energy, but that's not part of my paper. So I guess I should leave it out. But now I don't know how to explain that feeling of peacefulness without explaining how hard you have to work for it. It all fits together. It's not like just sitting down somewhere and watching the clouds roll by. That's different.

W: Then you'll have to include that in your point. The peacefulness of cross-country skiing is the kind you earn by effort. Why leave that out? Part of your point you knew before hand but part you discovered as you wrote. That's common, right?

M: Yeah, I guess so.

Questions 19 to 21 are based on the conversation you have just heard.

19) What is the topic of the man's writing assignment?

20) What problem does the man have while working on his paper?

21) What does the woman say is common in writing papers?

19. **D**) A sport he participates in

解析：题目问的是，男生论文的主题是什么?从talk about what particular sport means to me when I participate in一句中，可得对应选项D。

20. **D**) He can't decide whether to include the effort part of skiing.

解析：当男生打算将越野滑雪的艰辛剔除出论文时，教授说了一句"Then you'll have to include that in your point."，故选D。

21. **A**) New ideas come up as you write.

解析：在对话的最后，教授提到"Part of your point you knew before hand but part you discovered as you wrote. That's common, right?" 这句话意思是说，在写论文之前，论点的一部分我们已经有了，但另一部分在写的过程中才会发现，故选A。

Conversation Two

W: Good evening and welcome to this week's Business World. It program for and about business people. Tonight we have Mr. Angeleno who came to the US six years ago, and is now an established businessman with three restaurants in town. Tell us Mr. Angeleno, how did you get started?

M: Well I started off with a small diner. I did all the cooking myself and my wife waited on tables. It was really too much work for two people. My cooking is great. And word got around town about the food. Within a year, I had to hire another cook and four waitresses. When that restaurant became very busy, I decided to expand my business. Now with three places my main concern is keeping the business successful and running smoothly.

W: Do you advertise?

M: Oh yes. I don't have any TV commercials, because they are too expensive. But I advertise a lot on radio and in local newspapers. My children used to distribute ads. in nearby shopping centres, but we don't need to do that anymore.

W: Why do you believe you've been so successful?

M: Em, I always serve the freshest possible food and I make the atmosphere as comfortable and as pleasant as I can, so that my customers will want to come back.

W: So you always aim to please the customers?

M: Absolutely! Without them I would have no business at all.

W: Thank you Mr. Angeleno. I think your advice will be helpful to those just staring out in business.

Questions 23 to 25 are based on the conversation you have just heard.

22. What is the woman's occupation?

23. What do we learn about Mr. Angeleno's business at its beginning?

24. What does Mr. Angeleno say about advertising his business?

25. What does the man say contribute to his success?

22. **D**) Hostess of the weekly "Business World"

解析：从对话中可以听出，这是一个访谈节目，因此这个女士是节目主持人，故选D。

23. **B**) He and his wife did everything by themselves.

解析：题目问的是，刚开始的时候，Angeleno的生意怎么样？对话中提到，I did all the cooking myself and my wife waited on tables. Angeleno负责做菜，他妻子负责接待，故选B。

24. **B**) He advertises a lot on radio and in newspapers.

解析：从But I advertise a lot on radio and in local newspapers. 一句中，可知正确选项是B。

25. **B**) The restaurant atmosphere

解析：题目问的是，什么有助于餐厅的成功？对话中提到，I always serve the freshest possible food and I make the atmosphere as comfortable and as pleasant as I can, so that my customers will want to come back. 可见，Angeleno会提供尽可能新鲜的食物和舒适的用餐环境以吸引顾客，故选B。

Section B
Passage One

There are many commonly held beliefs about eye glasses and eyesight that are not proven facts. For instance, some people believe that wearing glasses too soon weakens the eyes. But there is no evidence to show that the structure of eyes is changed by wearing glasses at a young age. Wearing the wrong glasses, however, can prove harmful. Studies show that for adults there is no danger, but children can develop loss of vision if they have glasses inappropriate for their eyes. We have all heard some of the common myths about how eyesight gets bad. Most people believe that reading in dim light causes poor eyesight, but that is untrue. Too little light makes the eyes work harder, so they do get tired and strained. Eyestrain also results from reading a lot, reading in bed, and watching too much television. However, although eyestrain may cause some pain or headaches, it does not permanently damage eyesight.

Another myth about eyes is that they can be replaced, or transferred from one person to another. There are close to one million nerve fibres that connect the eyeball to the brain, as of yet it is impossible to attach them all in a new person. Only certain parts of the eye can be replaced. But if we keep clearing up the myths and learning more about the eyes, some day a full transplant may be possible.

Questions 26 to 28 are based on the passage you have just heard.

26. What does the speaker want to tell us about eyesight?

27. What do studies about wearing the wrong glasses show?

28.What do we learn about eye transplanting from the talk?

26. 答案：**C**) There are many false notions about it.

解析：从"eyesight" 可以把答案定位于第一句，关键词有"many commonly held beliefs" "that are not proven facts"，故选C。

27. 答案：**C**) It can lead to the loss of vision in children.

解析：本题关键词是"studies" "wearing the wrong glasses". 文章中第二句中关键词很明显："weakens the eyes"，故选C。

28.答案：**D**) It can only be partly accomplished now.

解析：本题关键词"eye transplanting"，迅速定位于听力后面部分。文章最后部分提到"Only certain parts of the eye can be replaced" "Only certain parts of the eye can be replaced", 故选D。

Passage Two

When people care for an elderly relative, they often do not use available community services such as adult daycare centers. If the caregivers are adult children, they are more likely to use such services, especially because they often have jobs and other responsibilities. In contrast, a spouse usually the wife, is much less likely to use support services or to put the dependent person in a nursing home. Social workers discover that the wife normally tries to take care of her husband herself for as long as she can in order not to use up their life savings. Researchers have found that caring for the elderly can be a very positive experience. The elderly appreciated the care and attention they received. They were affectionate and cooperative. However, even when caregiving is satisfying, it is hard work. Social workers and experts on aging offer caregivers and potential caregivers help when arranging for the care of an elderly relative. One consideration is to ask parents what they want before they become sick or dependent. Perhaps they prefer going into a nursing home and can select one in advance. On the other hand, they may want to live with their adult children. Caregivers must also learn to state their needs and opinions clearly and ask for help from others especially brothers and sisters. Brothers and sisters are often willing to help, but they may not know what to do

Questions 29 to 32 are based on the passage you have just heard.

29. Why are adult children more likely to use community services to help care for elderly parents?

30. Why are most wives unwilling to put their dependent husbands into nursing homes?

31. According to the passage, what must caregivers learn to do?

29. 答案：**D**) They have jobs and other commitments.

解析：细节题。本题询问原因，文章开头很快就给出了本题答案"because they often have jobs and other responsibilities." 注意D选项中的commitments的意思是"承诺，保证；承担义务" 和responsibilities意思相近，故选D。

30. 答案：**A**) They don't want to use up all their life savings.

解析：根据关键词"wives" "husbands"，可以在文章第七行直接找出答案 "in order not to use up their life savings"。故选A。

31. 答案：**B**) Be frank and seek help from others.

解析：关键词"caregivers" "learn to do"，问看护人应该要学会做的事情，然后迅速定位于最后部分，"One consideration is to ask..."，"Caregivers must also learn to state..." 主要有两件事情，只有B选项正确。

Passage Three

Since a union representative visited our company to inform us about our rights and protections. My coworkers have been worrying about health conditions and complaining about safety hazards in the workplace. Several of the employees in the computer department, for example, claim to be developing vision problems from having to stare at a video display terminal for about 7 hours a day. The supervisor of the laboratory is beginning to get headaches and dizzy spells because she says it's dangerous to breathe some of the chemical smoke there. An X-rays technician is refusing to do her job until the firm agrees to replace its out-dated equipment. She insists that it's exposing workers to unnecessarily high doses of radiation. She thinks that she may have to contact the Occupational Safety and Health Administration and asked that government agency to inspect the department. I've heard that at a factory in the area two pregnant women who were working with paint requested a transfer to a safer department, because they wanted to prevent damage to their unborn babies. The supervisor of personnel refused the request. In another firm the workers were constantly complaining about the malfunctioning heating system, but the owners was too busy or too mean to do anything about it. Finally, they all met an agree to wear ski-clothing to work the next day. The owner was too embarrassed to talk to his employees. But he had the heating system replaced right away.

Questions 32–35 are based on the passage you have just heard.
32. What does the talk focus on?
33. What did the X-ray technician ask her company to do?
34. What does the speaker say about the two pregnant women working with paint?
35. Why did the workers in the firm wear ski-clothing to work?

32. 答案：**A**) Health and safety conditions in workplace.
解析：本题比较简单，了解了文章主要内容后，就可以直接选出答案。

33. 答案：**A**) Replace its out-dated equipments.
解析：细节题。从文章的第七行"An X-rays technician is refusing... replace its out-dated equipment"一句可得出答案为A。

34. 答案：**A**) They requested to transfer to a safer department.
解析：细节题。文章倒数第八行"I've heard... a safer department "一句可得出答案。

35. 答案：**C**) To protest against the poor working conditions.
解析：推理题。通过"too embarrassed" "had the heating system replaced right away"从老板的反应及采取的措施可以推断出，员工们穿滑雪服的原因其实是对差的工作环境向老板提出抗议，故选C。

Section C Compound Dictation

Contrary to the old warning that time waits for no one, time slows down when you are on the move. It also slows down more as you move faster, which means astronauts（宇航员）someday may survive so long in space that they would return to an earth of the distant future.

If you could move at the speed of light, your time would stand still, if you could move faster than light, your time would move backward.

　　Although no form of matter yet discovered, moves as fast as or faster than light, scientific experiments has already confirmed that accelerated motion causes a traveler's time to be stretched. Albert Einstein predicted this in 1905, when he introduced the concept of relative time as part of his Special Theory of Relativity. A search is now under way to confirm the suspected existence of particles of matter that move at a speed greater than light, and therefore, might serve as our passports to the past. An obsession with time-saving, gaining, wasting, losing and mastering it— seems to have been a part of humanity for as long as humans have existed. Humanity also has been obsessed with trying to capture the meaning of time. Einstein used a definition of time for experimental purposes, as that which is measured by a clock. Thus time and time's relativity are measurable by any hour glass, alarm clock, or an atomic clock that can measure a billionth of a second.

36. survive
解析：根据文章内容我们知道，运动越快，时间变得越慢，这也就意味着宇航员有朝一日可以在太空中生存很久，因此这个空填survive。

37. distant
解析：这个空后面紧跟的单词是future，所以预判该填形容词。而常用搭配无非near, close, distant等，根据听力原文，确定是遥远的未来，因此这个空填distant。

38. backward
解析：根据常识我们可以推断，若速度快于光速，那么时间将后退，即move backward，因此这个空填backward。

39. discovered
解析：空缺部分作后置定语，从音频可知这个空填discovered，并用过去分词形式，表被动。

40. scientific
解析：该空后接名词experiments，所以应为形容词，从整篇文章推断，scientific最合适。

41. motion
解析：根据原文内容，实验已证明运动加快会使宇航员的时间延长，这里的运动为motion。

42. predicted

解析：因为爱因斯坦是在1905年时作出预测，所以该用过去式predicted。

43. introduced

解析：这是爱因斯坦提出的一个相对时间的概念，所以该用过去式introduced。

44. that move at a speed greater than light, and therefore, might serve as our passports to the past.

解析：整句汉语意思：当下进行的研究旨在证实，是否有这样的物质，它能以超光速运行，并可以作为我们回归过去的"通行证"。意思大概对上即可，无固定答案。

45. seems to have been a part of humanity for as long as humans have existed.

解析：整句汉语意思：人类对时间的节约，获取，浪费以及流失等的着迷，自人类诞生以来就一直是其生活的一部分。意思大概对上即可，无固定答案。

46. used a definition of time for experimental purposes, as that which is measured by a clock.

解析：整句汉语意思：人类也对时间的含义非常着迷，爱因斯坦就曾提出一个试验性的定义，这个定义下的时间可以用钟表来测量。意思大概对上即可，无固定答案。

下面是2010年6月份的大学英语四级听力考试题目

Section A

> Directions: *In this section, you will hear 8 short conversations and 2 long conversations. At the end of each conversation, one or more questions will be asked about what was said. Both the conversation and the questions will be spoken only once. After each question there will be a pause. During the pause, you must read the four choices marked A), B), C) and D), and decide which is the best answer. Then mark the corresponding letter on Answer Sheet 2 with a single line through the centre.*

注意：此部分试题请在答题卡2上作答。

11. A) He has proved to be a better reader than the woman.

　　B) He has difficulty understanding the book.

　　C) He cannot get access to the assigned book.

　　D) He cannot finish his assignment before the deadline.

12. A) She will drive the man to the supermarket.

　　B) The man should buy a car of his own.

C) The man needn't go shopping every week.

D) She can pick the man up at the grocery store.

13. A) Get more food and drinks.

B) Ask his friend to come over.

C) Tidy up the place.

D) Hold a party.

14. A) The talks can be held any day except this Friday.

B) He could change his schedule to meet John Smith.

C) The first-round talks should start as soon as possible.

D) The woman should contact John Smith first.

15. A) He understands the woman's feelings.

B) He has gone through a similar experience.

C) The woman should have gone on the field trip.

D) The teacher is just following the regulations.

16. A) She will meet the man halfway.

B) She will ask David to talk less.

C) She is sorry the man will not come.

D) She has to invite David to the party.

17. A) Few students understand Prof. Johnson's lectures.

B) Few students meet Prof. Jonson's requirements.

C) Many students find Prof. Johnson's lectures boring.

D) Many students have dropped Prof. Johnson's class.

18. A) Check their computer files.

B) Make some computations.

C) Study a computer program.

D) Assemble a computer.

Questions 19 to 22 are based on the conversation you have just heard.

19. A) It allows him to make a lot of friends.

B) It requires him to work long hours.

C) It enables him to apply theory to practice.

D) It helps him understand people better.

20. A) It is intellectually challenging.

    B) It requires him to do washing-up all the time.

    C) It exposes him to oily smoke all day long.

    D) It demands physical endurance and patience.

21. A) In a hospital.

    B) At a coffee shop.

    C) At a laundry.

    D) In a hotel.

22. A) Getting along well with colleagues.

    B) Paying attention to every detail.

    C) Planning everything in advance.

    D) Knowing the needs of customers.

Questions 23 to 25 are based on the conversation you have just heard.

23. A) The pocket money British children get.

    B) The annual inflation rate in Britain.

    C) The things British children spend money on.

    D) The rising cost of raising a child in Britain.

24. A) It enables children to live better.

    B) It goes down during economic recession.

    C) It often rises higher than inflation.

    D) It has gone up 25% in the past decade.

25. A) Save up for their future education.

    B) Pay for small personal things.

    C) Buy their own shoes and socks.

    D) Make donations when necessary.

Section B

> Directions: *In this section, you will hear 3 short passages. At the end of each passage, you will hear some questions. Both the passage and the questions will be spoken only once. After you hear a question, you must choose the best answer from the four choices marked A), B), C) and D). Then mark the corresponding letter on Answer Sheet 2 with a single line through the centre.*

注意：此部分试题请在答题卡2上作答。

Passage One

Questions 26 to 28 are based on the conversation you have just heard.

26. A) District managers.

    B) Regular customers.

    C) Sales dircctors.

    D) Senior clerks.

27. A) The support provided by the regular clients.

    B) The initiative shown by the sales representatives.

    C) The urgency of implementing the company's plans.

    D) The important part played by district managers.

28. A) Some of them were political-minded.

    B) Fifty percent of them were female.

    C) One third of them were senior managers.

    D) Most of them were rather conservative.

29. A) He used too many quotations.

    B) He was not gender sensitive.

    C) He did not keep to the point.

    D) He spent too much time on details.

Passage Two

Questions 30 to 32 are based on the passage you have just heard.

30. A) State your problem to the head waiter.

    B) Demand a discount on the dishes ordered.

    C) Ask to see the manager politely but firmly.

    D) Ask the name of the person waiting on you.

31. A) Your problem may not be understood correctly.
    B) You don't know if you are complaining at the right time.
    C) Your complaint may not reach the person in charge.
    D) You can't tell how the person on the line is reacting.

32. A) Demand a prompt response.
    B) Provide all the details.
    C) Send it by express mail.
    D) Stick to the point.

Passage Three
Questions 33 to 35 are based on the passage you have just heard.

33. A) Fashion designer
    B) Architect.
    C) City planner.
    D) Engineer.

34. A) Do some volunteer work.
    B) Get a well-paid part-time job.
    C) Work flexible hours.
    D) Go back to her previous post.

35. A) Few baby-sitters can be considered trustworthy.
    B) It will add to the family's financial burden.
    C) A baby-sitter is no replacement for a mother.
    D) The children won't get along with a baby-sitter.

Section C

Directions: *In this section, you will hear a passage three times. When the passage is read for the first time, you should listen carefully for its general idea. When the passage is read for the second time, you are required to fill in the blanks numbered from 36 to 43 with the exact words you have just heard. For blanks numbered from 44 to 46 you are required to fill in the missing information. For these blanks, you can either use the exact words you have just heard or write down the main points in your own words. Finally, when the passage is read for the third time, you should check what you have written.*

注意：此部分试题请在答题卡2上作答。

Almost every child, on the first day he sets foot in a school building, is smarter, more (36) _____, less afraid of what he doesn't know, better in finding and (37) _____ things out, more confident, resourceful（机敏的）, persistent and (38) _____than he will ever be again in his schooling or, unless he is very (39) _____ and very lucky for the rest of his life. Already, by paying close attention to and (40) _____ with the world and people around him, and without any school-type (41) _____instruction, he has done a task far more difficult, complicated and (42) _____ than anything he will be asked to do in school or than any of his teachers has done for years. He has solved the (43) _____of language. He has discovered it Babies do not even know that language exists and (44) _____He has done it by exploring, by experimenting, by developing his own model of the grammar of language, (45) _____ _____until it does work. And while he has been doing this, he has been learning other things as well, (46) _____ _____and many that are more complicated than the ones they do try to teach him.

听力原稿及答案：

Section A

11. W: Just imagine we have to finish reading 300 pages before Monday, how can the professor expect us to do it in such a short time?

M: Yeah, but what troubles me is that I can't find the book in the library or in the university bookstore.

Q: what does the man mean?

答案：**C**) He cannot get access to the assigned book.

解析：根据对话我们知道，该男士认为令他烦恼的是无论在图书馆还是在书店他都找不到那本书，故选C。

12. M: Do you think I could borrow your car to go grocery shopping? The supermarkets outside the city are so much cheaper. I'd also be happy to pick up anything you need.

W: Wow, I don't like to let anyone else to drive my car. Tell you what, why don't we go together?

Q: What does the woman mean?

答案：**A**) She will drive the man to the supermarket.

解析：根据对话我们知道，女士不喜欢别人开她的车。由 why don't we go

together?可知女士将开车与男士一同去超市，故选A。

13. M: Forgive the mess in here. We had a party last night. There were a lot of people and they all brought food.

    W: Yeah, I can tell. Well, I guess it's pretty obvious what you'll be doing most of today.

    Q: What does the woman think the man will do?

答案：**C**) Tidy up the place.

解析：根据I guess it's pretty obvious what you'll be doing most of today可知，女士想让他打扫房间，故选C。

14. W: What time would suit you for the first round talks with John Smith?

    M: Well, you know my schedule. Other than this Friday, one day is as good as the next.

    Q: What does the man mean?

答案：**A**) The talks can be held any day except this Friday.

解析：one day is as good as the next的意思是"任何一天都行"，因此男士的意思是除了本周五，其它任何一天都可以，故选A。

15. W: I was so angry yesterday. My biology teacher did not even let me explain why I missed the field trip. He just wouldn't let me pass.

    M: That doesn't seem fair. I'd feel that way too if I were you.

    Q: What does the man imply?

答案：**A**) He understands the woman's feelings.

解析：从"I'd feel that way too if I were you. "可知男士认为，如果他是那位女士的话他也会那样。因此他赞同女士的想法，表示理解女士的感受，故选A。

16. M: I really can't stand the way David controls the conversation all the time. If he's going to be at your Christmas party, I just won't come.

    W: I'm sorry you feel that way. But my mother insists that he come.

    Q: What does the woman imply?

答案： **D**) She has to invite David to the party.

解析：从文中女士的话我们知道，女士的母亲执意要David去参加圣诞party，因此她不得不请David，故选D。

17. W: You're taking a course with Professor Johnson. What's your impression so far?

    M: Well, many students can hardly stay awake in his class without first drinking a cup of coffee.

Q: What does the man imply?

答案：**C**) Many students find Prof. Johnson's lectures boring.

解析：由男士的话我们知道，很多同学如果课前没喝咖啡的话，几乎很难保持清醒状态，忍不住犯困，可见Prof. Johnson的课很无聊，故选C。

18. W: Have you ever put a computer together before?

    M: No, never. But I think if we follow these instructions exactly, we won't have much trouble.

    Q: What are the speakers going to do?

答案：**D**) Assemble a computer.

解析：assemble意为"组装，装配"，而"put a computer together"指"组装电脑"，故选D。

Conversation One

W: What sort of hours do you work, Steve?

M: Oh, I have to work very long hours, about 11 hours a day.

W: What time do you start?

M: I work 9 to 3. Then I start again at 5:30 and work until 11. Six days a week. So I have to work very unsocial hours.

W: And do you have to work at the weekend?

M: Oh, yes, that's our busiest time. I get Wednesdays off.

W: What are the things you have to do, and the things you don't have to do?

M: Eh, I don't have to do the washing-up, so that's good. I have to wear white and I have to keep everything in the kitchen totally clean.

W: What's hard about the job?

M: You're standing up all the time. When we're busy, people get angry and sharp. But that's normal.

W: How did you learn the profession?

M: Well, I did a two year course at college. In the first year, we had to learn the basics. And then we had to take the exams.

W: Was it easy to find a job?

M: I wrote to about six hotels. And one of them gave me my first job. So I didn't have to wait too long.

W: And what's the secret of being good at your job?

M: Attention to detail and you have to love it. You have to show passion for it. And what are your plans for the future?

M: I want to have my own place when the time is right.

Questions 19 to 22 are based on the conversation you have just heard.

19. What does the man say about his job?

20. What does the man think is the hardest part of his job?

21. Where did the man get his first job after graduation?

22. What does the man say is important to being good at his job?

19. **B)** It requires him to work long hours.

解析：一开始男士便说I have to work very long hours，故选B。

20. **D)** It demands physical endurance and patience.

解析：当女士问及工作哪个部分会比较难时，男士回答说他需要一直站着，同时在他们忙的时候，别人会变得易怒，也就是说这份工作需要体力和耐心，故选D。

21. **D)** In a hotel.

解析：由文中I wrote to about six hotels and one of them gave me my first job可知正确答案为D。

22. **B)** Paying attention to every detail.

解析：由男士的回答Attention to detail可知，B选项为正确答案。

Conversation Two

W: Now you've seen this table of figures about the pocket money children in Britain get?

M: Yes. I thought it was quite interesting, but I don't quite understand the column entitled "change". Can you explain what it means?

W: Well, I think it means the change from the year before. I'm not a mathematician, but I assume the rise from 72p to 90p, is the rise of 25%.

M: Oh, yes, I see. And the inflation rate is there for comparison.

W: Yes. Why do you think the rise in pocket money is often higher than inflation?

M: I'm sorry, I've no idea. Perhaps parents in Britain are too generous.

W: Perhaps they are. But it looks as if children were a lot better off in 2001 than they were in 2002. That's strange, isn't it? And they seemed to have been better off in 2003 than they are now. I wonder why that is.

M: Yes, I don't understand that at all.

W: Anyway, if you had children, how much pocket money would you give them?

M: I don't know. I think I probably give them two pounds a week.

W: Would you? And what would you expect them to do with it?

M: Well, out of that they have to buy some small personal things. But I wouldn't expect them to save to buy their own socks for example.

W: Yes. By the way, do most children in your country get pocket money?

M: Yeah, they do.

Questions 23 to question 25 are based on the conversation you have just heard.

23. What is the table of figures about?

24. What do we learn from the conversation about British children's pocket money?

25. Supposing the man had children, what would he expect them to do with their pocket money?

23. **A**) The pocket money British children get.

解析：根据第一句话Now you've seen this table of figures about the pocket money children in Britain get? 我们可以知道这个表格是关于英国孩子的零花钱情况的。

24. **C**) It often rises higher than inflation.

解析：原文中女士说"Why do you think the rise in pocket money is often higher than inflation?"意思是： "你觉得为什么零花钱通常要比通货膨胀涨的更高呢？ " 据此我们可以判断英国孩子的零花钱比通货膨胀涨的更高，故选C。

25. **B**) Pay for small personal things.

解析：原文中男士说"...out of that, they have to buy some small personal things, but I wouldn't expect them to save to buy their own socks, for example."意思是 "我希望他们用零花钱去买一些小的个人物品，但我不希望他们把钱存起来去买他们自己的短袜等"，故选B。

Section B
Passage One

As the new sales director for a national computer firm, Alex Gordon was looking forward to his first meeting with the company's district managers. Every one arrived on time and Alex's presentation went extremely well. He decided to end the meeting with a conversation about the importance of the district managers to the company's plans. "I believe we're going to continue to increase our share of the market", he began, "Because of the quality of the people in this room. The district manager is the key to the success of the sales representatives in his district. He sets the tone for everyone else. If he has ambitious goals and is willing to put in long hours, everyone in his unit will follow his example." When Alex was finished, he received polite applause but hardly the warm response he had hoped for. Later, he spoke with one of the senior managers. "Things were going so well until the end", Alex said disappointedly, "Obviously I said the wrong thing." "Yes", the district manager replied, " Half of our managers are women. Most have worked the way up from sales representatives and they are very proud of the role they've played in the company's growth. They don't care at all about the political correctness but they are definitely surprised and distressed to be referred to as "he" in your speech."

Questions 26 to 29 are based on the passage you have just heard.

26. Who did Alex Gordon speak to at the first meeting?

27. What did Alex want to emphasize at the end of his presentation?

28. What do we learn about the audience at the meeting?

29. Why did Alex fail to receive the warm response he had hoped for?

26. **A)** District managers

解析：原文开头说到Alex期盼着与district managers的会议，故选A。

27. **D)** The important part played by district managers

解析：原文中提到，Alex打算以 "the conversation about the importance of the district managers to the company plans" 来结束会议，可见他打算强调district managers在公司计划中所起的重要作用，故选A。

28. **B)** Fifty percent of them were female

解析：原文后面提到 "Half of our managers are women"，而参加会议的基本上都是district managers，由此可判断，会议的听众有一半是女性，故选B。

29. **B)** He was not gender sensitive

解析：文章最后一句说这些女性district managers听到Alex总用 "he" 来指代 "district managers" 感到surprised和distressed，由此可见Alex失败的原因是由于他对于涉及到性别的用词不够敏感所造成的，故选B。

Passage Two

The way to complain is to act business-like and important. If your complaint is immediate, suppose you got the wrong order at a restaurant, make a polite but firm request to see the manager. When the manager comes, ask his or her name and then state your problem, and what you expect to have done about it. Be polite. Shouting or acting rude will get you nowhere. But also be firm in making your complaint. Besides, act important. This doesn't mean to put on airs and say, "Do you know who I am?"

What it means is that people are often treated the way they expect to be treated. If you act like someone who expects a fair request be granted, chances are it will be granted. The worst way to complain is over the telephone. You are speaking to a voice coming from someone you can not see, so you can't tell how the person on the line is reacting. It is easy for that person to give you a run-around. Complaining in person or by letter is generally more effective. If your complaint does not require an immediate response, it often helps to complain by letter. If you have an appliance that doesn't work, send a letter to the store that sold it. Be business-like and stick to the point. Don't spend a paragraph on how your Uncle Joe tried to fix the problem and couldn't.

Questions 30 to 32 are based on the passage you have just heard.

30. What does the speaker suggest you do when you are not served properly at a restaurant?

31. Why does the speaker say the worst way to complain is over the telephone?

32. What should you do if you make a complaint by letter?

30. **C**) Ask to see the manager politely but firmly

解析：原文中提到在餐馆遇到上错菜时，应该"make a polite but firm request to see the manager",故选C。

31. **D**) You can't tell how the person on the line is reacting

解析：原文中提到"So you can't tell how the person on the line is reacting.",故选D。

32 . **D**) Stick to the point

解析：原文中提到"be business-like and stick to the point",即围绕自己的要点来说，而不要说些无关紧要的废话，故选D。

Passage Three

Barbara Santos is a wife and the mother of 2 children, ages 2 and 4. Her husband, Tom, is an engineer and makes an excellent salary. Before Barbara had children, she worked as an architect for the government, designing government housing. She quit her job when she became pregnant, but is now interested in returning to work. She's been offered an excellent job with the government. Her husband feels it's unnecessary for her to work since the family does not need the added income. He also thinks that a woman should stay home with her children. If Barbara feels the need to do socially important work, he thinks that she should do volunteer work one or two days a week. Barbara, on the other hand, has missed the excitement of her profession, and does not feel she would be satisfied doing volunteer work. She would also like to have her own income, so she does not have to ask her husband for money whenever she wants to buy something. She does not think it's necessary to stay at home every day with the children, and she knows a very reliable babysitter who's willing to come to her house. Tom does not think a babysitter can replace a mother, and thinks it's a bad idea for the children to spend so much time with someone who's not part of the family.

Questions 33 to 35 are based on the passage you have just heard.

33. What was Barbara's profession before she had children?

34. What does Barbara's husband suggest she do if she wants to work?

35. What does Tom think about hiring a babysitter?

33. B) Architect

解析：从原文"Before Barbara had children, she worked as an architect for the government, designing government housing"可知C为正确选项。

34. **A**) Do some volunteer work.

解析：从原文"If Barbara feels the need to do socially important work, he thinks that she should do volunteer work one or two days a week."可知C为正确选项。

35. **C**) A baby-sitter is no replacement for a mother.

解析：从原文"Tom does not think a baby-sitter can replace a mother"可知C为正确选项。

Section C Compound Dictation

Almost every child, on the first day he sets foot in the school building, is smarter, more curious, less afraid of what he doesn't know, better in finding and figuring things out, more confident, resourceful, persistent, and independent than he will ever be again in his schooling or unless he is very unusual and very lucky for the rest of his life. Already, by paying close attention to and interacting with the world and people around him, and without any school-type formal instruction, he has done a task far more difficult, complicated, and abstract than anything he will be asked to do in school or than any of his teachers have done for years. He has solved the mystery of language. He has discovered it. Babies do not even know that language exists and he has found out how it works and learned to use it appropriately. He has done it by exploring, by experimenting, by developing his own model of the grammar of language, by trying it out and seeing whether it works by gradually changing it and refining it until it does work. And while he has been doing this, he has been learning other things as well, including many of the concepts that the schools think only they can teach him and many that are more complicated than the ones they do try to teach him.

36. curious
37. figuring
38. independent
39. unusual
40. interacting
41. formal
42. abstract
43. mystery

44. and he has found out how it works and learned to use it appropriately
解析：意思大概对上即可，无固定答案。

45. by trying it out and seeing whether it works by gradually changing it and refining it
解析：意思大概对上即可，无固定答案。

46. including many of the concepts that the schools think only they can teach him
解析：意思大概对上即可，无固定答案。

Part IV Reading Comprehension (Reading in Depth) ⏱ (25 minutes)

在四级考试中，阅读理解做题时间为25分钟，包括两部分。一部分是选词填空题，即一篇长度为200单词左右的文章，考法是15选10的选词填空，考查考生对诸如连贯性、一致性、逻辑关系等语篇整体特征的理解以及单词在实际语境中的应用；另外一部分是篇章阅读题，包括2篇文章10道多项选择题。每篇文章的单词数在300–350之间，要求考生的阅读速度达到每分钟70词。下面我们就这两部分谈一下具体的做题技巧。

选词填空做题步骤：

一、阅读选项，按词性分类。选项中的15个单词是考查的关键，因此考生应该仔细理解这15个单词。熟悉单词后，再分别标明词性和词义。不熟悉或无法确定的单词，可以先搁置起来，并作出相应的标记。

二、跳读全文，抓住中心。由于仔细阅读考查的是考生对篇章的理解，因此在把词性分类后，应该略读整篇文章，确定文章的中心和主要说明的问题。

三、瞻前顾后，灵活选择。考生略读文章后，对文章意思已经有了大概的了解，这时候需要根据原文中空格前后的单词或者语句确定所要填的词性，然后从分类好的单词中选择出意思、语法都符合要求的最佳选项。解题时如果遇到复杂句式或涉及上下句的情况，需要理清句子的逻辑结构。

四、复读检查，谨慎调整。填空完成后，再次复读全文，检查上下文是否通顺、内在逻辑关系是否连贯、单词放在此处是否合适。如有问题，也需要谨慎地微调。

篇章阅读解题步骤：

一、快速浏览5个题目，划出标志词或关键词。在读文章前快速浏览题目，对5个题目有大概印象以便阅读时有侧重点。一般来说，对于本身已经明确其考查内容的题目，标志词和关键词是比较容易找到的，只看一下题干即可。

二、略读文章，适时做标记。略读时，先阅读第一段，因为第一段通常会告诉我们本文将要讨论的话题。然后阅读下面各段的第一句话，对每个段落的内容有个大概的了解。最后，阅读最后一段，以帮助我们对文章内容进行概括，或了解作者的评价、态度等。读的过程中，如果遇到关键词或标志词时，可以做出标记。另外，要关注考试原则句，即常出考点的地方。

三、解答试题，选定答案。根据试题中的标志词和关键词，找到试题在文章中对应的句子，并进行仔细阅读，然后对比四个选项，选出正确答案。通常情况下，正确选项就是文章对应句的同义改写。

下面是2011年6月份的大学英语四级精细阅读考试题目

Section A

> Directions: *In this section, there is a passage with ten blanks. You are required to select one word for each blank from a list of choices given in a word bank following the passage. Read the passage through carefully before making your choices. Each choice in the bank is identified by a letter. Please mark the corresponding letter for each item on Answer Sheet 2 with a single line through the centre. You may not use any of the words in the bank more than once.*

Questions 47 to 56 are based on the following passage.

The popular notion that older people need less sleep than younger adults is a myth, scientists said yesterday.

While elderly people _47_ to sleep for fewer hours than they did when they were younger, this has a(n) _48_ effect on their brain's performance and they would benefit from getting more, according to research.

Sean Drummond, a psychiatrist（心理医生）at the University of California, San Diego, said older people are more likely to suffer from broken sleep, while younger people are better at sleeping _49_ straight through the night.

More sleep in old age, however, is _50_ with better health, and most older people would feel better and more _51_ if they slept for longer periods, he said.

"The ability to sleep in one chunk（整块时间）overnight goes down as we age but the amount of sleep we need to _52_ well does not change," Dr Drummond told the American Association for the Advancement of Science conference in San Diego.

"It's _53_ a myth that older people need less sleep. The more healthy an older adult is, the more they sleep like they did when they were _54_ . Our data suggests that older adults would benefit from _55_ to get as much sleep as they did in their 30s. That's _56_ from person to person, but the amount of sleep we had at 35 is probably the same amount as we need at 75."

注意：此部分试题请在答题卡2上作答。

A) alert	I) formally
B) associated	J) function
C) attracting	K) mixed
D) cling	L) negative
E) continuing	M) sufficient
F) definitely	N) tend
G) different	O) younger
H) efficiently	

Section A

答案：

47. **N** tend

48. **L** negative

49. **H** efficiently

50. **B** associated

51. **A** alert

52. **J** function

53. **F** definitely

54. **O** younger

55. **E** continuing

56. **G** different

答案解析：

47. tend to 是固定搭配，表示"倾向于"，N符合句意。

48. 空格后是effect，前面是a(n)，因此该处需要填入一个形容词。题目给出的形容词有negative, sufficient, younger，根据语境，negative最为恰当，表示"少的睡眠时间对大脑的活动有负面的影响。"

49. 根据分析，该处应该填入一个副词，题目给出的副词有efficiently, definitely, formally. 前面提到，老年人在睡觉的时候更容易被打断，而后面的while有对比的意思，年轻人相比起来能获得更_____的睡眠，因此选用efficiently（有效率的）最为准确。

50. be associated with是固定搭配，表示"与……联系在一起"，本句话表示"更多的睡眠通常都与健康度联系在一起"。

51. 整句意思是，"如果他们能睡更长的时间，他们应该会感觉更好，更……"。该处应该填入一个褒义词，alert比较恰当，表示"更加警觉，机灵"。

52. 前后分析一下，此处应该填入一个动词，剩下的动词有cling, function. 整句话的意思是"当我们上了年纪的时候，我们一觉睡到天亮的能力下降了，但是，我们需要……的睡眠量并没有改变。"空格后的单词是well, cling一般与to连用，在这里并不合适，选用function最为适合。

53. 作者在首段已经提出这个观点是一个myth，那么显而易见最后一段中出现的myth是作为一种强调手段，应填入definitely。

54. 空格的前面是when they were...，"当他们年轻的时候"，应填入younger。

55. 本句的意思是"我们的数据显示老年人将从……获益"，空格的后面是"得到和他们在30多岁的时候能得到的睡眠一样多"。根据上下文意思，该处应填入"continuing"。

56. different from是固定搭配，表示"和……不同"。

Section B

Directions: *There are 2 passages in this section. Each passage is followed by some questions or unfinished statements. For each of them there are four choices marked A), B), C) and D). You should decide on the best choice and mark the corresponding letter on Answer Sheet 2 with a single line through the centre.*

Passage One

Questions 57 to 61 are based on the following passage.

Several recent studies have found that being randomly（随机地）assigned to a roommate of another race can lead to increased tolerance but also to a greater likelihood（可能性）of conflict.

Recent reports found that lodging with a student of a different race may decrease prejudice and compel students to engage in more ethnically diverse friendships.
An Ohio State University study also found that black students living with a white roommate saw higher academic success throughout their college careers. Researchers believe this may be caused by social pressure.

In a New York Times article, Sam Boakye—the only black student on his freshman year floor—said that "if you're surrounded by whites, you have something to prove." Researchers also observed problems resulting from pairing interracial students in residences.

According to two recent studies, randomly assigned roommates of different races are more likely to experience conflicts so strained that one roommate will move out.
An Indiana University study found that interracial roommates were three times as likely as two white roommates to no longer live together by the end of the semester.

Grace Kao, a professor at Penn said she was not surprised by the findings. "This may be the first time that some of these students have interacted, and lived, with someone of a different race," she said.

At Penn, students are not asked to indicate race when applying for housing.

"One of the great things about freshman housing is that, with some exceptions, the process throws you together randomly," said Undergraduate Assembly chairman Alec Webley. "This is the definition of integration."

"I've experienced roommate conflicts between interracial students that have both broken down stereotypes and reinforced stereotypes," said one Penn resident advisor (RA). The RA of two years added that while some conflicts "provided more multicultural acceptance and melding（融合），" there were also "jarring cultural confrontations."

The RA said that these conflicts have also occurred among roommates of the same race.

Kao said she cautions against forming any generalizations based on any one of the studies, noting that more background characteristics of the students need to be studied and explained.

注意：此部分试题请在答题卡2上作答。

57. What can we learn from some recent studies?

A) Conflicts between students of different races are unavoidable.

B) Students of different races are prejudiced against each other.

C) Interracial lodging does more harm than good.

D) Interracial lodging may have diverse outcomes.

58. What does Sam Boakye's remark mean?

A) White students tend to look down upon their black peers.

B) Black students can compete with their white peers academically.

C) Black students feel somewhat embarrassed among white peers during the freshman year.

D) Being surrounded by white peers motivates a black student to work harder to succeed.

59. What does the Indiana University study show?

A) Interracial roommates are more likely to fall out.

B) Few white students like sharing a room with a black peer.

C) Roommates of different races just don't get along.

D) Assigning students' lodging randomly is not a good policy.

60. What does Alec Webley consider to be the "definition of integration"?

A) Students of different races are required to share a room.

B) Interracial lodging is arranged by the school for freshmen.

C) Lodging is assigned to students of different races without exception.

D) The school randomly assigns roommates without regard to race.

61. What does Grace Kao say about interracial lodging?

A) It is unscientific to make generalizations about it without further study.

B) Schools should be cautious when making decisions about student lodging.

C) Students' racial background should be considered before lodging is assigned.

D) Experienced resident advisors should be assigned to handle the problems.

答案解析:

57. 答案：**D**. Interracial lodging may have diverse outcomes.

解析：题干中some recent studies提示答案定位在第一段第一句话。由此可知that后就是recent studies的内容，即being randomly assigned to a roommate of another race can lead to increased tolerance but also to a greater likelihood of conflict. 其中"being randomly assigned to a roommate of another race"对应了选项D中的 "interracial lodging"，"can...but also..."说明了interracial lodging是有利有弊的。因 此D选项符合文意。

58. 答案：**D**. Being surrounded by white peers motivates a black student to work harder to succeed.

解析：题干中出现的人名Sam Boakye提示答案定位在第三段第一句话。问题提问Sam Boakye的话是什么意思。通过定位可以找到Sam Boakye的那段话，即if you're surrounded by whites, you have something to prove. 这句话前面的插入语the only black student on his freshman year floor介绍了Sam Boakye作为黑人学生的背景，帮助我们理解了之前那句话：如果你的周围都是白人，那么你一定会去证明些什么，言下之意就是选项D："白人同伴的存在会激励黑人学生更加努力地去取得成功"。

59. 答案：**A**. Interracial roommates are more likely to fall out.

解析：题干中出现的机构名称Indian University提示答案定位在第四段第一句话。问题提问Indian University的研究显示了什么。通过定位可以发现研究结果显示Interracial roommate were three times as likely as two white roommates to no longer live together，与选项A中的more likely to fall out 对应，因此选择D。此处，fall out 应该理解为"散伙，分开"。

60. 答案：**D**. The school randomly assigns roommates without regard to race.

解析：题干中出现的人名Alec Webley提示答案定位在第七段第一句。通过定位找到人名，人名后出现"This is the definition of integration"，由"this"可知人名前就是我们要找的答案，即the process throws you together randomly，"throw you together randomly"与"randomly assign"对应。意思与选项D符合，故选D。

61.答案：**A**. It is unscientific to make generalizations about it without further study.

解析：题干中出现的人名Grace Kao以及generalizations提示答案定位在文章最后一段。根据最后一段意思：要得出Interracial lodging的一般规律，需要对学生的背景特征有更多的研究，与选项D的意思相同。

Passage Two
Questions 62 to 66 are based on the following passage.

Global warming is causing more than 300,000 deaths and about $125 billion in economic losses each year, according to a report by the Global Humanitarian Forum, an organization led by Annan, the former United Nations secretary general.

The report, to be released Friday, analyzed data and existing studies of health, disaster, population and economic trends. It found that human-influenced climate change was raising the global death rates from illnesses including malnutrition（营养不良）and heat-related health problems.

But even before its release, the report drew criticism from some experts on climate and risk, who questioned its methods and conclusions.

Along with the deaths, the report said that the lives of 325 million people, primarily in poor countries, were being seriously affected by climate change. It projected that the number would double by 2030.

Roger Pielke Jr., a political scientist at the University of Colorado, Boulder, who studies disaster trends, said the Forum's report was "a methodological embarrassment" because there was no way to distinguish deaths or economic losses related to human-driven global warming amid the much larger losses resulting from the growth in populations and economic development in vulnerable（易受伤害的）regions. Dr. Pielke said that "climate change is an important problem requiring our utmost attention." But the report, he said, "will harm the cause for action on both climate change and disasters because it is so deeply flawed（有瑕疵的）."

However, Soren Andreasen, a social scientist at Dalberg Global Development Partners who supervised the writing of the report, defended it, saying that it was clear that the numbers were rough estimates. He said the report was aimed at world leaders, who will meet in Copenhagen in December to negotiate a new international climate treaty.

In a press release describing the report, Mr. Annan stressed the need for the negotiations to focus on increasing the flow of money from rich to poor regions to help reduce their vulnerability to climate hazards while still curbing the emissions of the heat-trapping gases. More than 90% of the human and economic losses from climate change are occurring in poor countries, according to the report.

62. What is the finding of the Global Humanitarian Forum?

    A) Global temperatures affect the rate of economic development.

    B) Rates of death from illnesses have risen due to global warming.

    C) Malnutrition has caused serious health problems in poor countries.

    D) Economic trends have to do with population and natural disasters.

63. What do we learn about the Forum's report from the passage?

    A) It was challenged by some climate and risk experts.

    B) It aroused a lot of interest in the scientific circles.

C) It was warmly received by environmentalists.

D) It caused a big stir in developing countries.

64. What does Dr. Pielke say about the Forum's report?

    A) Its statistics look embarrassing.

    B) It is invalid in terms of methodology.

    C) It deserves our closest attention.

    D) Its conclusion is purposely exaggerated.

65. What is Soren Andreasen's view of the report?

    A) Its conclusions are based on carefully collected data.

    B) It is vulnerable to criticism if the statistics are closely examined.

    C) It will give rise to heated discussions at the Copenhagen conference.

    D) Its rough estimates are meant to draw the attention of world leaders.

66. What does Kofi Annan say should be the focus of the Copenhagen conference?

    A) How rich and poor regions can share responsibility in curbing global warming.

    B) How human and economic losses from climate change can be reduced.

    C) How emissions of heat-trapping gases can be reduced on a global scale.

    D) How rich countries can better help poor regions reduce climate hazards.

62. 答案：**B**. Rates of death from illnesses have risen due to global warming.

解析：在文章的第一段，第一行，"...300,000 deaths and about $ 125 billion..."，根据这里，考生可以把答案锁定在选项A (economic)和选项B (Rates of death)。然后接着往下看，可以发现，第二段就没有再提到金钱方面了，而都是在讲死亡和疾病的话题，如第二段的第三行 "...death rates from illnesses..."。所以，最后正确的选项是B。

63. 答案：**A**. It was challenged by some climate and risk experts.

解析：根据顺序原则，在接下来的第三段里考生就能找到63题的答案。第三段的第一行就讲到 "the report drew criticism from some experts on climate and risk"，这和A选项是完全相一致的，challenged是criticism的同义替换，故选A。

64. 答案：**B**. It is invalid in terms of methodology.

解析：在第五段，我们可以很快找到Pielke，然后找到他说的话，第二行"the Forum's report was 'a methodological embarrassment' "，然后在第七行"but the report, he said 'will harm the...it is so deeply flawed' "。根据这两句话，选项中invalid是flawed的同义替换，因此B选项是正确答案。

65. 答案：**D**. Its rough estimates are meant to draw the attention of world leaders.
解析：在第六段的第二行和第三行，可以看到"the number were rough estimates. He said the report was aimed at world leaders...". 根据这两句话可知正确答案是D选项。

66. 答案：**D**. How rich countries can better help poor regions reduce climate hazards.
解析：最后一段是Kofi Annan说的一段话，第二行，focus on后面"...from rich to poor regions to help reduce...", 而后面的内容就无需再花时间去看了，因为他focus（关注）的地方，在此就已经陈述清楚了，因此D选项为正确答案。

下面是2010年12月份的大学英语四级精细阅读考试题目
Section A

Directions: *In this section, there is a passage with ten blanks. You are required to select one word for each blank from a list of choices given in a word bank following the passage. Read the passage through carefully before making your choices. Each choice in the bank is identified by a letter. Please mark the corresponding letter for each item on Answer Sheet 2 with a single line through the centre. You may not use any of the words in the bank more than once.*

Questions 47 to 56 are based on the following passage.

What determines the kind of person you are? What factors make you more or less bold, intelligent, or able to read a map? All of these are influenced by the interaction of your genes and the environment in which you were_47_. The study of how genes and environment interact to influence_48_activity is known as behavioral genetics. Behavioral genetics has made important_49_to the biological revolution, providing information about the extent to which biology influences mind, brain and behavior.

Any research that suggests that_50_to perform certain behaviors are based in biology is controversial. Who wants to be told that there are limitations to what you can_51_based on something that is beyond your control, such as your genes? It is easy to accept that genes control physical characteristics such as sex, race and eye color. But can genes also determine whether people will get divorced, how_52_they are, or what career they are likely to choose? A concern of psychological scientists is the_53_to which all of these characteristics are influenced by nature and nurture（养育），

by genetic makeup and the environment. Increasingly, science 54 that genes lay the groundwork for many human traits. From this perspective, people are born 55 like undeveloped photographs: The image is already captured, but the way it 56 appears can vary based on the development process. However, the basic picture is there from the beginning.

注 意 ： 此 部 分 试 题 请 在 答 题 卡 2 上 作 答 。

A) abilities	I) extent
B) achieve	J) indicates
C) appeal	K) proceeds
D) complaints	L) psychological
E) contributions	M) raised
F) displayed	N) smart
G) essentially	O) standard
H) eventually	

答案：

47. **M)** raised

48. **L)** psychological

49. **E)** contributions

50. **A)** abilities

51. **B)** achieve

52. **N)** smart

53. **I)** extent

54. **J)** indicates

55. **G)** essentially

56. **H)** eventually

答案解析：

47. raise意思是"养育"，the environment in which you were raised表示"你成长的环境"。

48. "psychological activity"意思是"心理活动"，全句意思是："研究基因和外部环境如何相互作用影响人心理活动的学科被称为行为遗传学"。

49. "make contributions to"为固定搭配，意为"为……做贡献"。

50. "ability to..."意思是"做某事的能力"，全句意思是"任何一篇宣称人类做出某种行为的能力是基于生物学的研究都是有争议的"。

51. "limitations to what you can achieve"意思是 "你所能达到的水平的限制"。

52. 此处需填一个形容词，而且用来形容人。smart符合题意，表示 "机灵，可爱"。

53. 此处填extent，主要是因为后面有to，"to the extent..." 意为 "到……的程度"。

54. indicate 意思是 "表明，显示"。全句意为 "越来越多的科学（现象）表明基因对人类的很多特征有基础作用"。

55. essentially 的意思是 "实际上，本质上"。全句意为 "从这个角度来讲，人一出生，本质上就像是还没洗出来的照片：相已经照了，但是最终会呈现多少就在于显影的过程了"。

56. eventually意思是 "最终，最后"。

Section B

Directions: *There are 2 passages in this section. Each passage is followed by some questions or unfinished statements. For each of them there are four choices marked A), B), C) and D). You should decide on the best choice and mark the corresponding letter on Answer Sheet 2 with a single line through the centre.*

Passage One
Questions 57 to 61 are based on the following passage.

It is pretty much a one-way street. While it may be common for university researchers to try their luck in the commercial world, there is very little traffic in the opposite direction. Pay has always been the biggest deterrent, as people with families often feel they cannot afford the drop in salary when moving to a university job. For some industrial scientists, however, the attractions of academia（学术界）outweigh any financial considerations.

Helen Lee took a 70% cut in salary when she moved from a senior post in Abbott Laboratories to a medical department at the University of Cambridge. Her main reason for returning to academia mid-career was to take advantage of the greater freedom to choose research questions. Some areas of inquiry have few prospects of a commercial return, and Lee is one of them.

The impact of a salary cut is probably less severe for a scientist in the early stages of a career. Guy Grant, now a research associate at the Unilever Centre for Molecular Informatics at the University of Cambridge, spent two years working for a pharmaceutical（制药的）company before returning to university as a post-doctoral researcher. He took a 30% salary cut but felt it worthwhile for the greater intellectual opportunities.

Higher up the ladder, where a pay cut is usually more significant, the demand for scientists with a wealth of experience in industry is forcing universities to make the transition（转换）to academia more attractive, according to Lee. Industrial scientists tend to receive training that academics do not, such as how to build a multidisciplinary team, manage budgets and negotiate contracts. They are also well placed to bring something extra to the teaching side of an academic role that will help students get a job when they graduate, says Lee, perhaps experience in manufacturing practice or product development. "Only a small number of undergraduates will continue in an academic career. So someone leaving university who already has the skills needed to work in an industrial lab has far more potential in the job market than someone who has spent all their time on a narrow research project."

注意：此部分试题请在答题卡2上作答。

57. By "a one-way street" (Line 1, Para. 1), the author means _____.

   A) university researchers know little about the commercial world

   B) there is little exchange between industry and academia

   C) few industrial scientists would quit to work in a university

   D) few university professors are willing to do industrial research

58. The word "deterrent" (Line 2, Para. 1) most probably refers to something that _____.

   A) keeps someone from taking action

   B) helps to move the traffic

   C) attracts people's attention

   D) brings someone a financial burden

59. What was Helen Lee's major consideration when she changed her job in the middle of her career?

   A) Flexible work hours.

   B) Her research interests.

   C) Her preference for the lifestyle on campus.

   D) Prospects of academic accomplishments.

60. Guy Grant chose to work as a researcher at Cambridge in order to _____.

   A) do financially more rewarding work

B) raise his status in the academic world

C) enrich his experience in medical research

D) exploit better intellectual opportunities

61. What contribution can industrial scientists make when they come to teach in a university?

A) Increase its graduates' competitiveness in the job market.

B) Develop its students' potential in research.

C) Help it to obtain financial support from industry.

D) Gear its research towards practical applications.

57. 答案：**C**) few industrial scientists would quit to work in a university

解析："one-way street"字面意思是"单行道"，含有只能从一个方向前进却很难往相反方向前进的意思。文章第二句就解释说明了这个"one-way street"在文中的含义。大学里的学者去商界创业的现象不算稀奇，但是反过来就不怎么常见了，故选C。

58. 答案：**A**) keeps someone from taking action

解析："deterrent" 有妨碍物的意思，单词前的意思是"薪水永远是最大的……因为很多人觉得到大学里工作就会工资减少，从而无法养家糊口。"从后面半句，我们可以推断出deterrent的意思，故选A。

59. 答案：**B**) Her research interests.

解析：答案在第二段第三行可以找到。"Her main reason for...to take advantage of the great freedom to choose research questions."表明Helen Lee换行主要考虑到的是自己可以比较自由地选择研究领域，即个人的研究兴趣，故选B。

60. 答案：**D**) exploit better intellectual opportunities

解析：从第三段最后一句"felt it worthwhile for the great intellectual opportunities"可以知道，D为正确答案。

61. 答案：**A**) Increase its graduates' competitiveness in job market.

解析：最后一段话里，"the demand for scientists with a wealth of experience in industry in...that will help students get a job when they graduate"主要是在讲industrial scientists到大学教学后将为其毕业生就业做出的主要贡献，故选A。

Passage Two

Being sociable looks like a good way to add years to your life. Relationships with family, friends, neighbours, even pets, will all do the trick, but the biggest longevity（长寿）boost seems to come from marriage or an equivalent relationship. The effect was first noted in 1858 by William Farr, who wrote that widows and widowers（鳏夫）were at a much higher risk of dying than their married peers. Studies since then suggest that marriage could add as much as seven years to a man's life and two to a woman's. The effect holds for all causes of death, whether illness, accident or self-harm.

Even if the odds are stacked against you, marriage can more than compensate. Linda Waite of the University of Chicago has found that a married older man with heart disease can expect to live nearly four years longer than an unmarried man with a healthy heart. Likewise, a married man who smokes more than a pack a day is likely to live as long as a divorced man who doesn't smoke. There's a flip side, however, as partners are more likely to become ill or die in the couple of years following their spouse's death, and caring for a spouse with mental disorder can leave you with some of the same severe problems. Even so, the odds favour marriage. In a 30-year study of more than 10,000 people, Nicholas Christakis of Harvard Medical School describes how all kinds of social networks have similar effects.

So how does it work? The effects are complex, affected by socio-economic factors, health-service provision, emotional support and other more physiological（生理的）mechanisms. For example, social contact can boost development of the brain and immune system, leading to better health and less chance of depression later in life. People in supportive relationships may handle stress better. Then there are the psychological benefits of a supportive partner.

A life partner, children and good friends are all recommended if you aim to live to 100. The ultimate social network is still being mapped out, but Christakis says: "People are interconnected, so their health is interconnected."

注意：此部分试题请在答题卡2上作答。

62. William Farr's study and other studies show that _____.

    A) social life provides an effective cure for illness

    B) being sociable helps improve one's quality of life

    C) women benefit more than men from marriage

    D) marriage contributes a great deal to longevity

63. Linda Waite's studies support the idea that _____.

    A) older men should quit smoking to stay healthy

    B) marriage can help make up for ill health

    C) the married are happier than the unmarried

D) unmarried people are likely to suffer in later life

64. It can be inferred from the context that the "flip side" (Line 4, Para. 2) refers to _____.
    A) the disadvantages of being married
    B) the emotional problems arising from marriage
    C) the responsibility of taking care of one's family
    D) the consequence of a broken marriage

65. What does the author say about social networks?
    A) They have effects similar to those of a marriage.
    B) They help develop people's community spirit.
    C) They provide timely support for those in need.
    D) They help relieve people of their life's burdens.

66. What can be inferred from the last paragraph?
    A) It's important that we develop a social network when young.
    B) To stay healthy, one should have a proper social network.
    C) Getting a divorce means risking a reduced life span.
    D) We should share our social networks with each other.

62. 答案：D) marriage contributes to a great deal of longevity
解析：第一段提到"but the biggest longevity boost seems to come from marriage or an equivalent relationship."紧接着就说到"The effect was first noted in 1958 by William Farr...". 句中的boost和选项D中的contribute是近义词，故选D。

63. 答案：B) marriage can help make up for ill heath
解析：Linda Waite举例子说到一个有心脏病的已婚男人可以比未婚但是健康的男人多活4年。由此可知，婚姻可以弥补身体不健康带来的不利因素，因此B选项为正确答案。

64. 答案：A) the disadvantages of being married
解析：flip side的原意是唱片的另一面，前面已经分析过婚姻的好处，这里指的就是婚姻的不利方面，故选A。

65. 答案：A) They have effects similar to those of a marriage.
解析：从第二段最后一句how all kinds of social networks have similar effects可知，正确答案是A.

66. 答案：B) To stay healthy, one should have a proper social network.

解析：最后一段提到如果想生活到100岁，就要发展自己的社交网络，故选B。

Part V   Cloze   ⏱(15 minutes)

　　大学英语四级考试中的完形填空是在一篇题材熟悉、难度适中的短文（约220–250词）内留有20个空白，每个空白为一题，每题有4个选择项，要求考生在读懂原文的基础上，选择一个最佳答案，使短文的意思和结构恢复完整。完形填空所选文章的体裁涵盖了议论文、说明文和记叙文，但常考的都是议论文与说明文，记叙文所占的比重较小。最近几年的完形文章往往选取反映社会时事、介绍英美社会热点话题的内容。

　　四级考试中的完形填空综合了词汇、结构以及阅读理解部分的测试内容，不仅要测试考生词汇和句段中运用语言的能力，还测试考生在语篇上综合运用语言的能力。完形填空中所要填的词是与文章的上下文紧密联系的。因此，要做好完形填空，必须在通读全文、了解文章大意与结构的前提下，根据所提供的选项、句子的结构、语境等，进行逻辑推理、对比等，最后确定答案。

　　一般来说，完形填空的做题顺序要分3步：

　　一、通读文章，了解大意。做题之前，首先要快速通读全文，弄清文章的大意和结构，确立正确的背景知识，为正式的填空做好充分的准备。切忌读一句填一空、望文生义，盲目猜测，以致造成判断失误。阅读时尤其要注意每段的第一句话，第一句一般不留空，它既能让考生了解文章的主题，又是对下文的重要提示。尤其是第一段的第一句话，会介绍文章的背景知识或主题思想。

　　二、细读文章，初选答案。在阅读段落、了解基本内容的前提下，再自上而下逐一选择。这时，有些考生会遇到很难确定的选择，这时可先跳过此题，做其他相对简单的题目，待阅读到下文获取更多信息时，再回过头来处理未选之项。对某些选项把握不大时，尤其要注意捕捉信息词作为解题线索，利用已知线索推出未知信息。

　　三、检查全文，核实答案。20个选项全部完成后，要认真检查。用一两分钟的时间，将答案带入文中，通过语感来确定答案是否正确，与作者观点是否一致。

第一次就考好英语四级

下面是2011年6月份的大学英语四级完形填空考试题目

> Directions: *There are 20 blanks in the following passage. For each blank there are four choices marked A), B), C) and D) on the right side of the paper. You should choose the ONE that best fits into the passage. Then mark the corresponding letter on Answer Sheet 2 with a single line through the centre.*

注意：此部分试题请在答题卡2上作答。

When it comes to eating smart for your heart, thinking about short-term fixes and simplify life with a straightforward approach that will serve you well for years to come.

Smart eating goes beyond analyzing every bite ad you lift __67__ your mouth. "In the past we used to believe that __68__ amounts of individual nutrients（营养物）were the __69__ to good health," Linda Van Horn, chair of the American Heart Association's Nutrition Committee. "But now we have a __70__ understanding of healthy eating and the kinds of food necessary to __71__ not only heart disease but disease __72__ general," she adds.

Scientists now __73__ on the broader picture of the balance of food eaten __74__ several days or a week __75__ than on the number of milligrams（毫克）of this or that __76__ at each meal.

Fruits, vegetables and whole grains, for example, provide nutrients and plant-based compounds __77__ for good health. "The more we learn, the more __78__ we are by the wealth of essential substances they __79__," Van Horn continues, "and how they __80__ with each other to keep us healthy."

You'll automatically be __81__ the right heart-healthy track if vegetables, fruits and whole grains make __82__ three quarters of the food on your dinner plate. __83__ in the remaining one quarter with lean meat or chicken, fish or eggs.

The foods you choose to eat as well as those you choose to __84__ clearly contribute to your well-being. Without a __85__, each of the small decisions you make in this realm can make a big __86__ on your health in the years to come.

67. A) between   B) through   C) inside   D) to
68. A) serious   B) splendid   C) specific   D) separate
69. A) key   B) point   C) lead   D) center
70. A) strict   B) different   C) typical   D) natural
71. A) rescue   B) prevent   C) forbid   D) offend

72. A) in	B) upon	C) for	D) by
73. A) turn	B) put	C) focus	D) carry
74. A) over	B) along	C) with	D) beyond
75. A) other	B) better	C) rather	D) sooner
76. A) conveyed	B) consumed	C) entered	D) exhausted
77. A) vital	B) initial	C) valid	D) radical
78. A) disturbed	B) depressed	C) amazed	D) amused
79. A) retain	B) contain	C) attain	D) maintain
80. A) interfere	B) interact	C) reckon	D) rest
81. A) at	B) of	C) on	D) within
82. A) out	B) into	C) off	D) up
83. A) Engage	B) Fill	C) Insert	D) Pack
84. A) delete	B) hinder	C) avoid	D) spoil
85. A) notion	B) hesitation	C) reason	D) doubt
86. A) outcome	B) function	C) impact	D) commitment

答案解析：

67. **D** to第二段首句可翻译为：科学饮食远不止分析每一口放到嘴里的饭。这里要选择一个介词，lift的原意是高举，在这里的意思就是"放到嘴边"，to表示方向，故选D。

68. **C** specific根据上一句话的意思，接下来的一句话，是表达过去人们如何如何，是为了给出"靶子"加以批评。读到作者提倡的做法，然后反向理解一下，便可选出答案。

69. **A** key根据语法搭配，只有key才可以和后面的to相搭配，故选A。

70. **B** different句首的but表达对比之意，因此下文开始讲述"另一种""不同的"饮食习惯，故选B。

71. **B** prevent这里是个不定式短语，需要一个动词，由宾语heart disease可知，"prevent"（预防）是最佳搭配。

72. **A** in只有in能和general搭配，意为"一般，通常"故选A。

73. **C** focus语法上4个选项都可以和on搭配，但turn on表示打开，focus on表示注重，put on表示穿衣，carry on表示执行。根据宾语，"更广的层面"，可知应该选择focus on。

74. **A** over several days or a week 表示一段时间以来，故选A。

75. **C** rather这里表示"是什么而不是什么"，应该用rather than才能准确达意。

76. **B** consumed这是个分词短语作后置定语修饰前面的"this or that"，这里的this or that代指食物。只有consume符合题意，故选B。

77. **A** vital此处需要一个形容词做后置定语，和for good health搭配，这里只有vital能和for搭配，表示"对……重要"。

78. **C** amazed这里是the more...the more...的固定表达，表示"越……越……"，这里用amazed表达科研人员对新发现所产生的"惊奇之感"。

79. **B** contain这里的they表示食物，结合后面的动词，构成定语从句，修饰"必备营养元素"，只有contain最合适。

80. **B** interact 需要一个动词和with搭配，只能选择A和B，但从语义上判断，必备营养元素之间会相互影响，肯定不会相互干扰，故选B。

81. **C** on此处需要一个介词和track搭配，on the right track意为"做对了"，因此选C。

82. **D** up根据题意，"蔬菜、水果和谷物构成了饭菜的3/4"，这里make up表达"构成"之意。

83. **B** fill此处需要一个动词，宾语是"剩余的1/4"，从语义上理解，我们需要选择"填充"，因此应选fill in。

84. **C** avoid此处需要一个动词，结合题意，这个空应该表达"不吃"，才能和前面的eat形成对比，这里的avoid，表达避免的意思，故选C。

85. **D** doubt 文章的最后一句，是一个结论，这里用without a doubt 表达"毫无疑问"，符合题目要求。

86. **C** impact这里需要一个名词和on搭配，只有impact符合题意。

下面是2010年12月份的大学英语四级完形填空考试题目

> Directions: *There are 20 blanks in the following passage. For each blank there are four choices marked A), B), C) and D) on the right side of the paper. You should choose the ONE that best fits into the passage. Then mark the corresponding letter on Answer Sheet 2 with a single line through the centre.*

注意：此部分试题请在答题卡2上作答。

Over half the world's people now live in cities. The latest "Global Report on Human Settlements" says a significant change took place last year. The report_67_this week from U.N. Habitat, a United Nations agency.

A century ago, _68_ than five percent of all people lived in cities. _69_ the middle of this century it could be seventy percent, or _70_ six and a half billion people.

Already three-fourths of people in _71_ countries live in cities. Now most urban population _72_ is in the developing world.

Urbanization can _73_ to social and economic progress, but also put _74_ on cities to provide housing and _75_. The new report says almost two hundred thousand people move _76_ cities and towns each day. It says worsening inequalities, _77_ by social divisions and differences in _78_, could result in violence and crime _79_ cities plan better.

Another issue is urban sprawl (无序扩展的城区). This is where cities _80_ quickly into rural areas, sometimes _81_ a much faster rate than urban population growth.

Sprawl is _82_ in the United States. Americans move a lot. In a recent study, Art Hall at the University of Kansas found that people are moving away from the _83_ cities to smaller ones. He sees a _84_ toward "de-urbanization" across the nation. _85_ urban economies still provide many _86_ that rural areas do not.

67. A) came on   B) came off   C) came over   D) came out
68. A) more   B) other   C) less   D rather
69. A) By   B) Through   C) Along   D) To
70. A) really   B) barely   C) ever   D) almost
71. A) flourishing   B) developed   C) thriving   D) fertile
72. A) extension   B) addition   C) raise   D) growth
73. A) keep   B) turn   C) lead   D) refer
74. A) pressure   B) load   C) restraint   D) weight
75. A) surroundings   B) communities   C) concerns   D) services
76. A) onto   B) into   C) around   D) upon
77. A) pulled   B) driven   C) drawn   D) pressed
78. A) situation   B) wealth   C) treasure   D) category
79. A) when   B) if   C) unless   D) whereas
80. A) expand   B) split   C) invade   D) enlarge
81. A) in   B) beyond   C) with   D) at
82. A) common   B) conventional   C) ordinary   D) frequent
83. A) essential   B) prior   C) primitive   D) major
84. A) trend   B) style   C) direction   D) path
85. A) Then   B) But   C) For   D) While
86. A) abilities   B) qualities   C) possibilities   D) realities

答案解析：

67. **D** came out 表示"出版、公布"，此处表示报告的公布。

68. **C** less 根据上下文可知这里说的是都市人口的增长，强调之前的少和现在的多，所以用少于更合适。

69. **A** by 在这里表示"截止到某时间为止"。

70. **D** almost"几乎，将近"，对前面的解释，说明人口有多少。

71. **B** developed 根据上下文意思，以及后文相对的developing world可知此处应该是发达国家，即developed countries。

72. **D** growth这里讲的是都市人口的增长，所以用growth。

73. **C** lead. lead to表示"导致，通向"，本段末也有出现过，在这里是说都市化有助于社会和经济的进步。

74. **A** pressure 从下文的描述可以看出过快的都市化也给城市带来了巨大压力，所以选pressure。

75. **D** services 服务，即城市为人们提供住房和服务。

76. **B** into 介词选择，move into表示"移入，迁入"，是固定搭配。

77. **B** driven 表示"推动，驱动"，driven by "由……驱动，由什么原因引起的"。

78. **B** wealth. wealth表示"财富"，符合上下文的意思。

79. **C** unless 除非，这里的意思是除非城市规划更好，否则各部分财富分配不均的局面将可能导致犯罪问题。

80. **A** expand 指扩张，expand into rural areas 扩张到农村地区。

81. **D** at at a much faster rate固定搭配，表示"以更快的速度"。

82. **A** common 表示某事件很普遍，平常。

83. **D** major. major cities，大城市，与后文中的smaller cities形成对比。

84. **A** trend 趋势，这里是对前面情况的概括，a trend toward de-urbanization 表示一种逆城市化的发展趋势。

85. **B** But 表示转折，意为城市还是有自身优点的，与前面的"逆城市化"形成转折关系。

86. **C** possibilities 可能性，这里表示城市依然能够提供农村所不能提供的机会和可能性。

Part VI Translation ⏱(5 minutes)

四级考试中，翻译题是试卷的最后一部分，形式是汉译英，一共5个句子，一句一题，句长为15-30词。由于句中的一部分已用英文给出，考生只需根据全句意思将汉语部分译成英语，考试时间5分钟。这种题型重点考察考生对语法结构及常用英语表达习惯的掌握情况。由于英语和汉语是两种差异比较大的语言，英语重形合，汉语重意合，因此翻译时，根据表达习惯，英语、汉语的句子结构有时需要进行相应的转换。英汉语复合句中主句和从句之间的时间顺序和逻辑顺序也不完全一致，因此，翻译时，也时常需要根据表达习惯，对句序进行调整。要想取得高分，光有一定的英语基础还不行。在学习和复习时掌握一些翻译的基本常识和常用方法，针对考试中经常出现的一些语言现象，仔细分析一些翻译实例，总结出一些规律性的东西，再加以必要的练习，对考生来说是非常必要的，而且在短时间内提高自己在该部分的得分是完全有可能的。下面就来谈谈翻译的基本步骤：

一、理解。这一步骤要求考生通读全文，从整体上把握整篇文章的内容，弄清原文的意思，并且理解划线部分与文章其他部分之间的语法与逻辑关系。一般来说，划线部分句子结构都比较复杂。复杂的句子如果不搞清楚它的语法结构，很难正确完整地理解原文的要求。因此在分析划线部分的句子结构时，考生要着重分析句子的骨干结构，注意首先把句子的主语、谓语和宾语找出来。

二、表达。表达是重中之重，考生在弄清了句子的意思后，就要填上合适的词组或句子来完成翻译。填空时应清楚下列问题：

1. **固定搭配考点**：比如名词与动词搭配，形容词与名词搭配，动词与副词的修饰关系，名词与介词搭配，更为重要的是常见的固定词组以及固定表达。

2. **核心语法考点**：核心语法考点中最重要的是虚拟语气，其次是倒装结构、从句、虚拟语气、非谓语动词等。

三、校对。在填空完成后，要检查一下所填部分是否与整句一致，有无语法或拼写错误。

下面是2011年6月份的大学英语四级翻译考试题目

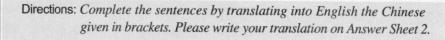

Directions: *Complete the sentences by translating into English the Chinese given in brackets. Please write your translation on Answer Sheet 2.*

注意：此部分试题请在答题卡2上作答，只需写出译文部分。

87. The university authorities did not approve the regulation, _____（也没有解释为什么）.

88. Jane is tired of dealing with customer complaints and wishes that she _____（能被分配做另一项工作）.

89. John rescued the drowning child _____（冒着自己生命危险）.

90. George called his boss from the airport but it _____（接电话的却是他的助手）.

91. Although he was interested in philosophy, _____（他的父亲说服他）majoring in law.

答案解析：

87. 答案：nor did they make any explanation
解析：本题考察了两个知识点：nor的倒装句用法，后半句表示"也不"的否定意义，注意助动词的时态与上半句保持一致；对某事做出解释的表达，考察了汉译英中动词转名词的技巧，explain→explanation。

88. 答案：could be assigned (to) another job
解析：本题考察了wish从句的虚拟语气用法（can→could）和"分配某人做某事"的词组搭配，assign sb. to sth. 或者assign sb. sth.。

89. 答案：at the risk of his own life
解析：本题考察了"冒着……的危险/风险做某事"的词组搭配，可以用at the risk / expense of one's own life（冒着某人的生命危险做某事）。

90. 答案：was his assistant who answered the phone
解析：该句比较灵活，在句法上，既可以使用强调句结构，也可以采用turn out的惯用搭配。

91. 答案：his father persuaded him into majoring in law
解析：本题考察"说服某人做某事"的表达，persuade sb. into doing sth.。

下面是2010年12月份的大学英语四级翻译考试题目

Directions: *Complete the sentences by translating into English the Chinese given in brackets. Please write your translation on Answer Sheet 2.*

注意：此部分试题请在答题卡2上作答，只需写出译文部分。

87. _____（为了确保他参加会议）, I called him up in advance.

88. The magnificent museum _____（据说建成于）about a hundred years ago.

89. There would be no life on earth _____ ___（没有地球独特的环境）.

90. _____（给游客印象最深的）was the friendliness and warmth of the local people.

91. They requested that _____（我借的书还回图书馆）by next Friday.

答案解析：

87. 答案：In order to ensure him to attend the meeting
解析：本题句子的主干 "I called him up in advance"已经给出，需要翻译部分为"为了确保他能参加会议"。该部分在句子中作目的状语，另外，确保某人做某事 ensure sb. to do sth.。

88. 答案：is said to have been built
解析：本题重点考查被动语态和be said to的用法。主语museum与动词build之间为被动关系，且build这一动作发生在过去，故用现在完成被动时。

89. 答案：without its unique environment
解析：本题重点考查：without的用法。without 是介词，后接名词或动名词。

90. 答案：What impressed the tourists most
解析：本题重点考查what引导的主语从句，what引导从句可充当主语。另外还考察impress的用法，impress sb. 给……留下印象。

91. 答案：books I borrowed (should) be returned to the library
解析：本题考察了request的用法。当request表示"要求"时，引导的宾语从句要使用虚拟语气，即(should) + 动词原形。另外还考察了定语从句，"我借的书"，the book (that) I borrowed。

第三部分

大学英语四级模拟试题及答案解析

Sample Test and the answer of analysis for College Enlish Test Band Four

大学英语四级模拟试题

Part I   Writing (30 minutes)

Directions: *For this part, you are allowed 30 minutes to write a composition on the topic Campus Thefts. You should write at least 120 words following the outline given below in Chinese:*
1)校园盗窃案件时有发生
2)物品被盗的原因
3)学生如何加强防盗意识

Part II   Reading Comprehension (Skimming and Scanning) (15 minutes)

Directions: *In this part, you will have 15 minutes to go over the passage quickly and answer the questions on Answer Sheet 1. For questions 1-7, choose the best answer from the four choices marked A), B), C) and D). For questions 8-10, complete the sentences with the information given in the passage.*

Will We Run Out of Water?

Picture a "ghost ship" sinking into the sand, left to rot on dry land by a receding sea. Then imagine dust storms sweeping up toxic pesticides and chemical fertilizers from the dry seabed and spewing them across towns and villages.Seem like a scene from a movie about the end of the world? For people living near the Aral Sea in Central Asia, it's all too real. Thirty years ago, government planners diverted the rivers that flow into the sea in order to irrigate (provide water for) farmland. As a result, the sea has shrunk to half its original size, stranding ships on dry land. The seawater has tripled in salt content and become polluted, killing all 24 native species of fish.

Similar large-scale efforts to redirect water in other parts of the world have also ended in ecological crisis, according to numerous environmental groups. But many countries continue to build massive dams and irrigation systems, even though such projects can create more problems than they fix. Why? People in many parts of the world are desperate for water, and more people will need more water in the next century.

"Growing populations will worsen problems with water," says Peter H. Gleick, an environmental scientist at the Pacific Institute for studies in Development, Environment, and Security, a research organization in California. He fears that by the year 2025, as many as one-third of the world's projected 8.3 billion people will suffer from water shortages.

Where Water Goes

Only 2.5 percent of all water on Earth is freshwater, water suitable for drinking and growing food, says Sandra Postel, director of the Global Water Policy Project in Amherst, Mass. Two thirds of this freshwater is locked in glaciers and ice caps. In fact, only a tiny percentage of freshwater is part of the water cycle, in which water evaporates and rises into the atmosphere, then condenses and falls back to Earth as precipitation (rain or snow).

Some precipitation runs off land to lakes and oceans, and some becomes groundwater, water that seeps into the earth. Much of this renewable freshwater ends up in remote places like the Amazon river basin in Brazil, where few people live. In fact, the world's population has access to only 12,500 cubic kilometers of freshwater—about the amount of water in Lake Superior. And people use half of this amount already. "If water demand continues to climb rapidly," says Postel, "there will be severe shortages and damage to the aquatic environment."

Close to Home

Water woes may seem remote to people living in rich countries like the United States. But Americans could face serious water shortages too, especially in areas that rely on groundwater. Groundwater accumulates in aquifers, layers of sand and gravel that lie between soil and bedrock. (For every liter of surface water, more than 90 liters are hidden underground.) Although the United States has large aquifers, farmers, ranchers, and cities are tapping many of them for water faster than nature can replenish it. In northwest Texas, for example, over pumping has shrunk groundwater supplies by 25 percent, according to Postel.

Americans may face even more urgent problems from pollution. Drinking water in the United States is generally safe and meets high standards. Nevertheless, one in five Americans every day unknowingly drinks tap water contaminated with bacteria and chemical wastes, according to the Environmental Protection Agency. In Milwaukee, 400,000 people fell ill in 1993 after drinking tap water tainted with cryptosporidium, a microbe that causes fever, diarrhea and vomiting.

The Source

Where do contaminants come from? In developing countries, people dump raw sewage into the same streams and rivers from which they draw water for drinking and cooking; about 250 million people a year get sick from water borne diseases.

In developed countries, manufacturers use 100,000 chemical compounds to make a wide range of products. Toxic chemicals pollute water when released untreated into rivers and lakes. (Certain compounds, such as polychlorinated biphenyls, or PCBs, have been banned in the United States.)

But almost everyone contributes to water pollution. People often pour household cleaners, car antifreeze, and paint thinners down the drain; all of these contain hazardous chemicals. Scientists studying water in the San Francisco Bay reported in 1996 that 70 percent of the pollutants could be traced to household waste.

Farmers have been criticized for overusing herbicides and pesticides, chemicals that kill weeds and insects but that pollute water as well. Farmers also use nitrates, nitrogen rich fertilizer that help plants grow but that can wreak havoc on the environment. Nitrates are swept away by surface runoff to lakes and seas. Too many nitrates "over enrich" these bodies of water, encouraging the buildup of algae, or microscopic plants that live on the surface of the water. Algae deprive the water of oxygen that fish need to survive, at times choking off life in an entire body of water.

What's the Solution?

Water expert Gleick advocates conservation and local solutions to water-related problems; governments, for instance, would be better off building small-scale dams rather than huge and disruptive projects like the one that ruined the Aral Sea.

"More than 1 billion people worldwide don't have access to basic clean drinking water," says Gleick. "There has to be a strong push on the part of everyone—governments and ordinary people—to make sure we have a resource so fundamental to life."

1. What caused the Aral Sea to shrink?

A) Government planners over pumped its water.

B) The rivers flowing into it have been diverted.

C) High temperature made its water badly evaporate.

D) Farmers used its water to irrigate their farmland.

2. The construction of massive dams and irrigation projects.

A) solves more problems than what they created

B) does more good than harm

C) brings more water to people than expected

D) does more harm than good

3. The chief causes of water shortage include.

A) population growth and water waste

B) water waste and pollution

C) population growth and water pollution

D) water pollution and dry weather

4. Americans could suffer from greatly serious water shortages?

A) bearing high standards of safe drinking water in mind

B) living in big cities but poor condition

C) depending on groundwater

D) living in rich areas

5. What is the main pollutant in developed countries?

A) Raw sewage into rivers and streams.

B) Untreated toxic chemicals from manufacturers.

C) Herbicides and pesticides used by farmers.

D) Household cleaners poured down the drain.

6. How does algae make threats to life of a body of water?

A) By competitively using oxygen life in water needs.

B) By covering the whole surface of the water.

C) By releasing hazardous chemicals into water.

D) By living more rapidly than other life in water.

7. According to Gleick, who should be responsible for solving water-related problems?

A) government and housewives.

B) farmers and manufacturers.

C) ordinary people and manufacturers.

D) government and every person.

8. According to Peter H. Gleick, by the year 2025, as many as _____ of the world's people will suffer from water shortages.

9. Two thirds of the freshwater on Earth is locked in _____.

10. In developed countries, before toxic chemicals are released into rivers and lakes, they should be treated in order to avoid _____.

Part III Listening Comprehension (35 minutes)

Section A

Directions: *In this section, you will hear 8 short conversations and 2 long conversations. At the end of each conversation, one or more questions will be asked about what was said. Both the conversation and the questions will be spoken only once. after each question there will be a pause. During the pause, you must read the four choices marked A), B), C) and D), and decide which is the best answer. Then mark the corresponding letter on Answer Sheet 2 with a single line through the centre.*

11. A) Get further information about the sale.
    B) Wait for the sale to start.
    C) Buy a new suit.
    D) Call the TV station to be sure if the ad is true.

12. A) He doesn't think that John has a very good knowledge of physics.
    B) He thinks that perhaps John is not in very good health.
    C) He doesn't think that John is ill.
    D) He is aware that John is ill.

13. A) Before six.   B) At six.
    C) After six.   D) After seven.

14. A) 11:25   B) 11:26
    C) 11:40   D) 11:46.

15. A) He doesn't want to live in the suburbs.
    B) He can't afford the high taxes.
    C) The rent is too high.
    D) It's too far away from his office.

16. A) No. He doesn't like going to the club.
    B) No. He has to finish his homework.
    C) Yes. He'll write his paper after he returns.

D) Yes. He'll go after he finishes his homework.

17. A) Johnson's classmate.

B) Johnson's father.

C) Johnson's friend.

D) Johnson's brother.

18. A) He was unharmed.

B) He was badly hurt.

C) He got a heart attack.

D) He has fully recovered from the shock.

Questions 19 to 22 are based on the conversation you have just heard.

19. A) The benefits of strong business competition.

B) Suggestions concerning new business strategies.

C) Complaints about the expense of modernization.

D) A proposal to lower the cost of production.

20. A) It costs much more than its worth.

B) It calls for immediate repairs.

C) It can still be used for a long time.

D) It should be brought up-to-date.

21. A) The personnel manager should be fired for inefficiency.

B) A few engineers should be employed to modernize the factory.

C) The entire staff should be retrained.

D) Better educated employees should be promoted.

22. A) Advertising in newspapers alone is not sufficient.

B) TV commercials attract more investments.

C) Their competitors have long been advertising on TV.

D) TV commercials are less expensive.

Questions 23 to 25 are based on the conversation you have just heard.

23. A) In the middle of the semester.

B) At the beginning of exams.

C) In the middle of summer vacation.

D) At the end of the school year.

24. A) To a rock and mineral show.

    B) To a popular music concert.

    C) To an opera at the concert hall.

    D) To a movie at the student center.

25. A) She gets a student's discount.

    B) Bob doesn't have very much money.

    C) She lost a bet and owes Bob money.

    D) Bob left his wallet at home.

Section B

Directions: *In this section, you will hear 3 short passages. At the end of each passage, you will hear some questions. Both the passage and the questions will be spoken only once. After you hear a question, you must choose the best answer from the four choices marked A), B), C) and D).Then mark the corresponding letter on Answer Sheet 2 with a single line through the centre.*

Passage One

Questions 26 to 28 are based on the passage you have just heard.

26. A) Three months.

    B) From three to five months.

    C) Four months.

    D) Five months.

27. A) Watch traffic.

    B) Obey commands.

    C) Cross streets safely.

    D) Guard the door.

28. A) Two weeks.

    B) Three weeks.

    C) Four weeks.

    D) Five weeks.

Passage Two

Questions 29 to 31 are based on the passage you have just heard.

29. A) Family violence.

   B) The Great Depression.

   C) Her father's disloyalty.

   D) Her mother's bad temper.

30. A) His advanced age.

   B) His second wife's positive influence.

   C) His children's efforts.

   D) His improved financial condition.

31. A) Divorce often has disastrous consequences.

   B) Happiness is hard to find in blended families.

   C) Love is blind.

   D) Love breeds love

Passage Three

Questions 32 to 35 are based on the passage you have just hear.

32. A) They haven't reached a decision yet.

   B) They have decided to go hunting bears.

   C) They want to go camping.

   D) They want to go exploring in the country.

33. A) Tom.

   B) The speaker.

   C) Susie.

   D) The speaker's husband.

34. A) They stayed outside the tent and did nothing.

   B) They chased the bear away.

   C) They climbed up a tree.

   D) They put some honey outside for the bear to eat.

35. A) He drank the beer.

   B) He ate the honey.

   C) He chased the people away.

   D) He turnde things upside down.

Section C

Directions: *In this section, you will hear a passage three times. When the passage is read for the first time, you should listen carefully for its general idea. When the passage is read for the second time, you are required to fill in the blanks numbered from 36 to 43 with the exact words you have just heard. For blanks numbered from 44 to 46 you are required to fill in the missing information. For these blanks, you can either use the exact words you have just heard or write down the main points in your own words. Finally, when the passage is read for the third time, you should check what you have written.*

Coal has not been used very extensively as an energy source recently. However, it (36)_____ will become a very important source of energy in the future because of dwindling (37)_____ of natural gas and oil. Although coal (38)_____to be black, it actually has black, yellow, orange, and red bands of color when it is examined under a powerful microscope.

Coal probably was formed about 300 million years ago by (39)_____ trees and other plant life growing in (40)_____. These trees and plants died and then fell into the water. They contained the elements oxygen, hydrogen, and (41)_____. As the earth changed its (42)_____, the weight of the ground (43)_____ down on the trees and plants. Thus seams of coal were formed.

(44)_____. Strip mining is quicker and safer than underground mining, but it can leave the surface of the earth bare and ugly. (45)_____. While both underground and strip mines still can be hazardous, there no longer are as many accidents in coal mining as there once were. (46)_____. Many of today's coal miners are earning good wages in an occupation which is quite safe and very important.

Part IV Reading Comprehension (Reading in Depth) (25 minutes)

Section A

Directions: *In this section, there is a passage with ten blanks. You are required to select one word for each blank from a list of choices given in a word bank following the passage. Read the passage through carefully before making your choices. Each choice in the bank is identified by a letter. Please mark the corresponding letter for each item on Answer Sheet 2 with a single line through the centre. You may not use any of the words in the bank more than once.*

Questions 47 to 56 are based on the following passage.

Wise buying is a positive way in which you can make your money go further. The way you go about purchasing an article or a service can actually__47__your money or can add to the cost. Take the__48__example of a hairdryer. If you are buying a hairdryer, you might think that you are making the__49__buy if you choose one whose look you like and which is also the cheapest__50__price. But when you get it home you may find that it takes twice as long as a more expensive__51__to dry your hair. The cost of the electricity plus the cost of your time could well make your hairdryer the most expensive one of all.

So what principles should you__52__when you go out shopping? If you keep your home, your car or any valuable__53__in excellent condition, you'll be saving money in the long run. Before you buy a new__54__, talk to someone who owns one. If you can, use it or borrow it to check it suits your particular purpose. Before you buy an expensive__55__, or a service, do check the price and what is on offer. If possible, choose__56__three items or three estimates.

A) save   B) from   C) element   D) best

E) appliance   F) reasonable   G) possession   H) material

I) simple   J) with   K) in   L) model

M) item   N) adopt   O) easy

Section B

Directions: *There are 2 passages in this section. Each passage is followed by some questions or unfinished statements. For each of them there are four choices marked A), B), C) and D).You should decide on the best choice and mark the corresponding letter on Answer Sheet 2 with a single line through the centre.*

Passage One
Questions 57 to 61 are based on the following passage.

Culture is one of the most challenging elements of the international marketplace. This system of learned behavior patterns characteristic of the members of a given society is constantly shaped by a set of dynamic variables: language, religion, values and attitudes, manners and customs, aesthetics, technology, education, and social institutions. To cope with this system, an international manager needs both factual and interpretive knowledge of culture. To some extent, the factual knowledge can be learned; its interpretation comes only through experience.

The most complicated problems in dealing with the cultural environment stem from the fact that one cannot learn culture—one has to live it. Two schools of thought exist in the business world on how to deal with cultural diversity. One is that business is business the world around, following the model of Pepsi and McDonald's. In some cases, globalization is a fact of life; however, cultural differences are still far from converging.

The other school proposes that companies must tailor business approaches to individual cultures. Setting up policies and procedures in each country has been compared to an organ transplant; the critical question centers around acceptance or rejection. The major challenge to the international manager is to make sure that rejection is not a result of cultural myopia or even blindness.

Fortune examined the international performance of a dozen large companies that earn 20 percent or more of their revenue overseas. The internationally successful companies all share an important quality: patience. They have not rushed into situations but rather built their operations carefully by following the most basic business principles. These principles are to know your adversary, know your audience, and know your customer.

57. According to the passage, which of the following is true?

A) All international managers can learn culture.

B) Views differ on how to treat culture in business world.

C) Most people do not know foreign culture well.

D) Business diversity is not necessary.

58. According to the author, the model of Pepsi_____.

A) is in line with the theories that the business is business the world around

B) is different from the model of McDonald's

C) shows the reverse of globalization

D) has converged cultural differences

59. The two schools of thought_____.

A) both propose that companies should tailor business approaches to individual cultures

B) admit the existence of cultural diversity in business world

C) both advocate that different policies be set up in different countries

D) both A and B

60. This article is supposed to be most useful for those_____.

A) who want to travel abroad

B) who are interested in researching the topic of cultural diversity

C) who have connections to more than one type of culture

D) who want to run business on International Scale

61. According to Fortune, successful international companies_____.

A) earn 20 percent or more of their revenue overseas

B) will follow the overseas local cultures

C) adopt the policy of internationalization

D) all have the quality of patience

Passage Two

Questions 62 to 66 are based on the following passage.

It is not often realized that women held a high place in southern European societies in the 10th and 11th centuries. As a wife, the woman was protected by the setting up of a dowry (嫁妆). Admittedly, the purpose of this was to protect her against the risk of desertion, but in reality its function in the social and family life of the time was much more important. The dowry was the wife's right to receive a tenth of all her husband's property. The wife had the right to with hold consent, in all transactions the husband would make, and more than just a right; the documents show that she enjoyed a real power of decision, equal to that of her husband. In no case do the documents indicate any degree of difference in the legal status of husband and wife.

The wife shared in the management of her husband's personal property, but the opposite was not always true. Women seemed perfectly prepared to defend their own inheritance against husbands who tried to exceed their rights, and on occasion they showed a fine fighting spirit. A case in point is that of Maria Vivas. Having agreed with her husband Miro to sell a field she had inherited, for the needs of the household, she insisted on compensation. None being offered, she succeeded in dragging her husband to the scribe to have a contract duly drawn up assigning her a piece of land from Miro's personal inheritance. The unfortunate husband was obliged to agree, as the contract says, "for the sake of peace." Either through the dowry or through being hot-tempered, the wife knew how to win herself, with the context of the family, a powerful economic position.

62. Originally, the purpose of a dowry is to_____.

A) give a woman the right to receive all her husband's property

B) help a woman to enjoy a higher position in the family

C) protect a woman against the risk of desertion

D) both A and C

63. According to the passage, the legal status of the wife in marriage was_____.

    A) higher than that of a single woman

    B) the same as that of her husband

    C) higher than that of her husband

    D) lower than that of her husband

64. Why does the author give us the example of Maria Vivas?

    A) To show that the wife shared in the management of her husband's personal property.

    B) To prove that women have powerful position.

    C) To illustrate how women win her property.

    D) To show that the wife can defend her own inheritance.

65. The compensation Maria Vivas got for the field is_____.

    A) some of the land Miro had inherited

    B) money for household expenses

    C) money form Miro's inheritance

    D) a tenth of Miro's land

66. The author's attitude towards Maria Vivas is_____.

    A) sympathetic   B) disapproval

    C) indifferent   D) objective

Part V Cloze (15 minutes)

Directions: *There are 20 blanks in the following passage. For each blank there are four choices marked A), B), C) and D) on the right side of the paper. You should choose the ONE that best fits into the passage. Then mark the corresponding letter on Answer Sheet 2 with a single line through the centre.*

Methods of studying vary; what works _67_ for some students doesn't work at all for others. The only thing you can do is experiment _68_ you find a system that does work for you. But two things are sure: _69_ else can do your studying for you, and unless you do find a system that works, you won't get through college. Meantime, there are a few rules that _70_ for everybody. The hint is "don't get _71_".The problem of studying, _72_ enough to start with, becomes almost _73_ when you are trying to do three _74_ in one weekend. _75_ the fastest readers have trouble _76_ that. And if you are behind in written work that must be 77 , the teacher who accepts it 78 late will probably not give you good credit. Perhaps he may not accept it 79 . Getting behind in one class because you are spending so much time on another is really no 80 . Feeling pretty virtuous about the seven hours you spend on chemistry won't 81 one bit if the history teacher pops a quiz. And many freshmen do get into trouble by spending too much time on one class at the 82 of the others, either because they like one class much better or because they find it so much harder that they think, they should 83 all their time to it. 84 the reason, going the whole work for one class and neglecting the rest of them is a mistake, if you face this 85 , begin with the shortest and easiest 86 . Get them out of the way and then go to the more difficult, time consuming work.

67. A) good	B) easily	C) well	D) sufficiently
68. A) after	B) while	C) until	D) so
69. A) somebody	B) nobody	C) everybody	D) anybody
70. A) follow	B) go	C) operate	D) work
71. A) after	B) slow	C) behind	D) later
72. A) hard	B) hardly	C) unpleasant	D) heavy
73. A) improbable	B) inevitable	C) impossible	D) necessary
74. A) week's work	B) weeks' works	C) weeks' work	D) week's works
75. A) If	B) Almost	C) Even	D) With
76. A) at doing	B) to do	C) doing	D) with doing
77. A) turned in	B) tuned up	C) turned out	D) given in
78. A) very	B) quite	C) such	D) too
79. A) at all	B) anyway	C) either	D) that
80. A) method	B) solution	C) answer	D) excuse
81. A) help	B) encourage	C) assist	D) improve
82. A) pay	B) expense	C) debt	D) charge
83. A) put	B) devote	C) spend	D) take
84. A) Whichever	B) However	C) Wherever	D) Whatever
85. A) attraction	B) decision	C) temptation	D) dilemma
86. A) assignments	B) arrangements	C) way	D) class

Part VI Translation (5 minutes)

87. _____（考虑到各种各样的因素）, our subjects should be rearranged to meet the requirements of the curriculum.

88. When the train came, _____（人们立即涌进站台）.

89. If we had set out earlier, _____（我们就不会在雨中行走）.

90. Living in the desert has many problems, _____（缺水并不是唯一的问题）.

91. The circulation figures have risen _____（自从我们在头版上采用了彩色照片后）.

大学英语四级模拟试题
答案解析

Part I Writing

【思路点拨】

> 这是一篇论述校园物品被盗和加强防盗意识的文章，这一话题比较接近考生的日常生活，学校也时常开展防盗知识的教育，因此难度不大。根据题目中所给的提纲，考生可在第一段主要陈述校园盗窃案件发生的情况。第二段主要分析校园物品被盗的原因。第三段主要阐述学生怎样增强防盗意识。

【范文】

Enhance Awareness to Guard Against Campus Thefts

"If you don't want to wake up and find you have no pants to wear, you'd better put them on in sleep," goes a popular joke among students. Obviously, campus thefts have become increasingly annoying as they occur far more often than before. And it seems that the thieves are less choosy these days, with their targets ranging widely from bikes, cell phones, purses, pre-paid IC cards to sunglasses, bags, and even underwear. In short, anything that worth a dime is likely to be stolen.

What makes students the easy targets? The reasons are not hard to find. But I believe of all these reasons, the lack of anti-theft alertness is the most important. For lack of alertness, the students tend to leave the doors and windows wide open during sleep at noon or at night in summer. For the same reason, they'll also leave their bikes unlocked before a store or by a road, or forget to take away their personal stuff before they go out of the classroom to make a phone call. These acts undoubtedly have increased their exposure to the light-fingered monsters.

In order to minimize possible losses, the students must stay on guard in the first place, as awareness of the thefts around often makes a big difference. To be more specific, the students should not hide any tempting amount of cash in the dorm. Put it in the bank instead. Besides, do not leave any valuable items unattended. Take them wherever you go. In addition, it's advisable to develop a neighbourhood watch programme with other students in the dorm and neighbouring dorms.

文章以诙谐幽默的语句开篇，指出校园盗窃案件时有发生且日益猖獗，失窃物品各种各样。

文章的第二段说明了被盗原因。指出最重要的原因就是学生缺少防范意识，随后列举了几种常见的缺少防范意识的表现：夏天中午或晚上睡觉时不关门窗；自行车放在商店门前或路边不上锁；出教室或打电话时忘带随身物品。这一切都给盗贼以可乘之机。

文章的最后一段阐述了如何加强防盗意识。首先要保持警惕，具体来说，如不要在宿舍里放大量现金；其次，贵重物品要随身携带；最后，可以和其他同学或其他宿舍结合起来做好防盗工作。

Part II Reading Comprehension (Skimming and Scanning)

【全文精译】

我们会陷入水资源枯竭的困境吗？

想象一只"幽灵船"沉入了沙土中，任其留在干旱的沙土中腐烂掉。再想象沙尘暴从干旱的海床上席卷起有毒的杀虫剂和化肥，呼啸着穿过城镇和村庄。看起来像关于世界末日的电影中的一个场景？对于居住在中亚咸海附近的居民而言，这一切都是真实的。【1】30年前，为了灌溉(提供水)农田，政府部门的规划专家们改道了引水入海的河流。【1】结果，咸海缩小为原来的一半，船只也搁浅在干旱的沙土上。海水受到污染，其盐含量增到了3倍，导致24种土生土长的鱼类灭绝。

根据众多环保组织的调查，世界其他地方与此类似的大规模的改道努力也是以生态危机而告终的。【2】尽管建造大坝和灌溉系统创造的问题要比它们解决的问题多，但是许多国家仍然继续这样的项目。为什么呢？世界许多地方的人都非常需要水；而且，随着人口的增长，下个世纪将有更多的人需要更多的水。来自于太平洋发展、环境和安全研究所(the Pacific Institute for Studies in Development, Environment, and Security)的环境科学家Peter H. Gleick说："不断增长的人口将会进一步恶化缺水问题"。该研究所是位于加利福尼亚的一个研究机构。【8】他担心，到2025年，在83亿世界预计人口中，将有1/3的人口面临缺水问题。

水去了哪里？

来自位于马塞诸塞州阿默斯特的全球水政策项目的Sandra Postel主任认为，地球上只有2.5%的水是适合饮用和种植食物的淡水，【9】其中的2/3属于冰川和冰盖。事实上，只有极小比例的淡水是水循环的一部分。在水循环中，水蒸发后上升到大气中，然后凝结并以降水的形式(雨或雪)回落到地球上。

一些降水流经陆地进入湖泊和海洋，另一些渗入地球变成地下水。大部分这样的再生淡水最后积聚在诸如巴西亚马逊河流域这样很少有人居住的偏远地方。事实上，世界人口能获得的淡水仅有12,500立方千米——相当于Superior湖的湖水量，其一半已为人类所使用。Postel说，"如果水的需求量不断快速攀升，水资源将严重短缺，水环境将受到极大破坏。"

问题就在家门口

对于生活在像美国这样富裕国家的人来说，水危机似乎很遥远。【4】但是美国人可能面临严重的缺水问题，尤其是那些依赖地下水的区域。地下水储存于地下含水层和位于泥土和岩床之间的沙石层中。（地球上的地表水与地下水的水量之比大约为1∶90。）虽然美国富有含水层，农民、农场主和城市居民的用水速度超过了自然界水资源的再生速度。例如，根据Postel的调查，在西北部的得克萨斯州，超量的抽取使得地下水供应减少了25%。

美国人可能会面临更紧迫的污染问题。在美国，饮用水普遍安全，符合高标准要求。不过，据环境保护署的调查，每天有1/5的美国人在不知不觉中饮用受到细菌和化学废物污染的自来水。1993年，密尔沃基有40万人因饮用受到隐孢子虫污染的自来水而患病。隐孢子虫是一种可引起高烧、腹泻和呕吐的微生物。

污染源

这些污染物从何而来呢？【10】在发展中国家，人们把污水倒入他们从中获取饮用和烹饪水的同一小溪和河流中，每年大约有250万人感染污水带来的疾病。

【5】在发达国家，制造商使用100,000种化合物来制造更多种类的产品。未经处理就被释放入河流和湖泊中的化学物质使水受到污染。（某些化合物，如多氯联苯，即PCBs，在美国已被禁用。）

但是，水污染几乎与每个人都有关。人们常常将清洁用品、汽车防冻剂、油漆稀释剂倒入下水道中，而所有这些用品都含有有害的化学物质。1996年，科学家们对旧金山海湾的水进行了研究，他们说，70%的污染物可以追溯到家居废物。

除草剂和杀虫剂既可以杀死杂草和昆虫，也会污染水源，因此农民们一直因过量使用除草剂和杀虫剂而备受批评。农民们还使用可以促进植物生长的硝酸盐和富含氮的化肥，但是它们也会严重破坏环境。硝酸盐类物质会被地表径流冲刷入湖泊和海洋之中。过多的硝酸盐使得水域"超级富有"，从而造成水藻或水面微小植物的大量繁殖。【6】藻类剥夺了鱼生存所必需的氧气，有时候会令整个水域中的生命窒息而亡。

解决的方法是什么呢？

水资源专家Gleick提倡保护水资源，通过因地制宜的方法来解决与水相关的问题。例如，政府最好建筑小规模的水坝，而不是像毁掉咸海那样具有破坏性的大水坝。

"全世界有超过10亿的人口缺乏基本的清洁饮用水，"【7】Gleick说，"每个人——政府人员和普通人——都要付诸努力，确保我们有一个最基本的生活源泉。"

【答案解析】

1.【答案】B

【解析】本题属于细节推断题。根据题干信息该题要求找出咸海海水量减少的原因。本文的第一段提到了咸海的具体情况，所以根据题干中的核心词"Aral Sea"，并结合第二段的具体内容，可以将答案定位到该段的第三、四句话"...government planners diverted the rivers that flow into the sea in order to irrigate (provide water for) farmland. As a result, the sea has shrunk to half its original size...",这与B"The rivers flowing into it have been diverted"表示的"流入其中的河流被改道"的意思相吻合。所以正确答案是B项。答案A和D均属于断章取义，偷换了句子中的部分内容，是迷惑项。答案C的内容按照常理来说，具有一定正确性，但文章并未提及，也是干扰项。

2.【答案】D
【解析】本题属于同义转换题。题干要求回答有关大坝建设和灌溉工程的情况，根据其中的核心词"massive dams and irrigation"可定位到文章的第二段。该段中的第二句话"...many countries continue to build massive dams and irrigation systems, even though such projects can create more problems than they fix"。这与D项意思"坏处多于好处"一致。所以正确答案是D。答案A和B的意思与原文相反；答案C在文中未提及，属于故意干扰项。

3.【答案】C
【解析】本题属于段落大意理解题。对于此类主旨大意题，可以先看各个选项的区别和联系，然后结合自己对文章的理解来予以选择或者排除。本题要求回答缺水的主要原因是什么。对比四个选项，其中共有四种情况的不同组合：人口增长、水资源污染、水资源浪费和气候干燥。其中的"人口增长"在第二段结尾和第三段开头"Growing population will worsen problems with water"中提到过，属于缺水的主要原因之一；"水资源污染"在小标题"the source"下面分别从发展中国家、发达国家、个人和农民的角度作出重要说明，也是造成缺水的主要原因之一；"水资源浪费和气候干燥"在文中均未提及，所以正确答案是C。

4.【答案】C
【解析】本题属于同义转换题。根据题干中的关键词"Americans"，可以定位在小标题"Close to home"下第一段的第二句话，"Americans could face serious water shortages too, especially in areas that rely on groundwater"，表明美国人，特别是依赖地下水的居民可能面临缺水问题，这与答案C的"depending on groundwater"意思一致，属于同义转换，所以答案选C。答案A、B、D都是文章中与题干内容相关的某句话的断章取义，属于干扰项。

5.【答案】B
【解析】本题属于细节推断题。根据题干中的关键词"pollutant"，可以将答案定位在小标题"The sources"之下，再根据"in developed countries"，可以定位于第二段前两句"In developed countries, ...Toxic chemicals pollute water when released untreated into rivers and lakes"。这与B"untreated toxic chemicals from manufacturers"完全吻合，所以答案是B。A是发展中国家水污染的主要来源，C和D分别说明的是农民和个人对水资源造成的污染，属于干扰项。

6.【答案】A

【解析】本题属于细节推断题。根据题干中的关键词algae可定位到小标题"The source"之下最后一段的最后一句，"Algae deprive the water of oxygen that fish need to survive, at times choking off life in an entire body of water"，这与A "与水域中的生物竞争氧气"相吻合，所以答案选A项。答案B是对文中部分内容的改写，与答案无关；C和D在文中均未提及。

7.【答案】D

【解析】本题属于细节推断题。根据题干中的关键词"Gleick"和"solving water related problems"可定位到文章最后一段的最后一句，"...says Gleick. 'There has to be a strong push on the part of everyone—governments and ordinary people—to make sure we have a resource so fundamental to life'"，这与D "government and every person"意思一致，所以答案选D项。其他选项意思与文章不符。

8.【答案】one-third

【解析】根据题干中的关键词 "Peter H. Gleick"和 "2025"可定位到文章第四段最后一句话：He fears that by the year 2025, as many as one-third of the world's projected 8.3 billion people will suffer from water shortages.

9.【答案】glaciers and ice caps

【解析】根据题干信息可定位到文章第五段的第二句话：Two thirds of this freshwater is locked in glaciers and ice caps.

10.【答案】water pollution

【解析】根据题干信息可定位到文章第十段的第二句话：Toxic chemicals pollute water when released untreated into rivers and lakes.

Part III Listening Comprehension (35 minutes)

Section A

11.W: I just saw an ad. on television that said men's suits were on sales today and
    tomorrow at Conrad's Me's Wear.

    M: Great! That's just what I've been waiting for.

    Q: What will the man probably do?

【答案】C

【解析】由选项可知该题询问的内容是某种动作或行为，男士说男士套装的特价销售正是他一直等待着的。所以从他的态度可判断，他要去买件男装。

12.W:Is John really ill?

M: It's hard to say. I doubt there's anything wrong with him physically.

Q: What does the man mean?

【答案】C

【解析】由选项可知该题询问的内容是男士对John某方面的看法，从男士的话"我怀疑约翰的身体没有任何问题"中可看出答案。

13. M: Do you know if the bookshop is still open?

W: Yes, it's open till six.

Q: When do you think this conversation took place?

【答案】A

【解析】由选项可知该题询问时间，因此要特别注意有关时间的信息。女士说书店现在还开着，一直开到6点呢，说明现在的时间是在6点之前。

14. M: The train is late. When will it arrive?

W: They say it's late for 25 minutes, so it should be here at 11:46.

Q: When will the train arrive?

【答案】D

【解析】由选项可知该题询问时间，因此要特别注意有关时间的信息。本题中女士提到火车晚点25分钟是个干扰项，她说的后半句话即是答案so it should be here at 11:46。

15. M: I would like to move to the suburbs, but I don't have enough money to pay the high taxis.

W: I wish you could. It's nice to live there.

Q: Why isn't the man moving to the suburbs?

【答案】D

【解析】本题为推理题，对话中没有直接给出答案，需要推理。男士说：我很想住郊区，但我没那么多钱付高额的打的费。打的费高只能是因为郊区离工作的地点太远的缘故。

16. W: Jack, would you like to go to the club with us tomorrow night?

M: I wish I could, but I have to work on my term paper.

Q: Is Jack going to the club?

【答案】B

【解析】各选项都是对一般问句的回答，后面是原因。女士问：杰克，明天晚上跟我们一起去俱乐部吧？男士说：我很想去，但是我必须写我的学期论文。由此可见，杰克是不会去俱乐部的。

17. M: Have you seen Johnson this afternoon? I can't find him anywhere in this school.

W: I saw your brother Johnson studying with Cindy in the library.

Q: Who is the man looking for Johnson?

【答案】D

【解析】此为推理题，从女士的话中做个简单的推理，女士说：我看见他的兄弟Johnson在图书馆和Cindy一起学习。所以找Johnson的男士是Johnson's brother。

18. W: Were you hurt in the accident?

　　M: I was shocked at the time, but wasn't hurt at all. My bike was totally damaged though.

　　Q: What do we know about the man?

【答案】A

【解析】男士说：我那时吓坏了，但是一点儿也没伤着。因此答案为He was unharmed。

Now you'll hear two long conversations.

Conversation One

W: Hello, Gary. How're you?

M: Fine! And yourself?

W: Can't complain. Did you have time to look at my proposal?

M: No, not really. Can we go over it now?

W: Sure. I've been trying to come up with some new production and advertising strategies. First of all, if we want to stay competitive, we need to modernize our factory. New equipment should have been installed long ago.

M: How much will that cost?

W: We have several options ranging from one hundred thousand dollars all the way up to half a million.

M: OK. We'll have to discuss these costs with finance.

W: We should also consider human resources. I've been talking to personnel as well as our staff at the factory.

M: And what's the picture?

W: We'll probably have to hire a couple of engineers to help us modernize the factory.

M: What about advertising?

W: Marketing has some interesting ideas for television commercials.

M:TV? Isn't that a bit too expensive for us? What's wrong with advertising in the papers, as usual?

W: Quite frankly, it's just not enough anymore. We need to be more aggressive in order to keep ahead of our competitors.

M: Will we be able to afford all this?

W: I'll look into it, but I think higher costs will be justified. These investments will result in higher profits for our company.

M: We'll have to look at the figures more closely. Have finance draw up a budget for these investments.

W: All right. I'll see to it.

Questions 19 to 22 are based on the conversation you have just heard.

19. What are the two speakers talking about?

20. What does the woman say about the equipment of their factory?

21. What does the woman suggest about human resources?

22. Why does the woman suggest advertising on TV?

19. 【答案】B

【解析】四个选项说的都是关于某方面的话题，可以推测此题可能是询问谈话的主题。女士问Did you have time to look at my proposal? 你有时间看看我的建议么。听完全文，可见是一个关于新的商业计划的提案，因此正确答案是Suggestions concerning new business strategies。

20. 【答案】D

【解析】女士说New equipment should have been installed long ago。即早就该给工厂装新的设备了。所以正确答案为工厂应该引进最新的设备。

21. 【答案】B

【解析】女士说We'll probably have to hire a couple of engineers to help us modernize the factory。女士建议雇用一些工程师帮助实现工厂的现代化。所以正确答案应是B项：A few engineers should be employed to modernize the factory。

22. 【答案】A

【解析】从女士的话it's just not enough anymore. We need to be more aggressive in order to keep ahead of our competitors中可看出，仅仅在报纸上做广告是不够的了。

Conversation Two

M: Hey, Ellen, how are you?

W: I'm fine, Bob. Aren't you glad the semester's over?

M: Yep. Are you going to the rock concert Friday night?

W: I haven't thought much about it. Are you?

M: Sure. Would you like to go with me?

W: Sounds like fun!

M: You'll have to buy your own ticket, though.

W: Are you broke again? Let me treat you!

M: Wow, where did you come into so much cash?

W: You know I am a waitress at the Student Center. Anyway, now that the final exams are almost over, I'd love a night out.

M: Since you've been so great about buying the tickets, why don't I take us out to dinner?

W: You've got a deal. Let's buy the tickets now.

Questions 23 to 25 are based on the conversation you have heard.

23. When does this conversation take place?

24. Where do Bob and Ellen want to go?

25. Why is Ellen buying the tickets?

23.【答案】D

【解析】由选项可知该题询问的是时间。从女生的话Aren't you glad the semester's over中可知，这是个学期的期末。

24.【答案】B

【解析】由选项可知该题询问的是地点。这题关键在于听出the rock concert，两个人打算去听摇滚音乐会。

25.【答案】B

【解析】由选项可知该题询问的内容跟钱有关。Ellen必须自己买票，因为Bob没有太多的钱。

Section B

Passage One

A guide dog is a dog especially trained to guide a blind person. Dogs chosen for such training must show good intelligence, physical fitness, and responsibility.

At the age of about fourteen months, a guide dog begins an intensive course that lasts from three to five months. It becomes accustomed to the leather harness and stiff leather handle it will wear when guiding its blind owner. The dog learns to watch traffic and to cross streets safely. It also learns to obey any command that might lead its owner into danger.

The most important part of the training course is a four-week program in which the guide dog and its future owner learn to work together. However, many blind people are unsuited by personality to work dogs. Only about a tenth of the blind find a guide dog useful.

Questions 26 to 28 are based on the passage you have just heard.

26. How long does the intensive course last?

27. Which of the following is not a necessary skill guide dogs have to learn?

28. How long does the most important training course last?

26. 【答案】B

【解析】由选项可知该题询问的是时间。文中明确提到an intensive course that lasts from three to five months，因此正确答案为B。

27. 【答案】D

【解析】答案依据是The dog learns to watch traffic and to cross streets safely. It also learns to obey any command that might lead its owner into danger. 从这两句中可看出看家不属于导盲犬训练范围内的技能。

28. 【答案】C

【解析】由选项可知该题也是询问时间。文中明确指出了本题答案。The most important part of the training course is a four-week program，最重要的训练课程持续四周。

Passage Two

"Loving a child is a circular business. The more you give, the more you get, the more you want to give." Penelope Leach once said. What she said proves to be true of my blended family. I was born in 1931. As the youngest of six children, I learned to share my parents' love. Raising six children during the difficult times of the Great Depression took its toll on my parents' relationship and resulted in their divorce when I was 18 years old. Daddy never had very close relationships with his children and drifted even farther away from us after the divorce. Several years later, a wonderful woman came into his life and they were married. She had two sons, one of them still at home. Under her influence, we became a blended family and a good relationship developed between the two families. She always treated us as if we were her own children. It was because of our other mother, Daddy's second wife, that he became closer to his own children. They shared over 25 years together before our father passed away. At the time of his death, the question came up of my mother, Daddy's first wife, attending his funeral. I will never forget the unconditional love shown by my stepmother. When I asked her if she would object to mother attending Daddy's funeral, without giving it a second thought, she immediately replied. "Of course not, honey. She is the mother of my children."

Questions 29 to 31 are based on the passage you have just heard.

29. According to the speaker, what contributed to her parents' divorce?

30. What brought the father closer to his own children?

31. What message does the speaker want to convey in this talk?

29. 【答案】B

【解析】由选项中的family, her father, her mother可推测本题与家庭和其成员有关，又由violence, disloyalty, bad temper可进一步推测家庭不和睦。实际问题是：父母离婚的原因是什么。文章开头提到Raising six children during the difficult times of the Great Depression took its toll on my parents' relationship and resulted in their divorce when I was 18 years old. （在经济大萧条的艰难时期，养6个孩子的艰难使父母的感情受到了伤害并导致了在我18岁的时候父母离异。）因此答案为B。

30. 【答案】B

【解析】由选项中的advanced, efforts, improved, positive可预测本题与某一情况的好转有关。实际问题是：什么使父亲与孩子的感情加深了？文中提到It was because of our other mother, Daddy's second wife, that he became closer to his own children. （由于我们的另一个母亲，爸爸的第二个妻子，他和他自己孩子的感情加深了。）因此答案为B。

31. 【答案】D

【解析】四个选项中A，B是关于离异的后果，C，D，是关于爱，可以推测本题是关于文章主旨的考查。文中后面提到I will never forget the unconditional love shown by my step mother. （我将永远不会忘记继母对我们无私的爱。）因此答案为D。

Passage Three

Our family is trying to decide where to go for a vacation this summer. Our son Tom wants to go to Yellow Stone Park again to see the bears. We did that last summer and what an experience it was! When we got there, we put up our tent and went to explore. As we returned, we heard our daughter Susie cry out and then we saw a bear enter our camp. Tom wanted his father to chase him away. His father said, "No, it's dangerous to chase a bear. And don't let him chase you." Susie said, "What shall we do?" "Maybe we ought to climb a tree." Tom said: "No, we've got to get him out of there. He might go to sleep in our tent." "Maybe we could make him leave if we put some honey outside for him to eat." Susie suggested. Then I said, "How are you going to get the honey? It's in the tent." We watched the bear enter the tent and heard him upset everything inside. "It's foolish for us to try to catch him," said my husband. "Leave him alone and wait for him to come out." We waited but the bear stayed inside. We had to sleep in the car.

Questions 32 to 35 are based on the passage you have just heard.

32. Where have the family decided to go in the vacation this summer?

33. Who do you think saw the bear first?

34. What did they do when they saw a bear enter their tent?

35. What did the bear do in the tent?

32.【答案】A

【解析】听完全文可以得知这个家庭还未决定好去哪里度假。所以正确答案为They haven't reached a decision yet。

33.【答案】C

【解析】短文中读到：As we returned, we heard our daughter Susie cry out and then we saw a bear enter our camp，因此显然是女儿Susie先看到了熊。

34.【答案】A

【解析】四个选项都是对熊的反应。文中也读到：他们站在外面一直在讨论该怎么对付这只熊，但最终什么都没做。因此，正确答案为They stayed outside the tent and did nothing。

35.【答案】D

【解析】显然，选项中的he指的是熊。文中读到：We watched the bear enter the tent and heard him upset everything inside。关键词在upset，意为"颠覆、翻倒"。熊把帐篷里的东西弄得乱七八糟。

Section C (听力原文参考333页文章及351页答案)

36.【答案】undoubtedly

【解析】undoubtedly意为"毋庸置疑地，的确"。煤毋庸置疑将成为重要的能源。

37.【答案】supplies

【解析】supply意为"供应，供给"。由于天然气和石油资源供应的逐渐减少，煤毋庸置疑将成为重要的能源。注意是复数形式。

38.【答案】appears

【解析】appear意为"出现，看来，似乎"。虽然煤看似黑色的，但是在高倍显微镜下，它还有黄色，橘色和红色。注意是第三人称单数。

39.【答案】giant

【解析】giant意为"巨大的"。煤大约形成于3亿年前，由巨大的树木和沼泽里的其他植物形成的。

40.【答案】swamps

【解析】swamp意为"沼泽"。煤大约形成于3亿年前，由巨大的树木和沼泽里的其他植物形成的。

41.【答案】carbon

【解析】carbon意为"碳"。它们包含的元素有氧、氢以及碳。

42.【答案】shape

【解析】shape意为"形状，形态"。随着地表形态的改变，树木和植物被埋在地下。

43.【答案】pressed

【解析】press意为"压，挤压"。地表的压力作用于树木和植物之上。注意是过去式。

44.【答案】Coal can be taken from underground mines found deep in the earth or from strip mines which are found near the earth's surface

【解析】空白处之后的一句话讲露天开采比地下开采更快、更安全，但是露天开采使地表变得光秃秃的而且很难看。可见该空与露天矿和地下矿有关。此句中的关键词汇有：underground mines, strip mines.

45.【答案】Although miners still are needed in any coal mining operation, today heavy machinery does much of the hard work

【解析】空白处之后的一句话讲尽管露天开采和地下开采两者都很危险，开采过程中的事故已不像以前那么多了。可推测该空可能与采矿工作有关。此句中的关键词汇有：operation, heavy machinery.

46.【答案】The coal miners of today owe much to the union to which they belong the United Mine Workers of America

【解析】结合前后句可推测此句与工人状况的改善有关。此句中的关键词汇有：owe... to, the United Mine Workers of America（美国矿工联合会）。

Part IV Reading Comprehension (Reading in Depth) (25 minutes)

【全文精译】

Section A

　　理智购买是一种积极的方式，可以让你的钱更值钱。你购买一件物品或者一份服务的方式真的可以给你节省钱或者多花钱。以吹风机作一个简单的例子。如果你要买一个吹风机，当你选了一个外观非常受喜欢而且价格又是最便宜的，你一定认为你买了最好的东西。但是，当你把它买回家，你才发现它要花两倍于较贵的吹风机所花的时间来吹干你的头发。电费加上你的时间成本很可能使你的吹风机成为最贵的一种。

　　当你外出购物时，你应该采取什么样的原则呢？如果你保持你的家、你的车，或者任何一件值钱的物品处于一种良好的状态中，从长远的眼光来看，你会省钱。在你买一个新的用品前，先与有这个物品的人交流一下。如果可能的话，你可以试试或者借来看看是否适合你的特殊要求。在购买一个贵重物品或者一项服务之前，要看好它的价格和功能。如果可能的话，一定要货比三家。

47.【答案】A) save
【解析】此空需要填入一个动词，所给选项中的动词只有save和adopt，另外根据句义来选本文主要讲理智的购物可以省很多钱的问题。你购买一件物品或者一份服务的方式真的可以给你省钱或者让你多花钱，所以此处空格填save，节省。

48.【答案】I) simple
【解析】就拿吹风机作一个简单的例子。空格处用simple形容例子符合文章所表达的意思。

49.【答案】D) best
【解析】如果你要买一个吹风机，当你选了一个外观你非常喜欢而且价格又是最便宜的，你一定认为你买了最好的东西。make the best buy意即买了最好的东西。

50.【答案】K) in
【解析】以怎样的价格用固定短语in price。最便宜的价格就是the cheapest in price。

51.【答案】L) model
【解析】意为"样式，型"。当你把它买回家，你才发现它要花两倍于较贵的吹风机所花的时间来吹干你的头发。a more expensive model更贵的一款。

52.【答案】N) adopt

【解析】此空考察动宾搭配。principles需要用adopt来搭配，adopt principles "采用原则"。那么你外出购物时应该采用什么样的原则呢？

53.【答案】G) possession

【解析】意为 "拥有物"。如果你保持你的家、你的车，或者任何一件值钱的物品处于一种良好的状态中，从长远的眼光来看你会省钱。

54.【答案】E) appliance

【解析】意为 "用品，器具"。在你买一个新的用品之前，先与有这个物品的人交流一下。

55.【答案】M) item

【解析】在买一个贵的东西之前，要看好价格和正在出售的物品。item可用来指一件商品（或物品）。文章最后一句中有显示。

56.【答案】B) from

【解析】此空考察动词与介词的搭配。这个空格前是动词choose，从中作出选择即用介词from来搭配。

Section B
Passage One

【全文翻译】

　　文化是国际商业中最具有挑战性的因素之一。作为一种体系，文化具有既定社会成员习得性行为模式的特点，不断受到一些动态变量的塑造，如：语言、宗教信仰、价值观、态度、行为方式和风俗习惯、美学、科技、教育和社会制度。为了应对这一体系，一个国际经理需要了解文化知识并对此作出诠释。在某种程度上，文化知识可以通过学习获得，但对文化的诠释只能通过实践获得。

　　应对文化环境最复杂的问题源于这样一个事实：人生在文化中但却不能学习文化。关于如何应对文化的多样性，商界中存在两种观点。一种认为，商业是世界性的，遵循百事(Pepsi)和麦当劳(McDonald)的模式。在某些情况下，全球化就是生活。但是，文化差异仍然难以趋同。

　　另外一种观点认为，企业必须调整其策略以适应特别的文化。在各个国家建立政策和程序就如同器官移植，关键的问题是以接受或排斥为中心。国际经理面临的主要挑战是要确认排斥不是由文化近视或者盲目所引起的。

　　财富(Fortune)对12个海外收入占其总收入20%或更多的大公司的国际业绩进行了研究。成功的国际公司都有一个重要的特征：耐心。它们不是冒失地闯入而是遵循最基本的商业原则认真地营造自己的经营活动。这些原则就是了解对手、了解观众以及了解顾客。

57.【答案】B

【解析】本题属于推断题。意为"在商业中怎样对待文化有着不同意见"。文化在商业中是一个很具挑战性的因素,不同的国家与地区可能会有不同的文化体系。在商业中,应该怎样对待不同的文化,商业界存在着不同的看法。

58.【答案】A

【解析】本题属于细节题。Pepsi采纳的是国际化的商业风格,这与那些主张国际化的派别的意见是相一致的。

59.【答案】B

【解析】本题属于推断题。意为"承认商业世界中文化的多元性"。两个派别都承认商业世界中文化的多元性。他们的不同在于,如何对待不同的文化,应该搞国际化还是对不同的文化采取不同的策略。

60.【答案】D

【解析】本题属于主旨题。由文中的例子可以知道,作者主要关心的并不是研究多种文化形态,而是文化背景对商业运作的影响。所以D是正确答案。

61.【答案】D

【解析】本题属于细节题。意为"都具有耐心这一素质"。即他们并不急于对号入座而是依据最基本的商业原则谨慎地建立自己的运行模式。

Passage Two

【全文翻译】

　　欧洲南部的妇女在十和十一世纪时享有较高的社会地位,这并未获得广泛认识。作为一个妻子,女性的地位受到其嫁妆的保护。诚然,嫁妆最初的目的是防止女性被抛弃;但是,它在当时家庭和社会现实生活中起着更重要的作用。妻子的嫁妆使她有权获得其丈夫1/10的财物。妻子有权利拒绝丈夫所做的任何交易,但这不仅仅只是一项权利而已;文件表明她与丈夫一样平等地享有真正的决定权。文件没有表明丈夫和妻子在法律地位上有任何差别。

　　妻子享有管理丈夫私人财产的权利,但是反之则不然。如果丈夫要越权侵犯她们的利益,女性们会时刻准备着捍卫自己的利益,有时她们还会表现出一种坚强的斗争精神。Maria Vivas就是一个典型的例子。为了家庭的需要,她同意其丈夫Miro出售一块属于她的土地,但是她坚持要求获得补偿。但是丈夫没有给她提供补偿,于是她把丈夫拖到一个文书处,起草了一份合同,成功地把他丈夫的一块私人土地划归自己。正如合同所写的,"为了和平", 这个不幸的丈夫不得不同意。要么借助嫁妆, 要么通过发脾气, 妻子都知道如何在家庭中为自己赢得强大的经济地位。

62.【答案】C

【解析】本题属于推断题。本文介绍了欧洲南部在十和十一世纪时嫁妆对女性在婚姻中地位的重要性。虽然嫁妆最初的目的是防止女性被抛弃, 但实际上它的作用远远不止于此。它使妻子在婚姻中的地位与丈夫平等, 并保障了妻子的经济利益。女性在维护自己的利益上, 是很坚定果敢的, Maria Vivas就是一个例子。见第一段第三句, "Admittedly, the purpose of this was to protect her against the risk of desertion.", 虽然在实际生活中嫁妆有更重要的作用, 但最初它的作用只是为了防范女性被丈夫抛弃, 所以C为正确答案。

63.【答案】B

【解析】本题属于细节题。根据本文, 妻子在婚姻中的法律地位和丈夫是平等的。见第一段最后一句, "In no case do the documents indicate any degree of difference in the legal status of husband and wife" 文件中并没有表明丈夫和妻子在法律地位上有任何的差别, 也就是说他们的地位是平等的, 所以B为正确答案。

64.【答案】D

【解析】本题属于推断题。作者举Maria Vivas的事例, 是为了说明妻子是能够捍卫自己的利益的。见第二段第二句, "Women seemed perfectly prepared to defend their own inheritance...they showed a fine fighting spirit." 如果丈夫要侵占自己的利益, 女性们就时刻准备着捍卫自己的利益, 有时她们还表现出很强的斗争精神。接下来作者就举了Maria Vivas的例子, 说明女性是有能力捍卫自己利益的。所以D为正确答案。

65.【答案】A

【解析】本题属于细节题。Maria Vivas得到的一份作为补偿的土地, 本来是属于Miro的个人财产。见第二段第五句, "None being offered, she succeeded in... assigning her a piece of land from Miro's personal inheritance" 由此知A为正确答案。

66.【答案】D

【解析】本题属于推断题。作者对Maria Vivas所持的态度是客观的。作者客观地介绍了Maria Vivas的事例, 并没有表示出同情、不满或者是漠不关心, 所以A、B、C都是错误答案。

Part V Cloze (15 minutes)

【全文翻译】

　　学习的方法大不相同，对一些学生有效的方法对其他人来说并不一定起作用。你唯一能做的就是要进行实验，直到找到一个适合自己的学习方法。但是有两件事是肯定的：没有人能替你学习，而且如果你找不到适合自己的学习方法，你就不会通过大学考试。同时，还有一些对每个人都起作用的规则，例如"不要落后"的规则。学习的问题是，一开始的时候是非常难的，而当你尝试在一周内完成3周的事情时则变得几乎不可能。即使是最好的读者也难以完成。如果你没有按时完成必须上交的书面任务或交得太迟，老师大概都不会给你打个高分，也许他根本就不接受它。在其他科目上花费太多的时间不是你在某个科目上落后的真正借口。在化学上花费7个小时感到非常有效，却对历史考试毫无帮助。许多大一新生的确陷入了困境，他们以牺牲其他课程为代价而在一门课程上花费了太多的时间，这么多因为他们喜欢一门课程超过其他各门课程，要么因为他们发现这门课程非常难，所以他们认为应该在这门课程上付出自己全部的时间。不管什么原因，对某门课程全力以赴而忽视其余的课程却是不正确的。如果你在面对这样的诱惑时，那么就应该从最短、最容易的课程开始入手。完成它们后，再去学习更困难的、费时的课程。

【答案解析】

67.【答案】C

【解析】此空缺少的是副词，而选项A中的good是形容词，所以A不对。此处要与后面的doesn't work at all形成对比，而B、D没有对比的意味。

68.【答案】C

【解析】此句的意思是你一直进行尝试，直到找到适合自己的学习方法。因而此处的连词要表达"直到"的意思。

69.【答案】B

【解析】线索是空格后的else，两个词连起来表示"（除了你自己），别的任何人都不能……"。

70.【答案】D

【解析】work常用于抽象的意义，表示"起作用"的意思。文章第一句中已多次使用这一动词。

71.【答案】C

【解析】get (fall, be) behind等都表示落后的意思，根据上下文，显然是说，我们在学习上不要落后。

72.【答案】A

【解析】此空要求填一个形容词，因此选项B可排除。又根据上下文，可以理解出这句话的意思应该是：学习的问题是，一开始的时候是非常难的，而当你想在一周内完成三周的事情时则变得几乎不可能。这时谈的是难度的问题，因此选其他的答案是不合适的。如果直接解此题有困难，可以先做后面的题。

73.【答案】C

【解析】可以根据从句中的意思来判断本题的答案。要在一周内做3周的事，毫无疑问，应当说这是几乎不可能的。improbable意为"不大可能，未必会发生的"，而impossible语气上更为决绝，说话者带有绝对否定的意思在里面"不可能的，做不到的"。

74.【答案】C

【解析】表面考的是所有格的用法，实际上考察的是名词的数。三周肯定是复数，week必须是复数形式；work是不可数名词。

75.【答案】C

【解析】此空考查的是篇章词汇。解题也有两种方法。第一种方法是从篇章的角度着手，上面一段说的是学习的困难，承接上文这里显然是说"即使"是读得最快的人也有困难，选项C正合此意。第二种方法是从句法着手。这是一个简单句，显然不能填连词和介词，A、D明显错误。单就本句来说，选almost也是不能的。

76.【答案】C

【解析】have trouble后接动名词。

77.【答案】A

【解析】turn in的意为"交上去，上交"，其他的选项是：turn up"出现"，turn out"出来；结果是"，give in"让步"。

78.【答案】D

【解析】此处表示"过晚"之意，用too。

79.【答案】A

【解析】考查常用句型not...at all。

80.【答案】D

【解析】这一句是说因为你在别的科花的时间太多而在另一科落后，前者不是后者的理由。所以此处要选表示"借口、理由"意思的词，即excuse。

81.【答案】A
【解析】表示笼统的"有用"的动词是help。assist指具体的帮助，强调在提供帮助时，以受助者为主，所给的帮助起第二位或从属的作用。其他的选项是：encourage"鼓励"，improve"改善，提高"。

82.【答案】B
【解析】此空考察短语用法。at the expense of的意思是"以……为代价"。

83.【答案】B
【解析】此空考察固定搭配。devote...to...意为"把……献于……；把……用于……"。

84.【答案】D
【解析】考查句型"What is the reason that."

85.【答案】C
【解析】前面所说的明显是一种诱惑，所以要选temptation。其他的选项是：attraction"吸引（力），有吸引力的人或事物"，decision"决定"，dilemma"困境"。

86.【答案】D
【解析】前面说的是上某课的事，所以选class。assignment"作业，任务"，arrangement"布置，安排"。

Part Ⅵ　Translation　(5 minutes)

87.【答案】With various factors considered
【解析】题中已给出部分的句子结构是完整的。所以该部分可译成短语或从句来作整个句子的状语。由于主句用的是被动语态，并没有明确指出施动者，所以所译的部分最好别使用含有施动者的主动句形式。可使用介词with来引导这一结构，而"考虑"和"因素"之间是动宾关系，所以应使用动词的过去分词来表示被动。

88.【答案】people poured into the platform immediately
【解析】本题的考点是"涌进"一词的译法，短语pour into与此含义相符。而题中给出的时间状语从句为过去时，因此主句也应为过去时。

89.【答案】we wouldn't have walked in the rain

【解析】本题的考点是虚拟语气的用法。分析句子结构和中文部分的内容可知，本句采用了虚拟语气，我们知道虚拟语气大致可分为三种情况：

一、如果所述与现在事实相反，那么虚拟条件句的从句谓语部分用过去时态，主句谓语部分用would / could / might / should + 动词原型。

二、如果所述与过去事实相反，则从句谓语用过去完成时态，主句谓语用would / could / might / should + 动词现在完成时态。三、如果所述与将来事实相反，则从句谓语用should / were to + 动词原型，主句谓语用would / could / should / might + 动词原型。再由从句为过去完成时可知，本句表示对过去事实的虚拟假设，因此主句谓语部分应为would have done的结构。

90.【答案】of which the lack of water is not the only one

【解析】根据中文提示，可译为the lack of water is not the only problem，但已给出的英文部分已经是个完整的句子，所以译文应以从句的形式出现。缺水是many problems中的一个问题，故使用表示所属关系的of which结构来引导。缺水也可译为water shortage。

91.【答案】since we introduced color photographs on the front page

【解析】本句用了现在完成时，再结合中文提示可知，该部分应译成since引导的时间状语从句。为了强调此处的"采用"是从无到有的运用，应将其译成introduce，而不是单纯表示"运用"的use。